CHILDREN

and YOUTH

in SPORT

CHILDREN and YOUTH in SPORT

A Biopsychosocial Perspective

Frank L. Smoll and Ronald E. Smith
University of Washington

Boston, Massachusetts   Burr Ridge, Illinois   Dubuque, Iowa
Madison, Wisconsin   New York, New York   San Francisco, California
St. Louis, Missouri

WCB/McGraw-Hill

A Division of The **McGraw·Hill** *Companies*

Basal Text: Times Roman
Display Type: Helvetica
Typesetting System: QuarkXPress for Macintosh
Paper Stock: 50# Phoenix
Production Services: Edwards Brothers, Inc.
Printing and Binding: Edwards Brothers, Inc.

Book Team

Publisher   *Bevan O'Callaghan*
Editor   *Scott Spoolman*
Publishing Services Coordinator   *Peggy Selle*
Proofreading Coordinator   *Carrie Barker*
Production Manager   *Beth Kundert*
Visuals/Design Freelance Specialist   *Mary L. Christianson*
Marketing Manager   *Pamela S. Cooper*
Copywriter   *M.J. Kelly*

President and Chief Executive Officer   *Thomas E. Doran*
Vice President of Production and Business Development   *Vickie Putman*
Vice President of Sales and Marketing   *Bob McLaughlin*
Director of Marketing   *John Finn*

Cover design and illustration by Ellen Pettengell Design

Copyedited by Laurie McGee; Proofread by Nancy Phan

Library of Congress Catalog Card Number: 94-73668

ISBN 0-697-22490-2

10 9 8 7 6 5 4 3

CONTENTS

PREFACE

The vast degree of involvement in sport, both vicariously and directly, is one of the most notable features of contemporary Western society. Indeed, sport has been an increasingly integral part of American culture and is regarded as a major social institution. This is particularly true for children and youth, as more and more participate in athletics each year. Without pursuing an in-depth analysis of the nature of play, games, or sport, it suffices to say that *youth sports* refer to adult-organized and controlled athletic programs for young people in the age range 6 to 18 years. The participants are formally organized into teams and leagues, and they attend practices and scheduled competitions under the supervision of an adult leader. These programs not only have clear social sanction in the United States but are also recognized as a worldwide phenomenon.

Although youth sports are firmly entrenched in our social and cultural milieu, concerns about their desirability have been expressed for some time. Those who favor youth sports emphasize that many aspects of the experience contribute to personal development. Proponents generally view youth sports as miniature life situations where participants can learn to cope with several of the important realities of life. Within sport, youngsters can compete and cooperate with others, they can learn risk taking and self-control, and they can deal with success and failure. Important attitudes are formed about achievement, authority, and persistence in the face of difficulty. In addition, the advocates point out, lifelong patterns of physical activity that promote health and fitness can be initiated through involvement in youth sports. Critics counter with claims that excessive physical and psychological demands are placed on young people and that programs exist primarily for the self-serving needs of coaches and parents. They suggest that children and youth would benefit far more if adults simply left them alone to participate in their own games and activities.

A realistic appraisal of youth sports indicates that participation does not automatically result in beneficial or detrimental effects. We believe that the sport environment affords a strong *potential* for achieving desirable objectives. The question is not whether youth sports should continue to exist. They are here to stay, and, if anything, they will continue to grow in spite of the criticisms that are sometimes leveled at them. The real question is how the programs can be effectively structured and conducted in ways that ensure attainment of positive outcomes.

One of the keys to unlocking the potential of youth sports lies in understanding their physical, psychological, and sociological dimensions. Since the mid-1970s the scientific community has studied the impact of highly structured sports on young athletes and on the complex social network comprising coaches, parents, and peers. The proliferation of research has given rise to youth sport conferences and symposia as well as academic courses on the subject at colleges and universities. The accumulation of empirical evidence has also resulted in a body of knowledge that spans several disciplinary areas, including psychology, sociology, and the sport sciences. The purpose of the present volume is to furnish a multidisciplinary view of youth sport issues. In developing *Children and Youth in Sport,* our goal has been to produce a volume that can provide sport scientists, students, coaches, administrators, and parents with an up-to-date survey of current scientific knowledge in the many facets of children's sports. It is also our hope that a better understanding of the multifaceted nature of youth sports, as well as the specific recommendations offered by our panel of experts, will stimulate and guide changes in current policies and practices. Improving the conditions under which youth sports are conducted should ultimately prove beneficial to all individuals involved—young athletes and adults alike!

We wish to thank Maureen R. Weiss, whose suggestions helped to shape the original organization of the book. And, of course, we are greatly indebted to the authors for contributing up-to-date syntheses of the literature in their respective areas of expertise. Finally, we would like to express our gratitude to the editorial and production staffs of Brown & Benchmark Publishers for their roles in designing and producing the book.

One of the joys of editing a book of this nature is the day-to-day contact with the contributors, who in this case also happen to be friends and colleagues. Thus we were deeply saddened by the death of one of our coauthors, Michael D. Smith, as the book was in production. We valued Mike as a friend and scholar, and we wish to dedicate this book to his memory.

Frank L. Smoll
Ronald E. Smith

HISTORY AND CURRENT STATUS

Although children and youth have always engaged in play and informal games, the twentieth century has witnessed the development of increasingly organized youth sport programs. Youth sports in the United States actually go back to the early 1900s. The first programs were instituted in public schools when it was recognized that physical activity was an important part of education. The programs emerged as after-school recreation activities, but they soon acquired a highly competitive "win-at-all-costs" orientation. This change resulted in condemnation and subsequent withdrawal of support by educators. Over time, sponsorship and control of some sports shifted to a host of local and national agencies. The diversified mix of autonomous organizations offered a wide array of sport programs that grew in scope and popularity.

In moving from the sandlot to the more-formalized programs that now exist, the youth sport explosion has touched youngsters and adults in increasing numbers. Estimates of the number of participants (ages 6 to 18 years) in agency-sponsored athletics in the United States are astonishing. A report presented at the 1984 Olympic Scientific Congress indicated that about 20 million of the 45 million young people in this age range participated in nonschool sports. At the same time, nearly 2.5 million men and women volunteered their time as coaches, league administrators, and officials. Such figures alone have established youth sports as important child and adolescent development activities.

Youth sports have continued to flourish during the past decade. There is no evidence that participation has either reached a peak or that a decline is likely to occur. Today more opportunities to play a greater variety of sports exist than ever before. This is not only true for young males; the rise of sport programs for girls and young women has been a relatively recent and highly significant development.

The growth of youth sports and the role that they play in the lives of children and youth are undeniable. But this expansion has generated persisting and, at times, bitter debate. Thoughtful persons have raised questions about the desirability of adult-organized sports. However, the answers to their queries are not simple. Just as medical doctors must have thorough histories of their patients, so must we understand the evolution of youth sports. By analogy, this knowledge assists us in effectively dealing with both the maladies and well-being of contemporary athletics and in contributing to a healthy and happy future.

The opening chapter by Jack W. Berryman provides a historical account of the growth of highly organized sport programs for young boys. In tracing the rise of boys' sports, Berryman focuses on two separate but interrelated developments in the social and cultural milieu of U.S. society at the turn of the century. The first was the inclusion of sport in the school curriculum, which brought organized athletics closer to the children of the nation than ever before and established the rationale for their acceptance and promotion. The second factor influencing the growth of boys' sports was recognition that childhood is an important stage in the development of an adult and that measures must be taken to ensure a happy and profitable period of growing up. As a result, an entirely new branch of social welfare, called boys' work groups, began using sports to provide wholesome leisure-time pursuits for young boys and to keep them out of trouble. Of particular interest are the alterations of philosophies and attitudes of professional educators and the associated shifts in sponsorship of youth sports to community-based organizations.

David K. Wiggins's chapter begins with an overview of the boys' playground movement of the mid–nineteenth century. He then chronicles the late-nineteenth-century transition from participation in less organized and more informal games to competing in highly organized sports directed by adults. Similar to Berryman's work, Wiggins's historical analysis indicates that despite the early influence of educational institutions, the highly competitive programs that emerged in the 1920s and 1930s were primarily in the hands of various churches, boys' work groups, civic groups, and community councils. Professional educators eventually relinquished any control they had over youth sports because of their growing belief that highly competitive athletics exposed children to great risks. It is important to note that participation was initially confined to boys and that attempts to eliminate sexual discrimination did not begin until the early 1970s. In this regard, Wiggins reviews significant legal cases that led to more equitable treatment for girls and young women in sport. The trend toward desegregation coincided with revised interest in youth sports on the part of academicians and professional educators. Among the most visible indications of this concern were the organization of conferences, the establishment of institutes, and the formulation of coach-training programs devoted specifically to youth sports. The final part of the chapter focuses on the growth in publications and research studies on both the benefits and hazards of highly competitive youth sport programs.

In the final chapter of this part, Martha E. Ewing and Vern Seefeldt examine the status of American agency-sponsored youth sport programs. Their report is based on data derived from a national survey of approximately 8,000 youth in the age range 10 to 18 years. Patterns of participation and attrition are summarized for the two largest categories of programs, namely, nonschool- and school-sponsored sports. Focusing on the 10 most popular sports in each of these categories, participation patterns are analyzed separately by gender and by race (African American, Asian American, Caucasian, Hispanic American, and Native American). Age-related patterns are then discussed for the total group. A unique feature of the chapter is the inclusion of information pertaining to youngsters' participation in "free-play" sports (i.e., activities that are not organized or supervised by adults). In addition to presenting a comprehensive picture of participation, Ewing and Seefeldt identify programmatic and research needs that should be addressed.

THE RISE OF BOYS' SPORTS IN THE UNITED STATES, 1900 TO 1970

—Jack W. Berryman

The rise of highly organized competitive sport programs[1] for boys under the age of 12 was a phenomenon of the first half of the twentieth century and indicated that sport had finally penetrated all levels of the American population.[2] To be sure, young children played games and enjoyed a variety of sports throughout America's history, but regulated and administered sport programs by interested individuals and organizations solely for the use of small boys did not begin until after 1900. In fact, the first instances of sport teams, leagues, championships, and other examples of highly organized children's sports outside of the schools were not evident until the 1920s and early 1930s. Even then, the programs were only local affairs, usually established by communities who wanted to provide something different and special for their children. Little did they know that in another 10 to 15 years nationally organized and administered sports for children would be spreading throughout the country to eventually become one of the most pervasive forces in the lives of many American youngsters.

Two separate but interrelated developments in the social and cultural milieu of American society during the early twentieth century provided the most direct influence on the rise and growth of boys' competitive sport programs. The first, of course, was the rise of sport itself in all parts of the country and the subsequent desire to participate and spectate by large numbers of the population. More specifically, though, the inclusion of sport in the school curriculum brought organized sport closer to the youth of the nation than ever before. Along with school sports came the rationale for their acceptance and promotion. This was most often provided by professional physical educators, recreation people, playground directors, and athletic coaches who were responsible for the majority of competitive sport situations during the first three decades of the twentieth century.[3] But when philosophies changed within this group during the 1930s, educators dropped any sponsorship of children's sport they had previously provided and refused to condone high-level competition for preadolescents. This change of outlook by professionally trained educators who were deeply involved with the early stages of sport competition for children was the first important development in conjunction with the overall rise of sport. Although it seemed to be antagonistic to the growth and development of children's sport, the alteration of philosophy would eventually lead to bigger, better, and more highly organized programs.

The second development influencing the growth of boys' sport programs was that Americans began to realize the need and importance of protecting and providing varied opportunities for children. Childhood became recognized as an important stage in the development of an adult, and concerned individuals and organizations took measures to ensure a happy and profitable period of growing up. By means of a variety of laws and policies enacted by national, state, and community organizations, children were provided with an abundance of free time, parents took a different view of their offspring, and national programs were organized to protect the child's welfare. An entirely new branch of social welfare, called boys' work, originated in the last decade of the nineteenth century.[4] Boys' work groups, originally composed of all voluntary members, were organized specifically to provide wholesome leisure-time pursuits for young boys and keep them out of trouble. These social workers began using sports and other recreational activities very early in their work and realized the importance of reaching the youthful minds and bodies of preadolescent boys. Leaders of this movement advocated the usefulness of sport for many of the same reasons that schools turned to sport. But when the schools refused to sponsor competitive sports for the young boys, the task was left to the voluntary boys' work groups. Therefore, the linking of the overall popularity of sport and its believed values, many of which were established by school personnel in the early twentieth century, as well as the sport sponsorship of boys' work agencies (along with the work groups' own modifications and gradual growth) did more to promote boys' sport competition than any other factor and led directly to America's emphasis on highly organized competitive sports for preadolescent boys.

Before the 1930s, the responsibility for providing recreational activities and organized sports for small children was shaped by the schools, playgrounds, and a few nationally organized youth membership agencies such as the YMCA, Boy Scouts, and Boys' Clubs. As specific alterations of goals and purposes occurred within the physical education and recreation profession, however, the provision of sport competition for preadolescent boys became more and more a primary function of national voluntary boys' work agencies. Beginning in the 1930s, physical educators and professional recreation leaders denounced the overt emphasis placed on winning, the physical and emotional strain that sport placed on children, and the attempt to organize competition into leagues for championship play, which were becoming common in many children's sport programs. Professionals also disagreed with providing competition for only the best athletes instead of allowing all children to participate. As a result, professionally trained leaders in sports and recreation retracted their support and relinquished their hold on organized competition for young boys.

By allowing highly organized children's sport to leave the educational context, professional educators presented a golden opportunity to the many voluntary youth-related groups in America. These groups had no educationally imposed restrictions on their work for children and many times had the funds and support from parents and communities to provide elaborate and well-organized sport programs. The volunteer workers and members of these groups often had no educational training in child development or child psychology and operated with little or no restraints in providing the best for the children. Consequently, by giving up their support of youth sports, school personnel could no longer enforce their rules and regulations for competition. Accordingly, the outside agencies capitalized on children's free time from school during the evenings, weekends, and summer months and provided numerous opportunities for competition. With very few limitations and a single goal of serving children and making them happy, boys' work groups saw no end to the sport situations they could provide.

The withdrawal of the schools' sponsorship came at a time when the values inherent to sport and its benefits to both children and society were becoming firmly established in the beliefs of most Americans. Parents, child welfare workers, and organizations established to serve youth were not easily convinced of what they believed were questionable detriments of sport competition for children. Therefore, child-related organizations, and specifically boys' work groups, stepped in to fill the void created by professional educators. The schools continued to be paramount in their sponsorship of interscholastic athletics for youth beyond the age of 12, but sport competition for preadolescent boys became the responsibility of child-oriented organizations outside of the educational framework. Their main objective was to provide wholesome character-building activities to occupy the leisure time of children to better enable them to make the transition from childhood to adulthood. Sport, these organizations believed, was the one activity that was capable of providing all of the necessary conditions for this successful growth and development. Thus, it was during the 1930s, under the sponsorship of boys' work organizations outside of the educational context, that highly organized sport competition for preadolescent boys began its ascendance to present-day heights.

Educators Discourage Highly Competitive Sports

The policy statements of the professional physical education and recreation groups, as well as other leading educators from the 1930s to the 1960s, illustrated their discouragement of highly competitive sports for children. A steady stream of proposals, guidelines, speeches, manuals, and periodical articles containing warnings against too much competition for elementary school children flowed from the ranks of professional educators. The statements reinforced their refusal to condone and administer such programs and were released at various times during the 1930s, 1940s, 1950s, and 1960s when children's sport in association with boys' work groups was making rapid progress.

The first formal statements by professional physical educators and recreational leaders declaring their concern about organized sports for elementary school children came during the early 1930s. The sport programs that were already in the schools came under attack because they were not in line with educational objectives and only a few of the highly skilled students were able to compete. Later in the decade, a determined effort was made to establish official policies to eliminate all interscholastic competition for elementary-age children both within and outside of the school ("Mid-West District News," 1937). The American Association for Health, Physical Education and Recreation (AAHPER) was quick in approving a resolution against highly organized sports for children at its 1938 convention in Atlanta, Georgia. Its statement, like many of the ones to follow, was based on the strenuous nature of competitive sports.

Inasmuch as pupils below tenth grade are in the midst of the period of rapid growth, with the consequent bodily weaknesses and maladjustments, partial ossification of bones, mental and emotional stresses, physiological adjustments, and the like, be it therefore resolved that the leaders in the field of physical and health education should do all in their power to discourage interscholastic competition at this age level, because of its strenuous nature. ("Two Important Resolutions," 1938, pp. 488–489)

Before the end of the decade, the Society of State Directors of Physical and Health Educators also prepared a formal statement on the subject. Its policy statement was directed to school board members and school administrators and suggested that interscholastic athletics had no place in elementary schools. The Society specifically discouraged postseason games and championships, extensive travel, and "all star" teams, all of which were becoming attractive aspects of organized sport programs outside of the school (Moss & Orion, 1939).

During the 1940s educational psychologists spoke out against the emphasis placed on competition for rewards (Duncan, 1951; Skinner, 1945), and AAHPER adopted another resolution condemning interscholastic competition for the first 8 grades ("Recommendations," 1947).[5] In 1947 a Joint Statement of Policy on Interscholastic Athletics by the National Federation of High School Athletic Associations and AAHPER recommended that the competitive needs of elementary-age children be met with a balanced intramural program (AAHPER, 1947).[6] Finally, in 1949 AAHPER and its Society of State Directors of Health, Physical Education and Recreation joined with representatives from the Department of Elementary School Principals, National Education Association, and the National Council of State Consultants in Elementary School Principals to form the Joint Committee on Athletic Competition for Children of Elementary and Junior High School Age. Their recommendations were more extensive than any of the previous statements but stayed with the same overall policy of no highly organized competitive programs (AAHPER, 1952).[7] They made an attempt to influence community agencies as well as school personnel but failed to realize that the very aspects of competitive sport they were condemning were the interesting and unique features that were attracting young, enthusiastic, and energetic boys. Leagues, championships, tournaments, travel, spectators, and commercial sponsors were viewed by parents, community leaders, and the boys' work agencies as examples of doing a great service for the children. In addition, young boys wanted to play on a level as close to the "big leagues" as possible and enjoyed the new form of attention provided by sport competition.

Evidence that the formal resolutions and professional policies that were passed during the 1930s and 1940s had some impact on school-sponsored programs became noticeable by the 1950s. Specifically, surveys reflected the transfer of sponsorship for children's sport programs from the schools to independent boys' work agencies. A National Recreation Association survey in 1950 of 304 departments throughout the United States indicated only 36 approved of high-level competition and championship play ("Competitive Athletics," 1951). The President's Committee on Interschool Competition in the Elementary School, representing AAHPER, found that 60 percent of the schools surveyed in 1950 had no competition for elementary-age children. Of the 40 percent that did sponsor some competitive sports, none had competition below the fourth-grade level (Wayman et al., 1950). The shift of support for children's programs was finally recognized and alluded to in a professional recreation journal in 1952, whereby the author successfully captured the nature of the contemporary scene.

> Although elementary schools continue to feel pressure to adopt the characteristics of the high school and college interscholastic sports program, most of the recent developments have taken place outside of the school system. . . . As a result, the recent development of "highly organized competitive athletics" for the elementary school age child has been sponsored largely by private independent groups not connected with the schools or the public recreation department. (National Recreation Congress, 1952, pp. 422–426)

Another survey (Scott, 1953) indicated the attitudes of adults toward athletic competition for young children. The results illustrated one of the major reasons that highly organized programs were growing rapidly outside of the educational realm. From a group of more than 1,000 respondents from seven states, which included parents, teachers, and administrators, the majority of all three groups were in favor of intensive competition. The parents were the most favorable, however, and within this group, the fathers were overwhelmingly supportive.[8] With this type of support from parents and even some school personnel, it was evident that professional physical education and recreation groups were competing against unfavorable odds.[9]

Boys' Work Groups Assume Leadership

Although organized sport competition at the elementary school level failed to gain support and therefore faltered after its seemingly robust beginnings during the first decades of the twentieth century, youth sport programs outside of the school grew rapidly in the number of total participants and in the variety of sports offered. With few exceptions, the stimuli behind these programs that arose all over the United States were parents and other interested adults associated with boys' work. Organizations identifying with the boys' work movement selected the promotion, sponsorship, and organization of sports as one of the best things they could do for children. To make children happy and to give them what they wanted became one of their major objectives. They progressed by paying little or no attention to the warnings from professional educators.

The boys' work movement had its beginnings in the last decade of the nineteenth century and resulted from efforts of concerned adults to improve the total environment for children. Citizens of the larger cities became greatly concerned with the effects of industrialization, urbanization, and immigration and, as a result of the general child study movement, were also beginning to realize the basic needs of children. Welfare and reform programs were therefore instituted to improve or alleviate such social problems as child labor, public health and sanitation, lack of wholesome play facilities, crime and delinquency, orphan and dependent children, and crowded housing. But the main factors that led adults to establish programs and organizations to aid the plight of the child were the increased amount of leisure and delinquency and a growing population of underprivileged and neglected children.[10] Leaders of the boys' work movement during the late nineteenth century explored the ideas of organizing boys into clubs and groups to better carry on training programs. These early programs were designed to occupy leisure time to keep the boys out of trouble, keep them off the streets, and evangelize them. Most of these early programs operated under the auspices of a religious education group or the social welfare program of agencies.[11] However, by the beginning of the twentieth century, the boys' work movement developed and achieved separate status from other welfare movements. This development represented the fact that at least a portion of American society had seen the need and value of special agencies to act as conservators and curators of child life.[12]

The use and encouragement of play, games, sports, and general recreational activities began quite early in the boys' work programs. As the emphasis moved from soul saving to one of boy guidance and concern for the "whole person" during the 1920s, organized sports became more and more popular as an acceptable method of filling leisure-time hours.[13] New organizations for boys came into existence as separate enterprises. They were recreational rather than evangelical in nature, primarily because of the character-building values thought to be inherent to play, games, and sport. The concepts of clean fun as a character builder and of play as creative education, rather than just something to keep boys out of trouble, led to the formation of more playgrounds, gymnasiums, swimming pools, and outdoor athletic fields. Accordingly, civic groups, fraternal orders, and businesses joined the ranks of established boys' work organizations that already included religious bodies, philanthropic groups, national and state governments, and general child welfare groups in sponsoring and promoting sporting activities for the younger set. The primary objective of the new sponsors was to use sport as a preventive measure for juvenile delinquency.[14]

During the 1920s and 1930s highly organized competitive sport programs for young boys began to be established outside the realm of the educational system by local groups representing the fundamental boys' work beliefs. As early as 1924 the Cincinnati Community Service started city baseball tournaments for boys under 13. Likewise, Milwaukee organized its "Stars of Yesterday" baseball leagues and began sponsoring a "Kid's Baseball School" in 1936. The *Los Angeles Times* conducted its Junior Pentathlon for the first time in 1928, the Southern California Tennis Association established its junior program two years later, and tackle football for boys under the age of 12 began in the Denver area in 1927 and in Philadelphia three years later. Two further developments that occurred in 1939, however, did more for the overall growth of this new trend in sport than the others.

The first development was an article entitled "*Life* Goes to a Kid's Football Game" that appeared in *Life* magazine. It concerned the Denver Young American League and included color photographs and descriptions depicting the values of such an activity. Themes such as nationalism, courage, character, the need for similar programs in other communities, and the disgrace of "turning yellow" were discussed in the article. The second major development in 1939 was the introduction of Little League Baseball in Williamsport, Pennsylvania. Formed by Carl Stotz, a local businessman, the organization grew from a few local teams at its inception to more than 300 leagues in 11 states by 1949. Part of Little League's success can also be linked to the publication of an article entitled "Small Boy's Dream Come True" in the *Saturday Evening Post* (Paxton, 1949). This article, like the *Life* article 10 years before, included beautiful colored photographs, proclaimed the values of such a program for small boys, and emphasized the rewards reaped by communities that had already established Little League teams. The author was correct in observing that "the Little League's chief mission in life is to give a lot of pleasure to a lot of little boys. With its realistic simulation of big-league playing conditions, with its cheering crowds, it is a small boy's baseball dream come true" (p. 140). From this point on, the "little league" concept spread to almost every sport on the American scene.

Interest in providing sporting competition for young children began to spread to a variety of other youth-related agencies after the 1940s. As continued emphasis was placed on providing fun and amusement for young boys and as organizations found ulterior motives for promoting sport competition, the sponsorship of children's sports began to come from previously unexpected sources. Nationally known business firms, professional sport organizations, Olympic committees, and colleges initiated particular aspects of sport sponsorship for young boys. Sponsorship came in the form of funds, facilities, workers, advertisements, and equipment. These new sponsors joined previously established sponsors such as civic groups, churches, community councils, local merchants, and some of the older youth membership organizations. They saw a chance to assist the development of young boys but, at the same time, realized that boys' sport programs could help them as well. This new sidelight to sponsorship, the idea of a "two-way street" or what could be termed a form of "ludic symbiosis" in this context, differed radically from the earlier voluntary groups' support and added the aspects of big business and more-pronounced competition to sport for young boys.

By the 1960s highly organized sport competition for preadolescents had grown to encompass millions of American boys. Little League Baseball, Pop Warner Football, and Biddy Basketball were joined on the national level by similar developments in other sports, such as Pee Wee Hockey and Little Britches Rodeo.[15] Most of these national sporting bodies had member teams and leagues throughout the United States, but the youthful participants in baseball, football, basketball, and other sports did not necessarily have to belong to one of the national controlling bodies. When this occurred, local boys' sports organizations were often just referred to as midget leagues, the "lollypop set," boys' leagues, youth leagues, junior leagues, small fry leagues, or tiny tot leagues. The important factor, however, was that regardless of title, sponsor, or organizational structure, young boys below the age of 12 were being introduced to highly organized competitive sports in just about every community in the United States.

As indicated, radical changes occurred in the sponsorship of boys' sports programs. By the 1960s the most prominent sponsors could be classified in six different categories: (a) private national sport bodies such as Little League Baseball; (b) youth-serving organizations composed of adult members such as the Jaycees; (c) youth membership organizations composed of child membership such as the YMCA; (d) youth sport development organizations such as Junior Golf; (e) quasi-commercial organizations like Ford's Punt, Pass and Kick; and (f) an individual or community like Jim's Small Fry's or Riverdale Junior Baseball. An analysis of each sponsor's stated objectives revealed the same idea of sport's inherent values that had existed since the turn of the century. Each sponsor claimed to support children's sport for one or more of the following reasons: physical fitness, citizenship, character, sportsmanship, leadership, fair play, good health, democratic living, and teamwork. It also was evident that a few of the sponsors took advantage of the "two-way-street" concept. Boys' sports were used as training grounds for future athletes, as methods to prevent juvenile delinquency, as proselytizing agents to attract new members, as methods of advertisement, as means of identification and glory, and as methods for direct financial gain.

Parents, too, began to get more deeply involved than ever before with the sports of their children. Eager mothers and fathers devoted more time to sports and actually began to take part in the sports themselves. Many reasons could be given to explain this increased interest of parents, but three major causes were believed to be the increasing awareness of the athlete as a viable professional endeavor, overly competitive mothers and fathers, and parents' desire of "sure victory" for their children. Earlier in the history of children's sports, parents were content to be only spectators, but the decades of the 1950s and 1960s became an era of parental entrance, with their child, into competition. Instances of parents constructing racers for the Soap Box Derby, fine-tuning engines for youthful go-cart drivers, and engineering new gear ratios for bike racers appeared as boys' sports became increasingly important to the entire family. This new emphasis placed on children's sport by the family unit, combined with the entrance of big business and other high-pressure tactics after the early 1950s, caused even the most avid sponsors to begin to take a serious look at what they had developed.

The literature after 1950 concerning highly organized competitive sports for young boys reflected the growing concern for the welfare of the young competitors.[16] Nationally circulated journals, magazines, and newspapers carried articles emphasizing the pros and cons of children's sport in an attempt to illustrate the current status of the ever-growing youth leagues and to present the most recent findings related to the subject. Similarly, those in favor of the highly competitive situations used the mass media to advertise the goodness and need for such programs and even went so far as to suggest new organizations in previously unchildlike sports such as yachting, motor boating, and airplane flying. Likewise, those strongly opposed to highly organized sports attacked their obvious detriments via the printed word. The issue became increasingly visible as the debate continued, but even in the 1970s, youth sport programs were showing no signs of decline. In fact, the decade of the 1970s ushered in a new and eager generation of youthful competitors.

Conclusions

The rise of highly organized sport competition for preadolescent boys was an important phase of the total involvement of Americans with sport and has blossomed into a new national sporting trend. Lowering the age for entrance into sport indicated the faith Americans had in it and reflected a desire to provide the young with something thought to be beneficial for their overall development. Besides illustrating the breadth and depth of the nation's involvement with sport, the guided entrance of children into sporting competition also influenced the overall growth of sport. Young children carried their interests and desires with them into adult life and subsequently passed them along to their own children. In addition, the joy, freeness, and innocence of the youthful competitors came to be seen as desirable characteristics of sport itself. These attributes were sought as highly desired traits by the adult population. The older portion of the population attached sport to the image of youth and consequently engaged in a variety of sports beyond the time when they normally would have ceased participation.

The provision of highly organized competitive sports for boys below the age of 12 and the accompanying introduction of more sporting opportunities and facilities for all young children was one of the most significant social and cultural events of recent times. It contributed an additional dimension to the age of childhood and marked the beginning of a new era in American sport. An analysis of the origins of this trend, however, is also important outside of its contributions to the realm of sport because the history of the developments in childhood is central to the study of overall social change and human behavior. The growth of sport for young boys illustrated a change in parental authority as well as an alteration in general child-rearing practices. The fact that sport teams were usually organized by age or weight groupings indicated the increased sensitivity to the various stages of childhood and became an important step in the growth of child welfare. Children's sport organizations led to changes in the American family structure and, in many instances, added a new aspect to the socialization of children. In addition, the sponsorship and use of sport by boys' work agencies contributed to the belief that Americans should organize the life and activities of their children. Finally, the degree to which children's sports became organized mirrored an often-proclaimed American characteristic of being overly regimented, businesslike, and competitive.

References

American Association for Health, Physical Education and Recreation and Committee on Athletic Competition for Children of Elementary and Junior High School Age. (1952). *Desirable athletic competition for children.* Washington, DC: Author.

American Association for Health, Physical Education and Recreation and the National Education Association. (1947). *Cardinal athletic principles.* Washington, DC: Author.

Competitive athletics for boys under twelve—Survey. (1951). *Recreation, 45,* 489–491.

DeGraff, H. O. (1933, March). Social factors in boys' work. *Association Boys' Work Journal,* p. 2.

Duncan, R. O. (1951). The growth and development approach. *Journal of Health, Physical Education and Recreation, 22,* 36–37.

Engle, W. L. (1919). Supervised amusement cuts juvenile crime by 96%. *American City, 20,* 515–517.

Holman, H. (1951). *Play ball: A study of Little League Baseball in operation.* Fresno, CA: Recreation Department.

Life goes to kid's football game. (1939, October). *Life,* pp. 90–93.

Lowman, C. L. (1947). The vulnerable age. *Journal of Health and Physical Education, 18,* 635; 693.

Mangold, G. B. (1924). *Problems of child welfare.* New York: Macmillan.

Mid-west district news. (1937). *Journal of Health and Physical Education, 8,* 382.

Moss, B., & Orion, W. H. (1939). The public school program in health, physical education, and recreation. *Journal of Health and Physical Education, 10,* 435–439; 494.

National Recreation Congress. (1952). Are highly competitive sports desirable for juniors? Conclusions from the committee on highly organized sports and athletics for boys twelve and under. *Recreation, 46,* 422–426.

North, C. C. (1931). *The community and social welfare.* New York: Recreation Department.

Paxton, H. T. (1949, May). Small boy's dream come true. *Saturday Evening Post,* pp. 26–27; 137–140.

Reckless, W. C., & Smith, M. (1932). *Juvenile delinquency.* New York: Recreation Department.

Recommendations from the Seattle convention workshop. (1947). *Journal of Health and Physical Education, 18,* 429–432; 556–557.

Schmidt, C. A. (1944). Elementary school physical education. *Journal of Health and Physical Education, 15,* 130–131, 161.

Scott, P. M. (1953). Attitudes toward athletic competition in elementary schools. *Research Quarterly, 24,* 352–361.

Shanas, E. (1942). *Recreation and delinquency.* Chicago: Recreation Commission.

Skinner, C. E. (1945). *Elementary educational psychology.* New York: Prentice-Hall.

Stone, W. L. (1931). *What is boys' work?* New York: Recreation Department.

Stone, W. L. (1932). *The place of activities in boys' work. Work with boys.* New York: Recreation Department.

Two important resolutions. (1938). *Journal of Health and Physical Education, 9,* 448–489.

Wayman, F., Hager, R., Hartwig, H., Houston, L., LaSalle, D., & McNeely, S. (1950). Report of the president's committee on interschool competition in the elementary school. *Journal of Health, Physical Education and Recreation, 21,* 279–280, 313–314.

Wickenden, E. (1960). Frontiers in voluntary welfare services. In E. Ginzberg (Ed.), *The nation's children: Vol. 3. Problems and prospects* (pp. 124–147). New York: Columbia University Press.

Notes

1. Highly organized competitive sports have been defined as: "any athletic activity which involves a considerable amount of the leisure time of the youngster in formalized practice, which encourages extensive attendance by adult spectators, which is limited to the outstanding players, and which involves the selection of winners on a state, regional, or national basis" (National Recreation Congress, 1952, p. 423).
2. This chapter is a revised and condensed version of an article titled "From the Cradle to the Playing Field: America's Emphasis on Highly Organized Competitive Sports for Preadolescent Boys," by J. W. Berryman, 1975, *Journal of Sport History, 2,* 112–131. The reader is directed to the original publication for a more-detailed account of the trends and factors under discussion as well as for supporting documentation.
3. By the close of the 1920s, sport had become quite popular in the United States. However, with few exceptions, organized sport competition was still for the middle-aged adult population, college students, and high school students in the upper grades. Organized competitive sport had not yet developed for the elementary school–aged population.
4. One person directly associated with the movement defined boys' work as "social engineering in the field of boyhood motivation . . . supervised leisure-time education, the purpose of which is social adjustment and creative living" (Stone, 1931, p. 28).
5. For a survey of common activities in elementary schools during this time see Schmidt (1944, p. 130).
6. Also see Lowman (1947, p. 635). A large percentage of orthopedists surveyed believed interscholastic competition should be discouraged for young boys because of its strenuous nature. They were particularly critical of swimming, tackle football, wrestling, and ice hockey.
7. They believed elementary schools should only provide intramural playdays, sportsdays, and informal games.
8. Similar results were found in a survey of parents having boys in Little League Baseball in Fresno, California, in 1951 (Holman, 1951). One hundred percent of the parents regarded the program as beneficial to their sons and repudiated the claims that competition was harmful physically, psychologically, or socially.
9. It should be noted that parents were very concerned that their sons excelled and held their own among the peer group. Sport competition offered a unique setting where young boys could be compared and evaluated with others of the same age.

10. Directly related to these developments were the play movement and the child welfare movement. The combination of objectives included in each of these two distinct aspects of the overall childhood reform movement assisted the development of organized sports and additional play facilities for young children.

11. It was realized early in boys' work that sport-related clubs and teams served as a better medium for organization than the earlier attempts at trying to reach large masses of boys at one time.

12. Basically the boys' work groups aided the overall society by protecting children through their dependency period, inducting children into the culture, and supplementing the family by providing for special needs and by sponsoring specific services. The work groups were committed to a specific social obligation toward children not yet accepted by the whole society. Consequently, boys' work agencies began to provide services in education, health, and recreation, all of which they believed could be improved by organized sport programs. See Mangold (1924) and Wickenden (1960).

13. Sport competition was believed to enhance personality adjustment and creative living in society. In addition, since boys' workers wanted to aid the transition from childhood to adulthood, they sponsored sport programs that combined association on a peer basis with adult leadership. See DeGraff (1933, p. 2) and Stone (1932, p. 5).

14. The belief that a boy busy with sports had little time to get into trouble influenced many organizations in local communities to begin sponsoring boys' sports. Psychological and sociological knowledge of the time indicated that problems of delinquency originated in early childhood and not during the actual time of delinquent acts. Therefore, it was deemed important to extend the age range lower for a positive delinquency prevention program. Civic clubs such as Rotary, Lions, Kiwanis, and Jaycees; fraternal orders like the Elks and Moose; and businesses such as Winchester, Curtis Publishing, General Electric, Pratt and Whitney, and John Wanamaker all turned to sport sponsorship in the interest of protecting young children from crime and providing them with wholesome alternatives for gang life in the streets. For more information see Engle (1919), North (1931), Reckless and Smith (1932), and Shanas (1942).

15. Some of the other popular children's sports were Midget Lacrosse, Junior Ski Jumping, Junior Nordic Skiing, National Junior Tennis League, Junior National Standard Racing, and the Junior Special Olympics for retarded children.

16. It is interesting to note that the *Readers' Guide to Periodical Literature* did not include a topical heading for "Sports for Children" until Volume 22 (March 1959–February 1961), p. 1564.

2

A HISTORY OF HIGHLY COMPETITIVE SPORT FOR AMERICAN CHILDREN

—David K. Wiggins

American children have always participated in their own play activities, games, and sports. Regardless of their economic station in life, living conditions, and physical abilities, children in this country carved out a world of sport that contributed to their overall growth as human beings while providing the sense of accomplishment and enjoyment necessary to be functioning members of society. Children of both sexes in such diverse settings as New York City, Puritan New England, southern slave communities, and western frontier towns organized sporting activities free from the surveillance of adults who did not exercise the same degree of control over young people as their contemporary counterparts. Marbles, crack-the-whip, capture-the-flag, soccer, variations of baseball, and a host of other games were played with unabated enthusiasm by children on city streets, urban sandlots, and open fields.

Children in this country could eventually choose between their own organized sports and those directed and controlled by adults. By the latter stages of the nineteenth century, adults were abandoning their traditional laissez-faire approach toward children's activities and establishing large-scale sport programs for America's youth (particularly boys). These initial programs came about largely through the efforts of the Young Men's Christian Association (YMCA). Established by evangelical Protestants in England in 1851 and transported to this country prior to the Civil War, the YMCA eventually responded to the precarious position of children in an increasingly industrialized American society by organizing sport leagues for boys and offering classes in physical culture.

By the beginning of the twentieth century various agencies—including playgrounds, schools, and national youth organizations—followed the YMCA's example and began sponsoring recreational activities and sport programs for children. These programs, while varying in both style and content, were part of the progressive era's effort to control the behavior and contribute to the moral development of children through organized play activities and sports administered by reform-minded adults. The public school athletic league and other reformist organizations established by various educators, recreation leaders, and philanthropists were intentionally designed to inculcate children with a particular set of values necessary to function properly in a democratic society.

The 1920s witnessed the emergence of children's sport programs that were decidedly different from those progressive reformers established. These programs, rather than ideologically based or intentionally reformist, were usually highly competitive and geared toward elite performers and championship play. Tellingly, the movement toward increased competitiveness drew heavy criticism from professional recreation leaders and physical educators who had previously been supporters of youth sport programs. The disenchantment of professional educators resulted in their eventual relinquishment of highly organized youth sport programs to various business firms, colleges, Olympic committees, professional sport organizations, and individual or community service groups. The withdrawal of professional educators' support from youth sport programs did not curb the debate over the value of highly competitive athletics for children. On the contrary, the last several decades have seen a continuing dialogue, centering on the negative effects or positive outgrowths of youth sport programs, among medical doctors, professional educators, and other sundry groups. This debate has been most vividly reflected in the founding of various youth sport institutes and coaching programs, development of policy statements and guidelines for those involved in children's sport, and the participation of academicians in various youth sport projects and research programs.

Christian Manliness and American Boys

In the mid–nineteenth century, American Protestants ignited a movement commonly known as Muscular Christianity. Alarmed by the debilitating effects of industrialization and other changes in American life, well-known clergymen and eastern intellectuals abandoned their traditional animosity toward vigorous physical activity and promoted the interconnectedness between sport and spiritual sacredness. Thomas Wentworth Higginson and other advocates of Christian manliness associated achievement with a vigorous childhood that stressed the Greek ideal of the harmonious development of mind, body, and spirit. It was imperative for "manly" youth to participate in sport while exercising Christian virtues and such character habits as self-control, candidness, and honesty (Lewis, 1966; Lucas, 1968; Rader, 1983).

The transmission of Christian manliness to American boys took place primarily through such well-known pieces of sports fiction as Thomas Hughes's *Tom Brown's School Days* (1857); G. W. Bankes's *A Day of My Life; or, Everyday Experiences at Eton* (1877); Bracebridge Heming's *Eton School Days* (1864); and Robert Grant's *Jack Hall, or The School Days of an American Boy* (1887). The YMCA, however, was the most important institution associated with the Muscular Christianity movement. Originally opposed to organized sport for children, the YMCA was luring more young men and boys into its program toward the latter years of the nineteenth century by establishing classes in gymnastics and promoting highly competitive athletics (Boyer, 1978; Forbush, 1901, 1904).

Although several people would be responsible for this transformation within the YMCA, it was Luther Gulick who spearheaded the organization's new interest in games and highly competitive sport. Born of missionary parents in Honolulu in 1865 and eventually both an instructor and superintendent of the Physical Training

Department at the YMCA Training School in Springfield, Massachusetts, Gulick was always committed to the basic tenets of Muscular Christianity and the compatibility between physical development and spiritual sacredness. Gulick's belief in Christian manliness was largely an outgrowth of the evolutionary theory of play he developed with his former mentor, G. Stanley Hall, the famous genetic psychologist from Clark University. The two men theorized that play activities of preadolescent children consisted of the same physical activities that had allowed primitive men and women to survive in a hostile environment. Such individual activities as running and hurling objects at targets were both relics of the struggle for survival and natural acts necessary for the physical and psychological development of young children. Older children's more-advanced games, such as football, basketball, and baseball, combined the earliest hunting instinct and the more recent instinct of cooperation while serving as the primary vehicle in developing moral character. Participation in team sports, therefore, provided an ideal opportunity for adults to develop in boys self-control, loyalty, obedience, selflessness, and other character traits rapidly vanishing from the increasingly industrialized American society (Dorgan, 1934; Forbush, 1901; Gerber, 1971; Gulick, 1898, 1899).

Gulick incorporated the new evolutionary theory of play in different ways at the YMCA Training School. He spearheaded the establishment of a graduate diploma in physical education. He also organized a sport program at the school for young men and adolescent boys. Perhaps most important, Gulick developed a pioneering course in the psychology of play, a class in which students were encouraged to create new games and sports appropriate for specific age groups (Dorgan, 1934; Forbush, 1901; Gerber, 1971).

Playgrounds, Sport, and Reform-Minded Adults

Gulick did not expend all his energy on the YMCA. He also contributed mightily, along with such other reform-minded adults as Joseph Lee, Henry Curtis, Jane Addams, and Clark Hetherington, to the playground movement in the early twentieth century. Resulting primarily from rapid urbanization and its attendant problems, the playground movement had as one of its primary purposes the moral development of children through sports. Progressive reformers, many of whom were officers in the Playground Association of America, considered organized play and sport a perfect medium for developing character among young people while socializing them into an increasingly complex industrialized society (Cavallo, 1981; Goodman, 1979; Hardy, 1982).

Progressive reformers involved in the playground movement recognized no ethnic boundaries, directing much of their efforts at immigrant children who inhabited America's inner cities. The same cannot be said for young girls. Progressive reformers were similar to many others in American society in that they held deep-seated stereotypical notions about the sexes, which greatly influenced the types of programs they established for girls. Although reformers viewed women as being in wretched health and in need of exercise, progressives promoted less competitive and more moderate sporting activities for girls because of their special emotional and physiological abilities. As Allen Guttmann (1988) has recently noted, reformers assumed that men and women were physiologically destined to play complementary social roles; accordingly, boys and girls had differing recreational needs.

The types of activities established for girls can be seen in the Public School Athletic League (PSAL). A massive sport program established in 1903 for New York City schoolchildren by Luther Gulick and other progressive reformers, the PSAL was designed to permit all schoolchildren an opportunity to participate in highly organized sport. The League had different forms of competition geared toward children of various age levels and athletic ability. In keeping with the beliefs of G. Stanley Hall, Luther Gulick, and other progressive reformers, the girls' branch of the PSAL provided a program that emphasized less strenuous group activities rather than highly competitive sports. Elementary-aged girls participated in informal games and walking events while high school girls in the program engaged in certain track and field events. Interschool athletic competitions were forbidden in the program (Jable, 1979).

Highly Competitive Sport Outside the Educational Domain

The sport programs established for children by progressive reformers were idealistic in nature and intentionally designed to influence social behavior and moral development. The same cannot be said of the highly competitive youth sport programs that emerged during the 1920s and 1930s. A result of both the continuing interest of adults in the welfare of children and increasing popularity of sport in American society, these programs were organized for boys only and usually involved elite championships, all-star play, and close parental involvement. Examples of these programs are many and varied. In 1924 the Cincinnati Community Service organized a Junior Baseball tournament for boys under age 13. The tournament involved 84 teams and received endorsement from Judge Kenesaw Mountain Landis, the Commissioner of Major League Baseball. In 1927 Denver organized a tackle football program for boys under age 12. The *Los Angeles Times* established its Junior Pentathlon program a year later. In 1930 Pop Warner began play in Philadelphia and the Catholic Youth Organization began its junior tennis program with sponsorship from the Southern California Tennis Association. The Milwaukee Recreation Department established its "Stars of Yesterday" baseball program in 1936 for boys under 15. Finally, in 1939 Carl Stotz founded his famous Little League Baseball program in Williamsport, Pennsylvania (Berryman, 1975; Cloyd, 1952; Monroe, 1946; Paxton, 1949).

No sooner had these programs been established when professional educators, particularly those from the health, physical education, and recreation fields, began criticizing and passing resolutions condemning highly competitive sports for children. Their concerns usually revolved around questions of notoriety, commercialism, intensity of competition, elite championship play, and emotional and physiological damage incurred by young athletes. For example, in 1938 the American Association for Health, Physical Education and Recreation passed a resolution at its national convention disapproving of youth sport programs. The Society of State Directors of Physical and Health Education made official announcements in both 1938 and 1946 denouncing highly competitive sport in elementary and junior high schools. In 1947

AAHPER issued another resolution condemning interscholastic sports for children below the ninth grade and also made a joint policy statement with the National Federation of High School Athletic Associations (NFHSAA) arguing for the development of intramural programs at the elementary school level. The following year the Joint Committee on Athletic Competition for Children of Elementary and Junior High School Age—an organization made up of representatives from AAHPER and other groups—recommended the abolishment of highly competitive youth sport programs. In the early 1950s similar proclamations were made by such groups as the National Recreation Congress, National Conference on Physical Education for Children of Elementary School Age, and National Conference of Program Planning in Games and Sport for Boys of School Age (AAHPER, 1938, 1947, 1952; Lowman, 1947; Moss & Orion, 1939; National Recreation Congress, 1952; Wayman, 1950).

The policy statements of professional educators ultimately contributed to the elimination of children's interschool athletic competitions. Professionals did not stop, however, the growth of already existing youth sport programs or the creation of new ones outside the educational setting. By the latter half of the 1960s, children's highly competitive sport programs were being sponsored by such organizations as business firms, religious groups, community service organizations, Olympic committees, colleges, and professional sport organizations (Berryman, 1975).

The continuing support of youth sport programs outside the educational setting resulted from a number of interrelated factors. One of the primary reasons was the lasting belief of parents that children benefited in a number of different ways from participation in highly competitive sport programs. Although cognizant of some of the negatives associated with youth sport programs, the large majority of parents believed that highly competitive athletics contributed to the fitness level, overall character development, and sportsmanship of children (Scott, 1953; Seymour, 1956; Skubic, 1955, 1956). Another factor in the continued growth of youth sport programs was the increased media coverage and adulation enjoyed by outstanding athletes, and American society's obsession with highly competitive sport. Children, and their parents, were aware of this adulation and the logical consequence was an early involvement in sport that might ultimately lead to their own fame and fortune.

Girls, Youth Sport, and the Quest for Equality

The growth of highly competitive youth sport programs during the middle decades of the twentieth century was a phenomenon involving boys only. Girls were not allowed to participate. Largely because of the continuing belief about their emotional and physiological weaknesses, girls were not given an opportunity to exhibit their athletic skills in organized settings. About the only options available to athletically gifted girls were participation with friends in informal games or school "play days" that stressed recreational activities rather than highly competitive sports.

In the early 1970s sweeping changes took place in American society that would lead to more equitable treatment for girls and women involved in sport. The passage of the Equal Rights Amendment, Title IX, and other federal and state legislation combined with changing social forces that resulted in the elimination of various forms of sexual discrimination in sport at different levels of competition. For instance, in 1971 New York City named its first woman golf pro. In 1972 Michigan appointed Jan Magee as the state's first woman official in football. In the same year, the Eastern Athletic Conference ruled that women could participate on men's teams. In 1973 the United States Open Tennis Championship became the first major tournament to provide equal prize money for men and women. The California Interscholastic Federation ruled in 1973 that all high school sport teams could be coeducational (Gerber et al., 1974).

The elimination of sexual discrimination would also filter down to the lower levels of competition involving young girls. The most noteworthy case involved Little League Baseball, one of the older and most-hallowed youth sport programs. In May 1973 Jenny Fuller, a young ballplayer from California, wrote a letter to President Richard Nixon lamenting the fact she was not allowed to participate on her local Little League team because of gender. The Office of Civil Rights responded to Fuller by explaining that steps were being taken to handle such discriminatory practices. Coinciding with Fuller's letter were a number of unsuccessful lawsuits brought against the National Little League by girls who had been denied an opportunity to participate for their local teams. The strongest of these suits was filed by a young girl named Carolyn King and the Ypsilanti, Michigan, American League and the city of Ypsilanti. This particular suit, like so many of those involving Little League Baseball and questions of sexual discrimination, centered on local and national jurisdiction. After King beat out more than 100 boys for a position as center fielder, the Ypsilanti City Council ordered the local League to either let her participate or suffer the loss of city financial aid, staff, and facilities. The local League acceded to the Council's order. The National Little League responded, in turn, by revoking the local League's charter (Jennings, 1981).

The Carolyn King affair in Ypsilanti preceded by a couple of months the sexual discrimination case that would ultimately lead to the desegregation of Little League Baseball. Maria Pepe, a young player from Hoboken, New Jersey, experienced the same pangs of discrimination many other girls suffered when she was denied the opportunity to participate on her local Little League team. The uniqueness of this case, however, is that it would culminate in an investigation by the New Jersey Division of Civil Rights and eventually in the integration of Little League Baseball. The Civil Rights Division, at the request of the Essex Chapter of the National Organization for Women (NOW), conducted an investigation in November 1973 on behalf of Pepe and a number of other girls who wanted to participate in Little League Baseball. During six days of deliberation, the National Little League defended its segregationist policies by having expert witnesses present evidence confirming that highly competitive sport was harmful to girls both emotionally and physiologically. The key witness for the National Little League was Creighton Hale, who was executive vice-president of the organization and an exercise physiologist. Hale cited a number of studies claiming that girls had slower reaction time and weaker bones than those of boys and, therefore, were unsuited for vigorous competitive sport. Hale also argued that girls could harm their breasts while participating in competitive athletics (Jennings, 1981).

The Civil Rights Division countered with its own expert testimony. Psychiatrist Antonia Giancotti claimed that mutual participation in sport by boys and girls contributed positively to the development of mental health. Joseph Torg, a pediatric-orthopedic surgeon, contended that the bone strength of preadolescent girls was actually greater than that of boys of comparable age. Torg also criticized Creighton Hale for basing his testimony on studies that examined adult cadavers rather than those of children (Jennings, 1981).

The testimony given by Torg and others proved crucial in the decision handed down by Sylvia Pressler, the Division's hearing officer. Pressler concluded that differences in athletic performance between girls and boys under the age of 12 resulted from an individual rather than "sexual class basis." Most important, she ruled that because Little League Baseball was given public financial support and used public accommodations, "it was indeed subject to state and federal laws preventing discrimination" (Jennings, 1981, p. 85).

Little League Baseball challenged Pressler's ruling by appealing to New Jersey's superior court in March 1974. Little League argued that its federal charter officially prohibited girls from participation and that New Jersey law allowed only boys on its local teams. Little League Baseball's arguments proved futile and ultimately unconvincing. The state's superior court ruled on March 29, 1974, that a local league chartered by Little League, Inc. was not exempt from federal legislation barring sexual discrimination. The conflict was finally put to rest in December 1974 when Congress amended the National Little League Charter, allowing girls as well as boys to participate (Jennings, 1981).

The decision Congress handed down did not translate into immediate desegregation of leagues across the country or stop people from expressing their opposition to girls' participation in highly competitive sport programs. Increasingly, however, girls found their way onto both integrated and nonintegrated teams in a variety of different sports at various levels of competition. The last two decades have seen a growth in the number of girls participating in youth sport programs sponsored by such diverse organizations as the United States Olympic Development Committee, Amateur Athletic Union, and the American Alliance for Health, Physical Education, Recreation and Dance (Figler & Whitaker, 1991).

Academicians, Professional Educators, and the Youth Sport Phenomenon

The desegregation of youth sport programs would coincide with an outpouring of interest in children's sport on the part of academicians and professional educators. The expansion of youth sport programs, combined with recognition of the importance of sport as a social institution, caused educators and scholars from such disciplinary areas as sport psychology and sport sociology to consider the implications of children's participation in highly competitive athletics. One of the most visible indicators of this interest was the increasing number of conferences that included posters, verbal presentations, and symposiums devoted specifically to youth sport participation. Such national organizations as the North American Society for the

Psychology of Sport and Physical Activity (NASPSPA), the North American Society for Sport Sociology (NASSS), the National Association for Physical Education in Higher Education (NAPEHE), and the American Alliance for Health, Physical Education, Recreation and Dance (AAHPERD) began including sessions at their annual conferences devoted to some aspect of children's involvement in sport. The 1989 NASPSPA Conference, as just one example, devoted a session to "children in sport and physical activity." Included in the session were presentations on topics ranging from the relationship of parental attitudes and levels of intrinsic motivation in young athletes to reasons for dropping out of youth sport programs (NASPSPA, 1989).

Even more significant were the organization of conferences and workshops devoted exclusively to children's participation in sport. In 1973 a conference was held at Queens University in Canada entitled "The Child in Sport and Physical Activity." Organized by John Albinson and George Andrew, two physical educators from the host university, the conference took a multidimensional approach in that it included papers from such disciplinary areas as motor learning, exercise physiology, motor development, psychology of sport, sports medicine, and sport sociology (1976). Four years later a similar conference was organized by Frank Smoll and Ronald Smith at the University of Washington entitled "Contemporary Research on Youth Sports." The conference was unique for a number of reasons, including the fact it was jointly sponsored and partly financed by the Safeco Insurance Company and involved all data-based presentations rather than speculative or opinion-oriented studies. Although business organizations had always provided financial support to youth sport programs, very seldom had a company such as Safeco helped fund a research conference devoted to the subject. The conference presentations touched on various topics dealing with youth sport participation and included as participants such well-known academicians as Jerry Thomas, Glyn Roberts, Lawrence Rarick, Tara Scanlan, Robert Malina, and Michael Passer (Smoll & Smith, 1978).

In 1985 the Big Ten Committee on Institutional Cooperation held a symposium at Michigan State University entitled "Effects of Competitive Sports on Children and Youth." Conceived of by leaders of the Youth Sport Institute at Michigan State and supported by several of the university's academic units, this symposium brought together noted scholars from several disciplines to share their research and knowledge relating to the effects of highly competitive sport on children (Brown & Branta, 1988). In the same year, the American Orthopaedic Society for Sports Medicine (AOSSM) held a workshop in Indianapolis, Indiana, entitled "Strength Training for the Prepubescent Athlete." This workshop, which included as participants physicians, physiologists, and other sports medicine professionals, focused on the ramifications of youth strength-training programs from a variety of disciplinary perspectives (Cahill, 1988). In 1990 the AOSSM held yet another workshop in Peoria, Illinois, addressing intensive training and participation in youth sports. Perhaps broader in scope and certainly different in format from its symposium three years earlier, this workshop included as participants some of the most noted scholars in the country who analyzed the various risks and benefits of youth sports from psychological, sociological, physiological, and clinical viewpoints. Participants in the workshop also made recommendations intended to maximize the positive contributions and minimize the negative outcomes of highly competitive youth sport programs (Cahill & Pearl, 1993).

Another indication of professional interest in youth sports was the establishment of guidelines and conduction of large-scale legislative studies. In 1976 AAHPERD led the drive toward healthier and more educationally sound youth sport programs by establishing the National Association for Sport and Physical Education Youth Sports Task Force. Made up of experts from the recreation, medical, and physical education professions, the task force analyzed the effects of children's participation in highly competitive sport programs and provided suggestions as to how those programs could be more satisfying and beneficial. Perhaps the most notable and far-reaching accomplishment of the task force was the drafting of a "Bill of Rights for Young Athletes," a document that attempts to guarantee, among other things, that children are given the right to have fun, enjoy equitable treatment, and share in the administration of youth sport programs (Martens & Seefeldt, 1979).

Larger in scope than AAHPERD's Task Force was Michigan's Joint Legislation Study Committee on Youth Sport Programs. An outgrowth of the state's concern about the educational value of youth sport participation, this special six-member committee conducted, in collaboration with several Michigan universities, a longitudinal study assessing the impact of highly competitive sports on the development of children. The results of the study, which were announced in November 1978, indicated that enjoyment and the chance to increase skill level were children's primary motivations for participation in youth sport programs. Coaches, administrators, and other support personnel indicated that their involvement in youth sports came about either because of their children's participation in the program or because they provided special skills needed by the particular organization (JLS, 1976, 1978a, 1978b).

Among the most significant outgrowths of the longitudinal study was the establishment of the Youth Sport Institute (YSI) at Michigan State University in 1978. Under the leadership of Vern Seefeldt, the institute was founded to ensure that children benefited positively from participation in youth sport programs. In an effort to achieve that goal, the institute has conducted scientific research on children's sport participation; provided in-service education, clinics, and workshops for youth sport administrators; and disseminated educational materials to parents, coaches, and officials involved in children's competitive sport programs (JLS, 1976, 1978a, 1978b).

The Youth Sport Institute at Michigan State set the stage for similar types of programs both inside and outside the formal educational setting. The National Council of Youth Sports Directors (NCYSD) was established in 1979 to secure mutual cooperation among executives of youth sport programs. Originally sponsored in cooperation with the Athletic Institute, the NCYSD included on its membership roll such groups as the American Amateur Baseball Congress, American Youth Soccer Organization, Babe Ruth Baseball, National Federation of State High School Associations, National Junior Tennis League, Pop Warner Football, U.S.A. Wrestling, U.S. Field Hockey Association, and YMCA (NCYSD, n.d.). The North American Youth Sport Institute (NAYSI) was organized the same year as the NCYSD in Kernersville, North Carolina. The NAYSI took on a number of projects, including the sponsorship of research studies and clinics for youth sport coaches (Cox, 1982). The National Youth Sports Coaches Association (NYSCA), the officially endorsed program of the National Recreation and Parks Association, was organized in 1981 to train youth sport coaches, educate the general public about youth sport programs, and conduct research on all aspects of youth sports (NYSCA, n.d.). Finally, in 1981 Rainer Martens, a well-known sport psychologist and now head of Human Kinetics Publishers, officially founded the American Coaching Effectiveness Program (ACEP). Certainly one of the most extensive coaching education programs in the country, ACEP offers courses that provide both the theoretical underpinnings and knowledge of sport techniques and fundamentals (ACEP, 1984).

Informing Parents, Participants, and the Public through Publications and Research

A growth in publications and research studies dealing with various aspects of highly competitive sports for children coincided with the establishment of institutes and coaching programs. Included in these studies and publications were a plethora of popular essays on youth sports written by well-known sportswriters, Little League parents, and famous professional athletes. These articles, which usually centered on questions concerning the value of youth sport programs, have appeared in such popular magazines as *Ladies Home Journal, The Atlantic Monthly, U.S. News and World Report, Today's Health, Sports Illustrated, Changing Times, Better Homes and Gardens, Look, Life,* and *New York Times Magazine* (Feller, 1956; Roberts, 1975; Tarkenton, 1970; Underwood, 1975).

Just as informative as the aforementioned essays were several reminiscences and popular books written on various aspects of youth sport programs. Catherine and Loren Broadus, parents of three former Little League players, describe the problems associated with youth sport programs in their book *Laughing and Crying with Little League* (1972). Al Rosen, a former major league player, provides a personal view of Little League Baseball in his book *Baseball and Your Boy* (1967). Rosen argues, among other things, that Little League Baseball can be a very positive experience for children who have supportive parents and enthusiastic as well as competent coaches. Emily Greenspan provides an insightful analysis of highly competitive youth sport programs in her book, *Little Winners: Inside the World of the Child Sports Star* (1983). She describes in detail the trials and tribulations of young athletes, including the effects of sport participation on family relationships. Martin Ralbovsky, a writer for the *New York Times,* provides a provocative oral history of the Schenectady, New York, Little League champions of 1954 in his book, *Destiny's Darlings* (1974). Ralbovsky's story of the Schenectady Club, which was based on interviews with nine players and the manager of the team 20 years after they captured the championship, was a mixture of positive reminiscences and lasting disillusionment. Larry Yablonsky and Jonathon Brower provide a journalistic summary of a Little League program in California in their 1979 book, *The Little League Game.* The authors suggest that changes should be made in Little League, including restrictions on the number of innings pitched by one player, elimination of scorebooks, and players' selection of coaches.

The more popular literature on children's sport was counterbalanced by a large body of publications emanating from previously mentioned conferences, professional organizations, institutes, and coaching education programs. For instance, John Albinson and George Andrew took seven papers from the conference they organized at Queens University in 1973 and edited a book entitled *Child in Sport and Physical Activity* (1976). In a similar vein, Frank Smoll and Ronald Smith published a collection of papers from their 1977 youth sport conference at the University of Washington. Entitled *Psychological Perspectives in Youth Sports* (1978), the book includes essays on everything from "Social Learning of Violence in Minor Hockey" to "Children's Assignment of Responsibility for Winning and Losing." Rainer Martens and Vern Seefeldt summarized the results of AAHPERD's 1976 Youth Sports Task Force in a book entitled *Guidelines for Children's Sports* (1979). Michigan State's Youth Sport Institute has put together an impressive list of titles, including Daniel Gould's *Motivating Young Athletes* (1980); Vern Seefeldt, Frank Smoll, Ronald Smith, and Daniel Gould's *A Winning Philosophy for Youth Sports Programs* (1981); and Frank Smoll and Ronald Smith's *Improving Relationship Skills in Youth Sport Coaches* (1979). One of the first youth coaching manuals published by a national association was Jerry Thomas's *Youth Sports Guide for Coaches and Parents* (1977). Published by AAHPERD, the manual discusses such topics as instructional strategies, motivating young athletes, psychological issues, physiological development, and philosophy of winning and losing. In 1981 Rainer Martens, Robert Christina, John Harvey, and Brian Sharkey came out with their *Coaching Young Athletes,* a book that served as the sports medicine and science resource book for ACEP. The following year Richard Cox edited another AAHPERD publication on youth sport entitled *Educating Youth Sports Coaches: Solutions to a National Dilemma* (1982).

Maureen Weiss and Daniel Gould (1986) provided an international perspective on youth sport participation with their edited proceedings of the 1984 Olympic Scientific Congress titled *Sport for Children and Youths.* The text, which included as contributors a number of well-known scholars from around the world, covered such topics as game modification, perceptions of stress, and injuries in youth sports. Eugene Brown and Crystal Branta (1988) edited the papers from the 1985 Big Ten Conference on Youth Sport at Michigan State in a book entitled *Competitive Sports for Children and Youth: An Overview of Research and Issues.* Included in the book are chapters dealing with such topics as psychological stress, physiological characteristics, strength training, and body composition among young athletes. Finally, Bernard Cahill and Arthur Pearl edited the papers from the 1990 youth sport conference organized by the American Orthopaedic Society for Sports Medicine (AOSSM) in Peoria, Illinois. Entitled *Intensive Participation in Children's Sports* (1993), the book includes eight chapters and topics ranging from competitive stress and burnout among young athletes to pathoanatomic change in youth sport participants.

A number of other specialized monographs have provided data and much needed insights into various aspects of children's highly competitive sport programs. These works, while varying in style and format, generally take a multidisciplinary approach to the study of youth sports by employing different methodologies and asking a host of questions. Terry Orlick and Cal Botterill analyze the importance of athletic competition for young children in their 1975 book *Every Kid Can Win.* The authors provide a number of practical suggestions for adults interested in changing the structure of organized games. Thomas Tutko and William Bruns provide a critique of sport programs, with special emphasis on youth sports, in their 1976 book *Winning Is Everything and Other American Myths.* In 1978 Rainer Martens came out with his well-known anthology, *Joy and Sadness in Children's Sports.* The book consists of 38 articles from both popular and scholarly sources and a number of practical applications drawn by Martens. Frank Smoll, Richard Magill, and Michael Ash provide a close look at youth sports from a variety of different perspectives in their 1988 book, *Children in Sport.* A compilation of 22 essays written by some of the best-known sport studies scholars in the country, the book includes topics ranging from the growth and development of young athletes to family influences in sport socialization of children. A similar type of publication is Daniel Gould and Maureen Weiss's 1987 *Advances in Pediatric Sport Sciences.* The second volume in a series by Human Kinetics Publishers, the book includes as contributors such noted academicians as Jay Coakley, Thelma Horn, Shirl Hoffman, Marjorie Woollacott, and Brenda Bredemeier. Perhaps more than any other work on the subject, the book integrates the scholarly literature from several behavioral science disciplines dealing with sport participation of children.

Providing additional insights into highly competitive children's sports are surveys and textbooks from the sport studies and exercise science fields. Sport sociology surveys perhaps serve as the best examples among this genre; virtually all of them include a chapter or section on some aspect of children's highly competitive sport programs. Jay Coakley, for instance, takes an interesting look at children's sport participation in his well-known text, *Sport in Society: Issues and Controversies* (1990). Coakley discusses, among other things, the differences between informal games and adult-directed sport programs for children, possible reasons for "dropping out" of youth sport programs, and the concept of idiocultures as described by Gary Fine (1987) and other academicians. Howard Nixon discusses such items as adult values in youth sports, the success ethic in "Little Leaguism," and girls' participation in competitive sport in his 1984 survey, *Sport and the American Dream.* Wilbert Leonard examined the emphasis on winning, elimination from participation, levels of maturity, influence of adults, and psychological ramifications of youth sport participation in his 1988 text, *A Sociological Perspective of Sport.* In their 1991 survey, *Sport & Play in American Life: A Textbook in the Sociology of Sport,* Stephen Figler and Gail Whitaker analyze the advantages and disadvantages of youth sports, alternative models for children's sports, and a host of other issues. Stanley Eitzen and George Sage examine the socialization process, sports alternatives, and other concerns in their 1991 text, *Sociology of North American Sport.*

Serving as theoretical underpinnings for the aforementioned works are a plethora of quantitative and qualitative research studies on youth sports published in academic journals and other outlets representing various disciplinary areas. Although defying easy classification, these studies fall most neatly into the psychological, sociological, physiological, anthropological, and motor development domains. Within these domains, the studies are further delimited to such topics as moral growth through physical activity, children and the sport socialization process, attrition in children's sport, motor skill performance in children, gender differences in sport participation of children, influence of coaching behavior on the psychological development of children, physiological impact of intensive training on young athletes, and self-esteem and achievement in children's sport. Examples of frequently cited research studies are the following: Heyward Nash, 1987, "Elite Child-Athletes: How Much Does Victory Cost?" *The Physician and Sportsmedicine, 15,* 129–133; Tara Scanlan and Rebecca Lewthwaite, 1986, "Social Psychological Aspects of Competition for Male Youth Sport Participants: IV: Predictors of Enjoyment," *Journal of Sport Psychology, 8,* 25–35; Maureen Weiss, Diane Weise, and Kimberly Klint, 1989, "Head Over Heels with Success: The Relationship between Self-Efficacy and Performance in Competitive Youth Gymnastics," *Journal of Sport and Exercise Psychology, 11,* 444–451; Thelma Horn, 1985, "Coaches Feedback and Changes in Children's Perceptions of Their Physical Competence," *Journal of Educational Psychology, 77,* 174–186; Janet Harris, 1984, "Interpreting Youth Baseball: Players' Understandings of Fun and Excitement, Danger and Boredom," *Research Quarterly for Exercise and Sport, 55,* 379–382; Gary Fine, 1985, "Team Sports, Seasonal Histories, Significant Events: Little League Baseball and the Creation of Collective Meaning," *Sociology of Sport Journal, 2,* 219–313; Diane Gill, John Gross, and Sharon Huddleston, 1983, "Participation Motivation in Youth Sports," *International Journal of Sport Psychology, 14,* 1–14; Damon Burton and Rainer Martens, 1986, "Pinned by Their Own Goals: An Exploratory Investigation into Why Kids Drop Out of Wrestling," *Journal of Sport Psychology, 8,* 183–197; Walter Rejeski, Charles Darracott, and Sally Hutslar, 1979, "Pygmalion in Youth Sports: A Field Study," *Journal of Sport Psychology, 1,* 311–319; Michael Passer, 1983, "Fear of Failure, Fear of Evaluation, Perceived Competence and Self-Esteem in Competitive Trait Anxious Children," *Journal of Sport Psychology, 5,* 172–188; and Joan Duda, 1987, "Toward a Developmental Theory of Children's Motivation in Sport," *Journal of Sport Psychology, 9,* 130–145.

Summary

The involvement of children in highly competitive sport has, as we have seen, changed dramatically over the course of American history. Initially participants in games and sports among themselves, American children could eventually choose between informal games and adult-directed sport programs both within and outside the educational domain. The organization of adult-directed sport programs resulted from a combination of factors, including concerns about the health and moral development of American children. Professional educators, however, would eventually relinquish any control they had over youth sport programs to nonschool agencies and business organizations because of their belief about the harmful effects of intense competition on children. Relinquishing control of youth sport programs to other organizations only seemed to intensify the interest of professional educators and academicians in children's sport participation. This was most evident in the establishment of youth sport institutes and coaching clinics as well as the publication of a myriad of studies dealing with highly competitive sport programs for children.

References

Albinson, J. G., & Andrew, G. M. (Eds.). (1976). *Child in sport and physical activity.* Baltimore: University Park Press.

American Association for Health, Physical Education and Recreation. (1938). Two important resolutions. *Journal of Health and Physical Education, 9,* 488–489.

———. (1947). *Cardinal athletic principles.* Washington, DC: Author and National Education Association.

———. (1952). *Desirable athletic competition for children.* Washington, DC: Author.

American Coaching Effectiveness Program. (1984). *Brochure.* Champaign, IL: Human Kinetics.

Bankes, G. W. (1877). *A day of my life; or, everyday experiences at Eton.* London: Stanley Paul.

Berryman, J. W. (1975). From the cradle to the playing field: America's emphasis on highly competitive sports for pre-adolescent boys. *Journal of Sport History, 2,* 112–131.

Boyer, P. (1978). *Urban masses and moral order in America, 1820–1920.* Cambridge, MA: Harvard University Press.

Broadus, C., & Broadus, L. (1972). *Laughing and crying with Little League.* New York: Harper and Row.

Brown, E. W., & Branta, C. F. (1988). *Competitive sports for children and youth: An overview of research and issues.* Champaign, IL: Human Kinetics.

Burton, D., & Martens, R. (1986). Pinned by their own goals: An exploratory investigation into why kids drop out of wrestling. *Journal of Sport Psychology, 8,* 183–197.

Cahill, B. R. (Ed.). (1988). *Proceedings of the conference on strength training and the prepubescent.* Chicago: American Orthopaedic Society for Sports Medicine.

Cahill, B. R., & Pearl, A. J. (1993). *Intensive participation in children's sports.* Champaign, IL: Human Kinetics.

Cavallo, D. (1981). *Muscles and morals: Organized playgrounds and urban reform 1880–1920.* Philadelphia: University of Pennsylvania Press.

Cloyd, J. (1952). Gangway for the mighty midgets. *American Magazine, 154,* 28–29, 83–85.

Coakley, J. J. (1990). *Sport in society: Issues and controversies.* St. Louis: Times Mirror/Mosby.

Cox, R. (Ed.). (1982). *Educating youth sport coaches: Solutions to a national dilemma.* Reston, VA: American Alliance for Health, Physical Education, Recreation and Dance.

Dorgan, E. J. (1934). *Luther Halsey Gulick, 1865–1918.* New York: Teachers College, Columbia University.

Duda, J. L. (1987). Toward a developmental theory of children's motivation in sport. *Journal of Sport Psychology, 9,* 130–145.

Eitzen, D. S., & Sage, G. H. (1993). *Sociology of North American sport.* Dubuque, IA: Brown & Benchmark.

Feller, B. (1956, August). Don't knock Little Leaguers. *Colliers,* pp. 78–81.

Figler, S. K., & Whitaker, G. (1991). *Sport & play in American life.* Dubuque, IA: Wm. C. Brown.

Fine, G. A. (1985). Team sports, seasonal histories, significant events: Little League Baseball and the creation of collective meaning. *Sociology of Sport Journal, 2,* 219–233.

———. (1987). *With the boys: Little League Baseball and preadolescent culture.* Chicago: The University of Chicago Press.

Forbush, W. B. (1901). *The boy problem: A study in social pedagogy.* Boston: Pilgrim Press.

———. (1904). Can the Y.M.C.A. do all the street boys' work? *Work with Boys, 4,* 182.

Gerber, E. W. (1971). *Innovators and institutions in physical education.* Philadelphia: Lea & Febiger.

Gerber, E. W., Felshin, J., Berlin, P., & Wyrick, W. (1974). *The American woman in sport.* Reading, MA: Addison-Wesley.

Gill, D. L., Gross, J. B., & Huddleston, S. (1983). Participation motivation in youth sports. *International Journal of Sport Psychology, 14,* 1–14.

Goodman, C. (1979). *Choosing sides: Playground and street life on the lower east side.* New York: Schocken Books.

Gould, D. (1980). *Motivating young athletes.* East Lansing, MI: Youth Sport Institute.

Gould, D., & Weiss, M. (Eds.). (1987). *Advances in pediatric sport sciences* (Vol. 2). Champaign, IL: Human Kinetics.

Grant, R. (1887). *Jack Hall, or the school days of an American boy.* New York: Scribner.

Greenspan, E. (1983). *Little winners: Inside the world of the child sports star.* Boston: Little, Brown.

Gulick, L. H. (1898). Physical aspects of group games. *Popular Science Monthly, 53,* 793–805.

———. (1899). Psychological, pedagogical, and religious aspects of group games. *Pedagogical Seminary, 6,* 144.

Guttmann, A. (1988). *A whole new ball game: An interpretation of American sports.* Chapel Hill: The University of North Carolina Press.

Hardy, S. (1982). *How Boston played: Sport, recreation, and community.* Boston: Northeastern University Press.

Harris, J. (1984). Interpreting youth baseball: Players' understanding of fun and excitement, danger and boredom. *Research Quarterly for Exercise and Sport, 55,* 379–382.

Hemings, B. (1864). *Eton school days.* London: Hutchinson.

Horn, T. (1985). Coaches feedback and changes in children's perceptions of their physical competence. *Journal of Educational Psychology, 77,* 174–186.

Hughes, T. (1857). *Tom Brown's school days.* New York: Harper and Brothers.

Jable, J. T. (1979). The public school athletic league of New York City: Organized athletics for city school children, 1903–1914. In W. M. Ladd & A. Lumpkin (Eds.), *Sport in American education: History and perspective* (pp. ix–18). Washington, DC: American Alliance for Health, Physical Education, Recreation and Dance.

Jennings, S. E. (1981). As American as hot dogs, apple pie and Chevrolet: The desegregation of Little League Baseball. *Journal of American Culture, 4,* 81–91.

Joint Legislative Study Committee. (1976). *Joint legislative study on youth sports: Agency-sponsored sports—phase I.* Lansing, MI: State of Michigan.

———. (1978a). *Joint legislative study on youth sports: Agency-sponsored sports: Agency—Phase II.* Lansing, MI: State of Michigan.

———. (1978b). *Joint legislative study on youth sports: Agency-sponsored sports: Agency—Phase III.* Lansing, MI: State of Michigan.

Leonard, W. M. (1988). *A sociological perspective of sport.* New York: Macmillan.

Lewis, G. (1966). The Muscular Christianity movement. *Journal of Health, Physical Education and Recreation, 37,* 27–28.

Lowman, C. L. (1947). The vulnerable age. *Journal of Health and Physical Education, 18,* 635, 693.

Lucas, J. A. (1968). A prelude to the rise of sport: Ante-bellum America, 1850–1860. *Quest, 2,* 50–57.

Martens, R. (1978). *Joy and sadness in children's sports.* Champaign, IL: Human Kinetics.

Martens, R., Christina, R. W., Harvey, J. S., Jr., & Sharkey, B. J. (Eds.). (1981). *Coaching young athletes.* Champaign, IL: Human Kinetics.

Martens, R., & Seefeldt, V. (1979). *Guidelines for children's sports.* Washington, DC: American Alliance for Health, Physical Education, Recreation and Dance.

Monroe, K. (1946). Hothouse for tennis champs. *Readers Digest, 49,* 22.

Moss, B., & Orion, W. H. (1939). The public school programs in health, physical education, and recreation. *Journal of Health and Physical Education, 10,* 435–439, 494.

Nash, H. L. (1987). Elite child-athletes: How much does victory cost? *The Physician and Sportsmedicine, 15,* 129–133.

National Council of Youth Sports Directors. (n.d.). *Brochure.*

National Recreation Congress. (1952). Are highly competitive sports desirable for juniors? *Recreation, 46,* 422–426.

National Youth Sport Coaches Association. (n.d.). *Brochure.* West Palm Beach, FL: Author.

Nixon, H. L. (1984). *Sport and the American dream.* New York: Leisure Press.

North American Society for the Psychology of Sport and Physical Activity. (1989). *Program bulletin.* Kent, OH: Kent State University.

Orlick, T., & Botterill, C. (1975). *Every kid can win.* Chicago: Nelson-Hall.

Passer, M. W. (1983). Fear of failure, fear of evaluation, perceived competence and self-esteem in competitive trait anxious children. *Journal of Sport Psychology, 5,* 172–188.

Paxton, H. T. (1949). Small boy's dreams come true. *Saturday Evening Post, 221,* 26–27, 137–140.

Rader, B. (1983). *American sports: From the age of folk games to the age of spectators.* Englewood Cliffs, NJ: Prentice-Hall.

Ralbovsky, M. (1974). *Destiny's darlings.* New York: Hawthorne Books.

Rejeski, W., Darracott, C., & Hutslar, S. (1979). Pygmalion in youth sports: A field study. *Journal of Sport Psychology, 1,* 311–319.

Roberts, R. (1975, July). Strike out Little League. *Newsweek,* p. 11.

Rosen, A. (1967). *Baseball and your boy.* New York: Funk and Wagnall.

Scanlan, T. K., & Lewthwaite, R. (1986). Social psychological aspects of competition for male youth sport participants: IV: Predictors of enjoyment. *Journal of Sport Psychology, 8,* 25–35.

Scott, P. (1953). Attitudes toward athletic competition in elementary schools. *Research Quarterly, 4,* 352–361.

Seefeldt, V., Smoll, F. L., Smith, R. E., & Gould, D. (1981). *A winning philosophy for youth sports programs.* East Lansing, MI: Youth Sport Institute.

Seymour, E. (1956). Comparative behavior characteristics of participant boys in Little League Baseball. *Research Quarterly, 27,* 338–346.

Skubic, E. (1955). Emotional responses of boys to Little League and Middle League competitive baseball. *Research Quarterly, 26,* 342–352.

———. (1956). Studies of Little League and Middle League baseball. *Research Quarterly, 27,* 97–110.

Smoll, F. L., Magill, R. A., & Ash, M. J. (1988). *Children in sport* (3rd ed.). Champaign, IL: Human Kinetics.

Smoll, F. L., & Smith, R. E. (1978). *Psychological perspectives in youth sports.* Washington, DC: Hemisphere.

———. (1979). *Improving relationship skills in youth sport coaches.* East Lansing, MI: Youth Sport Institute.

Tarkenton, F. (1970, October). Don't let your son play smallfry football. *Ladies Home Journal,* pp. 146–147.

Thomas, J. (Ed.). (1977). *Youth sports guide for coaches and parents.* Washington, DC: National Association for Sport and Physical Education.

Tutko, T., & Bruns, W. (1976). *Winning is everything and other American myths.* New York: Macmillan.

Underwood, J. (1975). Taking the fun out of games. *Sports Illustrated, 43,* 86–98.

Wayman, F. (1950). Report of the president's committee on interschool competition in the elementary school. *Journal of Health, Physical Education, and Recreation, 21,* 279–280, 313–314.

Weiss, M. R., & Gould, D. (Eds.). (1986). *The 1984 Olympic scientific congress: Vol. 10. Sport for children and youths.* Champaign, IL: Human Kinetics.

Weiss, M. R., Weise, D., & Klint, K. (1989). Head over heels with success: The relationship between self-efficacy and performance in competitive youth gymnastics. *Journal of Sport and Exercise Psychology, 11,* 444–451.

Yablonsky, L., & Brower, J. (1979). *The Little League game.* New York: Times Books.

PATTERNS OF PARTICIPATION AND ATTRITION IN AMERICAN AGENCY-SPONSORED YOUTH SPORTS

—Martha E. Ewing and Vern Seefeldt

Many benefits can be gained from participation in sports. For children, one of the main benefits may be to learn sports skills. With school systems struggling to survive economically, the reduction or elimination of physical education programs and interscholastic sports is a common occurrence. Under these circumstances, youth sport programs may be asked to provide even more of the instruction of sports skills in the future. In addition, personal characteristics, such as moral development (Chambers, 1991), perceptions of competence (Feltz & Ewing, 1987; Feltz & Petlichkoff, 1983), and self-esteem (Weiss, 1987) may be enhanced in children through sport participation. Evidence is also mounting that academic achievement can be fostered through sport participation (Landers et al., 1978; Spady, 1970).

The importance of sport within the American culture is evident from the number of groups involved in the business of providing sport opportunities for youth. Program opportunities can be divided into six categories: agency-sponsored programs, national youth service organizations, club sports, recreation programs, intramural programs, and interscholastic programs. Of these six categories, four are community based and two are promoted through the schools. For this chapter, however, the discussion of participation and attrition will be limited to patterns that exist within the two larger categories of school-sponsored and nonschool-sponsored sports. This limitation exists because few researchers differentiate nonschool-sponsored sports into more discrete categories.

When viewing trends in patterns of participation and attrition, the assumption often is that 100 percent of the youth in a community should be participating in a program. Obviously, many factors preclude all youth from participating, such as direct and indirect costs, practices and games held at times that are inconvenient to the prospective participants, and diverse interests of the youth. Therefore, this chapter will add the use of "free time" to the discussion, since many youth will find ways within their local neighborhoods to engage in sport and physical activity that are not organized or supervised by adults. The inclusion of "free-play" patterns of participation will provide a more comprehensive understanding of sport in the development of our youth.

Finally, the discussion of patterns of participation and attrition divides youth into pertinent subgroups. This avoids the pitfall of assuming that a singular sport experience or pattern of participation exists for all youth. For this chapter, the participation patterns will be presented for three groups of youth: boys and girls; youth of color (i.e., African American, Asian American, Native American, European American, and Hispanic American); and youth ages 10 to 18.

Rates of Participation in Youth Sports

Participation in organized sport has become a common rite of childhood in the United States. Since the introduction of highly competitive sports in the 1940s, organized athletics have grown so rapidly that nearly every community offers one or more forms of competitive athletics to its youth, and virtually every secondary school and many middle and junior high schools provide interscholastic athletic programs (National Federation of State High School Associations, 1990). The popularity of organized athletics for children and youth has resulted in estimates of participation ranging from 20 million (Michigan Joint Legislative Study on Youth Sports, 1978) to 35 million (Martens, 1986). Unfortunately, there is no precise account of the number of youth who participate in sport programs prior to the age of 12 or 13, the typical age youth enter interscholastic athletic programs. The inability to establish an accurate count of sport participants is one of the major drawbacks to tracking participation and attrition patterns within the United States.

The enumeration of participants is more accurate at the high school level, where the National Federation of State High School Associations has tracked the total number of participants each year. Unfortunately, youth are likely to participate in more than one sport, which confounds the accounting of participants. Interscholastic athletic competition includes the organized interschool sport participation of boys and girls at the middle school and junior and senior high school levels. A national study of eighth-grade students found that 48 percent participated in varsity sports, and 43 percent participated in intramural sports (National Education Longitudinal Study, 1988). According to the National Federation of State High School Associations (NFSHSA), which governs interscholastic competition within the United States, more than 10 million athletes are involved in interscholastic competition (NFSHSA, 1990). Table 3.1 provides information about the extent of involvement by boys and girls in the nation's interscholastic athletic programs. One of the shortcomings of the data presented in table 3.1 is the number of youth who participate in more than one sport. For many youth at the middle, junior, and senior high school levels, multiple sport participation is the norm. Often youth will participate in three to four sports each year. To illustrate this redundancy even more, the census data for 1990 reported that there were 13,237,000 youth between the ages of 14 and 17. Based on these data, 75.5 percent of all high school youth are participating in interscholastic sports. These data are incongruent with the percentages reported to be participating at the eighth-grade level.

A second problem exists in the reporting of participants when the numbers of youth participating in nonschool-sponsored sports are compared to census data.

TABLE 3.1 Projected School-Age Populations for Specific Years, Ages 5, 6, 5–13 and 14–17

Year	5-year-olds	6-year-olds	5–13-year-olds	14–17-year-olds
1985	3,548,000	3,428,000	30,000,000	14,865,000
1986	3,605,000	3,555,000	30,351,000	14,797,000
1987	3,651,000	3,612,000	30,823,000	14,467,000
1988	3,668,000	3,657,000	31,374,000	13,970,000
1989	3,604,000	3,674,000	31,793,000	13,476,000
1990	3,736,000	3,609,000	32,393,000	13,237,000
1991	3,719,000	3,741,000	32,827,000	13,334,000
1992	3,724,000	3,724,000	33,243,000	13,538,000
1993	3,734,000	3,729,000	33,549,000	13,774,000
1994	3,745,000	3,739,000	33,738,000	14,187,000
1995	3,730,000	3,750,000	33,864,000	14,510,000

Source: National Center for Education Statistics, U.S. Department of Education, December, 1989.

Seefeldt, Ewing, and Walk (1992) surveyed representatives from many national governing agencies, each of whom reported a general trend of increased participation in their programs during the last five years. These reports are surprising in light of the data presented in table 3.2, which indicate that the population of youth in the age group of 5 to 17 years has shown a steady decline since 1970 in proportion to some other age groups in the United States (U.S. Department of Commerce, 1985). These data suggest that any increases in youth sport participation are due to changes within a relatively stable pool. Potential explanations are that the increase is due to (1) a shift from participation in the less competitive recreational programs to the agency-sponsored programs that have national affiliations, (2) there is greater recruitment and involvement of the younger-aged clients, or (3) program sponsors are providing greater accessibility to youth sports, resulting in the participation of a higher proportion of the potential enrollees (Seefeldt, Ewing, & Walk, 1992). Although some truth may exist in each of the potential explanations, nonschool sport programs may also be accommodating greater numbers, especially those younger children within the 4- to 10-year-old age categories who were not included in the survey. Certainly a more accurate means of recording participation data is required to accurately assess participation rates.

Patterns of Participation in Youth Sports

The patterns of participation that will be discussed in the following pages are taken from data that were collected in a national survey of approximately 8,000 youth. The survey was conducted in 1988 by the Institute for the Study of Youth Sports with

TABLE 3.2 Total United States Population in Age Categories, by Percentage

Age Category	Percentage			
	1970	1975	1980	1984
Under 5 years	8.4	7.5	7.2	7.5
5–17 years	25.7	23.6	20.7	19.0
18–24 years	12.1	13.0	13.3	12.2
25–34 years	12.3	14.6	16.5	17.4
65 or over	9.8	10.5	11.3	11.8
Median age, all citizens	27.9	28.7	30.0	31.2

Source: U.S. Department of Commerce, Bureau of the Census, June, 1985.

funding support from the Athletic Footwear Council of the Sporting Goods Manufacturers Association. The youth ranged in age from 10 to 18. Fifty-one percent of the sample were girls and 49 percent were boys. Data were collected from intact classrooms randomly selected from 17 regional sites around the country. The data that are presented represent only a part of an extensive questionnaire that assessed participation and attrition patterns, reasons for participating, reasons for dropping out of sports and suggested changes that dropouts would make in sport that, if implemented, would cause them to stay involved in sport.

Participation Patterns in Nonschool-Sponsored Sport Programs

The assessment of participation by youth in nonschool sport programs can be accomplished in several ways. The best way to address participation patterns would be through longitudinal studies, which would involve tracking a number of youth through their childhood and adolescent years in different types of communities. Due to time and expense, however, no such studies have been reported in the literature. A more practical approach has been to assess the participation of youth of different ages and to compile from these data a pattern of participation that represents what youth of different ages are doing. With replication, the picture should become more stable and predictable. Certainly, shifts in a culture over time will alter the picture. One such shift within our culture has been the passage of Title IX, which resulted in a dramatic increase in the number of girls and women who participate in sport. Future researchers who track the patterns of participation should document the social and economic situation that exists at the time the data are collected to enhance an understanding of data that have been gathered at different times.

One such influence in our society at the time the following data were collected was the increasing popularity of soccer. A second factor that should be kept in mind was the economic depression that our country was experiencing. In addition, several myths existed that related to participation patterns of certain races within our country; for example, very few African Americans would be involved in expensive sports

TABLE 3.3 Participation in the 10 Most Popular Nonschool Sports for Boys and Girls

		Nonschool Sports		
Boys	**%**		**Girls**	**%**
Baseball	31.1		Swimming	26.7
Basketball	30.9		Softball	26.6
Football	27.3		Basketball	22.1
Soccer	22.7		Volleyball	21.2
Swimming	17.8		Gymnastics	17.7
Bowling	14.9		Soccer	17.4
Tennis	12.2		Tennis	16.4
Wrestling	11.7		Bowling	16.4
Flag Football	11.7		Baseball	12.5
Track	11.4		Skiing	10.8

such as gymnastics, tennis, or ice hockey. These factors and others may influence the number of participants as well as the type of sport in which they are engaged.

Of the approximately 8,000 youth surveyed (Ewing & Seefeldt, 1989), 55 percent reported having participated in a nonschool sport activity. The vast majority of the youth reported participating on a team sport. As was expected, most youth reported participating on more than one sport team. Table 3.3 presents the most popular nonschool sports for boys and girls. Boys participated most frequently in baseball (31%), basketball (31%), football (27%), and soccer (23%); the girls' greatest participation was in swimming (27%), softball (27%), basketball (22%), and volleyball (21%). Although the overall participation of boys was slightly higher than that of the girls, this difference was due to the boys' higher participation levels in the four top-ranked sports. Six of the ten most popular nonschool sports were common to boys and girls. Three of the sports that were popular with boys—football, flag football, and wrestling—are not offered to girls. Although girls did report playing in most of these sports, society's view of a girl's desire to be a member of these teams provides a sufficient barrier to most girls whose interests and skills would lead to enjoyment of these sports.

Sport participation by race was similar in some sports (baseball, basketball) but varied greatly in others such as tennis, golf, skiing, and swimming (see table 3.4). Of particular note was the low percentage of African American and Hispanic American youth involved in soccer and bowling compared to Caucasian, Asian American, and Native American youth. Although public facilities have made these sports available to many Americans, the reason that African American and Hispanic American youth did not participate at similar rates to other ethnic groups is unclear.

As was mentioned earlier, when reviewing participation data by race it is important to remember that not all minority youth come from poor, inner-city

TABLE 3.4 Percentage of Individuals, by Race, Who Joined or Planned to Join a Selected Nonschool Sport Team during the 1987–1988 School Year

	Caucasian	African American	Hispanic American	Asian American	Native American
Baseball	24.4	21.5	16.2	17.6	27.7
Basketball	29.0	37.6	14.1	20.3	27.7
Football	17.6	21.1	12.1	14.4	20.8
Swimming	27.3	20.7	9.9	25.7	28.3
Softball	21.3	22.5	10.0	15.0	23.1
Soccer	25.2	12.8	10.9	33.7	23.7
Volleyball	17.5	20.6	10.1	26.7	21.4
Gymnastics	13.4	14.1	7.3	12.3	16.8
Bowling	19.5	13.6	6.2	20.3	18.5
Tennis	17.1	12.7	6.6	33.2	13.3

communities. This is evident, for example, from the number of African American youth who reported participating in figure skating (6.0%) and gymnastics (14.1%). These are two of the more expensive sports; yet, the percentage of African American youth participants was comparable to the percentage of youth in other racial groups. Overall, however, African American and Hispanic American youth were underrepresented in individual sports such as bowling, golf, ice hockey, swimming, and tennis. These findings have several potential explanations. Perhaps the most plausible explanation is that for most African Americans, few role models exist in these sports, which may dissuade youth from wanting to participate in them. Another explanation that most of us would like to discount is that prejudice still exists among owners of the facilities that offer these sport opportunities, including public facilities, that discourage youth from becoming involved. This prejudice may take the subtle form of simply not informing certain members of the community of opportunities that exist. Future research should examine this pattern of selective participation in greater detail.

To understand participation patterns of youth by age, it is necessary to look at patterns by sport. Table 3.5 presents participation rates of youth ages 10 to 18 in the most popular sports for boys and girls. The basic trend is to have a higher rate of participation at age 10 and a rather steady decline in the participation rate from 10 to 18 years of age. The most dramatic display of this decline can be seen with baseball and swimming, where approximately 42 percent of the 10-year-olds reported participating on a nonschool sport team compared with 12.0 percent of the 18-year-olds. These data suggest a slightly different participation pattern to that reported by Sapp and Haubenstricker (1978), who noted that the decline in participation rates of the youth in Michigan was highest for children between the ages of 11 and 13 years. However, Sapp and Haubenstricker's data were obtained in 1976 and the difference may be attributed to a shift in the age at which competition began then as compared with the data gathered 10 years later.

TABLE 3.5 Percentage of Individuals, by Chronological Age, Who Joined or Planned to Join Selected Nonschool Sport Teams during the 1987–1988 School Year

	Chronological Age								
	10	11	12	13	14	15	16	17	18
Baseball	42.7	30.7	26.6	28.1	20.3	18.7	17.0	14.0	12.5
Basketball	40.5	33.4	31.5	30.5	27.2	25.8	25.2	20.5	17.8
Football	25.6	23.0	21.0	18.5	15.7	17.3	14.3	11.2	11.2
Swimming	41.6	32.2	27.3	26.2	21.3	20.8	19.6	16.0	12.1
Softball	26.9	21.7	20.2	22.5	20.6	19.7	19.9	15.9	11.2
Soccer	38.5	35.6	30.0	25.0	18.5	15.6	11.4	9.2	11.0
Volleyball	20.9	21.0	18.8	17.3	18.0	17.3	14.0	15.8	9.3
Gymnastics	25.3	20.3	15.1	17.9	11.1	9.2	6.3	5.2	3.3
Bowling	24.4	24.3	14.7	18.7	13.7	15.3	15.2	12.9	10.6
Tennis	16.7	22.2	15.2	18.9	14.6	14.4	13.1	11.2	7.8

The decline in nonschool-sponsored sport participation may reflect a lack of emphasis on older youth in these programs (most community and agency-sponsored programs are offered for youth 6 to 12) or the increased popularity of competitive opportunities provided by the scholastic sport programs. Certainly the interaction of school-sponsored and nonschool-sponsored sport programs needs further investigation. Perhaps the same youth are being served by both types of programs, rather than the needs of a larger number of youth being served with the different programs. Nonschool sport programs for youth 12 to 18 years of age may serve youth better by reducing the emphasis on elite competitors and focusing more on an intramural or adult recreation philosophy.

Participation Patterns in School-Sponsored Sport Programs

Perhaps one of the most dramatic findings in the school-sponsored sport participation rates was that the percentage of participants was reduced by approximately one-half of those who played nonschool sports. The reduction in participation applied to both boys and girls. This reduction may be attributable to the fact that most schools offer one team per grade (particularly during the middle school or junior high school years) and only one or two teams during the high school years. Thus, opportunities for sport participation are greatly reduced for youth when they enter the middle school and junior and senior high schools. Although there has been an increase of participation in interscholastic sports for girls over the past decade (NFSHSA, 1990), the number of boys participating continues to exceed the number of girls. Table 3.6 presents the sport participation rates for the 10 most popular sports by gender. The most popular sports for boys included football, basketball, track and field, and baseball. For the girls, the

TABLE 3.6 Percentage of Participation in the 10 Most Popular Interscholastic Sports for Boys and Girls during the 1987–1988 School Year

Interscholastic Sports

Boys	%	Girls	%
Football	22.7	Track & Field	12.3
Basketball	16.4	Basketball	12.2
Track & Field	15.5	Softball	10.9
Baseball	14.8	Volleyball	9.5
Soccer	9.5	Soccer	6.8
Gymnastics	6.6	Swimming	6.4
Tennis	6.4	Tennis	6.1
Cross Country	6.1	Cross Country	5.9
Skiing	5.4	Skiing	4.6
Flag Football	5.1	Baseball	1.6

TABLE 3.7 Percentage of Individuals, by Race, Who Joined or Planned to Join a Selected School Sport Team during the 1987–1988 School Year

	Caucasian	African American	Hispanic American	Asian American	Native American
Baseball	9.0	13.0	9.0	5.9	6.9
Basketball	13.9	26.0	7.3	14.4	12.1
Football	11.5	18.8	8.9	5.3	12.1
Track & Field	14.2	8.8	8.5	15.0	19.1
Softball	7.3	10.2	3.7	10.7	5.8
Soccer	8.7	6.9	5.3	22.5	6.9
Volleyball	8.0	9.3	6.3	18.2	7.5
Gymnastics	4.4	6.5	2.2	7.0	9.8
Swimming	5.6	7.0	3.1	6.4	9.2
Tennis	5.6	8.4	4.9	17.6	4.0

most popular sports were track and field, basketball, softball, and volleyball. Of the 10 most popular sports for both boys and girls, one-half were team sports.

Participation in school-sponsored sports by race revealed that Asian American and African American students participated to a greater extent, proportionately, than the Caucasian, Hispanic American, or Native American students. The most notable

TABLE 3.8 Percentage of Individuals, by Chronological Age, Who Joined or Planned to Join Selected School Sport Teams during the 1987–1988 School Year

	Chronological Age						
	12	13	14	15	16	17	18
Baseball	5.8	14.3	13.0	14.4	11.7	11.0	12.6
Basketball	14.6	23.7	25.9	22.1	16.0	10.9	11.0
Track & Field	10.5	24.0	20.9	20.6	17.6	14.0	14.3
Swimming	4.8	12.2	7.9	7.5	6.4	5.1	6.1
Softball	5.3	12.3	12.4	11.1	8.9	7.9	4.1
Soccer	9.1	14.3	13.0	11.6	7.2	6.9	9.9
Volleyball	10.8	15.1	13.7	10.2	6.7	6.3	7.6
Gymnastics	7.9	13.4	5.4	4.3	2.4	3.2	3.2
Football	6.1	14.1	15.4	20.7	17.2	16.8	14.5
Tennis	5.1	12.2	8.0	8.3	9.0	6.2	6.3

pattern among the data is the relatively large proportion of African American students (26%) who reported participating in basketball. (See table 3.7.)

The greatest percentage of participation in school sports was at 13, 14, and 15 years of age with a gradual reduction in percentage by age thereafter (see table 3.8). The availability of more opportunities through larger team rosters at the junior high and freshman levels may be one reason for the apparent attrition at the older ages. The highly competitive nature of many high school sport experiences may also dissuade moderately skilled junior and senior students from competing for positions on the teams.

Basketball was the most popular school-sponsored sport at almost all age levels. Participation in track and field, which can accommodate large numbers of participants, also ranked consistently high for all age levels. Tackle football presented an interesting pattern, with an increase in participation rates from 12 through 15 years and a decline occurring from ages 16 through 18. Paradoxically, the participation rates in football, where larger numbers of students can be accommodated, was lower than in basketball, where a very limited number of students are selected for a team because of the limitations imposed by team size. The difference in participation rates may suggest that more schools offer basketball than offer football. Certainly, talking to high school students about their choice of sports and the experiences they have as members of these various sports would clarify some of the confusion presented by the participation rates.

Participation Patterns in "Free-Play" Sport Activities

A less traditional view of sport participation patterns is to view what youth do in their unstructured, or free, time. The decision to participate in sport at this time may be the

TABLE 3.9 Sports Children Do in Their Free Time, by Chronological Age (Data from Total Sample)

	Chronological Age									Mean Percentage
	10	11	12	13	14	15	16	17	18	
Archery	8.4	7.6	7.0	5.3	5.6	5.9	4.9	6.5	6.9	6.2
Baseball	28.6	27.5	26.0	25.0	20.4	18.9	20.3	18.0	16.4	22.2
Basketball	29.7	35.0	34.5	34.7	30.0	27.7	28.6	26.3	24.9	30.2
Bowling	19.6	28.2	20.9	18.0	16.3	17.8	20.7	21.8	23.0	20.7
Cross Country	8.6	6.9	9.0	5.5	5.4	5.6	5.0	3.8	5.8	6.1
Field Hockey	5.1	4.6	4.2	2.2	2.3	2.6	1.3	1.2	2.6	2.7
Figure Skating	11.0	13.4	7.9	5.8	6.8	5.5	5.6	6.4	3.3	7.5
Flag Football	10.6	11.5	11.0	9.6	8.8	7.7	11.4	10.2	10.8	9.9
Tackle Football	18.3	24.9	23.2	18.8	17.8	17.7	17.3	18.3	17.7	19.2
Golf	11.9	16.2	12.0	7.9	7.7	8.6	7.7	8.9	6.7	9.9
Gymnastics	16.1	18.8	13.4	11.2	9.6	7.5	8.2	5.1	5.2	10.5
Ice Hockey	3.5	3.6	2.7	2.7	1.9	2.7	3.0	2.5	3.0	2.8
Lacrosse	2.9	3.5	3.1	1.7	2.8	2.9	3.4	2.6	2.6	2.9
Skiing	12.3	16.0	11.2	10.3	11.2	11.6	12.1	16.3	10.6	12.4
Soccer	26.9	33.1	26.8	23.4	18.4	16.1	15.2	11.9	14.1	20.8
Softball	20.7	19.3	20.4	19.4	21.5	19.8	21.7	20.7	17.7	20.0
Swimming	33.3	38.2	33.0	26.7	28.4	24.2	30.8	26.3	24.2	29.4
Tennis	13.4	22.7	16.2	15.8	16.7	14.8	18.3	16.8	14.1	17.1
Track & Field	10.4	11.7	9.5	9.4	6.6	9.2	8.8	7.5	6.5	8.8
Volleyball	20.9	22.8	21.6	18.4	22.3	19.8	21.6	21.2	17.8	21.0
Wrestling	11.0	13.9	12.3	8.7	8.0	8.3	9.6	5.7	1.8	9.5
Other	17.8	19.7	14.1	10.4	9.4	11.2	12.6	11.8	10.4	11.5

truest representation of the value that this society holds for sport activities. On the other hand, many changes in our society over the past few years may be detrimental to youth engaging in sport activities during their free time. For example, neighborhoods and community parks have become less safe, so parents may be less likely to allow children to spend time outside in pickup games.

The most popular sports to participate in during free time were basketball and swimming. Table 3.9 presents the participation rates of youth ages 10 to 18, as well as the average percentage of participants across ages. One of the interesting differences in the data between sport participation in one's free time and in organized non-school participation patterns is the increase in participation in virtually every sport

TABLE 3.10 Sports Children Do in Their Free Time, by Race

	Caucasian	African American	Hispanic American	Asian American	Native American
Archery	7.0	2.8	4.8	5.4	9.8
Baseball	22.9	15.7	27.5	20.3	19.7
Basketball	31.7	27.7	28.6	27.3	27.2
Bowling	22.6	15.7	18.4	20.3	15.0
Cross Country	6.5	3.6	4.9	10.2	9.8
Field Hockey	2.6	1.7	3.2	5.9	2.3
Figure Skating	8.0	5.3	6.0	12.8	4.6
Flag Football	9.3	9.8	13.6	11.8	13.3
Tackle Football	19.6	16.3	21.7	10.7	25.4
Golf	11.9	3.8	6.9	11.2	8.1
Gymnastics	11.2	10.2	7.6	7.5	12.1
Ice Hockey	3.5	0.8	1.8	3.7	1.2
Lacrosse	3.3	1.1	1.6	5.3	2.9
Skiing	16.3	2.9	4.8	8.6	8.7
Soccer	22.7	10.6	21.3	27.8	20.2
Softball	19.7	19.2	23.7	15.0	19.7
Swimming	32.6	19.7	26.1	30.5	28.9
Tennis	18.3	9.9	16.6	29.9	11.0
Track & Field	8.1	12.1	8.7	7.0	10.4
Volleyball	20.0	19.1	26.9	24.6	26.0
Wrestling	8.8	9.1	14.1	6.4	12.1
Other	15.0	5.5	10.5	6.9	12.2

from age 10 to age 11 during the free-time patterns. Age 11 represents the zenith of sport participation during a child's free time with a steady decline in participation from 11 to 18 years of age. In most sports, participation remains higher during one's free time than it is in nonschool-sponsored sports. This trend is stable across both team and individual sports, which may challenge the popular notion among physical educators that more individual sports skills should be taught during middle school and junior and senior high school to prepare youth to engage in active leisure pursuits during adulthood.

When viewed by race (see table 3.10), some interesting differences emerge in participation patterns during free time. Only basketball and gymnastics have comparable participation rates for all races (less than 5% difference). Basketball is the most popular free-time sport among all races. Some interesting differences emerge when viewed by specific sport. Figures 3.1 to 3.5 present the participation rates for three

FIGURE 3.1
Leisure sport participation
in baseball, by race.

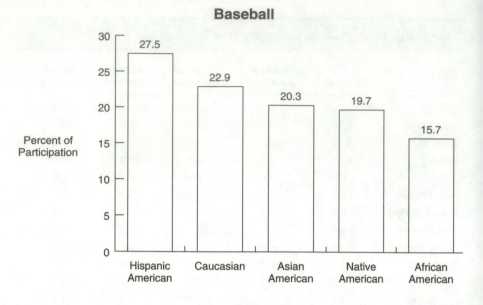

Baseball

FIGURE 3.2
Leisure sport participation
in soccer, by race.

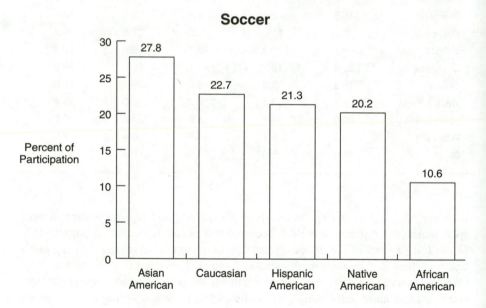

Soccer

team sports (baseball, soccer, and tackle football) and two individual sports (tennis and golf). These sports were selected to present the different patterns that emerge when race is a consideration. Too many times we have ignored race and assumed that all youth participate similarly. These data reveal the fallacy in this assumption. Why these differences in participation patterns exist remains a question to be addressed.

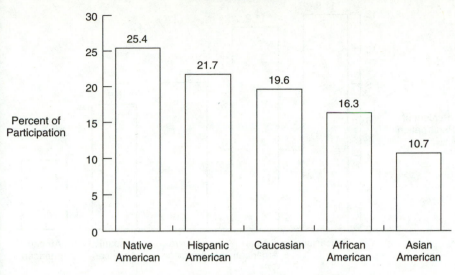

Tackle Football

FIGURE 3.3
Leisure sport participation in tackle football, by race.

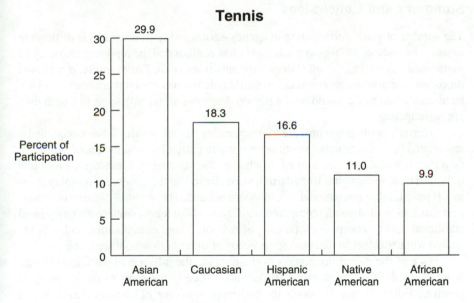

Tennis

FIGURE 3.4
Leisure sport participation in tennis, by race.

Additional factors that must be considered when trying to understand why these differing patterns exist are gender and economic status. These factors are best viewed as interactions rather than variables in isolation. Suffice it to say that youth of color make different choices than Caucasians (with the exception of basketball) as to which sport they will engage in during their free time.

FIGURE 3.5
Leisure sport participation
in golf, by race.

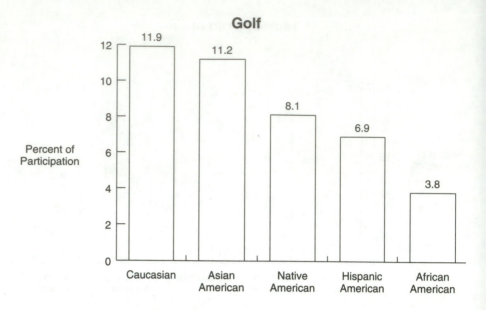

Summary and Conclusions

The number of youth participating in agency-sponsored sport programs is difficult to assess. The issue of multisport participants has confounded the reporting accuracy of participants as well as the number of dropouts from sport. For example, if a person drops out of one sport but continues to participate in one or two others, we would not be as concerned as we would be if a person drops out of the only sport in which they are participating.

Current sport programs are not appealing to all youth. What needs to be researched further is whether youth are not participating because the opportunities to be a member of a team are limited or whether the offering of competitive programs only is discouraging youth from participation. Based on the results of free-play sport involvement, more recreational offerings are needed. The attrition patterns also suggest that less-skilled youth (compared with their school team counterparts) may need additional sport opportunities outside of school. Thus, communities and schools should work together to meet the sport needs of older high school students.

One of the disturbing aspects of the data are the differential participation patterns of youth of different races. Basketball is clearly the sport of choice of most youth regardless of race. However, the underrepresentation of Hispanic Americans in all sports is disturbing and needs further study—particularly when this is the fastest-growing minority in the United States.

The participation pattern for females has become more comparable to those of males since the passage of Title IX. Girls and boys reported greater participation in team sports than individual sports, which may reflect both the economic demands associated with individual sports and that more team sport opportunities are offered in both school and nonschool situations.

References

Chambers, S. T. (1991). Factors affecting elementary school students' participation in sports. *The Elementary School Journal, 91*(5), 413–419.

Ewing, M. E., & Seefeldt, V. (1989). *Participation and attrition patterns in American agency-sponsored and interscholastic sports: An executive summary.* Final Report. North Palm Beach, FL: Sporting Goods Manufacturers Association.

Feltz, D. L., & Ewing, M. E. (1987). Psychological characteristics of elite young athletes. *Medicine and Science in Sports and Exercise, 19*(5), S98–S105.

Feltz, D. L., & Petlichkoff, L. (1983). Perceived competence among interscholastic sport participants and dropouts. *Canadian Journal of Applied Sport Sciences, 8,* 231–235.

Landers, D. M., Feltz, D. L., Obermeier, G. E., & Brouse, T. R. (1978). Socialization via interscholastic athletics: Its effects on educational attainment. *Research Quarterly, 49,* 475–483.

Martens, R. (1986). Youth sport in the USA. In M. Weiss & D. Gould (Eds.), *Sport for children and youth, vol. 10.* Champaign, IL: Human Kinetics.

Michigan Joint Legislative Study on Youth Sports. (1978). Lansing, MI: State of Michigan.

National Education Longitudinal Study. (1988). *A profile of the American eighth grader: NELS: 88 student descriptive summary.* Washington, DC: U.S. Government Printing Office.

National Federation of State High School Associations. (1990). *1990–91 handbook.* Kansas City, MO: Author.

Sapp, M., & Haubenstricker, J. (1978). *Motivation for joining and reasons for not continuing in youth sport programs in Michigan.* Paper presented at the meeting of the American Alliance for Health, Physical Education, Recreation and Dance, Kansas City, MO.

Seefeldt, V., Ewing, M. E., & Walk, S. (1992). *Overview of youth sports programs in the United States.* Washington, DC: Carnegie Council on Adolescent Development.

Spady, W. G. (1970). Lament for the letterman: Effects of peer status and extramural activities on goals and achievement. *American Journal of Sociology, 75,* 680–702.

U.S. Department of Commerce. (1985, June). *Bureau of the census.* Washington, DC: U.S. Government Printing Office.

Weiss, M. R. (1987). Self-esteem and achievement in children's sport and physical activity. In D. Gould & M. R. Weiss (Eds.), *Advances in pediatric sports sciences. Vol. 2: Behavioral issues* (pp. 87–119). Champaign, IL: Human Kinetics.

PART

2

READINESS FOR PARTICIPATION

Along with the trend of increasing numbers of participants, a trend toward children's entering youth sport programs at earlier ages has emerged. Often as a result of parental coercion, boys and girls as young as 3 and 4 years of age now compete in a broad range of activities, including swimming, gymnastics, and figure skating. The advent of early childhood education programs, expanded media coverage of youth sports, and schemes for the early identification of athletic talent undoubtedly have contributed to the situation. When should children begin competing in sports? The significance of this question is that it reflects a concern for the welfare of the child. Given that the overall objective of youth sports is to provide a positive developmental experience, it follows that the issue of readiness is of paramount importance.

In our society, as in others, many significant life events are organized according to chronological milestones. For example, initiation of formal education and attainment of voting privileges are geared solely to the amount of time that an individual has lived since birth. Yet it is well known that chronological age alone is a rather poor indicator of an individual's degree of progress toward maturity. Because biological clocks run at different rates, children of the same chronological age may differ tremendously. More exactly, boys in the age range 10 to 16 years may vary as much as 60 months in their physiological maturity, which translates into differences as great as 15 inches in height and 90 pounds in weight.

Biological processes obviously play a primary role in determining readiness for sport. But social, emotional, and cognitive development is also a major factor to consider. Children differ a great deal in their levels of physical maturation, their interests and motivation, and their abilities. For these reasons, it is impossible to recommend a specific age for participation of all children in all sports. Rather, the age of readiness depends on a child's characteristics, the tasks/demands of the sport, and the nature of the program. In this part of the book, the complex issue of readiness is addressed in three chapters that provide different yet complementary perspectives.

Chapter 4, by Vern Seefeldt, focuses on developmental mechanisms that relate to children's readiness to learn motor skills. Following a concise interpretation of the readiness construct, consideration is given to the interrelations between cognitive and motor processes and to the controversial issue of generality versus specificity of motor skills. Seefeldt then discusses the role of behavioral cues that foretell readiness to acquire specific skills. This essentially involves an understanding of the orderly sequence of motor development and the child's acquisition of necessary antecedent behaviors. Seefeldt's approach provides a much needed base for recognizing when a particular sports skill should be introduced to a child.

In a treatise that extends Seefeldt's chapter, Richard A. Magill and David I. Anderson propose a working model of the vital components involved in determining when a child is optimally ready to participate in a sport. Their multidimensional model takes into account the child's maturation level, prerequisite skill achievement, and motivation to learn. Critical periods are presented as intervals of time during which a person is best suited to acquire a particular skill. Optimal readiness occurs when the person's characteristics and experiences related to the three dimensions of the model are appropriate for learning a skill. An important feature of viewing readiness in this way is the knowledge that initial age of entry in a sport is not the key factor for predicting future success. The chapter concludes with a discussion of the readiness model in terms of specific implications for youth sport programs and for parental action.

In the final chapter of this part, Michael W. Passer deals directly with the age-based question about readiness for participation in youth sports. To establish age guidelines, three psychological criteria are examined: motivational readiness, cognitive readiness, and potential harmful consequences. Motivational readiness is seen as an aspect of children's development of an orientation toward social comparison. This dynamic process enables youngsters to assess their athletic prowess relative to that of their peers. The discussion of cognitive readiness focuses on children's information-processing capabilities, ability to attribute causality for their performance, and role-taking capabilities. In relation to the preceding, harmful consequences that may result from a lack of motivational and cognitive readiness are highlighted. Based on these key criteria, Passer concludes his chapter by offering some general age-related guidelines for youth sport participation.

4

THE CONCEPT OF READINESS APPLIED TO THE ACQUISITION OF MOTOR SKILLS

—Vern Seefeldt

The word *readiness* as it is used by specialists in human development implies that an individual has reached a certain point in an ongoing process. In learning, readiness implies that an accumulation of events or experiences has occurred that then places the learner in a position to acquire additional information, skills, or values.

The past half century has provided abundant information that gives us clear indications about when children are ready to learn many of the fine and gross motor skills of infancy and childhood (e.g., see reviews by Branta, Haubenstricker, & Seefeldt, 1984; Haywood, 1993; Payne & Isaacs, 1991; Seefeldt & Haubenstricker, 1982). This information has allowed us to become more confident about identifying the periods when young children are ready to learn movement skills. In addition, we are also relatively well informed about the sequence of events that must precede every instance of readiness when acquisition of motor skills is the objective (Roberton & Halverson, 1988; Seefeldt, 1980; Wickstrom, 1977).

Coaches of young athletes and teachers of movement skills make decisions daily about the readiness of children to learn skills. However, available materials in textbooks indicate that most activity programs are still based on tradition rather than on well-defined developmental progressions of fundamental movement skills (Rarick, 1989; Thomas, 1989). This situation exists in part because most definitions of readiness depend on an overt attempt on the part of the learner to perform a certain task. This action then indicates to the teacher or coach that the student is ready to refine the skill or to progress to a more complex level of performance. In other words, we depend on the observable behavior of the performer to tell us when the state of readiness exists. In contrast, if our predictive information was accurate and available to teachers and coaches, we would have at our disposal a series of signs that convey readiness. These signs would provide valuable information to teachers and coaches to tell them when learners are ready to move along the pathway from rudimentary to mature performance levels.

It is entirely feasible that children may be biologically or mentally ready to learn motor skills, yet not make any attempt at performing specific tasks because some of the components necessary for successful completion are not available in the

FIGURE 4.1
Model for the acquisition of
fundamental movement
skills.
(Redrawn from Seefeldt, 1980)

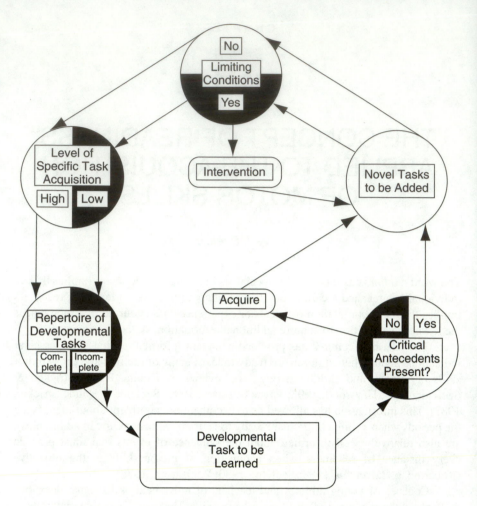

present environment. For that reason, teachers of movement must be aware of the antecedent variables that influence the acquisition of movement skills (see figure 4.1). Clearly, if we are to assist individuals in achieving their motor potential, we must be able to (a) identify the antecedent variables that provide the state of readiness for specific tasks, (b) recognize the behaviors that foretell the readiness of the learner for specific skill-learning situations, and (c) provide the appropriate environment that will permit or persuade the learner to advance to the next level of skill acquisition.

The construct of readiness has undergone some changes in its interpretation during the past several decades. During the first half of the twentieth century, physicians and educators believed that the biological maturation of children was the sole determiner of their ability to perform fine and gross motor skills (Gesell, 1946; Thelen & Adolph, 1992; Wild, 1938). However, subsequent research has produced abundant evidence concerning the significant contribution that the environment makes to children's learning (Connolly, 1970; Kugler, Kelso, & Turvey, 1982; Smith & Thelen, 1993).

An indication of the beginning of this transition in the definition of readiness for learning motor skills can be drawn from Bruner's (1965) statement regarding the ability to deal with cognitive information. His chapter "Readiness for Learning" was introduced with the statement: "We begin with the hypothesis that any subject can be taught effectively in some intellectually honest form to any children at any state of development" (p. 33). Bruner's interpretation of readiness removed the burden of prerequisite biological maturation from the learner and concurrently placed the responsibility for the assessment of developmental status and the provision of antecedent experiences on the teacher. Bruner's definition suggested that the child is always ready for some type of experience, but the selection and provision of the stimuli that elicit the desired responses are the responsibility of the teachers in charge of the child's environment. The implication to be drawn from Bruner's work is that the ability to learn motor skills was no longer solely attributable to the maturational level that the learner brought to the task. Rather, it was the previous proficiencies combined with current, appropriate experiences that led to advances in motor skill acquisition.

Interrelationship between Cognitive and Motor Functions

The teaching of motor skills has traditionally ignored the importance of learning styles and cognitive functions that may influence the rate of learning (Connolly, 1970). Recent attempts to identify and incorporate the hierarchy of cognitive structures into situations that involve motor skill learning are a welcome addition to the literature (Kelso & Clark, 1982; Kugler et al., 1982; Schmidt, 1975; Smith & Thelen, 1993). The relatively late incorporation of cognitive information into the theory and practice of motor skill acquisition may have been due to the strong influence that biologists had on the field during the first part of the twentieth century. For example, Piaget's developmental sequence, originally presented in 1952, has only received attention in the United States during the last two decades. Hebb's (1949) attempt to explain readiness to learn by incorporating earlier experiences into present actions is still a fundamental part of most theories of skill acquisition. Hebb's model suggests that experience in a variety of tasks aids the performer in (a) selecting more appropriate stimuli, (b) making finer discriminations concerning the accuracy of the response, (c) attending to a task for a longer period of time, (d) being able to depend more on transfer of elements, (e) being able to retain more of what was learned by integrating it with previous experience, and (f) eliminating faulty responses from the alternatives available.

The concurrent and inseparable development of cognitive and motor processes in early life was emphasized by Bruner (1969), who affirmed this relationship as a result of extensive research with children below 6 months of age. He noted that the ability to solve problems that require a motor response is a process that begins soon after birth. According to Bruner, the infant's initial movements are not random responses but represent the answers to hypotheses that are formed by problems that are unique to early development. Out of these early movements the infant develops a hierarchy of functions that provides the basis for future learning. The reflexes and reactions that are present at birth provide the repertoire from which the infant learns to *differentiate* the actions that are effective and efficient in completing a specific task. The second mechanism, which Bruner termed *modularization,* permits the infant to partition and recombine the movements into additional patterns. *Substitution* is a means whereby one action is used in place of another, thus adding variety to the responses available. *Sequential integration* permits the selection of a variant order, in lieu of solving the same problems with a rigid sequence of movements. *Place-holding* permits the infant to carry on two motor skills while devoting alternate degrees of attention to both of them. *Internalization of action* is the ability to carry out behavior symbolically.

The ability to perform complex motor operations and the transferability of these mechanisms to many motor tasks during the first two years of life underscore the importance of abundant stimulation in early infancy. This definition of abilities also illustrates the need for a concurrent study of cognitive and motor development during the periods of early and middle childhood.

Perhaps the most recent of the paradigm shifts to emerge in viewing the concept of readiness was that of dynamical systems, introduced by Kugler et al. (1982) in a book edited by Kelso and Clark (1982). The theory of dynamical systems evolved from contemporary theories of motor control. *Dynamical systems* theory suggests that the emerging movement is a product of the individual's cognitive status, neural maturation, and all the environmental elements to which the individual has been and is being exposed. The theory of dynamical systems views the contributing systems, whether neurological, biological, psychological, or environmental, as equally important, with no single factor being ultimately more important than any of the others. This all-encompassing theory combines the ontogenetic with the phylogenetic forces that influence the acquisition of motor skills. Its primary contribution may be the attention it focuses on variables that have heretofore been ignored as contributors to enhanced motor function.

The onset of locomotion increases the opportunities for sensory stimulation available to the child (for thorough reviews see Haywood, 1993 and Keogh & Sudgen, 1985). The motor repertoire is expanded when responses are made to an incessant desire for sensory stimulation. A cyclic process is initiated whereby an increase in sensory experiences contributes to the variety and frequency of motor responses. An enlarged repertoire of motor patterns provides more options to the performer, and a greater proportion of successful responses contributes to a desire for additional stimulation. This cycle is self-sustaining, with the provision that the environment contains appropriate stimuli and the child has the opportunity to formulate the motor responses. On the basis of this proposed sequence, it is evident that an abundance of experiences that culminate in successful motor responses early in life is an efficient way to establish the readiness necessary for subsequent learning.

Generality versus Specificity of Motor Skills

The controversy concerning the generality versus specificity of motor skills has waxed and waned through the decades. Although research favors those who contend that movement skills are specific, we lack conclusive evidence that the fundamental motor skills of infancy and childhood are unrelated one to another (Keogh, 1977). The evidence most often cited in support of specificity is based on correlational studies in which the data were derived via quantitative measures, with little regard for the neurological patterns of development used by the performers. Yet sound evidence indicates that the substrate of the basic movements and fundamental motor skills of infancy and childhood is composed of reflexes and reactions that are common to all human beings (Hellebrandt, Rarick, & Carns, 1961; Knott & Voss, 1968; Milina-Comparetti & Gidoni, 1967).

The role of reflexes that are associated with future skill acquisition has been the focus of several investigations. The reports of Knott and Voss (1968) and Shambes and Campbell (1973), based on the theory of proprioceptive neuromuscular facilitation, suggest the existence of four diagonal patterns that form the basis of all movement, whether reflexive, developmental, or ontogenetic. The authors contend that once the basic diagonal patterns are perfected, all future skills are acquired through a variation of these patterns in temporal-spatial relationships. Examples of other reports that trace the transition from reflexes and reactions to voluntary movement include such tasks as grasping and prehension (Twitchell, 1965), the use of the tonic neck reflex in writing (Waterland, 1967), and righting reactions in the achievement of erect posture (Milani-Comparetti & Gidoni, 1967). The sequential description of the reflexes and reactions that must be suppressed or built upon for normal motor development to occur during the first year of life—given by Milani-Comparetti and Gidoni—is an excellent example of the high level of prediction that can accompany motor function when qualitative assessment is used.

Order and Sequence in Motor Skill Acquisition

The orderly nature of early motor behavior has frequently led to the erroneous impression that infants or young children acquire their motor repertoires at approximately the same chronological age. However, because genetic endowment determines the boundaries within which the skills are expressed, a wide range exists in the ages at which children learn basic motor skills (Roberton & Halverson, 1988; Haubenstricker & Seefeldt, 1986). Consequently, classification of motor skills by age has less utility for teachers of movement than having them know the developmental sequences and the ability to provide the appropriate experiences when the child is ready for the next step toward maturity (Payne & Isaacs, 1991). Also, many scales that purport to assess motor performance for compensatory or remedial motor education lack the specificity that is necessary for prescriptive teaching. These scales were developed primarily by psychologists and physicians and have basic problems in defining the specificity in developmental patterns that are common to children beyond 1 year of age (Bruner, 1969).

The identification of an orderly sequence of development in various fundamental movement skills has provided teachers with practical guides concerning the readiness of children to move on to the next level of a particular skill. However, we do not yet have sufficient evidence to suggest when the introduction to specific skills should occur; nor do we have sufficient evidence to know which antecedent conditions are essential or helpful in moving the child into a position of readiness for specific skills. Apparently these movements have their origins in the reflexes and reactions displayed during the first year of life.

Predicting the Rate of Motor Skill Acquisition

The concept of maturation and the use of skeletal age and body size as criteria for readiness to engage in certain activities is discussed by Malina (this volume). Despite the fact that research evidence suggests that the selection and classification of performers for subsequent competition in sports and dance be determined by variables such as biological maturity, skill, body size, and experience, the grouping of young athletes has been primarily a season-by-season procedure based solely on chronological age. Virtually all of the investigators whose work was reviewed for this topic reported the retrospective prediction of success, often through the use of regression equations that were obtained from cross-sectional studies or computed at the termination of longitudinal studies. None of the investigators attempted to predict the success of individuals in specific athletic endeavors prior to their involvement in activity programs, nor did they conduct a longitudinal follow-up to determine the accuracy of the original predictions. In no case were the predictive equations applied to other samples as a test of their validity. This neglect is unfortunate in light of the national interest that is currently focused on organized sports and dance for young children, the well-defined objectives for success that are commonly associated with these programs, and the desire on the part of most coaches and teachers to foretell the success of their clients at the earliest possible age. Perhaps the most useful function of predictive criteria would be the determination of relative success, thus eliminating the need for children to engage in tasks with which they have a relatively low level of success.

The relationship between the various indicators of biological maturity, commonly classified under the phrase *primary* and *secondary sex characteristics,* is modest to high, depending on whether individuals mature early or late in relation to their chronological age peers. As might be expected, the relationship between skeletal age and the primary and secondary sex characteristics is also in the modest-to-high range. Thus, if skeletal age has a high positive relationship with height, weight, breadth, and measures of circumference, and also with the primary and secondary sex characteristics, it seems ironic that some form of predictive equation that incorporates some indicator of maturational age is not used more frequently as a means of predicting the readiness of children to engage in various sports. However, the ease of grouping children by chronological age and the expertise that is required to classify them by any other technique or formula causes the promoters of youth sports to routinely revert to the qualifying criterion of chronological age.

Part of the reluctance to use skeletal age as a predictor of motor performance is that teachers and coaches cannot easily obtain such an assessment. The determination of skeletal age requires special competencies in its procurement and assessment that are not required when obtaining other growth data. Additional deterrents may result from a reluctance to expose children to X-irradiation except for diagnostic purposes. However, the most logical reason for its exclusion from predictive equations involving motor performance is its high positive relationship to parameters that are considerably easier to assess. If it can be demonstrated that height, weight, or other bodily dimensions account for most or all of the variance in performance attributable to physical growth, there is no need to include an estimate of biological maturity. This is precisely what research reports have indicated. Espenschade in 1940, Rarick and Oyster in 1964, and our own longitudinal data (Howell, 1979; Seefeldt, Haubenstricker, & Milne, 1976) confirm that skeletal age adds little to the prediction of motor performance if chronological age, height, and weight are already part of the equation.

The difficulty in classifying children and youth for physical activity by criteria other than chronological age does not excuse promoters of youth sports from making an attempt to equalize composition as much as possible. Young athletes who dominate competitive situations or whose size is a threat to the safety of teammates or opponents should be reclassified according to criteria that include an estimate of biological age, body size, playing experience, skill level, and social maturity in relation to the youth of their age group and those in the age category to which the athlete is to be promoted.

Summary

In conclusion, there is still little evidence to suggest that the readiness to learn specific motor skills can be identified with accuracy through a combination of chronological age, body size, or the various assessments of biological maturation. The most feasible procedure for ensuring that young performers will be ready to learn motor skills involves a task analysis of the skills to be learned, accompanied by an opportunity for the learner to acquire the requisite antecedent skills. Although the order in which children learn the sequence in fundamental motor skills is invariant, great variation exists in the rate at which they move through the sequences to maturity.

References

Branta, C., Haubenstricker, J., & Seefeldt, V. (1984). Age changes in motor skills during childhood and adolescence. *Exercise and Sport Sciences Reviews, 12,* 467–520.

Bruner, J. (1965). *The process of education.* Cambridge, MA: Harvard University Press.

————. (1969). Processes of growth in infancy. In A. Ambrose (Ed.), *Stimulation in early infancy* (pp. 205–225). New York: Academic Press.

Connolly, K. (Ed.). (1970). *Mechanisms of motor skill development.* New York: Academic Press.

Espenschade, A. (1940). Motor performance in adolescence. *Monographs of the Society for Research in Child Development, 5,* 1–127.

Gesell, A. (1946). The ontogenesis of infant behavior. In L. Carmichael (Ed.), *Manual of child psychology* (pp. 295–331). New York: Wiley.

Haubenstricker, J., & Seefeldt, V. (1986). Acquisition of motor skills during infancy and childhood. In Seefeldt, V. (Ed.), *Physical activity and well being* (pp. 41–104). Reston, VA: American Alliance for Health, Physical Education, Recreation and Dance.

Haywood, K. M. (1993). *Life span motor development* (2nd ed.). Champaign, IL: Human Kinetics.

Hebb, D. (1949). *The organization of behavior.* New York: Wiley.

Hellebrandt, F., Rarick, G., & Carns, M. (1961). Physiological analysis of basic motor skills. *American Journal of Physical Medicine, 40,* 14–25.

Howell, R. (1979). *The relationship between motor performance, physical growth, and skeletal maturity in boys nine to twelve years of age.* Unpublished master's thesis, Michigan State University, East Lansing.

Kelso, J. A. S., & Clark, J. E. (Eds.). (1982). *The development of movement control and co-ordination.* New York: Wiley & Sons.

Keogh, J. F. (1977). The study of movement skill development. *Quest, 28,* 76–88.

Keogh, J., & Sudgen, D. (1985). *Movement skill development.* New York: Macmillan.

Knott, M., & Voss, D. (1968). *Proprioceptive neuromuscular facilitation.* New York: Harper & Row.

Kugler, P. N., Kelso, J. A. S., & Turvey, M. T. (1982). On the control and co-ordination of naturally developing systems. In J. A. S. Kelso & J. E. Clark (Eds.), *The development of movement control and co-ordination* (pp. 5–78). New York: Wiley & Sons.

Malina, R. M. (1995). The young athlete: Biological growth and maturation in a biocultural context. In F. L. Smoll & R. E. Smith (Eds.), *Children and youth in sport: A biopsychosocial perspective* (pp. 161–186). Dubuque, IA: Brown & Benchmark.

Milina-Comparetti, A., & Gidoni, E. (1967). Routine developmental examination in normal and retarded children. *Developmental Medicine and Child Neurology, 13,* 631–638.

Payne, V. G., & Isaacs, L. D. (1991). *Human motor development: A lifespan approach* (2nd ed.). Mountain View, CA: Mayfield.

Piaget, J. (1952). *The origins of intelligence in children.* New York: International Universities Press.

Rarick, G. L. (1989). Motor development: A commentary. In J. Skinner, C. Corbin, D. Landers, P. Martin, & C. Wells, *Future directions in exercise and sports science research* (pp. 383–391). Champaign, IL: Human Kinetics.

Rarick, G., & Oyster, N. (1964). Physical maturity, muscular strength and motor performance of young school-age boys. *Research Quarterly, 35,* 523–531.

Roberton, M. A., & Halverson, L. E. (1988). The development of locomotor coordination: Longitudinal change and invariance. *Journal of Motor Behavior, 20,* 197–241.

Schmidt, R. A. (1975). A schema theory of discrete motor learning. *Psychological Review, 82,* 225–260.

Seefeldt, V. (1980). Developmental motor patterns: Implications for elementary school physical education. In C. Nadeau, W. Halliwell, K. Newell, & G. Roberts, *Psychology of motor behavior and sport* (pp. 314–323). Champaign, IL: Human Kinetics.

Seefeldt, V., & Haubenstricker, J. (1982). Patterns, phases and stages: An analytical model for the study of developmental movement. In J. Kelso & J. Clark (Eds.), *The development of movement control and coordination* (pp. 309–318). New York: Wiley.

Seefeldt, V., Haubenstricker, J., & Milne, C. (1976, March). *Skeletal age and body size as variables in motor performance.* Paper presented at the Third Symposium on Child Growth and Motor Development, University of Western Ontario, London.

Shambes, G., & Campbell, S. (1973). Inherent movement patterns in man. In C. Widule (Ed.), *Kinesiology* (Vol. 3, pp. 50–58). Washington, DC: American Association for Health, Physical Education and Recreation.

Smith, L. B., & Thelen, E. (Eds.). (1993). *A dynamic systems approach to development: Applications.* Cambridge, MA: MIT Press.

Thelen, E., & Adolph, K. E. (1992). Arnold L. Gesell: The paradox of nature and nurture. *Developmental Psychology, 28,* 368–380.

Thomas, J. (1989). Naturalistic research can drive motor development theory. In J. Skinner, C. Corbin, D. Landers, P. Martin, & C. Wells, *Future directions in exercise and sport science research* (pp. 349–367). Champaign, IL: Human Kinetics.

Twitchell, T. (1965). Attitudinal reflexes. *Physical Therapy, 45,* 411–418.

Waterland, J. (1967). The supportive framework for willed movement. *American Journal of Physical Medicine, 46,* 266–278.

Wickstrom, R. (1977). *Fundamental motor patterns.* Philadelphia: Lea and Febiger.

Wild, M. (1938). The behavior pattern of throwing and some observations concerning its course of development in children. *Research Quarterly, 9,* 20–24.

5

CRITICAL PERIODS AS OPTIMAL READINESS FOR LEARNING SPORT SKILLS

—Richard A. Magill and David I. Anderson

A question parents of young children commonly ask is, If I want my child to be successful in a particular sport, is it important that he or she get involved in that sport at a very early age? This is a reasonable question given the frequent media stories about how young some champion athlete was when he or she began competing in that sport. The problem is we do not know whether this athlete is typical of all champion athletes or whether he or she is an exception. Unfortunately, we have no substantial data that tell us what percentage of champion athletes began competing in their sports at a given age. We do know, however, that although many champion athletes became involved in their sports at early ages, others became involved at much older ages. For example, Greg Norman, the Australian who is consistently one of the professional golf tour's leading money winners, didn't hit a golf ball until he was 16 years old. Early involvement is no guarantee of an advantage over those who begin participating in the sport at a later age.

Rather than focusing on what typifies or should be the age of initiating involvement in sport, the issue discussed in this chapter concerns what we know about characteristics of children that can give us insight into determining when they are optimally ready to get involved in sport. Two readiness-related questions must be addressed to adequately determine when a child is ready to get involved in a sport. One concerns the child's attitudes about competition and what that means for becoming involved in sport; that is, when is a child's attitude about competition in concert with the demands of the competitive situation related to a specific sport? This question will be discussed in the next chapter by Michael Passer. However, a question that is equally important to address, and will be discussed here, concerns a child's *readiness to learn* sports skills. Readiness to learn skills is an important issue because success in sports depends on acquiring the skills that comprise a sport. For parents, the benefit of answering both of these readiness questions is that they can feel some confidence about the decision to permit a child to begin competing in sport.

You were introduced to the readiness-to-learn concept in the preceding chapter by Vern Seefeldt. This chapter will amplify some of Seefeldt's points as well as add some different perspectives. Specifically, the approach taken here will be to look at readiness to learn by addressing two specific questions. First, do certain *critical periods* exist for learning sports skills that if not taken advantage of will lead to less success than would have been possible if these skills had been introduced during these critical periods? Second, how essential are early experiences for later success? That is, what do we know from research concerned with early experiences with general motor activities and specific sports skills that will provide a better understanding of when to initiate involvement in a sport?

Critical Periods for Learning

The term *critical periods* concerns growth and development and is commonly seen in the behavioral science literature. Unfortunately, this term is often misunderstood, misused, and even overused. Some of the confusion results from the lack of a consistent definition. Also contributing to the confusion is an apparent lack of understanding about what determines the onset and duration of a critical period. Further, there appear to be some discrepancies between what is defined as a critical period for animals compared with humans. One thing that has agreement is that critical periods exist for at least three different aspects of development: emotional development, social development, and learning. The bulk of the research addressing critical periods, which primarily has been animal research, has focused on the formation of basic social relationships. The focus of the present discussion, however, is on critical periods for learning, with particular attention given to implications for youth sport involvement. After discussing some of the different views that have been proposed to indicate what determines the onset of a critical period for learning skills, we will define the term critical period in a way that is appropriate for what we know about skill learning.

Determinants of Critical Periods

The person generally credited with first noticing the phenomenon of critical periods for children learning motor skills was Myrtle McGraw (1935, 1939). Her studies of the twins named Jimmy and Johnny are well known to all who have studied human development. McGraw pointed out that for certain activities, such as walking and tricycle riding, early practice was not beneficial. For example, Johnny was given considerable practice and instruction on tricycle riding beginning when he was 11 months old. Jimmy, on the other hand, was not exposed to a tricycle until he was 22 months old. Despite the later exposure, Jimmy actually learned to ride the tricycle faster than did his brother. But for other skills, such as roller skating, early exposure proved beneficial. Johnny was taught to roller-skate at about 1 year old. Jimmy did not begin until he was almost 2 and never achieved the same level of skill as Johnny. Based on observations such as these, McGraw concluded that critical periods for learning exist and vary from activity to activity. Further, an optimal period exists for rapid and skillful learning for each motor skill.

The evidence provided by McGraw, along with many others, leads to an important question: What determines the critical period? Some of the possible answers to this question will be discussed next, and then an answer will be proposed on which the remainder of this chapter will be based.

Maturation as the Primary Determinant

McGraw's (1939) answer to the critical period determinant question was that *maturation* is the primary determinant; that is, the neuromuscular system of the child must be mature enough to allow the activity to be performed. In this regard, she accounted for the ineffectiveness of early tricycle practice for Johnny by stating that the "activity was initiated before his neuro-muscular mechanisms were ready for such a performance" (p. 3). Later McGraw (1945) stated rather definitively that it is simply wasted effort to begin training before adequate "neural readiness."

McGraw's maturation viewpoint was actually an extension of a developmental theory that was prevalent at the time of her research. Influential child development theorists such as G. Stanley Hall (1921) and Arnold Gesell (1928) helped promote the growth-readiness model of development. This model proposed that certain organized patterns of growth must occur before learning can effectively contribute to development. In addition to McGraw's classic study with Jimmy and Johnny, experiments such as one by Gesell and Thompson (1929) were interpreted as providing evidence to support the maturation model.

In the Gesell and Thompson study, one twin was given special training in stair climbing at the age of 46 weeks. The identical other twin did not receive this training. Seven weeks later, the untrained twin did not climb the stairs as well as the trained twin. However, following only two weeks of training, which was five weeks less than the previously trained twin had received, the originally untrained twin surpassed her sister in climbing the stairs. Gesell and Thompson concluded that better learning with less training will result when the child's maturation level is adequate for the skill being learned.

More recently, this maturation view has been extended by motor development researchers who adhere to what has come to be known as a dynamic systems model of motor control. This model proposes that the interaction of multiple subsystems related to human movement determines the onset of new motor behaviors. For example, Esther Thelen and her colleagues (e.g., Kamm, Thelen, & Jensen, 1990; Thelen, 1987; Thelen & Fisher, 1982) argue that these various subsystems, including the skeletomotor apparatus, the perceptual apparatus, and postural control mechanisms, do not all mature at the same rate. And the maturation of any one of these subsystems can act as a trigger to enable the child to engage in a new form of behavior. For example, newborns demonstrate a stepping reflex that eventually disappears before returning when the child begins to walk. Thelen proposes that the disappearance of newborn stepping is due to changes in the skeletomotor apparatus. Because the rapid weight gain of the newborn in the first few months of life is not accompanied by a proportionate gain in muscle strength, lifting the legs against gravity becomes difficult for the child. Support for this proposal is based on research evidence that has shown that infants who gain weight the most rapidly also show the most rapid disappearance of the stepping reflex. And adding weights to newborn's legs inhibits stepping, whereas submersing the infant in water facilitates stepping. When the child's muscles eventually gain the appropriate strength, the legs can be lifted such that stepping activity can again be demonstrated.

A related perspective on the importance of maturation for learning skills was proposed by Newell (1986). He argued that body scale is an important component of the skill acquisition capability of the developing child. Changes in the absolute and relative size of body parts to each other and to environmental features lead to changes in the biomechanical constraints on the motor control system. Changes in body part size need to be accompanied by changes in strength if the child is to be able to adequately coordinate body parts to perform a skill. This maturation characteristic means that the coordination demands of a specific skill that can be achieved by one child may not be achieved by another child of a similar age because of body scale differences. Similarly, a child who was successfully performing a skill at one age may have difficulty performing that same skill at an older age because of body scale changes. Sometimes it is possible to accommodate body scale characteristics by adjusting sizes of objects with which the child interacts, such as adjusting ball sizes or heights of volleyball nets. It is possible that considerable effort may be required for later training if the coordination function for a particular skill continually changes with changes in body scale, or if body scale characteristics have not been adequately compensated for in the skill performance setting.

The physical characteristics of the body have not been the only aspects of development considered important in a maturational view of determining the onset of optimal learning periods. Laszlo and Bairstow (1983), for example, proposed that perceptual maturation is also an important consideration here as well. They showed that 6- to 8-year-old children who scored low on a test of kinesthetic sensitivity significantly improved their ability to draw shapes (without the use of vision) after a period of kinesthetic training. Furthermore, the kinesthetic training also led to improvements in printing and writing in normal classroom settings. The significance of the benefit of the kinesthetic training was seen when specific drawing training led to negligible improvements in drawing skill. Taken together, these results support McGraw's (1945) earlier contention that repeated practice on a particular skill may be useless if critical subsystems have not matured appropriately.

Maturation Plus Environment as Determinants

Other child developmental researchers and theorists have proposed that in addition to maturation as a determinant of the onset of critical learning periods, interaction with the environment must also be added as a significant key determinant. For example, Piaget (1952, 1969) credited maturation as a major contributor to development but also gave a considerable role to the child's interaction with the environment and to learning, although he gave learning a relatively minor role. Flavell (1963) described an adaptive model that accommodated both maturation and environment as key components for cognitive development. In this model, he proposed that development occurs as a result of the child adapting to the demands of his or her environment and intellectualizing that adjustment.

The intellectualizing part of this model is viewed as critical to cognitive development, which Piaget saw as strongly dependent on acquired movement capabilities. These movement capabilities were in turn seen as strongly dependent on intellectual capabilities. Piaget proposed that this developmental process occurred through two stages he called assimilation and accommodation. *Assimilation* involves the child attempting to interpret new experiences as they relate to the child's present stage of development. *Accommodation* involves adjusting thought processes to deal with these new experiences. That is, the child attempts to accommodate the new experience into his or her way of viewing the world. How children perceive the world at any given time depends on their developmental stage. These well-known stages, which relate to the cognitive capabilities of children during their preadolescent lives, are: the sensorimotor stage (birth to 2 years), the preoperational stage (2 to 7 years), the concrete operational stage (7 to 11 years), and the formal operational stage (12 years and older). According to Piaget, children perform tasks consistent with the stage of development they are in at the time of engaging in the task. However, new experiences constantly challenge children to make appropriate adaptations to the environment. The appearance of a new developmental stage can be facilitated, to a limited degree, by appropriate environmental interactions.

Another point of view espousing the interaction of maturation and environment as primary determinants of critical periods is one promoted by Robert Gagné (1968, 1970), although he argues that learning plays a more significant role in development than in the Piaget model. Gagné proposed the cumulative model, which states that the "child progresses from one point to the next in his development . . . because he learns an ordered set of capabilities which build upon each other in progressive fashion through the process of differentiation, recall, and transfer of learning" (1968, p. 181). In effect, this model classifies a skill to be learned into a particular category of learning, such as stimulus-response connections, multiple discriminations, concepts, and rules. These categories are hierarchically organized such that a lower-level category must be acquired before the next higher-level category can be successfully achieved. Thus for a rule to be learned, all of the various learning categories that underlie the rule category are prerequisite skills that must be acquired before effective rule learning can occur.

Although Gagné developed his model primarily to represent learning cognitive skills, he considered it applicable to motor skills as well. Of particular relevance here is the emphasis placed on transfer of learning in this developmental model. Gagné (1968) stated that "any learned capability, at any stage of a learning sequence, may operate to mediate other learning which was not deliberately taught" (p. 168). The significance of this view is seen by noting that it proposes an alternative interpretation for the results of the Gesell and Thompson (1929) stair-climbing study. While acknowledging maturation is a part of the reason for the originally untrained twin to require five weeks less training than the originally trained twin, the Gagné model proposes that it is possible that the originally trained twin did not have the appropriate prerequisite skills to successfully climb stairs at the time the original training took place. As a result, the training took longer than for the other twin who received training at a later time. It was possible, for example, that the previously untrained twin actually gained certain prerequisite stair-climbing skills during the seven weeks of training of the other twin. Thus the first twin had to learn both the stair-climbing skill and its prerequisite skills, whereas the second twin did not have to learn those same prerequisite skills, which were developed through her own play activity before formal stair-climbing training began.

A Multidimensional View

Unfortunately, no conclusive empirical evidence exists to exclusively support any one of the various views just discussed. Each has empirical support to which it can point, and each view appears to provide alternative interpretations of empirical results purported as supporting evidence by other views. One resolve to this issue of what determines a critical period is seen in a discussion of critical periods many years ago. Scott (1962) concluded that a critical period should be seen as a time when all physical, mental, perceptual, and motivational characteristics critical to performing a skill are present. This point of view argues that no one factor should be promoted as *the* primary determinant of a critical period. Instead, maturation, environmental interactions, and learning must be viewed as multidimensional factors. Each factor must be evaluated individually and as an aggregate to establish the onset of a critical period. Also, it is reasonable to consider a critical period for a person as a period of time during which these factors appropriately describe the person's characteristics and experiences such that the person is optimally ready to learn a particular skill or activity. This more reasonable view of the critical period for the development of human motor behavior is discussed next.

Critical Periods as Optimal Readiness Periods

According to a view of critical periods that takes into account the child's maturation level, environment, and learning experiences, critical learning periods should not be seen as times during which learning *must* be initiated. Rather, these time intervals should be viewed as periods during which the child is optimally ready to initiate learning a skill. This means that it is more appropriate to consider critical periods, when referring to skill learning, as *optimal readiness periods.* Some have referred to these as *sensitive periods* (e.g., Gallahue, 1989). These are periods when the child's maturation level is appropriate for the skill to be learned, when he or she has acquired the necessary prerequisite skills for the skill to be learned, and when he or she is adequately motivated to learn the skill. When skill learning is undertaken during an optimal readiness period, learning occurs with greater effectiveness and efficiency than it would at some other time in the child's life. Thus the key is to determine *when* a person is optimally ready to learn.

An Optimal Readiness Model for Initiating Skill Learning

In the multidimensional view of development described earlier, three factors need to be considered to determine when a person is optimally ready to learn a skill: *maturation, prerequisite skills,* and *motivation.* These three characteristics must be evaluated in terms of both the individual and the skill to be learned. The relative importance of any one factor in determining the onset of an optimal period will vary from skill to skill for the same person and will vary from person to person for a particular skill.

   For example, if the skill of pitching in baseball is to be learned, two children of the same chronological age may differ in physical maturation characteristics. As has been pointed out elsewhere in this book, chronological age does not equal maturation age. Children mature at different rates; thus, a child at age 12 could be physically more like a 10-year-old or more like a 14-year-old. Because pitching a baseball requires a certain degree of strength and coordination, the physical maturation of the child becomes a critical factor in determining whether the child is ready to learn this skill. Note here that the term *pitching* is being used as a sport-specific form of throwing. This distinction is important because the role of maturation takes on different degrees of importance for these two skills. A child may be physically mature enough to learn to throw a ball but may not be sufficiently mature to learn to pitch. The difference between throwing and pitching illustrates the prerequisite skill factor in the optimal readiness model and the significance of this factor. Throwing is a prerequisite skill for pitching. If a child has not had sufficient experience to learn to throw a ball well, then encouraging that child to learn to pitch in baseball would be premature. Before the child can learn to pitch, instruction and experiences related to basic throwing patterns must first be provided.

Before considering the motivation factor of the readiness model, it will be helpful to stop and look back at two research studies discussed earlier in this chapter. Recall that the results of the study of Jimmy and Johnny by McGraw (1935) and the study of the stair-climbing twins by Gesell and Thompson (1929) were used to support the maturation model of skill learning readiness. If we now interpret those studies according to the three-factor interaction readiness model, the explanation for those results will be different. For example, it is quite possible that neither Jimmy nor Johnny had the prerequisite skills needed for tricycle riding. Early training may not have benefited these children because they did not have the appropriate prior experiences needed to successfully ride a tricycle. Although maturation was undoubtedly a factor in the lack of a training benefit, possibly the lack of prerequisite skills was also an influential factor. A similar interpretation of the Gesell and Thompson study was described earlier.

At this point then, it should be evident that in terms of the roles of maturation and prerequisite skill achievement, neither can stand alone as a determinant of an optimal learning readiness period; both are important in their influence of skill learning. The child who is maturationally ready to learn a skill but has not acquired skills prerequisite for that skill will have difficulty learning the skill. Similarly, a child who has the prerequisite skills may lack the physical or mental maturity required to learn the skill.

The Role of Motivation

The one factor in the three-factor readiness model not discussed thus far is motivation. Although there is some general misunderstanding of the meaning of this term, motivation is best defined as it relates to learning readiness as a state of being energized to engage in an activity. Just as a battery-driven toy needs a charged battery to operate, people need to be appropriately energized to learn a skill. Sometimes this energy comes from within individuals, in which case they are intrinsically motivated to learn the skill. The motivation to participate in an activity often is the result of the person's own interest in the activity. As a result of this intrinsic interest, the person has a desire to learn the skills needed to be successful in the activity. However, in other situations, the person does not have an intrinsic desire to participate. In such cases, extrinsic sources of motivation can help to develop an interest.

The appropriateness of the source of initial motivation to learn a skill, whether intrinsic or extrinsic, has been debated for many years. However, a statement by Ausubel (1968) is pertinent to this issue and is in line with the view presented here. He stated that "the causal relationship between motivation and learning is typically reciprocal rather than unidirectional" (p. 365). This means that the motivation to learn does not have to originate in the child as an intrinsic motivation to learn a skill. Rather, it is possible that introducing the skill to a child who may not be intrinsically motivated to learn the skill can lead to developing an intrinsic motivation to learn the skill and to continue to perform it. This view argues that instruction should not necessarily be postponed until the child shows evidence of being sufficiently intrinsically motivated. Many children resist participating in an activity or learning a skill because of preconceived notions about the activity. These notions may in fact be unfounded and subject to change.

An example from my own teaching experience (Richard Magill) relates to this situation. I have taught badminton to college men who took the class only because they were required to. They had no intrinsic motivation to learn to play badminton. Typically, this lack of interest was due to a lack of knowledge of the game and the challenges it provides. Somewhere in their past, these students had developed an inappropriate view of badminton and had determined that this was not an activity for them. After being properly introduced to badminton and being instructed in the skills of the game, however, they developed a tremendous interest in badminton and became avid players long after the course ended. Here an extrinsic source of motivation, a college requirement, was the basis for learning an activity. But appropriate instruction and participation in the activity eventually developed into an intrinsic motivation to learn more and to maintain regular participation in the activity.

The Influence of Early Experiences

In the preceding section, the roles of maturation, previous experiences, and motivation were presented as factors influencing when a child is optimally ready to learn a particular sports skill. Certain questions that arise from that discussion are important to consider. For example, Will exposure to an activity prior to this optimal readiness period affect learning the skill? Can introducing a child to an activity as early as possible in life give that child an advantage for eventual success in that activity? Could it be possible that involving a child in an activity too early could actually have negative effects? Such questions are important and will form the basis for this section.

Based on the three-factor model of readiness to learn described earlier, it is possible to develop an argument for as well as against early exposure to certain sports skills. For example, even though a child may not be sufficiently mature to participate in a sport, it seems possible that exposing the child to performing certain skills of that sport would give the child an advantage when he or she achieves the appropriate level of maturity. And this early exposure could lead to an intrinsic desire to participate in the activity. On the other hand, it could be argued that early exposure could lead to injury, the development of inappropriate skills, or a lack of interest in participating in the skill. Both sides of the argument appear to have merit and warrant some consideration.

The Maturation Factor

There is no question about the importance of a child being mature enough to learn a skill. The classic experimental results discussed earlier from McGraw (1935) and Gesell and Thompson (1929) underscore this point. Providing instruction or training prior to a child's achieving a sufficient level of maturation, both physical and cognitive, does not benefit learning the skill or eventual level of performing the skill. In fact, it is possible that encouraging a child to participate in an activity before being mature enough to properly learn the skill can negatively influence the child's motivation to participate in the activity when he or she achieves an appropriate maturation level. On the other hand, if the activity can be structured so that essential prerequisite skills can be taught, the immature child can gain some benefit from early exposure by acquiring important skills that will be needed to achieve success in the activity. Here again, all three factors involved in the multidimensional model of readiness to learn must be considered.

An important characteristic of maturation is that children mature at different rates, both cognitively and physically. In Piaget's stages of cognitive development model, children experience each stage but not necessarily at the same age. Some children achieve certain stages earlier or later than others. A similar situation exists for physical maturation. All children seem to go through similar stages of physical development but at different rates. These rates appear to be most pronounced for the onset of puberty. Evidence exists that shows as much as a 2- to 4-year chronological age difference in when puberty begins. Thus, as pointed out earlier, some children who are 12 years old may be physically more like 14- or 15-year-olds, whereas other 12-year-olds may be more like 9- or 10-year-olds.

What does this difference in maturation rate mean for children and youth involved in sport? It means that some may achieve success early because they are more mature than those they compete with who are of the same chronological age. For example, it is well documented that teams who win the Little League World Series are filled with players who are maturationally two to three years older than their chronological age. The maturation rate difference also means that some children and youth will achieve no appreciable success when they are young because they are maturationally younger than those they compete with. A classic example of a late maturer can be seen in the story of basketball hall-of-famer Bob Pettit, a superstar at LSU in the 1950s and in the NBA in the late 1950s and early 1960s. As a high school freshman, when Pettit was 5 feet 10 inches tall and weighed 114 pounds, he played in only three games and scored no points. The next year he was cut from the varsity team. But he maintained his motivation to play basketball and worked hard at developing the component skills by practicing in his backyard and playing in a church league and at the YMCA. By the time he was a senior, Pettit was 6 feet 7 inches tall and led his high school team to a state championship. Lest you think that this wouldn't happen today, a similar story is told about current basketball superstar David Robinson, who was cut from his junior high school basketball team.

What this means is that chronological age is *not* a good indicator of when a child is mature enough to begin participating in an activity. Maturation rate is an individual characteristic that needs to be evaluated on an individual level. Rather than elaborating further on this issue, refer to the chapter by Seefeldt, which precedes this one, for a more detailed discussion of the maturation issue.

Early Exposure May Be Beneficial to Later Performance

Early exposure to certain types of physical activity has definite advantages. The important requirement here is that the activities are appropriate for the child's maturation level. The emphasis needs to be on prerequisite skills that the child can readily perform. At the most basic level, providing children with many experiences involving fundamental motor skills is important. Fundamental skills include locomotor skills such as walking, running, jumping, and hopping and manipulation, or ballistic skills, such as throwing, catching, striking, and kicking. Experience with these fundamental skills is essential for the later development of more sport-specific skills involving these fundamental skills.

At the next level of skill development are the skills that are prerequisites for successful sport participation. These involve the component skills of a specific sport. Whereas kicking is a fundamental motor skill, passing a soccer ball is a component skill of soccer that is a prerequisite skill for successful soccer playing. No child should be expected to successfully compete in a sport without achieving a certain level of competence in the component skills of that sport.

Here, then, the prerequisite skill dimension of our multidimensional learning readiness is given a high degree of importance in determining readiness to participate in sport. A child may not be sufficiently mature to compete in a particular sport, or the child may not be motivated to participate in that sport. But the child can be indirectly introduced to that sport by providing him or her with experiences involving the fundamental motor skills and the sport-specific component skills that are essential prerequisites for eventual participation in that sport.

Early Exposure May Be Detrimental to Later Performance

Although there has been little research evidence indicating that certain types of early skill experiences can have detrimental effects on later skill performance, some recent evidence involving posture control suggests that these detrimental effects are possible. Research evidence produced by Marjorie Woollacott and her colleagues (e.g., Woollacott, Debû, & Shumway-Cook, 1987) has shown that the development of posture control is an important fundamental skill that serves as a foundation for the execution of many complex skills. There appears to be an important age-related transition period in the development of posture control between the ages of 4 and 6 years. During this period, the child is experiencing the development of the ability to integrate and effectively use sensory information from the visual, vestibular, and proprioceptive sensory systems. This integration of information characterizes effective postural control in older children and adults. Prior to this period, children are primarily oriented to using visual information as the basis for controlling postural responses.

Certain activities or emphases during the 4- to 6-years-of-age period can increase the likelihood that the multisensory integration capability will not develop to the extent that it should. For example, this integration will be lessened if motor skill experience is restricted during this age period to participation in only one or a very few closed skills rather than to a variety of both closed and open skills. *Closed skills* are those in which the object being acted on, such as a ball or a gymnastics apparatus, is stationary. The person is free to determine when to initiate a movement to achieve the goal of the skill. Hitting a baseball off a tee, shooting a free throw in basketball, and performing on a balance beam are examples of closed skills. *Open skills* are those in which the object or performer is moving. For these skills, success depends on integrating information from various sensory systems. The movements performed must be selected and initiated to adapt to the ever-changing characteristics of the object. (See Magill, 1993, for a more detailed discussion of closed and open skills.)

Lessened multisensory integration also can occur if children are engaged in activities that emphasize specific achievement criteria during this critical sensory integration period. Under the pressure of achieving these criteria, children may find it easier to revert to a visual system basis for control and not progress beyond a rigid stereotypic pattern of movement. The dependence on visual information may actually inhibit the integration of visual information with the other sensory systems involved in posture control and subsequently inhibit the child's ability to refine present movement skills and to adapt and learn new skills.

Woollacott et al. (1987) recommended activities that emphasize play and exploration for 4- to 6-year-old children. Children in this age range should explore a wide range of movements and situations in which these movements must be used so that information can be gathered from as extensive a variety of conditions as possible. The benefit of this exploration is that it increases the likelihood that appropriate sensory integration development occurs. To restrict the type of activity in which a child participates can lead to developing a lack of behavioral flexibility, which is essential for enabling people to successfully adapt to a wide range of movement situations.

Early Exposure May Have No Effect on Later Performance

One of the possible results from getting a child involved in an activity prior to being optimally ready to participate in that activity is that there will be no real benefit. That is, waiting until a later age would yield the same eventual level of performance as earlier exposure. This effect appears to be typical of many children and many activities. Two interesting examples can be seen in the results reported from research investigating the effectiveness of two early-exposure programs, infant swim programs and the Suzuki violin program. These two programs offer interesting examples because they deal with two quite different skills, one a sports skill and the other a music skill requiring coordinated movement.

Swimming is an activity well known for early involvement. Infant swim programs are popular. Though every person who enrolls an infant in a swim program does not do so to gain an advantage for later competitive swimming, the notion of an advantage exists in terms of getting a head start on the skill of swimming. In terms of competitive swimming, it is not uncommon to see children in early elementary school engaged in several hours of practice each week throughout the year with an organized swim team. Here again, the goal is often to gain an advantage. Although it may make intuitive sense that early involvement in swimming as an activity will give a child an advantage for learning to swim and that early involvement in competitive swimming will give a child an advantage for later competition, no conclusive evidence supports the advantage of either program. For example, Langendorfer (1987) concluded after reviewing research related to early swim programs that no evidence indicates that infant swimming enhances later swimming achievement. There does not appear to be a "critical period" for swimming in the sense that if swimming skill is not achieved during this time, future success will be hindered. Here again, then, the notion of optimal readiness learning periods is a more appropriate concept.

A lack of conclusive evidence also exists for later advantages due to early involvement in the Suzuki program, in which children begin learning to play the violin as early as 2 years old. The process of preparing the child for learning is carefully planned in the Suzuki method and appears to take into account all three factors described in our readiness model. Children are first introduced to the sound of the violin as early as birth. Parents are instructed to provide well-played, tonal music to establish an interest as well as a base of understanding on which to operate at a later time. Using this approach, both the motivation to learn and certain prerequisite skills are developed before the child begins to learn the mechanics of playing the violin itself. When the child begins formal lessons, a violin of the appropriate size rather than the standard larger instrument, is provided. It seems reasonable to expect that this type of organized, developmentally based instruction program would be advantageous. Most would expect that a child who is trained in such a program would gain an advantage over children who do not participate in this type of program. But the empirical evidence for any advantage is equivocal. Some world-class violinists began by using the Suzuki method; however, many did not. Nor did they begin at such a young age. And some individuals began in the Suzuki program but failed to develop any success; others lost interest in playing the violin altogether.

Application to Youth Sport

If we go back to the question asked at the beginning of this chapter about the importance of a child's early involvement in sport, two points have emerged from the discussion thus far that help provide an answer to that question. First, it is important to recognize that certain periods exist in a child's life in which he or she is optimally ready to learn skills. The onset of these periods is characterized by appropriate levels of physical and cognitive maturation, adequate achievement of prerequisite skills, and a motivation to be involved in the activity.

Second, the variety of results reported from various early introduction programs indicates that it is impossible to predict who will benefit from early exposure and who will not. Consider some examples that illustrate this point. Shannon Miller began gymnastics training when she was 5 years old and became an Olympic medal winner. Kristie Phillips also began gymnastics training when she was very young, at

4 years old. Although she won a world championship at age 14, however, she failed to make the U.S. Olympic team one year later. One of the factors considered influential in not making the team was that her gymnastic performance began to suffer due to the onset of puberty. This influence contributed to her gaining 20 pounds, which was more weight than she could effectively lose and compensate for in training. Thus, for both girls, early exposure to gymnastics led to benefits for later performance. But, for one of them, these benefits were overridden by the unforeseen influence of maturation. Add to these two examples the many girls you may know who began gymnastics training at age 4 or 5 but never achieved any degree of competitive success. These examples point out that early exposure to a sport is not the key component that leads to eventual success in sport participation. Rather, many variables must be considered in determining what leads to sport success.

Parents must determine their goals for involving a child in sport programs. If the goal is to develop an interest in the activity to motivate the child to continue in the activity as he or she gets older, then early involvement has merit. Even so, it is important to be aware that the opposite could occur. Negative early experiences could influence a child's attitude about the activity and the child's desire to continue to participate in that activity. Early involvement also has merit if the goal is to develop certain prerequisite skill capabilities in the child. Keep in mind, however, that prerequisite skill achievement does not by itself predict that the child will or will not do well in the activity at some later time. The powerful influence of maturation must always be kept in mind. Finally, if the goal for early involvement is to gain a competitive advantage over other children, then early involvement has questionable merit. Although many successful athletes began their sport experience early in their childhood, many others did not.

Desirable Youth Sport Involvement Characteristics

The conclusions presented in the discussion concerning early involvement in sport allow for children to be involved in organized youth sport programs. However, these conclusions specify that such programs should have certain characteristics to make them desirable for children's participation. Likewise, parental actions should be characterized by certain attitudes and involvement characteristics. Five of these program and parental action characteristics are described here.

1. *Children should be encouraged to be involved in a variety of motor skill and sport activities.* No preadolescent or adolescent child should be required to specialize in one activity. In early childhood, especially, the primary parental goal for their children should be to provide as wide a variety of movement skill opportunities as possible. With respect to the question concerning the age of involvement in sport, it is interesting to note that research has shown that later success in specific sports skills is more related to involvement in a variety of skills than to early involvement in a specific skill (see McPherson & Brown, 1988).
2. *Youth sport programs should provide a performance environment that is scaled to the physical characteristics of its participants.* Consider the possible skill learning effects that can be associated with learning to

perform a sports skill when dimensions are not scaled to participant sizes. For example, if a child must learn to shoot a basketball at a basket that is 10 feet from the floor, quite likely the child will develop inappropriate coordination characteristics to generate the right amount of force to make shots go through the basket. As the child gets older and taller, he or she will have to relearn these coordination patterns to appropriately adapt to changes in scale. The 10-foot regulation height was designed for adults, not children. For an adult who is 6 feet tall, the regulation basket is only 40 percent taller than he or she is. But for the child who is only 4 feet tall, the regulation basket is 150 percent taller than he or she is. From the perspective of the importance of developing component skills of a sport, it makes sense to scale down the height of the basket to keep the body height to basket height ratio reasonably similar across age ranges. This same scaling principle should be applied to all sports so that component skills can be learned properly.

3. *Youth sport programs must emphasize training of component skills involved in the sport.* If, for example, a child is participating in baseball, it is essential that the child receive instruction and practice involving the component skills of the game, such as throwing, catching, batting, and running. And it is important that every child on the team receive this type of experience. Too often a child is assigned a specific position on the team and then receives instruction and experience related only to that position. Every child should learn to catch a ball in the outfield, experience fielding ground balls in the infield, have an opportunity to learn to pitch, and so on. Competition, although an important part of any sport, should not dominate the youth sport program. The competitive aspects of the game must always be secondary to skill instruction. Coaches in youth programs must provide adequate skill instruction and organize effective practice conditions so that their young athletes can acquire critical skills required to experience success in the sport. Eventual success in any sport depends on having learned the skills of that sport.

4. *Youth sport programs and parents must provide an environment in which children want to participate.* Recall the discussion earlier in this chapter in which we established that intrinsic motivation to participate in an activity, and to continue participation in an activity, depends on the child's experiences in the activity. As discussed in other chapters in this book, research investigating why children and youth drop out of organized youth sport programs has consistently shown that three critical factors influence dropping out: the lack of having fun, too much emphasis on competition, and the lack of learning the skills of the sport. The kinds of experiences that encourage children to want to continue participation are those that provide opportunities to learn the skills of the sport, opportunities to experience success in the sport, encouragement and evidence that progress is being made, and opportunities to have fun and enjoy the sport. If parents and coaches wish to have youth sport program participants

continue in sport, it is essential that they establish an environment in which experiences encourage continued involvement.

5. *Youth sport programs must not have policies that allow children to be "cut" from the programs.* Earlier in this chapter, you saw some examples of athletes who were cut from a youth program or a high school program but who eventually became world-class or professional athletes. Each of these examples emphasizes the importance of the role of maturation to success in sport. Maturation rate differences for children cannot be ignored. The lack of prerequisite skills and/or appropriate motivation are also factors that must be considered when evaluating the success or potential success of any child. Policies that allow children to be cut from sport programs work against those factors that are involved in eventual success in sport. To increase the likelihood that the program will take advantage of these factors, it is essential that youth sport programs provide opportunities for all children to participate in their programs. Programs can be organized on the basis of skill level rather than age. This approach helps to account for maturational differences and provides opportunities for lesser-skilled youth to learn appropriate skills. It also establishes an environment in which young athletes can experience success and develop interest in continuing participation. In this way, youth sport programs incorporate the concept of readiness to learn and recognize that children are individually different in when they are optimally ready to learn and to participate in sport.

References

Ausubel, D. P. (1968). *Educational psychology: A cognitive view.* New York: Holt, Rinehart, & Winston.

Flavell, J. H. (1963). *The developmental psychology of Jean Piaget.* Princeton, NJ: Van Nostrand.

Gagné, R. M. (1968). Contributions of learning to human development. *Psychological Review, 75,* 177–191.

———. (1970). *The conditions of learning* (2nd ed.). New York: Holt, Rinehart, & Winston.

Gallahue, D. L. (1989). *Understanding motor development: Infants, children, adolescents* (2nd ed.). Indianapolis: Benchmark.

Gesell, A. (1928). *Infancy and human growth.* New York: Macmillan.

Gesell, A., & Thompson, H. (1929). Learning and growth in identical twin infants. *Genetic Psychology Monographs, 6,* 1–124.

Hall, G. S. (1921). *Aspects of child life and education.* New York: Appleton.

Kamm, K., Thelen, E., & Jensen, J. L. (1990). A dynamical systems approach to motor development. *Physical Therapy, 70,* 763–775.

Langendorfer, S. (1987). Separating fact and fiction in preschool aquatics. *National Aquatics Journal, 3*(1), 2–4.

Laszlo, J. I., & Bairstow, P. J. (1983). Kinaesthesis: Its measurement, training and relationship to motor control. *Quarterly Journal of Experimental Psychology, 35A,* 411–421.

Magill, R. A. (1993). *Motor learning: Concepts and applications* (4th ed.). Dubuque, IA: Brown & Benchmark.

McGraw, M. B. (1935). *Growth: A study of Johnny and Jimmy.* New York: Appleton-Century.

———. (1939). Later developments of children specifically trained during infancy: Johnny and Jimmy at school age. *Child Development, 10,* 1–19.

———. (1945). *The neuromuscular maturation of the human infant.* New York: Hafner.

McPherson, B. D., & Brown, B. A. (1988). The structure, processes, and consequences of sport for children. In F. L. Smoll, R. A. Magill, & M. J. Ash (Eds.), *Children in sport* (3rd ed., pp. 265–286). Champaign, IL: Human Kinetics.

Newell, K. M. (1986). Constraints on the development of coordination. In M. G. Wade & H. T. A. Whiting (Eds.), *Motor development in children: Aspects of coordination and control* (pp. 341–360). Dordrecht: Martinus Nijhoff.

Piaget, J. (1952). *The origins of intelligence in children.* New York: International Universities Press.

———. (1969). *The psychology of the child.* New York: Basic Books.

Scott, J. P. (1962). Critical periods in behavioral development. *Science, 138,* 949–958.

Thelen, E. (1987). The role of motor development in developmental psychology: A view of the past and an agenda for the future. In N. Ersenberg (Ed.), *Contemporary topics in developmental psychology* (pp. 3–33). New York: Wiley.

Thelen, E., & Fisher, D. M. (1982). Newborn stepping: An explanation for a "disappearing reflex." *Developmental Psychology, 18,* 760–775.

Woollacott, M. H., Debû, B., & Shumway-Cook, A. (1987). Children's development of posture and balance control: Changes in motor coordination and sensory integration. In D. Gould & M. Weiss (Eds.), *Advances in pediatric sport sciences: Behavioral issues* (Vol. 2, pp. 211–234). Champaign, IL: Human Kinetics.

AT WHAT AGE ARE CHILDREN READY TO COMPETE?
Some Psychological Considerations

—*Michael W. Passer*

About 15 years ago an unusual newspaper photograph caught my eye; it showed a 1-year-old infant flying through the air, having been tossed aloft by her mother in one of the events at a "baby decathlon" competition held in the Midwest. I don't know whether winning was based on distance covered, target accuracy, or some other criterion, but the photo caption did note that the young competitors landed on soft foam pads and this particular infant "won" the event. It also claimed she was smiling, though her expression clearly seemed to me to be one of sheer fright.

In the ensuing years I learned of a few other adult-organized physical contests held for toddlers, but recently I saw TV news footage of an event that truly is in a league by itself: a crawling race for infants. Once the race began, few competitors moved far from the starting line, but one crawled at breakneck speed and zoomed across the finish line in what must have been world-record time. The absolutely astonishing fact about this race, however, was the prize: The winner received $3,000 to be used toward a college scholarship!

I readily confess that when I learn about "contests" like this, a part of me feels they are so ludicrous as to be funny. But in reality, they are not amusing. Sport scholars note that the dominant sport culture in contemporary Western society emphasizes achievement and winning, materialism, and the view that sport performance is a means to an end (e.g., Donnelly, 1993; Ingham & Hardy, 1993). Events such as the "baby crawl" take these societal themes to an absurd extreme. Although other infant "competitions" may not link material rewards to performance, they provide an equally telling commentary on just how eager some parents are to give their children an early thrust into the world of competition. The irony, however, is that from the participants' point of view these events do not represent sports, races, or contests of any kind. As my subsequent comments will indicate, whatever the parents intentions and motives for organizing such events may be, any belief that their babies really are "competing" simply is misguided.

Criteria for Determining Age Readiness for Competition

To my knowledge infant and toddler competitions thankfully are rare, but it is not too far a climb up the age ladder before we find very young children competing in more formal organized youth sports. For example, in the United States the earliest age of participation is 3 years for swimming and gymnastics, 5 years for track and field, wrestling, and baseball, and 6 years for soccer and bowling (Martens, 1988). Some 4-year-old Australian children become involved in organized sports (Robertson, 1986), in Brazil 6-year-olds compete in swimming, soccer, and gymnastics (Ferreira, 1986), and in Canada competition for 6- to 8-year-olds is offered in some sports as high up as the provincial level (Valeriote & Hansen, 1988). Although most children join the ranks of youth sport at a later age, participation by 3- to 6-year-olds in some sports has become accepted across the globe.

Should very young children be competing in organized sports? If not, then at what age are children ready and able to compete? What criteria can be used to make such a determination? Whether viewed at the level of the individual child or in terms of general age guidelines, children's readiness for competition depends on many factors: the child's level of physical, psychological, and social development, the task demands of the particular sport, parental readiness, and broader cultural and socialization factors (see reviews by Coakley, 1986; Malina, 1986; Seefeldt, this volume; Sharkey, 1986).

In this chapter I will examine three psychological issues relevant to the formation of general age guidelines for participation in youth sport. The first issue concerns children's motivational readiness for competition. Whether in sports, academics, music, or other domains, competition gives children the direct opportunity to test and evaluate their abilities against those of other youngsters. This is important to children because it is a key means by which they assess their competence (Horn & Hasbrook, 1986; Scanlan, this volume). This process of learning about our characteristics (e.g., gauging the level of our abilities or the accuracy of our opinions) by comparing ourselves with other people is called *social comparison* (Festinger, 1954). From a social comparison standpoint, motivational readiness for competition occurs when children become attracted to, seek out, and take advantage of opportunities for comparing their own physical abilities with those of their peers.

Children's cognitive readiness for competition represents the second general issue that will be examined to establish age guidelines for youth sport. It is all too easy for adults to take for granted the numerous reasoning skills and cognitive abilities that come into play during competition and that help make competition a psychologically meaningful and maximally rewarding experience. Among others, these cognitive factors include the ability to organize and store information (e.g., a coach's skill or game instructions, set plays, an opponent's behavioral or strategic tendencies) in memory and retrieve that information later on, the ability to accurately identify why one has performed well or poorly so that future adjustments can be made, and the ability to understand situations from another person's (e.g., a coach, teammate, or opponent) point of view.

Finally, parents, coaches, and administrators often ask about age guidelines for youth sport participation because they are concerned that children's involvement at too early an age might produce harmful physical or psychological consequences. Some of these potential negative consequences will be addressed as a third criterion for judging children's age readiness for formal athletic competition.

Motivational Readiness for Competition

At its heart, competition is a social comparison process. To determine whether I have the ability to run or swim a certain distance, or shoot or kick ball into a goal, I need only make the attempt and observe the outcome. To determine whether I run or swim *quickly,* or am *good* at shooting or kicking a ball into a goal, I must gauge how my performance compares with the performance of other people (Festinger, 1954).

Motivationally, delaying children's entrance into organized sport programs until they reach an age where the unique opportunities for ability comparison provided by competition become attractive and important to them makes sense. In other words, once children develop the motivation to compare their skills with those of their peers, participating in competition begins to serve a special psychological function for them. Several investigators have emphasized that very young children cannot and do not compete because they are either incapable of or uninterested in social comparison (Roberts, 1980; Scanlan, this volume; Sherif, 1976). Therefore, to assess children's motivational readiness for competition we must determine the age at which their social comparison motivation develops.

Before doing so, one very critical point must be emphasized. Children who are too young to engage in social comparison surely can participate in athletic activities, have fun, learn skills, attempt goals, and gain feedback about their abilities by examining whether they can physically accomplish certain tasks (e.g., hitting a ball). For that matter, even infants placed in a "crawling race" may find it a pleasurable experience. Thus, it might be argued that it is inappropriate to equate motivational readiness for competition with the development of social comparison motivation. This stance, however, fails to take into account one important fact: Every one of these benefits—pleasure and fun, skill development, goal accomplishment—can be obtained from noncompetitive instructional or play settings. If the activity truly is being conducted for the child's benefit and enjoyment, rather than for the satisfaction of parents or other adults, then there is absolutely no need to formalize and structure physical activities into highly organized competitive games for children to whom social comparison is meaningless or of little importance.

The Preschool Years

At what age do children become oriented toward social comparison? When they are about 1½ to 2½ years old, children develop a well-organized, autonomous achievement orientation that evolves from a more basic mastery or competence motivation (Veroff, 1969; White, 1959). The child masters new skills via exploration and play and readily evaluates the outcome of mastery attempts. Competence is judged based on autonomous standards, and satisfaction is derived from successful mastery attempts. From 3½ to 5½ years of age children increasingly act to maximize their self-gain at the expense of others when placed in conflict-of-interest situations (see Pepitone, 1980). For example, naturalistic observations made during indoor and outdoor free-play periods indicate that preschoolers periodically initiate attempts to take objects away from other children and defend themselves against such attempts by other children (Weigel, 1984).

To adults it often appears that these children are "competing" rather than sharing or cooperating because they vie with peers for desired objects or limited rewards. But this typically is not competition in a true social comparison sense. Rather, these children simply act to acquire or hold on to something they value (Pepitone, 1980), and in essence they are still pursuing autonomous achievement goals. Similarly, while they are working on achievement tasks very young children often may look at their peers' work—a behavior that adults may perceive as reflecting competitive interests—but such looking primarily stems from an individual mastery orientation (i.e., the desire to improve by observing others) rather than a desire for competitive ability comparison (Butler, 1989).

Although achievement motivation strongly centers around autonomous goals between the ages of 2 to 5, naturalistic observation studies of preschoolers at play indicate that they begin to engage in some types of social comparison when they are about 4 years old (Chafel, 1986, 1987; Mosatche, 1981). Much of this social comparison centers around rudimentary differences or similarities that children share (e.g., "My hair is brown, yours is red," "We are both 4½ years old"), and though some preschoolers engage in "besting statements" or verbal boasts, their comparisons often pertain to simple object possession (e.g., "My toy is bigger than yours," "I've got the most and you don't"). Some besting statements, however, do seem to serve a competitive function related to ability (e.g., "I can run faster than you").

Other researchers have placed preschoolers into competitive situations to determine whether they use social comparison information to assess their competence. The results of these studies are mixed. For example, Butler (1989) had children work on a picture-creation task and concluded that preschoolers assigned to perform in a competitive condition did not display greater interest in their peers' work than preschoolers who performed in a noncompetitive condition. Older children (fourth graders), however, showed greater interest in their peers' work when they performed in the competitive condition.

In a study by Pascuzzi (1981), second graders and preschoolers participated in races with two other children of the same sex and age. After each race children's emotional responses, self-concept of ability, and expectancy of future success were measured. All of these psychological variables had been shown in earlier research to be influenced by perceptions of success and failure. Thus, Pascuzzi reasoned that if the children's psychological responses after the race differed according to whether they finished first, second, or third, this would indicate that they judged their own performance relative to how well their peers did. If the children did not engage in social comparison, then the order of finish would have no bearing on their postrace responses. As predicted, second graders' responses varied according to their place of finish. The results for the preschoolers, however, depended on gender: The psychological responses of the preschool boys varied according to their order of finish but those of the preschool girls were similar regardless of placement.

In a recent study (Reissland & Harris, 1991), younger boys and girls (mean age 34 months) competed against their older siblings (mean age 58 months) in a "race" to fit objects into a wooden board. For each pair of siblings their mother was present during the race and the task was rigged so that the younger children would win the first race, with the older children winning the second. The results indicated that all of the 4- to 5-year-olds exhibited pride when they won and almost all of the approximately 2- to 4-year-olds did likewise; the few who didn't were quite young (mean age 23 months). Further, the younger children drew as much attention to their achievement as the older children.

At first glance the Reissland and Harris (1991) findings suggest the remarkable possibility that most preschoolers—even as young as 2½ to 3—use social comparison to judge whether they have "won" and gauge their emotional response accordingly. Unfortunately, the researchers note that the task of completing the puzzle elicits pride, yet there was no control group to examine children's pride reactions when they successfully completed the task in the absence of a race situation. It is entirely possible that the race meant nothing or little to the children and that their pride and desire for their mother's attention was based only on their individual achievement of completing the task. Stated differently, their pride may have been an indicant of autonomous achievement motivation, not social comparison motivation.

In summarizing the research results pertaining to preschoolers, it seems that some preschool-age children (most typically 4-year-olds) spontaneously engage in simple ability comparisons and make use of social comparison information to assess their abilities when placed in competitive situations; however, there is no consistent or clear evidence to indicate that, as a group, preschoolers are significantly oriented toward social comparison for the purpose of assessing their abilities. Rather, individualistic or autonomous achievement motivation is predominant during this age period.

Elementary School Years

Children's social comparison motivation develops significantly during the early elementary school years. Veroff (1969) notes that in general children do not begin to spontaneously compare themselves with peers for purposes of ability assessment until they are about 5 to 6 years old. Frey and Ruble (1985) conducted classroom observations and found that as children progressed from kindergarten to first grade there was a sharp increase in social comparison related to performance assessment. Using a different methodology, other researchers have exposed children to achievement tasks and found that at around the ages of 7 or 8 they start to make use of or seek out social comparison information to judge their own abilities (Butler, 1989; Ruble et al., 1980).

This rise in social comparison behavior during the early elementary school years corresponds nicely with other findings that show that, in contrast to preschoolers who generally value individualism and have difficulty understanding the concept of social comparison, early elementary school age children place greater social value on superiority (Knight, Dubro, & Chao, 1985) and have a better understanding of social comparison (Schoeneman, Tabor, & Nash, 1984). Some evidence also indicates that children's interest in competition stems directly from this burgeoning desire for social comparison. Naturalistic observation research (Rowen, 1973) indicates that around the ages of 6 or 7 children begin to transform all sorts of situations into competitive ones to determine who is "the best." Other research has found that around the age of 7 children will increase their competitive behavior when social comparison information is made available (Toda et al., 1978).

In sum, findings from diverse lines of research suggest that the early elementary school years are when most children develop an interest in social comparison for purposes of assessing their ability and begin to seek out competitive situations specifically for their social comparison value. During the middle and late elementary school years, children's interest in social comparison continues to grow (Butler, 1989; Keil et al., 1990; Ruble et al., 1980).

Although numerous qualities can serve as focal points for youngsters' social comparison interests, physical and athletic ability typically are valued attributes among children of elementary and secondary school age, particularly for boys (Adler, Kless, & Adler, 1992; Buchanan, Blankenbaker, & Cotten, 1976). Therefore, as social comparison motivation strengthens during the elementary school years, it would be expected that an increasing number of youngsters would seek out sport opportunities to develop and assess their athletic skills relative to their peers. This is, in fact, what happens. Depending on the sport, the average beginning age of participation in nonschool (i.e., nonmandatory) youth sport programs typically ranges from 8 to 12 years (Martens, 1988; Valeriote & Hansen, 1988), and the total number of participants across most sports grows steadily until it peaks at around the ages of 11 to 13 (State of Michigan, 1976).

This analysis suggests two conclusions. First, if motivational readiness for competition is the main criterion upon which general age guidelines in youth sport are to be based, then participation should not begin until children are about 7 years old. At this age the desire for and ability to use social comparison information should be reasonably well developed in most children. Second, for the vast majority of children, their age of initial involvement in youth sport currently falls well within this guideline.

Cognitive Readiness for Competition

Information-Processing Abilities

Participation in organized sports requires a host of cognitive skills and abilities. One very important set of cognitive factors concerns the child's information-processing capabilities. Young athletes must be able to attend to and remember considerable amounts of information such as rules of the sport, skill techniques and lessons, game or performance strategies, and specific instructions from coaches during practice and competition. In many sports, athletes also need to learn and remember various plays or performance options, as well as the characteristic strategies or plays used by one's opponent.

Before the age of 4 most children have relatively short attention spans and are easily distracted from achievement-related activities in which they are engaged (Ruff & Lawson, 1990; see Shaffer, 1993). As they progress through elementary school, children are able to focus their attention on tasks for longer periods of time and they become better at paying attention to and searching for task-relevant information. Research suggests that around the late elementary or early secondary school years children become much more sophisticated in gathering relevant information and ignoring task-irrelevant information (see Shaffer, 1993).

Even if young athletes successfully attend to task-relevant information, they must be able to retain and retrieve it later on. Sometimes this time duration is short (e.g., as when a baseball coach sends a player up to the plate with instructions to "bunt," or a wrestling coach discusses a last-minute change in strategy with an athlete); at other times the needed retention period is long (e.g., as when players learn rules or various plays or formations that will be used throughout a season or beyond).

Children's memory capabilities improve as they grow older. These changes appear to be brought about by increases in the speed and efficiency with which children process information into memory and their use of more sophisticated retrieval strategies rather than changes in the physical capacity of short-term and long-term memory (Bee, 1992; Shaffer, 1993). For example, one of the most common strategies that people use to remember information is to rehearse it. Another strategy is to group bits of information together into clusters or "chunks" (e.g., in trying to learn a play diagram of "X's" and "O's", a player would group related "letters" into larger units rather than trying to individually memorize the location of each one). Although children as young as 2 or 3 may use rehearsal and clustering under very simple and carefully arranged task conditions, these strategies are primitive and rarely appear spontaneously. Between the ages of 5 and 8 children use rehearsal more regularly but not in the same way as older children do. Further, they often have trouble using clustering and if they do use this strategy in one situation, they typically fail to generalize it to other situations. By late childhood and into adolescence it takes progressively less time to process information, memory strategies become more sophisticated, and they are used more flexibly (Bee 1992; Kail, 1991; Shaffer, 1993).

Attributional Abilities

The capacity to understand causal relationships is another cognitive ability highly relevant to the competition process. As noted earlier, children seek out competition because it provides social comparison information that helps them assess their competence. Yet competence cannot be judged accurately until one becomes aware that performance outcomes such as winning and losing are the products of interactive causal factors such as physical skill, strategy, preparation, effort, task (opponent) difficulty, and luck. A number of studies suggest that it may not be until the late elementary and early secondary school years that this cognitive ability becomes well developed (Nesdale & Pope, 1985; Nicholls, 1978; Roberts, 1980, 1986; Weiner & Kun, 1978). For example, Nesdale and Pope (1985) found that 4- to 7-year-old children attributed their successes and failures to the difficulty of the task and generally did not view ability, effort, and luck to be responsible for their performance outcomes. In fact, many of the explanations given by preschool- and kindergarten-aged children for why they can or cannot accomplish something bear little resemblance to the traditional attributional categories employed by adults or older children (see Burgner & Hewstone, 1993). Research by Ewing, Roberts, and Pemberton (cited in Roberts, 1986) with 9- to 14-year-old youth sport participants found that children younger than 12 were not able to differentiate between the relative contributions of effort and ability as determinants of success and failure, and a recent study by Walling (personal communication, April 11, 1994) of 5- through 13-year-old boys and girls also found a strong developmental trend; at both sport-related and academic tasks, only the 11- to 13-year-olds clearly differentiated between the concepts of effort and ability.

These developmental shifts in causal reasoning influence not only how children of different ages will assess their competence based on performance outcomes but also how they will respond emotionally to those outcomes, what their future performance aspirations and success expectancies will be, and how they will approve or disapprove of other children based on those children's outcomes. For example, Stipek and DeCotis (1988) studied 6- through 13-year-olds and concluded that not until age 12 were pride-shame reactions to success-failure exclusively linked to ability and effort attributions. Similarly, whereas by age 6 children's expectancies of future success begin to be influenced by their past success-failure outcomes, it may not be until 10 to 12 years of age that their success expectancies become linked to the diverse attributions they make for these outcomes (Weiner & Kun, 1978). As Weiner and Kun note, to develop realistic performance expectancies and achievement goals, children may first need to understand that how well one does in the future depends on the cause of having done well or poorly in the past. In this vein, Roberts (1986) suggests that children's attributional capacities influence their general achievement goals in sport.

Role-Taking and Other Cognitive Abilities

A host of other cognitive abilities are called into play during organized sport participation; among them are simple logical reasoning and problem-solving skills, the capacity to understand situations from various perspectives or roles, language comprehension, and the ability to infer other people's emotions from their nonverbal behavior. Similar to the age-related changes that occur in children's information-processing and attributional capabilities, these other cognitive abilities develop dramatically and become much more sophisticated by the end of the elementary school years (see Bee, 1992; Shaffer, 1993). Consistent with these age trends, several sport scientists propose that children's cognitive abilities are such that they do not develop a mature overall understanding of the competition process until they are about 12 years old (Coakley, 1986; Roberts, 1980).

Coakley (1986), for example, proposes that full comprehension of what it means to compete against an opponent cannot occur until children possess the ability to put themselves into the point of view or role of other participants. Coakley argues that before the age of 6 children's thinking is egocentric and from 6 to 8 years of age children begin to understand others' viewpoints. Between the ages of 8 and 10 children's role-taking abilities are sufficiently developed so that they can understand and accept another person's viewpoint. Finally, when they are 10 to 12 years old, children develop the capacity to comprehend more than just one other viewpoint and can readily adopt a group perspective. Based on more recent developmental research than that cited by Coakley, the specific ages at which these perspective-taking abilities develop may be subject to some debate; some studies show, for example, that even 3-year-olds are capable of adopting another child's perspective at very simple tasks (see Shaffer, 1993). Nevertheless, the overall age progression and implications of Coakley's analysis remain intact: In team sports young children will have diffi-culty understanding that a team is composed of interdependent positions that must simultaneously respond to one another's and the opposing players' movements (Coakley, 1986). Anyone who has watched 7-year-old youth soccer players continu-ally swarm to the ball from across the field like bees to nectar, rather than maintain field position and focus on strategically passing the ball as repeatedly instructed by the coach, can bear witness to Coakley's general point.

Potential Harmful Consequences

Are young children at risk for psychological harm when they participate in organized youth sports? Yes, they are. Among other risks, it is possible that their self-perceptions of physical competence may suffer, that their short-term and long-term competitive anxiety may increase, that they will be unpopular with teammates, and that their general self-esteem may decrease because of their sport involvement. It is absolutely essential, however, to keep two points in mind. First, other achievement activities in which young children participate—including typical academic experi-ences in elementary school—carry analogous risks. Second, even among older chil-dren sport competition can have negative psychological effects if the setting is aversive or managed inappropriately. For example, the psychological stress brought about by an overemphasis on competition and winning can adversely affect older children's and young adolescents' physical and psychological health, enjoyment of sport, and athletic performance (see Passer, 1988). Further, among both younger and older children, those who are poorer performers athletically usually will be less pop-ular among their teammates or other peers in the sport setting (Passer & Scanlan, 1980; Weiss & Duncan, 1992). There simply is no magic age beyond which partici-pation in youth sport programs can be delayed so as to guarantee that such outcomes will not occur.

Still, some special hazards must be considered prior to involving young chil-dren in organized sports, and many of them are an outgrowth of children's lack of motivational and cognitive readiness for competition. Several negative consequences may arise when children who are not motivationally ready are placed in competitive events. At best, the physical activity will be enjoyed, but the competitive component simply will be meaningless or irrelevant to children who are not oriented toward social comparison; they will focus instead on autonomous individual achievement goals. At worst, the children will not enjoy the activity for intrinsic reasons and may find themselves involved in sports, not because they want to be, but because others—such as their parents—have decided they ought to be. In turn, research suggests that children who feel it is not their own decision to participate in youth sport programs are less likely to be satisfied with their sport experience and more likely to discon-tinue their involvement (McGuire & Cook, 1983). Children who report participating in youth sports to please their parents have also been found to have higher competi-tive stress (Scanlan & Lewthwaite, 1984).

As noted earlier, young children do not understand complex causal relation-ships and may be especially likely to form inaccurate assessments of their physical competence based on success-failure outcomes in sport. Indeed, the correlation between perceived and actual competence is weaker among younger children (see Roberts, 1986). Inaccurate perceptions of ability subsequently may cause children to develop unrealistically high or low achievement goals.

This difficulty in assessing competence and the true causes of performance outcomes increases young children's dependence on performance-related feedback from adults. Thus young children are especially sensitive to comments and reactions by adults, sometimes in ways that adults do not realize. For example, young children may perceive constructive mild criticism from adults as evidence of failure rather than as helpful advice, the result being that the children experience stress (Roberts, 1986). Young children also may misinterpret adults' lack of reaction. Smith, Smoll, & Curtis (1978) studied 8- through 15-year-old Little League Baseball players; their findings suggested that when 8- to 9-year-olds performed well or did something positive and coaches ignored it (e.g., they failed to offer praise), the children interpreted the coaches' neutral behaviors as aversive or negative responses.

Youth sport participants also obtain considerable performance feedback by observing coaches', parents', and one another's nonverbal responses, such as facial expressions. Numerous studies indicate that young children are less skilled than older children in accurately inferring people's emotions from facial expressions. In particular, 3- through 8-year-olds are most accurate in identifying happiness from facial expressions but have more difficulty distinguishing between negative emotions (Fabes et al., 1991; see Gross & Ballif, 1991). Preschoolers tend to confuse expressions of anger and sadness, anger and disgust, and perceive neutral facial expressions as indicating sadness; even third graders often confuse anger and sadness and misjudge neutral expressions. Younger children are also more likely than older children to infer someone else's emotion based on the simple outcome of a situation (e.g., incorrectly judging that a coach looks angry because the player or team lost) rather than taking into account other situational factors or the other person's attribution for that outcome (e.g., correctly judging that a coach looks sad, not angry, because the child tried hard but was up against a superior opponent or had bad luck). Moreover, children are less accurate in using facial expressions to identify more complex emotions (e.g., pride, shame, guilt) than basic ones (see Gross & Ballif, 1991). Thus there is considerable potential for young children to misread coaches', parents', and teammates' nonverbal reactions to their performance. The finding that children have relative difficulty reading neutral facial expressions is especially interesting because it fits in with Smith et al.'s (1978) observation that young children may perceive a coach's nonresponse to positive player performance as punitive. Coaches may feel that they are verbally and nonverbally responding to players in a neutral fashion, but this may not be the players' interpretation.

Another potential hazard of sport participation at an early age is that young children, limited by language capacity and other relatively immature cognitive skills, cannot understand the directions or instructions of adults as well as older children can. This inability may cause frustration and stress not only for the child but also for parents and coaches who feel they are communicating clearly and become annoyed when their instructions are not obeyed. In some cases these adults may have unrealistic expectations of children's cognitive abilities and speak to them as if they are miniature adults (a tendency facilitated, perhaps, by the stylish uniforms and other adult trappings of many youth sport programs). In other cases, well-meaning parents and coaches may do a good job of adjusting task demands and their level of speech to the age of the child but may not be fully aware of the sometimes subtle limitations in children's cognitive abilities (e.g., very young children find it more difficult to understand negative instructions [Don't do X] than positive instructions [Do Y]). Thus the readiness of parents and coaches to work within the level of youngsters' cognitive abilities becomes another important consideration in determining the age at which children should become involved in youth sports (Malina, 1986).

Age Guidelines and Conclusions

Three broad issues bearing on children's preparedness for participating in youth sport programs have been discussed: motivational readiness, cognitive readiness, and potential harmful consequences. Of these, I view motivational readiness as the starting point for formulating age guidelines. As the "baby decathlon" and "infant scholarship crawl" contests mentioned at the beginning of this chapter illustrate, children of virtually any age can be placed in athletic events or physical contests that are organized and labeled by adults as "competition." But it is not until the early elementary school years that most children will have a fairly well developed orientation to respond to these contests as representing competition in a social comparison sense, much less spontaneously seek out competitive sport situations for their social comparison value. Based solely on the criterion of motivational readiness, I suggest that adults should delay children's participation in organized youth sports until the early elementary school years.

Several arguments can be made for setting a younger age limit, and others can be given for establishing an older one. With regard to a lower age limit, the first argument is that involving preschoolers in sport competition is necessary if the children are to become highly skilled performers or possibly champions when they grow older. However, I do not know of any good, nonanecdotal data to support this argument. In fact, even in countries such as Russia, where elite training programs in some sports begin as early as age 4 or 5, many sport specialists have begun to doubt whether the final level of skill achieved by athletes is proportional to the number of years spent in training (Jefferies, 1986). If preschool-age children are to be involved in adult-supervised physical activity—even for the alleged purpose of "grooming" them for potential elite performance—their time would be better spent on skill development than on competition.

A second argument for lower youth sport age limits is that some preschoolers are oriented toward social comparison and competition, as suggested by the studies I presented earlier. The counterpoint is that there is no good evidence that even a significant minority of preschoolers are oriented toward socially comparing their physical abilities, and those who are oriented toward such comparison typically make very basic comparisons.

A third and related argument is that involving very young children in organized sports will facilitate their interest in social comparison. Veroff (1969) contends that young children may become intrinsically socially comparative if their environment orients them toward this, and recent research indicates that children's understanding and use of social comparison is influenced by the degree of competitiveness in their general social-educational environment (Butler & Kedar, 1990; Butler & Ruzany, 1993). Whether accelerating children's interest in social comparison and competition is an inherently wise developmental goal can only be answered in relation to one's personal values about childhood. But even if the answer is affirmative, the potential costs must be weighed, and this is precisely where children's cognitive readiness and the potential harmful consequences of early involvement in sport competition must be considered.

Research on children's cognitive abilities suggests they typically will not have a reasonably mature understanding of the competition process until the middle to late elementary school years. Although numerous studies over the past decade or two have shown that many cognitive abilities develop more quickly than previously believed (see Bee, 1992; Shaffer, 1993), it is clear that during the elementary school years children's information-processing capabilities, attributional processes, role-taking abilities, and skill in inferring other people's emotional reactions all become much more sophisticated. When they compete, older children will have a better understanding of what they are doing, why they are doing it, the causes of their success-failure, and how other people feel about it.

The issue of readiness is complicated by the differences that exist in the rate of children's psychological development and in the kinds of competitive sport environments to which they are exposed. Nevertheless, based on criteria considered in this paper, I recommend that children younger than 7 or 8 be discouraged from participating in organized youth sports. By this age most children should have a general motivational readiness for competition and cognitive abilities sufficient for a basic understanding of the competition process. Even so, the competitive emphasis of sport should be phased in gradually as children get older, and it is essential that the parents and coaches of youth sport participants—especially 7- to 9-year-olds—be made aware of the ways in which children's cognitive capacities differ from those of adults. This educational goal should be a key component of coach and parent training programs.

References

Adler, P. A., Kless, S. J., & Adler, P. (1992). Socialization to gender roles: Popularity among elementary school boys and girls. *Sociology of Education, 65,* 169–187.

Bee, H. (1992). *The developing child* (6th ed.). New York: HarperCollins.

Buchanan, H. T., Blankenbaker, J., & Cotten, D. (1976). Academic and athletic ability as popularity factors in elementary school children. *Research Quarterly, 3,* 320–325.

Burgner, D., & Hewstone, M. (1993). Young children's causal attributions for success and failure: 'Self-enhancing' boys and 'self-derogating' girls. *British Journal of Developmental Psychology, 11,* 125–129.

Butler, R. (1989). Mastery versus ability appraisal: A developmental study of children's observations of peers' work. *Child Development, 60,* 1350–1361.

Butler, R., & Kedar, A. (1990). Effects of intergroup competition and school philosophy on student perceptions, group processes, and performance. *Contemporary Educational Psychology, 15,* 301–318.

Butler, R., & Ruzany, N. (1993). Age and socialization effects on the development of social comparison motives and normative ability assessment in kibbutz and urban children. *Child Development, 64,* 532–543.

Chafel, J. A. (1986). A naturalistic investigation of the use of social comparison by young children. *Journal of Research and Development in Education, 19*(3), 51–61.

———. (1987). Achieving knowledge about self and others through physical object and social fantasy play. *Early Childhood Research Quarterly, 2,* 27–43.

Coakley, J. (1986). When should children begin competing? A sociological perspective. In M. R. Weiss & D. Gould (Eds.), *Sport for children and youths* (pp. 59–63). Champaign, IL: Human Kinetics.

Donnelly, P. (1993). Subcultures in sport: Resilience and transformation. In A. G. Ingham & J. W. Loy (Eds.), *Sport in social development: Traditions, transitions, and transformations* (pp. 119–145). Champaign, IL: Human Kinetics.

Fabes, R. A., Eisenberg, N., Nyman, M., & Michealieu, Q. (1991). Young children's appraisals of others' spontaneous emotional reactions. *Developmental Psychology, 27,* 858–866.

Ferreira, M. B. R. (1986). Youth sport in Brazil. In M. R. Weiss & D. Gould (Eds.), *Sport for children and youths* (pp. 11–15). Champaign, IL: Human Kinetics.

Festinger, L. (1954). A theory of social comparison processes. *Human Relations, 7,* 17–140.

Frey, K. S., & Ruble, D. N. (1985). What children say when the teacher is not around: Conflicting goals in social comparison and performance assessment in the classroom. *Journal of Personality and Social Psychology, 48,* 550–562.

Gross, A. L., & Ballif, B. (1991). Children's understanding of emotion from facial expressions and situations: A review. *Developmental Review, 11,* 368–398.

Horn, T. S., & Hasbrook, C. (1986). Informational components influencing children's perception of their physical competence. In M. R. Weiss & D. Gould (Eds.), *Sport for children and youths* (pp. 81–88). Champaign, IL: Human Kinetics.

Ingham, A. G., & Hardy, S. (1993). Introduction: Sport studies through the lens of Raymond Williams. In A. G. Ingham & J. W. Loy (Eds.), *Sport in social development: Traditions, transitions, and transformations* (pp. 119–145). Champaign, IL: Human Kinetics.

Jefferies, S. C. (1986). Youth sport in the Soviet Union. In M. R. Weiss & D. Gould (Eds.), *Sport for children and youths* (pp. 35–40). Champaign, IL: Human Kinetics.

Kail, R. (1991). Processing time declines exponentially during childhood and adolescence. *Developmental Psychology, 27,* 259–266.

Keil, L. J., McClintock, C. G., Kramer, R., & Platow, M. J. (1990). Children's use of social comparison standards in judging performance and their effects on self-evaluation. *Contemporary Educational Psychology, 15,* 75–91.

Knight, G. P., Dubro, A. F., & Chao, C. (1985). Information processing and the development of cooperative, competitive, and individualistic social values. *Developmental Psychology, 21,* 37–45.

Malina, R. M. (1986). Readiness for competitive youth sport. In M. R. Weiss & D. Gould (Eds.), *Sport for children and youths* (pp. 45–50). Champaign, IL: Human Kinetics.

Martens, R. (1988). Youth sport in the USA. In F. L. Smoll, R. A. Magill, & M. J. Ash (Eds.), *Children in sport* (3rd ed., pp. 17–23). Champaign, IL: Human Kinetics.

McGuire, R. T., & Cook, D. L. (1983). The influence of others and the decision to participate in youth sports. *Journal of Sport Behavior, 6,* 9–16.

Mosatche, H. S. (1981). An observational study of social comparison in preschoolers. *Child Development, 52,* 376–378.

Nesdale, A. R., & Pope, S. (1985). Young children's causal attributions and performance expectations on skilled tasks. *British Journal of Developmental Psychology, 3,* 183–190.

Nicholls, J. G. (1978). The development of the concepts of effort and ability, perception of own attainment, and the understanding that difficult tasks require more ability. *Child Development, 49,* 800–814.

Pascuzzi, D. L. (1981). Young children's perception of success and failure. Abstract in *Psychology of Motor Behavior & Sport* (1981): 97.

Passer, M. W. (1988). Determinants and consequences of children's competitive stress. In F. L. Smoll, R. A. Magill, & M. J. Ash (Eds.), *Children in sport* (3rd ed., pp. 203–227). Champaign, IL: Human Kinetics.

Passer, M. W., & Scanlan, T. K. (1980). *A sociometric analysis of popularity and leadership status among players on youth soccer teams.* Paper presented at the meeting of the North American Society for the Psychology of Sport and Physical Activity, Boulder, CO.

Pepitone, E. A. (1980). *Children in cooperation and competition.* Lexington, MA: D.C. Heath.

Reissland, N., & Harris, P. (1991). Children's use of display rules in pride-eliciting situations. *British Journal of Developmental Psychology, 9,* 431–435.

Roberts, G. C. (1980). Children in competition: A theoretical perspective and recommendations for practice. *Motor Skills: Theory into Practice, 4,* 37–50.

———. (1986). The perception of stress: A potential source and its development. In M. R. Weiss & D. Gould (Eds.), *Sport for children and youths* (pp. 119–126). Champaign, IL: Human Kinetics.

Robertson, I. (1986). Youth sport in Australia. In M. R. Weiss & D. Gould (Eds.), *Sport for children and youths* (pp. 5–10). Champaign, IL: Human Kinetics.

Rowen, B. (1973). *The children we see: An observational approach to child study.* New York: Holt, Rinehart & Winston.

Ruble, D. N., Boggiano, A. K., Feldman, N. S., & Loebl, J. (1980). Developmental analysis of the role of social comparison in self-evaluation. *Developmental Psychology, 16,* 105–115.

Ruff, H. A., & Lawson, K. R. (1990). Development of sustained focused attention in young children during play. *Developmental Psychology, 26,* 85–93.

Scanlan, T. K. (1995). Social evaluation and the competition process: A developmental perspective. In F. L. Smoll & R. E. Smith (Eds.), *Children and youth in sport: A biopsychosocial perspective* (pp. 298–308). Dubuque, IA: Brown & Benchmark.

Scanlan, T. K., & Lewthwaite, R. (1984). Social psychological aspects of competition for male youth sport participants: I. Predictors of competitive stress. *Journal of Sport Psychology, 6,* 208–226.

Schoeneman, T. J., Tabor, L. E., & Nash, D. L. (1984). Children's reports of the sources of self-knowledge. *Journal of Personality, 52,* 124–137.

Seefeldt, V. (1995). The concept of readiness applied to the acquisition of motor skills. In F. L. Smoll & R. E. Smith (Eds.), *Children and youth in sport: A biopsychosocial perspective* (pp. 49–56). Dubuque, IA: Brown & Benchmark.

Shaffer, D. R. (1993). *Developmental psychology: Childhood and adolescence* (3rd ed.). Pacific Grove, CA: Brooks/Cole.

Sharkey, B. J. (1986). When should children begin competing? A physiological perspective. In M. R. Weiss & D. Gould (Eds.), *Sport for children and youths* (pp. 51–54). Champaign, IL: Human Kinetics.

Sherif, C. (1976). The social context of competition. In D. Landers (Ed.), *Social problems in athletics* (pp. 18–36). Urbana: University of Illinois Press.

Smith, R. E., Smoll, F. L., & Curtis, B. (1978). Coaching behaviors in little league baseball. In F. L. Smoll & R. E. Smith (Eds.), *Psychological perspectives in youth sports* (pp. 173–201). Washington, DC: Hemisphere.

State of Michigan. (1976). *Joint legislative study on youth sports programs: Phase I.* East Lansing, MI: Author.

Stipek, D. J., & DeCotis, K. M. (1988). Children's understanding of the implications of causal attributions for emotional experiences. *Child Development, 59,* 1601–1610.

Toda, M., Shinotsuka, H., McClintock, C. G., & Stech, F. J. (1978). Development of competitive behavior as a function of culture, age, and social comparison. *Journal of Personality and Social Psychology, 36,* 825–839.

Valeriote, T. A., & Hansen, L. (1988). Youth sport in Canada. In F. L. Smoll, R. A. Magill, & M. J. Ash (Eds.), *Children in sport* (3rd ed., pp. 25–29). Champaign, IL: Human Kinetics.

Veroff, J. (1969). Social comparison and the development of achievement motivation. In C. P. Smith (Ed.), *Achievement-related motives in children* (pp. 46–101). New York: Russell Sage Foundation.

Weigel, R. M. (1984). The application of evolutionary models to the study of decisions made by children during object possession conflicts. *Ethology and Sociobiology, 5,* 229–238.

Weiner, B., & Kun, A. (1978). *The development of causal attributions and the growth of achievement and social motivation.* Unpublished manuscript, University of California, Los Angeles.

Weiss, M. R., & Duncan, S. C. (1992). The relationship between physical competence and peer acceptance in the context of children's sports participation. *Journal of Sport & Exercise Psychology, 14,* 177–191.

White, R. W. (1959). Motivation reconsidered: The concept of competence. *Psychological Review, 66,* 297–334.

SOCIAL PROCESSES

For the most part, the antecedents and consequences of sport involvement, as well as sport participation itself, occur within a social context. The developing child's entry into the world of physical activity and sport is influenced not only by processes of biological and psychological maturation but also by the social context in which he or she develops. Once the child is involved in sports, the social environment of sport continues to exert a strong influence on developmental processes that occur as a result of participation. The four chapters in this part of the book focus on the familial and social influences that help to determine initial involvement in sports, continued participation, and the psychosocial effects of the sport environment on the child.

The role of the family in sport socialization of boys and girls is a timely and important topic of research in the field of sport sociology. In a penetrating analysis of this research, Susan L. Greendorfer, John H. Lewko, and Karl S. Rosengren address a paradoxical question: How can we reconcile the dramatically increasing involvement of girls in sports with a lack of research evidence for corresponding changes in sex-typing socialization practices that seem to encourage participation by boys and discourage "masculine" behavior on the part of girls? They conclude that an understanding of gender differences in sport participation and experiences requires that we take into account the dominant role of ideological beliefs and cultural values in determining socialization practices. Research shows that despite increasing participation by girls, they continue to value and experience sport participation quite differently than do boys from early childhood on, and they also continue to receive different behavioral messages from parents and the culture at large as to what is to be valued and pursued. Factors that challenge traditional gender-role ideology, such as the increase in working and single-parent mothers, may be expected to offer challenges to gender-role stereotypes and thereby influence child rearing and sport socialization practices over time. The authors offer a comprehensive theoretical model of sport socialization influences that accords cultural ideologies a central role. This model provides a basis for understanding current gender-role phenomena in youth sports, and it is certain to be a useful guide for future research.

Three important classes of significant others influence children's psychosocial development in sport. Parents, coaches, and peers all can exert strong influences on the child's desire and choice to participate, degree of enjoyment while participating, decision to terminate sport involvement, and on personality and social development that occurs as a result of sport participation. In chapter 8, Robert J. Brustad considers the role of parents and peers in children's psychological development through sport. The influence of parents and peers results in part from their provision of informational feedback to the athlete concerning skill levels and personal acceptability. Brustad shows that parent and peer behaviors influence self-concept development as well as the levels of enjoyment and stress experienced by the young athlete. Research indicates that parental influences are initially prominent but that peer influences become increasingly more important during later childhood and adolescence.

Coaches, the third class of significant others, are the focus of the chapter by Ronald E. Smith and Frank L. Smoll. In chapter 9, they present evidence that specific coaching behaviors can significantly affect children's enjoyment of their sport experience, their attitudes toward the coach, the degree of liking among teammates, and changes in self-esteem. Coaching behaviors have a particularly strong impact on children who are low in self-esteem. Smith and Smoll also describe research on the training of coaches to provide a more positive sport environment for children. Experimental studies indicate that one such training program has significant positive effects on children's liking for coach and teammates. Children who play for trained coaches also show significant increases in self-esteem, reduction in sport performance anxiety, and a greatly lowered likelihood of dropping out of sport. Thus, coaches join parents and peers as important figures in the youth sport environment.

As violence continues to escalate in our society, increasing concern has focused on sport as a possible influence on the learning and promotion of aggressive behavior. In the final chapter of this part, Norman Morra and Michael D. Smith examine the social learning of aggressive and violent behaviors in ice hockey. Their interview and observational studies clearly illustrate the roles that parents, coaches, professional hockey players, administrators, and the mass media play in the learning and encouragement of illegal aggression. Such aggression is not merely tolerated; it is actively promoted and has become such an important part of the game's fabric that it may be difficult to eradicate. There are clear indications that through participation and exposure to professional hockey, young athletes become more accepting of illegal aggression and more likely to engage in such behaviors. Morra and Smith's chapter shows how sport participation can produce negative as well as positive outcomes for children and youth. (See also the chapter by Bredemeier and Shields in Part V, which addresses moral development in greater detail.)

FAMILY AND GENDER-BASED INFLUENCES IN SPORT SOCIALIZATION OF CHILDREN AND ADOLESCENTS

—*Susan L. Greendorfer, John H. Lewko, and Karl S. Rosengren*

Previous reviews of research on children's sport socialization indicate that the process begins in early infancy and consciously encourages physical activity involvement for males (Lewko & Greendorfer, 1978, 1982, 1988). These reviews also suggest that subtle influences in child rearing tend to direct females away from physical activity involvement. Although never explicitly stated in these reviews, it seemed to us that subtle and inconspicuous types of discrimination underlie social-ization practices. Most easily identified as sex-typing, these socialization practices that occur early in life often lead to young females' lack of exposure to a variety of motor and physical activities, which in turn may result in a self-selection away from "inappropriate" and/or unfamiliar activities.

Social learning theory would support the premise that the family initiates much of this sex-typing—such as rewarding girls less than boys for developing motor skills; discouraging their participation in vigorous physical activity; and not making conscious efforts to provide basic skill instruction—and that these early socialization practices influence later sport involvement. Consequently, low rates of female partic-ipation would be a product of socialization. Yet, today, some 20 years after Title IX, figures pertaining to participation patterns reveal that more females are engaged in sport and physical activity than during any other period in American history. Approximately two million young women currently participate in interscholastic sports and more than one-third of all intercollegiate athletes are females (Kane & Greendorfer, 1994), figures that attest to some kind of change.

Present-day patterns tend to indirectly suggest that change has occurred in parental conceptions of sports as appropriate activities for girls as well as boys. Such an assumption suggests that parents now engage in more equitable child-rearing prac-tices. Yet we could find little evidence of such change in our last review on the topic of family influence (Lewko & Greendorfer, 1988). Toddler-infant-childhood play styles, game and toy selection/preferences, and gender labeling of physical activities continued to persist. The dilemma, then, is how to reconcile research findings with perceptions of reality. To address this dilemma, we continue to examine the issue of persistent gender differences and differential socialization practices.

In this chapter we present an overview of the most recent research pertaining to childhood socialization influences in general and sport socialization in particular. To accomplish this task we consider recent research, which emanates from social psychological and behavioral paradigms, from a more broad based perspective—that of cultural values and ideological belief systems. In taking this interpretive stance we make two assumptions: (1) that much of the content of socialization emanates from ideological beliefs and cultural values, and (2) that instead of reflecting social change, superficial shifts in behavior are more representative of cultural accommodation when deeply rooted ideological values are challenged.

We begin by suggesting a more critical analysis of how to view social change. Specifically, we might ask whether increased participation rates of females are reflections of either changing socialization practices or of major shifts in underlying ideological beliefs. An interesting example of this point is evident in a recent study of girls between 9 and 12 years of age that found that more than three-fourths of the physically active girls indicated that they received encouragement and motivation to participate from mother, father and friends. Equally noteworthy, however, is that a majority of these girls also reported they faced unfair treatment by peers and teachers as well as serious obstacles in the form of unequal opportunity (Jaffee & Manzer, 1992). These findings suggest a "mixed message"—replacement of overt exclusionary barriers with more subtle forms of discriminatory practices in the form of "resistance." If so, the question is why.

Before addressing this question, however, we need to understand more about the general process of socialization. Although socialization encompasses the acquisition of social psychological skills, the process represents a key means of integrating individuals into society by transmitting cultural values and traditions. This social learning is accomplished through a network of culturally agreed upon ideological beliefs, attitudes, values, and cultural practices (Aberle, 1961; Clausen, 1968; Goslin, 1969; Inkeles, 1968). Thus the process represents a complex and dynamic constellation of social practices, cultural beliefs, and value orientations. Several researchers have linked the process to play, games, physical activity, and sport, arguing that such activities serve as a primary medium for teaching children fundamental concepts, ideas, norms, rules, and expectations of society (Mead, 1934; Piaget, 1951; Roberts & Sutton-Smith, 1962). Nowhere do we experience the potency of this process more emphatically than when we learn our gender role.

After understanding this dynamic relationship, the next step is to examine the cultural meanings attached to children's motor skill development, games, and sport. All are symbolically and integrally connected to male identity and the meanings of masculinity (Messner, 1988, 1989; Whitson, 1990), and some researchers even argue that motor skills and sport function to teach boys how to perform their gender roles (Dewar, 1987; Griffin, 1988). They argue that perceptions of gender are deeply rooted, albeit nonconsciously, in physical activity participation and performance. Thus despite the presence of more effort toward equality in inculcating motor skills, few changes are evident and gender-biased perceptions continue, both in the family and in schools (Dewar, 1987; Greendorfer, 1992; Griffin, 1988).

The family as well as the school seem to continue to reproduce *ideological* beliefs about gender—namely, beliefs that tell us what males are, do, and should be in contrast to what females are, do, and should be. Such beliefs dominate our adult behavior in child rearing and form the basis of what we do when we socialize our children. The consequence is gender-role socialization, a process by which specific child-rearing practices (i.e., differential treatment of boys and girls and labeling activities as gender appropriate) are considered "natural" because they are taken for granted and are rarely questioned or closely examined. Thus, we are products of cultural values and ideas and in turn we perpetuate (reproduce) cultural ideology in our child-rearing practices.

Because gender-role socialization places greater emphasis on differences between the sexes rather than similarities, two significant outcomes result. First, distinctions are made between what is appropriate and inappropriate for each sex. Second, because judgment of appropriateness is an outgrowth of cultural ideology (beliefs) that is subtly interwoven in the socialization practices, we treat sons differently than daughters. Whenever we hold expectations that are *prescribed* according to one's biological sex, we are engaged in gender-role stereotyping. Unfortunately, in many child-rearing practices the biological sex of a child frequently determines which activities the child will and will not be exposed to as well as *how* the child will experience activities. In other words, socialization practices are products of a cultural belief system that values certain activities or skills for one sex but not for the other.

Consequently, we consider observable gender differences in a variety of behavioral preferences and styles to be socialization outcomes, products of differential treatment, rather than "natural." That is, interest and involvement in physical activity are not chance occurrences simply depending on a child's sex or on innate skill and motor talent. Both are closely related to the type and nature of early childhood social practices. Because family members are primarily responsible for early childhood socialization a reexamination of the developmental literature is in order, this time to determine whether changes in socialization practices have occurred, and if not, to gain insight into ways in which dominant ideological beliefs are reproduced in family socialization.

It was apparent from the start of this review that we would encounter difficulties if we attempted to explain findings in a framework other than that used in the original research. Thus, in addition to our criticism that several researchers failed to employ a theoretical framework, we found that even when some conceptual rationales were used, researchers continued to ignore more pervasive cultural factors that influence behavioral outcomes. Norms and cultural sanctions; racial, class, or ethnic values; and the relatedness of the socialization process to gender ideology, or the fundamental recognition that socialization practices represent cultural reproduction of the existing system of power and privilege, all continue to be ignored in most of the recent research.

Research Trends in Sport Socialization

In our earlier review of family influences in sport socialization (Lewko & Greendorfer, 1988) we noted that the research tends to shed more light on individuals remaining in sport rather than on the processes influencing initial involvement. We also noted that the literature was fragmented, focused mostly on preadolescence and adolescence, and virtually ignored younger children despite the fact that family dynamics suggest greater attention be paid to this earlier time frame. Finally, we concluded that ". . . we have not yet arrived at a clear understanding of how individuals become involved in sport" (p. 294).

In this section, we examine the progress sport socialization researchers have made since the 1988 review. In reviewing this literature, we made every attempt to identify trends or themes that could characterize an area of research in total, rather than focusing on specific research findings. We also kept in mind the major limitations that had been observed in the 1988 review (unsystematic nature of the research; lack of an adequate theory of sport participation; absence of research on young children) as well as the suggestions that had been put forth regarding future exploration of this topic (locating the research within a family system framework; treating sport involvement as a continuum; exploring the role of the peer group; use of more qualitative methodological approaches).

Unfortunately, a careful review of recent literature suggests that current sport socialization research continues to be fragmented in focus. Therefore, in our effort to provide a review that identifies possible trends, as well as address the earlier limitations, we have used age as an organizing principle. Although it would have been preferable to adopt a true developmental perspective toward sport socialization within the context of cultural and ideological influences, the range of conceptual approaches and number of variables identified in the literature made such a task impossible. The material is therefore organized into three time frames: the early years (ages 0–8 years); preadolescence (9–13 years); and adolescence (14–18 years). Though the age ranges of the samples in various studies may sometimes blur distinctions between these three divisions, they do capture the basic age clusterings encompassed in the studies. Also, in keeping with a general socialization framework, we paid particular attention to findings that addressed the influence of family, peers and school, parent versus sibling influence, and father influence (Lewko & Greendorfer, 1988, p. 288). We soon discovered, however, that no studies consider influences of significant others or socialization practices from a cultural perspective. In addition, few researchers have framed the process of socialization within the context of ideological belief systems (cf. Greendorfer & Bruce, 1991).

The Early Years

Limited progress has been made in directing research attention to sport socialization before 8 years of age. Moore et al. (1991) examined the relationship between activity levels of parents and their 4- to 7-year-old children. Bloch (1987) investigated sex differences in young children's (ages 0–6 years) involvement in various types of activities close to home. Eccles and Harold (1991) reported on a three-year longitudinal investigation of gender differences in sport involvement of children who were initially in kindergarten and first and third grades. The three studies reflect significantly different conceptual orientations and are united more by their focus on gender differences than on explaining sport involvement in the early years. They do, however, identify parental linkages in the process, thereby adding to our understanding of early activity involvement. Indirectly, such linkages suggest the advisability of including cultural and ideological values as critical aspects of sport socialization.

Bloch (1987) used Whitting's cultural-ecological model in her investigation of social context on activity involvement. The study is noteworthy in examining involvement from birth through the preschool years. Although the author reported more gender similarities than differences in activities (no differences in gross motor play, construction activities, rough-and-tumble play, and art), she also reported that all children spent large amounts of time with family. More specifically, she observed that 90 percent of the people in these activity settings were immediate family members, with mothers and fathers being present as often in boys' as in girls' settings. Unfortunately, little attention was given to more in-depth interactions within family constellations. Nor was any attention paid to value orientations of families or other cultural beliefs that might influence the observed behavior.

The study by Moore and colleagues (1991) reflects a pediatric research focus on early childhood determinants of physical activity and later health status, such as decreased risk of cardiovascular disease. The authors employed the Framingham Children's Study to examine the relationship between parental and child activity levels. Although the study subscribed to no particular theoretical framework, it provides strong descriptive data in support of parental activity levels being directly related to activity levels of their children. Using direct activity monitoring, Moore et al. (1991) observed that active fathers had a greater impact on their children than active mothers. Additionally, the greatest impact occurred when both parents were active, resulting in nearly a sixfold increase in the likelihood of the child being active. Parental activity appeared to impact more strongly on boys than on girls: If both parents were active, sons were 7.2 times and daughters 4.5 times more likely to be active. Although the authors suggested a number of mechanisms that might account for these findings, ranging from role-modeling to genetic predisposition, their focus was primarily on observable behaviors. They offered virtually no analysis of the process and totally ignored the broad cultural context that provides the conditions, "climate," and setting for the proposed mechanisms.

The most theoretically advanced work is reflected in the study by Eccles and Harold (1991). In fact, the *expectancy-value model* seems to be having significant impact on the current direction of sport socialization research. Eccles and Harold underscored the importance of investigating sport involvement during early childhood, emphasizing their basic finding that gender differences are evident by Grade 1 and persist over time on ratings of sport ability, how important it is to do well, enjoyment, and usefulness of what was learned. Girls see themselves as less able in sport, indicate that doing well in math and reading is more important than doing well in sport, and see sport as the least useful domain when ranked with math and reading.

These findings support those from earlier research suggesting that by the first grade, boys recognize sports as the most important attribute for popularity, whereas girls recognize that grades are (cf. Buchanan, Blankenbaker & Cotton, 1976; Caplan & Kinsbourne, 1974; Stein, Pohly, & Mueller, 1971). Despite the consistent pattern, however, we note that researchers offer little insight as to why females gravitate toward some activity or ways in which subject preferences may be related to gender perceptions of superiority and inferiority. To date researchers have ignored any examination of the relationship between cultural ideology and male development of motor skills, and explanations of findings fail to consider whether motor skill development (e.g., sport socialization) represents another domain for reproducing male power and privilege.

The Eccles and Harold (1991) study also sheds some light on the social influence that parents exert on their children. More specifically, they found that children attended to the importance they believed parents attached to their doing well and to their participating in sport activities. Again gender differences were found as males reported higher perceptions than females. Both males' and females' perceptions of the importance that parents attribute to doing well in sports were also found to relate to ratings of ability in sports. These findings underscore not only the importance of understanding ways in which family dynamics influence perceptions and choices of physical activity but also the significance of more subtle social influences such as value structure.

Preadolescence

By far the largest number of research studies on sport socialization have focused on the middle years of childhood. Findings from these studies are consistent with trends reported previously (Lewko & Greendorfer, 1988). Primary attention in the majority of these studies has been devoted to two areas: parental influences (Brustad, 1993; Cashmore & Goodnow, 1986; Colley, Eglinton, & Elliott, 1992; Dempsey, Kimiecik & Horn, 1993; McCullagh et al., 1993) and gender differences (Colley et al., 1992; Dubois, 1990; Eccles & Harold, 1991; Ignico, 1990). The parental influences studies provided only limited advances in our understanding of how children either become involved or remain involved in physical activities, and the gender difference studies seemed to reinforce earlier understanding that males and females experience sport differently. None of the studies examined the cultural conditions or reasons that might be contributing to these differential experiences.

The studies by Colley et al. (1992) and Dempsey et al. (1993) focused on children at approximately 9 years of age. Colley et al. adopted the Greendorfer perspective on socialization in framing their study. The authors indicated that parental participation (as reported by the child) accounted for a negligible amount of variance in reported sport participation of the child. Dempsey et al. adapted the Eccles expectancy-value model in their examination of parental influence. The authors found no relationships between parents' (self-reported) and children's (self-reported) moderate-to-vigorous physical activity participation (MVPA). These findings contrast with those of Moore et al. (1991), who used actual activity measurements with parents and younger (0–6 years) children. Dempsey et al. did find, however, that parents' beliefs about their children's MVPA competence accounted for a small amount of variance (6%) in their children's MVPA. The authors concluded that " . . . the relationship between parent and child belief systems about MVPA is probably more complex than the unidirectional one presented in this study" (Dempsey et al., 1993, p. 165). Although these findings suggest that ideological beliefs and values are significant aspects in sport socialization, unfortunately the authors limited their discussion to a social psychological framework.

McCullagh et al. (1993) and Brustad (1988) also addressed parental influences within the framework of Harter's competence motivation theory. The McCullagh et al. study focused on perceptions that parents and their 7- to 14-year-old children held regarding children's competencies and motives for participation. Although the authors found a positive relationship between parents' and children's perceptions of competencies, no relationship was reported between perceived competence and motives for participation. It should be noted that children rated all domains (fitness, skill/mastery, fun/excitement, affiliation, recognition, team factors, ego/competitiveness) more highly than did their parents. Exploration of the parental dimension was limited to the parallel questionnaires even though the authors had acknowledged Harter's emphasis on the role of significant others in the socialization process. The Brustad (1988) study addressed parental influences as a predictor of children's (9–13 years old) enjoyment in playing basketball. For both males and females, lower perceived parental pressure to participate and excel in basketball was associated with higher levels of enjoyment.

The final study we examined in the preadolescent time frame that focused on parental influences was conducted by Cashmore and Goodnow (1986). They used an attributional framework, which is of interest here because it considers the extent to which parents and their preadolescents agree with respect to beliefs about talent, effort, and teaching in a child's development of skill. Five areas of skill development were addressed: math, sport, art, writing a good essay, and science. In general, parents attributed greater importance to talent, whereas their children ranked effort relatively high. Both mothers and fathers responded in the same manner. In ranking math and science, children gave higher ratings to effort than to talent. With respect to sport, however, both parents and children made similar attributions to talent for skill development. Cashmore and Goodnow proposed that "vested interest" factors may have been operating such that parental attributions of their child's success to talent would reflect back on the parent in terms of heredity and own ability. Given the variability of findings regarding parental influences, more in-depth and contextualized examination of parental values would be in order. Although mediated by social class, race, and ethnicity, parental influences quite often correspond with dominant cultural values. Moreover, child-rearing practices include value climate and orientations that are integrally embedded in the cultural milieu.

Gender Differences

Because the topic of gender differences represents the largest focus of the sport socialization research across the three time frames, we have selected four studies in the preadolescent period for discussion. Although these studies vary in both their focus as well as their methodological sophistication, they do reflect the breadth of inquiry that is being pursued within the framework of "gender differences."

Colley et al. (1992) explored the impact of sex-typing of activities with a sample of 9-year-olds. Consistent with previous research on gender differences in play, the authors reported that boys appeared to be more rigidly sex-typed than girls: No boys played female sports whereas 20 percent of the females played male sports. Ignicio (1990) also examined sex-typing in a sample of 7- to 13-year-olds who were involved in a university-based activity program. Males were reportedly more stereotyped in their labeling of physical activities than were the females. Similar to previous research cited, however, the authors in both studies were unable to provide new insight or explanations of socialization mechanisms that might be sustaining this pattern. This may be because significant-other influences were addressed only indirectly via perceptions of the children. Thus, the consideration of more robust theoretical concepts—such as *hegemony* (a lived system of meanings and values that when experienced as practices become reciprocally confirming; rather than being forced upon subordinate groups, they are accepted as "natural" or commonsense), *patriarchy* (belief in male superiority and privilege), and *ideology* (belief system that conveys meanings and ideas about social life, particularly about how things should be)—could enrich our understanding of the complex dynamics encompassed in the process of socialization. Such notions suggest ways in which *power* and privilege are culturally reproduced through socialization practices.

In his study focusing on value orientations of a group of 8- to 10-year-olds, Dubois (1990) found that both males and females shifted orientations on a range of values depending on activity structure. The author stressed the gender difference found on a winning orientation, with young females more likely to reject a winning orientation. Although the author couched his study within the socialization rhetoric, no effort was made to address the factors that may be shaping the orientations of either the males or females. It would seem that attempts to explain how culture influences value formation, the links between values and gender socialization, and the connection between socialization experiences and game orientations are needed.

Perhaps the most-sophisticated study of gender differences in sport involvement was conducted by Eccles and Harold (1991). (Findings from their longitudinal investigation were previously reported in the section on "The Early Years.") As part of their overall testing of Eccles's expectancy-value model, the authors focused on males and females who were 11 and 12 years of age. Consistent with the gender differences literature, boys perceived themselves as more able in math and sports and viewed sports as more important, useful, and enjoyable than did the girls. In the same vein, girls perceived themselves as more able in English and viewed English as more important, more useful, and more enjoyable than did the boys. Although both boys and girls reported participating more in sports than in either math or English, boys reported being more involved than girls in sports, with girls reporting being more involved than boys in math and reading/writing.

Although the self-perception data are significant in their own right, Eccles and Harold took the involvement issue further by exploring free-time expenditure, as time is a necessary condition for skill development and the attainment of any level of accomplishment. Though they found a significant gender difference in reported free time spent in sport, the significant relationship between gender and free time disappeared when the three attitudinal variables of self-concept of ability, importance to do well, and usefulness of activity were included in the analysis. Given these findings, the question then arises as to the major forces that shape the development of the three attitudinal variables and how they impact on participation time. Although the expectancy-value model provides for inputs such as "socializers' beliefs and values," it does not appear to subscribe to a more elaborate treatment of family dynamics in general or the generative power of personal relationships. By the same token it does not appear to offer potential for explaining the formation of family attitudes, values, and practices.

In a recent study attempting to identify influences on children's attraction to physical activity, Brustad (1993) took the Eccles model one step further by obtaining data directly from parents as well as their 10-year-old children. The findings were tempered somewhat by the limited number of parental responses and the tendency for questionnaires to be completed more frequently by the mother. These methodological constraints notwithstanding, Brustad found that parents who experienced high levels of enjoyment of physical activity indicated that they encouraged their children's involvement in physical activity more so than parents who experienced less enjoyment in physical activity. Parents also differentiated between sons and daughters by providing sons with more encouragement to be physically active. In addition, Brustad found that parental encouragement also impacted on development of perceptions of competence for children. Although parental enjoyment/parental encouragement influence will require intensive investigation to understand the mechanisms that underpin the parent-child sport involvement relationship, another dimension should not be ignored: the role of hegemonic ideology (dominant beliefs and values) in providing the underpinnings for behavioral mechanisms.

Adolescence

In contrast to the number of studies dealing with socialization factors during preadolescence, the adolescent period continues to receive little research attention with respect to sport socialization even though the field of adolescent research is booming. The studies reported here emerge primarily from nonsport journals and the direction of research varies considerably. What is perhaps most striking about these studies is their atheoretical nature as well as their social psychological emphasis.

Two studies provide a strong descriptive base of activities that occupy the life space of adolescents. The most general case of adolescent activity is reported by Rekers and colleagues (1988). The authors administered a 133-item activity questionnaire to adolescents between 11 and 18 years of age. The study details a wide array of activity patterns of adolescents, ranging from "having romantic thoughts about girls/boys" to "member of a sports team" to "reading glamour and fashion magazines." Of the 37 activities where significant gender differences emerged, only 4 were clearly sport based: football, watch football on TV, member of a sports team, gymnastics. Factor analyses revealed clear-cut gender differences on the first two factors: Adolescent males involved themselves more in outdoor, aggressive activities, whereas adolescent females involved themselves in indoor, feminine activities. In addition to the gender differences, the Reker et al. study underscores an important discovery: Physical/sport activities do not dominate the life experiences of adolescents.

Obtaining similar results, Kirshnit, Ham, and Richards (1989) provided a more ecologically valid description of adolescent activity patterns. Using electronic pagers, adolescent females and males in Grades 5 through 9 completed self-report forms on their activities as well as on their subjective states. From this information, obtained at random intervals throughout the waking hours, the authors found that only a very small portion (6%) of the adolescents' total waking time was spent in sports. Of this time, a majority (69.9%) were involved primarily in informal sports. However, sport emerged as one of the most positive activities associated with higher levels of motivation, positive affect, and arousal. This positive affect could reflect the greater freedom of choice that accompanied participation in informal sports. Not surprisingly, gender differences also emerged, with girls spending less time overall in sports, particularly in informal sport participation. Perhaps the minimal time expenditure spent by adolescents in sports, as indicated in these studies, accounts for the limited amount of research on this age group.

The effects of parent child-rearing practices on sport participation were examined within a larger study of gender differences in soccer (Borman & Kurdek, 1987). Relevant to the process of socialization is the finding that motivation to play soccer was significantly related to low maternal control. This finding could be viewed as similar to Brustad's (1988) observation that low perceived parental pressure was associated with higher levels of enjoyment in playing basketball.

In a qualitative treatment of sport socialization, Coakely and White (1992) examined the dynamics of decision making about sport participation. Through in-depth interviews of young men and women in an industrial area southeast of London, England, the researchers noted that sport is represented as one of many activities that could impact on adolescents' transition to adulthood.

A number of socialization factors identified in earlier studies were also cited by Coakley and White. Specifically, participation in sport activities was more likely if it offered the opportunity to enhance one's perceived competence, the importance of which has been underscored in research emanating from the expectancy-value model that has focused on younger age groups (cf. Brustad, 1993; Eccles & Harold, 1991). In addition, parental constraints emerged as a factor limiting participation for females. Specifically, the monitoring of activity settings, the composition of groups, and the setting of time limits appeared to limit the opportunities for freedom of choice. Not unexpectedly, parental support and encouragement emerged as key factors influencing sport participation. Interviewees expanded the notion of encouragement to include the provision of money and transportation, items that are rarely addressed in research delving into the construct of parental support and encouragement.

What Have We Learned?

To help the reader reach some form of closure we have undertaken two exercises at this point. First, we developed a profile of research findings that summarizes our general understanding of socialization influences. In developing this profile, we have taken some liberties in both the use of particular studies and in the selection of findings. The reader should therefore treat this profile as more heuristic than factual. Second, we have revisited three of the major limitations that emerged from the 1988 review and provided a status report.

We begin with our profile of socialization research findings that emerged in a developmental progression:

- In the early years children spend large amounts of time with close family, including time in physical activities.
- Activities during the early years are more gender similar than gender differentiated.
- Active parents have active children, with boys being more active than girls.
- Parents who enjoy physical activity also encourage their children's involvement in physical activities.
- By Grade 1, children hold sport-based perceptions about their ability, enjoyment, and usefulness of sport that carry over time.
- By Grade 1, gender differences in sport ability, enjoyment, and perceived usefulness are evident.
- By Grade 1, children are monitoring their parents' behavior for cues that reveal the importance that parents attach to participating and doing well in sports.
- During middle childhood, parental participation seems to lose its impact as an influence on child's participation.
- Perceptions of competence that children have are related to parental perceptions of the child's competence.
- Lower parental pressure and lower maternal control in parenting are related to higher enjoyment in sport.
- Parents and children may hold different explanations for skill in sport that could influence further interaction.
- Boys continue to demonstrate greater rigidity in sex-typing of physical activities than do girls.
- In middle childhood, time spent on sports is affected by one's ability, self-concept, and the value attached to sport competence, with girls most negatively affected.
- Parents encourage sons more than daughters to be physically active and parental encouragement affects children's own perceptions of competence.
- Parental support and encouragement take on various forms, from verbal feedback to monetary support to transportation.
- Adolescents spend very little of their waking time in sports, even though sports is one of the most positive activities they experience.
- Adolescent activities continue to be highly gender stereotyped.

One of the limitations noted in the 1988 review was the lack of systematic research on sport socialization. We find, for the most part, this limitation still holds, particularly in research addressing the influence of significant others on sport involvement. Although a number of studies have attempted to address this issue, too often the scope of significant-other influence was delimited to "parents" only. Moreover, influences from the family/peer/school systems were not examined, no concerted attention was given to understanding the differential impact of mothers versus fathers, and the notion of reciprocity (Hasbrook, 1982, 1986) as well as consideration of socialization as an interactive process were completely ignored (Greendorfer, 1992). Compounding this situation was the dominant practice of relying on children's perceptions rather than approaching parents themselves as the source of data or rather than undertaking naturalistic research approaches.

A second limitation that emerged from the earlier review focused on the absence of an adequate theory of sport participation. One promising exception is research based on the Eccles expectancy-value model, which provides substantial examination of the relationship between parental expectations of their child's ability in physical activities and the child's own perceptions of ability. The model is constructed with the purpose of enabling researchers to differentiate between significant others' behaviors and significant others' belief systems. As Eccles and Harold (1991) noted, the ". . . model focuses attention on the role significant others play in shaping children's self-perceptions in two primary ways: (a) as interpreters of experience, and (b) as providers of experience" (p. 13).

Although Brustad (1993) underscored the importance of perceived physical competence in attraction to activity, only limited insight has been gleaned relative to the development of these perceptions in general and the dynamics of significant others as interpreters and providers in particular. To pursue this line of inquiry, researchers may have to entertain alternative methods. Qualitative methods that respect the social-cognitive development of children are one alternative, and one example might be the recursive interviewing methodology that is based on information-processing theory (cf. Bigelow, Tesson, & Lewko, in press).

We must mention, however, that methodological approaches are based on underlying theoretical assumptions. And since we have maintained that broader conceptual frameworks that include cultural reproduction of dominant belief systems are needed, we would argue that any theoretical conceptualization of cognitive developmental aspects of the sport socialization process would be incomplete were these influences to be ignored. The time has come for researchers to acknowledge the significant understandings that could be gained if research paradigms encompassed how meanings about sport are formulated in culture and reproduced in sport socialization practices. Obviously, such considerations of cultural contexts and meanings would have major implications for methodology.

Family Influence, Sport Socialization, and Gender

In developing this section on family socialization practices with reference to gender, we again were struck by the fact that not only have socialization practices remained relatively stable over the past 30 years but also that gender differences found in play styles of infants, toddlers, and older children continue to be quite similar to those found during earlier periods. Toy selection and preference as well as motor skill development are critical aspects of the socialization process. Toys are potent mechanisms of socialization, and while the selection of boys' and girls' toys represents an overt aspect of sex-typing, the subtle ways gender ideology and cultural values influence the socialization process remain virtually invisible. Regardless of how subtly the process operates, however, it typically begins in the family, which for the most part continues to treat boys and girls differently.

Gender-Typed Choices

Numerous studies examining gender-typed choices and behavior toward children suggest that very little has changed in the past 15 years. One indicator assessing differences in how boys and girls are treated is an inventory of the contents of children's rooms. The content and structure of children's bedrooms serves as an indirect measure of the socialization of boys and girls, and studies suggest that little has changed. Specifically, two sets of researchers, one in 1975 (Rheinghold & Cook, 1975) and one 15 years later (Pomerleau et al., 1990), examined the toys, decorations, and furniture contained in the bedrooms of boys and girls between 1 month and 6 years. In both studies, boys' rooms were more sports and action oriented than girls' rooms whereas girls' rooms were more family oriented than boys' rooms. Boys' rooms in these studies were found to contain more vehicles, machines, and sports equipment than girls' rooms; more dolls and patterned decorations were found in girls' rooms. Not surprisingly, given these results, other researchers have found that preferences for gender-typical toys are still quite strong in children in kindergarten through eighth grade (Etaugh & Liss, 1992). These researchers found that girls had a greater preference for masculine toys than boys had a preference for feminine ones. With increasing age, children showed an increasing preference for masculine toys. Since toy preference and play and sport behavior are *learned* activities, such preferences seem to be behavioral outcomes of a persistent gender ideology that subtly shows itself in everyday child-rearing practices that privilege one sex over the other. In the reproduction of cultural meanings, these practices convey messages relative to definitions of masculinity and femininity, images of gender superiority and inferiority, and gender appropriateness of activities. Unfortunately, little research attention has focused on the intersection of these meanings with motor skill development.

This relative stability of toy preference and sport behavior suggests that despite observation of some behavioral gender shifts, cultural values have remained virtually unchanged. Further evidence of a persisting gender ideology comes from research examining the manner in which parents view their sons and daughters. In a replication of the classic study of parents' descriptions of newborn sons and daughters by Rubin, Provenzano, and Luria (1974), Stern and Karraker (1989) found that parents still tend to describe daughters as smaller, softer, cuter, and more delicate than sons, regardless of the child's actual physical attributes. In both of these studies sons were described as stronger, more coordinated, and more alert than daughters.

Carson, Burks, and Parke (1993) have also reported little change in the behaviors fathers engage in with their children. Fathers have more physical contact with infant sons than with infant daughters. They engage in more rough-and-tumble play with their sons than with their daughters; in contrast, they are more likely to cuddle their infant daughters than sons. Thus, the dominant theme of the early gender-role socialization literature, that little change has occurred in parents' perceptions and behaviors toward their sons and daughters, still held in 1990. This finding suggests that despite some behavioral shifts observed over the past 15 to 20 years, the ideological context shaping the "culture of social development" has not changed.

Gender Differences in Early Motor Skills

Even though differential parental treatment places females at a disadvantage, early motor skills of girls are typically found to be more advanced than those of boys. Interestingly, a common belief held by both parents and researchers is that girls are more motorically and cognitively advanced during infancy and early childhood compared to boys. The empirical literature on this topic, however, is less clear. Some studies report that girls reach motor milestones generally ahead of boys, whereas other studies find few differences between boys and girls on motor skill performance prior to age 4 (Haywood, 1993). If a gender difference is found in young children, it typically favors girls over boys for both fine and gross motor skills (Schneider, 1993; Sovik, 1993; but see Anastasia, 1981). Girls, for example, have been reported to exhibit better balance, agility, accuracy of movements, and greater overall coordination of skills than boys prior to age 5 (Schneider, 1993). Additionally, in skills such as galloping and skipping, girls perform at consistently higher levels than boys (Clark & Whitall, 1989). In early to middle childhood, boys begin to gain an advantage in most activities involving gross motor skill, and this advantage increases through adolescence (Thomas & French, 1985). Though the source of these gender differences is not entirely clear, a meta-analytic study by Thomas and French (1985) suggests that socialization practices may play a significant role. These researchers found that the only skill where boys *appear* to have some sort of biological advantage is in throwing. In addition, the fact that any early motor competence on the part of girls does not automatically carry over to later athletic performance or interest suggests that socialization factors, more so than biological factors, have a very strong influence in this domain.

Changing Family Structure and Socialization into Sport

Although the overwhelming evidence suggests that since our last review not much has changed in general socialization practices and subsequent involvement in physical activity, some hints of limited change may be slowly emerging. Two family system trends, namely, increasing levels of maternal employment and greater father involvement in child rearing, may have the potential to lead to changes in basic socialization practices, which in turn may impact on levels of sport involvement. In contrast, the steady divorce rate and increase in single parenting could create greater barriers to sport participation. Specifically, greater economic pressures and time demands on a single parent may make it difficult for the family to afford participation in certain organized sport programs. Such constraints may also create the need for parents to juggle their own schedules around their children's sporting events. It is possible that such changing family conditions could indirectly, if not directly, impact on the childhood sport socialization process. For this reason we have devoted the following section to an examination of maternal employment and increases in father involvement.

Influence of Maternal Employment

One of the major trends in the family system over the last 40 years has been the increase in working mothers. In two-parent families, 71 percent of the mothers work outside the home (Hoffman, 1989). Likewise, Huston and Alvarez (1990) state that most adolescents have a mother who works out of the home at least part time. Although the impact of maternal employment on sport participation has not been directly examined, maternal employment does seem to have an important influence on gender-role development (Hoffman, 1989). Thus one can infer that maternal employment may have an indirect effect on sports, perhaps due to general changes in children's attitudes toward gender-role expectations, which occur as a consequence of having a working mother.

Throughout childhood, children of working mothers seem to have less-stereotyped views of female roles; they also have more positive attitudes toward non-traditional female roles (Chandler, Sawicki, & Stryffeler, 1981; Huston, 1983). Working women generally have higher educational and career aspirations for their daughters than women who do not work outside of the home (Huston & Alvarez, 1990). Influences of maternal employment are typically found to be strongest and most beneficial for daughters rather than sons (Hoffman, 1979, 1984, 1986). Regardless of the sex of the child, however, children of employed women compared with children of nonemployed women have been found to reject many aspects of traditional sex roles (Hoffman, 1989). In addition, working mothers are more likely than nonworking mothers to regard their daughters in very positive terms. Children of working mothers are also more likely to view women as competent members of society (Hoffman, 1989). Thus, maternal employment does seem to alter the socialization process in ways that are particularly beneficial for girls. We suspect such influences could carry over to sport as well.

Huston and Alvarez (1990) suggest that maternal employment influences the development of sex-typed concepts through three basic avenues. First, maternal employment provides a model of the "competent woman." Second, maternal employment leads to changes in the basic household roles and activities of family members. Clearly, if both parents are working outside the home, it becomes very difficult for the woman to perform all of the traditional female chores in the home without some help. To some extent, this means less is accomplished on the home front, but even the most pessimistic studies suggest fathers pick up a bit of the slack (see the following section). Finally, and perhaps most significant for socialization into values challenging gender ideology, maternal employment leads to increases in maternal power in the family. As a result, the working mother becomes an even stronger role model. How these influences come to play in sport participation has not yet been investigated. We suggest that children of working mothers are more likely to receive fewer gender-stereotypic sport socialization influences; therefore, such children might make significantly different sport involvement choices than children of nonworking mothers.

Changing Role of Fathers

Although some evidence suggests the same-sex parent is the most influential member of the family with regard to children's sport involvement (Lewko & Ewing, 1980; McPherson, 1978; Snyder & Spreitzer, 1973), other research has found that fathers appear to play the primary role in influencing both boys and girls to participate in sports (Lewko & Greendorfer, 1978). Furthermore, fathers have often been reported to be the primary socialization agent for gender-role development (Fisher-Thompson, 1990; Langlois & Downs, 1980). As mothers gain a larger role in the workplace and play a greater role in providing income for the family, the role of the father as sole breadwinner and primary source of power in the family could potentially change. Indeed, the popular culture for the last 10 to 15 years has presented images of an emergent "new father," one who is a nurturant, involved caregiver (Lamb, 1987). Next we briefly examine the evidence in support of this view of the father and suggest implications that this change in role might have for sport involvement.

The view of the father as a caring, nurturant, active participant in the family, especially with respect to child rearing, began to emerge in the 1970s. This new role was viewed as replacing earlier versions where the father was seen primarily as a moral teacher, breadwinner, or strong masculine role model (Lamb, 1987). It is possible that the increase in fathers' participation can be attributed in part to changes in maternal employment. In families where the mother works, fathers have been found to play a greater role in caregiving (Gottfried, Gottfried, & Bathurst, 1988).

Although research over the past decade does suggest that fathers are becoming more involved in child rearing, and the public perception of the active father has gained ground, the actual degree of male involvement with their children continues to lag far behind that of women (see Lamb, 1987 for a review). Changes in fathers' participation in child rearing appear to be rather modest, with mothers continuing to provide the majority of the basic caregiving needs of children (Lamb, 1987). Lamb also has pointed out that even though the media have been trumpeting the virtues of the nurturant, active father for the last 10 to 15 years, more traditional views of the role of fathers continue to prevail. Again we note the tendency to perpetuate a dominant gender ideology that appears somewhat resistant to cultural change despite some superficial behavioral shifts.

One might consider that the real change in the role of fathers in society would be in the creation of new options or greater dimensionality in the role of parent rather than in increased participation in child rearing. Stated somewhat differently, although fathers now have the option to play the nurturant caregiver in many families, at the same time most of the responsibility for feeding, clothing, and maintaining the health of the children remains primarily the mother's job. To some extent cultural ideology seems to present favorable views of fathers, who seem to be receiving more credit and have a wider variety of parenting options available to them. By the same token, cultural meanings obscure the fact that mothers who enter the workplace primarily increase their workload. As a consequence, we misinterpret the degree of change achieved due to the images created and tend to ignore the relatively unchanging nature of the underlying gender ideology.

Therefore, given only modest gains in father involvement in child rearing over the last decade or two, we wonder how increased father involvement in child rearing might impact on their children, especially on children's orientations and involvement in sport. The first question that must be addressed is whether fathers can be competent caregivers; if they cannot, we might expect negative outcomes in situations where fathers play the primary caregiving role. Studies indicate that fathers can be entirely competent as caregivers, which suggests that parenting skills seem to be learned "on the job" (Hipgrave, 1982; Levine, 1976; Russell, 1982, 1983) and not "in the genes." A second question is whether involved fathers act differently than noninvolved fathers act with their children. Research suggests that greater time spent in child care leads to greater parental sensitivity to the needs of children. Involved fathers tend to be more sensitive and responsive to their children than uninvolved fathers.

Regardless of the extent of father involvement, however, fathers have been found to play more with their children and provide less caregiving than mothers (Lamb, 1987). Of the time they spend with their children, fathers spend approximately four times as much time engaged in play than engaged in caregiving (Hetherington & Parke, 1993; Parke, 1990). Even when fathers are very involved in caregiving, they engage in more physically stimulating activities (rough-and-tumble) and play more with their children than mothers (Field, 1978). Children seem to like these activities, reacting more positively toward father play than mother play (Field, 1990). In one study by Clarke-Stewart (1978), 18-month-olds chose fathers rather than mothers as the preferred play partner. Thus, both fathers and children seem to enjoy playing together, and play continues to be an integral part of father-child relationships. Recent research has demonstrated that fathers' encouragement of rough-and-tumble play and degree of arousal during play with their 18-month-old children is significantly related to the children's rough-and-tumble play in first grade (McBride-Chang & Jacklin, 1993). These researchers also found that choice of more feminine toys was negatively related to the amount of rough-and-tumble play in boys and girls.

Given these findings and regardless of the degree of father involvement, we might expect to find no differences in the extent to which involved or noninvolved fathers may be primary socializers of their children's sport involvement. However, this issues has yet to be studied. On the other hand, greater father involvement and greater warmth and closeness between father and child have been found to be related to better adjustment and less traditional views of gender roles (Lamb, 1987; Radin & Sagi, 1982; Sagi, 1982). Although fathers still might be seen as primary socializers with regard to sport involvement, and given earlier findings regarding play, these results suggest that involved fathers may raise children with less traditional views of appropriate behavior for boys and girls. Although the effect of father involvement in caregiving on children's choice of sports and the amount of sport participation has not yet been investigated, this line of research offers a potential rupture in the traditional "culture" of socialization by introducing some degree of modification in gender value orientations.

One might ask, given the public perception of greater father involvement, why fathers haven't become more involved. As previously suggested, while overall levels of father involvement in child rearing have increased, these increases do not seem to pervade our culture as a whole. For example, the division of labor and the nature of parenting roles in dual-wage families seem to have changed over the last 15 years; however, in single-wage families the family structure has remained fairly constant (Hoffman, 1989). Mothers have also been somewhat reluctant to give up some of the child-rearing roles they have traditionally held (Beitel & Parke, 1990).

Indeed, this reluctance might seem quite justified if we consider that child rearing is one of the few domains in which women have had more power and control than men. Allowing men to take over some of these responsibilities not only reduces women's roles but also reduces any power they might have in the family structure. Thus, the model of father as breadwinner remains quite strong, especially in some sectors of society. For example, in blue-collar families where both parents work, the father is still expected to be the primary breadwinner. To the extent the mother works and earns as much (or more) income as the father, and the father's income is viewed as inadequate to support the family, the father is viewed as a failure (Hood, 1986). By the same token, the workplace continues to present many obstacles for father involvement with their children; few, if any, opportunities are available for paternity leave or flexible work schedules. Probably the clearest message that little has changed in the workplace is the recent $100,000 fine to David Williams, a lineman on the Houston Oilers football team, who chose to participate in his child's birth rather than play a professional football game.

Thus, even though public perception of the role of fathers has changed, actual levels of father-child interaction have remained relatively constant. However, in situations where fathers do take a more active role in child rearing, changes in gender-role attitudes have been found. Since fathers still remain largely playmates for their children, we would expect that they would continue to be a strong (if not the strongest) influence on sport involvement. In families with more-involved fathers the children tend to have less stereotypical gender-role attitudes than in families where the father is uninvolved. As a result we might expect these children to make *different* choices with regard to sport involvement than children in families with uninvolved fathers.

To summarize this section on changing family structure, we offer figure 7.1 as a partial "model of influences," which offers the potential for changes in sport socialization influences. We view this diagram as complex, dynamic, and multidirectional in flow. The larger oval can be interpreted as the pervasive cultural system of values, beliefs, attitudes, and behaviors that creates the underlying ideological belief system that influences sport socialization practices. We see the influences of the mass media and workplace as impacting on father involvement in the family and having implications for sport socialization. For example, positive portrayals/images of fathers as caregivers may lead to increasing options for fathers. Attitudes in the workplace could possibly place barriers to father involvement, as could lack of flexible work time, economic pressures to work overtime, and a cultural ideology that permits fathers to place work above family. On the other hand, economic constraints and desires to maintain a particular lifestyle (such as one that their parents enjoyed) seem to require two wage earners in the family. Consequently, an increasing number of working mothers has led to increases in father involvement with children. The presence of a working mother not only offers increased family income but also may lead to a perception of increased power in the family. This modified perception alone could result in less traditional gender-role socialization, which could mean an expanded range of "appropriate" sport activities for both boys and girls. These potential changes accompanied by an increased family income could lead to greater ability to afford fees, lessons, and perhaps more specialized sport equipment. Yet it is our opinion that change must occur at the cultural level and, through a dynamic, interactive exchange, filter through the media, workplace, and the family to truly bring about a change in sport socialization.

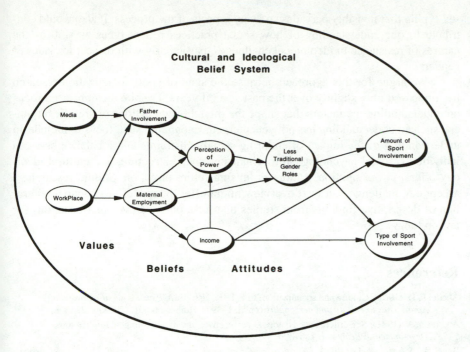

FIGURE 7.1
Model of influences.

Within the diagram:

Cultural and Ideological Belief System

Media

Father Involvement

Perception of Power

Less Traditional Gender Roles

Amount of Sport Involvement

WorkPlace

Maternal Employment

Income

Type of Sport Involvement

Values

Beliefs

Attitudes

Conclusion

Unlike our earlier reviews, our purpose in this update was to attempt to establish a sociocultural and ideological linkage to social psychological approaches to socialization in general and sport socialization in particular. To accomplish this goal, we need to analytically expand theoretical conceptualizations by introducing such notions as beliefs, values, and social forms of consciousness into the normative system of learning. Such an approach would allow us to view socialization in relationship to the development of cultural meanings that serve as the basis for formulating social constructions. This would allow us to view sport socialization as a negotiated reality that takes place within a more broadly defined social context than previously considered. From such a perspective we could conceptualize the process as fluid rather than fixed and as a cultural dynamic in which structured sets of preestablished interaction patterns and relationships are balanced with notions that allow for a range of differentiated interactions and exchanges that are negotiable and subject to interpretation.

We recognize that this type of reconsideration would critically change the nature of the topic in several ways. However, it suggests that sport socialization could be better understood by capturing a social totality—one that views the process as a product as well as reproduction of sociocultural practice. Such an ambitious goal becomes much more difficult given the narrow psychobehavioral paradigm that has dominated most sport socialization research. Yet such an approach offers potential for understanding emergence as well as persistence of gender difference and sex-typing that invisibly pervades so many aspects of the process. It also would contribute to our understanding of how social practices reflect types as well as the natures of resistance to ideological challenges, particularly with respect to issues of gender.

We argue for this approach because the state of sport socialization research has improved only slightly over the past several years. Despite the concerted focus on understanding the factors that shape the thoughts and actions of significant others, such an understanding has not yet emerged. Expanding such focus to include an understanding of the impact of enduring social constraints and a balance between individuals, social psychological mechanisms, social structure, and cultural ideology offers, in our opinion, a more promising future direction. Should researchers accept our challenge, our next overview might offer the reader more than a reiteration of descriptive findings from studies that have pursued the same questions for far too long.

References

Aberle, F. D. (1961). Culture and socialization. In F. L. K. Hsu (Ed.), *Psychological anthropology: Approaches to culture and personality* (pp. 381–397). Homewood, IL: The Dorsey Press.

Anastasia, A. (1981). Sex differences: Historical perspectives and methodological implications. *Developmental Review, 1,* 186–206.

Beitel, A., & Parke, R. D. (1990). *The role of maternal gatekeeping in father involvement.* Unpublished paper, University of Illinois, Urbana.

Bigelow, B. J., Tesson, G., & Lewko, J. H. (In press). *Children's social rules.* New York: Guilford Press.

Bloch, M. N. (1987). The development of sex differences in young children's activities at home: The effect of the social context. *Sex Roles, 16*(5/6), 279–301.

Borman, K. M., & Kurdek, L. A. (1987). Gender differences associated with playing high school varsity soccer. *Journal of Youth and Adolescence, 16*(4), 379–399.

Brustad, R. J. (1988). Affective outcomes in competitive youth sport: The influence of intrapersonal and socialization factors. *Journal of Sport & Exercise Psychology, 10,* 307–321.

————. (1993). Who will go out and play? Parental and psychological influences on children's attraction to physical activity. *Pediatric Exercise Science, 5,* 210–223.

Buchanan, H. T., Blankenbaker, J., & Cotton, D. (1976). Academic and athletic ability as popularity factors in elementary school children. *Research Quarterly, 47,* 320–325.

Caplan, P. J., & Kinsbourne, M. (1974). Sex differences in response to school failure. *Journal of Learning Disabilities,* 232–235.

Carson, J., Burks, V., & Parke, R. D. (1993). Parent-child physical play: Determinants and consequences. In. K. B. MacDonald (Ed.), *Parent-child play* (pp. 197–220). Albany, NY: SUNY Press.

Cashmore, J. A., & Goodnow, J. J. (1986). Parent-child agreement on attributional beliefs. *International Journal of Behavioral Development, 9,* 191–204.

Chandler, T. A., Sawicki, R. F., & Stryffeler, J. M. (1981). Relationship between adolescent sexual stereotypes and working mothers. *Journal of Early Adolescence, 1,* 72–83.

Clark, J. E., & Whitall, J. (1989). Changing patterns of locomotion: From walking to skipping. In M. H. Woollacott & A. Shumway-Cook (Eds.), *The development of posture and gait across the life span* (pp. 129–151). Columbia, SC: University of South Carolina Press.

Clarke-Stewart, K. A. (1978). And daddy makes three: The fathers' impact on mother and young child. *Child Development, 49,* 466–478.

Clausen, J. A. (Ed.). (1968). *Socialization and society.* Boston: Little, Brown.

Coakley, J., & White, A. (1992). Making decisions: Gender and sport participation among British adolescents. *Sociology of Sport Journal, 9,* 20–35.

Colley, A., Eglinton, E., & Elliott, E. (1992). Sport participation in middle childhood: Association with styles of play and parental participation. *International Journal of Sport Psychology, 23,* 193–206.

Dempsey, J. M., Kimiecik, J. C., & Horn, T. S. (1993). Parental influence on children's moderate to vigorous physical activity participation: An expectancy-value approach. *Pediatric Exercise Science, 5,* 151–167.

Dewar, A. M. (1987). The social construction of gender in physical education. *Women's Studies International Forum, 10*(4), 453–465.

Dubois, P. (1990). Gender differences in value orientation toward sports: A longitudinal analysis. *Journal of Sport Behavior, 13*(1), 3–14.

Eccles, J. S., & Harold, R. D. (1991). Gender differences in sport involvement: Applying the Eccles expectancy-value model. *Journal of Applied Sport Psychology, 3,* 7–35.

Etaugh, C., & Liss, M. B. (1992). Home, school, and playroom: Training grounds for adult gender roles. *Sex Roles, 26,* 129–147.

Field, T. M. (1978). Interaction behaviors of primary versus secondary caretaker fathers, *Developmental Psychology, 14,* 183–184.

———. (1990). *Infancy.* Cambridge, MA: Harvard University Press.

Fisher-Thompson, D. (1990). Adult gender typing of children's toys. *Sex Roles, 23,* 291–303.

Goslin, D. A. (Ed.). (1969). *Handbook of socialization theory and research.* Chicago: Rand McNally & Co.

Gottfried, A. E., Gottfried, A. W., & Bathurst, K. (1988). Maternal employment, family environment, and children's development: Infancy through the school years. In A. E. Gottfried & A. W. Gottfried (Eds.), *Maternal employment and children's development: Longitudinal research* (pp. 11–58). New York: Plenum.

Greendorfer, S. L. (1992). Sport socialization. In T. Horn (Ed.), *Advances in sport psychology* (pp. 201–218). Champaign, IL: Human Kinetics

Greendorfer, S. L., & Bruce, T. (1991). Rejuvenating sport socialization research. *Journal of Sport and Social Issues, 15*(2), 129–144.

Griffin, P. (1988). Gender as a socializing agent in physical education. In T. J. Templin & P. G. Schempp (Eds.), *Socialization in physical education: Learning to teach.* Champaign, IL: Human Kinetics

Hasbrook, C. A. (1982). The theoretical notion of reciprocity and childhood socialization into sport. In A. O. Dunleavy, A. W. Miracle, and C. R. Rees (Eds.), *Studies in the sociology of sport* (pp. 139–151). Fort Worth: Texas Christian University Press.

———. (1986). Reciprocity and childhood socialization into sport. In L. Vander Velden & J. H. Humphrey (Eds.), *Psychology and sociology of sport: Current selected research* (pp. 135–147). New York: AMS Press.

Haywood, K. (1993). *Life span motor development.* Champaign, IL: Human Kinetics.

Hetherington, E. M., & Parke, R. D. (1993). *Child psychology: A contemporary view.* New York: McGraw-Hill.

Hipgrave, T. (1982). Childrearing by lone families. In R. Chester, P. Diggory, & M. Sutherland (Eds.), *Changing patterns of child bearing and child rearing.* London: Academic Press.

Hoffman, L. W. (1979). Maternal employment: 1979. *American Psychologist, 34,* 859–865.

———. (1984). Maternal employment and the young child. In M. Perlmutter (Ed.), Parent-child interaction and parent-child relations in child development. *The Minnesota Symposia on Child Psychology,* (Vol. 7, pp. 223–282). Hillsdale, NJ: Erlbaum.

———. (1986). Work, family, and the child. In M. S. Pallak & R. O. Perloff (Eds.), *Psychology and work: Productivity, change and employment* (pp. 173–220). Washington, DC: American Psychological Association.

———. (1989). Effects of maternal employment in the two-parent family. *American Psychologist, 44,* 283–292.

Hood, J. C. (1986). The provider role: Its meaning and measurement. *Journal of Marriage and Family, 48,* 349–359.

Huston, A. C. (1983). Sex-typing. In E. M. Hetheriginton (Ed.), P. H. Mussen (Series Ed.), *Handbook of child psychology, vol. 4. Socialization, personality, and social development* (pp. 387–468). New York: John Wiley.

Huston, A. C., & Alvarez, M. M. (1990). The socialization context of gender role development in early adolescence. In R. Montemayor, G. R. Adams, & T. P. Gullotta (Eds.), *From childhood to adolescence: A transitional period?* (pp. 156–179). London: Sage Publications.

Ignico, A. A. (1990). The influence of gender-role perception on activity preferences of children. *Play & Culture, 3,* 302–310.

Inkeles, A. (1968). Society, social structure, and child socialization. In J. A. Clausen (Ed.), *Socialization and society* (pp. 73–130). Boston: Little, Brown.

Jaffee, L., & Manzer, R. (1992, Autumn). Girls' perspectives: Physical activity and self-esteem. *Melpomene Journal, 11*(3), 14–23.

Kane, M. J., & Greendorfer, S. L. (1994). The media's role in accommodating and resisting stereotyped images of women in sport. In P. J. Creedon (Ed.), *Women in sports: Challenging cultural values* (pp. 28–44). Newbury Park, CA: Sage.

Kirshnit, C. E., Ham, M., & Richards, M. H. (1989). The sporting life: Athletic activities during early adolescence. *Journal of Youth and Adolescence, 18*(6), 601–615.

Lamb, M. E. (1987). Introduction: The emergent American father. In M. E. Lamb (Ed.), *The father's role: Cross-cultural perspectives.* Hillsdale, NJ: Erlbaum.

Langlois, J. H., & Downs, A. C. (1980). Mothers, fathers, and peers as socialization agents of gender-typed play behaviors in young children. *Child Development, 51,* 1237–1247.

Levine, J. A. (1976). *And who will raise the children? New options for fathers (and mothers).* Philadelphia: Lippincott.

Lewko, J. H., & Ewing, M. E. (1980). Sex differences and parental influence in sport involvement of children. *Journal of Sport Psychology, 2,* 62–68.

Lewko, J. H., & Greendorfer, S. L. (1978). Family influence and sex differences in children's socialization into sport: A review. In D. M. Landers & R. W. Christina (Eds.), *Psychology of motor behavior and sport—1977* (pp . 434–447). Champaign, IL: Human Kinetics.

———. (1982). Family influence and sex differences in children's socialization into sport: A review. In R. A. Magill, M. J. Ash, & F. L. Smoll (Eds.), *Children in sport* (2nd edition, pp. 279–293). Champaign, IL: Human Kinetics.

———. (1988). Family influence in sport socialization of children and adolescents. In. F. L. Smoll, R. A. Magill, & M. J. Ash (Eds.), *Children in sport* (3rd edition, pp. 288–300). Champaign, IL: Human Kinetics.

McBride-Chang, C., & Jacklin, C. N. (1993). Early play arousal, sex-typed play, and activity level as precursors to later rough-and-tumble play. *Early Education and Development,* 99–108.

McCullagh, P., Matzkanin, K. T., Shaw, S. D., & Maldonado, M. (1993). Motivation for participation in physical activity: A comparison of parent-child perceived competencies and participation motives. *Pediatric Exercise Science, 5,* 224–233.

McPherson, B. D. (1978). The child in competitive sport: Influence of the social milieu. In R. A. Magill, M. J. Ash, & F. L. Smoll (Eds.), *Children in sport: A contemporary anthology* (1st ed., pp. 219–249). Champaign, IL: Human Kinetics.

Mead, G. H. (1934). *Mind, self, and society.* Chicago: University of Chicago Press.

Messner, M. A. (1988). Sports and male domination: The female athlete as contested ideological terrain. *Sociology of Sport Journal, 5*(3), 197–211.

———. (1989). Masculinities and athletic careers. *Gender and Society, 31,* 71–88.

Moore, L. L., Lombardi, D. A., White, M. J., Campbell, J. L., Oliveria, S. A., & Ellison, R. C. (1991). Influence of parents' physical activity levels on activity levels of young children. *The Journal of Pediatrics, 118*(2), 215–219.

Parke, R. D. (1990). In search of fathers: A narrative of an empirical journey. In I. Sigel & G. Brody (Eds.), *Methods of family research* (Vol. 1, pp. 153–188). Hillsdale, NJ: Erlbaum.

Piaget, J. (1951). *Play, dreams, and imitation in childhood.* London: Routledge, Kegan Paul.

Pomerleau, A., Bolduc, D., Malcuit, G., & Cossette, L. (1990). Pink or blue: Environmental gender stereotypes in the first two years of life. *Sex Roles, 22,* 359–367.

Radin, N., & Sagi, A. (1982). Childrearing fathers in intact families in Israel and the U.S.A. *Merrill-Palmer Quarterly, 28,* 111–136.

Rekers, G. A., Sanders, J. A., Rasbury, W. C., Strauss, C. C., & Morey, S. M. (1988). Differentiation of adolescent activity participation. *Journal of Genetic Psychology, 150*(3), 323–335.

Rheinghold, H. L., & Cook, K. V. (1975). The content of boys' and girls' rooms as an index of parent behavior. *Child Development, 46,* 459–463.

Roberts, J. M., & Sutton-Smith, B. (1962). Child training and game involvement. *Ethnology, 1,* 166–185.

Rubin, J. Z., Provenzano, F. J., & Luria, A. (1974). The eye of the beholder: Parent's views on the sex of newborns. *American Journal of Orthopsychiatry, 43,* 720–731.

Russell, G. (1982). Shared-caregiving families: An Australian study. In M. E. Lamb (Ed.), *Non-traditional families: Parenting and child development.* Hillsdale, NJ: Erlbaum.

———. (1983). *The changing roles of fathers?* St. Lucia, Queensland: University of Queensland Press.

Sagi, A. (1982). Antecedents and consequences of various degrees of paternal involvement in child rearing: The Israeli project. In: M. E. Lamb (Ed.), *Non-traditional families: Parenting and child development.* Hillsdale, NJ: Erlbaum.

Schneider, W. (1993). The longitudinal study of motor development: Methodological issues. In A. F. Kalverboer, B. Hopkins, & R. Geuze (Eds.), *Motor development in early and later childhood: Longitudinal approaches* (pp. 325–328). Cambridge: Cambridge University Press.

Snyder, E. E., & Spreitzer, F. (1973). Family influence and involvement in sports. *Research Quarterly, 44,* 249–255.

Sovik, N. (1993). Development of children's writing performance: Some educational implications. In A. F. Kalverboer, B. Hopkins, & R. Geuze (Eds.), *Motor development in early and later childhood: Longitudinal approaches* (pp. 243–244). Cambridge: Cambridge University Press.

Stein, A. H., Pohly, S., & Mueller, E. (1971). The influence of masculine, feminine and neutral tasks on children's achievement behavior, expectancies of success and attainment values. *Child Development, 42,* 195–208.

Stern, M., & Karraker, K. H. (1989). Sex stereotyping of infants: A review of gender labeling studies. *Sex Roles, 20,* 501–522.

Thomas, J. R., & French, K. E. (1985). Gender differences across age in motor performance: A meta-analysis. *Psychological Bulletin, 98,* 260–282.

Whitson, D. (1990). Sport in the social construction of masculinity. In M. A. Messner & D. F. Sabo (Eds.), *Sport, men and the gender order* (pp. 19–29). Champaign, IL: Human Kinetics.

PARENTAL AND PEER INFLUENCE ON CHILDREN'S PSYCHOLOGICAL DEVELOPMENT THROUGH SPORT

—Robert J. Brustad

For millions of youngsters, participation in organized sport programs is an essential part of childhood and adolescence. The widespread involvement of youngsters in sport, in combination with the fairly intensive nature of some programs, has raised concerns for the effects of sport participation on children's psychological development (Gould & Martens, 1979). As primary socialization influences on children's sport involvement, parents and peers assume key roles in shaping the psychological outcomes that children experience through their sport participation.

Psychological development refers to the process of qualitative change in psychological functioning that occurs as a consequence of maturation and experience. A particularly important dimension of psychological development pertains to the formation and refinement of the self-concept. This chapter will devote considerable attention to parental and peer influences on self-concept development through sport. Similarly, substantial attention will be focused on the influence of socialization agents in shaping the affective dimensions of children's psychological development. Included will be a discussion of favorable affective outcomes for youngsters in sport, such as enjoyment and peer acceptance, as well as a consideration of less favorable affective outcomes, such as anxiety and burnout.

Although parents and peers play important roles in shaping children's psychological development, it should be noted that the nature and extent of each source of influence varies greatly according to the age and developmental status of the child. During the early childhood years, parental influence on children's psychological development is quite strong for at least three reasons. First, a relatively large proportion of the child's time is spent within the context of the family. Second, prior to the age of about 8 years, children generally have not developed the necessary social skills, particularly role-taking abilities, to establish a solid network of social relations outside of the family (Selman, 1976). Third, as a consequence of cognitive developmental status, children younger than 8 years of age typically rely heavily on the feedback of parents and other adults in assessing personal competency (Horn & Hasbrook, 1986, 1987; Horn & Weiss, 1991; Stipek & MacIver, 1989). Consequently, it is apparent that parents are the most important socializing agents in shaping children's psychological development through sport during early childhood. This expectation is bolstered by research that indicates that children's early sport interest, initial sport involvement, and perceptions of physical ability are all strongly linked to parental beliefs and behaviors (Eccles & Harold, 1991; Felson & Reed, 1986; Lewko & Greendorfer, 1988).

With age and cognitive maturity, children demonstrate improved social skills and spend relatively more time in the company of their peers. Furthermore, they exhibit an increasing reliance on peer comparison and peer evaluation processes in assessing physical competence (Horn & Hasbrook, 1986, 1987; Horn & Weiss, 1991). If sport ability is highly valued by the child's peers, the peer group becomes a more prominent influence in shaping psychological development through sport during later childhood and adolescence. However, gender differences are also likely to emerge with regard to the relative influence of the peer group during this period of time, since sport ability is a much more highly prized personal characteristic for young males than young females in North America (Chase & Dummer, 1992; Zarbatany, Hartmann, & Rankin, 1990).

Since the relative influence of parents and peers varies according to the child's age and developmental status and since parents and peers impact different dimensions of children's psychological development, it will be beneficial to address these social influences separately.

Parental Influences on Children's Psychological Development

Parental influences will be discussed in this section, with particular attention devoted to assessing the role of parents in shaping children's self-concept and affective experiences in sport.

Children's Self-Concept Development

The formation and refinement of the *self-concept* is an important dimension of psychological development during childhood and adolescence. A growing body of research in psychology and education has identified self-concept variables as key mediating factors influencing children's achievement behaviors (e.g., Harter, 1981, 1988; Phillips, 1987). Furthermore, self-concept variables play a pivotal role in the most prominent current motivational theories in sport (e.g., Bandura, 1986; Harter, 1981; Nicholls, 1984). Consequently, understanding the processes underlying self-concept development is an important area of pursuit for youth sport researchers.

Researchers and theoreticians currently view the self-concept as multidimensional in nature (Fox & Corbin, 1989; Harter, 1988; Marsh & Peart, 1988; Weiss, 1987). *Multidimensionality* refers to the idea that the overall self-concept is composed of a number of distinct, domain-specific self-perceptions that contribute to one's overall sense of self. Harter's (1988) research reveals that the number and type of dimensions that compose the self-concept vary according to developmental status.

During the middle to late childhood years, children generally identify five specific dimensions of self-evaluation: scholastic competence, athletic competence, peer acceptance, physical appearance, and behavioral conduct. These self-perceptions are not necessarily related to any objective criteria of ability but merely reflect children's impressions of their capacities in each of these areas. Furthermore, a nonachievement dimension of the self-concept, self-esteem, also emerges at this time. *Self-esteem* represents an individual's global feelings of worth as an individual and refers to one's evaluative and affective beliefs about one's value as a person.

Research also indicates that children ascribe unequal importance to the various dimensions of the self (Harter, 1985a, 1985b). Self-evaluations in those dimensions that are most highly valued by the youngster have the greatest impact on the overall self-concept (Harter, 1985a). This finding is particularly important to understanding self-concept development in boys, since athletic ability is typically the most highly prized personal attribute of males during late childhood and adolescence (Adler, Kless, & Adler, 1992; Chase & Dummer, 1992).

Social psychological theory has long held that the self-concept is shaped through social interaction (Cooley, 1902/1956; Mead, 1934). Cooley originally proposed the image of the "looking glass self" through which individuals come to adopt views of themselves as they are reflected through the appraisals and behaviors of significant others. The image of the looking glass self is useful for this discussion of self-concept development because it highlights the role of significant others in shaping children's self-evaluations.

Significant others no doubt have a major influence in shaping the self-evaluations of young athletes because the public nature of sport provides extensive opportunities for social evaluation and feedback (Scanlan, this volume). As a consequence of children's reliance on adult sources of information in judging competence, in combination with the typically high levels of involvement of parents in their children's athletic competitions, it is logical to assume that parental behaviors and feedback significantly impact children's self-concept development during their early years of sport participation.

Research in the athletic domain indicates that children are likely to adopt their parents' appraisals of their physical ability and to hold similar expectations for future performance. For instance, Felson and Reed (1986) found a significant relationship between parental judgments of their children's physical abilities and the child's self-appraisals of ability, even when actual levels of physical ability were statistically controlled. More recently, McCullagh and colleagues (1993) also found a fairly strong correspondence between parent and child appraisals of the child's physical competence. Related research by Scanlan and Lewthwaite (1984) revealed that young wrestlers who perceived greater parental (and coach) satisfaction with their performance had higher personal expectancies for their future performance. These sport-related findings are bolstered by a similar pattern of results in academic settings (e.g., Parsons, Adler, & Kaczala, 1982; Phillips, 1984, 1987). For example, Phillips (1987) found that highly academically competent children (as assessed through objective achievement tests) who underestimated their ability generally had parents who also had low perceptions of the child's ability.

Eccles and Harold (1991) propose that parents assume two important functions in shaping children's ability perceptions. First, parents serve as interpreters of information about their children's achievement outcomes and thereby influence children's cognitions, attributions, and self-perceptions in each of the various achievement domains. Second, parents are likely to provide more opportunities for their child in those areas in which they hold high expectations for their son or daughter. This hypothesis is supported by recent research that indicates that children's perceptions of physical competence are significantly related to the amount of parental encouragement they receive to be physically active (Brustad, 1993b), and that parental perceptions of children's physical competence are related to actual levels of participation in physical activity by children (Dempsey, Kimiecik, & Horn, 1993).

Parental influence on children's self-esteem development through sport is a worthy topic but one that has yet to receive much research attention. In part, this is as expected, since self-esteem, a construct representing an individual's global sense of worth or value as a person, is a much broader construct than is perceived physical competence. Harter's (1988) research indicated that high self-esteem children could be distinguished from low self-esteem children on the basis of support they receive from significant others. Specifically, high self-esteem children report that parents (and peers) "accept them, support them, and hold them in high regard" (p. 69). In sport, parents have numerous opportunities to demonstrate acceptance and to provide or withhold support, thereby influencing children's self-esteem development. Therefore, there is potential benefit in examining parental influences on children's self-esteem development in the athletic domain, particularly since research indicates that coaches have a considerable effect on young athletes' self-perceptions and self-esteem characteristics (Black & Weiss, 1992; Horn, 1985; Smith, Smoll, & Curtis, 1979).

Affective Outcomes for Children

The topic of children's affective development through sport is a very important, and somewhat controversial, issue within the youth sport literature. A great deal of concern has focused on the causes and extent of negative affective outcomes such as stress, anxiety, and burnout for young athletes, with the assumption that these outcomes may impair children's psychological development. This concern for possible negative affective outcomes has been balanced somewhat by recent interest in the causes and correlates of more favorable affective outcomes for children in sport, such as enjoyment (e.g., Brustad, 1988; Scanlan et al., 1993; Scanlan & Lewthwaite, 1986).

Initial efforts at understanding the effects of sport participation on children and adolescents frequently resulted in the conclusion that sport involvement was highly stressful for many youngsters (Brower, 1978; Smilkstein, 1980) and that the competitive focus of youth sport programs was responsible for many youngsters dropping out of sport (Orlick, 1974). Subsequent research (e.g., Simon & Martens, 1979) has painted a somewhat different picture regarding children's emotional experiences in sport. As Passer (1988) and Smoll and Smith (this volume) argued, sport participation is not inherently stressful for many youngsters, but substantial individual differences appear to exist in youngsters' emotional responses to sport involvement. Parental attitudes and behaviors appear to be major contributors to these individual differences in children's affective responses to sport.

Parental influences have consistently been linked to children's emotional outcomes in sport. Virtually every published study on the topic has found a relationship between parental variables and children's affective experiences in sport (Brustad, 1993a). The bulk of the research has examined children's perceptions of parental influence according to various parental pressure, expectation, and evaluation characteristics. The most frequently examined affective outcomes for children have been anxiety and enjoyment.

A considerable body of research has been conducted on the correlates of competitive state and trait anxiety. The construct of competitive state anxiety represents a transitory and situation-specific form of anxiety, whereas competitive trait anxiety is conceptualized as the general tendency to view competition as threatening and to respond with correspondingly higher levels of state anxiety (Martens, 1977). Three studies have found a relationship between parental characteristics and children's precompetition state anxiety levels. In their research on young wrestlers, Scanlan and Lewthwaite (1984) found that youngsters who reported higher levels of parental pressure and who worried frequently about meeting parental (and coach) expectations experienced higher state anxiety prior to competition. Similarly, Gould and colleagues (1991) found that prematch state anxiety for youth wrestlers was significantly related to parental pressure to wrestle. Finally, Weiss, Weise, and Klint (1989), in their study of young male gymnasts, reported that the top two precompetition worries for these youngsters were about "what my parents will think" and "letting my parents down." Thus, this line of research seems to indicate that children who experience higher levels of precompetition anxiety do so, at least in part, because of concerns about how their performance outcomes may affect interactions with their parents.

Since competitive trait anxiety (CTA) represents a person's general tendency to appraise competitive situations as threatening, high-CTA children are of particular concern because they may experience enduring stress throughout their sport participation and, consequently, may be more likely to drop out of sport at an early age. Research also supports the link between parental influences and CTA levels. Investigators have found that high-CTA children are characterized in part by the tendency to worry more frequently about receiving negative evaluations from others (Brustad, 1988; Lewthwaite & Scanlan, 1989; Passer, 1983). These research findings on anxiety in youth sport parallel those in the educational literature that also indicate that concern about negative evaluation from parents is a major source of test anxiety for youngsters (Wigfield & Eccles, 1990).

Burnout in young athletes is an additional negative emotional consequence of concern but one that has received limited research attention. Burnout has been conceptualized as a negative emotional outcome that is the consequence of chronic stress and that results in a loss of interest in continuing sport involvement (Smith, 1986). Although it is unlikely that a large proportion of young athletes experience burnout, this outcome may significantly impact the psychological development of those who do experience this outcome.

Coakley (1992) argued that sport burnout must be examined with reference to the relationship between normal adolescent identity development, the structure of competitive sport, and the influence of significant others. During adolescence, youngsters typically report increasing differentiation and complexity to their identity (Thoits, 1983). This tendency to experience a greater sense of self-complexity during adolescence may not be evident for young athletes, whose identity may be constrained by their heavy focus on one dimension of achievement: sport. With continuing success, and as a consequence of the increasingly competitive structure of age group sport, young athletes are likely to become even more specialized in their sport role, thereby further narrowing their sense of self. A constricted self-identity has been linked to negative emotional consequences such as depression (Linville, 1985; Thoits, 1983) and, conceivably, to sport burnout.

Parents may contribute heavily, albeit unintentionally, to this identity constriction. In his research, Coakley (1992) reported that burnout was most frequently experienced by highly accomplished young athletes whose parents typically made great commitments of time and resources. As the family's level of investment in sport increases, the youngster may experience a sense of feeling "trapped" in the athlete role, thus contributing to burnout. Clearly a great deal of work remains to be done to understand the cause, correlates, and consequences of burnout in young athletes, but researchers should heed Coakley's recommendations to more closely consider the influence of significant others as indirect contributors to burnout.

Favorable affective outcomes for youngsters in sport have also been linked to parental influences; however, considerably less research has been done on this topic than on unfavorable outcomes such as anxiety. Favorable outcomes have typically been assessed in terms of enjoyment, which has generally been operationalized as the amount of fun youngsters report having over the course of a competitive season. The initial investigation into social influences on sport enjoyment was conducted by Scanlan and Lewthwaite (1986) in their study of young male wrestlers. They found that high levels of enjoyment for these athletes were predicted by high parental satisfaction with performance, favorable adult interactional and involvement patterns, and a low frequency of negative maternal interactions. Similarly, Brustad (1988) found that low perceived parental pressure was predictive of high perceived enjoyment among young male and female basketball players. Furthermore, former elite figure skaters reported that bringing pleasure or pride to their family was an important dimension of their sport enjoyment (Scanlan, Stein, & Ravizza, 1989). Finally, in their research with adolescent Norwegian soccer players, Ommundsen and Vaglum (1991) found that the positive emotional involvement of parents (and coaches) was significantly related to enjoyment for these young athletes.

Overall, a relatively clear picture emerges regarding the influence of parents on children's emotional experiences in sport. It seems apparent that the nature and quality of parent-child interactions is critical to understanding children's affective outcomes in sport. Young athletes who perceive that their parents have realistic expectations, will provide support and encouragement for their efforts, and rarely respond with negative evaluations of their performance outcomes will be much more likely to enjoy their sport involvement and to experience lower levels of state and trait anxiety than will children who do not receive these forms of parental support.

The research reviewed here strongly suggests that parents are instrumental in shaping their children's affective experiences in sport. What is less certain is the extent to which these sport-related affective experiences impact children's long-term psychological development. Since researchers have primarily studied children's sport at the nomothetic (group) rather than at the idiographic (individual) level, it is difficult to ascertain how these favorable and unfavorable affective experiences may influence an individual's development over time. Intuitively, it would seem that the enduring traitlike affective characteristics, such as competitive trait anxiety, would be more strongly related to affective development than would transitory or state characteristics.

Peer Influences on Children's Psychological Development

The knowledge base pertaining to peer influence on children's psychological development has lagged substantially behind research assessing parental influences on development. This outcome is apparent for both the sport and academic domains and is attributable to the complexity of studying children's peer cultures as well as to the shortage of theoretical frameworks from which to study children's peer interactions (Corsaro & Eder, 1990).

Unfortunately, lack of knowledge about peer influence greatly impairs our understanding of the developmental outcomes of youth sport involvement for at least three reasons. First, sport achievement is highly valued by children and adolescents in our culture (e.g., Chase & Dummer, 1992), and the relative importance of this achievement domain should logically affect children's social relations and self-concept development. Second, the participation motivation research clearly indicates that affiliation with others and the development of positive social relations are major motives underlying children's interest in sport involvement (see Weiss & Petlichkoff, 1989), further supporting the relationship between children's athletic involvement and the quality of their social interactions. Third, the peak years of sport involvement for youngsters coincide with the developmentally related tendency for youngsters to rely on peer social evaluation sources in assessing personal competence (Horn & Hasbrook, 1986, 1987; Veroff, 1969). For this reason, the reflected appraisals of peers are particularly instrumental in shaping children's self-concept in sport.

Two specific dimensions of peer influence on children's psychological development will be addressed in this chapter. Included will be a discussion of factors shaping children's acceptance by peers, which represents an important dimension of children's affective development. Second, peer influence on youngsters' self-concept development through sport will be addressed.

Peer Acceptance

Acceptance by one's peers has considerable influence on children's psychological development because it influences the types of social opportunities made available to youngsters, their ability to make friends, and the favorability of their self-concepts (Adler et al., 1992). Peer acceptance and popularity is also most likely to be gained by excelling in those achievement areas highly valued by one's peers (Chase & Dummer, 1992; Weiss & Duncan, 1992).

Recent research supports the link between the possession of physical ability and the attainment of peer acceptance. In their study of 8- to 13-year-old males and females enrolled in a summer sport program, Weiss and Duncan (1992) found that children higher in actual and perceived physical competence had higher levels of peer acceptance. In a similar vein, children who are relatively inactive and unfit report stronger feelings of loneliness than do more physically active and fit children (Page et al., 1992).

Researchers have concluded that the possession of sport ability is an important contributor to social status and peer acceptance for children and adolescents but that this relationship is much stronger for boys than for girls (Adler et al., 1992; Chase & Dummer, 1992; Eder & Parker, 1987). Research has found that during later childhood (ages 10–12 years), boys overwhelmingly identify athletic ability as the primary determinant of social status within their peer group, whereas physical appearance is viewed by girls as more strongly linked to peer acceptance (Adler et al., 1992; Chase & Dummer, 1992). Furthermore, the perceived importance of sport achievement as a determinant of peer acceptance seems to have increased for boys over the last 20 years but has decreased slightly for girls (Chase & Dummer, 1992). Thus, we may conclude that sport ability influences youngsters' popularity and acceptance by peers, but the extent of this influence is mediated by gender.

Recent reviews of the youth sport participation motivation literature have also concluded that for both boys and girls, affiliative motives are at least as strong as achievement motives in influencing children's interest in becoming involved in sport (Weiss & Chaumeton, 1992; Weiss & Petlichkoff, 1989). This interest in affiliation with others further reflects the extent to which youngsters view sport as a viable means of developing social relations and gaining peer acceptance. Peer acceptance also appears to underlie the development of a favorable self-concept for youngsters. Harter (1988) reported that children who reported higher perceptions of social support from peers (and parents) had higher self-esteem, intrinsic motivation, and positive affect in achievement situations such as sport.

Self-Concept Development

Of the five dimensions of self-concept identified by youngsters during later childhood (Harter, 1985b), perceptions of athletic competence and peer acceptance are influenced by sport involvement. Peer influences on these components of the self-concept are particularly evident. The imagery of the looking glass self (Cooley, 1902/1956) is useful in understanding the nature of peer group influence on youngsters' sense of self in later childhood and early adolescence. Whereas the reflected appraisals of parents were particularly important during early and middle childhood, the mirror of self provided by peers takes on increasing clarity during later childhood and through adolescence. This "transfer of loyalty to the peer group" (McCabe, Roberts, & Morris, 1991, p. 95) is attributable to the fact that, with age, children spend relatively more time in the company of their peers, as well as to cognitive developmental changes in youngsters' preferences for peer-based informational sources in assessing personal competencies.

Building on research conducted in academic settings (Frieze & Bar-Tal, 1980; Stipek & MacIver, 1989), Horn and colleagues (Horn & Hasbrook, 1986, 1987; Horn

& Weiss, 1991) have found a developmental pattern in children's preferences for various forms of evaluative feedback. This research reveals that at about age 8, children generally rely heavily on adult sources of information to assess their physical competence. Between the ages of 10 and 14 years, however, children demonstrate increasing reliance on peer-based sources of information including peer evaluation, which is the feedback provided by peers, as well as direct comparison of abilities with peers. It is also important to note that the peak levels of sport involvement occur at roughly 11 years of age (State of Michigan, 1978), which coincides with this reliance on peer-based evaluation sources.

As a consequence of this increasing reliance on peer-based evaluations of the self during the peak years of sport involvement, children's self-concepts are particularly likely to be influenced by peers' judgments. Furthermore, since peer acceptance is an important ingredient of a favorable self-concept, the relationship that has been established between physical ability and peer acceptance further points to the influence of peers in shaping self-concept.

In contrast to research that has examined the correspondence between parental and child judgments of children's abilities during childhood (e.g., Eccles & Harold, 1991; Phillips, 1984, 1987), researchers have yet to examine the influence of peer judgments on children's self-perceptions of ability. This outcome points to the general lack of attention that has been devoted to peer influence to date (Evans & Roberts, 1987). Clearly, a greater amount of research attention is needed to understand the nature and strength of peer influence on children's self-perceptions, particularly because of the established link between youngsters' self-perception characteristics and motivational patterns (see Weiss, 1993).

Recommendations for Future Research

An increasing amount of research attention is being focused on parental and peer influences on psychological outcomes for children in sport. This interest is very encouraging given the obviously important role that parents and peers play in shaping the quality of children's sport involvement. However, our understanding of these forms of social influence in sport still lags far behind the knowledge base regarding social influence in other dimensions of children's achievement. Furthermore, research on parental and peer influence has only extended to a few dimensions of psychological influence. Three recommendations will, therefore, be proposed to assist our understanding of this important topic.

To the present time, researchers have focused on a variety of psychological outcomes (e.g., anxiety, enjoyment) that children may experience in sport, but we do not yet have a strong sense for how sport participation influences children's long-term psychological development (Weiss, 1993). Consequently, first greater attention needs to be devoted to identifying the nature of parental and peer influence on youngsters' psychological development over time. To accomplish this goal, it will be necessary to focus on aspects of individual change rather than to rely solely on group data. Using longitudinal, as well as qualitative research methodologies will help to gain a better understanding of individual development through sport.

Second, researchers need to be fully aware of the importance of adhering to a developmental perspective in the study of children's psychological development through sport. The need for a developmental perspective has been stressed by other authors (e.g., Duda, 1987; Weiss & Bredemeier, 1983), but the necessity of such an approach should be particularly evident for the study of parental and peer influence, since the salience of each form of influence clearly depends on children's cognitive and social developmental status.

The third recommendation is that researchers should direct much greater attention to examining the nature of peer group influence on youngsters' psychological development through sport. Since the years of peak sport involvement correspond with a developmental stage in which peer feedback and peer comparison are quite salient to youngsters, we can be confident that peers play a key role in shaping the psychological, social, and affective outcomes that youngsters experience in sport. The lack of research attention given to peer influence to date is attributable in large part to the relative difficulty of studying children's peer interactions. Naturalistic research methods may be of particular benefit to understanding characteristics of peer influence. Fine's (1987) study of children's sport socialization is an excellent example of the benefits of a naturalistic approach to studying peer influence.

The study of children's psychological development through sport is a very complex undertaking because of the need to simultaneously consider cognitive, social, and developmental influences. However, a revitalized interest in examining the nature of parental and peer influences should greatly enhance our understanding of the developmental consequences of youth sport participation.

References

Adler, P. A., Kless, S. J., & Adler, P. (1992). Socialization to gender roles: Popularity among elementary school boys and girls. *Sociology of Education, 65*, 169–187.

Bandura, A. (1986). *Social foundations of thought and action: A social cognitive theory.* Englewood Cliffs, NJ: Prentice-Hall.

Black, S. J., & Weiss, M. R. (1992). The relationship among perceived coaching behaviors, perceptions of ability, and motivation in competitive age-group swimmers. *Journal of Sport and Exercise Psychology, 14*, 309–325.

Brower, J. J. (1978). Little league baseballism: Adult dominance in a "child's game". In R. Martens (Ed.), *Joy and sadness in children's sports* (pp. 39–49). Champaign, IL: Human Kinetics.

Brustad, R. J. (1988). Affective outcomes in competitive youth sport: The influence of intrapersonal and socialization factors. *Journal of Sport and Exercise Psychology, 10*, 307–321.

———. (1993a). Youth in sport: Psychological considerations. In R. N. Singer, M. Murphey, & L. K. Tennant (Eds.), *Handbook of research on sport psychology* (pp. 695–717). New York: Macmillan.

———. (1993b). Who will go out and play? Parental and psychological influences on children's attraction to physical activity. *Pediatric Exercise Science, 5*, 210–223.

Chase, M. A., & Dummer, G. M. (1992). The role of sports as a social status determinant for children. *Research Quarterly for Exercise and Sport, 63*, 418–424.

Coakley, J. (1992). Burnout among adolescent athletes: A personal failure or social problem? *Sociology of Sport Journal, 9*, 271–285.

Cooley, C. H. (1902/1956). *Human nature and the social order.* Glencoe, IL: Free Press.

Corsaro, W. A., & Eder, D. (1990). Children's peer cultures. *Annual Review of Sociology, 16*, 197–220.

Dempsey, J. M., Kimiecik, J. C., & Horn, T. S. (1993). Parental influence on children's moderate to vigorous physical activity participation: An expectancy-value approach. *Pediatric Exercise Science, 5*, 151–167.

Duda, J. L. (1987). Toward a developmental theory of children's motivation in sport. *Journal of Sport Psychology, 9,* 130–145.

Eccles, J. S., & Harold, R. D. (1991). Gender differences in sport involvement: Applying the Eccles expectancy-value model. *Journal of Applied Sport Psychology, 3,* 7–35.

Eder, D., & Parker, S. (1987). The cultural production and reproduction of gender: The effect of extracurricular activities on peer-group culture. *Sociology of Education, 60,* 200–213.

Evans, J. R., & Roberts, G. C. (1987). Physical competence and the development of peer relations. *Quest, 39,* 23–35.

Felson, R. B., & Reed, M. (1986). The effect of parents on the self-appraisals of children. *Social Psychology Quarterly, 49,* 302–308.

Fine, G. A. (1987). *With the boys.* Chicago: University of Chicago Press.

Fox, K. R., & Corbin, C. B. (1989). The physical self-perception profile: Development and preliminary validation. *Journal of Sport and Exercise Psychology, 11,* 408–430.

Frieze, I., & Bar-Tal, D. (1980). Developmental trends in cue utilization for attributional judgements. *Journal of Applied Developmental Psychology, 1,* 83–94.

Gould, D., & Martens, R. (1979). Attitudes of volunteer coaches toward significant youth sport issues. *The Research Quarterly, 50,* 369–380.

Gould, D., Eklund, R. C., Petlichkoff, L., Peterson, K., & Bump, L. (1991). Psychological predictors of state anxiety and performance in age-group wrestlers. *Pediatric Exercise Science, 3,* 198–208.

Harter, S. (1981). A model of intrinsic mastery motivation in children: Individual differences and developmental change. In W. A. Collins (Ed.), *Minnesota symposium on child psychology* (Vol. 14, pp. 215–255). Hillsdale, NJ: Erlbaum.

———. (1985a). Competence as a dimension of self-evaluation: Toward a comprehensive model of self-worth. In R. Leahy (Ed.), *The development of the self* (pp. 55–122). New York: Academic Press.

———. (1985b). Processes underlying the construction, maintenance, and enhancement of the self-concept in children. In J. Suls & A. Greenwald (Eds.), *Psychological perspectives on the self* (Vol. 3, pp. 132–182). Hillsdale, NJ: Erlbaum.

———. (1988). Causes, correlates, and the functional role of global self-worth: A life-span perspective. In J. Kolligan & R. Sternberg (Eds.), *Perceptions of competence and incompetence across the life-span* (pp. 67–98). New Haven, CT: Yale University Press.

Horn, T. S. (1985). Coaches' feedback and changes in children's perceptions of their physical competence. *Journal of Educational Psychology, 77,* 174–186.

Horn, T. S., & Hasbrook, C. A. (1986). Informational components underlying children's perceptions of their physical competence. In M. R. Weiss & D. Gould (Eds.), *Sport for children and youths* (pp. 81–88). Champaign, IL: Human Kinetics.

———. (1987). Psychological characteristics and the criteria children use for self-evaluation. *Journal of Sport and Psychology, 9,* 208–221.

Horn, T. S., & Weiss, M. R. (1991). A developmental analysis of children's self-ability judgments in the physical domain. *Pediatric Exercise Science, 3,* 310–326.

Lewko, J. H., & Greendorfer, S. L. (1988). Family differences in sport socialization of children and adolescents. In F. L. Smoll, R. A. Magill, & M. J. Ash (Eds.), *Children in sport* (3rd ed., pp. 287–300). Champaign, IL: Human Kinetics.

Lewthwaite, R., & Scanlan, T. K. (1989). Predictors of competitive trait anxiety in male youth sport participants. *Medicine and Science in Sports and Exercise, 21,* 221–229.

Linville, P. W. (1985). Self-complexity and affective extremity: Don't put all of your eggs in one cognitive basket. *Social Cognition, 3,* 94–120.

Marsh, H. W., & Peart, N. D. (1988). Competitive and cooperative physical fitness training programs for girls: Effects on physical fitness and multidimensional self-concepts. *Journal of Sport and Exercise Psychology, 10,* 390–407.

Martens, R. (1977). *Sport competition anxiety test.* Champaign, IL: Human Kinetics.

McCabe, A. E., Roberts, B. T., & Morris, T. E. (1991). Athletic activity, body image, and adolescent identity. In L. Diamant (Ed.), *Mind-body maturity* (pp. 91–103). New York: Hemisphere.

McCullagh, P., Matzkanin, K., Shaw, S., & Maldonado, M. (1993). Motivation for participation in physical activity: A comparison of parent-children perceived competencies and participation motives. *Pediatric Exercise Science, 5,* 224–233.

Mead, G. H. (1934). *Mind, self, and society.* Chicago: University of Chicago Press.

Nicholls, J. (1984). Achievement motivation: Conceptions of ability, subjective experience, task choice, and performance. *Psychological Review, 91,* 328–346.

Ommundsen, Y., & Vaglum, P. (1991). Soccer competition anxiety and enjoyment in young boy players. The influence of perceived competence and significant others' emotional involvement. *International Journal of Sport Psychology, 22,* 35–49.

Orlick, T. D. (1974, November/December). The athletic dropout: A high price of inefficiency. *Canadian Association for Health, Physical Education and Recreation Journal, 41,* 21–27.

Page, R. M., Frey, J., Talbert, R., & Falk, C. (1992). Children's feelings of loneliness and social dissatisfaction: Relationship to measures of physical fitness and activity. *Journal of Teaching in Physical Education, 11,* 211–219.

Parsons, J. E., Adler, T. F., & Kaczala, C. M. (1982). Socialization of achievement attitudes and beliefs: Parental influences. *Child Development, 53,* 310–321.

Passer, M. W. (1983). Fear of failure, fear of evaluation, perceived competence and self-esteem in competitive trait anxious children. *Journal of Sport Psychology, 5,* 172–188.

———. (1988). Determinants and consequences of children's competitive stress. In F. L. Smoll, R. A. Magill, & M. J. Ash (Eds.), *Children in sport* (3rd ed., pp. 203–228). Champaign, IL: Human Kinetics

Phillips, D. (1984). The illusion of incompetence among academically competent children. *Child Development, 55,* 2000–2016.

———. (1987). Socialization of perceived academic competence among highly competent children. *Child Development, 58,* 1308–1320.

Scanlan, T. K. (1995). Social evaluation and the competition process: A developmental perspective. In F. L. Smoll & R. E. Smith (Eds.), *Children and youth in sport: A biopsychosocial perspective* (pp. 298–308). Dubuque, IA: Brown & Benchmark.

Scanlan, T. K., Carpenter, P. J., Lobel, M., & Simons, J. (1993). Sources of enjoyment for youth sport athletes. *Pediatric Exercise Science, 5,* 275–285.

Scanlan, T. K., & Lewthwaite, R. (1984). Social psychological aspects of competition for male youth sport participants: I: Predictors of competitive stress. *Journal of Sport Psychology, 6,* 208–226.

———. (1986). Social psychological aspects of competition for male youth sport participants: IV: Predictors of enjoyment. *Journal of Sport Psychology, 8,* 25–35.

Scanlan, T. K., Stein, G. L., & Ravizza, K. (1989). An in-depth study of former elite figure skaters: II: Sources of enjoyment. *Journal of Sport and Exercise Psychology, 11,* 65–83.

Selman, R. L. (1976). Social-cognitive understanding: A guide to educational and clinical practice. In T. Lickona (Ed.), *Moral development and behavior* (pp. 299–316). New York: Holt, Rinehart, & Winston.

Simon, J., & Martens, R. (1979). Children's anxiety in sport and nonsport evaluative activities. *Journal of Sport Psychology, 1,* 160–169.

Smilkstein, G. (1980). Psychological trauma in children and youth in competitive sport. *The Journal of Family Practice, 10,* 737–739.

Smith, R. E. (1986). Toward a cognitive-affective model of athletic burnout. *Journal of Sport Psychology, 8,* 36–50.

Smith, R. E., Smoll, F. L., & Curtis, B. (1979). Coach effectiveness training: A cognitive behavioral approach to enhancing relationship skills in youth sport coaches. *Journal of Sport Psychology, 1,* 59–75.

Smoll, R. L., & Smith, R. E. (1995). Competitive anxiety: Sources, consequences, and intervention strategies. In F. L. Smoll & R. E. Smith (Eds.), *Children and youth in sport: A biopsychosocial perspective* (pp. 359–380). Dubuque, IA: Brown & Benchmark.

State of Michigan. (1978). *Joint legislative study on youth sport programs-Phase II.* East Lansing, MI: Youth Sport Institute.

Stipek, D., & MacIver, D. (1989). Developmental change in children's assessment of intellectual competence. *Child Development, 60,* 521–538.

Thoits, P. A. (1983). Multiple identities and psychological well-being: A reformulation and test of the social isolation hypothesis. *American Sociological Review, 48,* 174–187.

Veroff, J. (1969). Social comparison and the development of achievement motivation. In C. P. Smith (Ed.), *Achievement related motives in children* (pp. 46–101). New York: Sage Foundation.

Weiss, M. R. (1987). Self-esteem and achievement in children's sport and physical activity. In D. Gould & M. R. Weiss (Eds.), *Advances in pediatric sport sciences* (Vol. 2, pp. 87–119). Champaign, IL: Human Kinetics.

———. (1993). Psychological effects of intensive sport participation on children and youth: Self-esteem and motivation. In B. Cahill & A. Pearl (Eds.), *Perspectives on intensive participation in youth sports* (pp. 39–69). Champaign, IL: Human Kinetics.

Weiss, M. R., & Bredemeier, B. J. (1983). Developmental sport psychology: A theoretical perspective for studying children in sport. *Journal of Sport Psychology, 5,* 216–230.

Weiss, M. R., & Chaumeton, N. (1992). Motivational orientations in sport. In T. S. Horn (Ed.), *Advances in sport psychology* (pp. 61–99). Champaign, IL: Human Kinetics.

Weiss, M. R., & Duncan, S. C. (1992). The relationship between perceived competence and peer acceptance in the context of children's sport participation. *Journal of Sport and Exercise Psychology, 14,* 177–191.

Weiss, M. R., & Petlichkoff, L. M. (1989). Children's motivation for participation in and withdrawal from sport: Identifying the missing links. *Pediatric Exercise Science, 1,* 195–211.

Weiss, M. R., Weise, D. M., & Klint, K. A. (1989). Head over heels with success: The relationship between self-efficacy and performance in competitive youth gymnastics. *Journal of Sport and Exercise Psychology, 11,* 444–451.

Wigfield, A., & Eccles, J. S. (1990). Test anxiety in elementary and secondary school students. *Educational Psychologist, 24,* 159–183.

Zarbatany, L., Hartmann, D. P., & Rankin, D. B. (1990). The psychological functions of preadolescent peer activities. *Child Development, 61,* 1067–1080.

THE COACH AS A FOCUS OF RESEARCH AND INTERVENTION IN YOUTH SPORTS

—Ronald E. Smith and Frank L. Smoll

Youth sports are a firmly established part of contemporary Western society, and they directly touch the lives of many people (Berryman, this volume; Wiggins, this volume). Current figures indicate that approximately half of all youngsters between the ages of 10 and 18 years participate in agency-sponsored programs, such as Little League Baseball, Pop Warner Football, and community-based programs in soccer, basketball, and a variety of other individual and team sports (Ewing & Seefeldt, this volume). Millions more participate in interscholastic programs.

A corresponding increase in adult involvement has accompanied the rising participation rates of youngsters. Consequently, organized sport programs have become an extremely complex social system that has attracted the attention of researchers interested in studying the impact of sport competition on psychosocial development (see Brown & Branta, 1988; Cahill & Pearl, 1993; Gould & Weiss, 1987; Malina, 1988; Smoll, Magill, & Ash, 1988; Weiss & Gould, 1986).

Much of the controversy that surrounds youth sports concerns the roles that adults play in the process. However, general agreement exists that an important determinant of the effects of participation lies in the relationship between coach and athlete (Martens, 1987a; Seefeldt & Gould, 1980; Smoll & Smith, 1989). Coaches influence the effects that youth sport participation has on children through the interpersonal behaviors they engage in, the values and attitudes they transmit both verbally and through example, and the goal priorities they establish (for example, winning versus equal participation and fun). Coaches not only occupy a central and influential position in the athletic setting but their influence can extend into other areas of the child's life as well. For example, because of the high frequency of single-parent families, coaches sometimes find themselves occupying the role of a substitute parent.

Most athletes have their first sport experiences in programs staffed by volunteer coaches. Although many of these coaches are fairly well versed in the technical aspects of the sport, they rarely have had any formal training in creating a healthy psychological environment for youngsters. Moreover, through the mass media, these coaches are frequently exposed to college or professional coaches who model aggressive behaviors and a "winning is everything" philosophy that is highly inappropriate in a recreational and skill development context. Because the vast majority of youth coaches have desirable motives for coaching (Martens & Gould, 1979; Smith, Smoll, & Curtis, 1978), one can assume that their limitations result primarily from a lack of information on how to create a supportive interpersonal climate. Several educational programs have therefore been developed for the purpose of positively affecting coaching practices and thereby increasing the likelihood that youngsters will have positive sport experiences.

Four training programs currently available in the United States include curricular components designed to influence how volunteer coaches interact with young athletes. The American Coaching Effectiveness Program (Martens, 1987b), Coach Effectiveness Training (Smoll & Smith, 1993), the National Youth Sport Coaches Association program (Brown & Butterfield, 1992), and the Program for Athletic Coaches' Education (Seefeldt & Brown, 1992) have been administered to many thousands of youth coaches. The national coaching associations of Australia and Canada have also developed formal programs that provide training in sport psychology as well as other areas, such as sport pedagogy (teaching sports skills and strategies), sport physiology (conditioning, weight training, and nutrition), and sports medicine (injury prevention, care, and rehabilitation). Unfortunately, only one of the preceding programs, Coach Effectiveness Training (CET), has been subjected to systematic evaluation to determine its influence on coaches' behaviors and the effects of such behaviors on youngsters' psychosocial development (Brown & Butterfield, 1992). In this chapter, we present overviews of (a) the development of CET, (b) the content of CET and procedures for its implementation, and (c) empirical studies that assessed the efficacy of CET. A more comprehensive discussion of cognitive-behavioral principles and techniques used in conducting psychologically oriented coach training programs appears elsewhere (Smoll & Smith, 1993).

Developing a Coach Training Program

A crucial first step in developing a training program is to determine what is to be presented. In this regard, our work was guided by a fundamental assumption that a training program should be based on scientific evidence rather than on intuition and/or what we "know" on the basis of informal observation. An empirical foundation for coaching guidelines enhances the validity and potential value of the program and increases its credibility in the eyes of consumers. We now describe our approach to generating an empirical database for CET.

Theoretical Model and Research Paradigm

In the early 1970s, recognition of the potential impact of youth coaches on athletes' psychological welfare prompted several scientific questions that we felt were worth pursuing. For example, what do coaches do, and how frequently do they engage in such behaviors as encouragement, punishment, instruction, and organization? What are the psychological dimensions that underlie such behaviors? And, finally, how are observable coaching behaviors related to children's reactions to their organized

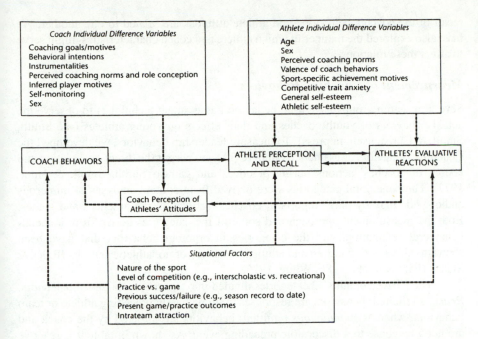

FIGURE 9.1
A model of coaching behaviors, their antecedents, and their effects on athletes, with hypothesized relations among situational, cognitive, behavioral, and individual difference variables.

Figure 1 (1534). Smoll, Frank L., & Smith, Ronald E. (1989). Leadership behaviors in sport: A theoretical model and research paradigm. *Journal of Applied Social Psychology*, **19**, 1522–1551. Copyright 1989 by V. H. Winston & Son, Inc. Reprinted by permission.

athletic experiences? Answers to such questions are not only a first step in describing the behavioral ecology of one aspect of the youth sport setting, but they also provide an empirical basis for the development of psychologically oriented intervention programs.

To begin to answer such questions, we carried out a systematic program of research over a period of several years. A mediational model of coach-athlete interactions guided the project. The basic elements of the model are represented as follows: Coach behaviors result in perceptions and memories in the minds of young athletes which, in turn, affect their emotional reactions to their experiences and, ultimately, the psychosocial impact of their sport experience. In other words, we are assuming that the ultimate effects of coaching behaviors are mediated by the meaning that athletes attribute to them; what athletes remember about their coach's behaviors and how they interpret these actions affect the way that athletes evaluate their sport experiences. Furthermore, a complex of cognitive and emotional processes are involved at this mediational level. That is, the athletes' perceptions and reactions are likely to be affected not only by the coach's behaviors but also by other factors, such as the athlete's age, what he or she expects of coaches (normative beliefs and expectations), and certain personality variables, such as self-esteem and anxiety. In recognition of these additional layers of complexity, the basic three-element model has been expanded to reflect these factors (Smoll & Smith, 1989). The expanded model, which is presented in figure 9.1, specifies a number of situational factors as well as coach and athlete characteristics that could influence coach behaviors and the perceptions and reactions of athletes to them. Using this model as a starting point, we have sought to determine how observed coaching behaviors, athletes' perception and recall of the coach's behaviors, and athlete attitudes are related to one another. We have also explored the manner in which athlete and coach characteristics might serve to affect these relations.

Measurement of Coaching Behaviors

Several research groups have used behavioral assessment techniques to observe the actual behaviors of youth coaches and their effects on young athletes (see Smith, Smoll, & Christensen, in press). To measure leadership behaviors, we developed the Coaching Behavior Assessment System (CBAS) to permit the direct observation and coding of coaches' actions during practices and games (Smith, Smoll, & Hunt, 1977). The behavioral categories were derived from content analyses of numerous audiotaped "play-by-play" reports of coaches' actions during practices and games. Both the measurement approach and some of the categories derive from a social-behavioral orientation, and the categories incorporate behaviors that have been shown to affect both children and adults in a variety of nonathletic settings (Bales & Slater, 1955; Komaki, 1986; White, 1975).

The CBAS contains 12 categories divided into two major classes of behaviors. *Reactive* (elicited) behaviors are responses to immediately preceding athlete or team behaviors, whereas *spontaneous* (emitted) behaviors are initiated by the coach and are not a response to a discernible preceding event. As shown in table 9.1, reactive behaviors are responses to either desirable performance or effort, mistakes and errors, or misbehaviors on the part of athletes; the spontaneous class is subdivided into game-related and game-irrelevant behaviors. The system thus involves basic interactions between the situation and the coach's behavior. Use of the CBAS in observing and coding coaching behaviors in a variety of sports indicates that the scoring system is sufficiently comprehensive to incorporate the vast majority of overt leader behaviors, that high interrater reliability can be obtained, and that individual differences in behavioral patterns can be discerned (Chaumeton & Duda, 1988; Cruz et al., 1987; Horn, 1984, 1985; Rejeski, Darracott, & Hutslar, 1979; Smith et al., 1983; Wandzilak, Ansorge, & Potter, 1988).

Basic Research Relating Coaching Behaviors to Children's Evaluative Reactions

Following development of the CBAS, a field study was conducted to establish relations between coaching behaviors and several athlete variables specified in the conceptual model (Smith et al., 1978). Fifty-one male Little League Baseball coaches were observed by trained coders during 202 complete games. A total of 57,213 individual coaching behaviors were coded into the 12 categories, and a behavioral profile based on an average of 1,122 behaviors was computed for each coach.

Several self-report measures were developed to assess coaches' beliefs, attitudes, and perceptions. These were combined into a questionnaire that the coaches completed at the end of the season. Coaches' self-perception of their behaviors was of primary importance. This was assessed by describing and giving examples of the 12 CBAS behaviors and asking coaches to indicate on a seven-point scale how often they engaged in the behaviors in the situations described.

TABLE 9.1 Response Categories of the Coaching Behavior Assessment System

Class I. Reactive Behaviors

Responses to Desirable Performance

Reinforcement (R)	a positive, rewarding reaction (verbal or non-verbal) to a good play or good effort
Nonreinforcement (NR)	failure to respond to a good performance

Responses to Mistakes

Mistake-Contingent Encouragement (EM)	encouragement given to a player following a mistake
Mistake-Contingent Technical Instruction (TIM)	instructing or demonstrating to a player how to correct a mistake he/she has made
Punishment (P)	a negative reaction, verbal or nonverbal, following a mistake
Punitive Technical Instruction (TIM + P)	technical instruction following a mistake which is given in a punitive or hostile manner
Ignoring Mistakes (IM)	failure to respond to a player mistake

Response to Misbehavior

Keeping Control (KC)	reactions intended to restore or maintain order among team members

Class II. Spontaneous Behaviors

Game-Related

General Technical Instruction (TIG)	spontaneous instruction in the techniques and strategies of the sport (not following a mistake)
General Encouragement (EG)	spontaneous encouragement which does not follow a mistake
Organization (O)	administrative behavior which sets the stage for play by assigning duties, responsibilities, positions, etc.

Game-Irrelevant

General Communication (GC)	interactions with players unrelated to the game

Note. From "A System for the Behavioral Assessment of Athletic Coaches" by R. E. Smith, F. L. Smoll, and E. B. Hunt, 1977, *Research Quarterly*, 48, 401–407. This table is adapted with permission from the *Research Quarterly for Exercise and Sport,* vol. 48 (1977). The *Research Quarterly for Exercise and Sport* is a publication of the American Alliance for Health, Physical Education, Recreation and Dance, 1900 Association Drive, Reston, VA 22091. The letters in parentheses are the scoring codes for each behavior category.

Data from 542 players were collected after the season during individual interviews and questionnaire administrations carried out in the children's homes. Included were measures of their recall and perception of the coaches' behaviors (on the same scales as the coaches had rated their own behaviors), their liking for the coach and their teammates, the degree of enjoyment they experienced during the season, and their general self-esteem.

At the level of overt behavior, three independent behavioral dimensions were identified through factor analysis: supportiveness (composed of reinforcement and mistake-contingent encouragement); instructiveness (general technical instruction and mistake-contingent technical instruction *versus* general communication and general encouragement); and punitiveness (punishment and punitive technical instruction *versus* organizational behaviors). The first two dimensions correspond closely to the classic leadership styles of relationship orientation and task orientation emphasized in leadership theories such as Fiedler's (1967) Contingency Model, Situational Leadership (Hersey & Blanchard, 1977), and the Vertical Dyad Linkage model of Graen and Schiermann (1978) and identified in other research on leadership behavior (e.g., Stogdill, 1959).

Relations between coaches' scores on these behavioral dimensions and player measures indicated that players responded most favorably to coaches who engaged in higher percentages of supportive and instructional behaviors. Players on teams whose coaches created a supportive environment also liked their teammates more. A somewhat surprising finding was that the team's won-lost record was essentially unrelated to how well the players liked the coach and how much they wanted to play for the coach in the future. On the other hand, players on winning teams felt that their parents liked the coach more and that the coach liked them more than did players on losing teams. Apparently, winning made little difference to the children, but they knew that it was important to the adults. It is worth noting, however, that winning assumed greater importance beyond age 12, although it continued to be a less important attitudinal determinant than coach behaviors.

Another important issue concerns the degree of accuracy with which coaches perceive their own behaviors. Correlations between CBAS observed behaviors and coaches' ratings of how frequently they performed the behaviors were generally low and nonsignificant. The only significant correlation occurred for punishment. Overall we found that children's ratings on the same perceived behavior scales correlated much more highly with CBAS measures than did the coaches' own reports! It thus appears that coaches have limited awareness of how frequently they engage in particular forms of behavior and that athletes are more accurate perceivers of actual coach behaviors. Obviously this finding has important implications for coach training, since behavior change requires an awareness on the part of the coach of how he or she is currently behaving.

Finally, analysis of the children's attraction responses toward the coaches revealed a significant interaction between coach supportiveness (the tendency to reinforce desirable performance and effort and to respond to mistakes with encouragement) and athletes' level of self-esteem (Smith & Smoll, 1990). Specifically, the low self-esteem children were especially responsive to variations in supportiveness in a manner consistent with a self-enhancement model of self-esteem (Shrauger, 1975; Swann, 1990; Tesser, 1988). As shown in figure 9.2, the low self-esteem children responded far differently to coaches who were either high or low in supportiveness, whereas the moderate and high self-esteem children were far less influenced by the coach's level of supportiveness. This finding is consistent with the results of other studies that, collectively, suggest that the desire of people low in self-esteem to experience enhanced feelings of self-worth makes them especially responsive to variations

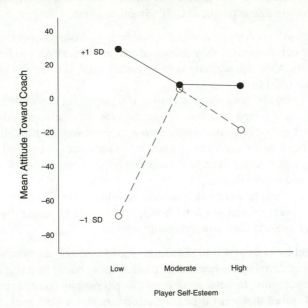

Supportiveness

FIGURE 9.2
Mean attraction factor
scores toward coaches
who were high and low in
(± 1 SD from the mean)
Coaching Behavior
Assessment System
supportiveness factor
scores (data from Smith &
Smoll, 1990).

in supportiveness because of their greater need for positive feedback from others (Dittes, 1959; Brown, Collins, & Schmidt, 1988; Tesser & Campbell, 1983).

The CET Program: Content and Procedures

CET was conceptualized and designed within a cognitive-behavioral framework (Bandura, 1986). The core of the program consists of a series of empirically derived behavioral guidelines (i.e., coaching *dos* and *don'ts*). The coaching guidelines are based primarily on social influence techniques that involve principles of positive control rather than aversive control, and the conception of success or "winning" as consisting of giving maximum effort. The behavioral guidelines, which are summarized in appendix A at the end of this chapter, emphasize the desirability of *increasing* four specific target behaviors: reinforcement (for effort as well as for good performance), mistake-contingent encouragement, corrective instruction (given in an encouraging and supportive fashion), and technical instruction (spontaneous instruction in the techniques and strategies of the sport). Coaches are also urged to *decrease* nonreinforcement, punishment, and punitive instruction, as well as to avoid having to use regimenting behaviors (keeping control). The guidelines are placed in a goal context of increasing positive coach-athlete and athlete-athlete interactions, developing team cohesion, and developing in athletes a positive desire to achieve rather than a fear of failure.

As far as winning is concerned, CET urges coaches to focus on athletes' effort and enjoyment rather than on success as measured by statistics or scoreboards.

Coaches are thus encouraged to emphasize "doing your best," "getting better," and "having fun" as opposed to a "win at all costs" orientation. More specifically, a four-part philosophy of winning is taught in CET (Smoll & Smith, 1981):

1. *Winning isn't everything, nor is it the only thing.* Young athletes cannot get the most out of sports if they think that the only objective is to beat their opponents. Although winning is an important goal, it is *not* the most important objective.
2. *Failure is not the same thing as losing.* It is important that athletes do not view losing as a sign of failure or as a threat to their personal value.
3. *Success is not synonymous with winning.* Neither success nor failure need depend on the outcome of a contest or on a won-lost record. Winning and losing pertain to the outcome of a contest, whereas success and failure do not.
4. *Children should be taught that success is found in striving for victory (i.e., success is related to effort).* Youngsters should be taught that they are never losers if they give maximum effort.

This philosophy is designed to maximize young athletes' enjoyment of sport and their chances of deriving the benefits of participation, partly as a result of combating competitive anxiety. In what ways does this philosophy combat stress? With respect to Point 1, given that sport is heavily achievement-oriented, seeking victory is encouraged. However, the philosophy attempts to reduce the ultimate importance of winning relative to other prized participation motives (e.g., skill development and affiliation with teammates). Most notably, in recognition of the inverse relation between enjoyment and competitive stress (Scanlan & Lewthwaite, 1984; Scanlan & Passer, 1978, 1979), *fun* is highlighted as the paramount objective.

Points 2 and 3 of the philosophy promote separation of the athlete's feelings of self-worth from the game outcome. This orientation is supported by Gallwey and Kriegel (1977), who emphasized that "the key to overcoming fear of failure is breaking one's attachment to results" (p. 85). Adults can help children develop healthy attitudes about competition by showing that winning and losing does not change children's value or adults' affection for them as individuals.

Finally, in Point 4, young athletes are encouraged to attribute their failures to an unstable, controllable factor (i.e., lack of effort) instead of lack of ability (a stable, less controllable factor). Considerable evidence exists that such an approach benefits children's motivation, performance, and feelings about themselves. For example, Dweck's (1975) highly successful attributional retraining program with low-achieving children involved nothing more complicated than explicitly attributing failure to a lack of effort and encouraging subjects to try harder. Children who received direct instruction in how to interpret the causes of their failures showed improved performance (in a math problem-solving task) and were better able to cope with failure. Within the realm of sport, one might expect this approach to lessen the effects of failure, thereby reducing stress for athletes.

In a CET workshop, which lasts approximately two and one-half hours, behavioral guidelines are presented both verbally and in written materials (a printed outline and a 12-page pamphlet) given to the coaches. The pamphlet supplements the guidelines with concrete suggestions for communicating effectively with young athletes, gaining their respect, and relating effectively to their parents. The importance of sensitivity and being responsive to individual differences among athletes is also stressed. The written materials serve to (a) help keep the workshop organized, (b) facilitate coaches' understanding of the information, (c) eliminate the need for coaches to take notes, and (d) give coaches a tangible resource to refer to in the future. Also, audiovisual aids, such as content slides and cartoons illustrating important points, are used to facilitate ease of comprehension and retention as well as to add to the organizational quality of the session.

We not only believe in the importance of establishing an empirical foundation for training guidelines, but we also feel that the ability to present supportive data increases the credibility of the guidelines for the coaches. A CET workshop therefore includes a description of the development and testing of the program. Using lay terms and avoiding scientific jargon, we place the empirical findings within the conceptual framework that has guided our work. As previously noted, this model emphasizes functional relations between coaching behaviors, athletes' perceptions of those behaviors, and athletes' reactions to their sport experiences. As a prelude to presenting behavioral guidelines, we customarily familiarize coaches with the core components of the mediational model and describe the CBAS. This provides coaches with a set of perceptual categories for organizing their own experiences and self-perceptions. After establishing a familiarity with potential behaviors, coaches are informed of how the various behaviors affect young athletes, and this, in turn, sets the stage for the presentation of coaching guidelines.

In introducing coaching guidelines, we emphasize that they should not be viewed as a "magic formula" and that mere knowledge of the principles is not sufficient. We stress that the challenge is not so much in learning the principles; they are relatively simple. Rather, the challenge is for coaches to integrate the guidelines into their own coaching styles. When coaches believe that adoption of the guidelines is a result of their own dedication and effort, they are more likely to attribute behavioral changes to themselves rather than to the trainer. This approach is supported by evidence that self-attributed behavioral changes are more enduring than those attributed to some outside causal agent (Deci & Ryan, 1987).

The most basic objectives of CET are to communicate coaching principles in a manner that is easily comprehended and to maximize the likelihood that coaches will adopt the information. As part of our approach to creating a positive learning environment, we encourage coaches to share their own experiences and associated practical knowledge with the group. CET workshops are thus conducted with an interactive format in which coaches are treated as an integral part of the session rather than a mere audience. The open atmosphere for exchange promotes active versus passive learning, and the dialogue serves to enhance the participants' interest and involvement in the learning process.

The didactic instruction just described contains many verbal modeling cues that essentially tell coaches what to do. To supplement the didactic verbal and written materials, coaching guidelines are transmitted via behavioral modeling cues (i.e., actual demonstrations showing coaches how to behave in desirable ways). In CET, such cues are presented by a live model (the trainer) and by symbolic models (coach cartoons), since many forms of modeling have been shown to be highly effective in changing behavior (Bandura, 1986; Perry & Furukawa, 1986). In addition, modeling is frequently used in conjunction with later role playing of positive behaviors (e.g., Edelstein & Eisler, 1976; Nay, 1975). Coaches are kept actively involved in the training process by presenting critical situations and asking them to role-play appropriate ways of responding. This form of behavioral rehearsal has great promise in enhancing acquisition of desired behaviors, in providing the opportunity to practice the behaviors, and in establishing an increased level of participant involvement during the workshops.

One of the striking findings from our initial research was that coaches had very limited awareness of how often they behaved in various ways (Smith et al., 1978). Thus, an important component of a training program should be an attempt to increase coaches' awareness of what they are doing as well as their motivation to comply with behavioral guidelines. In CET, coaches are taught the use of two proven behavioral change techniques, namely, behavioral feedback (Edelstein & Eisler, 1976; McFall & Twentyman, 1973) and self-monitoring (Kanfer & Gaelick-Buys, 1991; Kazdin, 1974; McFall, 1977). To obtain feedback, coaches are encouraged to work with their assistants as a team and share descriptions of each others' behaviors. Other potential feedback procedures include coaches soliciting input from athletes and provision of feedback by a league committee. With respect to self-monitoring, CET coaches are given a brief form that they are encouraged to complete immediately after practices and games (see Smoll & Smith, 1993, pp. 53–54). On the form, they indicate approximately what percentage of the time they engage in the recommended behaviors in relevant situations. For example, coaches are asked, "Approximately what percentage of the times they occurred did you respond to mistakes/errors with encouragement?" Self-monitoring is restricted to desired behaviors in light of evidence that tracking of undesired behaviors can be detrimental to effective self-regulation (Cavior & Marabotto, 1976; Gottman & McFall, 1972; Kirschenbaum & Karoly, 1977). Coaches are encouraged to engage in self-monitoring on a regular basis to achieve optimal results.

Applied Research Assessing the Efficacy of CET

Sweeping conclusions are often drawn about the efficacy of intervention programs in the absence of anything approximating acceptable scientific evidence. We therefore felt it was important not only to develop an empirical foundation for CET but also to measure its effects on coaches and the youngsters who play for them.

We have focused on five important classes of outcome variables in our program evaluation studies. First, we needed to know whether the program had effects on the behaviors of the trained coaches. Did coaches who were exposed to the program exhibit behaviors that conformed to the behavioral guidelines to a greater extent than was the case for untrained coaches? More specifically, would the trained and untrained coaches differ in observed behaviors and in their behaviors as perceived by their players?

A second set of outcome variables involved children's reactions to their athletic experience. Would children who played for trained coaches enjoy their experience more, like the coach more, feel more accepted by the coach, and like their teammates more? The program is designed to help coaches create an environment that would be expected to increase children's positive reactions to coach, teammates, and their sport experience.

Self-esteem is a central personality variable that affects people's level of well-being and the ways in which they interact with others, persist in goal-directed behavior, and cope with stressful events. As we have seen, children who are low in self-esteem are most highly affected by differences in supportive coaching behaviors. Moreover, children low in self-esteem have the most to gain from a positive sport experience. Thus we were particularly interested in whether exposure to a positive interpersonal environment created by trained coaches would result in an increase in general self-esteem, particularly among low self-esteem children.

A fourth outcome variable that we have focused on is performance anxiety. Many children find sports stressful because of fear of failure, and their anxiety can negatively affect their performance, reduce their enjoyment of their sport experience, and lead them to avoid sport competition or drop out of sport programs prematurely. On the assumption that coaching behaviors that create a supportive environment emphasize fun and personal improvement rather than winning and place effort above outcome in importance, we might expect that coaches could have a positive role in reducing anxiety by removing unnecessary sources of stress from the youth sport environment. We therefore have evaluated the effects of CET on children's sport performance anxiety.

Finally, putting these four outcome variables together, we reasoned that if trained coaches behave in ways that create a supportive environment in which children feel accepted and valued, teammates like and support one another, and a positive bond occurs between child and coach, we might expect an increase in self-esteem and reduced performance anxiety. Consequently, a fifth outcome variable, namely, attrition, should be affected. That is, children who play for trained coaches would be expected to value their experience more and therefore be less likely to drop out of sport programs.

These hypotheses have been tested in two controlled outcome studies of CET. In an initial field experiment (Smith, Smoll, & Curtis, 1979), 31 Little League Baseball coaches were randomly assigned to an experimental (training) or to a no-treatment control group. During a preseason CET workshop, trainers presented and modeled the behavioral guidelines. In addition to the information-modeling portion of the program, behavioral feedback and self-monitoring procedures were employed in an attempt to increase the coaches' self-awareness of their behaviors and to encourage them to comply with the coaching guidelines. To provide behavioral feedback, 16 observers trained in the use of the CBAS observed experimental group coaches for two complete games. Behavioral profiles for each coach were derived from these observations and were then mailed to the coaches so that they were able to see the distribution of their own behaviors. Also, trained coaches were given brief self-monitoring forms that they completed immediately after the first 10 games of the season.

To assess the effects of the experimental program, CBAS data were collected throughout the season, and behavioral profiles were generated for each coach in the experimental and control groups. Postseason outcome measures were obtained from 325 children in individual data collection sessions in their homes. On both observed behavior and player perception measures, the trained coaches differed from the controls in a manner consistent with the coaching guidelines. The trained coaches gave more reinforcement in response to good performance and effort, and they responded to mistakes with more encouragement and technical instruction and with fewer punitive responses. These behavioral differences were, in turn, reflected in their players' attitudes. The average won-lost percentages of the two groups of coaches did not differ, since success at this level is largely determined by the "luck of the player draft." Nevertheless, the trained coaches were better liked and were rated as better teachers. Additionally, players on their teams liked one another more and enjoyed their sport experience more. These results seemingly reflect the more socially supportive environment created by the trained coaches. Perhaps most encouraging was the fact that children who played for the trained coaches exhibited a significant increase on a measure of general self-esteem as compared with scores obtained a year earlier, whereas those who played for the untrained coaches showed no significant change.

A replication of our research on the efficacy of CET has recently been conducted. The subjects were 18 coaches and 152 children who participated in three Little League Baseball programs. Utilizing a quasi-experimental design, one league (8 teams) was designated the experimental group. The no-treatment control group included 10 teams from two other leagues. Prior to the season, the experimental group coaches participated in CET. To assess the effects of CET, preseason and postseason data were collected for 62 and 90 children in the experimental and control groups, respectively.

The study yielded four major results. First, we found that a brief but highly focused cognitive-behavioral intervention designed to increase the supportiveness and instructional effectiveness of coaches resulted in player-perceived behavioral differences between trained and untrained coaches that were in accordance with the behavioral guidelines. Thus, as in previous research (Smith et al., 1979), the experimental manipulation was successful in promoting a more desirable pattern of coaching behaviors. Second, the behavioral differences resulting from the CET program were accompanied by player evaluative responses that favored the trained coaches. They were better liked and were rated as better teachers by their players, their players reported that they had more fun playing baseball, and a higher level of attraction among teammates was found despite the fact that their teams did not differ from controls in won-lost records. Third, consistent with a self-esteem enhancement model, low self-esteem children who played for the trained coaches exhibited a significant increase in general self-esteem over the course of the season; low self-esteem youngsters in the control group did not change (Smoll et al., 1993). Fourth, the children who played for the CET coaches manifested lower levels of performance anxiety than did the control children (Smith, Smoll, & Barnett, in press).

An extension of the preceding study was completed one year following the CET intervention (Barnett, Smoll, & Smith, 1992). At the beginning of the next baseball season, dropout rates were assessed for youngsters who had played for the two groups of coaches. If a child was not playing baseball, a brief home interview was scheduled. During this session the children completed a questionnaire designed to assess their reasons for discontinuing participation. The results revealed a 26 percent dropout rate among the control group children, a figure that is comparable to those obtained in previous youth sport attrition studies (Gould, 1987). In contrast, an attrition rate of only 5 percent was found for the children who had played for the CET coaches. No difference in won-lost percentages was found between dropouts and returning players; thus the attrition was not a consequence of a lack of team success. Moreover, evidence suggested that the withdrawal was a response to the players' sport experience rather than something that occurred subsequently during the nine-month interim. Finally, the questionnaire responses revealed that dropouts in the control group more often reported reasons for withdrawing that were associated with having a negative reaction to their sport experience the previous year.

In summary, CET has proven to be an economical and effective program that alters coaching behaviors in a desirable fashion and thereby has positive psychosocial effects on the children who play for trained coaches. The training program has significantly influenced all five classes of outcome variables—coaching behaviors, children's attitudes, self-esteem, performance anxiety, and attrition. Nonetheless, a number of research questions remain. For example, dismantling studies are needed to assess the relative contributions of the various components of the training program, which included didactic instruction, modeling and role playing of desired behaviors, training in self-monitoring of coaching behaviors, and behavioral feedback. Such research could help to establish the necessary and sufficient components of an effective program and could facilitate the development of improved training programs.

The study of coaching behaviors and their effects on children is certain to yield more information in future research. Coaches play a central role in the sport environment, and they are a worthy target for interventions designed to enhance the youth sport experience.

References

Bales, R. F., & Slater, P. (1955). Role differentiation in small decision-making groups. In P. Parson & R. F. Bales (Eds.), *Family, socialization, and interaction process* (pp. 259–306). Glencoe, IL: Free Press.

Bandura, A. (1986). *Social foundations of thought and action: A social cognitive theory.* Englewood Cliffs, NJ: Prentice-Hall.

Barnett, N. P., Smoll, F. L., & Smith, R. E. (1992). Effects of enhancing coach-athlete relationships on youth sport attrition. *The Sport Psychologist, 6,* 111–127.

Brown, B. R., & Butterfield, S. A. (1992). Coaches: A missing link in the health care system. *American Journal of Diseases in Childhood, 146,* 211–217.

Brown, E. W., & Branta, C. F. (Eds.). (1988). *Competitive sports for children and youth: An overview of research and issues.* Champaign, IL: Human Kinetics.

Brown, J. D., Collins, R. L., & Schmidt, G. W. (1988). Self-esteem and direct versus indirect forms of self-enhancement. *Journal of Personality and Social Psychology, 55,* 445–453.

Cahill, B. R., & Pearl, A. J. (Eds.). (1993). *Intensive participation in children's sports.* Champaign, IL: Human Kinetics.

Cavior, N., & Marabotto, C. M. (1976). Monitoring verbal behaviors in a dyadic interaction. *Journal of Consulting and Clinical Psychology, 44,* 68–76.

Chaumeton, N. R., & Duda, J. L. (1988). Is it how you play the game or whether you win or lose?: The effect of competitive level and situation on coaching behaviors. *Journal of Sport Behavior, 11,* 157–173.

Cruz, J., Bou, A., Fernandez, J. M., Martin, M., Monras, J., Monfort, N., & Ruiz, A. (1987). Avaluacio conductual de les interaccions entre entrenadors isjugadors de basquet escolar. *Apunts Medicina de L'esport, 24,* 89–98.

Deci, E. L., & Ryan, R. M. (1987). The support of autonomy and the control of behavior. *Journal of Personality and Social Psychology, 53,* 1024–1037.

Dittes, J. (1959). Attractiveness of a group as a function of self-esteem and acceptance by group. *Journal of Abnormal and Social Psychology, 59,* 77–82.

Dweck, C. S. (1975). The role of expectations and attributions in the alleviation of learned helplessness. *Journal of Personality and Social Psychology, 31,* 674–685.

Edelstein, B. A., & Eisler, R. M. (1976). Effects of modeling and modeling with instructions and feedback on the behavioral components of social skills. *Behavior Therapy, 7,* 382–389.

Ewing, M. E., & Seefeldt, V. (1995). Patterns of participation and attrition in American agency-sponsored youth sports. In F. L. Smoll & R. E. Smith (Eds.), *Children and youth in sport: A biopsychosocial perspective* (pp. 31–46). Dubuque, IA: Brown & Benchmark.

Fiedler, F. E. (1967). *A theory of leadership effectiveness.* New York: McGraw-Hill.

Gallwey, W. R., & Kriegel, R. (1977, November). Fear of skiing. *Psychology Today,* pp. 78–85.

Gottman, J. M., & McFall, R. M. (1972). Self-monitoring effects in a program for potential high school dropouts: A time series analysis. *Journal of Consulting and Clinical Psychology, 39,* 273–281.

Gould, D. (1987). Understanding attrition in children's sport. In D. Gould & M. R. Weiss (Eds.), *Advances in pediatric sport sciences* (pp. 61–85). Champaign, IL: Human Kinetics.

Gould, D., & Weiss, M. R. (Eds.). (1987). *Advances in pediatric sport sciences: Vol. 2. Behavioral issues.* Champaign, IL: Human Kinetics.

Graen, G., & Schiemann, W. (1978). Leader member agreement: A vertical dyad linkage approach. *Journal of Applied Psychology, 63,* 206–212.

Hersey, P., & Blanchard, K. H. (1977). *Management of organizational behavior* (3rd ed.). Englewood Cliffs, NJ: Prentice-Hall.

Horn, T. S. (1984). Expectancy effects in the interscholastic athletic setting: Methodological considerations. *Journal of Sport Psychology, 6,* 60–76.

———. (1985). Coaches' feedback and changes in children's perceptions of their physical competence. *Journal of Educational Psychology, 77,* 174–186.

Kanfer, F. H., & Gaelick-Buys, L. (1991). Self-management methods. In F. H. Kanfer & A. P. Goldstein (Eds.), *Helping people change: A textbook of methods* (4th ed., pp. 305–360). New York: Pergamon.

Kazdin, A. E. (1974). Self-monitoring and behavior change. In M. J. Mahoney & C. E. Thoresen (Eds.), *Self-control: Power to the person* (pp. 218–246). Monterey, CA: Brooks/Cole.

Kirschenbaum, D. S., & Karoly, P. (1977). When self-regulation fails: Tests of some preliminary hypotheses. *Journal of Consulting and Clinical Psychology, 45,* 1116–1125.

Komaki, J. L. (1986). Toward effective supervision: An operant analysis and comparison of managers at work. *Journal of Applied Psychology, 71,* 270–279.

Malina, R. M. (Ed.). (1988). *Young athletes: Biological, psychological, and educational perspectives.* Champaign, IL: Human Kinetics.

Martens, R. (1987a). *Coaches guide to sport psychology.* Champaign, IL: Human Kinetics.

———. (1987b). *American coaching effectiveness program: Level 1 instructor guide* (2nd ed.). Champaign, IL: Human Kinetics.

Martens, R., & Gould, D. (1979). Why do adults volunteer to coach children's sports? In G. C. Roberts & K. M. Newell (Eds.), *Psychology of motor behavior and sport—1978* (pp. 79–89). Champaign, IL: Human Kinetics.

McFall, R. M. (1977). Parameters of self-monitoring. In R. B. Stuart (Ed.), *Behavioral self-management: Strategies, techniques and outcomes* (pp. 196–214). New York: Brunner/Mazel.

McFall, R. M., & Twentyman, C. T. (1973). Four experiments on the relative contributions of rehearsal, modeling, and coaching to assertion training. *Journal of Abnormal Psychology, 81,* 199–218.

Nay, W. R. (1975). A systematic comparison of instructional techniques for parents. *Behavior Therapy, 6,* 14–21.

Perry, M. A., & Furukawa, M. J. (1986). Modeling methods. In F. H. Kanfer & A. P. Goldstein (Eds.), *Helping people change: A textbook of methods* (3rd ed., pp. 66–110). New York: Pergamon.

Rejeski, W., Darracott, C., & Hutslar, S. (1979). Pygmalion in youth sport: A field study. *Journal of Sport Psychology, 1,* 311–319.

Scanlan, T. K., & Lewthwaite, R. (1984). Social psychological aspects of competition for male youth sport participants: I. Predictors of competitive stress. *Journal of Sport Psychology, 6,* 208–226.

Scanlan, T. K., & Passer, M. W. (1978). Factors related to competitive stress among male youth sports participants. *Medicine and Science in Sports, 10,* 103–108.

——— (1979). Sources of competitive stress in young female athletes. *Journal of Sport Psychology, 1,* 151–159.

Seefeldt, V., & Brown, E. W. (Eds.). (1992). *Program for athletic coaches' education.* Dubuque, IA: Brown & Benchmark.

Seefeldt, V., & Gould, D. (1980). *Physical and psychological effects of athletic competition on children and youth.* Washington, DC: ERIC Clearinghouse on Teacher Education.

Shrauger, J. S. (1975). Responses to evaluation as a function of initial self-perceptions. *Psychological Bulletin, 82,* 581–596.

Smith, R. E., & Smoll, F. L. (1990). Self-esteem and children's reactions to youth sport coaching behaviors: A field study of self-enhancement processes. *Developmental Psychology, 26,* 987–993.

Smith, R. E., Smoll, F. L., & Barnett, N. P. (in press). Reduction of children's sport performance anxiety through social support and stress-reduction training for coaches. *Journal of Applied Developmental Psychology.*

Smith, R. E., Smoll, F. L., & Christensen, D. S. (in press). Behavioral assessment and interventions in youth sports. *Behavior Modification.*

Smith, R. E., Smoll, F. L., & Curtis, B. (1978). Coaching behaviors in little league baseball. In F. L. Smoll & R. E. Smith (Eds.), *Psychological perspectives in youth sports* (pp. 173–201). Washington, DC: Hemisphere.

———. (1979). Coach effectiveness training: A cognitive-behavioral approach to enhancing relationship skills in youth sport coaches. *Journal of Sport Psychology, 1,* 59–75.

Smith, R. E., Smoll, F. L., & Hunt, E. B. (1977). A system for the behavioral assessment of athletic coaches. *Research Quarterly, 48,* 401–407.

Smith, R. E., Zane, N. W. S., Smoll, F. L., & Coppel, D. B. (1983). Behavioral assessment in youth sports: Coaching behaviors and children's attitudes. *Medicine and Science in Sports and Exercise, 15,* 208–214.

Smoll, F. L., Magill, R. A., & Ash, M. J. (Eds.). (1988). *Children in sport* (3rd ed.). Champaign, IL: Human Kinetics.

Smoll, F. L., & Smith, R. E. (1981). Developing a healthy philosophy of winning in youth sports. In V. Seefeldt, F. L. Smoll, R. E. Smith, & D. Gould (Eds.), *A winning philosophy for youth sport programs* (pp. 17–24). East Lansing, MI: Michigan Institute for the Study of Youth Sports.

———. (1987). *Sport psychology for youth coaches.* Washington, DC: National Federation for Catholic Youth Ministry.

———. (1989). Leadership behaviors in sport: A theoretical model and research paradigm. *Journal of Applied Social Psychology, 19,* 1522–1551.

———. (1993). Educating youth sport coaches: An applied sport psychology perspective. In J. M. Williams (Ed.), *Applied sport psychology: Personal growth to peak performance* (2nd ed., pp. 36–57). Mountain View, CA: Mayfield.

Smoll, F. L., Smith, R. E., Barnett, N. P., & Everett, J. J. (1993). Enhancement of coach's self-esteem through social support training for youth sport coaches. *Journal of Applied Psychology, 78,* 602–610.

Stogdill, R. M. (1959). *Individual behavior and group achievement.* New York: Oxford University Press.

Swann, W. B., Jr. (1990). To be known or to be adored? The interplay of self-enhancement and self-verification. In R. M. Sorrentino & E. T. Higgins (Eds.), *Handbook of motivation and cognition: Foundations of social behavior* (Vol. 2, pp. 408–488). New York: Guilford.

Tesser, A. (1988). Toward a self-evaluative maintenance model of social behavior. In L. Berkowitz (Ed.), *Advances in experimental social psychology* (Vol. 21, pp. 69–92). Orlando, FL: Academic Press.

Tesser, A., & Campbell, J. (1983). Self-definition and self-evaluation maintenance. In J. Suls & A. G. Greenwald (Eds.), *Psychological perspectives on the self* (Vol. 2, pp. 1–32). Hillsdale, NJ: Erlbaum.

Wandzilak, T., Ansorge, C. J., & Potter, G. (1988). Comparison between selected practice and game behaviors of youth soccer coaches. *Journal of Sport Behavior, 11,* 78–88.

Weiss, M. R., & Gould, D. (Eds.). (1986). *Sport for children and youths.* Champaign, IL: Human Kinetics.

White, M. A. (1975). Natural rates of teacher approval and disapproval in the classroom. *Journal of Applied Behavior Analysis, 8,* 367–372.

Appendix A: Summary of Coaching Guidelines

I. Reactive Coaching Behaviors: Responding to Athlete Behaviors and Game Situations

A. Good plays

Do: Provide *reinforcement!!* Do so immediately. Let the athletes know that you appreciate and value their efforts. Reinforce effort as much as you do results. Look for positive things, reinforce them, and you will see them increase. Remember, whether children show it or not, the positive things you say and do remain with them.

Don't: Take their efforts for granted.

B. Mistakes, screw-ups, boneheaded plays, and all the things the pros seldom do

Do: Give *encouragement* immediately after mistakes. That's when the youngster needs your support the most. If you are sure the athlete knows how to correct the mistake, then encouragement alone is sufficient. When appropriate, give *corrective instruction,* but always do so in an encouraging manner. Do this by emphasizing not the bad things that just happened, but the good things that will happen if the player follows your instruction (the "why" of it). This will make the athlete positively self-motivated to correct the mistakes rather than negatively motivated to avoid failure and your disapproval.

Don't: Punish when things are going wrong!! Punishment isn't just yelling. It can be any indication of disapproval, tone of voice, or action. Athletes respond much better to a positive approach. Fear of failure is reduced if you work to reduce fear of punishment.

Don't: Give corrective instruction in a hostile or harsh manner. That is, avoid *punitive instruction.* This is more likely to increase frustration and create resentment than to improve performance. Don't let your good intentions in giving instruction be self-defeating.

C. Misbehaviors, lack of attention

Do: Maintain order by establishing clear expectations. Emphasize that during a contest all members of the team are part of the activity, even those on the bench. Use reinforcement to strengthen team participation. In other words, try to prevent misbehaviors by using the positive approach to strengthen their opposites.

Don't: Get into the position of having to constantly nag or threaten athletes in order to prevent chaos. Don't be a drill sergeant. If an athlete refuses to cooperate, deprive him or her of something valued. Don't use physical measures, such as running laps. The idea here is that if you establish clear behavioral guidelines early and work to build team spirit in achieving them, you can avoid having to repeatedly *keep control*. Youngsters want clear guidelines and expectations, but they don't want to be regimented. Try to achieve a healthy balance.

II. Spontaneous Coaching Behaviors: Getting Positive Things to Happen and Creating a Good Learning Atmosphere

Do: Give *technical instruction*. Establish your role as a caring and competent teacher. Try to structure participation as a learning experience in which you are going to help the athletes develop their abilities. Always give instruction in a positive fashion. Satisfy your athletes' desire to become the best they can be. Give instruction in a clear, concise manner and, if possible, demonstrate how to do it.

Do: Concentrate on the activity. Be "in the game" with the athletes. Set a good example for team unity.

Don't: Give either instruction or encouragement in a sarcastic or degrading manner. Make a point, then leave it. Don't let "encouragement" become irritating to the athletes.

Note: These guidelines were excerpted from the printed materials that are given to CET workshop participants. They are discussed in greater detail elsewhere (see Smoll & Smith, 1987, pp. 23–39).

INTERPERSONAL SOURCES OF VIOLENCE IN HOCKEY: THE INFLUENCE OF THE MEDIA, PARENTS, COACHES, AND GAME OFFICIALS

—Norman Morra and Michael D. Smith

Prior research on sports violence has shown that parents and coaches strongly influence youths who play minor hockey (Smith, 1979, 1983, 1987; Vaz, 1982). These studies and others showed how coaches and parents, along with professional hockey players, instill highly aggressive attitudes in young men. The closer a youth advances to the professional ranks, the more likely he will use tactics such as fighting and illegal stick-work to play the sport (Colburn, 1985; 1986). Besides parents and coaches, we maintain that game officials and media members contribute indirectly to violence in minor hockey. Bandura (1986) affirms that children vicariously learn violence by emulating the macho behavior of their video idols. The media molds former athletes such as bodybuilder Arnold Schwarzenegger and martial arts black belt Jean Claude Van Damme into violent heroes for children. Likewise, in a less explicit way, professional hockey enforcers such as Bob Probert earn enormous salaries and serve as negative role models for younger players.

Method and Data

The understanding of any sociological problem requires some knowledge of its past. C. Wright Mills (1961) argued that social science helps to unravel complex issues by examining three intersecting elements—history, biography, and society. We have chosen Mills's method for two reason: (a) It allows us to look at the interpersonal relationships pertinent to hockey violence; (b) it forces us to question society's role in the matter.

The historical part of this study extends from the 1950s until the present. First we will outline some salient incidents of violence in the National Hockey League (NHL) within this time span. We include biographical descriptions of persons who helped formulate this history. Next we will show how particular individuals within the media benefit through the promotion of fighting. Before updating the interpersonal processes of these groups, we will examine earlier significant studies that have dealt with the sources of violence in hockey. Finally, we describe how some parents, coaches, and game officials influence the behavior of young hockey players at present.

Our research incorporates select data from previous studies in the 1970s and 1980s that addressed the issue of hockey violence. We also observed current professional matches on television and many minor league games at arenas within metropolitan Toronto. The children and youth we focused on were between the ages of 7 and 18. Besides parents, coaches, and referees, we interviewed arena managers and equipment handlers: individuals on the periphery of minor hockey. These adults gave us relatively unbiased accounts of hockey violence. Further discussions with two noted Canadian journalists helped us to clarify the nuances of violence in the sport. Interviews with two administrators in the Canadian Amateur Hockey Association (CAHA) made us aware of the difficulty in trying to eliminate this problem. Additional data came from sources such as videotapes, magazine articles, TV documentaries, and newspaper reports.

The Violent Past of Professional Hockey

Hockey has been an integral part of Canadian culture for nearly a century. Its violent aspect, however, is traceable to one source: the NHL. Traditionally the NHL has served as the model for hockey in North America and abroad (Tarasov, 1969; Tretiak, 1987). Although many of our young men dream of someday playing in the NHL, the sport is no longer exclusively Canadian. With the increasing numbers of American, European, and Scandinavian players in the NHL today, children from other countries also share this dream.

Today's star players, such as Wayne Gretzky and Mario Lemieux, have suffered injuries due to the cross-checks and slashes from their opponents' sticks. These two athletes serve as hockey's ambassadors and as exemplars for younger players. Todays superstars such as Gretzky and Lemieux rarely fight, but this has not always been the case. Professional hockey players during the 1950s and early 1960s considered it their duty to fight when others challenged them. Hockey players, whatever their status, viewed fighting as crucial for maintaining their honor. Failure to respond to an opponent's provocation was inexcusable. Those who backed down from a fight disgraced themselves and their teammates; it was conduct unbecoming a professional hockey player. Pundits of the sport maintained that fighting was a safety valve, a way to blow off steam, thus preventing serious injuries attributable to illegal stickwork (Colburn, 1986).

Fights, whether premeditated or not, followed a set of procedures. The primary rule required each player to drop his stick and gloves before exchanging blows (Colburn, 1985). Players who violated this code with such disreputable acts as "sucker punching" or spearing became the targets of a swift retribution by the other team. One administrator with the CAHA mentioned that young men in the Western Junior "A" Hockey League, for example, still act out this ritual. Because protective head and face gear is now mandatory in minor hockey, some players see this as a drawback to an even fight. For those combatants insistent on keeping fights fair, it is obligatory to remove their helmets before fighting. We observed this custom take place during a juvenile game in a Toronto house league.

Superstars of the 1950s, such as Maurice Richard and Gordie Howe, seldom backed away from a challenge. Detroit's Howe, among the game's finest players, commanded respect from his opponents. His career spanned four decades; he played, although with less and less intensity, until the age of 52. Howe also holds the distinction, besides his longevity, of being the only man to play a contact sport with his two adult sons. Howe's ability to fight, and the illegal use of his elbows and stick, are legendary in hockey lore. Today's players, regardless of their age, are familiar with the exploits of Gordie Howe.

Other talented but nonviolent superstars of the fifties, such as Montreal's Jean Beliveau and the New York Rangers's Andy Bathgate, were consummate professionals. Although these athletes were positive role models for the youth of their time, neither received their full measure of respect. Bathgate, because of his outspoken criticism of hockey violence, met with ridicule from team owners, the media, and his peers. Moreover, the NHL ruled that Bathgate's decrying of hockey violence in print was detrimental to the sport and fined him $500 (Dunnell, 1959).

Beliveau did earn the acclaim of fans and players, but intimidation was never a part of his game. The phlegmatic Beliveau, however, failed to receive the same adulation as his teammate, Maurice (Rocket) Richard. Richard was the first NHL player to score 50 goals in as many games. Followers of the sport remember him equally for his volatile temper and unbridled hatred of the opposition. Richard's charisma excited the Montreal fans who cheered any act of violence by him. In spite of his talent, Richard was responsible for one particularly abhorrent deed. In March 1955, irked by the close checking of Boston's Hal Laycoe, he slammed his stick across Laycoe's face. The blow shattered Laycoe's glasses and he fell to the ice where Richard hit him several more times with his stick. The NHL suspended Richard for the balance of the season and the following playoffs. In the aftermath of this incident, on St. Patrick's Day, the infamous Rocket Richard riot took place. Irate fans smashed windows and looted stores in the downtown section of Montreal (Frayne, 1973).

Once the league expanded into the lucrative U.S. sports market in 1967, team owners and managers realized how senseless it was to let star players fight. Hockey's superstars attracted the customers and it was ludicrous to have them inactive due to injuries or suspensions incurred through fights. Chicago's Bobby Hull was the prime example of this dilemma. Hull, with his introduction of the slap shot and the curved blade, helped to revolutionize the game. Despite being a productive and spectacular scorer, Hull had difficulty in fending off his rougher opponents. To protect the league's superstars, management devised a systematic division of labor. Owners hired players with marginal skills but fighting ability to protect their teams' top players. In the case of Hull, Chicago promoted a minor league tough guy, Reg Fleming, specifically for the job of enforcer.

Other teams recognized the benefit of this tactic and quickly adopted its format. Whenever an enforcer was unable to carry out his task, it became the responsibility of any player to assist his team's star. The Philadelphia Flyers of the 1970s were masters of this strategy. They stocked their club with several fighters to intimi-date other teams and enable their top playmaker, Bob Clarke, to execute his fiercely competitive game with impunity. Sportswriters labeled them "The Broad Street Bullies" and the Flyers asserted themselves as the most fearsome team of the seven-ties. Ontario's attorney general, Roy McMurtry, laid criminal charges against several Flyers after a particularly violent game in Toronto during the 1974–75 season. The Flyers were, according to McMurtry, "a very bad example for young kids who ape the professionals" (Schultz, 1981, p. 136).

With the increase in bench-clearing brawls and retaliatory acts with the stick, referees were unable to prevent games from getting out of control. Much of this vio-lence predicated itself on players' loyalty to one another. The NHL tried to curtail the rise in brawling with the "third man in" rule. The rule stated that any player attempt-ing to help a teammate already in a fight would face eviction from the game. In addi-tion, that same player would later receive a fine and suspension. Although this rule helped to prevent team brawls, it did not eradicate fighting. It reinforced instead the long-standing ritual of two men engaging in hand-to-hand combat. In brief, owners made token efforts to eliminate brawling but managed to preserve fighting as part of the game.

In spite of the NHL's rule changes and the increase in fines and suspensions, the demand for tougher enforcers persists. Some believe hockey is less violent today and that the time of the enforcer has passed. Nonetheless, teams still use specialty players to fill this role. For example, the Winnipeg Jets (1993) recently obtained ram-bunctious but highly popular Tie Domi from the New York Rangers. The Jets gave up a skilled player and guaranteed Domi a substantial salary to protect their team's sen-sational rookie, Finnish import Teemu Selanne. Domi's presence allowed Selanne to score at his record-shattering clip (Burman & Lee, 1993).

Selling Hockey Violence: TV, Videos, Magazines

Although fighting and dirty play have existed in professional hockey since it began in 1908, we think its continuance depends significantly on television. It is difficult to contest that television, from its inception, has affected entire segments of viewers (McLuhan & Fiore, 1967). TV and video are technological tools and represent the essential seductive force in our consumer culture (Baudrillard, 1983). Rarely do we dispute what we see on television. We have witnessed violence such as the Gulf War, strife in Bosnia, the beatings of Rodney King and Reginald Denny. These images document the reality of our present-day existence (Murphy & Choi, 1993). With con-tinuous sports channels such as ESPN in the United States and TSN in Canada, the violence of football, hockey, and boxing is instantly available for viewers at any time of the day.

Television shows us how professionals use intimidation as an expedient way to nullify an opponent's effectiveness. Violence, however, existed as a feature of the sport long before the introduction of television. TV simply brought it to countless viewers. Young boys avidly watch professional hockey on TV and simulate the good and bad actions of their sports heroes. Although the Canadian Federal Government's

Fair Play Commission and other agencies try to stop foul play, purveyors of fight videos, for example, are negating their efforts. Television, along with other media, are businesses in pursuit of financial gain. Their success relies heavily upon the cooperation of certain NHL players who are willing to play along with the condoning of violence. This complicity by players, perhaps unwitting, manifests itself in their discourse with certain sports journalists.

The foremost example of an individual who capitalizes on the promotion of violence is the former Boston Bruins coach, Don Cherry. For more than a decade, the ubiquitous Cherry has enjoyed the status of a Canadian celebrity. We cannot estimate the extent of his wealth, but Cherry's financial success is undeniable. He is the host of his own TV show and appears as a guest on various radio programs. He does commercials for automotive parts, trust companies, department stores, lotteries, colognes, and a slew of other products. Much of his prosperity is attributable to his tireless advocating for the retention of fighting in hockey.

The forum for most of Cherry's diatribe is the intermission segment "Coach's Corner" during telecasts of NHL games aired on CBC's "Hockey Night in Canada" (Harrison, 1993). For millions of Canadian viewers the ritual of watching this program is akin to the fervor many Americans have for "Monday Night Football" on ABC. With his entertaining, uninhibited speech style and his right-wing utterances, Cherry amuses some but antagonizes others. As his ratings soar the public anticipates his outbursts. Because of Cherry's immense popularity the CBC grants him considerable leeway to voice his contentious opinions.

Cherry especially harangues foreign players for taking NHL jobs away from Canadians. He singles out Soviets for their lack of fortitude and blames them for the dirty stick-work prevalent in today's hockey. His list of undesirables also includes Scandinavians, some Americans, and French-Canadians. He uses his TV and radio programs as outlets for others who share his conviction that slashing and spearing is a result of safety gear such as face masks. Cherry believes minor hockey regulations overprotect youngsters. As a result, they feel immune to injury and resort to illicit stick-work to control others. This argument contains some truth, but to call for the removal of protective equipment such as visors would surely jeopardize the welfare of young players. Many of his TV guests are current and past enforcers who delight in Cherry's showing film clips of their more savage battles. The TV studio audience reacts to these fights with howls of approval. Cherry has also compiled four editions of hockey's most brutal fight videos entitled "Rock Em Sock Em." These products are available in stores everywhere.

Although Cherry profits in the propagandizing of hockey violence, he is not alone in capitalizing on its promotion. Distributors in Minnesota, for instance, market a series of videotapes called *Sports Pages* (Combined Artists, 1992). "Killer Hockey" was the subtitle of the video that we analyzed. The cover of this videotape shows two players fighting. The blurb on the reverse side of the box advertises 30 minutes of "broken bones, the bloody gashes and the damage caused by flying pucks—and fists." It also lures young viewers with the names of their favorite NHL players, who fail to appear in the video. The message this product delivers is that hockey is a brutal sport meant only for tough men.

TABLE 10.1 Hockey Players' Perceptions of Their Parents' Approval of Hockey Fighting by Age and Level of Competition (in Percent)[1]

	Fathers' Approval			Mothers' Approval		
	Low	Medium	High[2]	Low	Medium	High
Age						
12–13 (*N* = 166)	77	20	3	89	8	3
14–15 (*N* = 196)	66	25	9	85	8	3
16–17 (*N* = 130)	47	31	22	81	14	5
18–21 (*N* = 112)	40	19	41	75	18	7
Level of Competition						
House League (*N* = 330)	76	18	6	94	6	0
Competitive (*N* = 274)	41	31	29	71	21	8
All players (*N* = 604)	60	24	16	83	13	4

[1]Adapted from Smith (1979, p. 113).
[2]Low = approval in no situations; medium = approval in one or two situations; high = approval in three or four situations.

The May 1993 edition of the magazine *Hockey Heroes* features fighting as its theme. In the top corner of its front cover is the caption "Blood on Ice!" The cover's photograph shows a bleeding Bob Probert of the Detroit Red Wings staving off a relentless Tie Domi. One article by Stan Fischler asserts "fighting is as much a part of the woof and warp of hockey as a stick and a puck" (1993, p. 11). Fischler argues that fighting is entertainment and must remain in the sport. He insists that without violence Americans will show little interest in hockey and stop attending games. Perhaps this is correct, but it is equally true that children, as well as adults, purchase these videos and magazines.

Previous Research on the Influence of Parents, Coaches, and Teammates

Parents

Data from a survey of Toronto hockey players conducted in the late 1970s reveal the extent to which hockey parents approve of violence (Smith, 1979). Six hundred and four players were asked if they thought their father and mother would approve of a minor hockey league player punching another player in four situations: (a) if ridiculed, (b) if threatened, (c) if shoved, or (d) if punched by the other player. Indexes of Parents' Approval of Hockey Fighting were constructed by summing the *yes* responses to these items. Table 10.1 shows variations in players' scores on these indexes by age and level of competition (house league or recreational versus competitive).

The majority of fathers (60%) rank low on the Fathers' Approval Index, which is to say these fathers would not, in the eyes of their offspring, approve of a player punching another player in any of the situations presented. But approval increases sharply with age and level of competition. In the older-age and competitive rows, the majority of fathers fall into the medium-approval (one or two situations) and high-approval (three or four situations) categories. Forty-one percent of the 18- to 21-year-olds felt their parents would approve of fighting in at least three of the situations, compared with only 3 percent of the 12- to 13-year-olds; 29 percent of the fathers of competitive-level players were seen as high approvers, compared with 6 percent of the house-league fathers. Mothers consistently were perceived as less approving than fathers; still, 25 percent and 29 percent in the 18- to 21-year-old and competitive rows are in the medium- and high-approval categories combined.

Coaches

How extensive is hockey coaches' approval of rough play? Almost all of 83 high school players interviewed by Smith (1975) stated that their coaches would approve (most of them "strongly") of "hard but legal body-checking." Over half of the more than 1,900 boys surveyed by Vaz (1982) reported that their coaches regularly emphasized "playing rough and being aggressive." When asked "What are the three most important qualities a coach looks for in selecting players for all-star teams?" 62 percent of the oldest boys (aged 15 and 16) included, out of nine possible response choices, "being aggressive at all times"; 56 percent included "physical size and strength"; 25 percent included "guts and courage." (More than half of these boys were house-leaguers, and their responses probably pulled these percentages down.)

Such findings are not surprising; much of what is called aggressive play is sanctioned by the official rules of the game. What of officially legal violence? Table 10.2 reveals that Toronto minor hockey players see coaches as somewhat more approving of violence than fathers, yet only 21 percent of all coaches come under the high-approval heading. Again, this overall figure obscures differences in age and level of competition. More than 50 percent of the 18- to 21-year-olds and 36 percent of the competitive-level players saw their coaches as high approvers.

Players' perceptions of coaches' sanctions for assaultive play do seem to have an impact on players' attitudes and conduct at all levels of hockey. Vaz (1982) reports statistically significant associations in all age divisions between players' perceptions of how much their coaches emphasized "playing rough and being aggressive" and players' approval of "taking out an opposing player any way you can to save a goal even though you risk injuring the opposing player." Smith (1979) has demonstrated statistically that the more coaches approve of fighting, the more players fight, and the more penalties they receive.

Teammates

The importance of peer approval in understanding violence in gangs, prisons, violent subcultures of all sorts, and among boys and men in general has long been recognized. Respect is what counts. You get it by demonstrating physical courage, gameness,

TABLE 10.2 Hockey Players' Perceptions of Their Coaches' Approval of Hockey Fighting by Age and Level of Competition (in Percent)[1]

	Coaches' Approval		
	Low	Medium	High[2]
Age			
12–13 (N = 166)	74	17	9
14–15 (N = 196)	59	30	11
16–17 (N = 130)	39	36	25
18–21 (N = 112)	25	23	52
Level of Competition			
House league (N = 330)	70	22	8
Competitive (N = 274)	32	32	36
All players (N = 604)	53	26	11

[1]Adapted from Smith (1979, p. 113)
[2]Low = approval in no situations; medium = approval in one or two situations; high = approval in three or four situations.

recklessness sometimes, disdain for injury, and a willingness to fight if necessary. You lose respect by revealing a lack of "heart" or "guts," by "chickening out."

Quantitative data on hockey players' violence approval—their own and the perceptions of their teammates—are shown in table 10.3. These data indicate that amateur hockey players perceive their teammates as considerably more approving of fighting than their coaches and parents. Sixty-four percent of the respondents viewed other team members as approving of fighting in at least three of the four situations presented. Comparisons with players' own attitudes, however, reveals an anomaly described by Matza (1964) in his research on delinquency. It is apparent in table 10.3 that individual violence approval is extensive, but not as extensive as that which individuals attribute to teammates collectively. It seems what individuals say and do about violence in the presence of peers is one thing, but their private attitudes are another. This results in a shared misunderstanding in which individuals think others value violence more than they actually do.

To what extent would players privately *prefer* less fighting and other sorts of illegal rough play? The foregoing players were asked "Would you like to see more, about the same, or less fistfighting in your games?" Forty-five percent said less. When asked "Would you like to see more, about the same, or less illegal stickwork in your games?" 82 percent said less. How many players quit hockey because of the violence? This question has yet to be adequately answered, but more than a few have done so, one suspects.

Closer inspection of the data in table 10.3 shows that the gap in violence approval between individuals and teammates closes with age, as does the gap between house-league and competitive-level players. Probably selection and socialization

	Players' Approval			Teammates' Approval		
	Low	Medium	High[2]	Low	Medium	High
Age						
12–13 (*N* = 166)	54	25	21	23	23	54
14–15 (*N* = 196)	37	39	24	11	27	61
16–17 (*N* = 130)	13	49	38	4	26	70
18–21 (*N* = 112)	17	24	59	9	13	78
Level of Competition						
House League (*N* = 330)	48	28	24	16	25	59
Competitive (*N* = 274)	15	42	43	8	21	71
All players (*N* = 604)	33	34	33	13	23	64

[1]Adapted from Smith (1979, p. 113).
[2]Low = approval in no situations; medium = approval in one or two situations; high = approval in three or four situations

processes jointly account for this. As the less pro-violent get older, they quit hockey at increasingly faster rates than the more pro-violent. In fact, the general dropout rate is precipitous after age 12. Further, as the less pro-violent who stay in hockey are socialized into the culture of the game with age, and in competitive-level as opposed to house-league competition, they bring their attitudes increasingly into line with the attitudes they impute to their peers.

Hockey players approve of violence, it seems, to the extent that it brings respect and works as a game tactic and career booster. Separable analytically, these uses merge empirically, each reinforcing the other. Though the latter becomes increasingly salient as players learn the occupational culture, the former remains important. Professional hockey players—grown men—cling to rituals of fighting (even when it is counterproductive in terms of winning) that most males leave behind in the schoolyard.

Recent Evidence of Violence in Minor Hockey

Parents Investing for Success

To understand fully how parents contribute to hockey violence, we must first consider their own involvement in their sons' hockey careers. The economic factor plays a significant part in parents attaching such importance to their sons' success in minor hockey. As the interest in competitive hockey rises so too does the expense of playing the sport. Parents today often feel an obligation to give their children the best equipment and training available.

In Canada the cost to outfit a 16-year-old is approximately $800. This amount includes the basic equipment: skates, pads, pants, helmets, and sticks. High-quality goaltender equipment costs more than $2,000. To provide a minor league hockey career for their children, parents must be financially secure. Children from single-parent homes seldom have the opportunity to pursue the sport. This financial commitment to minor hockey can undermine some parents' ability to cover their own auto and mortgage payments. Due to the recent recession, and the prohibitive costs associated with minor hockey, many parents find it difficult to meet their own expenses along with sustaining their boys' hockey careers. Once the best players advance to the Junior "A" level at the age of 18, parents no longer pay for their equipment and other expenses related to hockey. Young men in this division often play in cities away from home and receive modest salaries.

Lower-income parents are unable to subsidize necessary extras such as hockey schools and attendance at out-of-town tournaments. This excessive financial worry places a strain on the lives of family members. The daily routines of hockey families tend to revolve around tryouts, practices, and games. With this commitment to the boy's success in hockey, some parents sacrifice their own limited leisure time. Inevitably these parents gauge their success as parents in relation to how well their sons perform in hockey. At this stage certain parents become obsessive with their boys' achievements in hockey. One minor league coach told us that some parents reimburse their sons for scoring goals and winning fights.

Our field observations showed that a son's hockey game implicates the entire family. As a rule, hockey families arrive at the arena an hour before the game. Parents move around the lobby and chatter while nervously awaiting the opening face-off. Family members often sport their child's team colors and wear jackets emblematic of his club. Once the game begins parents demarcate their territories by sitting directly behind their boy's team bench. Immersion in the game is total and principally attuned to their own offspring. Booing and catcalls are directed at times at the referee and certain opposing players. From the stands, parents urge their children to hook, hold, slash, and use any illegal device to prevent the other team from scoring. The closer a team comes to scoring, the louder the parents shout and the more vicious the play becomes. It is around the goaltender's net where much of the high-sticking and hitting from behind takes place.

Some parents lose their composure and resort to abusive language. After a recent Bantam game (13-year-olds) at a North Toronto arena, one particularly irate father from a visiting Ottawa team berated the referee. His son's team had lost to an older, more-experienced Midget team (15-year-olds). Since this was an invitational tournament, the age discrepancy was irrelevant. If anything, the younger players may have welcomed this as a learning experience. This father, however, blamed the referee for the defeat of his sons' team. "You really blew this one, jerk," he shouted down at the referee. The players on the ice who were shaking hands noticed this father's display of temper as they exited to their respective dressing rooms. The referee shook his head in disbelief, but the angry father persisted by challenging the referee to meet him in the parking lot for a fight.

At times parents do resort to actual violence such as hitting other adults. A CBC documentary "The Spirit of the Game" (Burman, 1993) showed how some parents react when their children are hurt. A part of the documentary showed what happened to a 12-year-old Winnipeg boy during a Peewee game last January. An opponent rammed the boy heavily into the boards from behind, causing fractures to his left arm and shoulder. After the boy left for the hospital the game turned into a free-for-all and resembled a battle more than a sport. The referee wisely terminated the game and brought a halt to the violence. One father from the injured boy's team approached the opposing coach, spat in his face, and shoved him. When an interviewer inquired about this parent's conduct, the father replied that seeing the injured boy sprawled on the ice filled him with frustration and he lashed out at the coach.

Parental behavior such as this occurs in minor hockey to a certain extent. In its attempt to eliminate such irresponsible conduct the CAHA (1992) has created a videotape entitled "Hockey Parents Make the Difference." It simulates how some parents misbehave when they come to the arena to watch their sons' play. The CAHA believes that this video can teach parents how to behave while attending their sons' games. The message this video imparts is clear—abusive parents should stay away from the arena.

Coaches: In Search of the Right Stuff

Hockey coaches frequently encourage aggressive behavior. NHL teams seek out this quality when hunting for players who will advance to the professional ranks. Coaches are responsible for developing gameness and character in their players. These attributes lack importance if players are incapable of defending themselves against other more intimidating competitors. Scouts for NHL teams regard the combination of penalty minutes with high point totals as indicative of a junior player's ability to compete professionally. Coaches who foster these traits in their players also improve their chances of obtaining professional coaching jobs.

Unquestionably, combativeness can lead to success in hockey. Gaining possession of the puck, on offense and defense, is elementary to the game. For this reason coaches tend to select bigger, stronger boys who can outmuscle their rivals for the puck. Coaches will of course pick smaller talented players who display "guts." But if they must choose between a bigger and smaller player of equal ability, they invariably take the larger boy. This is true in minor and professional hockey. Youths with size, ability, and heart are the ones most likely to make it in major league hockey.

If players are reluctant to play an aggressive brand of hockey, a coach may set the initiative himself. He does this as a way to motivate his players. How professional coaches behave in emotionally charged situations may also serve as a model for their minor league counterparts. During the 1993 NHL playoffs the Toronto coach took exception to the way that several Los Angeles Kings players manhandled his smaller star forward. The Toronto coach appeared furious and rushed toward the Los Angeles bench while shouting at the opposing coach. This type of display is meant to wake up a team's more lethargic players. The Maple Leafs won this particular game because their coach's ploy worked. In cases where referees overlook the other team's fouls, coaches expect their players to retaliate and administer their own justice.

Any boy who fails to execute this highly aggressive brand of play can expect a reprimand from his coach. If the same boy allows an opponent to skate around him or does not defend his goaltender in a scuffle, the coach invariably benches him. Furthermore, should a young man continue to show a lack of desire in the following week's practice, the coach restricts his playing time in the next game. Although many coaches in minor hockey prefer that boys abide by the rules, they still demand a show of physical and mental toughness on the part of their players. The problem for inexperienced players is how to differentiate between aggressive and violent behavior.

Officials: The New Breed

The trend in hockey today is toward the elimination of fouls such as high-sticking and hitting from behind. The CAHA has guidelines for players to follow to ensure a balance between fun and the development of a child's skill in the sport. To counter unsportsmanlike attitudes the Canadian federal government's Department of Fitness and Amateur Sport has created a commission to encourage fair play among youths (Smith, 1987). Referees try to implement the commission's policies by mediating disputes with players and coaches in a sensible manner. The more recent introduction of women referees in minor hockey has also helped to modify the violent behavior of certain players. One coach informed us that a particular woman referee in the Metropolitan Toronto Hockey League (MTHL) was more proficient at officiating than any of her male peers. This referee could skate faster and understood the rules better than many of the men.

Game officials must now meet with team captains and coaches prior to the start of each match. This approach has been in effect in baseball and football for some time but is new to minor hockey. In the past, referees governed the sport with an iron fist and seldom tolerated any dialogue with the players. Referees frequently issued misconduct penalties to those players seeking clarification on a particular ruling. The policy in minor hockey now places much of the onus for responsible behavior squarely on the players and coaches. A player who commits an infraction such as butt-ending with his stick receives a match penalty and a suspension for three games.

Many referees, however, officiate minor hockey games as a way to supplement their incomes. Several of the referees whom we saw were overweight and struggled to keep pace with the speedier youths. As a result, these referees tended to find themselves out of position and unable to make proper calls on plays at the opposite end of the rink. Once players are beyond the referee's field of vision they have the opportunity to engage in vicious stick-work.

Referees can also be inconsistent in their interpretation of the rules and in assessing penalties to each team. Although most sports allow their officials discretion in making judgment calls, coaches and players still complain that referees seldom judge any recurring infraction in exactly the same way. Consequently some players feel that the referee will not penalize an opponent for committing a foul against them—so they retaliate. In attempting to maintain the flow of the game, referees tend to overlook the initial violation and catch the obvious act of retaliation.

Summary and Conclusion

The problem of violence persists in minor league hockey. We addressed previous important research dealing with the influence parents, coaches, and teammates had in contributing to how players learn violence as a way to succeed in the sport. In utilizing this research as our base, we have added to the understanding of this problem in three ways. First, by giving a historical account of violence in the NHL, we showed how past and present players have encouraged violence by acting as negative role models for young players. Second, our examination of game officials has pointed out the necessity for a more rigorous set of standards to upgrade referees' conditioning and knowledge of the rules. League officials must also recognize that certain women are equally capable of being referees and integrate them into minor hockey. Finally, we addressed the question of the media—television, especially— and how it profits by keeping violence alive throughout all of hockey.

This chapter has also concerned itself with the attitudes children and youth learn to succeed as adults in North American society. The larger social order stresses the importance of individualism and competitiveness as prime attributes for the achievement of success. We have tried to show that competition is basic to hockey but that it must divorce itself from violence in the pursuit of cultural rewards such as money and fame. Before all else, our society has to acknowledge that the priorities of amateur sport for young people are fun, sportsmanship, and the development of physical skills. It is the responsibility of adults to reinforce these values and to ensure that children freely enjoy sports without fear for their safety. Parents, coaches, and referees must ally themselves with those who accentuate fair play. Hockey is one of the world's most electrifying sports and can thrive without violence. We hope that the media and professional hockey will eventually alter their approach to the game.

References

Bandura, A. (1986). *Social foundations of thought and action: A social cognitive theory.* Englewood Cliffs, NJ: Prentice-Hall.

Baudrillard, J. (1983). *Simulations.* New York: Semiotext(e).

Burman, T. (Producer), & Lee, M. (Reporter). (1993). *The spirit of the game* [Videotape]. Toronto: Canadian Broadcasting Corporation.

Canadian Amateur Hockey Association (Producer). (1992). *Parents make the difference* [Videotape]. Calgary, Alberta: Hockey Canada.

Colburn, K., Jr. (1985). Honor, ritual and violence in ice hockey. *Canadian Journal of Sociology, 10*(2), 153–170.

———. (1986). Deviance and legitimacy in ice hockey: A microstructural theory of violence. *Sociological Quarterly, 27*(1), 63–74.

Combined Artists (Producer). (1992). *Sports pages: Killer hockey* [Videotape]. Plymouth, MN: Sitmar Entertainment Inc.

Dunnell, M. (1959, December 9). Jungle law in NHL—Bathgate. *The Toronto Star,* pp. 1, 17.

Fischler, S. (1993, May). Fighting belongs in hockey. *Hockey Heroes,* pp. 10–13.

Frayne, T. (1973). *Famous hockey players.* New York: Dodd, Mead & Co.

Harrison, R. (Producer). (1993). *Hockey night in Canada* [Videotape]. Toronto: Molstar.

Matza, D. (1964). *Delinquency and drift.* New York: Wiley.

McLuhan, M., & Fiore, Q. (1967). *The medium is the message: An inventory of effects.* New York: Bantam Books.

Mills, C. Wright. (1961). *The sociological imagination.* New York: Grove Press.

Murphy, J. W., & Choi, J. M. (1993). Imagocentrism and the Rodney King affair. *ETC: A Review of General Semantics, 49,* 478–484.

Schultz, D. (1981). *The hammer: Confessions of a hockey enforcer.* Toronto: Collins.

Smith, M. D. (1979). Towards an explanation of hockey violence: A reference-other approach. *Canadian Journal of Sociology, 4,* 105–124.

———. (1983). *Violence and sport.* Toronto: Butterworths.

———. (1987). *Violence in Canadian amateur sport: A review of literature.* Ottawa: Ministry for Fitness and Amateur Sport, Government of Canada.

Tarasov, A. (1969). *Road to Olympus.* Toronto: Griffin House.

Tretiak, V. (1987). *Tretiak: The legend.* S. & M. Budman (Trans.). Edmonton, Alberta: Plains Publishing.

Vaz, E. W. (1982). *The professionalization of young hockey players.* Lincoln, NE: University of Nebraska Press.

PART

IV

ANATOMICAL AND PHYSIOLOGICAL CONCERNS

The rise of youth sports at both national and international levels has been accompanied by the application of advanced training techniques. The training programs are designed to create stresses on the body systems through emphasis on extreme intensity and duration of activity. They are geared to specialization in a single sport, and they involve year-round participation. Because gaps exist in our understanding of the effects of exercise stress on children and youth, training programs for young athletes are often formulated on the basis of information obtained from adults. In spite of this practice, the general assumption that youngsters thrive on adult training regimes must be questioned.

Little doubt exists that a certain minimum of physical activity is necessary to support normal growth and that vigorous activity is essential for promoting optimal physical fitness. However, some physicians, educators, community leaders, and parents have opposed youth sports on the grounds that highly intense sport training may cause excessive physical stress and might be hazardous for youngsters. More specifically, many significant questions have been raised. What are the biophysical characteristics of young athletes, and what are the effects of strenuous physical activity on their growth and biological maturation? Do the stresses that endurance-type training regimes impose make excessive demands on the cardiovascular systems of children and youth? How do male-female morphological and physiological characteristics affect sex differences in sport performance during childhood and adolescence? What are the effects of endurance-type training on menstrual functioning? What are the effects of anabolic steroids on muscle strength and size, and what are the adverse effects of steroid use? What are the potential benefits of strength training for child and adolescent athletes, and are the risks excessively high? What is the nature of overuse injuries in youth sports, and what safeguards must be enacted to reduce their incidence? The chapters that follow address these questions as well as other salient issues.

157

In chapter 11, Robert M. Malina presents a comprehensive survey of the physical growth and maturation of young male and female athletes. A preliminary topic focuses on the complex interrelationships among maturity status, body size, physique, and body composition in children and adolescents. This information is vital in understanding associations between physical growth, biological maturity, and athletic performance. A summary is then presented of the growth and maturity characteristics of elite athletes in several individual and team sports. Next the topic of age at menarche is addressed, after which an in-depth analysis is provided concerning how biological and cultural factors interact to affect sport socialization. In this context, a two-part (biocultural) hypothesis is proposed as a plausible explanation for the later menarcheal status observed in athletes. Malina then reviews the effects of regular training for sport on indicators of growth and maturation. In the final part of the chapter, several issues are identified that merit further study and evaluation, including maturity matching, talent identification and selection, dietary and chemical manipulation, and the need for biological age limits in some sports.

Cardiovascular functioning is a major concern within the domain of exercise physiology. Donald A. Bailey and Roy L. Rasmussen approach this topic in chapter 12 by considering the cardiorespiratory differences between children and adults. Emphasizing that children are not simply miniature adults, the authors cite important adult-child differences in aerobic and anaerobic responses to strenuous physical exercise. The question of whether or not functional changes resulting from early sport training persist into adult years is addressed, along with an examination of problems inherent in investigating training effects in children. Next Bailey and Rasmussen explain why children are less efficient than adults with respect to temperature regulation. The authors point out that such differences have precautionary implications for children's sport programs conducted in climatic extremes of heat or cold. Concern is then given to the topic of exercise-induced amenorrhea and its harmful effect on skeletal integrity in extremely active young women. Finally, both physiological and philosophical perspectives are included in a discussion of factors contributing to the early identification and development of athletic potential.

The next chapter describes the biophysical characteristics of the postmenarcheal female athlete (14 to 16 years of age), who is emerging into full adulthood. In addition to examining real morphological sex differences that affect athletic performance, Christine L. Wells and Lynda B. Ransdell debunk several common myths, such as those associated with sex differences in pelvic width, center of gravity, and "carrying angle" of the arm. Consideration is also given to sex differences in various physiological parameters, including systemic oxygen transport, lactate threshold, and maximal oxygen uptake, which is the best single measure of cardiorespiratory efficiency. Sex differences in strength, swimming, and running performance are then analyzed relative to these biophysical differences. The final parts of the chapter are devoted to athletes' menstrual function. The hormonal characteristics of the menstrual cycle and the effects of its phases on sport performance are discussed. Conversely, the effects of intense athletic training are examined relative to risk factors, potential harm, and reversibility of menstrual cycle dysfunction. In this regard, the authors note that although athletic menstrual dysfunction poses no known danger to future reproductive function, it constitutes an important risk factor for long-term bone health.

Adolescent athletes use anabolic steroids to improve performance, improve physical appearance, and meet peer approval. In chapter 14, David A. Van de Loo and Mimi D. Johnson provide information concerning the physiologic effects, potential benefits, and complications of steroid use. Anabolic steroid use results in an increase in muscle strength and size in some individuals who use them under specific conditions. However, these individuals are at risk for numerous harmful consequences. After detailing the adverse physical effects of steroids, the authors describe untoward psychological effects, including increased aggressive behavior, mood swings, and irritability. The chapter includes consideration of the prevalence, dose, and manner of steroid use by adolescent athletes, and black market sources of these drugs. In addition to the importance of early identification of steroid users, emphasis is given to various forms of intervention, the goals of which are to induce complete abstinence, to restore physical and psychological health, and to prevent relapse. The final part of the chapter is devoted to prevention of steroid use via drug testing, law enforcement, and multifaceted educational approaches aimed at children and young adolescents.

Chapter 15 focuses on the controversial issue of whether or not children and adolescents should engage in strength training. In an authoritative and thorough review of the subject, David R. Webb begins by discussing the locker room and scientific vocabulary of strength training, as well as the implications of basic physiological concepts tied to the use of progressive resistance methods to increase strength. Next, because youngsters may be expected to become stronger in response to appropriate training, several potential benefits are identified, including enhanced self-image, enhanced athletic performance, and reduction of the incidence and severity of sport injuries. Unfortunately, however, strength training is not without risk. The author therefore addresses clinical concerns that relate mainly to acute and overuse injuries and to hypertension and associated diseases. The chapter concludes with a series of recommendations for initiating strength training with young athletes. In this regard, special attention is given to the importance of the following: proper supervision; proper exercise and spotting techniques; emphasis on mastering motor skills rather than on competition; avoidance of maximal lifts; "prehabilitation" of the back and shoulder; attention to any complaints of back, shoulder, and other joint pains; and gradual progression of the intensity and difficulty of exercises attempted.

In the last chapter of this part, Russell H. Lord and Bill Kozar present information pertaining to overuse injuries, which represent up to 50 percent of all sport injuries in young athletes. In describing the nature of this condition, the authors indicate that overuse injuries involve the musculoskeletal system, are chronic in nature, and result from repeated microtraumas that eventually overtake the structure's ability to adapt to the activity. Several factors that contribute to the occurrence of such injuries are identified, including (a) delayed maturation coupled with too rapid increases in duration, frequency, or intensity of training, (b) the absence of required and adequate preparticipation examinations to determine children's readiness for sport participation, (c) the fact that taller, heavier, and in many cases less physically fit youngsters are entering intensive training programs at a time when they are most vulnerable to overuse injuries, and (d) the lack of fit between the demands of specific sports and the participants' physiological makeups. Lord and Kozar conclude their chapter with practical recommendations for reducing the incidence of overuse injuries and for making the sport environment a safer place for children and youth to play.

11

THE YOUNG ATHLETE: BIOLOGICAL GROWTH AND MATURATION IN A BIOCULTURAL CONTEXT

—Robert M. Malina

Children and youth participate in competitive sport at many levels, ranging from free play and local leagues through national and international elite competitions. The social sanction given to childhood athletics and the necessary skills for successful participation in athletics grant sport awesome power not only in the youngster's world but also in the broader sociocultural complex within which the individual lives.

Interscholastic athletic competition at the junior and senior high school levels is an established feature of the American way of life with a long historical tradition. In addition, agency-sponsored, organized youth sports are well established not only in North America but also in most developed, and in many developing, countries. Further, the number of youth specializing in some sports, for example, gymnastics, figure skating, tennis, swimming, and diving, at relatively young ages and competing in these sports at national and international levels is increasing. "Women's gymnastics" in reality has become "girls gymnastics," a sport dominated by prepubertal girls.

The popularity of youth sport programs, both agency-sponsored and interscholastic, and the national or international success of youth in several sports at relatively young ages are not without problems. Some issues relate to equality of access to sport, readiness of children for sport, specialization at an early age, talent identification and selection, parental pressures, and so on. Others relate to potential influences of intensive training and the demands of sports, especially high-performance sports, on the growth and maturation of young athletes. Further, the media's microscopic analysis and evaluation of sport per se and sport figures add to the stresses imposed on young athletes. For example, Kim Zmeskal finished 10th in the world in gymnastics at the 1992 Barcelona Olympic Games and was essentially labeled a failure by the media. Indeed, the treatment and some of the techniques of training young athletes for high-performance sports may fall within the bounds of child abuse.

Globally, interest in high-performance sports, with their economic and political implications, is reaching almost maniacal proportions. Changes in the political systems of Eastern European countries and reevaluation of the role of sport in their national agendas have placed these elaborate sport systems in jeopardy. However, the practices developed in some Eastern European countries, especially those related to early talent identification and selection, have influenced corresponding programs in many parts of the world.

Thus, youth sports span the local through international landscapes. The success of youth sport programs and of youth in sport generates much discussion, pro and con, concerning the physical and emotional well-being of young athletes. It is in this context that several issues will be addressed in this chapter: (1) the growth and maturity characteristics of young athletes, (2) age at menarche in female athletes, (3) interactions of biological and cultural factors in sport, (4) the effects of regular training for sport on growth and maturation, and (5) issues in youth sports that merit further study and evaluation.

Who Is an Athlete?

The young athlete is different from his or her peers in that he or she is successful in sport. Young athletes are usually defined by success on agency or interscholastic teams and in age-group or select competitions for individual sports. Young athletes are thus a select group, usually based on skill but sometimes on size and physique. (The issue of selection is discussed later in the chapter.) Most of the available data on the growth and maturation of young athletes are based on samples that can be classified as select, elite, junior national, or international caliber. Corresponding information for athletes at the local level are not extensive.

Growth and Maturation

Growth refers to increase in the size of the body or its parts, including body composition, physique, and specific systems. Biological *maturation* refers to the tempo and timing of progress to the mature state. Skeletal age (bone age), sexual age (secondary sex characteristics), and somatic age (age at peak height velocity during the adolescent spurt) are the commonly used indicators of maturity status. Details of growth and maturity assessment and changes that occur during childhood and adolescence are described in Malina and Bouchard (1991).

The interrelationships between growth and maturation must be emphasized. Children who differ in maturity status also differ in size, physique, body composition, strength, and motor performance. The differences are especially marked just before and during the adolescent growth spurt and sexual maturation, that is, the circumpubertal years, about 9 to 14 in girls and 11 to 16 in boys. Boys who are advanced in maturity status (i.e., skeletal age is advanced relative to chronological age by a year or more, early sexual maturation for their chronological age) are generally taller and heavier, have more weight for stature, are more mesomorphic, are stronger, and perform motor tasks requiring speed and power better than boys who are delayed in maturity status (i.e., skeletal age lags behind chronological age by a year or more, sexual maturation occurs at a later chronological age). Later-maturing boys tend to be more linear in build than early-maturing boys. Later in adolescence, that is, about 17 to 18 years of age, the size, strength, and performance differences between boys of contrasting maturity status are reduced or disappear. The differences between boys of contrasting maturity status are most apparent at the time when participation in sports is perhaps most important in the culture of youth (i.e., 11 to 14 years), and it is the early-maturing boy who often has the advantage in many sports at these ages.

Girls advanced in biological maturity (i.e., advanced skeletal age relative to chronological age, earlier sexual maturation, early menarche) also are taller and heavier and have more weight for stature than later-maturing girls (delayed skeletal age, later sexual maturation, late menarche). Early-maturing girls tend to be somewhat endomorphic, whereas late-maturing girls are more linear (ectomorphic) in build. Early-maturing girls are also somewhat stronger early in puberty, but by 13 to 14 years of age the differences virtually disappear compared with late-maturing girls. In contrast to boys, motor performance of adolescent girls is poorly related to maturity status, and it is often the later-maturing girls who attain better performances in later adolescence.

The preceding has compared children who are advanced (early) or delayed (late) in the tempo and timing of biological maturation. However, the majority of children fall between the extremes and are classified as average in maturity status. They have skeletal ages that fall within one year plus or minus of their chronological ages, and they attain sexual and somatic maturity within one year plus or minus of the population average. Their growth, strength, and performance characteristics generally fall between the extreme groups and there is considerable overlap.

Growth and Maturity Characteristics of Young Athletes

The following is extracted from a more comprehensive review (Malina, 1994), which includes the primary references. For the sake of convenience, the data are summarized by sex and by type of sport (team or individual). The discussion is limited to stature, weight, and indicators of maturity status; menarche is treated separately because of the methodological variation in estimating the age at attaining this maturational event. Stature and weight are compared with the percentiles of reference data (growth charts) for American children and youth (Hamill et al., 1977). Physique and body composition are briefly considered initially.

Physique

Physique refers to the configuration of the body as a whole. It is most often viewed in the context of the somatotype concept, which summarizes an individual's physique through the varying contributions of endomorphy (relative fatness, laterality), mesomorphy (relative muscularity and skeletal robustness), and ectomorphy (relative linearity). Although some variation during adolescence exists due to individual differences in the timing and intensity of the adolescent growth spurt, an individual's somatotype is relatively stable during growth. It is also not significantly influenced by intensive training, except for local changes associated with heavy resistance training, which may not be sufficient to markedly alter an individual's somatotype (see Malina & Bouchard, 1991).

Physique is a selective factor in many sports; that is, youngsters are selected in part on the basis of their body build. Physique is also a limiting factor; that is, certain physiques are simply not suitable for some sports. Further, young athletes in a given sport tend to have somatotypes similar to those of successful adult athletes in the sport. This is especially apparent in the somatotypes of gymnasts (Carter & Brallier, 1988; Claessens et al., 1991, 1992; Eiben et al., 1986), divers (Geithner & Malina, 1993), and athletes in several winter sports (Orvanova, 1987). Carter (1988) provides a comprehensive overview of the somatotype characteristics of children and youth participating in sport at various competitive levels.

Body Composition

The composition of the body is most often viewed in the context of the two-compartment model, which partitions body mass into lean (fat-free mass) and fat components. Both components change with normal growth and maturation; for example, fat-free mass is related to growth in stature and body weight. On the other hand, training can influence body composition. Fatness is more affected by training; ordinarily no change or only minimal change in fat-free mass is associated with training in childhood and adolescence, and it is difficult to partition these changes from those that accompany normal growth and maturation (see Malina & Bouchard, 1991).

Since fat-free mass is related to overall body size, many studies of young athletes focus on relative fatness. Males, both athletes and nonathletes, decline in relative fatness during adolescence, but athletes in several sports have less fatness than nonathletes. Among females, relative fatness increases with age during adolescence in nonathletes but does not show as much change across age in cross-sectional samples of athletes from several sports (Malina & Bouchard, 1991). Thus differences in relative fatness are greater between young female athletes and nonathletes than between male athletes and nonathletes.

Team Sports

Males

Data are primarily available for baseball, basketball, football (American), ice hockey, soccer (European football), and volleyball. Young athletes in baseball, basketball, and football tend to be, on average, taller and heavier than the reference data. The size advantage reflects the generally advanced maturity status of successful participants in these sports, especially between 11 and 15 years of age. In later adolescence, the growth and maturation of early maturers nears termination whereas that of average and late maturers continues, thus reducing the size differences that were so apparent in early adolescence. Thus the size and maturity status of athletes is of less significance for success in sport in later adolescence, although physique differences likely remain. Note, however, that some sports, specifically basketball and football, place a premium on size, and young males are often identified and selected on this basis. It is surprising that, apparently, no growth data on young American basketball players are available. Data for male volleyball players are limited to later adolescence, and the taller statures of participants indicate the premium that this sport places on size.

Young athletes in soccer and ice hockey show a similar pattern in body size. During childhood and early adolescence, statures tend to approximate, on average, the median of the reference data, whereas after about 15 years of age statures tend to be at or below the median. Body weights, on the other hand, are more variable in soccer players from childhood through adolescence; however, mean weights of hockey players tend to approximate the reference median from 8 to 15 years and are above the median in older players. The trend toward somewhat greater weight for stature in late adolescent participants in these sports perhaps reflects the importance placed on two tactical demands of these sports, that is, tackling in soccer and body checking in ice hockey.

The maturity status of soccer and ice hockey players parallels that of their statures. The data suggest that youngsters regularly involved in soccer are of average maturity status during childhood and early adolescence, but more elite players at older ages (13+ years) are generally advanced in biological maturity status. These trends thus suggest that the population of successful participants in these two sports in later adolescence may be quite different from that in childhood and early adolescence.

The preceding raises a question that needs more careful consideration in youth sports for both sexes. Success in sport during childhood or early adolescence is no guarantee of success at older ages. Many youngsters drop out of a sport (and probably move into another sport) as the level of competition increases, more specialization is required, and/or the demands of a sport are more rigorous. And individual differences in the timing and tempo of the adolescent growth spurt and sexual maturation, with concomitant changes in body composition, strength, and power, are probably a major component of the so-called "dropout" problem.

Females

Information on female athletes in team sports is limited to basketball and volleyball. One study of volleyball players indicates tall girls (near the 75th percentile) have body weights that approximate the reference median from 9 to 13 years, whereas at older ages basketball and volleyball players are considerably taller and generally heavier than average. Limited maturity data indicate growth rates, skeletal ages, and secondary sex characteristic development that approximate the average. Hence, these athletes' larger size is not a function of accelerated growth rates or advanced maturation; it likely reflects the demands of the sports.

Individual Sports

Data are most available for swimming and gymnastics, two characteristically early entry sports, and then for track. Data for other sports—for example, ballet, tennis, figure skating, diving, skiing, and rowing, in both sexes, and cycling, wrestling, and weight lifting, in males—are less extensive. Since male and female participants in several individual sports often show similar growth and maturational trends, this section is partitioned by sport.

Swimming

Studies of young swimmers treat the athletes as a group without attention to stroke. Statures and weights of age-group swimmers of both sexes are, on average, at and often above the reference medians. As might be expected, variation occurs among samples. For example, swimmers 14 to 17 years from the U.S. Swimming Select Camp Program have statures that approximate the 90th percentile of the reference data. The select males tend to be heavier than other samples of male swimmers, but the select females have average weights that are not different from other samples of female swimmers. Statures and weights of age-group swimmers from Eastern and Western European programs are more variable than those from the United States.

Male and female swimmers show somewhat different trends in biological maturation. Male age-group swimmers tend to have skeletal ages that are concentrated in the average and advanced categories with relatively few late-maturing boys. In addition, better performers during late childhood and early adolescence tend to be advanced in maturity status. The trends in later adolescence are, of course, confounded to some extent by the catch-up of average- and late-maturing boys who are successful in swimming.

In contrast, female age-group swimmers tend to be average in skeletal maturation during early adolescence, about 10 to 13 years. At older ages the data are more variable, and the differences between skeletal and chronological ages are generally in the average range. Note that the majority of girls attain skeletal maturity by 16 years of age, so skeletal age is limited as a maturity indicator in later adolescence. Less extensive data indicate similar breast and pubic hair development in age-group swimmers and nonswimmers. Among girls under 12 years of age, the more successful swimmers tend to be somewhat advanced in biological maturation. Data for menarche are variable, depending on how and when it was collected (see the later section, "Methods of Estimating Menarche").

Gymnastics

In contrast to swimmers, gymnasts of both sexes are shorter and lighter than the reference data. Data, however, are more extensive for females than males. Reported mean statures and weights for gymnasts from Europe and the Americas tend to vary between the median and 10th percentile of the reference data, but those for European samples and participants in international competitions are more often nearer to the latter.

Skeletal ages of male and female gymnasts indicate no clear pattern of delay in childhood (6 to 10 years); subsequently, skeletal age tends to lag behind chronological age during adolescence. Data for secondary sex characteristics are consistent with those for skeletal maturation, and among girls, more-talented gymnasts are later in sexual maturation than participants at the local club level. Age at menarche is also quite late in gymnasts (see the later section, "Menarche in Athletes").

Track

Data for athletes participating in track were grouped as distance runners (one mile or further, cross-country) and sprinters. Data for jumpers and throwers are less available and are limited to later adolescence; hence, they are not considered.

Statures of male distance runners 10 to 18 years tend to fluctuate above and below the reference median, whereas those of female distance runners are at or above the reference median. In contrast, mean weights of distance runners of both sexes are below the respective reference medians. Statures of young male and female sprinters tend to be at or above sex-specific reference medians. Weights of male sprinters tend to be at or above the median; those of female sprinters are quite close to the median. Thus, young distance runners of both sexes tend to have less weight for stature than sprinters, that is, they are more linear; and the tendency is more apparent in adolescent females than in males.

Maturity data for track athletes are less extensive and samples are not always specified by event. Male distance runners under 12 years of age do not differ in skeletal maturity from nonathletes. Subsequently, successful male track athletes tend to be advanced in skeletal maturation, especially between 12 and 16 years of age. Some data indicate that later-maturing boys are often successful in track at 16 to 18 years, which emphasizes the reduced significance of maturity-associated variation in body size in the track performance of boys in late adolescence. Corresponding data for female track athletes 12 to 18 years suggest generally average skeletal maturity status.

The samples of track athletes in the preceding comparisons most likely included participants in all track and field events. Data for elite male and female distance runners 9 to 15 years indicate a slight delay in skeletal age (Seefeldt et al., 1988). Information on the sexual maturation of track athletes is not available except for menarche (see "Menarche in Athletes").

Diving

Data are limited to a sample of Junior Olympic divers 10 to 18 years. Mean statures of males approximate the 25th percentile, whereas body weights are only slightly below the reference median 11 to 15 years and at the median 16 to 18 years. Corresponding trends for female divers indicate statures and weights that are only slightly below the respective reference medians. Single-year longitudinal observations on 22 male and 29 female divers indicate growth rates for stature that are well within the range for the nonathletic reference population.

Figure Skating

Limited data for figure skaters of both sexes indicate statures and weights that are well below the respective reference medians, with the mean statures of four samples of males being at or below the 10th percentile. Several indicators point to later biological maturation in figure skaters of both sexes.

Tennis

Data for young tennis players are quite limited given the popularity of the sport. Statures and weights of males vary among studies. Data from Italy, Finland, and the United States indicate mean statures generally below the reference median with weights at the median; two samples of Czechoslovak players are considerably taller and heavier. In contrast, statures of female tennis players are generally above the reference median, whereas weights are near the median. Limited data for small samples indicate average skeletal maturity status; that is, skeletal and chronological ages do not differ.

Skiing

Mean statures and weights of male skiers fluctuate about the respective reference medians; statures of female skiers are generally above the median with weights at the median.

Rowing/Canoeing

Limited data for males and females indicate statures and weights greater than the respective reference medians. Data for a select sample of Czechoslovak rowers 12 to 15 years indicate advanced skeletal and somatic maturation.

Ballet

Data for children and youth training in ballet are largely available for females. Statures of U.S. and European samples are variable relative to the reference data, whereas body weights are uniformly low, approximating the 10th percentile especially in later adolescence. Late adolescent ballet dancers have statures that are not different from reference median for nondancers. The data suggest later attainment of adult stature (i.e., later maturation), which is consistent with indicators of skeletal and sexual maturation.

Small samples of male dancers 12 to 15 years had mean statures and weights below the respective reference medians. However, in late adolescence, statures are at or above the reference median while weights are more variable.

Cycling

Data are limited to European youth. Statures are at or above the median 11 to 16 years but are more variable in late adolescence; for example, samples from Czechoslovakia and Denmark are above while those from Belgium are below the median. Mean weights, on the other hand, generally cluster at the reference median. A sample of six select Czechoslovak cyclists 12 to 15 years shows advanced skeletal and somatic maturation.

Wrestling

During childhood and early adolescence, the limited data for wrestlers are variable; however, from 14 to 18 years, statures of U.S. wrestlers tend to be below the reference median, whereas weights are at or below the median. Wrestling, of course, is a weight category sport, which influences the trends. A sample of Finnish wrestlers shows delayed skeletal maturation, more so in early than in late adolescent boys.

Weight Lifting

Limited data from Europe indicate short statures just above the 10th percentile and body weights, with few exceptions, above the reference median in late adolescence.

Age at Menarche

Menarche, the first menstrual period, is a late event in the sexual maturation of females. It occurs, on average, about one year after peak height velocity, maximum growth in stature during the adolescent spurt.

This indicator of maturation is discussed separately for two reasons. First, several methods are available for estimating the age when it occurs, and they differ in their accuracy. Second, much of the sport science and popular literature associate later ages at menarche commonly observed in athletes with the inference that training "causes" the lateness.

Methods of Estimating Menarche

Age at menarche can be estimated with prospective, status quo, or retrospective methods. The *prospective method* is based on longitudinal studies in which girls are examined at close intervals during adolescence, usually every three months. The girl is interviewed as to whether menarche has occurred and when. Given that the interval between examinations is relatively short, age at menarche can be reliably estimated for individual girls. Sample sizes in longitudinal studies, however, are not ordinarily large enough to derive population estimates and may not reflect the normal range of variation.

To estimate age at menarche in a sample of girls, the *status quo method* is used. The resulting estimate applies only to the population and does not apply to individual girls. A large, representative sample of girls that covers the age range in which menarche normally occurs, 9 to 17 years, is surveyed. Two bits of information are required: first, the exact age of each girl, and second, whether or not she has attained menarche, that is, simply yes or no. The percentage of girls in each age class who attained menarche is calculated, probits for each percentage are plotted for each age group, and a straight line is then fitted to the points (see Malina & Bouchard, 1991). The point at which the line intersects 50 percent is the estimated median age at menarche for the sample.

The *retrospective method* requires the individual to recall the age at which she attained menarche. If the interview is done at close intervals, as in longitudinal studies, the method is quite accurate. If it is done some time after menarche, it is affected by error in recall. However, with careful interview procedures, for example, attempting to place the event in the context of a season or event of the school year or holiday, reasonably accurate estimates of the age at menarche can be obtained from most adolescents and young adults. The method should not be used with cross-sectional samples of adolescent girls under 16 or 17 years of age because the resulting estimate will be biased; that is, girls who have not attained menarche will be excluded from the calculations.

Menarche in Athletes

Prospective and status quo data for young athletes are very limited. The presently available data include the following estimates:

1. Prospective—select Polish gymnasts, 15.1 ± 0.9 years (Ziemilska, 1981); select Swiss gymnasts, 14.5 ± 1.2 years (Theintz et al., 1993); elite British gymnasts, 14.3 ± 1.4 years; elite British swimmers, 13.3 ± 1.1 years; elite British tennis players, 13.2 ± 1.4 years (Baxter-Jones et al., 1994); athletes at a Polish sports school for track, 12.3 ± 1.1 years (Malina, 1995a); elite ballet dancers in New York, 15.4 ± 1.9 years (Warren, 1980); athletes in a Polish sports school for rowing, 12.7 ± 0.9 years (Malina, 1995a). The British data are based on a combination of prospective and retrospective procedures in a mixed-longitudinal sample 8 to 16 years of age at the start of the study; and 26 of the 200 athletes (13 gymnasts, 11 tennis players, and 2 swimmers), 13.5 to 19.6 years of age, had not yet attained menarche by the end of the study (Baxter-Jones et al., 1994). Hence, the mean ages at menarche will be a bit higher.

2. Status quo—elite age group swimmers in the United States, 13.1 ± 1.1 and 12.7 ± 1.1 years (Malina, 1994); Hungarian gymnasts, 15.0 ± 0.6 years (Eiben et al., 1986); participants at the 1987 world gymnastics championships, 15.6 ± 2.1 years [this sample did not include girls under 13 years of age, thus the estimate may be biased toward an older age] (Claessens et al., 1992); Hungarian track athletes, 12.6 years (Farmosi, 1983); United States Junior Olympic divers, 13.6 ± 1.1 years (Malina & Geithner, 1993); ballet schools in Novi Sad, Yugoslavia, 13.6 and 14.1 years (Gavrilovic, 1983; Gavrilovic & Tokin, 1983).

    Reference mean or median ages at menarche for North American and European girls based on prospective and status quo methods range between 12.5 to 13.4 years (Malina & Bouchard, 1991).

3. Retrospective—mean ages at menarche for late adolescent and adult athletes in a variety of sports are shown in table 11.1. They tend to be later than the average. The means vary among athletes in different sports and tend to be later in athletes within a sport who are at a higher competitive level. Standard deviations are between one and two years, which emphasizes that not all athletes experience late menarche (see Beunen & Malina, in press; Claessens et al., 1991; Malina, 1983, 1991; Malina & Bouchard, 1991).

Allowing for variation among samples within a sport, the prospective and status quo estimates for gymnasts, divers, and ballet dancers are reasonably consistent with the retrospective data, indicating later ages at menarche. On the other hand, the prospective and status quo data for track athletes, the status quo data for swimmers, and the prospective data for rowers are earlier than the retrospective estimates for late adolescent and adult athletes.

It is well recognized that gymnastics and ballet have rigorous selective criteria, including physical characteristics associated with late maturation (see the "Biological Maturation and Sport Socialization" section). Female divers have many physical characteristics in common with gymnasts, and many divers have experience in gymnastics (Malina & Geithner, 1993). Thus it is no surprise that the different methods of determining menarche provide reasonably similar estimates.

TABLE 11.1 Retrospective Estimates of Ages at Menarche in Athletes by Sport

	n	Mean	SD
Individual Sports			
Ballet			
U.S.	67/89*	13.7	1.2
Diving			
U.S. Junior Olympians 17–18 yrs	28	14.1	1.3
U.S. Outdoor National Championships 1983	40	13.7	
U.S. national team 1991	13	13.7	1.5
University	21	14.1	1.7
Former East Germany, national	26	14.0	1.1
Gymnastics			
Olympic, Montreal	11	14.5	0.8
Former East Germany, national	25	15.0	1.1
Belgian, national	13/18*	15.1	1.7
Hungarian, national	13	13.7	0.9
World Championships, Rotterdam	121/200*	15.2	1.4
Figure Skating			
Former East Germany, national	30	15.0	1.1
Canada, elite	15/18*	14.0	1.3
Rowing/Canoeing			
Olympic, Montreal	59	13.7	1.1
Former East Germany	32	13.0	1.1
Swimming			
Olympic, Montreal	32	13.1	1.3
Former East Germany, national	52	13.1	1.0
Sweden, national	29/30*	12.9	
University	21	13.9	
University	89	14.3	1.5
Tennis			
Hungary, national	12	14.0	1.4
Track and Field, Events Combined			
Olympic, Montreal	31	13.8	1.8
Former East Germany, national	102	13.1	1.0
Hungary, national	42	13.5	1.0
University	66	13.6	1.3
High school	37	13.2	1.3

continued

TABLE 11.1 (*continued*)

	n	Mean	SD
Individual Sports			
Track and Field, Runners			
Olympic, sprint & middle distance, Montreal	17	14.3	1.6
University, distance	54	13.6	1.8
University, middle distance	12	13.6	1.0
University, spring	24	13.5	1.3
Track and Field, Jumpers			
Olympic, Montreal	11	13.4	2.1
University	11	13.7	1.3
Track and Field, Throwing Events			
University, shotput	9	13.4	1.7
University, discus, javelin	10	13.6	1.5
Team sports			
Basketball			
International, nine countries	107	13.9	
Hungary, national	50	13.3	1.0
High school	51	13.1	1.0
European Handball			
Former East Germany, national	98	13.0	1.0
Hungary, national	28	13.3	1.0
Volleyball			
Former East Germany, national	63	13.1	0.9
Hungary, national	16	13.7	0.7
U.S., Olympic (1976)	18	14.2	0.9
High school	81	12.7	1.0

*The first number indicates the number who attained menarche; the second number refers to the total sample surveyed. Based on data summarized in Malina (1983), Claessens et al. (1991), Malina and Bouchard (1991), Malina and Geithner (1993) and unpublished data for university athletes. High school and university athletes are from the United States.

On the other hand, late adolescent (17 to 18 years) and adult swimmers, track athletes, and rowers tend to attain menarche later than those involved in these sports during the circumpubertal years, about 9 to 15 years of age. The difference probably represents the interaction of several factors, including the longer growth period associated with later maturation (many do not attain adult body size until the late teens or early 20s), selective success of late-maturing girls, selective dropout of early-maturing girls, and probably others. This is considered in more detail in the subsequent sections.

Biocultural Interactions

The preceding has focused on the growth and maturation characteristics of young athletes in a variety of sports. Growth (e.g., size attained) and maturation (e.g., skeletal age, age at menarche), however, are outcomes of underlying biological processes. In healthy, adequately nourished children, growth and maturation are genotypically regulated (Malina & Bouchard, 1991; Tanner, 1962). Growth and maturation, however, cannot be treated in isolation from the cultural or social conditions into which an individual is born and under which he or she is reared. The processes underlying growth and maturation, including, for example, socioeconomic status, family size, diet, rearing styles, emotional states, health status, physical activity and training, and others, are responsive to these environments, but the individual's genotype can influence how he or she responds to specific environmental stresses. In other words, not everyone responds to the same environmental stress in the same manner. Some of these issues will become more apparent when the training for sport is evaluated later in the chapter as a possible factor influencing the growth and maturation of young athletes.

The sociocultural environments into which individuals are born and in which they are reared are of primary importance in sport. These environments are the matrices within which opportunity for sport is made available and in which talent for sport is realized. Thus any discussion of youth sport from the local to international levels can be done neither in a purely biological manner nor in a purely social or cultural manner. Biology and culture must be viewed in concert, in a biocultural or biosocial perspective. Sport may be a social or cultural phenomenon; however, individuals physically/biologically perform within a particular cultural context. The term *biocultural* is preferred because the term *culture* encompasses more than social relationships. Several examples of biocultural interactions in youth sports are subsequently discussed.

Social Circumstances

Social circumstances may either interact with or vary with a youngster's growth and maturation and, in turn, influence his or her opportunities and experiences in sport. Many individuals have the potential to succeed in sport, but not all have the opportunity or the environment in which to realize this potential. Outstanding young athletes are thus not a random sample and are not ordinarily representative of the general population of children and youth.

Parental encouragement and support often influence the youngster's early experiences in competitive sport. Parental attitudes, in turn, were probably affected by their own early experiences in sport. In some sports, such as gymnastics, figure skating, swimming, diving, and tennis, socioeconomic factors play a significant role. These sports are commonly associated with private clubs and have special facility needs that are often expensive (e.g., ice time, gym time, swimming and diving facilities, etc.). Given the opportunity and encouragement, those most suited to the demands of a sport and capable of adapting to them physically, emotionally, and psychologically presumably will experience some degree of success, persist in the sport, and perhaps attain elite status.

On the other hand, a child who has the requisites to be an Olympic figure skater or swimmer but who does not have access to skating and swimming facilities, good coaches, and so on will likely not reach his or her potential or may be diverted to a sport for which the child is not suited. For example, how many elite gymnastic, swimming, diving, tennis, or figure skating programs have their facilities located in inner cities? In other words, how many potentially elite gymnasts, swimmers, divers, skaters, or tennis players are being overlooked due to lack of opportunity?

Physical Characteristics and Opportunity

The physical characteristics (e.g., skill and size) of a youngster are probably important factors affecting performance and early success in sport. This success may provide other advantages, for example, being noticed and early access to expert coaching, that build on the youngster's talent. This is an example of an individual's physical characteristics interacting with social circumstances to secure access to expert coaching and, in turn, improved performance, further success, heightened motivation, and so on, all of which may lead to persistence in sport. In a retrospective study of Olympic swimmers, Bloom (1982) emphasized the importance of physical characteristics in providing early competitive advantages:

> Natural physical characteristics that give an individual some initial advantage over his or her age mates are likely to function to motivate the individual to enter and compete in a sport. They also help him or her secure the teaching and training needed to convert an individual with small initial advantages into a world-class athlete. (p. 515)

Biological Maturation and Sport Socialization

The processes of growth and maturation do not occur in a social vacuum. Changing relationships with peers, parents, and coaches accompany the adolescent growth spurt and sexual maturation. Individual variation in the timing and tempo of the growth spurt and sexual maturation, including changes in size, body composition, strength, performance, and behavior, are the backdrop against which youth evaluate and interpret their status among peers. Participation and perhaps success in sport are important components of this evaluative process.

Such an interaction between biological maturation and social circumstances regarding sport may occur among adolescent girls. As indicated earlier, retrospectively reported ages at menarche for late adolescent and young athletes indicate, on average, later ages at menarche in many sports. A two-part hypothesis, a biocultural interpretation, for the later menarche observed in athletes has been suggested (Malina, 1983).

First, the physique characteristics associated with later maturation, especially the tendency toward linearity, lower weight for stature, less fatness, relatively longer legs, and relatively narrow hips compared to shoulders (Malina & Bouchard, 1991; Tanner, 1962), are generally more suitable for success in athletic performance. Later maturers also tend to perform better on many motor tasks, and the differences between contrasting maturity groups of girls are more apparent in later adolescence, about 16 to 18 years of age (Beunen et al., 1978). Conversely, the physique characteristics associated with earlier maturation—a lateral build, greater weight for stature, higher fatness, relatively shorter legs, and relatively broad hips—may not be ideal for successful athletic performance, especially in tasks in which the body must be rapidly moved or projected (e.g., runs and jumps). The preceding does not preclude the fact that some early-maturing girls will have a physique suitable for athletic performance and perform well. However, on average, late-maturing girls more often have such characteristics.

Second, the process of socialization into or away from sport may interact with the girl's biological maturity status: Early-maturing girls are perhaps socialized away from sport while late-maturing girls are socialized into sport. Among girls, as in boys, earlier maturation may represent a performance advantage in some sports in early adolescence, 9 to 11 years. The larger body size of early maturers may be an advantage in sports that place a premium on size and strength; however, the larger body size may be a disadvantage in sports such as gymnastics, diving, and figure skating. And with the attainment of menarche (usually before 12 years of age), the early-maturing girl experiences new social roles and changing interests that may contribute to the process of being socialized away from sport. The structure of the sport system may be a contributory factor; that is, the status of a young teenager in her social group is linked to her femininity, and until quite recently, sport has not been considered feminine in some quarters of society. Early-maturing girls often have decreased self-esteem and are at a disadvantage socially compared with later-maturing peers.

In contrast, the late-maturing girl may be socialized into sport partly because of her lateness, that is, through her physical characteristics and skill. She has the opportunity to continue in athletics and thus more time to learn the skills and experience success in sport before attaining menarche. Since late-maturing girls are older chronologically when they attain menarche (usually after the 14th birthday), they perhaps have not experienced social pressures about competitive athletics for girls and/or are more able to cope with the pressures. In contrast to early maturers, late-maturing girls generally have an elevated sense of self-esteem. Late-maturing girls thus may have heightened motivational levels because of success in athletics, and this success may carry over into social interactions.

Another possible explanation for the success of late-maturing girls in sport is that late-maturing girls are more in phase in a developmental sense with early- and average-maturing boys of the same chronological age; late-maturing girls thus may have a more favored position in the adolescent social setting. This is illustrated in table 11.2. A late-maturing girl who attains menarche at 14 years of age is biologically closer to early- and average-maturing boys, who are more often good athletes. Early-maturing girls, on the other hand, are out of phase in a developmental sense with female and male chronological age peers. An early-maturing girl who attains menarche before 12 years of age is three to four years advanced biologically relative to most of her male chronological age peers. Such a difference in maturational and in turn developmental status is a considerable maturity distance. Early-maturing girls thus commonly seek out associations with older age groups. In this way, biological earliness or lateness may influence socialization away or into sport within a given chronological age group.

TABLE 11.2 Timing of Peak Height Velocity (PHV) and Menarche

	Ages (yrs) at Attaining Maturity Indicators		
	Early	Average	Late
GIRLS			
PHV	<11	**11–13**	>13
Menarche	<12	**12–14**	>14
BOYS			
PHV	**<13**	**13–15**	>15

Based on composite data for North American and European youth (Malina & Bouchard, 1991). Approximate mean ages of PHV in girls and boys are, respectively, 12.0 and 14.0 years, and approximate mean age of menarche is 13.0 years, with standard deviations of about one year. Values in bold print indicate the maturational similarity (developmentally in phase) of average- and late-maturing girls with early- and average-maturing boys.

Hata and Aoki (1990) have modified this two-part hypothesis (Malina, 1983) based on observations of Japanese athletes. These authors propose, first, that the increasing age at menarche associated with advancement in level of athletic competition is a result of selection ". . . in the socialization process into (or away from) sports participation . . . ," and, second, that the variation in mean ages at menarche by sport at a given competitive level is ". . . mainly a reflection of the diversity of suitable physiques by sport" (p. 181).

Talent Identification

A popular term in discussions of youth sports, especially high-performance sports, is *talent identification,* that is, the identification of individuals who have the physical, behavioral, and psychological requisites for a given sport. This identification is obviously a biocultural process. How talent identification and its corollary selection are carried out, however, varies with the objectives of sport programs.

The majority of youth sport programs emphasizes mass participation. Age and willingness to participate are the criteria and probably involve a parent-child decision. The primary motivations for children in such youth sport programs are to have fun, to be with friends and to make new friends, to learn skills, to be physically fit, and to compete and win (Seefeldt, 1987; Smith et al., 1983). The only selection here is parental selection of a program, which is potentially important because at this level the majority of coaches are volunteers with variable backgrounds and experiences in working with children in the context of sport. As some programs become competitive and specialized, however, identification and selection of talented youngsters systematically occurs both informally (e.g., observing youngsters in game situations, noting those who are more skilled and inviting them for a specific team) and formally (e.g., regular tryouts).

In contrast, high-performance programs that emphasize the elite have as their objective the identification, selection, and training of individuals with potential for success in the regional, national, and international arenas (see Regnier, Salmela, & Russell, 1993). A good deal of the information presented earlier on the growth and maturation of young athletes is derived from samples that can be classified as select, elite, junior national, or international caliber. Many of them have probably come through formal or informal talent identification programs.

Much discussion about the identification and selection of young athletes has focused on the success of sport systems in several Eastern European countries, which was based in part on systematic identification and selection at relatively young ages (Bompa, 1985; Brane & Leskosek, 1990; Hartley, 1988; Karacsony, 1988; Komarova & Rashimshanova, 1980). Many of these practices have been extended, with modification, to some sports in Western countries (Bajin, 1987; Feigley, 1987; Jiang, 1993; Poppleton & Salmoni, 1991) and have been incorporated into those of other countries, with China, perhaps, presently the most visible example (Ho, 1987; Lawrence, 1992; Reilly, 1988). The objective of such selection program is quite clear:

> Priority is given to selection of those children and young people thought most likely to benefit from intensive sports training and to produce top-class results in national and international competition. (Hartley, 1988, p. 50)

Although the identification and selection pattern varies by sport, the general pattern refined in many Eastern European countries includes initial evaluation of physical (physique, anthropometric, and motor) and behavioral characteristics, often as early as 3 to 8 years for some sports (e.g. gymnastics, diving, swimming, and figure skating). Secondary evaluations vary with sport. For example, in Romania secondary selections were made at 9 to 10 years for gymnastics, figure skating, and swimming and at 10 to 15 years for girls and 10 to 17 years for boys in other sports (Bompa, 1985). Potential rowers, basketball players, and weight lifters were not selected until after puberty in the former Soviet Union and German Democratic Republic (Hartley, 1988).

Ballet, though considered primarily as an art form, also has rather rigorous, selective anatomical criteria that rival those of some sports (Hamilton, 1986). Emphasis is commonly on extreme linearity and thinness.

Obviously the physical, motor, and behavioral requisites vary among sports, and the process of selection is ongoing. Selection is based on the assumption that the requisites for a given sport can be identified at a young age and subsequently perfected through specific training. In a perhaps simplistic view, the equation has two parts, the demands of a sport and the characteristics of the performer deemed suitable for the sport. The former are ordinarily described in technical manuals and can be summarized into three components: objectives, tasks (skills and tactics) and rules. The latter are more difficult to describe but may be operationally defined as ability, the biocultural matrix that includes the growth, maturational, and developmental characteristics of the individual. The preceding has been related to the concept of readiness for sport (Malina, 1986, 1993). That is, readiness occurs when a child's ability is commensurate with or exceeds the demands of a sport; unreadiness occurs when the demands of a sport exceed the child's ability.

Thus, success or failure in sport, or of a talent identification and selection program, can be viewed as dependent upon the balance between the individual's ability and the demands of a sport. The latter are relatively constant (i.e., high-level performance). Ability is dynamic, changing as the child grows, matures, and develops.

Does Training for Sport Influence Growth and Maturation?

Although regular physical activity, including training for sport, is often viewed as necessary to support normal growth and maturation, recent opinions more often focus on possible negative influences of training for sport on growth and maturation, more so in females than in males. For example, a recent report of the American Medical Association and American Dietetic Association (1991) cautions:

> Some fitness programs may be detrimental to adolescents if they mandate prolonged, strenuous exercise and/or very low body fat to maximize their competitive edge. . . . These regimes may delay sexual maturation, decrease bone growth and ultimate height. . . . (p. 4)

Therefore, how can the available data for young athletes in a variety of sports be interpreted? Does training for sport affect size attained (growth) and skeletal, sexual, and somatic maturation? The following discussion is based on Malina (1994), which includes the primary references (see also Beunen & Malina, in press). It is limited to stature and indices of biological maturation. The influence of training for sport on physique and body composition have been briefly described earlier.

Growth in Stature

The size attained by athletes of both sexes in most sports compares favorably with reference data. Further, longitudinal data for athletes in several sports indicate mean statures that maintain their position relative to reference values over time, whereas short-term longitudinal studies indicate growth rates in stature that are within the range of rates observed in the nonathlete population. Thus, intensive training for sport does not apparently affect growth in stature.

Gymnastics, figure skating, and weight lifting are exceptions. Gymnasts of both sexes are the only athletes who present a profile of short stature in both sexes. Figure skaters of both sexes and male divers and weight lifters also present, on average, shorter statures, though the data are not as extensive as for gymnasts. Female ballet dancers have shorter stature during early adolescence, but late adolescent statures do not differ from the reference median, indicating a growth pattern characteristic of late maturers.

The data for gymnasts must be considered in the context of extremely selective criteria applied to this sport, including selection at an early age for small body size and physique characteristics associated with later maturation. The short stature of gymnasts is in part familial; their parents are shorter than those of swimmers and nonathletes. Growth data for gymnasts in early childhood also indicate statures that are about one standard deviation score below the average by 2 years of age, long before gymnastics training was begun. The short stature is also related to slower skeletal and sexual maturation; data on the age at peak height velocity for gymnasts are not available. Longitudinal observations on elite East German male gymnasts from 12 to 14 years indicate similar gains in skeletal age, chronological age, and stature, leading the authors to conclude that the delayed growth and maturation are ". . . more a sequelae of selecting than caused by the influence of sports activities" (Keller & Frohner, 1989, p. 18). It is thus difficult to implicate the stress of training as the causative factor in the slower growth and smaller size of gymnasts.

Researchers have also recently suggested that growth rate of leg length is stunted in highly trained gymnasts (Theintz et al., 1993), leading to disproportionately short legs and short stature. However, cross-sectional data for several samples of male and female gymnasts, including international competitors, indicate sitting height/stature ratios that are quite similar to reference data for European and American White youth. Although gymnasts are absolutely shorter, the results suggest similar proportional relationships of the legs and trunk relative to nonathletes.

Diet is a confounding factor in evaluating the growth status of gymnasts, figure skaters, and ballet dancers. These sports share a common concern for maintenance of a relatively low body weight even though the normal progression of growth and maturation is to gain weight. Elite young East German female gymnasts, for example, were on a dietary regime ". . . intended to maintain the optimal body weight, i.e., a slightly negative energy balance, and thus (had) a limited energy depot over a long period" (Jahreis et al., 1991, p. 98). This may in fact be chronically mild undernutrition.

Other factors that interact with marginal caloric status must also be considered, including the psychological and emotional stress associated with maintaining body weight when the natural course of growth is to gain weight, year-long training (often before school in the morning and after school in the late afternoon), frequent competitions, altered social relationships with peers, and perhaps overbearing and demanding coaches. Altered eating habits, perhaps disordered eating, in young gymnasts and other athletes need closer attention.

Maturation

Indicators of biological maturation include skeletal age, age at peak height velocity, and age at development of secondary sex characteristics. Short-term longitudinal studies of boys and girls in several sports indicate similar gains in both skeletal age and chronological age, which would imply no effect of training on skeletal maturation. Similarly, the available data indicate no effect of training on the age at PHV in boys in several sports. Presently no corresponding estimates of age at peak height velocity of young female athletes exist.

Sexual maturation data are more available for young female than male athletes. The data, however, are largely cross-sectional, so inferences about the effects of training are hazardous. The trends in the development of secondary sex characteristics in pubertal athletes—breasts and pubic hair in girls and the genitals and pubic hair in boys—are consistent with data for other maturity indicators.

Menarche

As indicated earlier, prospective and status quo estimates of age at menarche indicate later ages in female gymnasts and ballet dancers. The late menarche and late attainment of adult stature in select ballet dancers is similar to the pattern of growth characteristic of late-maturing children. Like gymnastics, ballet has rigid selection criteria that place an emphasis on thinness and linearity (Hamilton, 1986), and significant numbers of young ballerinas have problems with disordered eating (Hamilton et al., 1988). In contrast to ballet, gymnastics selects for shorter statures and perhaps a somewhat more muscular physique.

In contrast, limited prospective and status quo data for athletes in other sports indicate ages at menarche that approximate those for the general population, whereas retrospective data for late adolescent and adult athletes generally indicate later mean ages at menarche. This discrepancy is especially evident in swimmers. Data for young swimmers, Olympic swimmers, and national-level swimmers from several countries collected in the 1950s to 1970s indicate mean ages at menarche that approximate the mean of the general population (Malina, 1983); however, university-level swimmers from elite programs in the United States in the mid-1980s had mean ages at menarche of 14.3 and 14.4 years.

This trend probably reflects increased opportunities for girls in swimming. In the 1950s to 1970s, female swimmers commonly retired by 16 or 17 years of age. With the advent of Title IX legislation in the United States, however, many universities added and/or improved their swim programs so that more opportunities are available. Also, later-maturing age-group swimmers, catching up to their peers in size and strength in late adolescence, probably experience more success in swimming and persist in the sport. Another factor that may account for later mean ages at menarche is change in the size and physique of female swimmers. A comparison of university-level female swimmers in the late 1980s with those in the mid-1970s indicated that the former were taller and more linear (Malina, 1995b), a physique characteristic of later maturers.

The later recalled mean ages at menarche of athletes in a variety of sports and correlations with years of training before menarche are often used to infer that training prior to menarche "delays" this physiological event. Association does not imply a cause-effect sequence between training and sexual maturation. Further, athletes who take up regular training in a sport after menarche are excluded in such analyses.

Other factors that are known to influence menarche also need to be considered. In families of athletes, for example, mother-daughter and sister-sister correlations for age at menarche are identical with those in the general population (Brooks-Gunn & Warren, 1988; Malina, Ryan, & Bonci, 1994; Stager & Hatler, 1988). This would suggest a significant genotypic contribution. Another factor is number of siblings in the family. Girls from larger families tend to attain menarche later than those from smaller families, and the estimated magnitude of the sibling number effect is similar in athletes and nonathletes (Malina, 1991).

As indicated earlier, in adequately nourished individuals, size attained, physique, and sexual maturation are primarily regulated by the genotype. Dietary practices associated with an emphasis on thinness or an optimal weight for performance may possibly influence growth and maturation, especially if they involve energy deficiency for prolonged periods. The demands of training may compete with those of the cellular processes underlying growth and maturation for available energy. The psychological and emotional stresses associated with training and competition are additional concerns. They may possibly affect neural centers in the hypothalamus associated with the regulation of sexual maturation. Nevertheless, if training for sport is related to later menarche—and no prospective data to date directly imply a causative role for training—it most probably interacts with or is confounded by other factors; consequently, the specific effect of training per se may be impossible to extract. The following conclusion from a review of exercise and the female reproductive system is appropriate in this regard:

> Thus, although menarche occurs later in athletes than in nonathletes, it has yet to be shown that exercise delays menarche in anyone. (Loucks et al., 1992, p. S288)

The literature on menarche is confused in part by altered menstrual function, which is common in athletes. Menarche refers only to the first menstrual period. Cessation of menstrual cycles after menarche has occurred, secondary amenorrhea, is a different issue beyond the scope of this discussion (see Shangold, 1994). Nevertheless, in the context of normal sexual maturation, menstrual cycles immediately following menarche tend to be anovulatory and quite irregular. The development of more or less regular menstrual cycles takes place over several years after menarche. Hence, some of the menstrual irregularities observed in adolescent athletes may in fact reflect the normal process of sexual maturation involved in the establishment of regular menstrual cycles (see Malina & Bouchard, 1991).

Sexual Maturation of Boys

The effects of training on the sexual maturation of boys does not receive the same attention as that given to girls. This is not surprising, since early and average maturation are characteristic of the majority of male athletes, and late maturers are represented in only several sports. Somewhat puzzling, however, is why one would expect training to influence the sexes differently. The underlying neuroendocrine processes that trigger sexual maturation are similar in both sexes, and other environmental stresses related to sport, such as anxiety and sleep problems, undoubtedly affect boys as well as girls. With the exception of wrestling, however, emphasis on extreme weight regulation is not characteristic of sports for boys.

Issues in Youth Sports

The experience of athletic training and competition does not have harmful effects on the growth and maturation of the vast majority of youngsters. However, the potential for detrimental effects on the growth, maturation, and development of children and youth exists. Several of these possible effects are addressed next.

Maturity Matching

Matching children—to equalize competition, to enhance chance for success, and to reduce injury in youth sports—is a worthwhile objective. However, the incorporation of measures of biological maturity status is logistically not practical on a widespread basis. Skill, stature, and weight within relatively narrow chronological age groups will probably match the majority of children under 11 to 12 years of age.

Subsequently during puberty, individual differences in biological maturation must be taken into consideration, perhaps more so for boys than for girls (see Malina & Beunen, in press). Nevertheless, the consequences of matching for sport need further study. What is the effect of maturity matching on behavioral development when, for example, an older child is biologically more suited to compete with younger children, or a younger child is biologically more suited to compete with older children?

Instead of matching children for sport, sport should be matched to the youthful participants. Serious consideration should be given to potential modifications of sports to meet the needs and characteristics of children and youth. For example, elimination of body checking in youth ice hockey significantly reduces the number of injuries (Roy et al., 1989).

Injury

Epiphyseal injuries and epiphysitis in the young athlete, though not extremely common, do represent a potential growth-influencing factor and might contribute to unevenness of growth. A common cause is overuse; for example, Little League elbow, tennis elbow or shoulder, and swimmer's shoulder. Fortunately, most epiphyseal injuries that occur in young athletes are amenable to clinical treatment and correction. In many cases, rest and proper training techniques are the key factors.

A relatively high prevalence of lower back problems has been reported in young gymnasts (Micheli, 1985). This is a different kind of injury situation that includes back pain associated with a variety of conditions from hyperlordosis, problems with intervertebral discs, stress fractures of the vertebrae, and spondylosis. A related issue in gymnastics is a high rate of reinjury (Caine et al., 1989), which would imply that many young competitors are not satisfactorily recovering from their original injuries.

Injuries to the skeleton of growing athletes always present the possibility of permanent effects. The data reported, however, are largely clinical cases, and growth of the skeletal element involved or of the young athlete is not usually considered or followed after recovery or repair. Nevertheless, in spite of the best medical care, injuries to the growing bones of young athletes may result in problems that do not surface until later in adult life. Epidemiological data are needed on the incidence of injuries in youth sports at all levels of competition.

Skeletal Integrity

Excessive training associated with altered menstrual function can compromise the integrity of skeletal tissue leading to a loss of bone mineral and increasing the risk of stress fractures (Dhuper et al., 1990; Drinkwater et al., 1984). Disordered eating and, specifically, restrictive diets are a contributory factor (Frusztajer et al., 1990). Thus, a threshold may exist for some female adolescent athletes. Regular physical activity generally has a beneficial effect on the integrity of skeletal tissue; however, when training is excessive, menstrual function is altered, and perhaps diets are deficient, the integrity of skeletal tissue may be compromised.

Talent Identification and Selection

Identification and selection programs have problems related to decision making, elimination or cutting, and manipulation, among others. Does the child have a voice in the selection process? Are parents involved? (Accounts in the electronic and print media often highlight parents who are seemingly more interested in their child's success than is the child.) Are decisions made independently by coaches or other sports authorities? What kind of guidance is available for the child, or parents, when the child is selected? What are the implications of being labeled "talented" for individual and parental expectations?

Selection initially involves elimination of many individuals and subsequently cutting of others as competition becomes more specialized and rigorous. The merit of selection programs is usually cast in the context of the number of successful athletes (gold medals). Little, if anything, is ever indicated about the individuals who do not make it through the process, and they are the vast majority.

Manipulation of Young Athletes

Manipulation of talented young athletes can be a problem and takes several forms; for example, altered familial patterns, separation from parents, preferential treatment, differential access to resources and travel, and so on. Issues related to dietary and chemical manipulation surface on a more or less regular basis, for example, caloric restriction with young gymnasts (Jahreis et al., 1991) and steroid use, perhaps with athletes as young as 13 years of age (Dickman, 1991; Fisher, 1991), in the former German Democratic Republic. Needless to say, dietary and chemical manipulation may alter the pattern of growth and maturation. A more recent potential form of chemical manipulation to enhance success in sport is the use of synthetic growth hormone to increase the stature of normal children. In addition to ethical concerns, metabolic risks and long-term benefits of growth hormone use in normal children and youth are not known (see Rogol, 1989).

Age Limits in National and International Competition

In sports that have an early age at entry and specialization, for example, gymnastics, figure skating, and tennis, the issue of chronological age and biological age limits needs careful evaluation, particularly in the context of potential for child abuse in sport. Should chronological age limits be raised for national and international competitions? Should biological age limits be imposed (e.g., a skeletal age of 15.0 years) in sports as gymnastics? Such limits may provoke outcries from those involved in coaching and administering high-level performance and competition for children. Nevertheless, such changes may be desirable for the sake of the health and well-being of the children involved. They are, after all, not miniature adults!

References

American Medical Association/American Dietetic Association. (1991). *Targets for adolescent health: Nutrition and physical fitness.* Chicago: American Medical Association.

Bajin, B. (1987). Talent identification program for Canadian female gymnasts. In B. Petiot, J. H. Salmela, & T. B. Hoshizaki (Eds.), *World identification for gymnastic talent* (pp. 34–44). Montreal: Sports Psyche Editions.

Baxter-Jones, A., Helms, P., Baines-Preece, J., & Preece, M. (1994). Menarche in intensively trained gymnasts, swimmers and tennis players. *Annals of Human Biology, 21,* 407–415.

Beunen, G., de Beul, G., Ostyn, M., Renson, R., Simons, J., & Van Gerven, D. (1978). Age at menarche and motor performance in girls aged 11 through 18. In J. Borms & M. Hebbelinck (Eds.), *Pediatric work physiology* (pp. 118–123) Basel: Karger.

Beunen, G., & Malina, R. M. (in press). Growth and biological maturation: Relevance to athletic performance. In O. Bar-Or (Ed.), *The encyclopedia of sports medicine: The child and adolescent athlete.* Oxford: Blackwell Scientific Publications.

Bloom, B. S. (1982). The role of gifts and markers in the development of talent. *Exceptional Children, 48,* 510–522.

Bompa, T. O. (1985). Talent identification. In *Sports: Science periodical on research and technology in sport, physical testing,* GN-1. Ottawa: Coaching Association of Canada.

Brane, D., & Leskosek, B. (1990). Racunalnisko podprt sistem iskanja visokih in motoricno sposobnih in njihova usmer janje v kocarko (computer aided system for identifying tall and motor-capable children and their direction into basketball). In *Sport Mladih (Sport and the Young, Proceedings of IV Congress of Sports Pedagogues of Yugoslavia and I International Symposium)* (pp. 623–628). Ljubljana-Bled: University of Ljubljana.

Brooks-Gunn, J., & Warren, M. P. (1988). Mother-daughter differences in menarcheal age in adolescent girls attending national dance company schools and non-dancers. *Annals of Human Biology, 15,* 35–43.

Caine, D., Cochrane, B., Caine, L., & Zemper, E. (1989). An epidemiologic investigation of injuries affecting young competitive female gymnasts. *American Journal of Sports Medicine, 17,* 811–820.

Carter, J. E. L. (1988). Somatotypes of children in sports. In R. M. Malina (Ed.), *Young athletes: Biological, psychological, and educational perspectives* (pp. 153–165). Champaign, IL: Human Kinetics.

Carter, J. E. L., & Brallier, R. M. (1988). Physiques of specially selected young female gymnasts. In R. M. Malina (Ed.), *Young athletes: Biological, psychological, and educational perspectives* (pp. 167–175). Champaign, IL: Human Kinetics.

Claessens, A. L., Malina, R. M., Lefevre, J., Beunen, G., Stijnen, V., Maes, H., & Veer, F. M. (1992). Growth and menarcheal status of elite female gymnasts. *Medicine and Science in Sports and Exercise, 24,* 755–763.

Claessens, A. L., Veer, F. M., Stijnen, V., Lefevre, J., Maes, H., Steens, G., & Beunen, G. (1991). Anthropometric characteristics of outstanding male and female gymnasts. *Journal of Sports Sciences, 9,* 53–74.

Dhuper, S., Warren, M. P., Brooks-Gunn, J., & Fox, R. (1990). Effects of hormonal status on bone density in adolescent girls. *Journal of Clinical Endocrinology and Metabolism, 71,* 1083–1088.

Dickman, S. (1991). East Germany: Science in the disservice of the state. *Science, 254,* 26–27.

Drinkwater, B. L., Nilson, K., Chestnut, C. H., Bremner, W. J., Shainholtz, S., & Southworth, M. B. (1984). Bone mineral in amenorrheic and eumenorrheic athletes. *New England Journal of Medicine, 311,* 277–281.

Eiben, O. G., Panto, E., Gyenis, G., & Frohlich, J. (1986). Physique of young female gymnasts. *Anthropologiai Kozlemenyek, 30,* 209–220.

Farmosi, I. (1983). Data concerning the menarche age of Hungarian female athletes. *Journal of Sports Medicine, 23,* 89–94.

Feigley, D. S. (1987). Characteristics of young elite gymnasts. In B. Petiot, J. H. Salmela, & T. B. Hoshizaki (Eds.), *World identification for gymnastic talent* (pp. 94–112). Montreal: Sports Psyche Editions.

Fisher, M. (1991). Massive E. German steroid use revealed: Elite athletes used high dosages in '80s. *Austin American Statesman,* Sept. 7, F3 and F11.

Frusztajer, N. T., Dhuper, S., Warren, M. P., Brooks-Gunn, J., & Fox, R. P. (1990). Nutrition and the incidence of stress fractures in ballet dancers. *American Journal of Clinical Nutrition, 51,* 779–783.

Gavrilovic, Z. (1983). Uticaj telesne aktivnosti na vreme pojave menarhe. In M. Milojevic & B. Beric (Eds.), *Zena i Sport* (pp. 53–59). Novi Sad, Yugoslavia: Fakultet Fizicke Kulture, OOUR Institut, Fizicke Kulture Univerziteta.

Gavrilovic, Z., and Tokin, S. (1983). Neke antropometrijske mere i menarha ucenica baletske skole u Novom Sad. In *Zena u Fizicko Kulturi: Zbornik Radova* (pp. 199–206). Novi Sad, Yugoslavia: Fakultet Fizicke Kulture, OOUR Institut, Fizicke Kulture Univerziteta.

Geithner, C. A., & Malina, R. M. (1993). Somatotypes of junior olympic divers. In R. M. Malina & J. Gabriel (Eds.), *Proceedings of the 1993 United States diving sports science seminar* (pp. 36–40). Fort Lauderdale, FL: U.S. Diving.

Hamill, P. V. V., Drizd, R. A., Johnson, C. L., Reed, R. D., & Roche, A. F. (1977). NCHS growth charts for children, birth–18 years, United States. *Vital and Health Statistics,* Series 11, No. 165.

Hamilton, L. H., Brooks-Gunn, J., Warren, M. P., & Hamilton, W. G. (1988). The role of selectivity in the pathogenesis of eating problems in ballet dancers. *Medicine and Science in Sports and Exercise, 20,* 560–565.

Hamilton, W. G. (1986). Physical prerequisites for ballet dancers: Selectivity that can enhance (or nullify) a career. *Journal of Musculoskeletal Medicine, 3,* 61–66.

Hartley, G. (1988). A comparative view of talent selection for sport in two socialist states—the USSR and the GDR—with particular reference to gymnastics. In *The growing child in competitive sport* (pp. 50–56). Leeds: The National Coaching Foundation.

Hata, E., & K. Aoki. (1990). Age at menarche and selected menstrual characteristics in young Japanese athletes. *Research Quarterly for Exercise and Sport, 61,* 178–183.

Ho, R. (1987). Talent identification in China. In B. Petiot, J. H. Salmela, & T. B. Hoshizaki (Eds.), *World identification for gymnastic talent* (pp. 14–20). Montreal: Sports Psyche Editions.

Jahreis, G., Kauf, E., Frohner, G., & Schmidt, H. E. (1991). Influence of intensive exercise on insulin-like growth factor I, thyroid and steroid hormones in female gymnasts. *Growth Regulation, 1,* 95–99.

Jiang, J. (1993). How to select potential Olympic swimmers. *American Swimming Magazine,* Feb/March, 14–18.

Karacsony, I. (1988). The discovery and selection of talented athletes and talent management in Hungary. In *The growing child in competitive sport* (pp. 34–49). Leeds: The National Coaching Foundation.

Keller, E., & Frohner, G. (1989). Growth and development of boys with intensive training in gymnastics during puberty. In Z. Laron & A. D. Rogol (Eds.), *Hormones and sport* (pp. 11–20). New York: Raven Press.

Komarova, A., & Rashimshanova, K. (1980). Identification of female throwing talent. In J. Jarver (Ed.), *The throws* (pp. 55–56). Los Altos, CA: Tafnews, Book Division of Track and Field News.

Lawrence, S. V. (1992, February 17) China's sporting dreams. *U.S. News & World Report, 112,* 59.

Loucks, A. B., Vaitukaitis, J., Cameron, J. L., Rogol, A. D., Skrinar, G., Warren, M. P., Kendrick, J., & Limacher, M. C. (1992). The reproductive system and exercise in women. *Medicine and Science in Sports and Exercise, 24* (6, supp.), S288–S293.

Malina, R. M. (1983). Menarche in athletes: A synthesis and hypothesis. *Annals of Human Biology, 10,* 1–24.

———. (1986) Readiness for competitive sport. In M. R. Weiss & D. Gould (Eds.), *Sport for children and youths* (pp. 45–50). Champaign, IL: Human Kinetics.

———. (1991). Darwinian fitness, physical fitness and physical activity. In C. G. N. Mascie-Taylor & G. W. Lasker (Eds.), *Applications of biological anthropology to human affairs* (pp. 143–184). Cambridge: Cambridge University Press.

———. (1993). Youth sports: Readiness, selection and trainability. In J. W. Duquet & J. A. P. Day (Eds.), *Kinanthropometry IV* (pp. 285–301) London: E. & F. N. Spon.

———. (1994). Physical growth and biological maturation of young athletes. *Exercise and Sport Sciences Reviews, 22,* 389–433.

———. (1995a). [Age at menarche for athletes at Polish sports schools]. Unpublished raw data.

———. (1995b). [Anthropometric measures for university-level female swimmers]. Unpublished raw data.

Malina, R. M., & Beunen, G. (in press). Matching of opponents in youth sports. In O. Bar-Or (Ed.), *The encyclopedia of sports medicine: The child and adolescent athlete*. Oxford: Blackwell Scientific Publications.

Malina, R. M., & C. Bouchard. (1991). *Growth, maturation, and physical activity*. Champaign, IL: Human Kinetics.

Malina, R. M., & Geithner, C. A. (1993). Attained size and rate of growth in Junior Olympic Divers. In R. M. Malina & J. Gabriel (Eds.), *Proceedings of the 1993 United States diving sports science seminar* (pp. 26–35). Fort Lauderdale, FL: U.S. Diving.

Malina, R. M., Ryan, R. C., & Bonci, C. M. (1994). Age at menarche in athletes and their mothers and sisters. *Annals of Human Biology, 21*, 417–422.

Micheli, L. J. (1985). Back injuries in gymnastics. *Clinical Sports Medicine, 4*, 85–93.

Orvanova, E. (1987). Physical structure of winter sports athletes. *Journal of Sports Sciences, 5*, 197–248.

Poppleton, W. L., & Salmoni, A. W., (1991). Talent identification in swimming. *Journal of Human Movement Studies, 20*, 85–95.

Regnier, G., Salmela, J., & Russell, S. J. (1993). Talent detection and development in sport. In R. N. Singer, M. Murphey, & L. K. Tennant (Eds.), *Handbook of research on sport psychology* (pp. 290–313). New York: Macmillan.

Reilly, R. (1988, August 15). Here no one is spared. *Sports Illustrated, 69*, 70–77.

Rogol, A. D. (1989). Growth hormone: Physiology, therapeutic use, and potential for abuse. *Exercise and Sport Sciences Review, 17*, 353–377.

Roy, M. A., Bernard, D., Roy, B., & Marcotte, G. (1989). Body checking in Pee Wee hockey. *Physician and Sportsmedicine, 17*, 119–126.

Seefeldt, V. (Ed.) (1987). *Handbook for youth sport coaches*. Reston, VA: American Alliance for Health, Physical Education, Recreation and Dance.

Seefeldt, V., Haubenstricker, J., Branta, C. F., & Evans, S. (1988). Physical characteristics of elite distance runners. In E. W. Brown & C. F. Branta (Eds.), *Competitive sports for children and youth* (pp. 247–258). Champaign, IL: Human Kinetics.

Shangold, M. M. (1994). Menstruation and menstrual disorders. In M. Shangold & G. Mirkin (Eds.), *Women and exercise: Physiology and sports medicine* (pp. 152–171). Philadelphia: F. A. Davis.

Smith, N. J., Smith, R. E., & Smoll, F. L. (1983). *Kidsports: A survival guide for parents*. Reading, MA: Addison-Wesley.

Stager, J. M., & Hatler, L. K. (1988). Menarche in athletes: The influence of genetics and prepubertal training. *Medicine and Science in Sports and Exercise, 20*, 369–373.

Tanner, J. M. (1962). *Growth at adolescence* (2nd ed.). Oxford: Blackwell Scientific Publications.

Theintz, G. E., Howald, H., Weiss, U., & Sizonenko, P. C. (1993). Evidence for a reduction of growth potential in adolescent female gymnasts. *Journal of Pediatrics, 122*, 306–313.

Warren, M. P. (1980). The effects of exercise on pubertal progression and reproductive function in girls. *Journal of Clinical Endocrinology and Metabolism, 51*, 1150–1157.

Ziemilska, A. (1981). *Wplyw intensywnego treningu gimnastycznego na rozwoj somatyczny i dojrzewanie dzieci*. Warsaw: Akademia Wychowania Fizycznego.

CHAPTER

12

SPORT AND THE CHILD: PHYSIOLOGICAL AND SKELETAL ISSUES

—Donald A. Bailey and Roy L. Rasmussen

During the growing years, physical activity is an important contributing factor if normal development of the child is to be maintained and encouraged. This fact is now well accepted. However, in recent years a debate has arisen regarding the potential benefits or risks of excessive physical training on the physical growth and development of children. With the increasing national and international prestige attached to athletic success, we are seeing more and more training and sport programs being developed for progressively younger children. Although not well documented, little question exists that the number of highly skilled young athletes involved in rigorous training programs is increasing (Rowland, 1993). This is particularly true in sports like swimming, gymnastics, figure skating, and tennis. Some of the training programs for specific sports are of extreme intensity and duration. Indeed, some young children today are involved in training programs that are more intense than would have been believed possible even for adults 30 years ago. Do these programs have an effect on the dynamics of human growth? When are children ready for the rigors of intense sport training and competition? Are there critical times during which a training stimulus may be more important in eliciting increases in functional capacity? These and many more questions are waiting for answers. But answers are not easy to come by for a variety of reasons, including the difficulty in isolating the training stimulus from the multiplicity of other factors that affect the growing organism. Although we recognize that gaps exist in our knowledge about the physiological responses of children to extreme exercise, we do know certain things about the effects of sport training on physiological and skeletal development in growing children. This chapter reviews some of the issues related to this topic.

Perspective

From a physiological point of view, concern has been voiced from some quarters that the stresses imposed by certain competitive sport-training regimes, particularly those of an endurance nature, may make excessive demands on the cardiovascular systems of children or early adolescents. In healthy children, little evidence exists to substantiate this concern. Under certain circumstances heavy exercise can have dele- terious effects on a child's health, but these negative effects can usually be attributed to sport injuries (Garrett, 1993) or overuse syndromes (Kibler & Chandler, 1993). These conditions are discussed elsewhere in this book (Lord & Kozar, this volume).

It is true that some cases of sudden death or cardiac arrest have occurred in young athletes during or immediately following games or practices, but, invariably, underlying pathology has been identified as the cause of death. Even in young car- diac patients sudden death during exertion is not as high as might be expected. Lambert et al. (1974) examined pooled data from nine countries on cardiac deaths in girls under age 21. Only 10 percent died while engaged in sport, 32 percent while playing, and 58 percent during sleep or rest. The investigators concluded that catas- trophe was not prevented by the avoidance of physical exertion in young cardiac patients. For this age group at least, Jokl's contention that exercise never caused death in a normal heart is probably correct (Jokl & McClellan, 1971). More recently Epstein and Maron (1986) report that the chances of a young athlete, with previously unrecognized heart disease, dying during training or competition is small, in the range of 1 per 200,000 participants. Clearly the chances of sudden death during exer- cise from undetected heart disease in children is exceedingly small.

Similarly there is little reason to believe that the physical demands of sport have deleterious effects on physiological function in the young athlete. Numerous studies have verified that in the absence of injury or disease, athletic training or sport participation do not seem to adversely affect the growth and development of the car- diorespiratory and metabolic capacities of children. To the contrary, young athletes or highly active children generally attain a high functional efficiency (Cunningham & Paterson, 1988; Rowland, 1990). In studying the physiological characteristics of children during the adolescent period, the wide variability in the onset, magnitude, and duration of the adolescent growth spurt imposes severe problems. A comprehen- sive review of the growth and maturity characteristics of young athletes is beyond the scope of this chapter but appears elsewhere in this book (Malina, this volume). In general, it can be said with some assurance that in terms of functional physiological characteristics, young athletes of both sexes develop as well as nonathletes. The experience of athletic competition and training is probably beneficial to the develop- ment of the cardiorespiratory capacity.

However, two areas of concern having to do with the child and sport training are currently receiving considerable attention. One has to do with the possibility of injury to the growth plate cartilage in the young athlete. As suggested by Caine (1990), concern exists that the tolerance limits of the growth plate in growing chil- dren might be exceeded by the mechanical stresses imposed by contact (shear forces) or repetitive loading sports. This could lead to a disturbance in bone growth. At risk are the lower extremities of young athletes who participate in contact sports such as tackle football, or the upper extremities and spine of young competitive gymnasts who may experience chronic growth plate injuries (Caine, 1990). Recent studies, however, suggest that occurrences like this are rare and that in most cases child and youth sports are relatively safe, with most injuries being mild and self-limiting (Baxter-Jones, Maffulli, & Helms, 1993; Micheli & Klein, 1991).

A second area of concern has to do with the skeletal integrity of extremely active young female women experiencing menstrual dysfunction. Early studies observed a relationship between intense chronic exercise and delayed menarche in young women (Malina, 1983) and subsequent activity-related amenorrhea (Cumming & Belcastro, 1982). Although the relationship between training, menarche, and amenorrhea is still in need of a satisfactory endocrine explanation, it is clear that a large negative energy balance, resulting from reduced caloric intake coupled with a high energy expenditure, seems to be involved in the problem. Whatever the cause, the situation has led to a concern that bone loss, secondary to an estrogen deficit that accompanies amenorrhea, is a potential cause of stress fractures in the short term and osteoporosis in later years. The topic of exercise-related amenorrhea and bone density will be discussed later in this chapter and elsewhere in this book (Wells & Ransdell, this volume).

For the present, it can be said that healthy children have few adverse physiological responses to exercise; on those rare occasions when they do occur, they are usually reversible and can be minimized with proper precautions. The body of a youngster is a wonderful machine with sophisticated built-in controls and instinctive limit-defining sensors. In the absence of externally created pressure or stress, a young body functions very effectively. However, children are not scaled-down adults, and a number of basic physiological differences between children and adults affect the ability to perform. Recognition and consideration of this fact are basic to any acceptable sport program involving growing children.

Children Are Not Scaled-Down Adults

The ability to sustain physical performance while competing in or training for a sport activity depends to a large degree on the ability of the organism to transfer oxygen from the atmosphere to the working tissues. Maximal aerobic power or maximal oxygen uptake ($\dot{V}O_2$max) represents the greatest volume of oxygen that can be utilized per unit of time under conditions of maximal exertion. To this end, maximal aerobic power is considered to be the best measure of cardiorespiratory efficiency because it depends on the interrelationships of all the body systems concerned with oxygen transport and is independent of motivation.

Maximal aerobic power in children can be significantly increased in response to sport training programs. This response is similar to changes seen in adults as a result of intensive training (Krahenbuhl, Skinner, & Kohrt, 1985). Values for relative maximal aerobic power expressed per kilogram of body weight ($\dot{V}O_2$max)/kg) are quite high in children who are involved in athletics (Hakkinen, Mero, & Kauhanen, 1989; Van Huss et al., 1988). However, if one looks at metabolic reserve—that is, the difference between maximal oxygen uptake and oxygen uptake needed for a given task—children are shown to be at a disadvantage (Rowland, 1990). The relative oxygen cost of walking or running is higher in children (Rowland & Green, 1988). The higher oxygen cost in young children in performing a given task has been suggested to be the result, probably, of mechanical inefficiency (Daniels et al., 1978). In addition, a continuum of improved running economy with growth has been shown during both childhood and adolescence (Bar-Or, 1983). For example, an 8-year-old child running at a pace of 180 meters per minute is operating at 90 percent of maximal aerobic power, whereas a 16-year-old running at the same speed is operating at only 75 percent of maximum. Thus, in comparison to an adult, the child is not as aerobically efficient as might be expected from looking at the high relative maximal aerobic power values (MacDougall et al., 1979).

Curiously, in spite of the above consideration, children grade physical effort lower than adolescents, and adolescents perceive the same effort as being less strenuous than do adults. Bar-Or (1977) conducted a study on more than 1,000 male subjects, ranging in age from 7 to 68 years, who performed an identical cycle ergometry test. The younger the individual, the lower the subjective perceived effort, although the relative intensity of effort demonstrated by heart and circulatory reactions was equally great. These data suggest that a given physiologic strain is perceived to be less by children than by older individuals. The reasons for this are discussed at length elsewhere (Bar-Or & Ward, 1989). These results raise an interesting question: Is it possible that young children under external pressure may be pushed too far?

Differences between children and adults also occur with respect to the anaerobic energy system. This system can be employed by the working muscles in the absence of oxygen. Work that results from anaerobic reactions can only be sustained for short periods of time, in contrast to aerobic work, which can be carried on for many minutes, even hours. Accumulating evidence supports the contention that the ability to derive energy from the anaerobic lactate pathway is not as developed in the preadolescent child as it is in the adult (Eriksson, 1980; Inbar & Bar-Or, 1986; Reybrouck, 1989). Further, gains in anaerobic capacity in growing children do not appear to be closely related to increasing size or increasing aerobic power, indicating a wide range of variation in the development of this pathway (Paterson, Cunningham, & Bumstead, 1986).

A detailed discussion of child–adult differences with respect to the individual components of the aerobic and anaerobic systems has been provided elsewhere (Bailey, Malina, & Mirwald, 1986; Bar-Or, 1983; Cunningham et al., 1984; Reybrouck, 1989; Rowland, 1990). It is sufficient here to refer to a statement by Astrand and Rodahl (1986):

> It may be concluded that children are physically handicapped compared with adults (and fully grown animals of similar size). When related to the child's dimensions, its muscular strength is low and so are its maximal oxygen uptake and other parameters of importance for the oxygen transport. Furthermore, the mechanical efficiency of children is often inferior to that of adults. The introduction of dimensions in the discussion of children's performance clearly indicates that they are not mature as working machines. (pp. 401–402)

Adaptability of Children to a Training Stimulus

Sport competition and training subjects the developing organism to a variety of stresses that may give rise to any number of significant responses. Whether adapting to repeated training sessions or to a single game situation, the growing child undergoes changes. The magnitude of these changes varies with the timing, duration, and intensity of the training stimulus. The physical exertion associated with sport training is only one of many factors that may affect the growing child. Thus our knowledge of children's adaptation to exercise is difficult to define and not completely understood. Notwithstanding, when the literature is critically analyzed, some facts are apparent.

Until recently, it was felt that regular sport training had no apparent effect on linear growth variables (e.g., stature) in children and youth (Malina & Bouchard, 1991). However, some recent reports have provided suggestive evidence indicating a reduction of growth potential in elite adolescent female gymnasts who trained an average of 22 hours per week (Theintz et al., 1993). This study supports an earlier report by Ziemilska (1985) on girls and boys involved in intensive gymnastic training. Thus the issue of the effect of intensive training for sports like gymnastics on the growth of children has been reopened and further investigation is warranted (Mansfield & Emans, 1993). And although skeletal maturity, as assessed in growth studies, does not appear to be influenced by physical training in young adolescent boys and girls (Bailey, Malina, & Mirwald, 1986; Malina & Bouchard, 1991), clearly professionals need to reevaluate the effects of very high intensity training programs for young athletes. The regulation and maintenance of body weight is certainly affected by regular physical activity. Youngsters regularly engaged in sport programs, be they formal or recreational in nature, have proportionally more lean body mass and less fat than those who are less regularly involved (Malina & Bouchard, 1991; Malina, Meleski, & Shoup, 1982). One question remains open: Do these training-associated changes in body composition persist into the adult years?

In studying the physiological response of the oxygen transport system to sport training, another dimension is added beyond simple quantitative change. Qualitative changes may occur in children during growth and/or training with or without quantitative alteration. Qualitative changes at the cellular level are not easily observed or measured; therefore, major gaps exist in our understanding of the processes involved in the physiological response to exercise. The traditional approach to studying the influence of sport training and physical activity on functional growth of the oxygen transport system has been to compare athletes with nonathletes. Most of these studies have been of short duration, involving pretest and posttest measurement, and many have failed to control for maturational differences. Taking into consideration all the constraints and limitations inherent in studying training-mediated responses in growing children, what conclusions can be drawn?

A number of early studies suggested that sport training or high activity prior to adolescence had a small or limited effect on maximal aerobic power (Ilmarinen & Rutenfranz, 1980; Mirwald et al., 1981; Weber, Kartodihardjo, & Klissouras, 1976). However, as the intensity of training programs for young children has increased, it has become apparent that maximal aerobic power can be significantly improved in response to an intense training stimulus and that the response in children does not appear to be much different from that seen in adults (Krahenbuhl, Skinner, & Kohrt, 1985; Rowland, 1993). Because most of the sporting tasks at this age are performed at less than maximal work rates, some researchers have suggested that the use of maximal aerobic power as a measure for evaluating the oxygen transport system in prepubescent children may be misleading (Stewart & Gutin, 1976). Sport training or a high level of physical activity has been shown to lead to improvements in submaximal efficiency that are independent of changes at maximal effort (Lussier & Buskirk, 1977; Mirwald & Bailey, 1984).

Some investigators have suggested that the effectiveness of aerobic training in adolescence may be greatest at or around the time of peak height velocity in boys (Kobayashi et al., 1978; Mirwald et al., 1981). Biologically this would seem reasonable in view of the marked changes taking place in endocrine function during this stage of development. Research is needed to confirm this hypothesis.

What happens when training ceases in growing children? Here again studies are needed, but it appears that, as in adults, adaptations to short-term training are not permanent (Michael, Evert, & Jeffers, 1972). Similarly, the aerobic response to long-term training in children appears to be lost in adult years with the cessation of training (Eriksson, 1976).

A major consideration in studies looking at the effects of sport training in children is the role of heredity. Early data from twin studies suggested that the principal determinant of variability in maximal aerobic power among individuals who lived under similar environmental conditions was genetic (Howald, 1976; Komi, Klissouras, & Karvinen, 1973; Weber et al., 1976). Though no doubt exists that genetically acquired characteristics contribute greatly to physiological capacity, recent studies are more cautious in their interpretation of the interaction between the environment and heredity. Estimates of the contribution of genetic effects to maximal aerobic power range from 30 percent to 50 percent (Bouchard, 1986; Malina & Bouchard, 1991).

Why is our understanding of the growing child's response to sport training still so fragmentary in spite of the surge of interest in the child as an elite young athlete? The gaps in our understanding are primarily attributable to an inherent methodological constraint that has been and continues to be a major challenge for investigators working in this area. As Bar-Or (1983) states:

> In adults, changes in function between pre- and post-intervention can be attributed with fair certainty to the conditioning program. Not so with children or adolescents. Here, changes due to growth, development, and maturation often outweigh and mask those induced by the intervention. It is intriguing that many of the physiologic changes that result from conditioning and training also take place in the natural process of growth and maturation. (p. 38)

Thermodynamics and Children

Not all sporting events or training sessions are held under ideal climatic conditions. In many regions of the world, climate can play a crucial role in terms of an individual's ability to perform. Climate is an especially important consideration in regard to sport programs for children, where many activities are performed outside, sometimes under less than ideal weather conditions. In general, children are not as efficient as adults in terms of temperature regulation, especially under conditions of extreme heat or cold (Bar-Or, 1983; Rowland, 1993).

A child has a smaller absolute surface area than an adult. However, when surface area is expressed per unit of body mass, the situation is reversed. Because heat loss is related to surface area and heat production to body mass, children should, theoretically, be at a disadvantage in a cold climate and favored in a warm one. However, other considerations place children at a disadvantage in a hot climate as well, in spite of their relatively large surface area. Children have a lower sweating rate than adults; consequently, their evaporative capacity is deficient (Davies, 1981; Inbar et al., 1981). The effect of a deficient evaporative capacity is to raise skin temperature and create a less favorable temperature gradient between the body core and the periphery, which in turn inhibits heat transfer by convection. The lower sweating rate in children is apparent both in absolute terms and when normalized per unit of body surface area (Bar-Or, 1983) and results from a lower output per sweat gland rather than a reduced number of glands. Sweat excretion per gland is two and one-half times greater in the adult compared with the child (Bar-Or, 1980). In summary, although low sweat production conserves water in the exercising child, it inhibits heat transfer in a hot climate.

Another age-related difference in adaptation to exercise in heat is the rate of acclimatization. The process of adaptation to heat takes considerably longer in children than in adults (Inbar et al., 1981). Further, children do not instinctively drink enough fluids to replenish fluid loss. Bar-Or (1983) reports that children exercising in dry heat will voluntarily become dehydrated even if allowed to drink ad libitum.

The American Academy of Pediatrics Committee on Sports Medicine (1982) has published a position paper, "Climatic Heat Stress and the Exercising Child," that reflects the importance attached to this topic. All leaders involved in sport programs for children should be made aware that in climatic extremes of heat or cold, children are less efficient in terms of temperature regulation than adults and that precautions are warranted.

Delayed Maturation, Menstrual Dysfunction, and Skeletal Integrity

Disturbances of the menstrual cycle have long been associated with an energy imbalance resulting from high levels of physical activity and/or low levels of nutritional intake, both in growing girls and mature women (Cumming & Belcastro, 1982; Wells & Ransdell, this volume; Yeager et al., 1993). Until recently these disturbances have generally been regarded as benign because the dysfunction is readily reversible with a restoration of a proper balance between energy expenditure and caloric intake. However, it is now clear that the low levels of endogenous estrogen associated with menstrual dysfunction in young women may lead to a decrease in bone mineral density or retard normal rates of bone accretion during growth (Bailey & Martin, in press; Loucks & Horvath, 1985). This in turn increases the probability of stress fractures in the short term and osteoporotic fractures in later life (Martin & Bailey, 1987).

Many reports document the delayed menarche of girls who train intensively in activities that require leanness for elite performance (Malina, this volume). This suggests the possibility of a delay in skeletal protection afforded by estrogen. Even after menarche such girls often display irregular or absent menses, compounding the skeletal hazard (Lloyd et al., 1988). The high incidence of disordered eating in athletic girls further aggravates the problem, as menstrual dysfunction seems to arise from some adverse combination of low body fat, low caloric intake, and high energy expenditure (Yeager et al., 1993). Regardless of its origin, prolonged amenorrhea in young females presents a serious potential hazard to the skeleton, and the bone loss associated with it may not be reversible (Bacharach, Katzman, & Litt, 1991; Baum et al., 1987).

In men with a history of delayed puberty, reduced levels of bone mineral density have been observed (Finkelstein et al., 1992). This suggests that in males, as well as females, pubertal delay may be an important determinant of bone density. The effects of intensive training on hormonal status in boys has not been fully investigated, but the few studies carried out in young men suggest that serum testosterone levels may be chronically reduced (Arce & de Souza, 1993). If this effect is confirmed, then heavy training during adolescence in boys possibly may have an effect on maturation and therefore bone density. Clearly this unexamined possibility should be given high priority by researchers.

Is Earlier Better?

On the theory that if some training is good, vast amounts must be better, we are seeing youngsters at increasingly earlier ages being subjected to intensive training regimes, in the hopes of developing world champions. In some countries of the world, exceptional talent is identified at an early age, and children are put through intensive programs on the speculation that they will eventually arrive at the top. We are not told what happens to the youngsters who do not make it.

The theory that the younger we start a child, the better the chances of his or her becoming an adult champion deserves close scrutiny. Some studies have suggested that early success offers no promise of the same later on. Clarke (1971), for example, found that outstanding elementary school athletes may not be outstanding in junior or senior high school and vice versa. Could it be that intensive participation and competition in the under-11 age group is not the great spawning ground it is purported to be? True, some child athletes later set world records, but the examples are not nearly as numerous as we may have been led to believe.

Many world class runners, for instance, were not acclaimed internationally as juniors. Scores of names come to mind of Olympic medalists who were not outstanding child athletes. In fact, an argument can be put forward that too much success too early makes future success less certain. Of the all-time top junior men's 100 meter performers, only one went on to win a world championship or an Olympic medal as a senior (Matthews, 1993). In this example, early success was no guarantee of future stardom. As in all human endeavors, there are exceptions to this observation, but the exceptions are rare enough not to discredit the hypothesis. The point to be made is that all that can safely be said with confidence about fast young runners is that they are fast young runners.

Swimming is often cited as another example of what can be accomplished if training is started at an early age. Shane Gould, the famous Australian swimmer, for example, was only 15 when she held every world freestyle record from 100 to 1,500 meters, an unparalleled achievement. But swimmers not only start early, they also tend to quit early—as young as 18 or 19 in the case of top women performers. The assistant U.S. swimming coach at the Montreal Olympics in 1976 is quoted as saying, "In some ways, the age-group program is backfiring. Sure it gets young kids into swimming, but it also burns them out before they are even close to their potential peak" (Kirshenbaum, 1977, p. 49). It is certainly reasonable to hypothesize that more success would be achieved if the people involved in the sport stayed with it longer. In many sports, children "dropping out" is a major concern.

A number of years ago, Dr. Gabe Mirkin, who was then medical editor for *Runner's World* magazine and author of a number of books on sports medicine, documented the case of his young running son. As a 9-year-old, the boy ran the mile in under 5 minutes and he held 12 age-class world records before he was 10. At age 10 he quit running. Mirkin's (1984) observation as a sports medicine physician and as a former advocate of running training at an early age is still pertinent to the discussion today:

> Kids burn out. They don't get injured. Of the hundreds of kids who came through, I didn't see a single long term injury. Some of these kids were running 70 or 80 miles a week, hard. You'd see a few injuries then—but, boy, the drop-out rate was frightening. Too much too soon. (p. 24)

Even granting the opposite point of view—that is, to get a world-beater of tomorrow we must train and crown young champions at an early age (an unverified premise)—and further assuming that it is possible to identify and select potential champions at an early age (a dubious assumption), the primary mandate of people working in children's sport programs should still be to respond to the long-term activity needs of all children. If athletic potential can be identified at an early age, it is logical to assume that a lack of potential should be just as easy to identify. If this is the case, should we not devote more time to the unskilled youngsters who have no motivation or encouragement toward physical activity? Perhaps what is needed in programs for the very young is to pay less attention to the selection of athletes and provide more encouragement to all youngsters to take an active interest in sports, games, and activities. If this occurs, every child has a chance to realize his or her potential, and the talent pool will be enlarged.

In North America a significant number of children who are late maturing and following a slower-than-average developmental timetable are denied a chance to even try to participate in sport, because most competitions for youngsters and adolescents are based on chronological age. Because size is an important determinant in many activities, youngsters who are small for their age are often discriminated against or discouraged, though they may have potential and may eventually be of average or even above-average adult size. Somehow we need to organize physical activity and sport programs so that more children can experience the feeling of success that comes from someone saying, "Well done."

Conclusion

Only selected aspects of the physiological response of the child to the rigors imposed by sport training and competition have been considered in this chapter. Other areas of research are undoubtedly relevant and important. For instance, a more-detailed examination needs to be done of hormonal responses to sport training, especially as they relate to bone mineral content in young female endurance athletes. Further studies are obviously necessary, as there are still many gaps in our knowledge of the underlying biological processes involved in the response of the growing child to sport participation. From a physiological perspective, the following quotation, drawn from a position statement prepared by the Canadian Association of Sports Sciences, summarizes material presented in this chapter and represents an appropriate guideline for adults involved in sport programming for children (Hughson, 1986).

> From a physiological and medical point of view, it should be recognized that each child is different in his/her response and tolerance to exercise, due to a great range of variability in growth rates, anthropometric indices, gender, and state of health, even in children of a similar chronological age. Younger pre-pubertal children should be encouraged to participate in a wide variety of motor skills, whereas older post-pubertal children can become more specialized in their training and sport participation. A child's performance and adaptation to training should not be directly compared to an adult's, as significant differences exist, especially during the years of accelerated growth. Environmental exercise tolerance is also more limited in children than adults. (p. 162)

Are young children ready for sport? Perhaps the question should be rephrased. Are adults, represented by parents, coaches, teachers, and spectators, ready to be involved in children's sport? Sport participation can be healthy for children, but unfortunately this is not always the case. Adults involved in sport programs for children, be they local recreational leagues or elite championship venues, have a responsibility to ensure that a child's happy participation is not jeopardized by unrealistic adult expectations. It is imperative that adults make the distinction between encouraging children to gain satisfaction from doing their best and pushing children beyond their capabilities and levels of interest. At this age the burden is on the leadership. Adults should have a thorough understanding of structural and functional differences that exist between children and adults. Sport programs for children should be designed accordingly.

References

American Academy of Pediatrics Committee on Sport Medicine. (1982). Climatic heat stress and the exercising child. *Pediatrics, 69,* 808–809.

Arce, J. C., & de Souza, M. J. (1993). Exercise and male infertility. *Sports Medicine, 15,* 146–169.

Astrand, P.-O., & Rodahl, K. (1986). *Textbook of work physiology* (3rd ed.). New York: McGraw-Hill.

Bacharach, L. K., Katzman, D. K., and Litt, I. F. (1991). Recovery from osteopenia in adolescent girls with anorexia nervosa. *Journal of Clinical Endocrinology and Metabolism, 72,* 602–606.

Bailey, D. A., Malina, R. M., & Mirwald, R. L. (1986). Physical activity and growth of the child. In F. Falkner & J. M. Tanner (Eds.), *Human growth—Postnatal growth neurobiology* (Vol. 2, pp. 147–170). New York: Plenum Press.

Bailey, D. A., & Martin, A. D. (in press). Physical activity and skeletal health in adolescents. *American Journal Diseases of Childhood.*

Bar-Or, O. (1977). Age-related changes in exercise perception. In G. Berg (Ed.), *Physical work and effort* (pp. 255–266). Oxford: Pergamon Press.

———. (1980). Climate and the exercising child—A review. *International Journal of Sports Medicine, 1,* 53–65.

———. (1983). *Pediatric sports medicine for the practitioner.* New York: Springer-Verlag.

Bar-Or, O., & Ward, D. S. (1989). Rating of perceived exertion in children. In O. Bar-Or (Ed.), *Advances in pediatric sport sciences* (pp. 151–168). Champaign, IL: Human Kinetics.

Baum, M. L., Kramer, E. L., Sanger, J. J., & Pena, A. (1987). Stress fractures and reduced bone mineral density with prior anorexia nervosa (letter). *Journal of Nuclear Medicine, 9,* 1506–1507.

Baxter-Jones, A., Maffulli, N., & Helms, P. (1993). Low injury rates in elite athletes. *Archives of Disease in Childhood, 68,* 130–132.

Bouchard, C. (1986). Genetics of aerobic power and capacity. In R. M. Malina & C. Bouchard (Eds.), *Sport and human genetics* (pp. 55–98). Champaign, IL: Human Kinetics.

Caine, D. J. (1990). Growth plate injury and bone growth: An update. *Pediatric Exercise Science, 2,* 209–229.

Clarke, H. H. (1971). *Physical and motor tests in the Medford Boys' Growth Study.* Englewood Cliffs, NJ: Prentice-Hall.

Cumming, D. C., & Belcastro, A. N. (1982). The reproductive effects of exertion. *Current Problems in Obstetrics and Gynecology, 5,* 3–41.

Cunningham, D. A., & Paterson, D. H. (1988). Physiological characteristics of young active boys. In E. W. Brown & C. F. Branta (Eds.), *Competitive sports for children and youth* (pp. 159–169). Champaign, IL: Human Kinetics.

Cunningham, D. A., Paterson, D. H., Blimkie, C. J., & Donner, A. P. (1984). Development of cardiorespiratory function in circumpubertal boys: A longitudinal study. *Journal of Applied Physiology, 56,* 302–307.

Daniels, J., Oldrige, N., Nagle, F., & White, B. (1978). Differences and changes in VO_2 among young runners 10 to 18 years of age. *Medicine and Science in Sports, 10,* 200–203.

Davies, C. T. M. (1981). Thermal responses to exercise in children. *Ergonomics, 24,* 55–61.

Epstein, S. E., & Maron, B. J. (1986). Sudden death and the competitive athlete, perspectives on preparticipation screening studies. *Journal of the American College of Cardiology, 7,* 220–230.

Eriksson, B. O. (1976). The child in sport and physical activity—Medical aspects. In J. G. Albinson & G. M. Andrews (Eds.), *Child in sport and physical activity* (pp. 43–65). Baltimore: University Park Press.

———. (1980). Muscle metabolism in children—A review. *Acta Paediatrica Scandinavica, 283* (Suppl.), 20–27.

Finkelstein, J. S., Neer, R. M., Biller, B. M., Crawford, J. D., & Klibanski, A. (1992). Osteopenia in men with a history of delayed puberty. *New England Journal of Medicine, 326,* 600–604.

Garrett, W. E. (1993). Clinical/pathological perspectives. In B. R. Cahill & A. J. Pearl (Eds.), *Intensive participation in children's sports* (pp. 195–201). Champaign, IL: Human Kinetics.

Hakkinen, K., Mero, A., & Kauhanen, H. (1989). Specificity of endurance, sprint, and strength training on physical performance capacity in young athletes. *Journal of Sports Medicine, 29,* 7–35.

Howald, H. (1976). Ultrastructure and biochemical function of skeletal muscle in twins. *Annals of Human Biology, 3,* 80.

Hughson, R. (1986). Children in competitive sports—A multidisciplinary approach. *Canadian Journal of Applied Sport Sciences, 11,* 162–172.

Ilmarinen, J., & Rutenfranz, J. (1980). Longitudinal studies of the changes in habitual physical activity of schoolchildren and working adolescents. In K. Berg & B. O. Eriksson (Eds.), *Children and exercise IX* (pp. 149–159). Baltimore: University Park Press.

Inbar, O., & Bar-Or, O. (1986). Anaerobic characteristics in male children and adolescents. *Medicine and Science in Sports and Exercise, 18,* 264–269.

Inbar, O., Bar-Or, O., Dotan, R., & Gutin, B. (1981). Conditioning versus exercise in heat as methods for acclimatizing 8- to 10-year-old boys to dry heat. *Journal of Applied Physiology: Respiratory, Environmental and Exercise Physiology, 50,* 406–411.

Jokl, E., & McClellan, J. (1971). *Exercise and cardiac death.* Baltimore: University Park Press.

Kibler, W. B., & Chandler, T. J. (1993). Musculoskeletal adaptations and injuries associated with intense participation in youth sports. In B. R. Cahill & A. J. Pearl (Eds.), *Intensive participation in children's sports* (pp. 203–216). Champaign, IL: Human Kinetics.

Kirshenbaum, J. (1977, April 25). Gimmicks, gadgets, goodby records. *Sports Illustrated,* pp. 40–49.

Kobayashi, K., Kitamura, K., Miura, M., Sodeyama, H., Murase, Y., Miyashita, M., & Matusi, H. (1978). Aerobic power as related to growth and training in Japanese boys: A longitudinal study. *Journal of Applied Physiology, 44,* 666–672.

Komi, P. V., Klissouras, V., Karvinen, E. (1973). Genetic variation in neuromuscular performance. *Internationale Zeitschrift fur Angewandte Physiologie, 31,* 289–304.

Krahenbuhl, G. S., Skinner, J. S., & Kohrt, W. M. (1985). Developmental aspects of maximal aerobic power in children. *Exercise and Sport Sciences Reviews, 13,* 503–538.

Lambert, E. C., Menon, V. A., Wagner, H. A., & Vlad, P. (1974). Sudden unexpected death from cardiovascular disease in children. *American Journal of Cardiology, 34,* 89–96.

Lloyd, T., Myers, K., Buchanan, J. R., & Demers, L. M. (1988). Collegiate women athletes with irregular menses during adolescence have decreased bone density. *Obstetrics and Gynecology, 72,* 639–642.

Lord, R. H., & Kozar, B. (1995). Overuse injuries in young athletes. In F. L. Smoll & R. E. Smith (Eds.), *Children and youth in sport: A biopsychosocial perspective* (pp. 281–294). Dubuque, IA: Brown & Benchmark.

Loucks, A., & Horvath, S. (1985). Athletic amenorrhea—A review. *Medicine and Science in Sports and Exercise, 17,* 45.

Lussier, L., & Buskirk, E. R. (1977). Effects of an endurance training regimen on assessment of work capacity in pre-pubertal children. *Annals of the New York Academy of Sciences, 301,* 734–747.

MacDougall, J. D., Roche, P. D., Bar-Or, O., & Moroz, J. R. (1979). Oxygen cost of running in children of different ages: Maximal aerobic power of Canadian school-children [Abstract]. *Canadian Journal of Applied Sport Sciences, 4,* 237.

Malina, R. M. (1983). Menarche in athletes: a synthesis and hypothesis. *Annals of Human Biology, 10,* 1–24.

———. (1995). The young athlete: Biological growth and maturation in a biocultural context. In F. L. Smoll & R. E. Smith (Eds.), *Children and youth in sport: A biopsychosocial perspective* (pp. 161–186). Dubuque, IA: Brown & Benchmark.

Malina, R. M., & Bouchard, C. (1991). *Growth, maturation and physical activity.* Champaign, IL: Human Kinetics.

Malina, R. M., Meleski, B. W., & Shoup, R. F. (1982). Anthropometric, body composition and maturity characteristics of selected school-aged athletes. *Pediatric Clinics of North America, 29,* 1305–1323.

Mansfield, M. J., & Emans, S. J. (1993). Growth in female gymnasts: Should training decrease during puberty? *Journal of Pediatrics, 122,* 237–240.

Martin, A. D., & Bailey, D. A. (1987). Athletic amenorrhea and skeletal integrity. *Australian Journal of Science and Medicine in Sport, 19,* 3–7.

Matthews, P. (Ed.). (1993). *Athletics 1993: The international track and field annual.* Windsor, UK: Harmsworth Active.

Michael, E., Evert, J., & Jeffers, K. (1972). Physiological changes of teenage girls during 5 months of detraining. *Medicine and Science in Sports, 4,* 214–218.

Micheli, L. J., & Klein, J. D. (1991). Sports injuries in children and adolescents. *British Journal of Sports Medicine, 25,* 6–9.

Mirkin, G. (1984, December). A conversation with Gabe Mirkin. *Runner's World,* p. 24.

Mirwald, R. L., & Bailey, D. A. (1984). Longitudinal comparison of aerobic power and heart rate responses at submaximal and maximal workloads in active and inactive boys aged 8 to 16 years. In J. Borms, R. Hauspie, A. Sand, C. Susanne, & M. Hebbelinck (Eds.), *III International congress of auxology: Human growth and development* (pp. 561–570). New York: Plenum Press.

Mirwald, R. L., Bailey, D. A., Cameron, N., & Rasmussen, R. L. (1981). Longitudinal comparison of aerobic power on active and inactive boys aged 7.0 to 17.0 years. *Annals of Human Biology, 8,* 405–414.

Paterson, D. H., Cunningham, D. A., & Bumstead, L. A. (1986). Recovery O_2 and blood lactate acid: Longitudinal analysis in boys aged 11 to 15 years. *European Journal of Applied Physiology and Occupational Physiology, 55,* 93–99.

Reybrouck, T. M. (1989). The use of anaerobic threshold in pediatric exercise testing. In O. Bar-Or (Ed.), *Advances in pediatric sport sciences* (pp. 131–149). Champaign, IL: Human Kinetics.

Rowland, T. W. (1990). *Exercise and children's health.* Champaign, IL: Human Kinetics.

———. (1993). The physiological impact of intensive training on the prepubertal athlete. In B. R. Cahill & A. J. Pearl (Eds.), *Intensive participation in children's sports* (pp. 167–193). Champaign, IL: Human Kinetics.

Rowland, T. W., & Green, G. M. (1988). Physiological response to treadmill exercise in females: Adult-child differences. *Medicine and Science in Sports and Exercise, 20,* 474–478.

Stewart, K. J., & Gutin, B. (1976). Effects of physical training of cardiorespiratory fitness in children. *Research Quarterly, 47,* 110–120.

Theintz, G. E., Howald, H., Weiss, U., & Sizonenko, P. C. (1993). Evidence for a reduction of growth potential in adolescent female gymnasts. *Journal of Pediatrics, 122,* 306–313.

Van Huss, W., Evans, S. A., Kurowski, T., Anderson, D. J., Allen, R., & Stephens, K. (1988). Physiological characteristics of male and female age-group runners. In E. W. Brown & C. F. Branta (Eds.), *Competitive sports for children and youth* (pp. 143–158). Champaign, IL: Human Kinetics.

Weber, G., Kartodihardjo, W., & Klissouras, V. (1976). Growth and physical training with reference to heredity. *Journal of Applied Physiology, 40,* 211–215.

Wells, C. L., & Ransdell, L. B. (1995). The maturing young female athlete: Biophysical considerations. In F. L. Smoll & R. E. Smith (Eds.), *Children and youth in sport: A biopsychosocial perspective* (pp. 200–225). Dubuque, IA: Brown & Benchmark.

Yeager, K., Agostini, R., Nattiv, A., & Drinkwater, B. (1993). The female athlete triad: Disordered eating, amenorrhea, osteoporosis. *Medicine and Science in Sports and Exercise, 25,* 775–777.

Ziemilska, A. (1985). Effects of intensive gymnastic training on growth and maturation of children. *Biology of Sport, 2,* 279–294.

13

THE MATURING YOUNG FEMALE ATHLETE: BIOPHYSICAL CONSIDERATIONS

—Christine L. Wells and Lynda B. Ransdell

The child athlete does not forever remain preadolescent. In the case of the young girl, puberty begins mysteriously; menarche occurs, and the young girl becomes a woman. This chapter will discuss the characteristics of this period—the morphological and physiological changes and the hormonal demands of a maturing reproductive system—and how serious athletic training affects these biophysical functions. But, where to begin? Pubescence is a period of rapid change. It is a period of confusion. Is the female teenage athlete still a girl? A postadolescent "young woman?" Or a fully reproductive adult woman? Is her appropriate counterpart a prepubertal boy? A postadolescent young man? Or a fully grown reproductive adult male?

The first section of this chapter describes the emerging young female athlete with particular regard to how her morphological and physiological characteristics differ from a similarly aged male and how these characteristics affect her performance. Following sections describe how the menstrual cycle affects the young female athlete's peformance and how athletic training affects her menstrual cycle.

The Postmenarcheal Female Athlete

This chapter focuses on the postmenarcheal female athlete who is 14 to 16 years of age. She has experienced peak height velocity and menarche and will grow in height only slightly more. She has had two to three years of "menstrual cycles," although she has most likely not had many fully ovulatory cycles until recently in her life. Most bony dimensions of her body—sitting height, arm length, leg length, shoulder and hip widths, foot and hand size—are very near full adult size, but her estrogen sensitive body tissues will continue to mature for several years.

Most postmenarcheal girls do not train seriously to become athletes. Many enjoy sports and play on recreational teams at school, church, or a youth agency. Some participate on club teams. Some girls experienced early maturation, developed breasts and "womanly" hips early in puberty, became "socialized out of sport," developed "other interests," and no longer pursue sport in earnest. A few tasted athletic success, were fortunate to display early talent, and thrived in competitive settings.

Some of these girls experienced a late maturation, which favored them with relatively tall height, long limbs, slim hips, low body fat, good muscular form, and an efficient cardiovascular system. (See Malina [this volume] for a discussion of a two-part hypothesis, a biocultural interpretation, for the later menarche commonly observed in talented athletes.) With few exceptions, this chapter is about these latter few girls . . . those with exceptional talent, or an unusual genetic disposition, or the driving "will to succeed"—young female athletes emerging into full adulthood.

Morphological Characteristics

Some prepubescent and early adolescent girls are very successful in sport at the national and international levels. In such activities as gymnastics, ballet, figure skating, and swimming, it is not unusual for adolescent girls to participate in international competitions and to win high awards, including Olympic medals and World Championships. Most likely these sports are begun *very* early in life, and by the time the young girl has reached such skill levels, she is a seasoned competitor. It is also likely that, depending on the particular sport, she would be morphologically described as very lean and compact and as displaying few secondary sex characteristics. Very likely, too, she will have a late age at menarche (Malina, 1994, this volume). These girls, contrary to popular opinion, do not suddenly blossom into voluptuous women and drop out of sport. Rather, they are morphologically well suited to their sports, and while they mature (develop breasts and hips as other girls do) their bodies remain well suited to their sports.

A more common scenario is that the young female athlete develops her skills and trains for team sports while of secondary school age. She excels late in high school and perhaps wins an athletic scholarship to college. For most sports, further physical maturation is an advantage because it allows the athlete to build more strength, to develop more coordination and grace, and to garner the experience needed for team play. Of course, as her body becomes more mature, some of the nymphlike qualities are lost. This is most often attributed to attainment of the *gynecoid* pelvis. So many misunderstandings accompany this notion that some explanation is in order. The true female pelvis has a round and roomy birth canal that, theoretically, allows for an easy delivery and, so the myth goes, gives women wider hips than men. This is the pelvis typically pictured in anatomy books for comparison with a typical male pelvis (the *android* pelvis). However, only about 50 percent of women have this type of pelvis. In reality, there are many perfectly normal pelvic shapes, and it is difficult to tell a male pelvis from a female pelvis. With respect to *absolute* anthropometric dimensions, the typical man has a slightly wider pelvis (greater breadth across the iliac crests) than a typical woman. Additionally, in terms of *proportional* dimensions, a man has a wider pelvis relative to his height, leg length, or thigh length. The typical woman, however, has broader hips relative to her shoulders (greater ratio of bicristal to biacromial breadth) (Malina & Bouchard, 1991; Roche & Malina, 1983). This proportional sex difference may be the actual root of the myth that women have wider hips than men.

During the postmenarcheal period of life a number of myths arise in regard to male and female morphological differences relative to sport and athletic performance.

Most of these myths stem from the false notion that a woman has a wider pelvis than a man, when, in fact, her absolute pelvic width is less than a man's. One such myth regards the *center of gravity* (or center of mass), a balance point of the body located at the intersection of the three primary planes, the sagittal, frontal, and transverse. Many sport technique books, and even sports medicine textbooks, state that a woman's center of gravity is significantly lower than a man's and imply that she is consequently less skilled in jumping, changing directions quickly, and running. Atwater (1990) reviewed the literature and reported a difference of about 1 percent in the average height of the center of gravity for men and women. Her biomechanic analysis led her to conclude that one's center of gravity is determined more by relative leg length (i.e., ratio of leg length to height), absolute height, and body type than it is by sex.

Another mythological sex difference that supposedly develops with morphological maturity is that the female will have a larger *Q angle,* and thus her risk of injury is greater than that of a male (Goldberg, 1989). The notion here is that the female's wider pelvis (a myth) and her shorter femur result in a smaller angle between the neck of the femur and the shaft of the femur. This is called the *femoral angle.* A smaller femoral angle may cause the shaft of the femur to slope more inward (medially). If the femur slopes inward, the Q angle, which is "the intersection of two lines in the midpatellar region, one drawn down the femur in the direction of the quadriceps pull and the other drawn up the tibia from the tibial tuberosity," will increase (Wells, 1991, p. 11). A Q angle larger than 15 degrees (which leads to "knock-kneed" positioning of the legs) is thought to cause the patella to track laterally in the patellofemoral groove (Francis, 1988; Hunter, 1988) and, consequently, predispose women to knee problems in sport (Amo, 1990; Cox, 1985). The Q angle is also thought to cause a lateral shift of the pelvis during running. Although little doubt exists that the Q angle is an important biomechanical determinant of patellofemoral dysfunction, or knee pain associated with patellofemoral articulation (Atwater, 1990; Cross & Crichton, 1987; Swenson, Hough, & McKeag, 1987), there is no data-based evidence that female athletes have larger Q angles than male athletes, more knee injuries than males, or run with a lateral pelvic shift that is absent in men. Of the injury data that exist, shortcomings have been exposed by Atwater (1990), and Nilson (1986). For example, some researchers have hypothesized that injury differences between men and women may be a result of training deficiencies rather than sex differences (Atwater, 1990; Francis, 1988; Nilson, 1986; Wells, 1991). Additionally, conclusions that women have a higher rate of knee injuries than men are not based on data from athletic populations. Data on athletes reveal that male athletes actually have a higher rate of knee injury than female athletes (Atwater, 1990; Francis, 1988; Nilson, 1986; Wells, 1991). A recent study has shown that a sample of Division 1A male ($n = 44$) and female athletes ($n = 43$) (age range 18–23 years) who participated in track, baseball, softball, basketball, and gymnastics did *not* differ in Q angle or prevalence of knee problems (Gastembebe, 1993).

Still another false belief that is a consequence of the mythological "wider female pelvis" is that the forearms of a woman must angle outward more sharply to "clear" the hips. This is referred to as the "carrying angle" of the arm and supposedly limits women's throwing ability. X-ray examination of four age groups, however, failed to reveal sex differences in carrying angle of the arm (Beals, 1976); therefore, throwing differences cannot be attributed to this.

Some *real* morphological sex differences appear during the secondary school years, however, that may considerably affect athletic performance. The most important has already been mentioned—linear growth in the female stops shortly after menarche. This gives the male about two additional growing years beyond the growing years of the female. The result is that the maturing young female athlete has shorter limb length, smaller foot and hand size, lesser shoulder width, and a less massive chest structure compared with the male secondary school athlete. Although the young female will continue to develop some lean body mass, particularly if she utilizes weight or resistance training, she will never develop the muscle mass that the postpubertal male is capable of developing. Small sex differences in body size and muscle mass are evident during the childhood years, and they become accentuated with the onset of puberty. Any advantage that the prepubertal girl had relative to the more slowly developing prepubertal boy is lost rather quickly. Although sex differences in motor performance are not extensive prior to puberty, at the onset of puberty, the male secondary school athlete will run faster, throw farther and more powerfully, jump farther and higher, and be capable of greater feats of strength than the female secondary school athlete (Haubenstricken & Seefeldt, 1986; Haywood, 1993; Smoll & Schutz, 1985, 1990; Thomas & French, 1985). The secondary sex characteristics typical of the "raging hormones" of adolescence are now evident. In the girl, this is characterized by stages 3, 4, and 5 breast development and stages 3, 4, and 5 pubic and axillary hair development (Rogol, 1988). In the boy, this is characterized by corresponding stages of penis and testes development, of axillary and pubic hair development, a deepening voice, and a receding hair line.

Changes in body composition are often rather extreme at this period of life. Young boys lose their "baby fat" and become slim, muscular, and well toned. Their leg, arm, and chest musculature takes on a much heavier quality, and chest hair and facial hair may appear. On the contrary, young girls may deposit considerable thigh and gluteal subcutaneous fat. The gynecoid body fat distribution pattern develops in those who are genetically predisposed. Even in those not destined to have an obvious thigh-gluteal fat distribution, the lesser muscle mass and the "softer" appearance of the typical female body is obvious (Malina & Bouchard, 1988, 1991; Malina & Roche, 1983).

Tables 13.1 and 13.2 report the body composition of trained and untrained 14- to 16-year-old females and males. In both genders, the athletes have less body fat and higher lean mass relative to their fat mass (lean:fat) than the untrained subjects. Female adolescent athletes have higher relative fat (percent body fat) and less lean body mass than their male counterparts, as is true of fully mature athletes. The male secondary school athlete is obviously more muscular than the female.

Physiological Characteristics

Until pubertal development, there is little sex difference in maximal oxygen uptake ($\dot{V}O_2$max), the best single measure of cardiorespiratory efficiency or maximal aerobic power. With her lesser development of muscle mass and her larger deposition of

TABLE 13.1 Body Composition of Trained and Untrained 14- to 16-Year-Old Females

Athletic Group or Sport	Level[a]	Age (y)	Height (cm)	Weight (kg)	Relative Fat (%)	Lean: Fat[b]	Reference
Untrained*	—	15.0	160.0	52.4	22.9	3.4	Forbes (1972)
Untrained	—	14–16	162.1	52.0	18.7	4.3	Novak (1963)
Ballet	HT	15.0	161.1	48.4	16.4	5.5	Clarkson et al. (1985)
Basketball	S	16.3	165.2	57.5	18.0	4.6	Shoup & Malina (1982) in Malina et al. (1982)
Figure Skating	HT	16.5	158.8	48.6	12.5	7.0	Niinimaa (1982)
Gymnastics	—	14.0	—	—	17.0	—	Parizkova (1973)
Gymnastics	S	15.2	161.1	50.4	13.1	6.6	Moffatt et al. (1984)
Cross-Country Running	S	15.6	163.3	50.9	15.4	5.5	Butts (1982)
Distance Running	S	15.9	162.6	51.9	13.0	7.0	Cunningham (1990)
Middle-Distance Runners	JO	16.6	—	51.4	12.5	7.0	Thorland et al. (1981)
Sprinters/Hurdlers	JO	16.7	—	56.4	13.4	6.5	Thorland et al. (1981)
Track	E	~16.0	—	55.1	15.5	5.5	Housh et al. (1984)
Track	S	16.8	162.2	54.3	17.5	4.7	Shoup & Malina (1982) in Malina et al. (1982)
Swimming	N	14.6	163.4	52.0	15.9	5.2	Haan (1979)
Swimming	O	16.3	164.4	56.9	14.5	5.9	McArdle, Katch, & Katch (1981)
Swimming	AG	13.9	158.9	48.6	16.0	5.3	Malina et al. (1982)
Swimming	AG	16.7	166.5	56.4	15.6	5.4	Malina et al. (1982)
Swimming	JO	~16.0	—	58.5	19.8	4.0	Housh et al. (1984)
Tennis	R	15.8	168.7	58.0	23.3	3.3	Powers & Walker (1982)
Volleyball	S	16.0	165.0	59.4	20.6	3.9	Shoup & Malina (1982) in Malina et al. (1982)
Cross-country running and skiing	HT	14.6	158.1	47.7	20.0	4.0	Wells et al. (1973)
Multisport (swimming, gymnastics, dancing, or running)	S	14.5	164.2	56.7	19.2	4.2	Willows et al. (1993)

*Data have been averaged.
[a]Levels of performance: E = Elite, HT = Highly Trained, N = National, O = Olympic, R = Ranked, S = Scholastic, JO = Junior Olympics, AG = Age-Group
[b]Lean: Fat calculated from data

adipose tissue, the postmenarcheal female's rate of improvement in $\dot{V}O_2$max usually declines, whereas the male's continues to increase. Thus, sex differences are not often seen before ages 11 or 12, but consistent differences are evident by age 14. Tables 13.3 and 13.4 present the aerobic power of trained and untrained 14- to 16-year-old females and males. The table shows that $\dot{V}O_2$max values of secondary school athletes are comparable to those of adult athletes, particularly in sports not

TABLE 13.2 Body Composition of Trained and Untrained 14- to 16-Year-Old Males

Group or Sport	Level[a]	Age (y)	Height (cm)	Weight (kg)	Relative Fat (%)	Lean: Fat[b]	Reference
Untrained*	—	15.0	169.1	59.8	13.3	6.5	Forbes (1972)
Untrained	—	14–16	171.8	66.8	11.2	7.9	Novak (1963)
Cycling	HT	16.2	171.0	58.8	10.6	8.4	Rico et al. (1993)
Distance Running	SCC	16.6	177.8	62.7	5.3	17.9	Cunningham (1990)
Distance Running	E	14.8	169.7	53.0	6.8	13.7	Thorland et al. (1990)
Gymnasts/Divers	JO	16.2	167.2	58.5	8.4	10.9	Thorland et al. (1981)
Sprinters	E	15.0	170.3	58.0	6.9	13.5	Thorland et al. (1990)
Sprinters	S	14–16	173.6	59.2	11.2	7.9	Tittel & Wutscherk (1972) in Malina et al. (1982)
Swimming	HT	14.3	167.5	53.9	9.4	9.6	Malina et al. (1982)
Swimming	HT	16.6	175.7	65.4	8.0	11.5	Malina et al. (1982)
Swimming*	AG	15.0	170.8	58.1	11.7	7.5	Tittel & Wutscherk (1972) in Malina et al. (1982)
Swimming	AG	13–15	172.8	61.0	9.7	9.3	Dessein (1981) in Malina et al. (1982)
Swimming	O	16.7	175.4	66.2	9.0	10.1	Malina et al. (1982)
Wrestling	S	15.3	171.2	61.6	8.0	11.4	Housh et al. (1991)
Wrestling	S	16.3	171.8	66.1	10.8	8.3	Housh et al. (1990)
Wrestling	JO	16.9	167.1	60.2	9.7	9.3	Thorland et al. (1981)
Wrestling	S	15.9	—	—	4.5	—	Katch & McArdle (1975)
	S	16.7	—	—	5.3	—	
	S	16.8	—	—	11.7	—	
Wrestling	S	16.2	168.8	66.6	7.4	12.5	Roemmich & Frappier (1993)
Multisport (canoeing, ice hockey, lacrosse)	HT	16.4	176.8	65.5	18.5	4.4	Wells et al. (1973)
Multisport (swimming, gymnastics, dancing, or running)	S	15.9	178.9	68.8	14.2	6.0	Willows et al. (1993)

*Data have been averaged
[a]Levels of performance: E = Elite, HT = Highly Trained, N = National, O = Olympic, R = Ranked, S = Scholastic, JO = Junior Olympics, SCC = State Championship Caliber
[b]Lean: Fat calculated from data

highly dependent on oxidative capacity. In sports for which success is highly dependent on high $\dot{V}O_2$max (middle- and long-distance running, cross-country skiing), adolescent athletes have somewhat lower values than elite adult athletes. Apparently a long period of training is necessary to develop world-class levels of $\dot{V}O_2$max for endurance sports.

TABLE 13.3 Aerobic Power of Trained and Untrained 14- to 16- Year Old Females

Sport or Activity	Level[a]	Age (y)	$\dot{V}O_2$max (1 min^{-1})	$\dot{V}O_2$max (ml • kg^{-1} • min^{-1})	Reference
Untrained	—	14.6	2.02	38.0	Armstrong et al. (1991)
Ballet	HT	15.0	2.37	48.9	Clarkson et al. (1985)
Canoeing	HT	16.0	3.13	48.2	Bunc & Heller (1993)
Gymnastics	S	15.0	2.28	45.2	Moffatt et al. (1984)
Runners					
Cross-Country	S	15.6	2.59	50.8	Butts (1982)
	S	15.9	3.20	61.7	Cunningham (1990)
	S	16.3	3.05	58.2	Bunc & Heller (1993)
Mid-Distance	HT	16.6	2.90	56.1	Bunc & Heller (1993)
Sprinters	S	15.0	—	43.9	Raven et al. (1972)
	S	16.0	—	58.5	Raven et al. (1972)
Track	E	9–15	—	59.9	Van Huss et al. (1988)
Unspecified	S	14–15	2.53	48.5	Drinkwater & Horvath (1971)
	HT	16.2	3.07	63.2	Burke & Brush (1979)
Figure Skating	HT	16.5	2.38	48.9	Niinimaa (1982)
Swimmers	N	14.6	2.93	56.4	Haan (1979)
	—	15.0	—	40.5	Cunningham & Eynon (1973)
Synchronized Swimmers	E	14.4	2.22	45.2	Poole et al. (1980)
Tennis	E	15.8	2.78	48.0	Powers & Walker (1982)
Cross-country running and skiing	HT	14.6	2.47	51.3	Wells et al. (1973)

[a]Levels of performance: E = Elite, HT = Highly Trained, N = National, O = Olympic, S = Scholastic

Puberty affects several factors important to cardiorespiratory efficiency. Changing proportions of muscle mass and fat mass directly affect the metabolically active tissue mass, which directly affects $\dot{V}O_2$max. As muscle mass increases in the postpubertal male, so does the metabolically active tissue mass; consequently, $\dot{V}O_2$max will most likely increase even without training. But muscle mass remains relatively constant, and adipose tissue mass increases in most postmenarcheal females; consequently, the relative proportion of metabolically active tissue mass will not increase significantly. Fat weight is essentially "dead weight" that contributes to the workload, but not to the work effort. At full adult stature, the male is about 25 pounds heavier and has about 10 percent less body fat than the female. This accounts for a major portion of the sex difference in $\dot{V}O_2$max.

Another factor important to $\dot{V}O_2$max is systemic oxygen transport. This involves at least two variables—maximal cardiac output and oxygen-carrying capacity. Both factors are altered by pubertal development. Maximal cardiac output ($\dot{Q}$) is a function of heart rate (HR) and stroke volume (SV). Both $\dot{Q}$, the quantity of blood

TABLE 13.4 Aerobic Power of Trained and Untrained 14- to 16-Year-Old Males

Sport or Activity	Level[a]	Age (y)	$\dot{V}O_2$max (1 min^{-1})	$\dot{V}O_2$max (ml $\cdot$ kg^{-1} $\cdot$ min^{-1})	Reference
Untrained	—	14.5	2.85	49.5	Armstrong et al. (1991)
Untrained	—	14.5	2.93	55.4	Binkhorst et al. (1981)
		15.5	3.26	55.7	
		16.8	3.43	54.2	
Runners					
Cross-Country	S	16.6	—	74.6	Cunningham (1990)
Middle-Distance	S	13.8	3.10	62.1	Maffulli et al. (1991)
Multisport (canoeing, ice hockey, and lacrosse)	HT	16.4	3.94	59.1	Wells et al. (1973)

[a]Levels of performance: S = Scholastic, HT = Highly Trained

pumped by the heart per minute, and SV, the quantity of blood pumped per heart beat, are partially limited by heart size. Following pubertal development, the female's heart is smaller than the male's mostly as a result of her generally smaller body size. Although the woman's heart rate will attempt to compensate for its smaller volume by beating more rapidly at submaximal cardiac output, this mechanism does not apply at maximal workloads (there is no sex difference in HRmax), and the male's maximal cardiac output is higher (Astrand et al., 1964).

The maximum oxygen-carrying capacity of the blood is determined primarily by hemoglobin (Hb), an iron-containing molecule in the red blood cells. Men have approximately 6 percent more red blood cells than women, and 10 percent to 15 percent more Hb per 100 milliliters of blood than women (Astrand & Rodahl, 1977; DeVries, 1980). Although it is usually assumed that these differences develop partly as a result of smaller body size and partly as a result of the monthly menstrual blood loss experienced by the female following menarche, when these differences first develop is not entirely clear. Taken all together, these differences generally mean that if all other factors remain equal, the postmenarcheal female will stabilize in $\dot{V}O_2$max while her male counterpart will continue to increase in $\dot{V}O_2$max even without training. Unless considerable training to increase skeletal muscle oxidative capacity and cardiac output is coupled with little (if any) gain in adipose tissue, few postmenarcheal girls will experience gain in $\dot{V}O_2$max.

Other physiological sex differences that may affect performance include anaerobic power, lactate threshold, and performance (running) economy. However, these variables have not been systematically studied in pre- or postpubertal athletes. Most assume that because postmenarcheal females have lesser muscle mass than males, that their corresponding anaerobic power will be less, and that appears to be true. Bar-Or (1983, p. 313) has presented normative data that indicate considerable sex difference in peak power output as measured by the Wingate Anaerobic Power Test

TABLE 13.5 Anaerobic Power of Trained and Moderately Active 14- to 16-Year-Old Females

Sport or Activity	Level[a]	Age (y)	Peak Power (W)[b]	PP:BM[c] (W • kg^{-1})	PP: FFM[d] (W • kgFFM^{-1})	Reference
Moderately Active	—	14.5	437.5 (L)	—	—	Blimkie et al. (1986)
	—	15.5	524.7 (L)	—	—	
	—	16.4	617.3 (L)	—	—	
Long-Distance Runners	HT	14.5	531 (L)	—	—	Tharp et al. (1984)

[a]Level of performance: HT = Highly Trained
[b]Anaerobic power test (L = leg ergometry)
[c]Ratio of peak power (W) to body mass (kg)
[d]Ratio of peak power (W) to fat free mass (kg)

by age 14. Tables 13.5 and 13.6 report what little data were located in the literature on 14- through 16-year-old trained and moderately active females and males. Nearly all these values exceed the normative values of Bar-Or.

Lactate threshold (LT) refers to the level of exercise at which blood lactate rises above 4 mM and is usually expressed as a percentage of $\dot{V}O_2$max. Although no sex differences in terms of percentage of $\dot{V}O_2$max have been noted in adults, LT is usually reached at a lower absolute power output (running pace or ergometer power output) by women. This means that at a given absolute workload, a larger anaerobic component may be required of the postpubertal female athlete than of the male. However, when exercise power outputs are expressed in terms of percent $\dot{V}O_2$max, the relative aerobic-anaerobic metabolic contributions are similar.

Performance economy (most often referred to as running economy, cycling economy, or swimming economy) is the oxygen uptake required to perform a submaximal exercise bout. Running economy in adult athletes does not differ between the sexes if subjects are equally trained or performance matched (Joyner, 1993, p. 118; Wells, 1991, pp. 28–29). It seems likely that considerable variation in performance economy occurs during periods of rapid growth and/or rapid motor development, but presumably those periods have passed by age 14 and are not a factor of sexual dimorphism in postpubertal athletes. However, this area needs further research at all levels of performance.

Performance Differences

Differences in Strength Performance

During the pubertal years, male strength performance moves significantly ahead of female strength performance. Ransdell and Wells (in press) calculated performance ratios and percentage differences in performance for bench press in the Teenage and Open Divisions of the Natural Athletic Strength Association (drug-free training and competition). The teenage girls' performance averaged 70 percent of the teenage

TABLE 13.6 Anaerobic Power of Trained and Moderately Active Adolescent Males

Sport or Activity	Level[a]	Age (y)	Peak Power (W)[b]	PP:BM[c] (W • kg^{-1})	PP: FFM[d] (W • kgFFM^{-1})	Reference
Moderately Active	—	14.5	579.3 (L)	—	—	Blimkie et al. (1986)
		15.6	679.0 (L)	—	—	
		16.5	774.9 (L)	—	—	
Moderately Active	—	16.2	833.0 (L)	13.2	—	Falk & Bar-Or (1993)
Long Distance Runners	E	13.8	614.0 (L)	10.1	11.3	Tharp et al. (1984)
Middle-Distance Runners	E	14.8	483.0 (L)	9.1	—	Thorland et al. (1990)
Sprinters	E	15.0	574.0 (L)	8.4	9.9	Thorland et al. (1990)

[a]Levels of performance: E = Elite, S = Scholastic
[b]Anaerobic Power Test (L = leg ergometry)
[c]Ratio of peak power to body mass
[d]Ratio of peak power to fat free mass

boys' performance for a percentage difference of 30 percent in the 52 kilogram through 82.5 kilogram weight classes. In the Open Division, the women's performance was 55 percent of the men's (same weight classes) for a percentage difference of 45 percent. Presumably these sex differences in strength occur because of differences in body composition, notably the increased muscular development and lean body mass of the male. Because boys have about two more years of growth than girls, sex differences in strength increase with maturity.

Tables 13.7 and 13.8 present the men's and women's American records of the U.S. Powerlifting Federation Junior Division. Results are shown for two lifts from seven common weight classes in the 14 to 15 and 16 to 17 age groups. The bench press requires predominantly upper body strength, a variable in which men notably dominate women. The squat requires predominantly leg and lower body strength, a variable in which sex differences are generally less evident. Several impressions can be gleaned from tables 13.7 and 13.8. First, and not surprisingly, both absolute strength and relative strength (weight lifted per kg body weight) increase with advanced maturity in both sexes. Second, percentage difference in performance changed very little across these age groups at this level of training—which implies that the increase in strength was approximately the same for each sex. For the squat, the mean percentage difference in performance was 37.5 percent in the 14 to 15 age group (excluding the unusual performance in the 52 kg weight class) and 35.7 percent in the 16 to 17 age group. For the bench press, the mean percentage difference in performance was 46.4 percent for the 14- to 15-year-olds and 46.5 percent for the 16- to 17-year-olds. Third, as these mean values point out, the female athletes were stronger relative to the males in the squat than in the bench press.

TABLE 13.7 Sex Differences in U.S. Powerlifting Federation American Records, Men's and Women's Junior Division, ages 14–15 (as of 11/12/93)

Weight Class (kg) and Event	Weight Lifted Men (kg)	Weight Lifted Women (kg)	Performance Ratio (W:M)	Percentage Difference	Weight Lifted per kg BW (Men)	Weight Lifted per kg BW (Women)
52.0						
Squat	138	125	91	9	2.65	2.40
Bench	120	75	63	37	2.31	1.44
56.0						
Squat	183	123	67	33	3.27	2.20
Bench	103	68	66	34	1.84	1.21
60.0						
Squat	215	128	60	40	3.58	2.13
Bench	123	63	51	49	2.05	1.05
67.5						
Squat	210	133	63	37	3.11	1.97
Bench	148	73	49	51	2.19	1.08
75.0						
Squat	240	140	58	42	3.20	1.87
Bench	144	70	47	53	1.92	.93
82.5						
Squat	215	143	67	33	2.61	1.73
Bench	135	73	54	46	1.64	.88
90.0						
Squat	231	138	60	40	2.57	1.53
Bench	141	63	45	55	1.57	.70

Performance ratio $= \dfrac{\text{Women's record}}{\text{Men's record}} \times 100$

Percentage difference $= \dfrac{\text{Men's record} - \text{Women's record}}{\text{Men's record}} \times 100$

Differences in Swimming Performance

Table 13.9 presents current U.S. national records for the 13- to 14- and 15- to 16-year-old age groups, plus percentage differences and performance ratios for swimming speed. The table reveals very little sex difference in swimming performance at these ages, with smaller percentage differences and larger performance ratios than for fully mature swimmers as reported by Ransdell and Wells (in press). Nevertheless, the greater height and longer arms and legs of the adolescent male provide a morphological advantage by providing more projection over the water at the

TABLE 13.8 Sex Differences in U.S. Powerlifting Federation American Records, Men's and Women's Junior Division, ages 16–17 (as of 11/12/93)

Weight Class (kg) and Event	Weight Lifted Men (kg)	Weight Lifted Women (kg)	Performance Ratio (W:M)	Percentage Difference	Weight Lifted per kg BW (Men)	Weight Lifted per kg BW (Women)
52.0						
Squat	181	123	68	32	3.48	2.37
Bench	128	75	59	41	2.46	1.44
56.0						
Squat	198	151	76	24	3.54	2.70
Bench	128	81	63	37	2.29	1.45
60.0						
Squat	250	148	59	41	4.17	2.47
Bench	138	77	56	44	2.30	1.28
67.5						
Squat	255	155	61	39	3.78	2.30
Bench	160	95	59	41	2.37	1.41
75.0						
Squat	265	173	65	35	3.53	2.31
Bench	173	88	51	49	2.31	1.17
82.5						
Squat	275	170	62	38	3.33	2.06
Bench	183	93	51	49	2.22	1.13
90.0						
Squat	283	168	59	41	3.14	1.87
Bench	193	68	35	65	2.14	.76

$$\text{Performance ratio} = \frac{\text{Women's record}}{\text{Men's record}} \times 100$$

$$\text{Percentage difference} = \frac{\text{Men's record} - \text{Women's record}}{\text{Men's record}} \times 100$$

start and a longer reach at the finish of a race. The male's larger muscle mass also provides more explosive power off the starting blocks. The male's larger $\dot{V}O_2$max provides an advantage for the middle-distance (400m free) and longer races. However, as in adult (open) performance, sex differences in middle-distance swimming performance are less than at sprint distances. As shown here, sex differences in performance for 400-meter through 1,500-meter freestyle swimming are very small for adolescent swimmers—less than 5 percent.

In the adult open division, sex differences in performance are closer to 7 or 8 percent. Note that the current 1,500-meter freestyle U.S. age-group record for 15- to

TABLE 13.9 Sex Differences in Swimming Events, U.S. National Age-Group Records (as of 10/12/93)

Age	Event	Women's Record (minutes)	Men's Record (minutes)	Women's Speed (meters per second)	Men's Speed (meters per second)	Percentage Difference	Performance Ratio
13–14	100m Free	0:56.61	0:51.59	1.77	1.94	9	91
	400m Free	4:07.15	4:03.20	1.62	1.64	2	98
	800m Free	8:29.35	8:22.99	1.57	1.59	2	98
	1,500m Free	16:12.57	15:31.03	1.54	1.61	4	96
15–16	100m Free	0:55.63	0:50.24	1.80	1.99	10	90
	400m Free	4:05.45	3:53.69	1.63	1.71	5	95
	800m Free	8:17.12	8:00.71	1.61	1.66	3	97
	1,500m Free	15:52.10	15:16.10	1.58	1.64	4	96

$$\text{Percentage difference} = \frac{\text{Men's speed (m} \cdot \text{s}^{-1}) - \text{Women's speed (m} \cdot \text{s}^{-1})}{\text{Men's speed (m} \cdot \text{s}^{-1})} \times 100$$

$$\text{Performance ratio} = \frac{\text{Women's speed (m} \cdot \text{s}^{-1})}{\text{Men's speed (m} \cdot \text{s}^{-1})} \times 100$$

16-year-old women is also the current women's world record! It is notable that Olympic swimming teams often have outstanding young women who are only 13 to 16 years of age. The men's teams are usually older.

Differences in Running Performance

U.S. national age-group records for a full range of running events are given in table 13.10 for 14-, 15-, and 16-year-olds. The percentage differences and performance ratios for running speed are very similar for fully mature runners (as reported by Ransdell & Wells, in press). In running, there is less sex difference in performance at the sprint distances than at middle (1,500 m) or long distances (10,000 m and 42 km). The male's larger muscle mass, lesser percentage of body fat, and higher $\dot{V}O_2$max provide him with greater driving force and higher oxidative capacity than the female of comparable age. However, these outstanding performances illustrate that biological differences between the sexes do not result in large performance differences either in adolescence or at full maturity.

Effects of the Menstrual Cycle on Athletic Performance

The menstrual cycle is the single most unique function of the human female. It is the only function that is completely unmatched by the male. The maturation of the reproductive system and the onset of the menstrual cycle is surely the most significant physiological event of puberty. From just before menarche (the first

TABLE 13.10 Sex Differences in Track Events, U.S. National Age-Group Records (as of 1/22/94)

Age	Event	Women's Record	Men's Record	Women's Speed (m • sec^{-1})	Men's Speed (m • sec^{-1})	Percentage Difference[a]	Performance Ratio[b]
14	100m	0:11.62	0:10.64	8.60	9.39	8	92
	400m	0:53.82	0:47.16	7.43	8.48	12	88
	800m	2:02.43	1:55.90	6.53	6.90	5	95
	1,500m	4:24.17	4:04.10	5.67	6.14	8	92
	5,000m	16:43.47	15:46.80	4.98	5.28	6	94
	10,000m	40:22.60	32:46.00	4.12	5.08	19	81
	42km	2.50:21	2.31:24	4.12	4.64	11	89
15	100m	0:11.17	0:10.46	8.95	9.56	6	94
	400m	0:51.70	0:46.55	7.73	8.59	10	90
	800m	2:02.29	1:57.03	6.54	7.20	9	91
	1,500m	4:19.80	3:51.50	5.77	6.47	11	89
	5,000m	16:34.70	14:32.80	5.02	5.72	12	88
	10,000m	34:01.10	31:43.20	4.89	5.25	7	93
	42km	2.46:23	2.29:11	4.22	4.71	10	90
16	100m	0:11.14	0:10.27	8.97	9.73	8	92
	400m	0:51.45	0:45.40	7.77	8.81	12	88
	800m	2:03.54	1:48.44	6.47	7.37	12	88
	1,500m	4:16.80	3:48.30	5.84	6.57	11	89
	5,000m	16:14.69	14:12.30	5.12	5.86	13	87
	10,000m	33:26.53	29:27.2	4.98	5.65	12	88
	42km	2.34:24	2.23:47	4.55	4.89	7	93

Percentage difference $= \dfrac{\text{Men's speed (m • s}^{-1}) - \text{Women's speed (m • s}^{-1})}{\text{Men's speed (m • s}^{-1})} \times 100$

Performance ratio $= \dfrac{\text{Women's speed (m • s}^{-1})}{\text{Men's speed (m • s}^{-1})} \times 100$

Acknowledgment. Information from table 13.10 (Sex Differences in Track Events, U.S. National Age-Group Records) was excerpted from "High School Track 1994," compiled, edited, and published by Jack Shepard, Men's High School Editor for *Track and Field News.*

menstrual period) through menopause (the last menstrual period), the woman's hormonal environment is characterized by cyclic fluctuations that result in numerous and significant changes in various target organs and tissues. During this time she is capable of maintaining a pregnancy should fertilization of an ovum occur. This section briefly describes how the three phases of the menstrual cycle differ from one another and, further, examines how these different phases affect athletic performance. We will first examine how the menstrual cycle influences physiological variables known to be important to performance and then examine whether the menstrual cycle enhances or hinders athletic performance.

The Menstrual Cycle

The menstrual cycle, which lasts approximately 28 days (but may vary from 20 to 38 days), is divided into three distinct phases. *Menses,* which occurs from days 1 through 4 to 7, is menstrual bleeding that sheds the endometrial lining when the ovum is not fertilized and no need exists to provide a rich environment for growth of a fetus. This phase is characterized by low levels of the steroid hormones, estrogen and progesterone, from the ovary. The *follicular phase* occurs from approximately day 5 until ovulation occurs on approximately day 14 or 15. This phase is characterized by the proliferation of tissues lining the endometrium (the beginning of the uterine cycle) and by maturation of a primary follicle in the ovary (the ovarian cycle). The follicular phase occurs under the direct influence of the gonadotropins from the pituitary gland, follicle stimulating hormone (FSH) and luteinizing hormone (LH). As the follicle develops, it secretes increasing amounts of estrogen, which eventually stimulates the LH surge resulting in ovulation. The *luteal phase* begins following ovulation and lasts until menstrual flow begins (approximately days 15 through 28). During this phase, there is continued growth and development of the endometrial layer in preparation for the implantation of a fertilized ovum. This includes the development of secretory glands and the storage of glycogen in the endometrial lining. The ruptured follicle becomes the corpus luteum, which secretes progesterone, the dominant hormone of this phase. If fertilization does not occur, the corpus luteum regresses and hormone secretion plummets. Without hormonal support, the rich endometrial lining can no longer be supported. It gradually collapses, which results in menstrual bleeding, and the cycle begins over again. Table 13.11 and figure 13.1 illustrate the plasma hormone concentrations and endometrial and ovarian changes characteristic of each menstrual phase.

Many biological variables show a regularly repeating pattern or periodicity. Most *biological rhythms* show a 24-hour or circadian rhythm, but some, besides those already described, show a circalunar or 28-day variability in accordance with the menstrual cycle. The variable to show the most consistent circalunar rhythm is basal body temperature, which is elevated during the luteal phase. Other variables that *may* show a circalunar periodicity include the following:

- Weight gain late in the luteal phase
- Hyperemia of the breast with a corresponding increase in breast volume late in the luteal phase
- Increased capillary and red blood cell fragility, and decreased hemoglobin concentration (Hb) and red blood cell count during menses
- Increased resting respiratory minute volume ($\dot{V}_E$) in the luteal phase

However, the 14- to 16-year-old female athlete may not experience many, if any, of these periodic variations because her menstrual cycle may still be irregular in occurrence and is often anovulatory. The periodicity described exists only when there are distinct hormonal differences among phases, and particularly when there is

TABLE 13.11 Characteristics of the Menstrual Cycle Phases

Phase of Cycle	Events	Hormonal Environment
Menses		
(Days 1 through 4–7)	*Uterus* Menstrual bleeding Shedding of endometrial lining	Low estrogen Low progesterone Low LH
	Ovary Disintegration of corpus luteum	Low FSH
Follicular Phase		
(Days 4 through ovulation on approximately days 14–16)	*Uterus* Proliferation of endometrial lining	Rising FSH Rising estrogen levels
	Ovary Development of mature follicle Secretion of increasing amounts of estrogen Ovulation	LH surge (sharp rise just prior to ovulation)
Luteal Phase		
(From ovulation until 1st day of flow, approximately days 15 to 28)	*Uterus* Development of secretory glands in endometrium	High progesterone High estrogen (until final days)
	Ovary Formation of corpus luteum	

high plasma progesterone in the luteal phase. Anovulatory menstrual cycles do not display distinct hormonal fluctuations. No data are available on phase periodicity in the adolescent girl.

Effect of the Menstrual Cycle on Physiological Variables Important to Athletic Performance

What little is known about menstrual cycle periodicity and variables known to be of importance to athletic performance has been gleaned from the study of fully adult women. These factors simply have not been studied in the younger female athlete.

Basal Body Temperature and Responses to Heat Stress

The elevation in basal body temperature during the luteal phase is thought to reflect a higher hypothalamic "set point" and to cause a delay in the sweating response in women exposed to high environmental temperatures during their luteal phase. However, numerous studies have failed to show menstrual phase differences in body core or mean skin temperatures, body heat content, sweating rate, evaporative heat

FIGURE 13.1

Plasma hormone concentrations, endometrial and ovarian changes, and basal body temperatures characteristic of each menstrual phase.

Note: Adapted from "Menstruation" by M. M. Shangold, in *Women and Exercise: Physiology and Sports Medicine* (p. 132) by M. M. Shangold and G. Mirkin (Eds.), 1988, Philadelphia: F. A. Davis, Copyright 1988 by F. A. Davis Co., adapted from *Human Physiology: The Mechanisms of Body Function* (4th Ed., p. 572) by A. J. Vander, J. H. Sherman, and D. S. Luciano, 1985, New York: McGraw-Hill, copyright 1985 by McGraw-Hill, Inc. Adapted by permission of McGraw-Hill, Inc.; adapted from *Women, Sport & Performance: A Physiological Perspective* (2nd Ed., p. 65) by C. L. Wells, 1991, Champaign, IL: Human Kinetics Publishers, copyright 1991 by Human Kinetics Publishers. Adapted by permission of Human Kinetics Publishers.

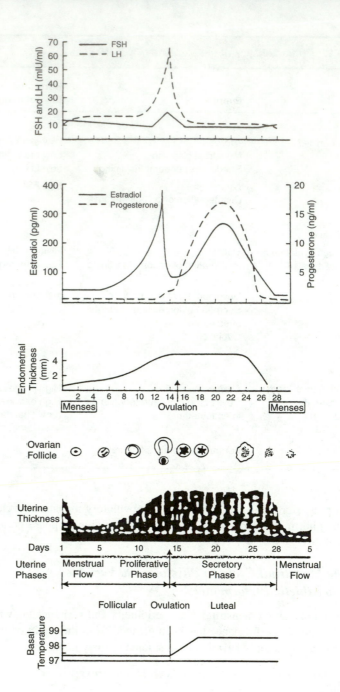

loss, oxygen uptake, ventilation volume, or oxygen pulse (oxygen uptake per heart beat) during exercise (Horvath & Drinkwater, 1982; Wells, 1977; Wells & Horvath, 1973, 1974). In addition, no differences were found, either before or after heat acclimation, in amenorrheic women (absent menstrual cycles) or women with normal menstrual cycles (Frye, Kamon, & Webb, 1982). Thus, no grounds exist to believe that the menstrual cycle affects temperature regulation during exercise in postmenarcheal athletes.

Respiratory Ventilation ($\dot{V}_E$)

Progesterone stimulates ventilatory drive and elevates $\dot{V}_E$ during pregnancy and the luteal phase of the menstrual cycle. In normally menstruating trained and sedentary subjects, exercise ventilation was elevated in the luteal phase (Schoene et al., 1981), but highly trained athletes showed a blunted response compared to other subjects. At 55 percent and 80 percent of maximal performance, Williams (1992) reported that highly trained young adult runners had elevated luteal phase $\dot{V}_E$ values. Other studies have failed to show a difference in $\dot{V}_E$ with menstrual phase (Eston & Burke, 1984; Hall-Jurkowski et al., 1981; Stephenson, Kolka, & Wilkerson, 1982).

Maximal Aerobic Power and Performance Economy

Two investigations of maximal aerobic power ($\dot{V}O_2$max) relative to menstrual cycle phase have been conducted, one in college athletes (Allsen, Parsons, & Bryce, 1977) and the other in amenorrheic and regularly menstruating athletes (Schoene et al., 1981). Neither reported cyclic differences in $\dot{V}O_2$max with menstrual phase. In addition, performance economy ($\dot{V}O_2$submax) at various menstrual phases has been examined during bicycle ergometry and running. No cyclic differences were found (Lamont, 1986; Schoene et al., 1981; Williams, 1992). Table 13.12 summarizes the preceding information on physiological variables important to athletic performance.

Effect of the Menstrual Cycle on Athletic Performance

Considering the interest in physiological variability occurring with the menstrual cycle, it is surprising so few objective investigations of athletic performance have been done. Brooks-Gunn, Gargiulo, and Warren (1986) carried out the only well-controlled study on performance in adolescent athletes (mean age 16 ± 1.4 years). They timed six menstruating national-level swimmers in 100-yard freestyle and their 100-yard "best event" twice a week for 12 weeks. Average performance times were calculated for the entire menstrual cycle, the follicular phase (a 10-day period after flow stopped), the luteal phase (a 4-day period before onset of flow), and menses. For four of the swimmers, fastest times occurred during menses, and slowest times occurred during the luteal phase. Basal body temperature (BBT) was obtained to verify menstrual phase. For two girls, BBT did *not* show the characteristic rise during the luteal phase indicating that their cycles were anovulatory.

Other investigators have reported no periodic differences in objectively measured performance in menstruating athletes. In highly trained college swimmers, Quadagno et al. (1991) reported no menstrual phase differences in repeated time trials for 100-meter and 200-meter freestyle. Schoene et al. (1981) reported no differences in time to exhaustion on a bicycle ergometer with menstrual phase in trained young adult women.

TABLE 13.12 The Effect of the Menstrual Cycle on Physiological Variables Important to Athletic Performance

Variables	Subjects	Results	Exercise Mode	Phase Verification	Reference
Strength	Young adult recreational weight lifters	No cyclic difference in strength	Bench and Leg Press	C	Quadagno et al. (1991)
$\dot{V}_E$	Sedentary and trained young adult women	Increased in both non-athletes and athletes during luteal phase but no significant effect on performance	BE to Exhaustion	T	Schoene et al. (1981)
$\dot{V}_E$	Highly trained young adult women runners	Higher in runners during midluteal phase (in comparison to early follicular phase)	Submax Exercise on Treadmill (55 and 80% of $\dot{V}O_2$max)	H	Williams (1992)
$\dot{V}O_2$max	Highly trained college athletes	No cyclic difference in college athletes	TM run	C	Allsen et al. (1977)
$\dot{V}O_2$max	Sedentary and trained young adult women	No cyclic difference in nonathletes or athletes	BE to Exhaustion	T	Schoene et al. (1981)
$\dot{V}O_2$submax	Sedentary and trained young adult women	No cyclic difference in nonathletes or athletes	BE to Exhaustion	T	Schoene et al. (1981)
$\dot{V}O_2$submax	Sedentary and active young adult women	No cyclic difference in active and untrained women	BE: 60 minutes, 70% of $\dot{V}O_2$max	H	Lamont (1986)
$\dot{V}O_2$submax	Highly trained young adult women runners	Athletes showed no cyclic difference in running economy	Submax Exercise on Treadmill (55 and 80% $\dot{V}O_2$max)	H	Williams (1992)

Table adapted from Wells (1991), pp. 79–80.

Note. TM = treadmill, BE = bicycle ergometer, C = calendar day, T = oral temperature chart, H = hormonal analysis, $\dot{V}O_2$max = maximum oxygen uptake, $\dot{V}_E$ = minute ventilation volume.

Many women claim they experience variations in body weight, breast tenderness, bloating, psychological mood and motivation, food cravings, ability to concentrate and make decisions, and incidence of headaches and backache with menstrual phase. In most instances, these "subjective complaints" are not verified by statistically significant findings when studied "objectively." In nearly all instances, between-subject variance exceeds within-subject variance, resulting in nonsignificant findings. The few athletes who truly experience cyclic variations in either their physical or mental well-being, particularly those who experience dysmenorrhea (painful menses) or premenstrual syndrome (weight gain, bloating, headache, mood shifts, etcetera late in the luteal phase), should consult a specialist in sport gynecology or endocrinology. We conclude that there is little need to adjust training or competition schedules because of the menstrual cycle.

Effects of Athletic Training on Menstrual Function

Considerable documentation supports that highly trained young women athletes in their 20s and 30s have a higher prevalence of menstrual dysfunction than the nonathletic population (Drinkwater, Bruemner, & Chesnut, 1990; Loucks et al., 1992; Wells, 1991). Although the prevalence of menstrual dysfunction in young adolescent athletes is unknown, they are considered particularly vulnerable because their reproductive systems have not fully matured. In many instances, menarche may have occurred in this population at a later age than in the nonathletic population (for a full discussion of this topic see chapter 11 by Malina, this volume); thus, the athletes described here may have a lower gynecological age (years between menarche and menopause) than their nonathletic counterparts. No doubt exists that heavy exercise stresses the hypothalamic-pituitary-ovarian (and adrenal) axes sufficiently to influence circulating levels of gonadotropic and ovarian hormones. Various menstrual irregularities such as luteal phase deficiency, anovulatory cycles, oligomenorrhea (irregular menses), and full-blown amenorrhea (menses less than three times per year) may result. Full descriptions of these menstrual dysfunctions are beyond the scope of this chapter but can be found in Wells (1991) or Shangold (1988).

Who Is at Risk for Athletic Menstrual Dysfunction?

Although the basic cause of athletic menstrual dysfunction is unknown, several associated factors are well documented. These include low gynecological and chronological age, a strenuous training regimen, and nutritional insufficiency (low caloric intake with/without low protein intake). The latter two factors have been coupled into a general model often referred to as "energy drain," which relates to excessive energy expenditure relative to energy intake (Warren, 1983; Wells & Gilman, 1990). An adolescent driven to excel in a demanding sport may be at particular risk for developing poor nutritional habits leading to disordered eating. At this age, major morphological changes may take place very rapidly. Many pubertal athletes are faced with rapid weight gain and increases in breast volume and gluteal-thigh subcutaneous fat characteristic of adult maturity. These athletes' lithe, relatively undeveloped bodies suddenly become cumbersome. Some respond by adopting severe dietary practices, including disordered eating behaviors such as anorexia nervosa and bulimia. Athletes who participate in sports in which a lean physique and low body fat are considered advantageous (gymnastics, ballet, figure skating, distance running) appear to be at highest risk. Pathogenic weight-control behaviors have been reported in 15 percent to 62 percent of young female athletes (Dummer et al., 1987; Rosen et al., 1986), and nutritional deficiencies are not uncommon (Loosli & Benson, 1990). Athletes with menstrual dysfunction often have a very low percentage of body fat, but this characteristic should be considered a symptom rather than mistaken as the "cause" or root of the problem.

Is Athletic Menstrual Dysfunction Harmful?

Adult oligomenorrheic and amenorrheic athletes are characterized by low levels of circulating ovarian and gonadotrophic hormones (Drinkwater et al., 1984; Loucks,

1986; Loucks & Horvath, 1985; Marcus et al., 1985). Baer (1993) recently verified that adolescent amenorrheic runners are similarly deficient in estrogen and gonadotrophic hormones.

Athletic menstrual dysfunction appears to have no lasting effect on future reproductive function. With reduction or discontinuation of training, menstruation usually resumes in two months or less, and anecdotal evidence suggests that formerly amenorrheic athletes are fully capable of bearing children. Thus, athletic menstrual dysfunction does not appear to be harmful to reproductive function.

However, all forms of athletic menstrual dysfunction, but particularly amenorrhea, are characterized by *hypoestrogenemia*. Normal levels of estrogen are essential for the normal deposition of bone mineral in the bone matrix. From puberty on, inadequate estrogen exposure is followed by a net loss of bone mineral (osteopenia) and a thinning of bone tissue (Chestnut, 1984; Dhuper et al., 1990; Drinkwater et al., 1990; Emans et al., 1990). This puts athletes with menstrual dysfunction at increased risk for low bone mineral content of both trabecular (cancellous bone of the spine and ends of long bones) and cortical bone (compact bone of the appendicular skeleton) (Myburgh et al., 1993). In addition, there is evidence that peak bone mineral density, a factor thought to be highly predictive of osteoporosis, occurs at a much earlier age than previously thought and may correspond with cessation of longitudinal growth and epiphyseal closure (Gilsanz et al., 1988). Thus the most important complication of athletic menstrual dysfunction is loss of bone mineral mass and increased risk for low peak bone mineral density and early postmenopausal osteoporosis. Several studies have verified that with return of menses, bone mineral density improves but remains below mean age-group levels (Drinkwater et al., 1986; Jonnavithula et al., 1993; Lindberg et al., 1987); thus, amenorrheic athletes may have compromised bone mineral density throughout the remainder of their lives.

Lloyd et al. (1986) was one of the first to document that athletes with menstrual disorders had more musculoskeletal injuries than athletes with regular menses. Warren et al. (1986) reported that young amenorrheic ballerinas had an exceptionally high prevalence of scoliosis and stress fractures and described femoral head collapse in a 20-year-old with an eating disorder and hypoestrogenism dating from age 13 (Warren et al., 1990). Femur fractures have been described in hypoestrogenic athletes of varying ages (Dugowson, Drinkwater, & Clark, 1991; Kadel, Teitz, & Kvonmal, 1992; Leinberry et al., 1992).

Athletic menstrual dysfunction should be considered an acute risk to long-term health. Parents, coaches, and physicians must recognize the connection between inadequate dietary intake, the high stress of intensive training, menstrual dysfunction, and musculoskeletal injury. Prevention and early identification are the best treatments for athletic menstrual dysfunction. Once identified, a multidisciplinary network of professionals should be utilized to plan and implement treatment (Nattiv, 1994).

References

Allsen, P. E., Parsons, P., & Bryce, G. R. (1977). Effect of the menstrual cycle on maximum oxygen uptake. *The Physician and Sportsmedicine, 5*(7), 53–55.

Amo, S. (1990). The A angle: A quantitative measurement of patella alignment and realignment. *The Journal of Orthopedic and Sports Physical Therapy, 12*(6), 237–242.

Armstrong, N., Williams, J., Balding, J., Gentle, P., & Kirby, B. (1991). The peak oxygen uptake of British children with reference to age, sex, and sexual maturity. *European Journal of Applied Physiology, 62*(5), 369–375.

Astrand, P. -O., Cuddy, T. E., Saltin, B., & Stenberg, J. (1964). Cardiac output during submaximal and maximal work. *Journal of Applied Physiology, 19,* 268–274.

Astrand, P. -O., & Rodahl, K. (1977). *Textbook of work physiology* (2nd ed.). New York: McGraw-Hill.

Atwater, A. E. (1990). Gender differences in distance running. In P. Cavanagh (Ed.), *Biomechanics of distance running* (pp. 321–361). Champaign, IL: Human Kinetics.

Baer, J. T. (1993). Endocrine parameters in amenorrheic and eumenorrheic adolescent female runners. *International Journal of Sports Medicine, 14,* 191–195.

Bar-Or, O. (1983). *Pediatric sports medicine for the practitioner.* New York: Springer-Verlag.

Beals, R. K. (1976). The normal carrying angle of the elbow. *Clinical Orthopaedics, 119,* 194–196.

Binkhorst, R. A., de jong-van de Kar, M. C., & Vissers, C. A. (1981). Growth and aerobic power of boys aged 11–19 years. In J. Ilmarinen & I. Valimaki (Eds.), *Children and sport* (pp. 99–105). Berlin: Springer-Verlag.

Blimkie, C. J. R., Roche, P., & Bar-Or, O. (1986). The anaerobic-to-aerobic power ratio in adolescent boys and girls. In J. Rutenfranz, R. Mocellin, & F. Klimt (Eds.), *Children and exercise XII* (pp. 31–37). Champaign, IL: Human Kinetics.

Brooks-Gunn, J., Gargiulo, J. M., & Warren, M. P. (1986). The effect of cycle phase on the performance of adolescent swimmers. *The Physician and Sportsmedicine, 14*(3), 182–192.

Bunc, V., & Heller, J. (1993). Ventilatory threshold in young and adult female athletes. *Journal of Sports Medicine and Physical Fitness, 33*(3), 233–238.

Burke, E. R., & Brush, F. C. (1979). Physiological and anthropometric assessment of successful teenage female distance runners. *Research Quarterly for Exercise and Sport, 50,* 180–187.

Butts, N. K. (1982). Physiological profiles of high school female cross-country runners. *Research Quarterly for Exercise and Sport, 53,* 8–14.

Chestnut, C. H., III. (1984). Treatment of postmenopausal osteoporosis. *Comprehensive Therapy, 10,* 41–47.

Clarkson, P. M., Freedson, P. S., Keller, B., Carney, D., & Skrinar, M. (1985). Maximal oxygen uptake, nutritional patterns and body composition of adolescent female ballet dancers. *Research Quarterly for Exercise and Sport, 56,* 180–184.

Cox, J. S. (1985). Patellofemoral problems in runners. *Clinics in Sports Medicine, 4,* 699–707.

Cross, M. J., & Crichton, K. J. (1987). *Clinical examination of the injured knee.* Baltimore: Wilkins and Wilkins.

Cunningham, L. N. (1990). Relationship of running economy, ventilatory threshold, and maximal oxygen consumption to running performance in high school females. *Research Quarterly for Exercise and Sport, 61*(4), 369–374.

Cunningham, D. A., & Eynon, R. B. (1973). The working capacity of young competitive swimmers, 10–16 years of age. *Medicine and Science in Sports, 5,* 227–231.

DeVries, H. (1980). *Physiology of exercise for physical education and athletics* (3rd ed.), Dubuque, IA: Wm. C. Brown.

Dhuper, S., Warren, M. P., Brooks-Gunn, J., & Fox, R. (1990). Effects of hormonal status on bone density in adolescent girls. *Journal of Clinical Endocrinology and Metabolism, 71,* 1083–1088.

Drinkwater, B. L., Bruemner, B., & Chestnut, C. H., III. (1990). Menstrual history as a determinant of current bone density in young athletes. *Journal of the American Medical Association, 263,* 545–548.

Drinkwater, B. L., & Horvath, S. M. (1971). Responses of young female track athletes to exercise. *Medicine and Science in Sports, 3,* 91–95.

Drinkwater, B. L., Nilson, K., Chestnut, C. H., III, Bruemner, W. J., Shainholtz, S., & Southworth, M. B. (1984). Bone mineral content of amenorrheic and eumenorrheic athletes. *New England Journal of Medicine, 311,* 277–281.

Drinkwater, B. L., Nilson, K., Ott, S., & Chestnut, C. H., III. (1986). Bone mineral density after resumption of menses in amenorrheic athletes. *Journal of the American Medical Association, 256*(3), 380–382.

Dugowson, C. E., Drinkwater, B. L., & Clark, J. M. (1991). Nontraumatic femur fracture in an oligomenorrheic athlete. *Medicine and Science in Sports and Exercise, 23,* 1323–1325.

Dummer, G. M., Rosen, L. W., Heusner, W. W., Roberts, P. J., & Counsilman, J. E. (1987). Pathogenic weight-control behaviors of young competitive swimmers. *The Physician and Sportsmedicine 15*(5), 75–84.

Emans, S. J., Grace, E., Hoffer, F. A., Gundberg, C., Ravnikar, V., & Woods, E. R. (1990). Estrogen deficiency in adolescents and young adults: Impact on bone mineral content and effects of estrogen replacement therapy. *Obstetrics and Gynecology, 76,* 585–592.

Eston, R. G., & Burke, E. J. (1984). Effects of the menstrual cycle on selected responses to short constant-load exercise. *Journal of Sports Sciences, 2,* 145–153.

Falk, B., & Bar-Or, O. (1993). Longitudinal changes in peak aerobic and anaerobic mechanical power of circumpubertal boys. *Pediatric Exercise Science, 5,* 318–331.

Forbes, G. B. (1972). Growth of the lean body mass in man. *Growth, 36,* 325.

Francis, P. R. (1988). Injury prevention through biomechanical screening: Implications for female athletes. In J. L. Puhl, C. H. Brown, & R. O. Voy. (Eds.), *Sport science perspectives for women* (pp. 97–110). Champaign, IL: Human Kinetics.

Frye, A. L., Kamon, E., & Webb, M. (1982). Responses of menstrual women, amenorrheal women, and men to exercise in a hot, dry environment. *European Journal of Applied Physiology, 48,* 279–288.

Gastembebe, D. G. (1993). *The Q angle and patellofemoral dysfunction in men and women athletes.* Unpublished master's thesis, Arizona State University, Tempe.

Gilsanz, V., Gibbens, D. T., Carlson, M., Boechat, M. I., Cann, C. E., & Schulz, E. E. (1988). Peak trabecular vertebral density: A comparison of adolescent and adult females. *Calcified Tissue International, 43,* 260–262.

Goldberg, V. (1989, November 29). Women warned of possible injury if early workouts are too intense. *NCAA News, 41,* 18.

Haan, A. L. (1979). *An anthropometrical and physiological study of outstanding female swimmers.* Unpublished master's thesis, Arizona State University, Tempe.

Hall-Jurkowski, J. E., Jones, N. L., Toews, C. J., & Sutton, J. R. (1981). Effects of the menstrual cycle on blood lactate, oxygen delivery and performance during exercise. *Journal of Applied Physiology: Respiratory, Environmental and Exercise Physiology, 51,* 1493–1499.

Haubenstricker, J. L., & Seefeldt, V. (1986). Acquisition of motor skills during childhood. In V. Seefeldt (Ed.), *Physical activity and well-being* (pp. 41–102). Reston, VA: American Alliance for Health, Physical Education, Recreation and Dance.

Haywood, K. M. (1993). *Life span motor development* (2nd ed.). Champaign, IL: Human Kinetics.

Horvath, S. M., & Drinkwater, B. L. (1982). Thermoregulation and the menstrual cycle. *Aviation, Space, and Environmental Medicine, 53,* 790–794.

Housh, T. J., Johnson, G. O., & House, D. J. (1991). Muscular power of high school wrestlers. *Pediatric Exercise Science, 3,* 43–48.

Housh, T. J., Highes, R. J., Johnson, G. O., Housh, D. J., Wagner, L. L., Weir, J. P., & Evans, S. A. (1990). Age-related increases in shoulder strength of high school wrestlers. *Pediatric Exercise Science, 2,* 65–72.

Housh, T. J., Thorland, W. G., Johnson, G. O., Tharp, G. D., Cisar, C. J., Refsell, M. J., & Ansorge, C. J. (1984). Body composition variables as discriminators of sports participation of elite adolescent athletes. *Research Quarterly for Exercise and Sport, 55,* 302–304.

Hunter, L. Y. (1988). The frequency of injuries in women's sports. In J. L. Puhl, C. H. Brown, & R. O. Voy (Eds.), *Sport science perspectives for women* (pp. 49–58). Champaign, IL.: Human Kinetics.

Jonnavithula, S., Warren, M. P., Fox, R. P., & Lazaro, M. I. (1993). Bone density is compromised in amenorrheic women despite return of menses: A 2-year study. *Obstetrics and Gynecology, 81,* 669–674.

Joyner, M. J. (1993). Physiological limiting factors and distance running: Influence of gender and age in record performance. *Exercise and Sport Sciences Reviews, 21,* 103–133.

Kadel, N. J., Teitz, C. C., & Kronmal, R. A. (1992). Stress fractures in ballet dancers. *The American Journal of Sports Medicine, 20,* 445–449.

Katch, F. I., & McArdle, W. D. (1975). Validity of body composition prediction equations for college men and women. *American Journal of Clinical Nutrition, 28,* 105–109.

Lamont, L. S. (1986). Lack of influence of the menstrual cycle on blood lactate. *The Physician and Sportsmedicine, 14*(11), 159–163.

Leinberry, C. F., McShane, R. B., Stewart, W. G., & Hume, E. L. (1992). A displaced subtrochanteric stress fracture in a young amenorrheic athlete. *The American Journal of Sports Medicine, 20*, 485–487.

Lindberg, J. S., Powell, M. R., Hunt, M. M., Ducey, D. E., & Wade, C. E. (1987). Increased vertebral bone mineral in response to reduced exercise in amenorrheic runners. *Western Journal of Medicine, 146*, 39–42.

Lloyd, T., Triantafyllou, S. J., Baker, E. R., Houts, P. S., Whiteside, J. A., Kalenak, A., & Stumpf, P. G. (1986). Women athletes with menstrual irregularity have increased musculoskeletal injuries. *Medicine and Science in Sports and Exercise, 18*, 374–379.

Loosli, A. R., & Benson, J. (1990). Nutritional intake in adolescent athletes. *Pediatric Clinics of North America, 37*, 1143–1163.

Loucks, A. B. (1986). Does exercise training affect reproductive hormones in women? *Clinics in Sports Medicine, 5*, 535–557.

Loucks, A. B., & Horvath, S. M. (1985). Athletic amenorrhea: A review. *Medicine and Science in Sports and Exercise, 17*, 56–72.

Loucks, A. B., Vaitukaitis, J., Cameron, J. L., Rogol, A. D., Skrinar, G., Warren, M. P., Kendrick, J., & Limacher, M. C. (1992). The reproductive system and exercise in women. *Medicine and Science in Sports and Exercise, 24*, S288–S293.

Maffulli, N., Testa, V., Lancia, A., Capasso, G., & Lombardi, S. (1991). Indices of sustained aerobic power in young middle distance runners. *Medicine and Science in Sports and Exercise, 23*(9), 1090–1096.

Malina, R. M. (1994). Physical growth and biological maturation of young athletes. *Exercise and Sport Sciences Reviews, 22*, 389–433.

———. (1995). The young athlete: Biological growth and maturation in a biocultural context. In F. L. Smoll & R. E. Smith (Eds.), *Children and youth in sport: A biopsychosocial perspective* (pp. 161–186). Dubuque, IA: Brown & Benchmark.

Malina, R. M., & Bouchard, C. (1988). Subcutaneous fat distribution during growth. In C. Bouchard & F. E. Johnston (Eds.), *Fat distribution during growth and later health outcomes* (pp. 63–84). New York: Liss.

———. (1991). *Growth, maturation, and physical activity*. Champaign, IL: Human Kinetics.

Malina, R. M., Meleski, B. W., & Shoup, R. (1982). Anthropometric, body composition, and maturity characteristics of selected school-aged athletes. *Pediatric Clinics of North America, 29*, 1305–1323.

Malina, R. M., & Roche, A. F. (1983). *Manual of physical status in childhood: Vol. 2. Physical performance*. New York: Plenum.

Marcus, R., Cann, C., Madvig, P., Minkoff, J., Goddard, M., Bayer, M., Martin, M., Gaudiani, L., Haskell, W., & Genant, J. (1985). Menstrual function and bone mass in elite women distance runners. *Annals of Internal Medicine, 102*, 158–163.

McArdle, W. D., Katch, F. I., & Katch, V. L. (1981). *Exercise physiology: Energy, nutrition, and human performance*. Philadelphia: Lea & Febiger.

Moffatt, R. J., Surina, B., Golden, B., & Ayres, N. (1984). Body composition and physiological characteristics of female high school gymnasts. *Research Quarterly for Exercise and Sport, 55*, 80–84.

Myburgh, K. H., Bachrach, L. K., Lewis, B., Kent, K., & Marcus, R. (1993). Low bone mineral density at axial and appendicular sites in amenorrheic athletes. *Medicine and Science in Sports and Exercise, 25*(11), 1197–1202.

Nattiv, A. (1994). The female athlete triad. *The Physician and Sportsmedicine, 22*(1), 60–68.

Niinimaa, V. (1982). Figure skating: What do we know about it? *The Physician and Sportsmedicine, 10*(1), 51–56.

Nilson, K. L. (1986). Injuries in female distance runners. In B. Drinkwater (Ed.), *Female endurance athletes* (pp. 149–160). Champaign, IL: Human Kinetics.

Novak, L. P. (1963). Age and sex differences in body density and creatinine excretion of high school children. *Annals of the New York Academy of Science, 110*, 545.

Parizkova, J. (1973). Body composition and exercise during growth and development. In G. L. Rarick (Ed.), *Physical activity, human growth and development* (pp. 97–124). New York: Academic Press.

Poole, G. W., Crepin, B. J., & Sevigny, M. (1980). Physiological characteristics of elite synchronized swimmers. *Canadian Journal of Applied Sport Sciences, 5*(3), 156–160.

Powers, S. K., & Walker, R. (1982). Physiological and anatomical characteristics of outstanding female junior tennis players. *Research Quarterly for Exercise and Sport, 53,* 172–175.

Quadagno, D., Faquin, L., Lim, G. N., Kuminka, W., & Moffatt, R. (1991). The menstrual cycle: Does it affect athletic performance? *The Physician and Sportsmedicine, 19*(3), 121–124.

Ransdell, L. B., & Wells, C. L. (in press). Sex differences in physical performance. In T. Fahey (Ed.), *Encyclopedia of sports medicine and exercise physiology.* New York: Garland.

Raven, P. B., Drinkwater, B. L., & Horvath, S. M. (1972). Cardiovascular responses of young female track athletes during exercise. *Medicine and Science in Sports, 4,* 205–209.

Roche, A. F., & Malina, R. M. (1983). *Manual of physical status and performance in childhood: Vol. 1. Physical status.* New York: Plenum.

Roemmich, J. N., & Frappier, J. P. (1993). Physiological determinants of wrestling success in high school athletes. *Pediatric Exercise Science, 5,* 134–144.

Rico, H., Revilla, M., Villa, L. F., Gomez-Castresana, F., & Alvarez Del Buergo, M. (1993). Body composition in postpubertal boy cyclists. *Journal of Sports Medicine and Physical Fitness, 33* (3), 278–281.

Rogol, A. D. (1988). Pubertal development in endurance-trained female athletes. In E. W. Brown & C. F. Branta (Eds.), *Competitive sports for children and youth* (pp. 173–193). Champaign, IL: Human Kinetics.

Rosen, L. W., McKeag, D. B., Hough, D. O., & Curley, V. (1986). Pathogenic weight-control behavior in female athletes. *The Physician and Sportsmedicine, 14*(1), 79–86.

Schoene, R. B., Robertson, H. T., Pierson, D. J., & Peterson, A. P. (1981). Respiratory drives and exercise in menstrual cycles of athletic and nonathletic women. *Journal of Applied Physiology: Respiratory, Environmental, and Exercise Physiology, 50,* 1300–1305.

Shangold, M. M. (1988). Menstruation. In M. M. Shangold & G. Mirkin (Eds.), *Women and exercise: Physiology and sports medicine* (pp. 129–144). Philadelphia: F. A. Davis.

Smoll, F. L., & Schutz, R. W. (1985). Physical fitness differences between athletes and nonathletes: Do changes occur as a function of age and sex? *Human Movement Science, 4,* 189–202.

———. (1990). Quantifying gender differences in physical performance: A developmental perspective. *Developmental Psychology, 26,* 360–369.

Stephenson, L. A., Kolka, M. A., & Wilkerson, J. E. (1982). Metabolic and thermoregulatory responses to exercise during the human menstrual cycle. *Medicine and Science in Sports and Exercise, 14,* 270–275.

Swenson, E. J., Hough, D. O., & McKeag, D. B. (1987). Patellofemoral dysfunction. *Postgraduate Medicine, 82*(6), 125–141.

Tharp, G. D., Johnson, G. O., & Thorland, W. G. (1984). Measurement of anaerobic power and capacity in elite young track athletes using the Wingate test. *Journal of Sports Medicine and Physical Fitness, 24,* 100–105.

Thomas, J. R., & French, K. E. (1985). Gender differences across age in motor performance: A meta-analysis. *Psychological Bulletin, 98,* 260–282.

Thorland, W. G., Johnson, G. O., Cisar, C. J., Housh, T. J., & Tharp, G. D. (1990). Muscular strength and power in elite young male runners. *Pediatric Exercise Science, 2,* 73–82.

Thorland, W. G., Johnson, G. O., Fagot, T. G., Tharp, G. D., & Hammer, R. W. (1981). Body composition and somatotype characteristics of Junior Olympic athletes. *Medicine and Science in Sports and Exercise, 13,* 332–338.

Van Huss, W., Evans, S. A., Kurowski, T., Anderson, D. J., Allen, R., & Stephens, K. (1988). Physiological characteristics of male and female age-group runners. In E. W. Brown & C. F. Branta (Eds.), *Competitive sports for children and youth* (pp. 143–158). Champaign, IL: Human Kinetics.

Warren, M. P. (1983). The effects of undernutrition on reproductive function in the human. *Endocrinology Reviews, 4,* 363–377.

Warren, M. P., Brooks-Gunn, J., Hamilton, L. H., Warren, L. F., & Hamilton, W. G. (1986). Scoliosis and fractures in young ballet dancers. *New England Journal of Medicine, 314,* 1348–1356.

Warren, M. P., Shane, E., Lee, M. J., Lindsay, R., Dempster, D. W., Warren, L. F., & Hamilton, W. G. (1990). Femoral head collapse associated with anorexia nervosa in a 20-year-old ballet dancer. *Clinical Orthopaedics and Related Research, 251,* 171–176.

Wells, C. L. (1977). Sexual differences in heat stress response. *The Physician and Sportsmedicine, 5*(9), 78–90.

Wells, C. L. (1991). *Women, sport, and performance: A physiological perspective* (2nd ed.). Champaign, IL.: Human Kinetics.

Wells, C. L., & Gilman, M. (1990). An ecological approach to training. *American Academy of Physical Education Papers, 24,* 15–29.

Wells, C. L., & Horvath, S. M. (1973). Heat stress responses related to the menstrual cycle. *Journal of Applied Physiology, 35,* 1–5.

———. (1974). Responses to exercise in a hot environment as related to the menstrual cycle. *Journal of Applied Physiology, 36,* 299–302.

Wells, C. L., Scrutton, E. W., Archibald, L. D., Cooke, W. P., & de LaMothe, J. W. (1973). Physical working capacity and maximal oxygen uptake of teenaged athletes. *Medicine and Science in Sports, 5*(4), 232–238.

Williams, T. J. (1992). *Menstrual cycle phase and running economy.* Unpublished doctoral dissertation, Arizona State University, Tempe.

Willows, N. D., Grimston, S. K., Roberts, D., Smith, D. J., & Hanley, D. A. (1993). Iron and hematologic status in young athletes relative to puberty: A cross-sectional study. *Pediatric Exercise Science, 5,* 367–376.

ANABOLIC STEROID USE IN ADOLESCENT ATHLETES

—David A. Van de Loo and Mimi D. Johnson

More than 35 years ago, elite athletes began using anabolic steroids in an attempt to improve athletic performance in sports that require great strength and size (Lamb, 1984). Since that time, the use of anabolic steroids has spread to professional, college, and high school athletics (Corder et al., 1975; Lamb, 1984). Up to 65 percent of high school anabolic steroid users participate in school-sponsored sports (Buckley et al., 1988). We who are involved with young athletes should understand the physiologic effects and potential adverse effects of steroids, how and why adolescents use steroids, and the role we can play in identifying and preventing steroid use.

Anabolic and Androgenic Effects of Steroids

Anabolic steroids are synthetic derivatives of the natural male sex steroid hormone, testosterone. Testosterone is synthesized in normal male testes and is the major hormone responsible for the androgenic and anabolic effects noted during male adolescence and adulthood. The androgenic and anabolic effects of testosterone cannot be totally separated as they are due to the same action of the hormone in different tissues, not to different actions of the hormone (Kruskemper, 1968; Wilson & Griffin, 1980). Although synthetic steroids are usually referred to as anabolic steroids, they have both anabolic and androgenic properties.

Testosterone's androgenic properties influence the growth of the male reproductive tract and the development of secondary sexual characteristics. In the pubertal male, androgenic effects include the increase in length and diameter of the penis; appearance of pubic, axillary, and facial hair; and the development of the prostate gland and scrotum (Rogol, 1985).

Testosterone's anabolic properties affect the nonreproductive tract tissues. Anabolic effects include the stimulation of long bone growth with subsequent induction of epiphyseal closure at puberty, the enlargement of the larynx and thickening of the vocal cords, an increase of skeletal muscle mass and strength, an increase in protein synthesis, a decrease in body fat, and the development of libido and sexual potential (Rogol, 1985).

Developers of synthetic steroids have modified the testosterone molecule in an attempt to minimize its unwanted androgenic effects. Nevertheless, all synthetic steroids have androgenic effects (Kruskemper, 1968; Wilson & Griffin, 1980) and are properly referred to as anabolic-androgenic steroids.

Effects of Steroids on Muscle Strength and Size

Many factors, including heredity, intensity of training, diet, and the status of the psyche (Wright, 1980) contribute to the development of muscle strength. Studies that have attempted to determine the effects of anabolic steroids on muscle strength in humans have yielded conflicting results. Half of the studies demonstrated that steroid use increased muscle strength and size, whereas the other half showed no increase in muscle strength or size with steroid use (American College of Sports Medicine, 1984; Haupt & Rovere, 1984). Haupt and Rovere (1984) have postulated that these inconsistencies resulted from differences in study protocols. Not all individuals who use anabolic steroids experience significant effects (American College of Sports Medicine, 1984). However, improvements in muscle strength and size may result from steroid use in individuals who (1) intensively train in weight lifting immediately before using anabolic steroids and continue intensive weight lifting during the steroid regimen, (2) maintain a high-protein, high-calorie diet, and (3) measure their strength improvement using the same single repetition, maximal weight technique (i.e., bench press) they used in training (American College of Sports Medicine, 1984; Haupt & Rovere, 1984).

In addition to their anabolic effects in athletes, anabolic-androgenic steroids have both anticatabolic and motivational effects. Anabolic steroids may increase muscle strength and size through one or more of the following proposed mechanisms:

1. Anabolic steroids may antagonize the increased protein breakdown that usually occurs during the muscular stress of athletic training. Intense weight training can lead to a catabolic state or negative nitrogen balance (Haupt & Rovere, 1984). Steroids convert a negative nitrogen balance to a positive one by improving the use of ingested protein and increasing nitrogen retention (Kruskemper, 1968).
2. Anabolic steroids may have the ability to induce protein synthesis in skeletal muscle cells (Murad & Haynes, 1985). This effect continues indefinitely during steroid treatment and occurs in both the healthy and the catabolic state (Haupt & Rovere, 1984).
3. Anabolic steroids may block the glucocorticosteroid-induced depression of protein synthesis that occurs during stressful events such as training. Glucocorticosteroids, which have a catabolic effect, are released during training. Anabolic steroids compete for glucocorticosteroid receptor sites and may reverse the catabolic effect (Haupt & Rovere, 1984; Kruskemper, 1968).
4. Anabolic steroids may affect an athlete's training habits. Athletes using steroids claim to experience a state of euphoria, increased aggressive

behavior, and diminished fatigue, all of which can have a positive effect on weight training (Wilson & Griffin, 1980). Athletes also report the ability to train more frequently and intensively while using the drugs and to recover more rapidly from workouts (Crawshaw, 1985). Whether this perception has a psychological basis (placebo effect) or a physiological basis is not clear.

In 1972 Ariel and Saville reported that athletes who took a placebo thinking that it was an anabolic steroid increased their strength over what would have been expected in the absence of an anabolic steroid. Rozenek et al. (1990) reported a lower plasma lactate concentration following exercise in steroid users than in nonusers. If a difference in lactate concentration exists, it may explain the subjective feelings of faster recovery in individuals taking anabolic steroids.

5. Finally, an increase in growth hormone may accentuate the anabolic effect of steroids (Alen et al., 1987). In growing adolescents, exogenous testosterone has been shown to promote an increase in the frequency and magnitude of growth hormone secretory bursts (Cowart, 1989). A 5- to 60-fold increase in serum growth hormone concentration has been seen in some power athletes who use steroids, but this has not been a consistent finding (Alen et al., 1987).

How Anabolic Steroids Are Used

Anabolic steroids are available as oral and injectable agents. Testosterone undergoes rapid degradation following both oral and parenteral (injectable) administration. Therefore, molecular changes have been made to increase the oral bioavailability and the half-life of the synthetic drugs (Murad & Haynes, 1985). Molecular changes have also been made in an attempt to decrease the unwanted androgenic effects of the drugs (Murad & Haynes, 1985). Anabolic steroids have legitimate medical uses, but athletes use them because of their potential anabolic effects. Athletes have developed several patterns of use, and even young athletes have found these drugs easy to obtain.

Most of the orally administered anabolic steroids are alkylated at the 17-alpha position, rapidly absorbed, and associated with an increased risk of hepatotoxicity (Kruskemper, 1968). The parenteral (injectable) steroids, which include the testosterone esters and the 19-nortestosterone derivatives, are injected intramuscularly and are slowly absorbed. Modification of some synthetic steroids has resulted in a partial dissociation between the androgenic and anabolic actions of the drugs, but complete separation of these activities has never been fully achieved. All synthetic steroids have some androgenic effects (Kruskemper, 1968; Wilson, 1988). The testosterone esters have the highest androgenic potency (androgenic:anabolic ratio of 1:1), whereas many of the 19-nortestosterone esters and the oral steroids have decreased androgenicity (Gribbin & Matts, 1976). Some of the commonly used anabolic steroids are listed in table 14.1.

Synthetic steroids are employed in the treatment of several medical conditions. Anabolic steroids are used as hormone replacement therapy in boys and men whose

TABLE 14.1 Anabolic Steroids Used by Athletes

ORAL ANABOLIC STEROIDS		INJECTABLE ANABOLIC STEROIDS	
Generic name	*Trade name*	*Generic name*	*Trade name*
Oxymetholone*	Anadrol	Nandrolone decanoate†	Deca-Durabolin
Oxandrolone*	Anavar	Nandrolone phenpropionate†	Durabolin
Methandrostenolone*	Dianabol	Testosterone cypionate‡	Depo-testosterone
Ethylestrenol*	Maxibolin	Testosterone enanthate‡	Delatestryl
Stanozolol*	Winstrol	Testosterone propionate‡	Oreton
Fluoxymesterone*	Halotestin	Methenolone enanthate	Primobolan depot
Norethandrolone	Nilevar	Boldenone undecyclenate	Equipoise
Methenolone acetate	Primobolan	Trenbolone acetate§	Finajet
Mesterolone	Proviron	Trenbolone§	Parabolan
Testosterone undecanoate		Stanozolol	Winstrol V

*17-alpha alkylated steroids
†19-nortestosterone esters
‡testosterone esters
§European veterinary steroids, reported in underground handbooks.
Reprinted with permission from M. D. Johnson, Anabolic Steroid Use in Adolescent Athletes. In A. C. Hergenroeder, J. G. Garrick (Eds.),
Sports Medicine. The Pediatric Clinics of North America. Philadelphia: W. B. Saunders, Vol. 37:6, 1990.

testes fail to secrete androgens normally. They are also used to stimulate pubertal development in some young men with marked developmental delay (Rogol, 1985) and to treat short stature in individuals with Turner syndrome (Moore, 1988). Synthetic steroids have also been used to treat osteoporosis in women, hereditary angioneurotic edema, and late stages of breast cancer. Researchers are currently studying slow release testosterone as a male contraceptive (Strauss, 1993).

Anecdotal reports suggest that athletes take doses that are from two to more than 100 times greater than those recommended for medical purposes (Lamb, 1984; Shikles, 1989). Handbooks are available to athletes that describe steroids and offer suggestions on how to use them (Anabolic Reference Guide, 1989; Duchaine, 1989). Steroid users have developed several patterns of use in an attempt to maximize the anabolic effects of steroids and minimize the side effects. Athletes often use more than one steroid at a time, referred to as *stacking*. The stack or "array" of drugs often includes at least one oral and one injectable agent. Some individuals begin using steroids at low doses, increase them gradually, and then taper them (sometimes called *pyramiding*) (Duchaine, 1989; Frankle, Cicero, & Payne, 1984). Users decide to stop, add, change, or increase the dose of a drug when increases in strength and size are no longer being attained through weight lifting (sometimes called a *plateau*). Although some users take the drugs year-round, most users cycle the steroids by taking them for 4 to 18 weeks, then undergo a drug-free period that averages two to three months. An example of a steroid cycle is shown in table 14.2.

TABLE 14.2 An Example of a Steroid Cycle

Week	Testosterone cypionate 200 mg/cc injection	Testosterone enanthate 200 mg/cc injection	Oxandrolone 2.5 mg/tab
1	2 cc/wk	2 cc/wk	10 tab/day
2	2 cc/wk	2 cc/wk	9 tab/day
3	1½ cc/wk	1½ cc/wk	8 tab/day
4	1½ cc/wk	1½ cc/wk	7 tab/day
5	1 cc/wk	1 cc/wk	6 tab/day
6	1 cc/wk	1 cc/wk	5 tab/day
7	½ cc/wk	½ cc/wk	4 tab/day
8	½ cc/wk	½ cc/wk	3 tab/day
9	¼ cc/wk	¼ cc/wk	2 tab/day
10	¼ cc/wk	¼ cc/wk	1 tab/day

Therapeutic doses of testosterone cypionate and enanthate range from 50–400 mg every 2–4 weeks (Murad & Haynes, 1985). The therapeutic dose of oxandrolone is 5–10 mg/day (Murad & Haynes, 1985). Reprinted with permission from M. D. Johnson, Steroids. In P. G. Dyment (Ed.), *Sports and the Adolescent. Adolescent Medicine: State of the Art Reviews*. Philadelphia: Hanley & Belfus, Vol. 2:1, 1991.

Terney and McLain (1990) reported that one-third of high school students surveyed said it would be easy to obtain steroids. Friends, other athletes, coaches, doctors, pharmacists, veterinarians, dealers, mail-order catalogues, and gym pushers have been reported as sources for anabolic steroids (Buckley et al., 1988; Office of Inspector General, 1990; Whitehead, Chillag, & Elliot, 1992). The majority of anabolic steroid users obtain the drugs from black market sources (Buckley et al., 1988; Windsor & Dumitru, 1989). The Department of Justice estimates that the annual black market sales of anabolic steroids is approximately $300 to $400 million dollars. Officials believe that the source of black market steroids is evenly divided between clandestinely manufactured goods, smuggled products, and diverted legally manufactured products (Shikles, 1989). Some of the drugs are manufactured in the United States, but many are smuggled into the country from Europe or Mexico (Shikles, 1989).

"Counterfeit" steroids are making up an increasing proportion of anabolic steroids on the black market. Counterfeited drugs include mislabeled drugs, drugs that are subpotent or adulterated with other substances, and bogus drugs that contain none of the substances they purport to contain. Since 1986, the Department of Justice and the FDA have uncovered more than 35 different counterfeit steroid products and more than 85 different labels used in their distribution (Shikles, 1989). The safety of these drugs is questionable, since they are often manufactured in underground labs (Anabolic Reference Guide, 1989; Duchaine, 1989). Steroid users may attempt to counter the side effects of steroids by using other drugs available on the black market such as human chorionic gonadotropin (HCG) to stimulate natural testosterone production and anti-estrogenic agents (tamoxifen) to decrease gynecomastia (Duchaine, 1989; Taylor, 1987).

Adverse Effects of Steroid Use

The adverse effects that one might experience from using steroids depend on the age, sex, and health of the user; the particular drugs and doses being used; and the frequency of use (Wilson & Griffin, 1980). Many of the short-term side effects of anabolic steroids appear to be reversible once they are discontinued. However, long-term adverse effects have not been well studied and most of the information comes from reports of individuals who have taken anabolic steroids in therapeutic doses (Shikles, 1989). Chronic anabolic steroid use has the potential to lead to deleterious long-term effects. Presently, there are very few life-threatening effects of steroid use, and these have been rarely seen. Potential complications of anabolic steroid use are summarized in table 14.3 and discussed in the following section.

Endocrine Effects

Anabolic steroids affect the endocrine and reproductive systems of both male and female users. Decreased spermatogenesis (Mauss et al., 1975), gynecomastia (development of male breast tissue) (Friedl & Yesalis, 1989), prostatic hypertrophy and priapism (prolonged painful erections) (Rogol, 1985), and carcinoma of the prostate (Roberts, 1986) have been reported in association with anabolic steroid use by males. In females, excess androgens may result in irreversible signs of masculinization and menstrual irregularities (Kruskemper, 1968). Some of these effects might prove to be more serious in prepubertal and pubertal users because of their developing endocrine and reproductive systems. Problems with glucose tolerance (Cohen & Hickman, 1987) and thyroid hormone disturbances (Kruskemper, 1968) have also been reported in association with anabolic steroid use.

In the male, excessive amounts of exogenous androgens in the serum result in negative feedback to the hypothalamus and anterior pituitary gland, causing a decrease in the secretion of follicle-stimulating hormone (FSH) and luteinizing hormone (LH). The decrease of these hormones results in decreased testosterone production, testicular atrophy, and a decrease in spermatogenesis. Although these changes appear to be reversible, abnormal sperm and decreased numbers of sperm have been noted for up to six months following discontinuation of steroids (Mauss et al., 1975).

Gynecomastia, the occurrence of mammary tissue in the male, is generally a sign of estrogen-androgen imbalance. As many as half of all boys exhibit some degree of transient breast swelling during normal pubertal development. In steroid users, gynecomastia may result from the conversion (aromatization) of exogenous androgens (i.e., the testosterone esters) to estradiol (Friedl & Yesalis, 1989). Gynecomastia may be even more pronounced in persons with altered hepatic (liver) function because of decreased clearance of the parent steroid or estrogenic metabolites by the liver (Kley, Strohmeyer, & Kruskemper, 1979). In steroid users, the breast tissue may become less prominent and less painful once steroids are stopped, but the problem may worsen with further steroid use and may not disappear entirely even with complete cessation of steroids (Friedl & Yesalis, 1989).

TABLE 14.3 Potential Complications of Anabolic Steroid Use

Endocrine

Male
- Decreased reproductive hormones
- Testicular atrophy
- Oligospermia/azospermia
- Gynecomastia
- Prostatic hypertrophy
- Prostatic carcinoma*
- Priapism

Female
- Masculinization
- Hirsutism*
- Deepening of voice*
- Clitoral hypertrophy*
- Menstrual irregularities

Adolescent
- Accelerated maturation*
- Altered glucose tolerance

Renal
- Elevated BUN, creatinine
- Wilms' tumor*

Musculoskeletal

Adolescent:
- Premature epiphyseal closure*
- Increased risk of musculotendinous injury

Dermatologic
- Acne
- Alopecia*
- Temporal hair recession*

Cardiovascular
- Decreased HDL cholesterol
- Increased LDL cholesterol
- Hypertension
- Clotting abnormalities

Hepatic
- Elevated liver function test values
- Cholestatic jaundice
- Tumor formation*
- Peliosis hepatitis*

Psychological
- Aggressive behavior
- Mood swings
- Increased or decreased libido
- Dependency
- Acute psychosis
- Manic and/or depressive episodes

Subjective Effects[†]
- Edema
- Muscle spasm
- Nervous tension
- Increased urine output
- Headache
- Dizziness
- Nausea
- Euphoria
- Skin rash
- Urethritis
- Scrotal pain
- Irritability

Table adapted from Johnson MD: Pediatr Clin North Am 37:1111–1123, 1990.
*Considered irreversible.
[†]Adapted from Haupt HA, Rovere GD: Anabolic steroids: A review of the literature. *Am J Sports Med* 12:477, 1984.
Reprinted with permission from Johnson M D: Steroids. In P. G. Dyment (Ed.), *Sports and the Adolescent. Adolescent Medicine: State of the Art Reviews.* Philadelphia: Hanley & Belfus, Vol. 2:1, 1991.

In females, signs of excess androgens include hirsutism (excessive body and facial hair) and deepening of the voice (Wilson & Griffin, 1980). As with other anabolic steroid effects, considerable variation occurs in the frequency and the degree to which these signs develop. If the use of anabolic steroids is discontinued as soon as these adverse effects are noted, they may slowly subside; but with prolonged steroid use, these effects may worsen and become irreversible. Clitoral hypertrophy, which is irreversible, has been reported (Wilson & Griffin, 1980). Amenorrhea and other menstrual irregularities have also been associated with anabolic steroid use (Kruskemper, 1968).

In prepubertal or pubertal males, steroid use accelerates maturation, with the premature development of secondary sexual characteristics and changes in physique (Kruskemper, 1968). Wilson and Griffin (1980) have stated that "florid virilization" may occur in children even when anabolic steroids are used in small amounts and for relatively limited periods of time. Some of these effects that are felt to be inconsequential or reversible in adults may affect biologically immature males differently.

Cohen and Hickman (1987) have reported increased insulin resistance with altered glucose tolerance in athletes using anabolic steroids. A decrease in serum concentrations of thyroxine (T4), triiodothyronine (T3), free thyroxine (FT4), and thyroid-stimulating hormone (TSH) have also been observed (Alen et al., 1987; Kruskemper, 1968). Alen et al. (1987) suggested that decreased concentrations of these hormones may be due to a decrease in thyroid-binding globulin (TBG). Thyroid hormone is apparently available at the cellular level, and clinical thyroid function is normal (Alen et al., 1987).

Cardiovascular Effects

Anabolic steroid use may affect myocardial structure and function. Urhausen, Holpes, and Kindermann (1989) reported increased left ventricular wall thickness and impaired diastolic function in steroid-using body builders. Sachtleben et al. (1993) found that myocardial thickness in steroid users was greater than that in nonusers. A significant increase in myocardial thickness also occurred in steroid users on-cycle as compared with users who were off-cycle. No evidence exists to suggest that steroids improve aerobic capacity. Sachtleben et al. (1993) reported decreased maximum oxygen consumption in users as compared with nonusers and suggested that cardiac contractility may decrease as a result of chronic steroid use.

Anabolic steroid use results in a decrease in the HDL cholesterol level and may result in an increase in the LDL cholesterol level (Hurley et al., 1984). The resulting increased LDL/HDL cholesterol ratio may signify an increased risk for coronary artery disease (Strauss, 1993). Cholesterol levels appear to return to baseline once steroid use is discontinued (Cohen, Noakes, & Benade, 1988). No occurrences of accelerated arteriosclerosis have been reported in anabolic steroid-using athletes, but two cases of myocardial infarction (heart attack) have been reported in young steroid users (Bowman, 1990; McNutt et al., 1988)

Anabolic steroids may increase red blood cell mass, therefore elevating the hemoglobin and hematocrit in users (Murad & Haynes, 1985). Normally, adult males have higher hematocrits than females as a result of the positive effect of testosterone on red blood cell production. Administration of androgens to women increases red cell production. Long-term androgen therapy, as in treatment for breast cancer, has resulted in polycythemia (an increase of red blood cells above normal) (Wilson & Griffin, 1980), but significant polycythemia has not been reported in athlete steroid users.

Other adverse cardiovascular effects reported in association with anabolic steroid use include: edema (swelling) due to the retention of fluid and sodium (Kruskemper, 1968); reversible hypertension (Messerli & Frohlich, 1979); and a decrease in clotting factors, increase in fibrinolytic activity, and enhanced platelet aggregation in association with the use of specific steroids (Ferenchick, 1990). Cerebrovascular accidents (strokes) in young steroid users have been reported (Frankle, Eichberg, & Zachariah, 1988; Mochizuki & Richter, 1988). In addition, some steroid users use diuretics to lose excess fluid and increase muscle definition. This may cause abnormal levels of serum potassium and place the individuals at greater risk for cardiac arrythmias.

Hepatic Effects

Hepatotoxicity is most commonly associated with the 17-alpha alkylated steroids, which are taken orally (Kruskemper, 1968). Use of these steroids may result in an elevation of liver function test values (Wilson & Griffin, 1980), indicating liver damage. The muscle damage incurred by weight lifting alone may cause an elevation in serum aspartate aminotransferase (AST) and alanine aminotransferase (ALT) (Strauss et al., 1983), but more specific measurements of liver function, including alkaline phosphatase, conjugated bilirubin, and liver isoenzymes of lactate dehydrogenase, have been elevated in some steroid users (Haupt & Rovere, 1984). Lamb (1984) reported that abnormally elevated liver function tests typically revert to normal following cessation of steroid use but that continued administration of steroids could result in obstruction of the bile canals (cholestasis) and jaundice. Steroid-induced cholestatic jaundice typically resolves within several months of discontinuing the drugs (Kruskemper, 1968).

Both benign and malignant liver tumors (Johnson et al., 1972; Sweeney & Evans, 1976) and peliosis hepatitis, a rare disease causing blood-filled sacs in the liver (Bagheri & Boyer, 1974), have been associated with steroid use. Athletes with histories of extensive steroid use have died of hepatocellular carcinoma (Goldman, 1985; Overly et al., 1984). One steroid-using bodybuilder developed hepatocellular carcinoma and died of uncontrolled bleeding following hepatic rupture (Creagh, Rubin, & Evans, 1988).

Renal Effects

Although an increase in serum creatinine may be seen in steroid-free weight lifters due to the increase in skeletal muscle mass (Strauss et al., 1983), steroid use may cause an increase in serum BUN, creatinine, and uric acid (Crawshaw, 1985). Elevation of these values in steroid users indicates that the drugs may have a negative effect on kidney function, although the abnormal values typically return to normal once the drugs are discontinued.

Fatal kidney tumors (Wilms tumors), which are uncommon in adults, have been reported in adult athletes using steroids (Prat et al., 1977; Strauss et al., 1983). Determining whether these tumors were related to steroid use or occurred coincidentally is not possible (Strauss et al., 1983). Nevertheless, evidence suggests that steroids may be weak carcinogens and capable of initiating tumor growth or promoting tumor growth in the presence of other carcinogens (Lamb, 1984).

Musculoskeletal Effects

The prepubertal or pubertal adolescent using excessive amounts of steroids for a prolonged period of time may experience premature epiphyseal closure with resulting stunted growth (Murad & Haynes, 1985). Children with poorly controlled diseases of androgen excess are initially taller than their peers but become relatively short adults (Rogol, 1985). This can result from accelerated advancement of bone age relative to acceleration in height velocity and from early onset of puberty with premature closure of the epiphyses (Moore, 1988).

Anabolic steroid use may result in an increased risk of musculotendinous injuries. McKillop et al. (1989) reported that creatine phosphokinase, the most sensitive enzyme index of muscle damage, was abnormally elevated in steroid users. Michna and Stang-Voss (1983) noted degenerative changes in the tendon fibers of female mice following administration of anabolic steroids. Cases of atypical spontaneous tendon ruptures in bodybuilders using steroids have also been reported (Hill et al., 1983; Kramhoft & Solgaard, 1986).

Dermatologic Effects

Acne is a commonly reported side effect of anabolic steroid use. The prevalence of acne at puberty is related to the growth and secretory activity of the sebaceous glands (Murad & Haynes, 1985). Sebaceous glands are very sensitive to androgenic stimulation (Kruskemper, 1968). The high doses of testosterone and anabolic steroids that are self-administered by athletes can increase the amount of sebum excretion from sebaceous glands (Kiraly et al., 1987). Furthermore, acne lesions resulting from steroid use, commonly on the chest and back, do not always respond to routine treatment. The use of tetracycline or isotretinoin for treatment of refractory acne could have additional adverse consequences in steroid users who have decreased hepatic clearance.

Other cutaneous manifestations associated with steroid use include: alopecia (hair loss), folliculitis (inflammation of hair follicles), hirsutism (presence of excessive body and facial hair, especially in women), and striae (stretch marks) (Scott, M. J., Jr., & Scott, M. J., III, 1989). Temporal hair recession and alopecia may be seen in men and women using steroids for a prolonged period of time (Houssay, 1976). In females, the scalp alopecia is usually not total, but considerable sparseness of hair is readily visible and may be permanent (Scott, M. J. Jr., & Scott, M. J., III, 1989).

Infections and Immune Response

Steroid users who share needles increase their risk of transmitting infections such as hepatitis B and acquired immune deficiency syndrome (AIDS). In a recent study, 25 percent of adolescent anabolic steroid users shared needles to inject drugs during the previous 30 days (DuRant et al., 1993). Adolescent steroid users may not perceive themselves as being at risk for infections; however, the human immunodeficiency virus (HIV) sero-status of individuals who inject steroids is not known. Two cases of AIDS have been reported in steroid users who shared needles with HIV-infected cohorts (Scott, M. J., & Scott, M. J., Jr., 1989; Sklarek et al., 1984).

Steroid users may also be at risk for other bacterial and viral infections. Skin or systemic infections could be caused by impure drugs or by contaminated vials, syringes, or needles. In addition, reduced serum immunoglobulins could lead to a reduced resistance to infection. A decrease in immunoglobulins, particularly IgA, has been reported in steroid-using bodybuilders (Calabrese et al., 1989).

Psychological Effects

Numerous psychological changes have been associated with anabolic steroid use. In most steroid users, psychological changes are minor, but in some steroid users, psychological changes may be severe and sufficient to cause significant morbidity and even mortality (Perry, Yates, & Anderson, 1990; Pope & Katz, 1992). Whether or not anabolic steroid users develop dependency remains controversial (Brower, 1992). Unfortunately, adolescents may be at an increased risk for development of the psychological effects associated with steroid use (Windsor & Dumitru, 1989; Yesalis et al., 1989).

Anabolic steroid use has been associated with increased aggressive behavior, mood swings, and irritability (Pope & Katz, 1988; Strauss et al., 1983). Other psychological changes that may result from steroid use include somatization (Perry et al., 1990), distractibility, forgetfulness and confusion (Su et al., 1993), and increased self-esteem and changes in libido (Strauss et al., 1983). Taylor (1987) reported a study in which 90 percent of health club athletes with a history of steroid use experienced episodes of overaggresiveness and violent behavior ("roid rage") that they believed were induced by steroids. Su et al. (1993) noted significant, albeit subtle, increases in irritability, mood swings, violent feelings, anger, and hostility following the administration of steroids to individuals with no previous steroid use or history of psychiatric problems in a placebo-controlled prospective study. Yates, Perry, and Anderson (1990), who found that the steroid users in their study displayed increased antisocial traits, suggested that antisocial traits may in themselves contribute to the aggressive behavior noted in steroid users. However, the discovery of neuronal androgen receptors in the brain (Sheridan, 1983) suggests there may be a neurochemical basis for aggressive behavior associated with steroid use and that individuals with antisocial traits may be especially sensitive to the effects of anabolic steroids.

Overt psychotic symptoms and manic or depressive episodes have been reported during steroid use in persons who were symptom-free prior to initiating steroids (Pope & Katz, 1988). Su et al. (1993) reported one case of mania, one case of hypomania, and one case of major depression following administration of relatively small doses of steroids to individuals in their prospective study. Indeed, the psychologic effects seen in individuals who use supraphysiologic doses may be markedly greater than those observed in many studies where only physiologic doses have been administered. Several legal cases have involved previously nonviolent persons who committed violent acts, including murder, while using steroids

(Pope & Katz, 1990). Steroid use has also been associated with suicide (Brower, Blow, Eliopulos, et al., 1989; Elofson & Elofson, 1990; Pope & Katz, 1992).

Evidence suggests that anabolic steroid use may result in dependency (Brower, Blow, Beresford, et al., 1989; Brower et al., 1990). Some steroid users fulfill the *Diagnostic and Statistical Manual,* 3rd edition, revised criteria for psychoactive substance dependence (Brower, Blow, Beresford, et al., 1989; Brower et al., 1991; Brower et al., 1990). Steroid users report that they have difficulty discontinuing the drugs and have a strong desire to reinitiate use once they have discontinued (Brower et al., 1990; Brower et al., 1991; Office of Inspector General, 1990). Users report continued steroid use despite adverse consequences (Brower, Blow, Beresford, et al., 1989).

Following cessation of steroids, users may experience fatigue, depression, anorexia, dissatisfaction with body image (Brower et al., 1990), decreased self-esteem (Hays, Littleton, & Stillner, 1990), restlessness, insomnia, decreased libido, headaches, and suicidal thoughts (Brower et al., 1991). Tennant, Black, and Voy (1988) reported a case in which physical withdrawal symptoms, such as those seen in opiate withdrawal, occurred upon cessation of extremely high doses of steroids. Some individuals may be psychologically dependent on steroids because of its muscle building effects and the resulting social reinforcement (Brower, 1992). Others who quit may resume steroid use to self-treat their withdrawal depression. It has not been established that anabolic steroid dependence results from a psychoactive or neurochemical effect on the brain (Brower, 1992).

The psychological effects of steroids on adolescents may be the most devastating of all the potential side effects. The developing nervous system of the teen may be especially vulnerable to these effects. The adolescent may lack the maturity to handle drug-induced mood changes. In addition, the development of the appropriate social skills and controls necessary to deal with pubertal changes may be made more difficult when the changes are occurring more rapidly than usual. Yesalis et al. (1993) reported that the strong association between steroid use and aggressive acts or crimes against property was most pronounced in the 12- through 17-year-old age group.

In addition, adolescents may be at greater risk for addiction. Those who take larger than therapeutic doses over longer periods of time appear more likely to become addicted (Brower, 1992). Signs of steroid habituation have been noted in adolescents (Yesalis et al., 1989). Yesalis et al. (1989) reported that, despite knowledge of possible dire health consequences, one-quarter of adolescent steroid users in their study were unwilling to discontinue steroid use, even if everyone else did. These "heavy users" were characterized by initiation of steroid use at a younger age than most, completion of a greater number and length of steroid cycles, having used multiple anabolic steroid drugs simultaneously, and having used injectable anabolic steroids (Yesalis et al., 1989).

Adolescent Anabolic Steroid Use

Corder et al. first reported the use of anabolic steroids by adolescent athletes in 1975. Results of early self-reported surveys published in the medical literature revealed that between 5 and 11 percent of male high school students (Buckley et al., 1988;

Johnson et al., 1989; Terney & McLain, 1990; Windsor & Dumitru, 1989) and between 0.5 and 2.5 percent of female high school students used anabolic steroids (Johnson et al., 1989; Terney & McLain, 1990; Windsor & Dumitru, 1989). In a recent study, Blessing, Health, and Escobeda (1993) reported that 3.1 percent of a nationally representative sample of 12,272 students in Grades 9 to 12 used anabolic steroids. Demographic data of users and reasons for anabolic steroid use differed somewhat between these studies.

Some authors have reported that white males were more likely to use steroids than black males (Blessing et al., 1993; Komoroski & Rickert, 1992), whereas others reported a greater minority representation in the user group when compared with the nonuser group (Buckley et al., 1988), with a significantly higher percentage of Hispanic than non-Hispanic adolescents reporting the use of anabolic steroids (DuRant et al., 1993). Windsor and Dumitru (1989) reported that use was signifi-cantly greater in high school districts with students of predominantly upper socio-economic status, whereas Komoroski and Rickert (1992) found that socioeconomic status did not differ between male users and nonusers in their study. Whitehead et al. (1992) reported that the rate of steroid use did not vary significantly based on high school enrollment or city size. They stated that schools with fewer than 100 students and towns of fewer than 2,000 people had similar use rates when compared with ear-lier studies of major metropolitan areas.

Studies of adolescent steroid users have found that between 63 and 85 percent were involved in sports (Buckley et al., 1988; Johnson et al., 1989; Terney & McLain, 1990; Whitehead et al., 1992), and many reported using steroids to improve athletic performance. Blessing et al. (1993) indicated that sport participation may increase the likelihood of anabolic steroid use. Sports with the highest prevalence of steroid use were football and wrestling (Buckley et al., 1988; Terney & McLain, 1990), but steroid use was present in all sports (Terney & McLain, 1990). Adolescent steroid users may believe that other professional and nonprofessional athletes use steroids (Komoroski & Rickert, 1992). Possibly, the values and behaviors demon-strated by elite athlete role models who have used steroids reinforce similar values and behaviors in young athletes. The pressure to win that parents, coaches, and peers place on athletes may motivate some to look for an advantage in their sport. Some young athletes may perceive that their only chance to compete with steroid-using peers is to use steroids themselves.

According to Buckley et al. (1988), 35 percent of adolescent steroid users were not involved in organized sport activities. Many of these adolescents were using steroids to improve appearance. In a recent study, Whitehead et al. (1992) reported that the predominant reason for steroid use was to improve appearance, indicating that adolescent insecurity with body image may be a major factor in those individu-als who use anabolic steroids to improve appearance. This is not surprising when one considers the importance society places on appearance, in addition to the adoles-cent's heightened concern about body image. As male adolescents become increas-ingly aware of their bodies and compare themselves with others, they may become impatient with the normal rate of muscle development. Their concern about appear-ance may motivate them to pursue a shortcut toward increased size. The experience of being "big" seems to carry special significance in making some adolescents feel good about themselves. In this way, use of anabolic steroids may become a method of improving self-esteem. This underlying agenda may be prevalent in many adolescent steroid users, even those involved in sports.

Some teens use steroids because friends use them (Buckley et al., 1988; Johnson et al., 1989). Achieving independence from parents and adopting peer codes and lifestyles are normal developmental tasks during adolescence. Peer pressure is known to be a strong force in illicit drug and alcohol use (Robinson et al., 1987). Whitehead et al. (1992) have suggested that anabolic steroids may be a part of the recognized pattern of adolescent drug use. They reported that the prevalence of illicit drug use and cigarette use was significantly higher in steroid users than in nonusers. Others have reported a significant association between the use of anabolic steroids and the use of cocaine, marijuana, smokeless tobacco, cigarettes, and alcohol (DuRant et al., 1993; Yesalis et al., 1993).

Adolescents have reported using anabolic steroids for other reasons, including injury prevention or treatment (Buckley et al., 1988), increasing strength or size, improving sexual performance, improving body definition, increasing penile size, and increasing ligament strength (Johnson et al., 1989). Finally, the adolescent's characteristic perception of his or her own invincibility may lead to risk-taking behavior, such as using anabolic steroids, without considering the long-term consequences.

Identifying Adolescent Steroid Users

Many sports organizations consider steroid use unethical and illegal. For this reason, it is unusual for an adolescent to volunteer information regarding personal steroid use. Coaches, trainers, educators, parents, nurses, and physicians must become aware of the level of steroid use, maintain a high index of suspicion, and look for subtle side effects to detect anabolic steroid use in adolescent athletes. Early identification of an adolescent who displays the more common but less severe side effects may allow for evaluation and intervention before the individual places himself or herself at significant risk for side effects that are less common but more severe and potentially fatal. If steroid use is suspected or confirmed, the adolescent should be referred to a knowledgeable, nonjudgmental physician for an appropriate history, physical examination, and laboratory evaluation to detect evidence of complications.

Recognizable adverse effects due to anabolic steroid use may include: rapid weight gain, especially if lean body mass has increased; a disproportionate development of the upper torso; marked muscular growth; premature maturation in prepubertal males; yellow coloring of the eyes or skin; puffy face or extremities; mood changes; increased aggressiveness; needle marks in large muscle groups; increased growth of body or facial hair in females; and a deepened or raspy voice in females. Breast enlargement in males and severe acne can be normal occurrences during puberty but also are possible signs of steroid use. Steroid use might also be suspected in a male who complains of urinary dribbling or pain with urination.

It is important to be knowledgeable, yet nonjudgmental, when inquiring about steroid use. Suspicion of steroid use might prompt one to ask the adolescent if he or she is involved in weight training. The adolescent may then be asked about legal performance aids such as protein powders or amino acid supplements. One may then inquire whether the individual knows anyone who uses or has used steroids; then ask whether he or she has ever thought about using them or has tried them. Confirmation of anabolic steroid use by the adolescent should prompt a referral for appropriate evaluation and intervention.

Intervention

Intervention may include monitoring of steroid users, encouraging them to pursue alternatives to steroid use, and supporting treatment for those who are dependent on steroid use. Some physicians feel that by monitoring steroid use, one is supporting it. Others feel that monitoring steroid users for potential side effects is no different from monitoring alcoholics for cirrhosis. Some professionals claim that the athlete will use steroids anyway and that testing periodically for serious effects is preferred to no testing at all. One might even use monitoring as a step in persuading the user to discontinue steroid use. For example, one could obtain a panel of laboratory tests, gain the steroid user's confidence, then persuade the individual to take a "drug holiday." One could then repeat the laboratory tests during the drug holiday and review the improved laboratory results with the steroid user (Strauss, 1993).

A nonjudgmental inquiry of the reasons for an adolescent's steroid use will allow the physician or other professional to assess the adolescent's fund of knowledge regarding steroids and correct any false information about physiologic effects or complications. Both the potential risks and the merits of anabolic steroid use must be presented to adolescents. It is not helpful to attempt to talk a teenager out of using steroids by saying they do not work or by exaggerating the potential adverse effects. That approach will decrease the credibility of the professional and potentially alienate the adolescent. Instead, the teen can be encouraged to think of alternatives to steroid use, including appropriate nutrition, strength training, and development of talents or attributes that might improve self-esteem.

The adolescent who is addicted to steroids may not be able to stop using in response to education. Treatment for these individuals may include detoxification, rehabilitation, and relapse prevention. Initial goals of treatment are to provide relief for withdrawal symptoms; to prevent complications such as suicide; to restore the function of the hypothalamic-pituitary-gonadal axis, which may have been suppressed during steroid use; and to foster a therapeutic alliance (Brower, 1992). Both supportive therapy and pharmacotherapy may be used. Rehabilitation goals are to induce complete abstinence from anabolic steroids, to restore health and psychosocial functioning, and to prevent relapse. A combination of individual counseling, peer-group supportive therapy and family therapy may be effective. Relapse prevention is complicated by the users' strong internal and external urges to resume use (Brower et al., 1991). These urges must be addressed through individual counseling around issues of self-esteem. In addition, alternatives to steroid use must be encouraged and facilitated. Finally, relapse prevention techniques must help the individual predict risky situations and develop avoidance strategies.

Prevention

Drug testing and law enforcement may impact the use of anabolic steroids by adolescent athletes. However, education by informed, nonjudgmental professionals may have a greater impact on young adolescents' decisions regarding personal use of anabolic steroids. Well-informed parents, coaches, and educators may aid in the prevention of inappropriate anabolic steroid use by adolescents.

Testing

Scheduled drug testing for anabolic steroids is not effective because the advance warning allows athletes to cycle off the drugs prior to the testing date (Strauss, 1993), but random short-notice testing in which athletes have only a few hours' notice before they provide a sample may be a more effective deterrent (Strauss, 1993). Numerous collegiate and professional organizations test for anabolic steroid use (Shikles, 1989). Unfortunately, drug testing is prohibitively expensive at the high school level, and few laboratories have the equipment to perform accurate testing. Testing of individuals by physicians for the purpose of proving use may only alienate the adolescent and make anticipatory guidance difficult, but if testing is performed, it should be done with a reputable lab.

Testing is initiated with a urine screen for anabolic steroids using radioimmunoassay (Hatton & Catlin, 1987). The testosterone to epitestosterone ratio is used to screen for exogenous testosterone use. This ratio is normally 1:1 and considered positive for steroid use at 6:1. If screening is positive, the drug or its metabolites are identified by performing gas chromatography with mass spectrometry (Hatton & Catlin, 1987). Oral steroids are usually detectable for several weeks after discontinuation (Hatton & Catlin, 1987). Parenteral agents are usually detected for up to three months after they are discontinued, but Hatton and Catlin have reported detection six months following discontinuation of their use.

Enforcement

In 1990, the U.S. Congress passed legislation to regulate anabolic steroids as controlled substances (Anabolic Steroids Control Act of 1990). However, the inability to control the import, distribution, and sale of other illicit substances regulated at the national level indicates that law enforcement alone may not be effective in preventing further steroid use. Enforcement must also involve schools, coaches, and parents to be successful. An enforced school policy for adolescent athletes and their parents that outlines consequences for steroid use may impact on adolescents' use of steroids. Yet until genuine penalties for steroid use are implemented, especially for college, professional, and olympic athletes who serve as role models for adolescents, there may be little deterrence to steroid use in the adolescent age group.

Education

Some educational strategies directed toward adolescents have been assessed for effectiveness in altering adolescents' potential for using anabolic steroids. An effective program must include the education of coaches, parents, trainers, and educators, as well as adolescents.

In one study that assessed the effectiveness of educational intervention, Bents et al. (1990) reported that athletes who participated in a program that provided information about anabolic steroid use, nutrition principles, and strength-training techniques were less likely to use steroids than athletes who had not participated in the program. However, Goldberg et al., (1991) reported that young athletes' attitudes toward anabolic steroid use were not altered following educational intervention, and Bents et al. (1989) reported that high school athletes showed a higher potential for steroid use after educational intervention using a lecture/handout format. Informational approaches to education on illicit drugs and alcohol have failed to decrease their use (Comerci & Macdonald, 1990). Programs that use these approaches, however, assume that teenagers use drugs and alcohol because they are not aware of the side effects and social consequences of such use; they do not address the reasons for teenage drug use (Comerci & Macdonald, 1990).

Educational intervention may be more effective if it is aimed at young adolescents before they begin use and while they are at the experimental-use phase (Buckley et al., 1988; Moore, 1988; Yesalis et al., 1990). Including strategies that emphasize alternatives to drug use such as proper nutrition and strength-training techniques may be necessary (Bents et al., 1990). Varied educational strategies may need to be employed to address the varied motivations for use (Yesalis et al., 1990). Peer counseling, which has been used effectively in other settings, may provide an effective intervention to limit anabolic steroid use in adolescents (Johnson et al., 1989). Older adolescents who are not using anabolic steroids may be more able than adults to dissuade younger adolescents from initiating use (Komoroski & Rickert, 1992). Since an association may exist between anabolic steroid use and the use of other drugs (DuRant et al., 1993), it may be appropriate to include general drug abuse prevention material in an educational program for anabolic steroid users. Educational strategies that present factual information and incorporate activities designed to increase self-esteem, promote responsible decision making and problem solving, teach assertiveness skills and stress reduction techniques, and provide exciting recreational opportunities have been proposed for prevention of drug abuse (Engs & Fors, 1988). Similar programs may be considered for prevention of anabolic steroid use, although the effectiveness of such a strategy has not been determined.

Educational programs must also be provided for parents, educators, trainers and coaches who serve as positive role models for adolescents. In one study, 26 percent of the inquiries for steroid use were made by parents for their sons (Salva & Bacon, 1991). From this study, it is evident that some athletes must cope with parental as well as personal and societal pressures. Parents should be informed of the potential adverse effects of steroid use and encouraged to support fair play in their teenagers' sports activities. Educators and coaches are in daily contact with adolescent athletes and could play an important part in effective prevention programs.

Educators could provide factual information and promote increased self-esteem by guiding adolescents toward realistic goals. Coaches and trainers could channel individuals into sports that are suited to their projected adult body sizes and strength. This may remove the temptation to use steroids in an attempt to attain size or strength incompatible with genetic potential. Society places tremendous importance on values that influence anabolic steroid use in today's adolescents—winning and appearance. Concerted efforts of educators, coaches, parents, and adolescents to deemphasize these values and reinforce a healthy steroid-free lifestyle could potentially curb the use of anabolic steroids by adolescents.

Summary

Evidence confirms that anabolic steroids used under certain circumstances can enhance size and strength in some individuals. Short-term adverse effects of anabolic steroid use have been studied in adults but have not been well studied in adolescents. The risk of long-term consequences of steroid use is unknown. In a society where athletes are so heavily rewarded for winning, eliminating steroid use will be difficult. A multifaceted approach to educate children at a younger age with broad-based programs that address the reasons for steroid use and emphasize alternatives to drug use such as proper nutrition and strength training may impact adolescent's use of these agents.

Further research is needed to determine potential benefits of steroid use, risks of steroid use by adolescents, and effectiveness of educational programs. Unfortunately, the illicit status and potential adverse effects of steroids impede the development of well-controlled, prospective studies regarding potential benefits and risks of these drugs used by adolescents at supraphysiologic doses. Until we can follow steroid-using athletes over a long period, determine precisely what steroids were taken, and how much for how long, many of our questions will remain unanswered.

References

Alen, M., Rahkila, P., Reinila, M., & Vihko, R. (1987). Androgenic-anabolic steroid effects on serum thyroid, pituitary and steroid hormones in athletes. *The American Journal of Sports Medicine, 15,* 357–361.

American College of Sports Medicine. (1984). Position stand on the use of anabolic-androgenic steroids in sports. *Sports Medicine Bulletin, 19,* 13–18. (Available from American College of Sports Medicine, P. O. Box 1440, Indianapolis, IN, 46206-1440)

Anabolic Reference Guide (4th ed.). (1989). Golden, CO: Mile High Publishing.

Anabolic Steroids Control Act of 1990 (P. L. 101–647, Sec. 1901–1907) (1990). United States Code Congressional and Administrative News (Vol. 4, pp. 104 STAT. 4851-104 STAT. 4854). St. Paul: West Publishing.

Ariel, G., & Saville, W. (1972). Anabolic steroids: The physiological effects of placebos. *Medicine and Science in Sports and Exercise, 4,* 124–126.

Bagheri, S. A., & Boyer, J. L. (1974). Peliosis hepatitis associated with androgenic-anabolic steroid therapy. *Annals of Internal Medicine, 81,* 610–618.

Bents, R., Trevisan, L., Bosworth, E., Boyea, S., Elliot, D., & Goldberg, L. (1989). The effect of teaching interventions on knowledge and attitudes of anabolic steroids among high school athletes. *Medicine and Science in Sports and Exercise, 21* (Suppl.), S26. (Abstract No. 152)

Bents, R., Young, J. Bosworth, E. Boyea, S. Elliot, D., & Goldberg, L. (1990). An effective educational program alters attitudes toward anabolic steroid use among adolescent athletes. *Medicine and Science in Sports and Exercise, 22* (Suppl.), S64. (Abstract No. 382)

Blessing, D. L., Health, G. W., & Escobeda, L. (1993). Prevalence of anabolic steroid use among American adolescents. *Medicine and Science in Sports and Exercise, 25* (Suppl.), S128. (Abstract No. 707)

Bowman, S. (1990). Anabolic steroids and infarction [Letter to the editor]. *British Medical Journal, 300,* 750.

Brower, K. J. (1992). Clinical assessment and treatment of anabolic steroid users. *Psychiatric Annals, 22,* 35–40.

Brower, K. J., Blow, F. C., Beresford, T. P., & Fuelling, C. (1989). Anabolicandrogenic steroid dependence. *The Journal of Clinical Psychiatry, 50,* 31–33.

Brower, K. J., Blow, F. C., Eliopulos, G. A., & Beresford, T. P. (1989). Anabolic androgenic steroids and suicide [Letter to the editor]. *American Journal of Psychiatry, 146,* 1075.

Brower, K. J., Blow, F. C., Young, J. P., & Hill, E. M. (1991). Symptoms and correlates of anabolic-androgenic steroid dependence. *British Journal of Addiction, 86,* 759–768.

Brower, K. J., Eliopulos, G. A., Blow, F. C., Catlin, D. H., & Beresford, T. P. (1990). Evidence for physical and psychological dependence on anabolic androgenic steroids in eight weight lifters. *American Journal of Psychiatry, 147,* 510–512.

Buckley, W. E., Yesalis, C. E., III, Friedl, K. E., Anderson, W. A., Streit, A. L., & Wright, J. E. (1988). Estimated prevalence of anabolic steroid use among male high school seniors. *JAMA, 260,* 3441–3445.

Calabrese, L. H., Kleiner, S. M., Barna, B. P., Skibinski, C. I., Kirkendall, D. T., Lahita, R. G., & Lombardo, J. A. (1989). The effects of anabolic steroids and strength training on the human immune response. *Medicine and Science in Sports and Exercise, 21,* 386–392.

Cohen, J. C., & Hickman, R. (1987). Insulin resistance and diminished glucose tolerance in powerlifters ingesting anabolic steroids. *Journal of Clinical Endocrinology and Metabolism, 64,* 960–963.

Cohen, J. C., Noakes, T. D., & Benade, A. J. S. (1988). Hypercholesterolemia in male power lifters using anabolic-androgenic steroids. *The Physician and Sportsmedicine, 16*(8), 49–56.

Comerci, G. D., & Macdonald, D. I. (1990). Prevention of substance abuse in children and adolescents. In V. C. Strasburger & D. E. Greydanus (Eds.), *Adolescent medicine: State of the art reviews* (Vol. 1, pp. 127–143). Philadelphia: Hanley & Belfus.

Corder, B. W., Dezelsky, T. L., Toohey, J. V., & DiVito, C. L. (1975). Trends in drug use behavior at ten central Arizona high schools. *Arizona Journal of Health, Physical Education, and Recreation, 18,* 10–11.

Cowart, V. S. (1989). If youngsters overdose with anabolic steroids, what's the cost anatomically and otherwise? *JAMA, 261,* 1856–1857.

Crawshaw, J. P. (1985). [Interview with John A. Lombardo, Christopher Longcope, & Robert O. Voy]. Recognizing anabolic steroid abuse. *Patient Care, 19*(14), 28–47.

Creagh, T. M., Rubin, A., & Evans, D. J. (1988). Hepatic tumours induced by anabolic steroids in an athlete. *Journal of Clinical Pathology, 41,* 441–443.

Duchaine, D. (1989). *Underground steroid handbook II.* Venice, CA: HLR Technical Books.

DuRant, R. H., Rickert, V. I., Ashworth, C. S., Newman, C., & Slavens, G. (1993). Use of multiple drugs among adolescents who use anabolic steroids. *The New England Journal of Medicine, 328,* 922–926.

Elofson, G., & Elofson, S. (1990). Steroids claimed our son's life. *The Physician and Sportsmedicine, 18*(8), 15–16.

Engs, R. C., & Fors, S. W. (1988). Drug abuse hysteria: The challenge of keeping perspective. *Journal of School Health, 58,* 26–28.

Ferenchick, G. S. (1990). Are androgenic steroids thrombogenic? [Letter to the editor]. *The New England Journal of Medicine, 322,* 476.

Frankle, M. A., Cicero, G. J., & Payne, J. (1984). Use of anabolic androgenic steroids by athletes [Letter to the editor]. *JAMA, 252,* 482.

Frankle, M. A., Eichberg, R., & Zachariah, S. B. (1988). Anabolic androgenic steroids and a stroke in an athlete: Case report. *Archives of Physical Medicine and Rehabilitation, 69,* 632–633.

Friedl, K. E., & Yesalis, C. E. (1989). Self-treatment of gynecomastia in bodybuilders who use anabolic steroids. *The Physician and Sportsmedicine, 17*(3), 67–79.

Goldberg, L., Bents, R., Bosworth, E., Trevisan, L., & Elliot, D. L. (1991). Anabolic steroid education and adolescents: Do scare tactics work? *Pediatrics, 87,* 283–286.

Goldman, B. (1985). Liver carcinoma in an athlete taking anabolic steroids [Letter to the editor]. *Journal of the American Osteopathic Association, 85,* 56.

Gribbin, H. R., & Matts, S. G. (1976). Mode of action and use of anabolic steroids. *The British Journal of Clinical Practice, 30,* 3–9.

Hatton, C. K., & Catlin, D. H. (1987). Detection of anabolic androgenic steroids in urine. *Clinics in Laboratory Medicine, 7,* 655–668.

Haupt, H. E., & Rovere, G. D. (1984). Anabolic steroids: A review of the literature. *The American Journal of Sports Medicine, 12,* 469–484.

Hays, L. R., Littleton, S., & Stillner, V. (1990). Anabolic steroid dependence [Letter to the editor]. *American Journal of Psychiatry, 147,* 122.

Hill, J. A., Suker, J. R., Sachs, K., & Brigham, C. (1983). The athletic polydrug abuse phenomenon: A case report. *The American Journal of Sports Medicine, 11,* 269–271.

Houssay, A. B. (1976). Effect of anabolic-androgenic steroids on the skin, including hair and sebaceous glands. In C. D. Kochakian (Ed.), *Anabolic-androgenic steroids* (pp. 155–190). New York: Springer-Verlag.

Hurley, B. F., Seals, D. R., Hagberg, J. M., Goldberg, A. C., Ostrove, S. M., Holloszy, J. O., Wiest, W. G., & Goldberg, A. P. (1984). High-density-lipoprotein cholesterol in bodybuilders vs. powerlifters. *JAMA, 252,* 507–513.

Johnson, F. L., Lerner, K. G., Siegel, M., Feagler, J. R., Majerus, P. W., Hartmann, J. R., & Thomas, E. D. (1972). Association of androgenic-anabolic steroid therapy with development of hepatocellular carcinoma. *Lancet, 2,* 1273–1276.

Johnson, M. D. (1990). Anabolic steroid use in adolescent athletes. In A. C. Hergenroeder & J. G. Garrick (Eds.), *The pediatric clinics of North America* (Vol. 37, pp. 1111–1123). Philadelphia: W. B. Saunders.

———. (1991). Steroids. In P. G. Dyment (Ed.), *Adolescent medicine: State of the art reviews* (Vol. 2, pp. 79–92). Philadelphia: Hanley & Belfus.

Johnson, M. D., Jay, M. S., Shoup, B., & Rickert, V. I. (1989). Anabolic steroid use by male adolescents. *Pediatrics, 83,* 921–924.

Kiraly, C. L., Alen, M., Rahkila, P., & Horsmanheimo, M. (1987). Effect of androgenic and anabolic steroids on the sebaceous gland in power athletes. *Acta Dermato-Venereologica (Stockh), 67,* 36–40.

Kley, H. K., Strohmeyer, G., & Kruskemper, H. L. (1979). Effect of testosterone application on hormone concentrations of androgens and estrogens in male patients with cirrhosis of the liver. *Gastroenterology, 76,* 235–241.

Komoroski, E. M., & Rickert, V. I. (1992). Adolescent body image and attitudes to anabolic steroid use. *American Journal of Diseases of Children, 146,* 823–828.

Kramhoft, M., & Solgaard, S. (1986). Spontaneous rupture of the extensor pollicis longus tendon after anabolic steroids. *Journal of Hand Surgery, 11,* 87.

Kruskemper, H. L. (1968). *Anabolic steroids* (C. H. Doering, Trans.). New York: Academic Press.

Lamb, D. R. (1984). Anabolic steroids in athletics: how well do they work and how dangerous are they? *The American Journal of Sports Medicine, 12,* 31–38.

Mauss, J., Borsch, G., Bormacher, K., Richter, E., Leyendecker, G., & Nocke, W. (1975). Effect of long-term testosterone oenanthate administration on male reproductive function: Clinical evaluation, serum FSH, LH, testosterone, and seminal fluid analyses in normal men. *Acta Endocrinologica, 78,* 373–384.

McKillop, G., Ballantyne, F. C., Borland, W., & Ballantyne, D. (1989). Acute metabolic effects of exercise in bodybuilders using anabolic steroids. *British Journal of Sports Medicine, 23,* 186–187.

McNutt, R. A., Ferenchick, G. S., Kirlin, P. C., & Hamlin, N. J. (1988). Acute myocardial infarction in a 22-year-old world class weight lifter using anabolic steroids. *The American Journal of Cardiology, 62,* 164.

Messerli, F. H., & Frohlich, E. D. (1979). High blood pressure: A side effect of drugs, poisons and food. *Archives of Internal Medicine, 139,* 682–687.

Michna, H., & Stang-Voss, C. (1983). The predisposition to tendon rupture after doping with anabolic steroids. *International Journal of Sports Medicine, 4,* 59. (Abstract)

Mochizuki, R. M., & Richter, K. J. (1988). Cardiomyopathy and cerebrovascular accident associated with anabolic-androgenic steroid use. *The Physician and Sportsmedicine, 16*(11), 109–114.

Moore, W. V. (1988). Anabolic steroid use in adolescence. *JAMA, 260,* 3484–3486.

Murad, F., & Haynes, R. C., (1985). Androgens. In A. G. Gilman, L. S. Goodman, T. W. Rall, & F. Murad (Eds.), *The pharmacological basis of therapeutics* (7th ed., pp. 1440–1458). New York: Macmillan.

Office of Inspector General, Office of Evaluation and Inspections (1990). *Adolescents and steroids: A user perspective* (DHHS Publication No. OEI-06-90-01081). Washington, DC: U.S. Government Printing Office.

Overly, W. L., Dankoff, J. A., Wang, B. K., & Singh, U. D. (1984). Androgens and hepatocellular carcinoma in an athlete [Letter to the editor]. *Annals of Internal Medicine, 100,* 158–159.

Perry, P. J., Yates, W. R., & Anderson, K. H. (1990). Psychiatric symptoms associated with anabolic steroids: A controlled, retrospective study. *Annals of Clinical Psychiatry, 2,* 11–17.

Pope, H. G. Jr., & Katz, D. L. (1988). Affective and psychotic symptoms associated with anabolic steroid use. *American Journal of Psychiatry, 145,* 487–490.

———. (1990). Homicide and near-homicide by anabolic steroid users. *The Journal of Clinical Psychiatry, 51,* 28–31.

———. (1992). Psychiatric effects of anabolic steroids. *Psychiatric Annals, 22,* 24–34.

Prat, J., Gray, G. F., Stolley, P. D., & Coleman, J. W. (1977). Wilms tumor in an adult associated with androgen abuse. *JAMA, 237,* 2322–2323.

Roberts, J. T. (1986). Adenocarcinoma of prostate in 40-year-old body-builder [Letter to the editor]. *The Lancet, 2,* 742.

Robinson, T. N., Killen, J. D., Taylor, C. B., Telch, M. J., Bryson, S. W., Saylor, K. E., Maron, D. J., Maccoby, N., & Farquhar, J. W. (1987). Perspectives on adolescent substance use: A defined population study. *JAMA, 258,* 2072–2076.

Rogol, A. D. (1985). Drugs to enhance athletic performance in the adolescent. *Seminars in Adolescent Medicine, 1,* 317–324.

Rozenek, R., Rahe, C. H., Kohl, H. H., Marple, D. N., Wilson, G. D., & Stone, M. H. (1990). Physiological responses to resistance-exercise in athletes self-administering anabolic steroids. *The Journal of Sports Medicine and Physical Fitness, 30,* 354–360.

Sachtleben, T. R., Berg, K. E., Elias, B. A., Cheatham, J. P., Felix, G. L., & Hofschire, P. J. (1993). The effects of anabolic steroids on myocardial structure and cardiovascular fitness. *Medicine and Science in Sports and Exercise, 25,* 1240–1245.

Salva, P. S., & Bacon, G. E. (1991). Anabolic steroids: Interest among parents and nonathletes. *Southern Medical Journal, 84,* 552–556.

Scott, M. J., & Scott, M. J., Jr. (1989). HIV infection associated with injections of anabolic steroids [Letter to the editor]. *JAMA, 262,* 207–208.

Scott, M. J., Jr., & Scott, M. J., III (1989). Dermatologists and anabolic-androgenic drug abuse. *Cutis, 44,* 30–35.

Sheridan, P. J. (1983). Androgen receptors in the brain: What are we measuring? *Endocrine Reviews, 4,* 171–178.

Shikles, J. L. (1989). *Drug misuse: Anabolic steroids and human growth hormone* (GAO/HRD-89-109). Washington, DC: United States General Accounting Office.

Sklarek, H. M., Mantovani, R. P., Erens, E., Heisler, D., Niederman, M. S., & Fein, A. M. (1984). AIDS in a bodybuilder using anabolic steroids [Letter to the editor]. *The New England Journal of Medicine, 311,* 1701.

Strauss, R. H. (1993). [Interview with Don Catlin, Jim Wright, Harrison Pope, Jr., & Mariah Liggett]. Assessing the threat of anabolic steroids. *The Physician and Sports Medicine, 21*(8), 37–44.

Strauss, R. H., Wright, J. E., Finerman, G. A. M., & Caitlin, D. H. (1983). Side effects of anabolic steroids in weight-trained men. *The Physician and Sportsmedicine, 11*(12), 87–96.

Su, T., Pagliaro, M., Schmidt, P. J., Pickar, D., Wolkowitz, O., & Rubinow, D. R. (1993). Neuropsychiatric effects of anabolic steroids in male normal volunteers. *JAMA, 269,* 2760–2764.

Sweeney, E. C., & Evans, D. J. (1976). Hepatic lesions in patients treated with synthetic anabolic steroids. *Journal of Clinical Pathology, 29,* 626–633.

Taylor, W. N. (1987). Synthetic anabolic-androgenic steroids: A plea for controlled substance status. *The Physician and Sports Medicine, 15*(5), 140–150.

Tennant, F., Black, D. L., & Voy, R. O. (1988). Anabolic steroid dependence with opioid-type features [Letter to the editor]. *The New England Journal of Medicine, 319,* 578.

Terney, R., & McLain, L. G. (1990). The use of anabolic steroids in high school students. *American Journal of Diseases of Children, 144,* 99–103.

Urhausen, A., Holpes, R., & Kindermann, W. (1989). One- and two-dimensional echocardiography in bodybuilders using anabolic steroids. *European Journal of Applied Physiology, 58,* 633–640.

Whitehead, R., Chillag, S., & Elliott, D. (1992). Anabolic steroid use among adolescents in a rural state. *The Journal of Family Practice, 35,* 401–405.

Wilson, J. D. (1988). Androgen abuse by athletes. *Endocrine Reviews, 9,* 181–199.

Wilson, J. D., & Griffin, J. E. (1980). The use and misuse of androgens. *Metabolism, 29,* 1278–1295.

Windsor, R., & Dumitru, D. (1989). Prevalence of anabolic steroid use by male and female adolescents. *Medicine and Science in Sports and Exercise, 21,* 494–497.

Wright, J. E. (1980). Anabolic steroids and athletics. *Exercise and Sport Sciences Reviews, 8,* 149–202.

Yates, W. R., Perry, P. J., & Anderson, K. H. (1990). Illicit anabolic steroid use: A controlled personality study. *Acta Psychiatrica Scandinavica, 81,* 548–550.

Yesalis, C. E., Kennedy, N. J., Kopstein, A. N., & Bahrke, M. S. (1993). Anabolic-androgenic steroid use in the United States. *JAMA, 270,* 1217–1221.

Yesalis, C. E., Streit, A. L., Vicary, J. R., Friedl, K. E., Brannon, D., & Buckley, W. (1989). Anabolic steroid use: Indications of habituation among adolescents. *Journal of Drug Education, 19,* 103–116.

Yesalis, C. E., Vicary, J. R., Buckley, W. E., Streit, A. L., Datz, D. L., & Wright, J. E. (1990). *NIDA Research Monograph, 102,* 196–214.

15

STRENGTH TRAINING IN CHILDREN AND ADOLESCENTS

—David R. Webb

Whether or not children and adolescents should engage in strength training has been a matter of surprisingly heated controversy. Are there any real benefits to be derived? Is the risk of injury excessively high? Opinions have differed widely (American Academy of Pediatrics Committee on Sports Medicine, 1983; American Orthopaedic Society for Sports Medicine, 1988; Faigenbaum, 1993; Fleck, Henke, & Wilson, 1989; Jesse, 1979; Maitland, 1986; National Strength and Conditioning Association, 1985; Rians, 1987; Risser, 1990; Webb, 1990; Weltman, 1989). Some equipment manufacturers' advertisements have suggested that "pumping plastic," if not iron, should begin in infancy (Matchbox Toys [USA] Ltd., 1985). At the other extreme, some physicians have taken the stance that "thou shalt not, until thou art adult."

The controversy notwithstanding, more and more American children and adolescents are lifting weights or engaging in some form of strength training (Neill, 1988; Risser, 1990). In recent years, a number of prospective studies have been carried out that demonstrate the efficacy and safety of appropriately designed and supervised strength-training programs (Baumgartner & Wood, 1984; Blimkie, 1989; Brown et al., 1992; Clarke, Vaccaro, & Andresen, 1984; Faigenbaum et al., 1993; Funato et al., 1987; McGovern, 1984; Nielsen et al., 1980; Pfeiffer & Francis, 1986; Ramsay et al., 1990; Rians, 1987; Sailors & Berg, 1987; Sale, 1989; Servedio et al., 1985; Sewall & Micheli, 1986; Siegal, Camaione, & Manfredi, 1989; Weltman et al., 1986; Wescott, 1992; Williams, 1991). It can be hoped that at least some of the controversy will be resolved as well-intentioned but ill-informed opinion yields to scientific inquiry.

This chapter provides a thorough review of the subject for parents, coaches, teachers, health care professionals, and others concerned with the health, well-being, and development of young athletes. First the locker room and the scientific vocabulary of strength training is presented. Special attention is given to the clinical implications of basic physiological concepts. Next the potential benefits and risks of greatest concern are reviewed, and the relevant data, or lack thereof, is discussed. Finally, from the author's perspective as a physician, as well as a parent and a former coach, specific, practical recommendations are made regarding beginning strength training for young athletes.

Basic Concepts and Terminology

Strength

In the context of exercise science, *strength* may be defined as the ability to exert muscular force against resistance.

In the more general context of sports, strength is sometimes used imprecisely as a synonym for athletic ability or prowess. A track coach, for example, may refer to a runner with exceptional stamina as a "strong" runner. Such casual usage of the term, however, should not be confused with the scientific definition.

Most daily physical activities of children and adults require muscular strength. It is a fundamental attribute of athletes in most competitive sports. Indeed, the only athletic activities in which it is not a factor in performance are the pure endurance events, such as long-distance running and swimming.

Types of Muscle Action

Exertion of muscular force does not necessarily produce skeletal movement or accomplish positive external mechanical work. A skeletal muscle has three basic functions: acceleration, fixation (stabilization), and deceleration of the skeleton. The external mechanical work accomplished (work equals force times distance) may thus be positive, zero, or negative. The corresponding actions of the muscle are described as concentric, isometric, and eccentric (Cavanagh, 1988).

A *concentric* muscle action is one in which the muscle shortens (contracts) as it exerts force. Skeletal movement is produced. The external mechanical work accomplished is positive.

Isometric means "same length." The term is used precisely to describe the *in vitro* action of an isolated muscle preparation in which the total length of the muscle does not change as force is exerted (Van Huss & Heusner, 1970). The term is also commonly used to describe *in vivo* muscle actions in which, even though considerable muscle shortening may occur, the total length of the muscle tendon unit does not change, and no skeletal movement occurs. The external mechanical work accomplished is zero.

An *eccentric* muscle action is one in which the muscle lengthens as it exerts force. Skeletal movement is controlled or slowed. The external mechanical work accomplished is negative.

Exercise with weights may involve all three types of muscle action. A barbell or dumbbell arm curl is a typical example (see fig. 15.1). As the weight is raised, elbow flexion is produced by the concentric action of the elbow flexor muscles. As the weight is slowly lowered, elbow extension is effected simply by the force of gravity. The motion is controlled, however, by the eccentric action of the elbow flexors. If the weight were held in any fixed position of elbow flexion, the force of gravity would be exactly offset by the isometric action of the elbow flexors.

In contrast, use of hydraulic resistance equipment and most isokinetic equipment involves only concentric muscle action. Again, the arm curl exercise provides

FIGURE 15.1

Barbell curl exercise. The elbow flexor muscles act concentrically when the weight is raised and eccentrically when the weight is lowered under control. They would act isometrically if the weight were held in a fixed position of elbow flexion.

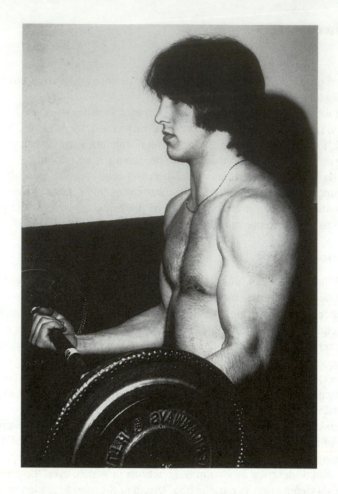

an illustrative example. As the elbow is flexed, the elbow flexor muscles act concentrically. On the return, however, as the elbow is extended, the elbow extensor muscles act concentrically.

At comparable speeds of shortening and lengthening, respectively, and against comparable external force, less tension in a muscle tendon unit will occur during concentric than during eccentric exercise (Olson, Schmidt, & Johnson, 1972). Also, with concentric exercise, as speed increases, the maximum amount of tension that can be developed in the muscle tendon unit decreases, whereas the opposite is true with eccentric exercise (Komi & Buskirk, 1972; Thorstensson, 1988).

Understandably, professionals may have some concern about children's doing eccentric resistance exercises (American Orthopaedic Society for Sports Medicine, 1988). However, most physical activities of children, as well as adults, involve eccentric muscle action. In throwing a ball, for example, eccentric loads are placed on the shoulder and scapular stabilizing muscles during deceleration of the throwing arm. Similarly, in landing a jump, eccentric loads are placed on the muscles of the lower limb, especially the quadriceps. Indeed, the only sports in which little or no eccentric muscle action occurs are cycling and swimming (Faria & Cavanagh, 1978). Thus, for example, it does not make good sense to tell a youngster with Osgood-Schlatter's disease that he or she may not lift weights (because of the eccentric muscle action involved) but that he or she may go out and play basketball or soccer "as long as it doesn't hurt."

Conversely, it cannot be assumed that because an exercise is concentric it is inherently "safe." In the author's experience, concentric isokinetic devices used at low speeds frequently cause musculotendinous injuries (strains). A few years ago, an exercise device intended to enhance leaping ability gained considerable notoriety for causing an "epidemic" of spinal injuries in young athletes (Brady, Cahill, & Bodnar, 1982). The device basically provided resistance against powerful concentric action of the hip and knee extensors. Used incorrectly, it placed excessive compression loads on the spine. Other such devices have been similarly implicated (Torg et al., 1976). Many authors have inveighed against Olympic-style lifting for children and adolescents (American Academy of Pediatrics Committee on Sports Medicine, 1983; American Orthopaedic Society for Sports Medicine, 1988; Jesse, 1977). Yet these lifts involve mainly concentric muscle action—a barbell is rapidly lifted and then dropped, rather than slowly lowered.

The risk of musculoskeletal injury would seem to be related mainly to the magnitude of repetitive and peak loads imposed and not necessarily to how the load is imposed. Eccentric as opposed to concentric exercise is just one way of imposing greater loads (Atha, 1981; Komi & Buskirk, 1972).

Power

In physics, *power* is defined as the rate at which work is performed, expressed mathematically as the first derivative of work with respect to time. If the work performed is mechanical and the force applied is constant, power simply equals force times the first derivative of distance with respect to time or force times speed.

As applied to exercise, power is a function of both the amount of muscular force exerted and the rate of body or limb movement (Van Huss & Heusner, 1970). This concept of power is quite analogous to many athletes' and coaches' intuitive sense of the "explosive strength," for example, of a powerful football running back or a powerful baseball batter.

Most "strength athletes" are in fact "power athletes." A few situations in sports do require mainly static strength and/or static muscular endurance, as opposed to power. Examples are gripping a racquet in tennis and bridging to avoid a pin in wrestling. Ironically, the only competitive "pure strength" sport is misnamed power lifting (see "Competitive Events"). Most athletic activities, for example, sprinting, jumping, throwing, hitting a ball, and taking down an opponent, require power, as opposed to pure strength. Strength, however, is a fundamental prerequisite of power.

Muscular Endurance

Static muscular endurance is the ability of a muscle or group of muscles to exert force continuously (without producing skeletal movement). *Dynamic muscular endurance* is the ability of a muscle or group of muscles to exert force repetitively (while producing or resisting skeletal movement).

Muscular endurance may be further classified as *short-, medium-,* or *long-term,* depending on the duration and energetics of the muscular action. In short-duration (less than 30 seconds), high-intensity work, such as the 100-meter dash in track, muscle energy requirements are largely supplied by creatine phosphate. In medium-duration (from 30 seconds up to 4 minutes), intermediate-intensity work, such as an 800-meter dash, muscle energy requirements are largely met by glycolysis. In long-duration (over 4 minutes), lower-intensity work, such as a 10-kilometer run, muscle energy requirements are met by oxidative phosphorylation.

Most athletic activities require at least short-term muscular endurance. A few notable exceptions are competitive weight lifting, some of the field events in track and field, vaulting in gymnastics, and hitting a baseball, all of which involve just single maximal efforts. Most strength and power events, even, for example, football line play, involve sustained or repeated high intensity efforts.

Measurements of Strength and Power

As tested, strength is the maximum effective force a muscle or group of muscles can exert one time (Van Huss & Heusner, 1970). Strength may be considered *dynamic* or *static,* depending on whether or not the muscular force exerted is associated with skeletal movement. The most commonly employed test of dynamic strength is the *one repetition maximum (1RM) lift* (DeLorme & Watkins, 1948), that is, the maximum amount of weight that can be lifted once in a prescribed way.

An important clinical consideration is that athletes of all ages, not to mention their peers, coaches, and scouts, frequently want to test their strength by seeing how much they can lift. Attempts at maximal lifts, however, clearly involve greater peak forces, frequently involve compromised lifting technique ("form breaks," "cheating"), and consequently, especially in the inexperienced lifter, involve increased risk of musculoskeletal injury. Alternative means of testing strength would therefore seem desirable (American Academy of Pediatrics Committee on Sports Medicine, 1983; American Orthopaedic Society for Sports Medicine, 1988; Faigenbaum, 1993; Kraemer & Fleck, 1993; National Strength and Conditioning Association, 1985; Risser, 1991; Webb, 1990).

Various formulae for estimating *one repetition maximum equivalent* lifts have been proposed (Brzycki, 1993; Hoeger et al., 1987; Landers, 1985; Mayhew, Ware, & Prinster, 1993). All have in common the use of multiple repetition maximum lifts (e.g., 10RM) to predict one repetition maximums. By definition, with any maximum lift, exercise is continued to the point of "failure" to be able to do one more repetition. Although the peak loads are less with a 10RM lift than with a 1RM lift, compromised lifting technique, especially on the last repetition, is still a problem. In the author's experience, both as a treating physician and a lifter, maximal lift attempts, regardless of the number of repetitions, are associated with substantially increased risk of injury.

One practical alternative is to use hydraulic resistance equipment rather than weights to assess strength. The maximum number of repetitions that can be accomplished in a specified time, for example, 30 seconds, is actually a mixed test of dynamic strength, power, and short-term muscular endurance. This method has been shown, however, to be a satisfactory way of measuring the response to training in prepubescent boys (Weltman et al., 1986). Also, it was found to be quite satisfactory for keeping the boys motivated, satisfying their competitive desires, and not causing injuries (Rians, 1987).

Power, as tested clinically, is the maximum effective force a muscle or group of muscles can exert at a given speed. Most commonly, muscular power is tested using an isokinetic device (discussed in "Types of Resistance Equipment"). Isokinetic testing has become a widely used research tool and has been shown to be reliable for assessing muscular power in children as well as adults (Weltman et al., 1987). As previously noted, however, maximum efforts at low speeds may involve increased risk of acute musculoskeletal injury.

Strength Training

The term *strength training* may be precisely defined as the use of *progressive resistance exercise* methods specifically to increase one's ability to exert muscular force against resistance.

The desired *training effect,* measurably increased strength, will represent a successful muscular and/or neuromuscular *adaptation* to the imposed exercise *overload* (Selye, 1970; Selye, 1974; Van Huss & Heusner, 1970). In this context, overload does not imply harmful excess or overuse but, rather, an increase above baseline. To be effective, the exercise program must be *specific* and of sufficient frequency and intensity.

The term *resistance training* encompasses all uses of progressive resistance exercise. The resistance may be provided by opposing muscle groups, the individual's body weight, free weights, elastic bands or tubing, or various types of machines. The intended training effect(s) may be increased strength, power, and/or muscular endurance. As adaptation occurs, the duration of exercise (number of repetitions) and then intensity of exercise (amount of resistance) are progressively increased.

As may be surmised, exercises done to increase dynamic strength and those done to increase power are qualitatively quite similar. They differ mainly in the speed with which they are performed. Any such exercises involving sets of two or more repetitions will also tend to increase short-term muscular endurance. Although purists may object to the imprecise use of the term, all of these exercises are commonly referred to as "strength training."

The term *weight training* properly refers to any progressive resistance exercise program in which the resistance is provided by free weights (dumbbells and barbells) and/or weight machines (National Strength and Conditioning Association, 1985). It has been suggested that the term be applied only to submaximal exercise of three or four repetitions (American Academy of Pediatrics Committee on Sports Medicine, 1983). However, such use of the term is artificially constrained and unnecessarily confusing. To athletes, coaches, and exercise scientists, "weight training" or "lifting weights" does not imply a specific intensity or duration of exercise. The distance runner doing a set of 200 one-pound arm curls and the football player bench pressing 200 pounds one time are both engaged in weight training.

Types of Resistance Exercise

The terms *isometric, isotonic, isokinetic, variable resistance,* and *plyometric* are used to describe various types of resistance exercise.

Isometric has already been defined. Resistance may be provided by opposing muscle groups (e.g., of the same or opposite limb), held weights, or immovable objects. Because no joint movement occurs, isometric exercises are often relatively well tolerated by injured athletes and have been found to be very useful in rehabilitation to maintain and to increase strength (Garrick & Webb, 1990). A limitation is that gains in strength are to a large extent specific to the joint angle at which the exercise is done.

The imprecise term *isotonic* has become very much ingrained in the parlance of sports and exercise as a synonym for any resistance exercise in which the resistance is provided by an individual's body weight, free weights, or simple weight machines. Isotonic literally means "same tension." As commonly used, however, it might better be construed as meaning "same mass." For example, even though the mass of a barbell does not change during a lift, the external force to be opposed (a vector quantity) will vary depending on the joint angle and angular joint velocity. Muscle tension will vary not only with the variable external force but also with muscle length, type of muscle action (concentric or eccentric), and speed of muscle shortening or lengthening. Although not a consideration for the beginner, it should be noted that some "explosive" movements in sports can indeed be very closely simulated by isotonic exercises done with free weights.

Isokinetic means "same speed." The term is used to describe dynamic resistance exercise performed at constant angular joint velocity. Resistance is provided and the speed of movement is controlled electromechanically. For both training and testing purposes, isokinetic devices are relatively safe, effective, and reliable. However, few, if any, natural movements are isokinetic, and no isokinetic device approaches the speeds commonly attained in athletic endeavors.

In virtually all dynamic resistance exercise, the external force opposed by muscle action varies during the exercise. The term *variable resistance exercise,* however, implies that the resistance can be programmed mechanically or electromechanically, for example, to match increases and decreases in muscular strength throughout the range of motion of the exercise or to simulate the biomechanics of certain athletic movements. Again, mechanical devices utilizing cams and weights cannot approach the speeds of movement commonly attained in most athletic activities. "High-tech" electromechanical devices in which both resistance and speed of movement can be programmed to simulate athletic movements have been touted for elite athletes but are hardly appropriate for young or inexperienced athletes.

Plyometrics is a method of training comprising various exercises in which concentric muscle action is immediately preceded by eccentric loading of the muscle (Chu, 1983). The exercises include hops, bounds, depth jumps, jumping with weights, medicine ball drills, and so forth. Eccentric loading has the effect of taking the slack out of the noncontractile elements of the muscle tendon unit and activating stretch reflexes. The close coupling of eccentric and concentric muscle actions has been shown to increase the amount of force that can be developed in the concentric phase of the movement (Bosco et al., 1981; Komi, 1988). Plyometric training has been shown to enhance performance in certain power events (Chu, 1983; Thorstensson, 1988; Veroshanski, 1967). However, even among mature, elite power athletes, a very high injury rate appears to be associated with this type of training. Skipping rope and doing jumping jacks are some plyometric exercises that in moderation would seem appropriate for children, but more strenuous exercises such as depth jumps should probably not be done at all by young or inexperienced athletes (Maitland, 1986).

Competitive Events

Although weight training may be done to enhance performance in many sports, it is integral to three competitive sports: Olympic weight lifting, power lifting, and body building.

Olympic weight lifting is a skilled power sport, requiring balance, agility, and speed, as well as dynamic strength. The sport comprises two competitive lifts, the *clean and jerk* and the *snatch.* The clean and jerk involves lifting a barbell from the floor to shoulder height in one move (clean) and then overhead in a second move (jerk). The snatch involves lifting a barbell from the floor to overhead in a single move. In both lifts, tremendous acceleration of the barbell is effected, mainly by powerful action of the hip and knee extensors. Many advanced strength and power athletes in various sports incorporate modified Olympic-style lifts, such as power cleans, into their regular training programs.

Power lifting is essentially a strength sport. It comprises three competitive lifts, the *bench press,* the *squat,* and the *dead lift.* The bench press begins with the athlete supine on a bench, holding a barbell above with the athlete's elbows fully extended. The barbell is then lowered to the chest and raised back up. In the squat and dead lift, the same muscle groups are used as in the Olympic lifts, but in a different manner. A squat begins with the athlete standing with a barbell supported on the shoulders. In a full squat, the hips and knees are flexed until the thighs are parallel to the floor. The athlete then stands back up. A dead lift begins similarly to a clean. The athlete stands up holding onto the barbell but without raising the arms.

Bodybuilding is an aesthetic sport and does not involve any competitive lifts. It is, however, dependent on weight training to achieve the desired level of muscular hypertrophy and definition.

In North America, the recommendation has usually been that children not participate in competitive weight lifting (American Academy of Pediatrics Committee on Sports Medicine, 1983; American Orthopaedic Society for Sports Medicine, 1988; Jesse, 1977). However, Soviet children reportedly begin competitive lifting as early as age 9 and Bulgarian children as early as age 7 (Kulund & Töttössy, 1983). Initially the children are judged mainly on technique, rather than the amount of weight lifted. Not surprisingly, the Soviet Union and Bulgaria usually garner most of the Olympic medals in the strength events. More important, however, some evidence suggests that Olympic-style lifting can be undertaken by prepubescent children without deleterious health effects (Servedio et al., 1985). It would also appear that adolescents can undertake power lifting without an associated high incidence of injury (Brown & Kimball, 1983).

Training Progression

Training is advanced as an individual adapts to his or her exercise program. Exercise demands are gradually increased both with respect to the amount of resistance used and with respect to the motor skills (neuromuscular coordination) required. The following represents a complete sequence of increasingly demanding resistance exercises:

1. Electrical muscle stimulator, isometrics with or without weights
2. High-repetition, light-resistance, mainly concentric strength/endurance exercises using elastic bands, hydraulic resistance equipment, isokinetic devices, and/or weight machines
3. Heavier resistance, concentric and eccentric strength exercises using elastic bands, hydraulic resistance equipment, isokinetic devices, weight machines, and/or free weights
4. "Explosive" Olympic-style lifts using free weights
5. Maximal lift workouts, negative (eccentric) lift workouts, and plyometrics

With increasingly demanding exercise, the potential is greater for gains in strength but also is greater for risk of injury.

It is important to note that all that is required for successful adaptation to occur is sufficient overload with respect to frequency, duration, and intensity of exercise. As with other types of training, strength gains can be achieved with submaximal overload. As a rule, however, *within the limits of exercise tolerance,* that is, without producing injury, the greater the overload, the greater will be the rate of strength gain (Van Huss & Heusner, 1970). For mature, elite strength athletes, sufficient overload may imply 1RM lifts, negative lifts, plyometrics, and so forth. For an acutely injured athlete, on the other hand, even simple isometric exercises may not be tolerated. For most children and inexperienced athletes, appropriate overload can probably be provided by submaximal, simple hydraulic or weight machine exercises done two to three times per week (Faigenbaum et al., 1993; McGovern, 1984; Pfeiffer & Francis, 1986; Ramsay et al., 1990; Sewall & Micheli, 1986; Weltman et al., 1986; Wescott, 1992; Williams, 1991).

Potential Benefits

Increased Strength

It will seem obvious to countless parents, coaches, and physical educators, and to children themselves, that they can achieve improvements in strength through strength training and sport participation. It will also seem obvious to many clinicians, physical therapists, and again the youngsters themselves that muscular size, tone, strength, endurance, flexibility, and function are "use it or lose it" phenomena. In the author's clinical practice, in children, just as in adults, disuse muscular atrophy and weakness following immobilization or injury and subsequent return of strength with specific progressive resistance rehabilitation exercises are common, everyday observations.

Common experience notwithstanding, some professionals have surmised and presented as fact that, because of insufficient circulating androgens, Tanner stage I and II individuals (Tanner, 1962) cannot significantly improve strength (American Academy of Pediatrics Committee on Sports Medicine, 1983; Kulund & Töttössy, 1983). Apparently supporting this notion were two early studies that failed to demonstrate any effect of weight training on limb muscle strength in prepubescents (Hetherington, 1976; Vrijens, 1978).

The controversy should now, however, be laid to rest. In recent years a number of prospective studies have well demonstrated that Tanner stage I and II boys and girls can indeed achieve measurable increases in strength as a result of training (Baumgartner & Wood, 1984; Blimkie, 1989; Brown et al., 1992; Clarke et al., 1984; Faigenbaum et al., 1993; Funato et al., 1987; McGovern, 1984; Nielsen et al., 1980; Pfeiffer & Francis, 1986; Ramsay et al., 1990; Rians, 1987; Sailors & Berg, 1987; Sale, 1989; Servedio et al., 1985; Sewall & Micheli, 1986; Siegal et al., 1989; Weltman et al., 1986; Wescott, 1992; Williams, 1991). Over 8 to 14 weeks of training with hydraulic resistance equipment, weight machines, and free weights (Faigenbaum et al., 1993; Servedio et al., 1985; Sewall & Micheli, 1986; Weltman et al., 1986), strength-trained subjects increased strength by 22 to 74 percent in various tests, compared with 3 to 14 percent for nonstrength-trained controls. Before puberty, increases in strength may be more the result of neuromuscular adaptation (motor learning) than muscular adaptation (hypertrophy) (Ramsay et al., 1990). However, the dramatic muscular hypertrophy and strength gains observed in some postpubertal athletes may be directly related to prepubertal motor learning.

Enhanced Self-Image and Self-Esteem

Many children and especially adolescents are motivated to undertake strength training to improve their physical appearance. Some studies have found that strength training can positively affect the self-concept of college-age students (Stein & Motta, 1992; Tucker, 1982), and some professionals have surmised this holds true for children as well (American Orthopaedic Society for Sports Medicine, 1988; National Strength and Conditioning Association, 1985). Parents and investigators have also noted improved work habits, self-confidence, and fitness awareness (Faigenbaum, 1993; Weltman et al., 1986). A common observation of the author and others (Kraemer & Fleck, 1993) is the sense of satisfaction children derive from mastering new motor skills. The pride of accomplishment in being able to lift a piece of iron confidently and cleanly overhead can be quite comparable to that of sticking a dismount or hitting a home run.

Enhanced Athletic Performance

The question of whether or not strength training can enhance athletic performance in children and adolescents resolves itself into three more fundamental questions: Can training make the young athlete stronger? Does his or her sport require strength? Is the strength-training program specific to the strength requirements of the sport?

The first question has been addressed and the second need not be belabored. In no sport is muscular strength the only determinant of success. Nonetheless, in any but the pure endurance sports, it is an asset. All other factors being equal, stronger individuals will run and swim faster, jump higher, and hit balls farther than their less strong counterparts. An illustrative case in point is Vasily Alexeyev, the great Soviet heavyweight weight lifter. His tremendous bulk notwithstanding, he could run 100 meters in 11.2 seconds and had a standing vertical jump of 26 inches (Yessis, 1987)—athleticism unmatched by world-class endurance athletes less than half his size.

In all of the previously referenced studies that demonstrated increased strength with appropriate training, flexibility was also either increased or unchanged. In some of the studies (Servedio et al., 1985; Sewall & Micheli, 1986; Weltman et al., 1986; Williams, 1991), strength-trained subjects also demonstrated significant improvement in power/skill tests such as vertical jump. In two of the studies (Brown et al., 1992; Faigenbaum et al., 1993), no such improvement was noted.

In children, as in adults, the specificity of training has been demonstrated (Nielsen et al., 1980). The inconsistent results of strength training with respect to motor performance tests probably relate mainly to the specificity of the training. For example, as training effects of doing elbow curls, one might reasonably expect increased size, tone, and strength of the biceps brachii but not improved running speed or vertical jump.

Prevention of Sports Injuries

A rational approach to prevention of sports-related injuries depends on an understanding of the epidemiology and mechanisms of injury and on reliable injury surveillance (Garrick, 1972). In this context, the question of whether or not strength training can prevent sports-related injuries resolves into several more fundamental questions: What injuries are incurred? Who is at risk for sustaining the injuries? Under what circumstances? Is lack of strength a likely causative factor? If so, can increased strength through appropriate training be shown to result in fewer injuries?

Experience suggests, and it is generally conceded, that preseason conditioning, including strength training, can reduce the incidence of musculotendinous injuries in sports (American Orthopaedic Society for Sports Medicine, 1988; Cahill & Griffith, 1978; Dominguez, 1978; Garrick & Requa, 1980; Hejna et al., 1982; National Strength and Conditioning Association, 1985). This may be true in part simply because some of the injuries usually associated with beginning a new activity are shifted from the early season to the period of preseason conditioning. The likelihood of acute injury increases whenever new motor skills are being learned and practiced, and the likelihood of overuse injuries increases whenever the level of physical activity increases abruptly (Garrick & Webb, 1990). Nonetheless, because conditioning can be carried out in a very orderly way, starting easily and advancing gradually, it is reasonable to suppose that the overall incidence of injuries, especially overuse injuries, can be reduced. It would also seem reasonable that a stronger, less easily fatigued muscle would be less likely to be injured and might be more protective of the joint(s) at which it acts.

One of the best predictors of sports injury is prior injury (Garrick, Gillien, & Whiteside, 1986). Certainly in this context, rehabilitation to repair any strength deficits can be preventive of subsequent overuse injury.

Such considerations, however, beg the questions of greatest concern. It is generally acknowledged that abrasions, contusions, muscle soreness, sprains, and strains occur in sports and that such injuries are acceptable costs of children's sport participation. Much more worrisome is the possibility of fatal, catastrophic, or other serious, acute injury. How can such injuries be prevented? Prevention must be the paramount concern, especially for spinal cord injury, as there is no satisfactory "definitive" treatment.

Several authors have called attention to the occurrence of severe cervical spine injuries in ectomorphic ("goose-necked") individuals and have suggested that strength training may be a key to injury prevention (Cantu, 1988; Crouch, 1979; Maroon, 1981; Maroon et al., 1977; Pearl & Mayer, 1979; Schneider, 1965, 1973; Sovio et al., 1984; Tator et al., 1984; Tator & Edmonds, 1984). Evidence has shown that appropriate rehabilitation can reduce the probability of subsequent nonsevere injury (Albright et al., 1985), but it has not been shown that increased strength protects against severe injury. Indeed, in both football and gymnastics, the more-advanced, stronger athletes are the more likely to sustain acute injuries (Clarke & Powell, 1982; Lindner & Caine, 1993; Schneider, 1965). Presumably this is because these athletes have increased exposure to high-risk situations, for example, more playing time in football games, more difficult skills attempted in the gym. Nonetheless, their strength per se does not lessen their risk of serious, acute injury.

Case report and epidemiological studies have helped clarify the pathomechanics of severe spinal injury in sports (Clarke & Powell, 1979, 1982; Maroon, 1981; McCoy et al., 1984; Mennen, 1981; Scher, 1981a, 1981b, 1983; Schneider, 1965, 1973; Sovio et al., 1984; Tator et al., 1981, 1984; Tator & Edmonds, 1984; Thompson & Morris, 1982; Torg, 1982; Torg et al., 1977, 1979a, 1979b). Axial loading is by far the most common mechanism. When the neck is slightly flexed, the normal cervical lordosis is lost, and the cervical spine becomes a straight column. Impact to the crown of the head can then produce axial loading of the cervical spine with excessive energy absorption, fracture and/or dislocation, and cord injury. The slightly built defensive back attempting an open field tackle of a larger opponent may indeed be at risk for severe injury. However, his risk derives not from insufficient neck girth but, rather, because he is liable to attempt head-down or "spear" tackling. This is also the mechanism by which diving into shallow water and striking the bottom or a submerged object can produce spinal injury.

These studies suggest that elimination of those practices that cause axial loading of the cervical spine could result in fewer severe injuries. Subsequent epidemiological studies have revealed that, for football at least, this is indeed the case (Albright et al., 1985; Clarke & Powell, 1979; Mueller & Blyth, 1979, 1982). In 1975 use of the helmet or face mask in blocking and tackling was outlawed. In 1977 and

1980 other rule changes were made that allowed offensive players more liberal use of the hands and arms for blocking. Following these rule changes, the incidence of catastrophic spinal injuries in football has dropped to an all-time low.

These and other studies (McCoy et al., 1984; Rapp & Nicely, 1978; Roy, 1979; Scher, 1982, 1983; Thompson & Morris, 1982; Torg et al., 1976; Torg & Das, 1984) reveal that imprudent or illegal practices are the major causes of severe spinal injury in recreational and organized sports. It would seem, therefore, that safety education and appropriate modification and strict enforcement of the rules of play are the keys to injury prevention. Torg (1982) states, "It is not sufficient for coaches to refrain from teaching techniques utilizing the top or the crown of the helmet as a primary point of contact. Coaches must teach the players *not* to use such techniques" (p. 8).

Similar considerations apply to other serious, acute sports injuries. For example, in most cases of serious knee injuries in sports such as football, fixation of the foot on the ground is a necessary element in the mechanism of injury. Cleat penetration, and thus foot fixation, is enhanced by the fewer number and greater length of cleats found on conventional football shoes. It has been shown that the risk of injury can be decreased by using multicleated, molded-sole, soccer-style shoes (Torg & Quedenfeld, 1974). It has not been satisfactorily shown that conditioning can prevent such injuries.

Most acute sports injuries would seem to result from being in the wrong place at the right time, rather than from some intrinsic weakness of the injured part. Promoting strength training as protection against such injuries does not seem appropriate. Insisting on proper coaching, safety education, strict enforcement of rules, proper equipment, and so forth as means of preventing such injuries does seem important.

Lifelong Fitness

As with other activities, strength training would seem most likely to be continued in adulthood by individuals who had learned the basic motor skills and enjoyed the activity in childhood. This may have important health and fitness implications.

Low back pain, for example, is an endemic problem in the adult population. The severity and duration of episodes have been shown to be correlated with decreased strength of the trunk muscles (Addison & Schulz, 1980; Jackson & Brown, 1983). Studies have also shown that workers who do not possess adequate strength relative to their job demands suffer a higher incidence of back injury (Jackson & Brown, 1983; Nachemson, 1976).

Another problem, especially in adult women, is osteopenia, the prevention of which should begin in childhood (Loucks, 1988). Several investigators have found long-term strength training to be an effective stimulus for bone mineralization in young populations (Conroy et al., 1990; Virvidakis et al., 1990; Whalen, Stillman, & Boileau, 1993).

Obesity is a problem in both children and adults (Kuntzleman & Reiff, 1992). Favorable changes in body composition as a result of strength training have been reported in both populations (Faigenbaum et al., 1993; Siegal et al., 1989; Wilmore, 1974).

Endurance training has long been emphasized as an appropriate lifelong preventive health measure for cardiovascular diseases. Probably, strength training beginning in childhood should be similarly emphasized as a preventive health measure.

Risks

As with any undertaking of childhood or adolescence, strength training is not without risk. However, to decide whether it is "safe" or "unsafe," one needs to quantify the risks as much as possible in terms of the probability of occurrence (rate) of injury and the consequences (severity) of injury. Proven concerns should be distinguished from theoretical ones. Safety issues (e.g., acute injury caused by dropping a dumbbell on the foot) and social issues (e.g., temptation to use illicit drugs) should be differentiated from the biological effects of training (e.g., stress fracture caused by repetitive compression loading of the lumbar spine). Finally, the risks of doing the activity should be weighed against the risks of not doing it, that is, one should try to determine a risk:benefit ratio.

Injuries

Although investigators have previously reported weight training–related musculoskeletal injuries in children and adolescents (Jesse, 1977; Kulund et al., 1978; Mason, 1977; Ryan & Salciccioli, 1976; Vrijens, 1978), the problem of these injuries first received widespread attention as a result of the 1979 Consumer Product Safety Commission's report (U.S. Consumer Product Safety Commission. National Electronic Injury Surveillance System, 1980). The report's authors estimated that among 10- to 19-year-olds, more than 17,000 "weight lifting" injuries requiring emergency room visits occurred annually. Since then one fatality has been reported (George, Stakiw, & Wright, 1989). By and large, these injuries were the result of accidents in the home, not the result of supervised weight training or competitive weight lifting. The most appropriate inference to be drawn from these reports probably is that parents and older siblings ought not leave weight equipment lying about, possibly to be misused in play by younger children.

No studies exist from which an injury index (combined rate and severity of injury) can be determined for strength training in children or adolescents. An injury rate for power lifting in adolescents can be estimated from one study (Brown & Kimball, 1983). A survey of 71 contestants entered in the 1981 Michigan Teenage Powerlifting Championship found that the average subject had participated in 4.1 training sessions per week for 17.1 months. The average training session lasted 99.2 minutes. The subjects incurred 98 time-loss injuries. The rate of injury can thus be calculated as 0.3 injuries per 100 hours of participation or, perhaps more meaningfully, as 0.97 injuries per participant year. Because of the retrospective nature of the study, the inaccuracy of recall over the time period involved, and the fact that the study population excluded individuals who might have succumbed to injury and were unable to compete, the calculated rate of injury might be an underestimate. Nonetheless, it is comparable with the reported 0.25 to 0.35 injuries per participant season for high school basketball, soccer, and track, and lower than the reported 0.39 to 0.81 injuries per participant season for high school football, women's gymnastics, and wrestling (Garrick & Requa, 1981).

In another one-year study of sports-related injuries in school-aged children, football, wrestling, and gymnastics had the highest incidence of injuries (Zaricznyj et al., 1980). Weight lifting accounted for only 0.7 percent of all reported injuries.

In most of the previously referenced studies that demonstrated increased strength with appropriate training, no injuries were reported. In one study, during 14 weeks of training, one strength training–related injury, a muscle strain, occurred that resulted in three missed training sessions. In contrast, during the same time period, six injuries were incurred in other activities of daily living that resulted in 47 missed training sessions (Rians, 1987).

Investigators have reported acute physeal (growth plate) injuries (Salter fractures) in young weight lifters (Brown & Kimball, 1983; Gumbs et al., 1982; Herrick, 1982; Jenkins & Mintowt-Czyz, 1986; Rowe, 1979; Ryan & Salciccioli, 1976). These, however, were either isolated case reports or small series. Moreover, the reported injuries were for the most part the result of unsupervised activity and/or disregard of proper technique.

A theoretical concern given great attention in various position papers is that the growing bones of children and adolescents might be less resilient to repetitive stress than the bones of skeletally mature individuals (American Academy of Pediatrics Committee on Sports Medicine, 1983; American Orthopaedic Society for Sports Medicine, 1988; Faigenbaum, 1993). In fact, however, during the many years in which attention has been focused on this potential problem, no cases of strength training–related physeal or epiphyseal overuse injury comparable to that of "Little Leaguer's elbow" (osteochondrosis dissecans of the humeral capitellum) have been reported. The physiology and biomechanics of strength training, a nonballistic, low-repetition activity, are not very similar to those of a ballistic, high-repetition activity such as baseball pitching. As noted earlier, several prospective studies have demonstrated that prepubescents can undertake well-supervised strength training, utilizing hydraulic resistance equipment, weight machines, free weights, and even Olympic-style lifts, without incurring clinically evident skeletal injury. In the one study in which subclinical evidence of skeletal injury was sought by radionuclide scintigraphy—all participants had bone scans done after 14 weeks of training—no physeal or epiphyseal injuries were found (Rians, 1987). This is not to say that one should not remain attentive to the possibility of physeal injuries. As will be discussed later, apophyseal growth plate injuries (e.g., Osgood-Schlatter's "disease") and vertebral end-plate (vertebral body growth plate) injuries (e.g., Scheuermann's "disease") can be caused or exacerbated by strength training. Available evidence, however, does not implicate strength training as posing an inordinate risk of physeal injury.

In actual clinical experience, the problem of greatest concern is that of low back injury (Aggrawal et al., 1979; Brady et al., 1982; Brown & Kimball, 1983; Jackson et al., 1982; Mason, 1977). In the previously noted study of adolescent power lifters, for example, one-half of all the reported time-loss injuries were to the low back. Individuals engaged in strength training are liable both to lumbar flexion/torsion-related injuries (e.g., herniated intervertebral disc, vertebral end-plate injury, and paraspinous muscle strain) and to lumbar extension-related injuries (e.g., "facet syndrome" and pars interarticularis stress fracture). Skeletally immature individuals would seem especially susceptible to pars interarticularis stress fracture, spondylolysis, and spondylolisthesis (Jackson et al., 1982). In young weight lifters, as in young ballerinas, football linemen, and gymnasts, a high index of suspicion for these injuries should be maintained. Persistent lumbar extension-related low back pain needs to be evaluated. Activity-related pain and positive scintigraphic examination ("hot" bone scan) represent a contraindication to continuation of the activity (Garrick & Webb, 1990). Similarly, flexion-related back pain localized to the thoracolumbar junction should raise one's index of suspicion for vertebral end-plate injury (Micheli, 1979; Wilcox & Spencer, 1986). This less common problem is also managed conservatively with activity modification, physical therapy, and rehabilitation (Garrick & Webb, 1990; Wilcox & Spencer, 1986).

Also of real concern are shoulder overuse injuries, including injuries to the anterior joint capsule, acromioclavicular joint, and rotator cuff (Cahill, 1982; Rians, 1987; Vrijens, 1978). Other joint injuries are of somewhat lesser concern. "Curler's elbow" (flexor-pronator strain/tendinitis) is a named weight training–related sports injury. Knee meniscal injuries have been reported both with use of weight machines and free weights (Brady et al., 1982), but most knee injuries would seem to be less serious overuse injuries, for example, patellofemoral pain, quadriceps strain/tendinitis, patellar tendinitis, and Osgood-Schlatter's disease (traction apophysitis of the anterior tibial tubercle). Nonetheless, any persistent activity-related pain in or around joints certainly needs to be evaluated and the activity modified or discontinued accordingly.

Interestingly, the observed relatively high incidence of back and shoulder injuries, especially in beginners, correlates with a Soviet report of a developmental lag of the abdominal wall, trunk, and shoulder abductor muscles in youngsters engaged in strength training (Yessis, 1987). Personal experience also suggests that in less than very well supervised programs, these muscle groups are usually neglected in favor of arm and chest exercises. Accordingly, the author recommends that beginning strength-training programs include prehabilitation of the torso, scapular stabilizing, and intrinsic shoulder muscles (see "Strength-Training Recommendations for Young Athletes").

In summary, both acute and overuse injuries do occur, some of which (e.g., physeal, meniscal, and pars interarticularis injuries) are indeed medically serious. However, the rate of injury does not seem to be excessively high and is probably comparable to many other usually condoned physical activities of childhood and adolescence. Moreover, the incidence and severity of injury can probably be minimized by adherence to guidelines (to be presented) with regard to proper supervision and technique, back and shoulder prehabilitation, attention to complaints of back, shoulder, and other joint pain, and avoidance of maximal lifts.

Medical Problems

The risks of strength training with respect to hypertension and related diseases have been matters of controversy and concern (American Academy of Pediatrics

Committee on Sports Medicine, 1983; Nau et al., 1990). To sort out the problem, one needs first to differentiate between the acute and longitudinal cardiovascular effects of strength training.

A dramatic acute increase in systemic arterial blood pressure with heavy resistance exercise has been well demonstrated (MacDougall et al., 1983). In a study of adult bodybuilders, direct intra-arterial pressure in a nonexercised limb was measured during heavy resistance exercise. The highest peak pressure was 450/310 mmHg during a double leg press. The lowest peak pressure recorded was 293/230 mmHg during a single arm curl. Peak pressures were higher when performing 7 to 10 repetitions ("to failure") than when performing a one repetition maximum. Over a 90-minute training session, mean arterial pressures averaged 131 mmHg. Similar blood pressure responses to bench press weight lifting have been reported in children (Nau et al., 1990). Accordingly, conditions that could be seriously adversely affected by acute increases in blood pressure (e.g., A-V malformation, congestive heart failure, and cystic medial necrosis of the aorta) should be considered absolute contraindications to heavy resistance training.

Although chronic hypertension has been reported in adults doing high-intensity anaerobic training (Hunter & McCarthy, 1983), no evidence exists that the observed acute, transient increases in blood pressure associated with resistance exercise lead to chronic elevation of blood pressure in previously normotensive children and adolescents. To date, studies in children have shown either favorable or no effects of short-term (8 to 14 weeks) strength training on various cardiovascular parameters including blood pressure (Faigenbaum et al., 1993; Rians, 1987; Servedio et al., 1985).

The effect of strength training on already hypertensive individuals is less predictable. However, it has been reported that in hypertensive adolescents, reductions in blood pressure achieved through endurance training can be maintained and possibly further reduced with strength training (Hagberg et al., 1984). In contrast, subjects who did not strength train reverted back to their previous baseline (hypertensive) levels.

Screening for hypertension and/or abnormal cardiovascular response to exercise as part of the preparticipation examination would seem appropriate. Moderate hypertension in the absence of serious end-organ disease should not be considered a contraindication to strength training. Rather, moderately hypertensive children should be followed to determine the longitudinal (training) effect of exercise on their hypertension, and the exercise program modified, discontinued, or encouraged as indicated.

Various phenomena (e.g., "weight lifter's blackout," "weight lifter's headache," transient ischaemic attack, and stroke) have been reported in adult weight lifters (Compton et al., 1973; Lehman, 1984; Paulson, 1983; Tuxen et al., 1983). These phenomena, however, have been noted mainly with hyperventilation and performance of Valsalva maneuvers during maximal lift attempts. As with musculoskeletal injury, avoidance of maximum lifts would seem to be preventative in most cases.*

---

*Whether or not breath holding during lifts should be discouraged or encouraged is debatable and should probably be individualized. Performing a Valsalva maneuver decreases venous return and consequently cardiac output. However, it also permits the torso to become a rigid muscular cylinder, stabilizing and protecting the spine.

Growth

Another theoretical concern that has not proven to be an actual problem is the possible adverse effect of strength training on growth. To date, studies in children and adolescents have shown either favorable or no effects of strength training on stature (Ekblom, 1969; Faigenbaum et al., 1993; Ramsay et al., 1990; Siegal et al., 1989; Weltman et al., 1986).

Drug Abuse

It has been well documented that weight rooms and training facilities are common sources of illicit drugs (Duchaine, 1989; Frankle et al., 1984; Lombardo et al., 1985; Yesalis et al., 1988). It has also been well demonstrated that in adolescent males, the use of anabolic steroids is addictive (Yesalis et al., 1989). In the author's opinion, the use and abuse of anabolic steroids, growth hormone, and "nutritional" supplements constitute at least as great a potential strength training–related health problem as do the various preceding biological and safety issues discussed. Discussion of this topic is beyond the scope of this chapter but is well covered elsewhere (Haupt & Rovere, 1984; Johnson, 1990; Van de Loo & Johnson, this volume; Yesalis, Wright, & Bahrke, 1989).

Strength Training Recommendations for Young Athletes

The following guidelines are in general agreement with previously published guidelines, position papers, and texts (American Orthopaedic Society for Sports Medicine, 1988; Faigenbaum, 1993; Fleck & Kraemer, 1987; Kraemer & Fleck, 1993; Maitland, 1986; National Strength and Conditioning Association, 1985). Specific differences derive from the author's clinical experience in the treatment and prevention of strength training–related injuries. Thus, for example, recommendations regarding prehabilitation of the shoulder and torso muscles, avoidance and/or modification of certain lifts, avoidance of maximal lift attempts, and limitation of range of motion of certain lifts reflect the author's bias in favor of maximizing the benefit:risk ratio of the exercise program. This approach will accordingly be most applicable to the beginning or fitness and recreational lifter, less so to the advanced strength or competitive athlete. Specific exercises that the author recommends be incorporated into most strength-training programs are described and illustrated as follows:

1. Children and adolescents should begin strength training only if they believe it to be a worthwhile undertaking. They should be encouraged to continue with it only if it continues to be fun, challenging, satisfying, and not seriously injurious.
2. A preparticipation examination should be carried out. Special attention should be paid to preexisting conditions that could be made worse by exercise, especially cardiovascular disease and unrehabilitated prior injury (Garrick & Webb, 1990; Kulund et al., 1978). Efficient screening examinations have been well described elsewhere (Harvey, 1982; Myers & Garrick, 1984).

Conditions that could be seriously adversely affected by acute increases in blood pressure, for example, A-V malformation, congestive heart failure, and cystic medial necrosis of the aorta, should be considered absolute contraindications to heavy resistance training. Moderate hypertension in the absence of serious end-organ disease should *not* be considered a contraindication to strength training. Children should be followed to determine the longitudinal (training) effect of exercise on their blood pressures, and the exercise program modified, discontinued, or encouraged as indicated.

3. Children should be mature enough to be "coachable" and to follow prescribed safety rules. Coaches should be competent, conscientious, and concerned about the children's health, safety, and overall development.

   Choosing a coach is an important parental responsibility. Some suggested criteria are certification by the National Strength and Conditioning Association, certification by the National Athletic Trainers Association, education (e.g., a college degree in physical education), experience (e.g., as a YMCA instructor or as a scholastic teacher or coach), and, perhaps most important, recommendations by other parents.

4. Close supervision is essential. Generally, the student:instructor ratio should be no greater than 10:1 (American Orthopaedic Society for Sports Medicine, 1988; National Strength and Conditioning Association, 1985). When athletes are less experienced, when new motor skills are being taught/learned, or when free weights are being used, higher levels of supervision are warranted.

5. Proper "safety spotting" is mandatory for training with free weights (Kraemer & Fleck, 1993). The spotter's chief responsibility is to prevent injury by helping the lifter perform the exercise safely. A second responsibility is to summon help should an accident occur. The spotter must know the proper exercise technique, know the proper spotting technique, be strong enough to carry out the proper spotting technique for the exercise being done, be attentive to the lifter at all times, and stop the exercise if any breach of exercise technique, breach of safety rules, or equipment malfunction occur (see fig. 15.2). As an intrinsic part of the overall strength-training program, children and adolescents should be instructed in the importance of and techniques of spotting.

6. Young athletes and their parents, coaches, and physicians should pay close attention to any exercise-related back, shoulder, or other joint pain. Pain during a particular exercise precludes continuation of that exercise. Pain afterward, including the next day, precludes doing the exercise at the next session. By the following session, if the symptoms have resolved, the exercise may again be attempted, but at a lower level of intensity. Symptoms that persist longer than two days merit medical evaluation. A high index of suspicion should be maintained for lumbar vertebral pars interarticularis stress reaction of bone (spondylolysis). If symptoms do not respond promptly to standard treatment measures for soft tissue injury,

FIGURE 15.2
Safety spotting for bench press exercise. The spotter assists the lifter to ensure that each repetition, especially including the last, is done with the proper form and at the same velocity. After the last repetition, the spotter also assists in racking the weight.

radionuclide scintigraphy (bone scan) should be considered to rule out stress reaction of bone or physeal (growth plate) injury.

7. Because of the developmental lag of the shoulder, abdominal wall, and trunk muscles and the incidence of shoulder and back overuse injuries (Aggrawal et al., 1979; Brady et al., 1982; Brown & Kimball, 1983; Jackson et al., 1982; Mason, 1977; Vrijens, 1978; Webb, 1990), prehabilitation of the shoulder and torso muscles should be carried out; that is, stretching and progressive resistance exercises as done for rehabilitation of shoulder and back injuries should be done beforehand as preventive measures. Recommended progressive resistance exercises for the intrinsic shoulder muscles (anterior deltoid, supraspinatus, middle deltoid, posterior deltoid, and internal rotators) are shown in figures 15.3 to 15.5. They may first be done just against gravity resistance or with a one-pound weight. Recommended resistance exercises for the upper back (scapular stabilizing muscles) include shrugs, bent over lateral raises (reverse flies), bent over rows, bench rows, seated rows, and modified "lat" (latissimus dorsi) pull-downs (to the chest not behind the neck). In the author's experience, the Cybex™ U.B.E. machine is the single most effective device for endurance training of the intrinsic shoulder and scapular stabilizing muscles and is well tolerated, even by athletes with shoulder injuries (see fig. 15.6). Recommended exercises for the lower back include lumbar paraspinous stretching, three direction "crunch" sit-ups (for the rectus and oblique abdominals), and "reverse" sit-ups (for the lumbar paraspinous muscles), as shown in figures 15.7 and 15.8.

FIGURE 15.3
Prehabilitation exercises for the shoulder: specific exercises for the anterior deltoid (a), supraspinatus (b), middle deltoid (c), and posterior deltoid (d). Note that in the supraspinatus exercise, the shoulder is fully internally rotated, and the arm is raised in the plane of the scapula, i.e., at a 45° angle anterior to the coronal plane of the body. In all of the deltoid exercises, the shoulder is in neutral rotation.

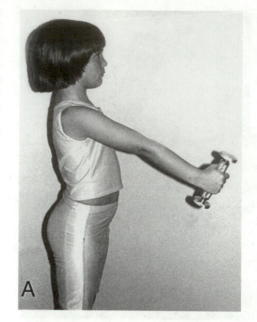

A

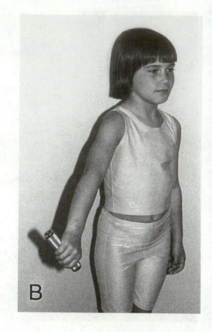

B

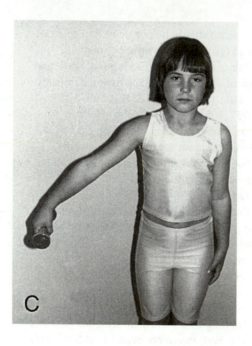

C

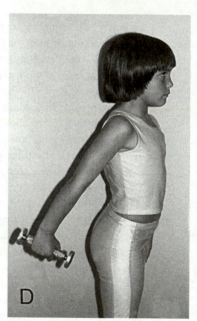

D

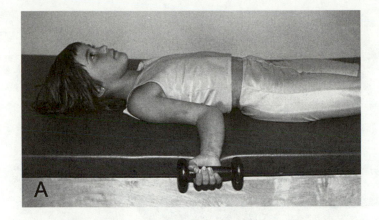

FIGURE 15.4
"Prehabilitation" exercises
for the shoulder: specific
exercises for the internal
rotators (a and b).

A

B

8. Resistance training should be submaximal, comprising combined strength and muscular endurance exercises, rather than pure strength exercises.

Primary emphasis should be given to learning and mastering new motor skills. Initially exercises should be done with minimal resistance, for example, just a bar without added weights. Only after proper exercise technique has been learned and mastered should the resistance be increased. Throughout the training program, coaches should stress adherence to proper technique.

Weight exercises should be of moderate intensity, for example, three sets of 10 to 15 repetitions per set. If a child cannot do at least 10 repetitions per set with a given weight, the weight is too heavy. When 15 repetitions become "too easy," the next weight increment can be attempted. On each set, muscular "fatigue," not "failure," is the desired end point. Fatigue may be judged by the child's perception that the repetitions are becoming difficult or the coach's perception that proper form is not being maintained. Repetitions should not be continued to the point that the child cannot do one more without help or without compromising technique.

(Even advanced lifters are well advised to avoid one repetition maximum lifts. A 1RM equivalent formula or other tests as discussed

FIGURE 15.5

"Prehabilitation" exercises for the shoulder: specific exercises for supraspinatus and infraspinatus, especially useful for throwing athletes. With shoulders abducted to 90° and elbows flexed to 90°, the weights are lowered and raised by rotating the shoulder internally and externally.

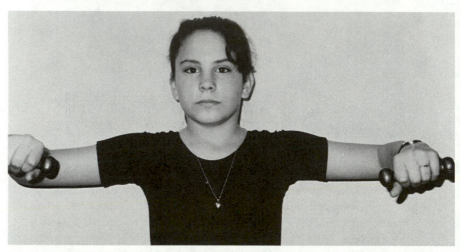

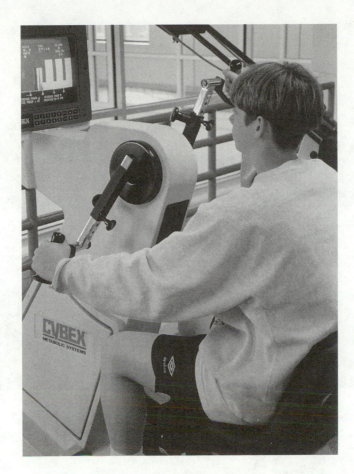

FIGURE 15.6
"Prehabilitation" exercises for the shoulder: Cybex™ U.B.E. machine. Saddle height is adjusted so that axis of rotation of shoulder is level with axis of arm cranks. Crank length is adjusted so that there is moderate shoulder girdle as well as arm motion. Cranks are turned at high (290) rpm. At intervals (e.g., 30 seconds), direction of cranking is reversed.

earlier should be used to assess strength gains. To be done safely, working "to failure," that is, to the point of not being able to continue the exercise, requires a mastery of motor skills and careful attention to technique by both lifter and spotter. The spotter should appropriately assist the lifter to ensure that the last repetition is done with the same form and at the same velocity as the previous repetitions. With lifts such as a barbell bench press, the spotter should also assist in racking the weight.)

9. With certain important exceptions, resistance exercises should be done through a full range of joint motion, both to develop strength throughout the range of motion and to prevent loss of flexibility (i.e., to avoid becoming "muscle bound"). However, if injury precludes doing an exercise through a full range of motion without pain, the exercise may be done through a limited but pain-free range of motion.

   Dips, deep bench presses and push-ups in which the bar touches the chest or the chest touches the floor, and full-arc bench flies are lifts that place undue stress on the anterior capsule of the shoulder. These exercises, if done at all, should not be done through an extreme range of motion.

FIGURE 15.7

"Prehabilitation" exercises for the torso: pelvic-tilt, shoulder-lift sit-ups (crunches). (a) Starting position—knees flexed, feet not held down; (b) To exercise the lower rectus abdominis, the pelvis is tilted posteriorly, "eliminating the hollow under the back"; (c) To exercise the upper rectus, both shoulders are slowly lifted off the floor, the position is held for a count of six, and then the shoulders are slowly lowered to the floor;

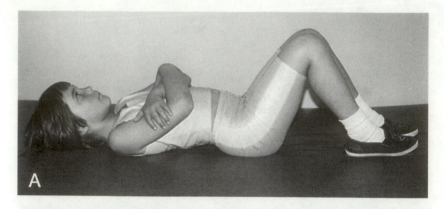

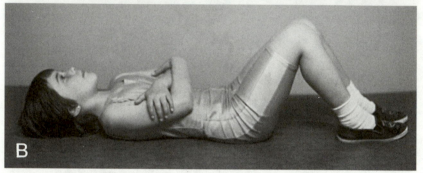

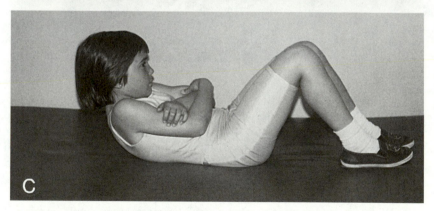

They are contraindicated in individuals with abnormal anterior glenohumeral laxity (recurrent shoulder dislocation or subluxation, thrower's shoulder, swimmer's shoulder).

Similarly, leg extension and leg press exercises begun from a position of full knee flexion place undue stress on the quadriceps mechanism, including the patellofemoral joint. These types of exercises should also be done through a less extreme range of motion.

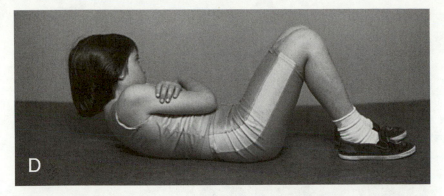

D

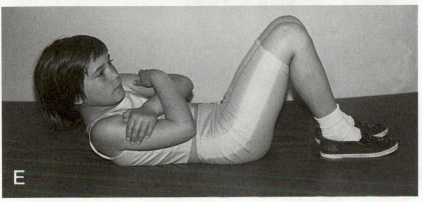

E

FIGURE 15.7 (*continued*)
(d and e) To exercise the oblique abdominal muscles, alternatively one shoulder, then the other, is lifted off the floor.

10. Strict attention should be paid to maintaining the normal lordotic curve of the lumbar spine during any exercise in which compression loads are placed on the spine, for example, military presses, squats, and dead lifts. Exercises that involve both compression loading and flexion or torsion of the lumbar spine (e.g., straight leg dead lifts and "good mornings") should be avoided altogether.

11. Training programs should include exercises for all major muscle groups, and there should be a good balance between exercises for opposing muscle groups.

    In addition to the prehabilitation exercises listed, recommended basic exercises include: shoulder abduction and adduction, bench press and bench row (for chest and upper back), arm curl and triceps pull down, wrist curl and reverse wrist curl, hip abduction and adduction, leg press (for knee and hip extensors), leg extension and leg curl (for quadriceps and hamstrings), and toe raise. Complete programs for beginners, utilizing weights and hydraulic resistance devices, have been well described (Fleck & Kraemer, 1987; Kraemer & Fleck, 1993; Maitland, 1986; Rians, 1987).

FIGURE 15.8
"Prehabilitation" exercises for the torso: trunk extensor strengthening. The torso is lifted from a flexed (a) to a neutral (b) position. Active hyperextension (extension past neutral) is not recommended.

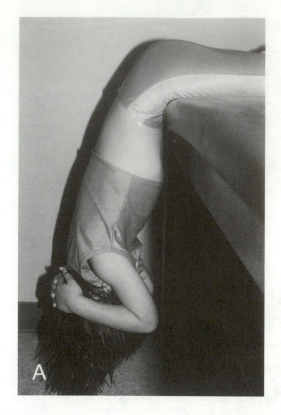

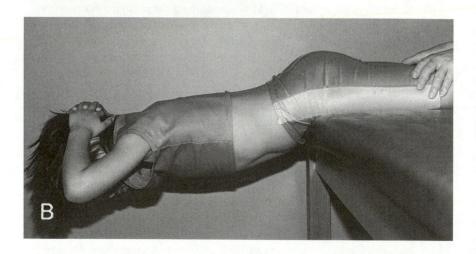

(Hydraulic resistance training has some important advantages for beginners (Rians, 1987). A single piece of equipment, for example, bench press and bench row, can be used at one time to exercise opposing muscle groups. Compared with using free weights, fewer motor skills are required. Compared with eccentric exercises, peak tensile loads are less. Accordingly, the risk of musculoskeletal injury may be less. The advantages, however, also reflect the drawbacks. There is less motor skill development, and muscles are not as well prepared for eccentric exercise in other activities.)

12. Training sessions ("workouts") should be done two or three days a week. The trainee should be well recovered from one session to the next.

    Training sessions should comprise warm-up, stretching, resistance exercises, fun/skill activity, stretching, and cooldown. Warm-up may be accomplished by jogging, riding an exercycle, skipping rope, or doing jumping jacks. These should be done until the child begins to sweat. Stretching should be done before the resistance exercises but after the child is well warmed up. Stretching should be done again, either after the resistance exercises or after the fun activity.

13. Training should be advanced in small increments, both with respect to amount of resistance used and with respect to motor skills required. With weight training, for example, a child should be able to do three sets of 15 repetitions of a given exercise on three consecutive sessions before more weight is attempted. Both child and coach should feel confident that the new weight can be handled. Basic strength lifts should be mastered before more complex power lifts are attempted.

References

Addison, R., & Schulz, A. (1980). Trunk strengths in patients seeking hospitalization for chronic low back disorders. *Spine, 5,* 539–544.

Aggrawal, N. D. et al. (1979). A study of changes in the spine in weight lifters and other athletes. *British Journal of Sports Medicine, 13,* 58–61.

Albright, J. P. et al. (1985). Head and neck injuries in college football: An eight year analysis. *American Journal of Sports Medicine, 13,* 147–152.

American Academy of Pediatrics Committee on Sports Medicine. (1983). Weight training and weightlifting: Information for the pediatrician. *The Physician and Sportsmedicine, 11,* 157–161.

American Orthopaedic Society for Sports Medicine. (1988). *Proceedings of the conference on strength training and the prepubescent.* Chicago: Author.

Atha, J. (1981). Strengthening muscle. *Exercise and Sport Science Reviews, 9,* 1–73.

Baumgartner, T., & Wood, S. (1984). Development of shoulder-girdle strength-endurance in elementary children. *Research Quarterly for Exercise and Sport, 55,* 169–171.

Blimkie, C. J. R. (1989). Age- and sex-associated variation in strength during childhood: Anthropometric, morphologic, neurologic, biomechanical, endocrinologic, genetic, and physical activity correlates. In C. V. Gisolfi & D. R. Lamb (Eds.), *Perspectives in exercise science and sports medicine: Youth and exercise in sport* (pp. 99–163). Indianapolis: Benchmark Press.

Bosco, C. et al. (1981). Prestretch potentiation of human skeletal muscle during ballistic movement. *Acta Physiologica Scandinavica, 111,* 135.

Brady, T. A., Cahill, B., & Bodnar, L. (1982). Weight training-related injuries in the high school athlete. *American Journal of Sports Medicine, 10,* 1–5.

Brown, E., Lillegard, W., Henderson, R., Wilson, D., Lewis, E., Hough, D., & Stringer, K. (1992). Efficacy and safety of strength training with free weights in prepubescents to early post-pubescents [Abstract]. *Medicine and Science in Sports and Exercise, 24,* S82.

Brown, E. W., & Kimball, R. G. (1983). Medical history associated with adolescent power lifting. *Pediatrics, 72,* 636–644.

Brzycki, M. (1993). Strength testing: Predicting a one-rep max from reps-to-fatigue. *Journal of Physical Education, Recreation and Dance, 64,* 88–90.

Cahill, B. R. (1982). Osteolysis of distal part of clavicle in male athletes. *Journal of Bone and Joint Surgery, 64A,* 1053–1058.

Cahill, B. R., & Griffith, E. H. (1978). Effect of preseason conditioning on the incidence and severity of high school football knee injuries. *American Journal of Sports Medicine, 6,* 180–184.

Cantu, R. C. (1988). Head and spine injuries in the young athlete. *Clinics in Sports Medicine, 7,* 459–472.

Cavanagh, P. R. (1988). On "muscle action" vs. "muscle contraction." *Journal of Biomechanics, 22,* 69.

Chu, D. (1983). Plyometrics: The link between strength and speed. *National Strength and Conditioning Association Journal, 5,* 20.

Clarke, D., Vaccaro, P., & Andresen, N. (1984). Physiologic alterations in 7- to 9-year-old boys following a season of competitive wrestling. *Research Quarterly for Exercise and Sport, 55,* 318–322.

Clarke, K. S., & Powell, J. W. (1979). Football helmets and neurotrauma—an epidemiologic overview of three seasons. *Medicine and Science in Sports, 11,* 138–145.

———. (1982). An epidemiologic view. In J. S. Torg (Ed.), *Athletic injuries to the head, neck, and face* (pp. 15–25). Philadelphia: Lea & Febiger.

Compton, D. et al. (1973). Weightlifters blackout. *Lancet, 2,* 1234–1237.

Conroy, B. P., Kraemer, W. J., Dalsky, G. P., Miller, P. D., Fleck, S. J., Kearney, J. T., Stone, M. H., Warren, B., & Maresh, C. M. (1990). Bone mineral density in elite junior weightlifters [Abstract]. *Medicine and Science in Sports and Exercise, 22,* S77.

Crouch, L. (1979). Neck injuries: Prevention to avoid rehabilitation. *National Strength and Conditioning Association Journal, 1,* 29–31.

DeLorme, T. L., & Watkins, A. L. (1948). Techniques of progressive resistance exercise. *Archives of Physical Medicine, 29,* 263–273.

Dominguez, R. H. (1978). Shoulder pain in age group swimmers. In B. Ericksson & B. Furong (Eds.), *Swimming medicine* (pp. 105–109). Baltimore: University Park Press.

Duchaine, D. (1989). *Underground steroid handbook II.* Venice, CA: HLR Technical Books.

Ekblom, B. (1969). Effects of physical training in adolescent boys. *Journal of Applied Physiology, 27,* 350–355.

Faigenbaum, A. D. (1993). Strength training: A guide for teachers and coaches. *National Strength and Conditioning Association Journal, 15,* 20–29.

Faigenbaum, A., Zaichkowsky, L., Wescott, W., Micheli, L., & Fehlandt, A. (1993). The effects of a twice per week strength training program on children. *Pediatric Exercise Science, 5,* 339–346.

Faria, I. E., & Cavanagh, P. R. (1978). *The physiology and biomechanics of cycling.* New York: Wiley.

Fleck, S. J., Henke, C., & Wilson, W. (1989). Cardiac MRI of elite junior Olympic weight lifters. *International Journal of Sports Medicine, 10,* 329–333.

Fleck, S. J., & Kraemer, W. J. (1987). *Designing resistance training programs.* Champaign, IL: Human Kinetics.

Frankle, M. A. et al. (1984). Use of androgenic anabolic steroids by athletes. *Journal of the American Medical Association, 252,* 482.

Funato, K., Fukunaga, T., Asami, T., & Ikeda, S. (1987). Strength training for prepubescent boys and girls. In *Proceedings of the Department of Sports Science* (pp. 9–19). University of Tokyo: Department of Sports Science.

Garrick, J. G. (1972). Prevention of sports injuries. *Postgraduate Medicine, 51*(1), 125–129.

Garrick, J. G., Gillien, D. M., & Whiteside, P. (1986). The epidemiology of aerobic dance injuries. *American Journal of Sports Medicine, 14,* 67–72.

Garrick, J. G., & Requa, R. K. (1980). The epidemiology of women's gymnastics injuries. *American Journal of Sports Medicine, 8,* 261–264.

———. (1981). Medical care and injury surveillance in the high school setting. *The Physician and Sportsmedicine, 9,* 115–120.

Garrick, J. G., & Webb, D. R. (1990). *Sports injuries: Diagnosis and management.* Philadelphia: W. B. Saunders.

George, D. H., Stakiw, K., & Wright, C. J. (1989). Fatal accident with weight-lifting equipment: Implications for safety standards. *Canadian Medical Association Journal, 140,* 925–926.

Gumbs, V. L., Segal, D., Halligan, J., & Lower, G. (1982). Bilateral distal radius and ulnar fractures in adolescent weight lifters. *American Journal of Sports Medicine, 10,* 375–379.

Hagberg, J. M. et al. (1984). Effect of weight training on blood pressure and hemodynamics in hypertensive adolescents. *Journal of Pediatrics, 104,* 147–151.

Harvey, J. (1982). The preparticipation examination of the child athlete. *Clinics in Sports Medicine, 1,* 353–369.

Haupt, H. A., & Rovere, G. D. (1984). Anabolic steroids: A review of the literature. *American Journal of Sports Medicine, 12,* 469–484.

Hejna, W. F., Rosenberg, A., Buturusis, D. J., & Krieger, A. (1982). The prevention of sports injuries in high school through strength training. *National Strength and Conditioning Association Journal, 4,* 28–31.

Herrick, R. T. (1982). Bilateral distal radius and ulnar shafts in adolescent weight lifters (letter). *American Journal of Sports Medicine, 11,* 354–356.

Hetherington, M. R. (1976). Effect of isometric training on the elbow flexion force torque of grade five boys. *Research Quarterly, 47,* 41–47.

Hoeger, W. et al. (1987). Relationship between repetitions and selected percentages of one repetition maximum. *Journal of Applied Sports Science Research, 1,* 11–13.

Hunter, G., & McCarthy, J. (1983). Pressor response associated with high-intensity anaerobic training. *The Physician and Sportsmedicine, 11,* 151–162.

Jackson, C. P., & Brown, M. D. (1983). Is there a role for exercise in the treatment of patients with low back pain? *Clinical Orthopaedics and Related Research, 179,* 39–45.

Jackson, D. W. et al. (1982). Stress reactions involving the pars interarticularis in young athletes. *American Journal of Sports Medicine, 9,* 304–312.

Jenkins, N. H., & Mintowt-Czyz, W. (1986). Bilateral fracture-separations of the distal radial epiphyses during weight-lifting. *British Journal of Sports Medicine, 20,* 72–73.

Jesse, J. P. (1977). Olympic lifting movements endanger adolescents. *The Physician and Sportsmedicine, 5,* 61–67.

———. (1979). Misuse of strength development programs in athletic training. *The Physician and Sportsmedicine, 7,* 46–52.

Johnson, M. D. (1990). Anabolic steroids. *Pediatric Clinics of North America, 37*(5), 1111–1123.

Komi, P. V. (1988). The musculoskeletal system. In A. Dirix et al. (Eds.), *The Olympic book of sports medicine* (pp. 15–39). Oxford, England: Blackwell Scientific Publications.

Komi, P. V., & Buskirk, E. R. (1972). Effect of eccentric and concentric muscle conditioning on tension and electrical activity of human muscle. *Ergonomics, 15,* 417–434.

Kraemer, W. J., & Fleck, S. J. (1993). *Strength training for young athletes.* Champaign, IL: Human Kinetics.

Kulund, D. N. et al. (1978). Olympic weightlifting injuries. *The Physician and Sportsmedicine, 6,* 111–119.

Kulund, D. N., & Töttössy, M. (1983). Warm-up, strength, and power. *Orthopedic Clinics of North America, 14,* 427–448.

Kuntzleman, C., & Reiff, G. (1992). The decline in American children's fitness levels. *Research Quarterly for Exercise and Sport, 63,* 107–111.

Landers, J. (1985). Maximum based on reps. *National Strength and Conditioning Association Journal, 6,* 60–61.

Lehman, M. (1984). Incidents of hypertension in 810 male sportsmen. *Zeitschrift Kardiologie, 73,* 137–141.

Lindner, K. J., & Caine, D. J. (1993). Physical and performance characteristics of injured and injury-free gymnasts. *Journal of Human Movement, 25,* 69–83.

Lombardo, J. A. et al. (1985). Recognizing anabolic steroid abuse. *Patient Care, 19,* 28–47.

Loucks, A. (1988). Osteoporosis prevention begins in childhood. In E. Brown & C. Brown (Eds.), *Competitive sports for children and youth* (pp. 213–223). Champaign, IL: Human Kinetics.

MacDougall, D. et al. (1983). Direct measurement of arterial blood pressure during heavy resistance training. *Medicine and Science in Sports and Exercise, 15,* 158.

Maitland, W. J. (1986). *Beginning weight training for young athletes.* Phoenix: Maitland Enterprises.

Maroon, J. C. (1981). Catastrophic neck injuries from football in western Pennsylvania. *The Physician and Sportsmedicine, 9,* 83–86.

Maroon, J. C. et al. (1977). A system for preventing athletic neck injuries. *The Physician and Sportsmedicine, 5,* 77–79.

Mason, T. A. (1977). Is weight lifting deleterious to the spines of young people? *British Journal of Sports Medicine, 5,* 61.

Matchbox Toys (USA) Ltd. (1985). BabyCise™. In *Kidsports,* (p. 3). Mount Laurel, NJ: Children's Business and Sportstyle.

Mayhew, J. L., Ware, J. R., & Prinster, J. L. (1993). Using lift repetitions to predict muscular strength in adolescent males. *National Strength and Conditioning Association Journal, 15,* 35–38.

McCoy, G. F. et al. (1984). Injuries of the cervical spine in schoolboy rugby football. *Journal of Bone and Joint Surgery, 66B,* 500–503.

McGovern, M. (1984). Effects of circuit weight training on the physical fitness of prepubescent children. *Dissertation Abstracts International, 45,* 452A–453A.

Mennen, U. (1981). Survey of spinal injuries from diving: A study of patients in Pretoria and Capetown. *South African Medical Journal, 59,* 788–790.

Micheli, L. J. (1979). Low back pain in the adolescent: Differential diagnosis. *American Journal of Sports Medicine, 6,* 362–364.

Mueller, F. O., & Blyth, C. S. (1979). Catastrophic head and neck injuries. *The Physician and Sportsmedicine, 7,* 71–74.

———. (1982). Fatalities and catastrophic injuries in football. *The Physician and Sportsmedicine, 10,* 135–140.

Myers, G. C., & Garrick, J. G. (1984). The preparticipation examination of the child athlete. In R. H. Strauss (Ed.), *Sports medicine.* Philadelphia: W. B. Saunders.

Nachemson, A. L. (1976). The lumbar spine: An orthopaedic challenge. *Spine, 1,* 59–71.

National Strength and Conditioning Association. (1985). Position paper on prepubescent strength training. *National Strength and Conditioning Association Journal, 7,* 27–31.

Nau, K., Katch, V., Beekman, R., & Dick, M. (1990). Acute intraarterial blood pressure response to bench press lifting in children. *Pediatric Exercise Science, 2,* 37–45.

Neill, M. (1988, May 2). All workout and no play? As any of these kids will tell you, it's a real jungle gym out there. *People,* pp. 135–137.

Nielsen, B., Nielsen, K., Behrendt-Hansen, M., & Asmussen, E. (1980). Training of "functional muscular strength" in girls 7–19 years old. In K. Berg & B. Eriksson (Eds.), *Children and exercise* (pp. 69–77). Baltimore: University Park Press.

Olson, V. L., Schmidt, G. L., & Johnson, R. C. (1972). The maximum torque generated by eccentric, isometric, and concentric contractions of the hip muscles. *Physical Therapy, 52,* 148–149.

Paulson, G. W. (1983). Weightlifter's headache. *Headache, 23,* 193–194.

Pearl, A. J., & Mayer, P. W. (1979). Neck motion in the high school football player. *American Journal of Sports Medicine, 7,* 231–233.

Pfeiffer, R., & Francis, R. (1986). Effects of strength training on muscle development in prepubescent, pubescent, and postpubescent males. *The Physician and Sportsmedicine, 14,* 134–143.

Ramsay, J., Blimkie, C., Smith, K., Garner, S., MacDougall, J., & Sale, D. (1990). Strength training effects in prepubescent boys. *Medicine and Science in Sports and Exercise, 22,* 605–614.

Rapp, G. F., & Nicely, P. G. (1978). Trampoline injuries. *American Journal of Sports Medicine, 6,* 269–271.

Rians, C. B. (1987). Strength training for prepubescent males: Is it safe? *American Journal of Sports Medicine, 15,* 483–489.

Risser, W. L. (1990). Musculoskeletal injuries caused by weight training. Guidelines for prevention. *Clinical Pediatrics, 29,* 305–310.

———. (1991). Weight-training injuries in children and adolescents. *American Family Physician, 44,* 2104–2108.

Rowe, T. A. (1979). Cartilage fracture due to weight lifting. *British Journal of Sports Medicine, 13,* 130–131.

Roy, S. P. (1979). Intercollegiate wrestling injuries. *The Physician and Sportsmedicine, 7,* 83–94.

Ryan, J. R., & Salciccioli, G. G. (1976). Fractures of the distal radial epiphysis in adolescent weight lifters. *American Journal of Sports Medicine, 4,* 26–27.

Sailors, M., & Berg, K. (1987). Comparison of responses to weight training in pubescent boys and men. *Journal of Sports Medicine, 27,* 30–37.

Sale, D. (1989). Strength training in children. In C. V. Gisolfi & D. R. Lamb (Eds.), *Perspectives in exercise science and sports medicine: Youth and exercise in sport* (pp. 165–216). Indianapolis: Benchmark Press.

Scher, A. T. (1981a). Diving injuries to the spinal cord. *South African Medical Journal, 59,* 603–605.

———. (1981b). Vertex impact and cervical dislocation in rugby players. *South African Medical Journal, 59,* 227–228.

———. (1982). "Crashing" the rugby scrum: Avoidable cause of cervical spinal injury. *South African Medical Journal, 61,* 919–920.

———. (1983). Rugby injuries of the upper cervical spine: Case reports. *South African Medical Journal, 64,* 456–458.

Schneider, R. C. (1965). Serious and fatal neurosurgical football injuries. *Clinical Neurosurgery, 12,* 226–236.

———. (1973). *Head and neck injuries in football.* Baltimore: Williams & Wilkins.

Selye, H. (1970). The evolution of the stress concept. *American Journal of Cardiology, 26,* 289–299.

———. (1974). *Stress without distress.* New York: Lippincott and Crowell.

Servedio, F. J., Bartel, R., Hamlin, R., Teske, D., Shaffer, T., & Servedio, A. (1985). The effects of weight training, using Olympic style lifts, on various physiologic variables in pre-pubescent boys [Abstract]. *Medicine and Science in Sports and Exercise, 17,* 288.

Sewall, L., & Micheli, L. J. (1986). Strength training for children. *Journal of Pediatric Orthopedics, 6*(2), 143–146.

Siegal, J., Camaione, D., & Manfredi, T. (1989). The effects of upper body resistance exercise in prepubescent children. *Pediatric Exercise Science, 1,* 145–154.

Sovio, O. M. et al. (1984). Cervical spine injuries in rugby players. *Canadian Medical Association Journal, 130,* 735–736.

Stein, P., & Motta, R. (1992). Effects of aerobic and nonaerobic exercise on depression and self-concept. *Perceptual Motor Skills, 74,* 79–89.

Tanner, J. M. (1962). *Growth at adolescence* (2nd ed.). Oxford, England: Blackwell Scientific Publications.

Tator, C. H. et al. (1981). Diving: Frequent and potentially preventable cause of spinal cord injury. *Canadian Medical Association Journal, 124,* 1323–1324.

———. (1984). Spinal injuries due to hockey. *Canadian Journal of Neurological Sciences, 11,* 34–41.

Tator, C. H., & Edmonds, V. E. (1984). National survey of spinal injuries in hockey players. *Canadian Medical Association Journal, 130,* 875–880.

Thompson, A. J., & Morris, I. M. (1982). Neck injury with quadriplegia: Avoidable training hazard. *British Journal of Sports Medicine, 16,* 59–60.

Thorstensson, A. (1988). Speed and acceleration. In A. Dirix et al. (Eds.), *The Olympic book of sports medicine* (pp. 218–229). Oxford, England: Blackwell Scientific Publications.

Torg, J. S. (1982). Problems and prevention. In J. S. Torg (Ed.), *Athletic injuries to the head, neck, and face* (pp. 3–13). Philadelphia: Lea & Febiger.

Torg, J. S. et al. (1976). Collision with spring-loaded football tackling and blocking dummies. *Journal of the American Medical Association, 236,* 1270–1271.

———. (1977). Severe and catastrophic neck injuries resulting from tackle football. *Journal of the American College Health Association, 25,* 224–226.

————. (1979a). National football head and neck injury registry: Report and conclusions, 1978. *Journal of the American Medical Association, 241,* 1477–1479.

————. (1979b). National football head and neck injury registry: Report on cervical quadriplegia, 1971–1975. *American Journal of Sports Medicine, 7,* 127–132.

Torg, J. S., & Das, M. (1984). Trampoline-related quadriplegia: Review of the literature and reflections on the American Academy of Pediatrics' Position Statement. *Pediatrics, 74,* 804–812.

Torg, J. S., & Quedenfeld, T. (1974). The shoe-surface interface and its relationship to football knee injuries. *American Journal of Sports Medicine, 2,* 261.

Tucker, L. (1982). Effects of a weight training program on the self-concepts of college males. *Perceptual and Motor Skills, 54,* 1055–1061.

Tuxen, D. V. et al. (1983). Brainstem injury following maximal weight lifting attempts. *Medicine and Science in Sports and Exercise, 15,* 158.

U.S. Consumer Product Safety Commission. National Electronic Injury Surveillance System. (1980). *Report for January 1 through December 31, 1979.* Washington, DC: Author.

Van de Loo, D. A., & Johnson, M. D. (1995). Anabolic steroid use in adolescent athletes. In F. L. Smoll & R. E. Smith (Eds.), *Children and youth in sport: A biopsychosocial perspective* (pp. 226–247). Dubuque, IA: Brown & Benchmark.

Van Huss, W. D., & Heusner, W. W. (1970). Strength, power, and muscular endurance. In H. J. Montoye (Ed.), *An introduction to measurement in physical education.* Indianapolis: Phi Epsilon Kappa.

Veroshanski, Y. (1967). Are depth jumps useful? *Track and Field, 12,* 9.

Virvidakis, K., Georgiou, E., Korkotsidis, A., Ntalles, K., & Proukakis, C. (1990). Bone mineral content of junior competitive weightlifters. *International Journal of Sports Medicine, 11,* 244–246.

Vrijens, J. (1978). Muscle strength development in the pre-and postpubescent age. *Medicine and Sport, 11,* 152–158.

Webb, D. R. (1990). Strength training in children and adolescents. *Pediatric Clinics of North America, 37,* 1187–1210.

Weltman, A. (1989). Weight training in prepubertal children: Physiologic benefit and potential damage. *Advances in Pediatric Sports Sciences, 3,* 101–129.

Weltman, A. et al. (1987). Measurement of isokinetic strength in prepubertal males. *Journal of Orthopaedic and Sports Physical Therapy, 9,* 345–351.

Weltman, A., Janney, C., Rians, C., Strand, K., Berg, B., Tippit, S., Wide, J., Cahill, B., & Katch, F. (1986). The effects of hydraulic resistance strength training in pre-pubertal males. *Medicine and Science in Sports and Exercise, 18,* 629–638.

Wescott, W. (1992). A new look at youth fitness. *American Fitness Quarterly, 11,* 16–19.

Whalen, R. L., Stillman, R. J., & Boileau, R. A. (1993). Physical activity level and bone mineral mass in prepubescent males [Abstract]. *Journal of Applied Sport Science Research, 5,* 170.

Wilcox, P. G., & Spencer, C. W. (1986). Dorsolumbar kyphosis or Scheuermann's disease. *Clinics in Sports Medicine, 5,* 343–351.

Williams, D. (1991). The effect of weight training performance in selected motor activities for preadolescent males [Abstract]. *Journal of Applied Sport Science Research, 5,* 170.

Wilmore, J. (1974). Alterations in strength, body composition, and anthropometric measurements consequent to a 10-week training program. *Medicine and Science in Sports, 6,* 133–138.

Yesalis, C. E. et al. (1988). Self-reported use of anabolic-androgenic steroids by elite power lifters. *The Physician and Sportsmedicine, 16,* 91–100.

————. (1989). Anabolic steroid use: Indications of habituation among adolescents. *Journal of Drug Education, 19,* 103–116.

Yesalis, C. E., Wright, J. E., & Bahrke, M. S. (1989). Epidemiological and policy issues in the management of the long term health effects of anabolic-androgenic steroids. *Sports Medicine, 8,* 129–138.

Yessis, M. P. (1987, April). *Pre- post-pubescent weight training.* Paper presented at the conference of the California Strength and Conditioning Clinic, Los Angeles, CA.

Zaricznyj, B., Shattuck, L., Mast, T., Robertson, R., & D Elia, G. (1980). Sports-related injuries in school-aged children. *American Journal of Sports Medicine, 8,* 318–324.

16

OVERUSE INJURIES IN YOUNG ATHLETES

—Russell H. Lord and Bill Kozar

Since the formation of Little League Baseball in 1939, the number of young Americans participating in organized sport has increased tremendously and "new injury patterns are developing as the number of children and adolescents in organized sports increases" (American College of Sports Medicine, 1993, p. 1). Although a variety of concerns have been expressed about the impact of youth sport participation on developing children, ranging from moral and social development to physiological and psychological development during the formative years, the concern in this chapter is the "overuse injury." Overuse injuries have been a common experience for sport participants at all age and competition levels, but attention to overuse injuries in young athletes has a shorter, more recent history (O'Neill & Micheli, 1988). Sport scientists and sports medicine practitioners have begun to focus on overuse injuries in young athletes in recent years—for good reason.

Children as young as 6 years of age are running up to 80 miles per week and completing full marathons (Lopez & Pruett, 1982). One hundred ninety children ages 7 to 17 ran in the 1981 Big M marathon in Melbourne (Dalton, 1992), young gymnasts in elite programs spend hours perfecting routines (Walsh, Huurman, & Shelton, 1985), ballet dancers work for hours practicing "en pointe" position and jumps (Micheli, Sohn, & Solomon, 1985), and young swimmers churn 20,000 meters per day (Dominquez, 1980), completing about half a million strokes per arm per year (Dalton, 1992).

Camps for aspiring athletes in virtually every sport abound—clear evidence of the increasing emphasis placed on earlier and earlier sport specialization. These sport specific camps involve youngsters in six- to eight-hour training regimens per day (Stanish, 1984)—a radical departure from traditional "summer camp" experiences where children participated in a variety of activities ranging from crafts to strenuous sports. Today's sport camps are worlds removed from the free-play situation that prevailed in children's physical activities before the advent of organized youth sport programs. Micheli (1983) has concluded that specialized sport camps are one of the main causes for the dramatic increase in overuse injuries in youngsters.

At younger ages, children are being subjected to more physiologically, psychologically, and socially taxing training regimens than were previously expected of older athletes. Where even a few decades ago, sports were "in season" or "out of season," with athletes participating in season, today's athletes not only specialize in one sport but that sport often has no off season. This, combined with the pressure from parents, community, peers, the media, and society in general to practice long hours, "pay the price," compete, and win, can and is leading to what has been recognized as an epidemic in overuse injuries in young athletes (Micheli, 1983) that constitutes "a great challenge for physicians and allied health personnel" (Renstrom, 1990, p. 365).

With organized practices and competitions, young athletes' activities become much more focused than in free play. No longer does boredom (often occurring quite quickly) produce a shift from one activity to another. No longer is being tired of a certain activity sufficient cause to stop. Instead, the range of activity is narrowed and extended in pursuit of enhanced skill development. The acute trauma accidents that are such an integral part of growing up give way to injuries without an identifiable acute trauma. Although adult athletes have always been susceptible to overuse injuries because of the nature of training—virtually all (91%) of the 95 competitors in the 1986 Hawaii triathlon sustained at least one overuse injury during the year of training leading up to the triathlon (O'Toole et al., 1989)—children and youth are more recent "victims."

In a study of 87,000 Massachusetts children aged 19 years or less in 1980–1981, 22 percent (19,140) experienced an injury requiring a visit to a hospital emergency room. Sport participation was the second leading cause of those injuries (Gallagher et al., 1984). Though those injuries were not specifically overuse injuries, such numbers clearly indicate the liability of young athletes for sports-related injuries. Researchers estimated that had visits to doctors' offices, clinics, and HMOs, and so forth been included, the number would have nearly doubled. Though no comparable nationwide data are available, the number of youngsters involved in organized youth sport programs in the United States has been estimated at well over 20 million (Martens, 1988). If the Massachusetts pattern is approximated in other states, the number of youth experiencing sports-related injuries in the United States each year represents an extremely large problem. This picture of traumatic injuries requiring a hospital visit for youth involved in sports is complicated by another study. Kannus, Niittymaki, & Jarvinen (1988) reported that approximately one-third of the youngsters who suffered an overuse injury waited more than six months before seeking help for the problem.

The concern raised by such studies is twofold. First, the vast majority of sport activity by youth occurs in programs outside of the schools (McGinnis, 1985), and is conducted by volunteers not under the same kinds of guidelines that direct coaches who are hired by schools. Not only are volunteers who direct nonschool youth sport programs seldom held to the same kinds of educational prerequisites as are school coaches, but the programs themselves seldom have the same kinds of preparticipation examination requirements, participation criteria, and so forth. Second, the kinds of traumatic injuries that are "available" to studies such as these are *not* the pervasive overuse injuries that have led several professional organizations (e.g., the American College of Sports Medicine [1993] and the American Academy of Pediatrics [1981]) to publicize their concern and are the focus of this chapter.

Despite continuing expressions of concern about children and youth in sports from the preceding groups, accurate assessment of the incidence of injuries to young athletes remains difficult. Studies have often used different definitions of injury (i.e., first aid administered by the school's athletic trainer, admittance to a hospital emergency room). Some studies have been school based and others based in sports clinics so that the injury profiles differ markedly (as do demographic, economic, and other variables). Nearly all studies have been "after the fact" instead of predictive or experimental, relying upon "samples of convenience" (i.e., many studies examine athletes who have already "shown up for some kind of treatment" because "they have suffered some kind of injury"). It is difficult, therefore, to accurately describe or understand the problem of overuse sport injuries in young athletes at this time. Nevertheless, it is an important area in which to expand concern and understanding, and studies conducted over the past 30 years have provided important information (Goldberg, 1989).

Nature and Incidence of Overuse Injuries

More recent references to "overuse syndrome" have not altered the defining characteristics of what was previously referred to as "overuse injuries." Boland's (1982) definition of overuse injury as a "chronic inflammatory condition caused by repeated microtrauma from a repetitive activity" (p. 116) provides a good point from which to develop an accurate, contemporary definition. Kannus, Niittymaki, and Jarvinen (1988) altered Boland's earlier definition in rephrasing Orava and Puranen's 1978 definition of overuse injury as "longstanding or recurring orthopedic trouble or pain in the musculoskeletal system, which had started without an acute trauma" (p. 334). Kiefhaber and Stern (1992) added still a little more when they adapted Pitner's (1990) definition of overuse injury as "a level of repetitive microtrauma sufficient to overwhelm the tissues' ability to adapt" that "usually [it] results from repetitive loading episodes at a force or elongation level well within the physiologic range" (p. 39).

To differentiate overuse injury from other injuries it seems critical that (a) a clear, precipitating trauma be absent, (b) tissue inflammation be recurrent or chronic rather than acute, and (c) tissue inflammation be connected to repetitive, "subclinical" assault rather than one-time, clinically significant trauma. Thus the diagnosis of overuse injury, as distinct from other injury, must "rest(s) with identification not only of the affected tendinous unit, but also *of the underlying predisposing condition or conditions*" (emphasis ours) (Renstrom, 1990, p. 365).

With the necessity to identify underlying, predisposing conditions, a major focus must be the identification of factors causing the injury. In identifying the cause of the injury, it is important to determine whether the likely cause is unique to the athlete (internal) or common to the tasks or situation under which the tasks are being performed (extrinsic).

Included among intrinsic causes of overuse injuries in young athletes are physical immaturity, anatomical malalignment, muscle strength and flexibility and the balance between them and skeletal maturity, asynchronies in development, psychological factors, and other idiosyncratic variables. Among extrinsic causes are factors such as training activities and schedules, equipment suitability for immature athletes, playing surfaces and environments, and similar conditions. Clearly, some of these "threats" to young athletes are highly preventable (e.g., delaying training for events such as marathons until the athlete is sufficiently mature, avoidance of adult levels of training intensity for immature athletes, adaptations of adult equipment for young athletes).

Environmental factors related to equipment, the intensity and duration of training, mismatched competitors, and similar factors might also be causal or contributive. For example, excessive racket string tension and adult-sized instruments would predispose any young athlete to overuse injuries.

However, "the most common significant factor leading to overuse injuries is the training program" (Stanitski, 1993, p. 91). Rapid changes in training frequency, intensity, duration, or activities are high-risk factors for overuse injuries. Under the pressure of highly organized competitive sports, young athletes will not have the same sensitivity to the symptoms that would lead them to stop an activity in an unstructured, free-play situation. The young athlete's enthusiasm combines with the too-adult nature of certain training situations to produce overuse injuries.

Additional focus on overuse injuries in young athletes can be gained by classifying such injuries into two categories: (a) those related to the immaturity of the athlete; and (b) those that are also found in physically mature athletes. Such injuries obviously differ and should not be confused. Some injuries related to the athlete's physiological immaturity may have little potential for disabling, long-term effects and "may simply reflect the manifestation of 'growing pains' seen in a normal growing population: for example, Osgood-Schlatter" (Dalton, 1992, p. 60). In marked and important contrast, other injuries related to the young athlete's physical immaturity, such as osteochondritis disease in a gymnast's or pitcher's elbow, can lead to permanent disability. Both of these types of injuries, being unique to the status of the young athlete as a growing individual, differ from those overuse injuries found in common with athletes who are skeletally mature. Either of these types of overuse injuries occur under two different circumstances: (a) when inadequately prepared athletes encounter high demands on their musculoskeletal systems; or (b) when already fit athletes overtrain. These circumstances apply to both mature and immature athletes and lead to overuse injuries in both cases. These overuse injuries are not simply transient problems that will resolve themselves with a little time while the young athlete "grows through them." They have been called "the most troublesome problem of the musculoskeletal system" (Stanish, 1984, p. 1).

Although children respond in basically the same way as adults to intense training (Seefeldt & Steig, 1986), those persons involved with young athletes must remember that a growing child is not simply a scaled-down adult. Teeple (1978) noted that while an adult's leg length represents almost half of the overall height, in a child it is considerably less. Consequently, for a young athlete to run the same distance as an adult places greater stress on the youngster. Further, growth rates in children are basically nonlinear (Haywood, 1986; Teeple, 1978); therefore, a training load that is acceptable during a nongrowth period may prove excessive during a growth spurt. Because of the presence of growth cartilage and the process of growth, the child, unlike the adult, is putting energy into growth as well as training (Wilkerson, 1981). Micheli and Fehlandt (1992) indicated that growth (and especially the growth spurt) enhances the risk for overuse injury in children and adolescents.

As youngsters mature, the ratio of muscle and tendon strength to bone length is constantly changing. Caine and Lindner (1984) pointed out that a youngster is more susceptible to overuse injury than an adult "because of the difference in the ratio of contractile muscle strength and static tendon strength to bone length" (p. 120). In children this ratio is lower and unidirectional because muscular strength lags behind bone length throughout the prepubertal years. Tabin, Gregg, and Bonci (1985) supported this contention by reporting that during prepubescence, quadriceps strength is equal to 70 percent of lean body weight in both sexes. This increases to 80 percent for girls and 90 percent for boys in the postpubescent period.

Weight training for the prepubescent does not provide an unequivocal solution. Although evidence suggests that strength gains do occur (see Webb, this volume), it is important to remember that making the muscular system stronger results in an increase in stress that the biological structures must withstand. At this point in the child's development, the weak link in the musculoskeletal system is the epiphysis (Singer, 1986). Bone growth that outdistances muscle and tendon growth can also lead to tightness about the joint. This loss of flexibility can lead to a further risk of overuse injury.

Ligamentous tissue in children is often as much as three times stronger than the cartilage and bone of the growth plate (Micheli, Santore, & Stanitski, 1980), which makes epiphyseal fractures much more likely than an injury to the ligament. Wilkerson (1981) claimed that overtraining a youngster can cause premature closure of the epiphyseal plate and, depending on the athlete's mechanics of movement, the long bones may stop growing at different times. Caine et al. (1992), who reviewed numerous studies and conducted a radiographic survey of 60 young gymnasts, concluded that abnormal changes to the distal radial physis do occur as a result of overuse. These long-term changes, according to Caine et al. (1992), "may include symmetrical or asymmetrical retardation of halted growth at the affected site" (p. 290). Swärd (1992) reported that higher rates of disc degeneration (and consequently back pain) were found in young elite wrestlers and gymnasts than in nonathletes.

Whereas the reporting of overuse injuries in young athletes has increased in the sports medicine literature over the last decade, the epidemiological procedures to study the cause and prevention of these injuries have not been thoroughly developed. This lack is not surprising, as the concentrated commitment to a sport by youngsters is a fairly recent phenomenon. The studies that are available deal primarily with highly successful national-level participants (Bailey & Martin, 1988). The fact that a limited number of genetically exceptional individuals are capable of withstanding strenuous long-term training loads (Sharkey, 1986) does not mean that less-endowed youngsters will not suffer from overuse injuries that may prevent further participation for an extensive time.

Even the exceptional young athlete may not escape overuse injury. Bill Masucci, the winning pitcher in the 1954 Little League World Series, has stated that because he threw so often as a Little Leaguer he could hardly throw a ball in later years (Michener, 1976). In addition, it is likely that excessive pitching at a young age prematurely ended the career of Sandy Koufax (Singer, 1986). Micheli (1983) suggested that repeated microtrauma to the proximal humerus in the growing skeleton is the etiology of Little League shoulder. Lipscomb (1975) maintained that the most serious injury incurred by young pitchers is osteochondritis of the capitellum, with the end result of "varying degrees of traumatic arthritis and permanent joint impairment" (p. 31).

Adams (1965), who was one of the first to report Little League shoulder problems, found that virtually all pitchers he studied had suffered some degree of injury to the medial epicondyle epiphysis. His findings contributed significantly to the decision by Little League officials to restrict the number of innings a youngster could pitch. However, despite the rule changes, the problem of overuse injuries still seems to be present. Mcmanama et al. (1985) reported that elbow surgery was deemed necessary to correct osteochondritis of the capitellum due to repetitive microtrauma in seven patients, six of whom reported considerable involvement in Little League and Pony League Baseball. Walsh et al. (1985), though they presented no specific data, indicated that the majority of injuries they treated in girls' gymnastics dealt with overuse of the knee and spine. Additional reports of runners (Caine & Lindner, 1984; Godshall, Hansen, & Rising, 1981), ballet dancers (Micheli et al., 1985), tennis players (Rettig & Beltz, 1985), and swimmers (Dominguez, 1980) have attested to the prevalence of overuse injury in children's sport.

Contributing Factors and Responses to Them

Besides just the increased population of serious young athletes, many other factors contribute to overuse injuries among young athletes. A complete list of all possible contributing factors cannot be provided for overuse injuries in young athletes any more accurately than such a list could be provided for any other injury for any other cohort group. However, several of the factors that contribute to the overuse injuries in young athletes are of sufficient magnitude to merit individual attention.

Athletes' Developmental Readiness

Teachers have long been able to rely on various "indicators" of a child's "developmental readiness" in planning, teaching, and evaluating children's lessons. Researchers have provided extensive background for a long time to help teachers match instruction to their students' levels of development.

The situation in youth sports is quite different. Unlike education, youth sports lack a sufficient history to provide much guidance to coaches, parents, and athletes. Youngsters had not been *intensely* involved in organized, competitive, year-round sport practice and competition until recently. Consequently, little background research and theory is available to direct the practices of those charged with supervising youth sports. Additionally, many of those who supervise youth sports are subject to inordinate social and emotional pressures by virtue of being parents of participating athletes, coaches whose camps and clinics depend on "their" athletes winning, or young volunteers with too little "distance" between themselves and the athletes and too little experience managing even competition uncomplicated by development variables. The lack of a deep research base combines with these additional pressures to exacerbate the problem of overuse injuries in young athletes. Although there may not be a "developmental readiness quotient" that could be used as a general indicator as to how "ready" an athlete is for sport participation at certain levels of intensity, frequency, and duration, several "markers" exist to help guide the decisions that coaches, parents, and athletes still have to make.

The physical maturity of the athlete is a primary concern. In a study of exertion injuries in young athletes (age 15 or less), Orava and Puranen (1978) found that about 33 percent of the injuries were growth disturbances, whereas 50 percent were typical of overuse injuries that also occur in adult athletes. Kannus, Niittymaki, and Jarvinen (1988) reported that 32 percent of the boys' and 15 percent of the girls' injuries were "exercise-induced growth disorders" (p. 335). Growth cartilage is less resistant to either acute forces or repetitive microtrauma than is adult cartilage (Dalton, 1992), and microtrauma to the ends of a youth's long bones is more likely to result in epiphyseal plate injury than ligamentous injury (Speer & Braun, 1985; Zito, 1983). In contrast, overuse injuries to the epiphyseal growth plate are uncommon in older adolescent athletes, though apophyseal avulsions and traction apophysitis are significant problems in adolescents (Dalton, 1992). Less physically mature young athletes are at different risk of overuse injury.

Recent research indicates several factors that should be considered when determining the extent and intensity of a young athlete's sport participation. Muscle weakness, ligamentous laxity, and muscle tightness were found in one investigation to predispose the 185 athletes studied to overuse injuries (Lysens et al., 1989). These factors also were found to interact with large body weight and length, high explosive strength, and malalignment of the lower limbs to create greater risk. Though these athletes were 18 years old on average, and thus more mature than younger athletes, these data still provide useful information for evaluating younger athletes' sport readiness. It would seem that the greater risk of growth cartilage, epiphyseal plate, and apophyseal injuries in younger athletes might be compounded by these factors identified by Lysens et al. (1989).

Some additional aspects of physical maturity, despite their not having been the subject of specific research studies aimed at connecting them with overuse injuries in young athletes, also seem appropriate for inclusion in any evaluation of an athlete's readiness. Clear differences between adults and children in areas such as body volume-to-surface ratios, aerobic and anaerobic work capacities, cardiovascular work capacities, length ratios of limbs and torso to overall height, percent body fat (especially young girls), bone density, and similar physical parameters should be considered.

Since some recent studies (ACSM, 1993) indicate that "a normal child" experiences an increased risk of injury during periods of accelerated growth such as the adolescent growth spurt, a general estimate as to the onset of this growth spurt seems advisable. At their best, estimates as to the status of this spurt are general, but Tanner's (1962) delineation of stages of genital development and Shaffer's more recent (1980) work looking at secondary sexual development can help estimate skeletal maturity. In addition to such work, some other general indicators (e.g., increases in female percent body fat) might be used. Though specific quantitative values for these physiological parameters have not yet been established by research, athletes who exhibit "more" indicators of delayed maturity should be guided toward less intense, less frequent participation that is also of shorter durations with more rest time between participation.

Athletes' Developmental History

As every working definition of overuse injury makes clear, "predisposing conditions" and lack of acute, easily identifiable trauma (the "history" unique to each individual athlete) are essential in understanding overuse injury. The very definition of overuse injury establishes the importance of personal history in understanding the problem. Certainly anyone attempting to evaluate a young athlete's readiness for sport participation must include the athlete's personal history. Guidelines for taking this history do not presently exist, but some starting points seem warranted.

First, previous history of any injuries/accidents should obviously be assessed. Second, previous participation should be evaluated for duration, frequency, and intensity. Third, the young athlete's personal history of physical fitness should be determined. The training program is the single most common source of overuse injuries (Zaricznyj et al., 1980), and since "probably the most important and perhaps the most correctable risk factor in the development of overuse injuries in all ages is *training error*" (emphasis ours) (Dalton, 1992, p. 64), the young athlete's personal history in terms of training must be carefully evaluated. Sudden changes (especially increases) in training regimens should raise particular concern. The data needed to establish a meaningful personal history for the young athlete might easily be obtained by using or modifying any of the several sports injury report forms available in athletic training texts (Arnheim & Prentice, 1993; Ray, 1994).

Although an assessment of the youngster's level of fitness is not included in a typical injury report, we feel it should be included. Items measuring strength, flexibility, and endurance could be included from one of several standardized fitness measures available, for example, the 1988 American Alliance for Health, Physical Education, Recreation, and Dance Physical Best Test, or Institute for Aerobics Research Fitnessgram Test (1987). In all cases, athletes' personal histories must be an integral part of any evaluation of overuse injury, determination as to readiness for participation, or return to participation following an injury.

Preparticipation Exam

The preparticipation exam and an athlete's injury history can go a long way in helping to determine the readiness of a youngster for sport participation. However, a preparticipation exam is often not even required for programs other than those organized through schools. Even when required, these once-a-year exams where dozens of athletes are screened on a given day are inadequate according to sports medicine practitioners (Johnson, Kibler, & Smith, 1993). Not only are these exams inadequate in detail, they tend not to be sport or activity specific; that is, one sport may place greater/different demands on the youngster and thus increase the chance of an overuse injury. Kibler recommends sport-specific exams for a youngster, preferably before or very early in the preseason, so potential problems can be identified and, if needed, appropriate preventative/remedial measures can be taken. The legal and insurance concerns associated with sport participation and the inherent dangers of injury make the preparticipation exam a "necessity" in today's society. Johnson et al. (1993) also stress that, as recommended earlier, a thorough history of sport participation and injury be obtained. They feel this history is as important if not more so than the actual physical exam.

Fitness Level

Though some recent research challenges the popularly held notion that today's youngsters are less fit than children 10 or 20 years ago (Corbin & Pangrazi, 1992), the evidence clearly shows that children have gotten heavier, fatter, and taller over the last 50 years (Kuntzleman & Reiff, 1992; Hamill, Johnson, & Grams, 1970). At the same time that educators and researchers are attempting to establish minimal levels of fitness, taller, heavier, and perhaps less fit youngsters are entering into ever increasingly strenuous repetitive training at a time when they are most susceptible to overuse (or as Micheli [1983] terms them—"over growth") injuries. The American College of Sports Medicine (1993) lists general fitness development as one of the most important strategies that may prevent and/or reduce the number of overuse (as well as other) injuries in youth sports. Rather than focusing only on sport skills and fitness activities deemed important for a specific sport, ACSM recommends a more general fitness program approach that will develop overall strength, flexibility, and endurance. These fitness activities should be started well before the particular sport season begins and should also follow the 10 percent rule of increasing distance, repetitions, intensity, etcetera, no more than 10 percent each week.

The Young Athlete's "Fit" to a Specific Sport

A critically important variable affecting young athletes is the extent to which the demands of the sport "match" the individual athlete's idiosyncratic physiological makeup. Matching young athletes to the skills, abilities, and demands of different sports is analogous to matching young competitors for age, size, skill level, etcetera.

Perhaps the "obvious" examples would be the slight, frail youngster trying to play football or become a power weight lifter, or the short, slow youngster spending hours practicing basketball or volleyball. However, more subtle mismatches certainly have a higher chance of going unnoticed and perhaps doing more damage to more young athletes.

A young athlete with little flexibility will not only perform poorly in a sport skill requiring a high degree of flexibility (e.g., pitching a baseball), but that athlete will also be at higher risk of overuse injury. So it would be for athletes having low bone density (e.g., amenorrheic females) participating in sports that require high bone density because of the extent of pounding that the athlete absorbs (e.g., gymnastics, endurance running). Various malalignments can also combine with the demands of specific sports to increase overuse injury occurrences and severity. Consider the athlete who is experiencing the rapid growth that characterizes the adolescent growth spurt. Anatomical malalignments that occur naturally at different points in the growth cycle can present serious risks. One example is the tightness and loss of flexibility across the joints that occur as lengthening of the bones increases faster than the musculotendinous unit involved (Dalton, 1992). This leads to imbalances across the joints, exposing the athlete to *increased stresses* that a younger or older athlete engaging in the same sport task would not experience. This is not an "abnormal" condition or situation but is the result of the normal growth pattern when the effects of that growth pattern interact with the anatomical and physiological demands of various sport tasks.

Social Facilitation

Research by Geen and Gange (1977) and others has established that the presence of coaches, competitors, and evaluators exerts a tremendous influence on motor performance. Similar effects on the perception and reporting of pain are not as well documented. Young athletes experiencing pain when alone or with friends in a free-play situation may respond quite differently in the presence of their coach, parents, fellow competitors, and spectators. Lord and Kozar (1986) found that second- and third-grade children tolerated significantly more cold pressor pain in the presence of peers than when alone. Do young athletes, therefore, because of their enthusiasm for sport, systematically tolerate greater levels of pain because of the social facilitation effects often present in the youth sport environment? Further research is needed to answer that question.

Social Comparison

Another major factor affecting young athletes is the extent to which all of us rely upon "social comparisons" when trying to judge ourselves (see Scanlan, this volume). As expressed so powerfully so long ago (Festinger, 1954), we strive to judge (evaluate) ourselves, and, given the absence of objective standards, we turn to social comparisons. That is, we judge our abilities by comparing ourselves with others. When we want to judge our abilities, people similar to or slightly higher in ability than ourselves provide the most informative comparison (Suls & Miller, 1977). These social comparison processes are pervasive, affecting all of us all of the time, and they differ markedly in adults and children and adolescents (Frieze, 1981). For adult athletes, all of whom are "equally mature physiologically," and for young athletes, with their incredible variability in physical maturity, social comparison processes should be expected to exert very different influences. Imagine the potential for excessive training demand when an adolescent athlete compares him- or herself with a competitor who is "winning" simply by virtue of being more physically mature, at an earlier age. The "loser" can easily suffer serious overuse injuries from training too intensely and too frequently in a futile attempt to "catch up" with a competitor who will only be "catchable" when the present maturational disparity disappears. How often does this subtle but powerful psychological factor lead to overuse injuries in young athletes?

Recommendations

Despite recent increases in research, there are still more questions than definite answers concerning overuse injuries in youth sports. Long-term effects range from being nonexistent (e.g., "normal growing pains" that resolve without intervention) through a range of benign results (the "bumpy knees" of Osgood-Schlatter's disease) and on to infrequent chronic, disabling consequences (e.g., osteochondritis disease of the capitellum or Little League elbow, growth plate injuries). Assessment of long-term effects is problematic because the effects are obviously so far removed from causes, but uncertainty about the prevalence and consequences of overuse injuries has not and will not slow the spread of youth sport programs. Thus some reasonable guidelines are needed for those who will continue to direct youth sport programs. Where applicable, the following recommendations are informed by research data. Where research is insufficient to support specific recommendations, our recommendation is based on reasonable inference from established research that is related to the topic.

1. A preparticipation exam and injury history that includes assessment relevant to the youngster's idiosyncrasies and the physical demands unique to the particular sport should be mandatory at every level of participation.
2. Adults who work directly with youngsters must meet certain minimum knowledge and experience requirements. Clinics and workshops that teach the latest applied sport science information relative to growth and development, exercise physiology, biomechanics, pedagogy, care and prevention of injuries, and social and psychological guidelines need to become an integral part of all organized sport programs. Specifically educate athletes, and the adults responsible for supervising their participation, about overuse injuries. Focus on developmental aspects of overuse injuries unique to a particular sport.
3. Since "maltraining" is the leading factor contributing to overuse injuries, proper training schedules and loads need to be adhered to. Follow the 10 percent rule referred to earlier governing the week-to-week increase in training loads. Any increase should be limited to one parameter per week, for example, a 10 percent increase in distance one week *followed* by a 10 percent increase in speed the next week.
4. Educate athletes, coaches, and parents as to the amount of time that should be allowed for the adaptive processes required for the specific training regimen. Impatient athletes and their coaches increase overuse injuries by undertaking increases in training too quickly and allowing insufficient time for adaptation. In certain situations where control of training schedules is possible (e.g., schools), minimum time periods for training are desirable. Many state athletic associations already do this, requiring, for instance, 10 practices before a cross-country runner can compete.
5. Training should be varied in terms of duration, amount, frequency, intensity, and specificity so that performance can still be enhanced but risk of overuse injury reduced through what Stone (1990) has labeled "periodization." Periodization appears to provide the rest that various body structures need between periods of overload, which are required if the training is to elicit the physical adaptation that is its purpose.
6. Include general as well as specific stretching, strength, and endurance exercises in the training regimen to allow for overall as well as specific

development of these important components. Always follow the best scientific guidelines available, for example, static rather than ballistic stretching.

7. Adapt playing equipment, court/field dimensions, distances, surfaces, rules, environment, and others, so they are developmentally appropriate. Lighter bats, shorter tennis racquets with reduced string tension, and others, are available and should be used when and where appropriate.

8. Discuss social comparison effects with athletes and responsible adults so that everyone involved can work toward less "inappropriate" comparisons and toward comparisons that are more closely tied to each athlete's individual abilities, efforts, and developmental level. Be watchful of social facilitation effects that may prompt some youngsters to "tough it out" rather than admit to a persistent pain that may signal an overuse injury.

References

AAHPERD. (1988). *Physical best test manual.* Reston, VA: American Alliance for Health, Physical Education, Recreation, and Dance.

Adams, J. E. (1965). Injury to the throwing arm: A study of traumatic changes in the elbow joints of boy baseball players. *California Medicine, 102,* 127–132.

American Academy of Pediatrics. (1981). Committee on pediatric aspects of physical fitness, recreation, and sports: Competitive athletics for children of elementary school age. *Pediatrics, 67,* 927–928.

American College of Sports Medicine. (1993, August). "Current Comment" by A. D. Smith, J. T. Andrish, & L. J. Micheli. Supplement to *Medicine and Science in Sports and Exercise, 25* (Supplement), 1–7.

Arnheim, D. A., & Prentice, W. E. (1993). *Principles of athletic training.* St. Louis: Mosby.

Bailey, D. A., & Martin, A. D. (1988). The growing child and sport: Physiological considerations. In F. L. Smoll, R. A. Magill, & M. J. Ash (Eds.), *Children in sport* (3rd ed., pp. 103–117). Champaign, IL: Human Kinetics.

Boland, A. L. (1982). Upper-extremity injuries: Overuse syndromes of the shoulder. In R. C. Cantu (Ed.), *The exercising adult* (pp. 115–120). Lexington, MA: Collamore Press.

Caine, D. J., Roy, S., Singer, K. M., & Broekhoff, J. (1992). Stress changes of the distal radial growth plate. *The American Journal of Sports Medicine, 20,* 290–298.

Caine, D. J., & Lindner, K. J. (1984). Growth plate injury: A threat to young distance runners? *The Physician and Sportsmedicine, 12,* 118–124.

Corbin, C. B., & Pangrazi, R. P. (1992). Are American children and youth fit? *Research Quarterly for Exercise and Sport, 63,* 96–106.

Dalton, S. E. (1992). Overuse injuries in adolescent athletes. *Sports Medicine, 13*(1), 58–70.

Dominguez, R. H. (1980). Shoulder pain in swimmers. *The Physician and Sportsmedicine, 8,* 37–42.

Festinger, L. (1954). A theory of social comparison processes. *Human Relations, 7,* 117–140.

Frieze, I. H. (1981). Children's attributions for success and failure. In S. S. Brehm, S. M. Kassin, & F. X. Gibbons (Eds.), *Developmental social psychology: Theory and research* (pp. 51–71). New York: Oxford University Press.

Gallagher, S. S., Finison, K., Guyer, B., & Goodenough, S. (1984). The incidence of injuries among 87,000 Massachusetts children and adolescents: Results of the 1980–81 Statewide Childhood Injury Prevention Program Surveillance System. *American Journal of Public Health, 74,* 1340–1347.

Geen, R. G., & Gange, J. J. (1977). Drive theory of social facilitation: Twelve years of theory and research. *Psychological Bulletin, 84,* 1267–1288.

Godshall, R. W., Hansen, C. A., & Rising, D. C. (1981). Stress fractures through the distal femoral epiphysis in athletes: A previously unreported entity. *American Journal of Sports Medicine, 9,* 114–116.

Goldberg, B. (1989). Injury patterns in youth sports. *The Physician and Sportsmedicine, 17*(3), 175–185.

Hamill, P. V. V., Johnson, F. E., & Grams, W. (1970). Height and weight of children. *United States Vital and Health Statistics, 104*(11), 1–46. Rockville, MD: U.S. Dept. of Health, Education and Welfare, National Center for Health Statistics.

Haywood, K. M. (1986). Modification in youth sport: A rationale and some examples in youth basketball. In M. R. Weiss & D. Gould (Eds.), *Sport for children and youths* (pp. 179–185). Champaign, IL: Human Kinetics.

Institute for Aerobics Research. (1987). *FITNESSGRAM user's manual.* Dallas: Institute for Aerobics Research.

Johnson, M. D., Kibler, W. B., & Smith, D. (1993). Keys to successful preparticipation exams. *The Physician and Sportsmedicine, 21,* 109–123.

Kannus, P., Niittymaki, S., & Jarvinen, M. (1988). Athletic overuse injuries in children. *Clinical Pediatrics, 27,* 333–337.

Kiefhaber, T. R., & Stern, P. J. (1992). Upper extremity tendinitis and overuse syndromes in the athlete. *Injuries of the Hand and Wrist, 11,* 39–55.

Kuntzleman, C. T., & Reiff, G. G. (1992). The decline in American children's fitness levels. *Research Quarterly for Exercise and Sport, 63,* 107–111.

Lipscomb, A. B. (1975). Baseball pitching injuries in growing athletes. *The Journal of Sports Medicine, 3,* 25–34.

Lopez, R., & Pruett, D. M. (1982). The child runner. *Journal of Physical Education, Recreation and Dance, 53,* 78–81.

Lord, R. H., & Kozar, B. (1986, April). *Social facilitation and pain attenuation: Implications for youth sports.* Paper presented at the conference of the American Alliance for Health, Physical Education, Recreation, and Dance, Cincinnati, OH.

Lysens, R. J., Ostyn, M. S., Auweele, Y. V., Lefevre, J., Vuylsteke, M., & Renson, L. (1989). The accident-prone and overuse-prone profiles of the young athlete. *American Journal of Sports Medicine, 17,* 612–619.

Martens, R. (1988). Youth sport in the USA. In F. L. Smoll, R. A. Magill, & M. J. Ash (Eds.), *Children in sport* (3rd ed., pp. 17–23). Champaign, IL: Human Kinetics.

McGinnis, J. M. (1985). The national children and youth fitness study: Introduction. *Journal of Physical Education, Recreation and Dance, 56,* 44.

Mcmanama, G. B., Micheli, L. J., Berry, M. V., & Sohn, R. S. (1985). The surgical treatment of osteochondritis of the capitellum. *American Journal of Sports Medicine, 13,* 11–19.

Micheli, L. J. (1983). Overuse injuries in children: The growth factor. In M. W. Korn (Ed.), Symposium on special considerations in sports medicine. *The Orthopedic Clinics of North America, 14,* 337–360.

Micheli, L. J., & Fehlandt, A. F. (1992). Overuse injuries to tendon and apophyses in children and adolescents. *Clinics in Sports Medicine, 11,* 713–726.

Micheli, L. J., Santore, R., & Stanitski, C. L. (1980). Epiphyseal fractures of the elbow in children. *American Family Physician, 22,* 107–116.

Micheli, L. J., Sohn, R. S., & Solomon, R. (1985). Stress fractures of the second metatarsal involving lisfranc's joint in ballet dancers. *The Journal of Bone and Joint Surgery, 67*(A), 1372–1375.

Michener, J. A. (1976). *Sport in America.* Greenwich, CT: Fawcett.

O'Neill, D. B., & Micheli, L. J. (1988). Overuse injuries in the young athlete. *Clinics in Sports Medicine, 7,* 591–610.

Orava, S., & Puranen, J. (1978). Exertion injuries in adolescent athletes. *British Journal of Sports Medicine, 12,* 4–10.

O'Toole, M., Hiller, D. B., Smith, R., & Sisk, T. (1989). Overuse injuries in ultra-endurance tri-athletes. *American Journal of Sports Medicine, 17,* 514–518.

Pitner, M. A. (1990). Pathophysiology of overuse injuries in the hand and wrist. *Hand Clinic, 6,* 355–364.

Ray, R. (1994). *Management strategies in athletic training.* Champaign, IL: Human Kinetics.

Renstrom, P. A. F. H. (1990). Overuse injuries in athletes. *Current Opinion in Orthopaedics, 1,* 365–373.

Rettig, A. C., & Beltz, H. F. (1985). Stress fracture in the humerus in an adolescent tennis tournament player. *American Journal of Sports Medicine, 13,* 55–58.

Scanlan, T. K. (1995). Social evaluation and the competition process: A developmental perspective. In F. L. Smoll & R. E. Smith (Eds.), *Children and youth in sport: A biopsychosocial perspective* (pp. 298–308). Dubuque, IA: Brown & Benchmark.

Seefeldt, V., & Steig, P. (1986). Introduction to an interdisciplinary assessment of competition on elite young distance runners. In M. R. Weiss & D. Gould (Eds.), *Sport for children and youths* (pp. 213–217). Champaign, IL: Human Kinetics.

Shaffer, T. E. (1980). The uniqueness of the young athlete: Introductory remarks. *American Journal of Sports Medicine, 8,* 370–371.

Sharkey, B. J. (1986). When should children begin competing? A physiological perspective. In M. R. Weiss & D. Gould (Eds.,), *Sport for children and youths* (pp. 51–54). Champaign, IL: Human Kinetics.

Singer, K. (1986). Injuries and disorders of the epiphysis in young athletes. In M. R. Weiss & D. Gould (Eds.), *Sport for children and youths* (pp. 141–150). Champaign, IL: Human Kinetics.

Speer, D. P., & Braun, J. K. (1985). The biomechanical basis of growth plate injuries. *The Physician and Sportsmedicine, 13,* 72–78.

Stanish, W. D. (1984). Overuse injuries in athletes: A perspective. *Medicine and Science in Sports and Exercise, 16,* 1–7.

Stanitski, C. L. (1993). Combating overuse injuries: A focus on children and adolescents. *The Physician and Sportsmedicine, 21,* 87–106.

Stone, M. H. (1990). Muscle conditioning and muscle injuries. *Medicine and Science in Sports and Exercise, 22,* 457–462.

Suls, J. M., & Miller, R. L. (Eds.). (1977). *Social comparison processes: Theoretical and empirical perspectives.* Washington, DC: Hemisphere.

Swärd, L. (1992). The thoracolumbar spine in young elite athletes. *Sports Medicine, 13,* 357–364.

Tabin, G. C., Gregg, J. R., & Bonci, T. (1985). Predictive leg strength values in immediately prepubescent and postpubescent athletes. *American Journal of Sports Medicine, 13,* 387–389.

Tanner, J. M. (1962). *Growth at adolescence* (2nd ed.). Oxford, England: Blackwell.

Teeple, J. (1978). Physical growth and maturation. In M. V. Ridenour (Ed.), *Motor development: Issues and application* (pp. 3–27). Princeton, NJ: Princeton Book Co.

Walsh, W. M., Huurman, W. W., & Shelton, G. L. (1985). Overuse injuries of the knee and spine in girls' gymnastics. *The Orthopedic Clinics of North America, 16,* 329–350.

Webb, D. R. (1995). Strength training in children and adolescents. In F. L. Smoll & R. E. Smith (Eds.), *Children and youth in sport: A biopsychosocial perspective* (pp. 248–280). Dubuque, IA: Brown & Benchmark.

Wilkerson, J. (1981). Strength and endurance training of the youthful performer. In C. H. Strong & D. D. Ludwig (Eds.), *Directions in health, physical education, and recreation: Proceedings of the national olympic academy IV, the olympic ideal: 776 B.C. to the 21st century* (Vol. 2, pp. 589–609). Bloomington: School of Health, Physical Education, and Recreation, Indiana University.

Zaricznyj, B., Shattuck, L. J. M., Mast, T. A., Robertson, R. V., & Delia, G. (1980). Sports-related injuries in school-aged children. *American Journal of Sports Medicine, 8,* 318–324.

Zito, M. (1983). The adolescent athlete: A musculoskeletal update. *Journal of Orthopaedic and Sports Physical Therapy, 4,* 20–25.

PART

PSYCHOLOGICAL ISSUES

In ever-increasing numbers, boys and girls are participating in sports. How does such participation affect their psychological development, and which psychological processes determine these effects? This part provides some provocative answers to these questions.

To begin this part, Tara Kost Scanlan establishes the significance of competitive sport experiences in the psychosocial development of children between the ages of 4 and 12 years. By means of a four-stage model of the processes involved, Scanlan shows the centrality of the process of social evaluation, and the role of competition in the socialization process. She cautions that a complete understanding of the sport experience requires that competition be understood within the broader context of children's socialization and psychosocial development. She also discusses the long-term developmental consequences of competitive sport experiences on children.

In an achievement-oriented society such as ours, a critical aspect of the self-concept is one's judgments of personal competence in various achievement domains. In chapter 18, Thelma S. Horn and Amy Harris discuss the determinants and consequences of perceived sport competence from early childhood through adolescence. Perceptions of physical or sport competence are related not only to actual sport performance but also to motivation, persistence, and emotional reactions to the sport experience. Horn and Harris's comprehensive review of their own and others' research indicates that the types of information that children use to make competence judgments change in important ways from early childhood through late adolescence; these changes are attributable not only to maturational processes but also to the changing characteristics of the sport situations to which children of various ages are exposed. On the basis of what we now know about these processes, the authors offer specific recommendations to coaches and parents for facilitating self-perceptions of competence in children of varying ages.

In a provocative counterpoint to the competitive nature of most youth sport programs, Terry D. Orlick and Louise Zeitzelberger emphasize the damaging effects that such an environment can have on the child's enjoyment of sport and on self-concept development. Common complaints made by children include too much emphasis on winning, not enough on fun, and inadequate playing time for many children. An alternative structure is provided by cooperative games, which remove the need to compete against others, include all athletes for the duration of the game, promote fun-filled interaction, and encourage consideration for others. The authors believe that cooperative structures provide a more psychologically healthy environment for children. They also suggest that the sport environment can be used as a setting for the learning of psychological skills that not only enhance sport performance but also serve as general life skills that can enrich the quality of daily life. Skill training of this type has become commonplace in the training of elite athletes, but Orlick and Zeitzelberger show how it can also be adapted for child athletes.

A major objective of youth sports is to teach the skills of the particular sport. How is this best accomplished? In chapter 20, Jere D. Gallagher, Karen E. French, Katherine T. Thomas, and Jerry R. Thomas review what is known about the mental and physical processes that turn sport novices into experts. Skill improvement includes motor control, decision making, and skill execution. Research indicates that experts and novices differ in perceptual and cognitive abilities as well as in physical skill levels. Of particular importance are memory strategies involving selective attention to the relevant cues in the sport environment, retention of relevant information in both short-term (working) and long-term memory, rehearsal of movements and strategies stored in memory, and the organization of knowledge so that it can easily be accessed. Athletes must have cognitive representations of the efficient motor patterns associated with the sport and be able to execute these patterns to become experts. Appropriate teaching and practice strategies can enhance both cognitive and motor skill development. Based on what is currently known about the development of expertise in sport, the authors propose specific coaching strategies that can be applied at various age levels.

In chapter 21, Frank L. Smoll and Ronald E. Smith analyze the nature of athletic stress and what can be done to reduce it. The adverse psychological, behavioral, and health-related consequences of sport stress are addressed, as is the controversial issue of whether sports are unduly stressful for youngsters. The authors present a conceptual model of stress that emphasizes relations between stressful situations, cognitive appraisal processes, physiologic responses, and attempts to cope with the demands of the situation. This model helps to organize empirical findings on the situational and intrapersonal determinants of anxiety experienced by young athletes prior to, during, and following competition. The model also suggests points at which intervention strategies might be employed to reduce unnecessary stress. Specifically, guidelines and procedures are offered that have proven effective in decreasing situational sources of stress associated with the nature of the sport, coaching roles and relationships, and parental roles and responsibilities. Next the authors describe a stress management training program that has been used to teach young athletes cognitive and physiologic coping skills. Finally, stress reduction at the behavioral level is explored with respect to young athletes' level of physical skill.

For many years we have heard the assertion that "sport builds character." In a provocative finale to this section, Brenda Jo Light Bredemeier and David Lyle Light Shields consider a body of literature that indicates that in some instances, sport participation is actually associated with lower levels of moral reasoning and a greater acceptance of immoral acts within the sport context. To understand the factors that might mediate the impact of sport experiences on moral behavior, the authors present a theoretical model that specifies a set of psychological competencies that undergird moral action. The authors suggest that the impact of sport on moral development actually involves four separate but related questions: (1) How does sport affect participants' role-taking and perspective-taking abilities? (2) How does sport affect the development of moral reasoning? (3) How is the development of the self-structure, particularly its motivational and moral value components, influenced by sport experiences? (4) How does sport affect children's development of self-regulatory and problem-solving skills? All of these determinants of moral behavior may potentially be affected, either positively or negatively, by the nature of the child's sport experiences. Depending on the nature of the environment created by adult supervisors, sport may indeed create character—or, alternatively, characters.

All of the papers in this part serve as urgent reminders that those who structure and supervise youth sport programs, particularly parents and coaches, have a strong but often unrecognized responsibility for the impact that athletic experiences can have on virtually all aspects of psychosocial functioning. They also demonstrate the important role that scientific research can play in providing practical guidelines for increasing the likelihood that children will be affected in a positive manner by their sport participation.

SOCIAL EVALUATION AND THE COMPETITION PROCESS: A DEVELOPMENTAL PERSPECTIVE

—Tara Kost Scanlan

Almost half of our nation's youth spend a large amount of their time participating in an achievement arena of considerable importance to them—competitive sport. The significance of this achievement experience to the developing child needs to be determined, and the complex relations between competition and social-psychological development require understanding. This chapter takes a first step in this direction by presenting a conceptualization of the competition process typically encountered by youth in the naturalistic competitive sport environment. Of primary interest are children between the ages of 4 and 12 years. The focus is on the examination of *social evaluation* as a key element of the competition process because of its centrality, pervasiveness, and developmental importance. Related discussion concerns whether social evaluation is actually perceived by participants and, if so, whether the evaluative information is actively sought. Finally, potential long-term, developmental consequences of the socially evaluative sport experience are considered.

Selection of a Viable Approach to Study Competition

To understand the complex competition process, it is necessary to determine a viable basic approach to serve as a starting point for its study. Two major approaches to the study of competition are the traditional reward approach and a more recent formulation articulated by Martens (1975, 1976). The reward approach defines competition as a situation in which rewards are distributed unequally among participants based on their performance in an activity (Church, 1968). The problems with the reward approach that have limited its scientific viability have been enumerated extensively by Martens (1975, 1976) and will be reviewed only briefly.

The major limitation of the reward approach is that the competitive situation defined on a reward basis cannot be clearly operationalized. It is difficult to achieve "consensus on the criteria for the distribution of rewards, on the subjective value of the rewards, and on the goal to be achieved" (Martens, 1975, p. 70). The goals strived for and the rewards sought might be entirely different for each competitor involved in the competition. Therefore, use of the reward definition forces the experimenter to make critical assumptions and inferences about the individual's perceptions, responses, and response consequences regarding the competitive situation.

The more viable approach to the study of competition, conceptualized by Martens (1975, 1976), has overcome the major deficiencies of the reward definition and provides a more workable alternative for scientific inquiry. Hence, this approach will be used to provide the underlying framework for the ensuing discussion. Martens provides clear operational definitions and makes no assumptions regarding how the individual perceives the competitive situation, the response made to it, or the consequences of the response. Instead, these factors have been divided into stages to be examined systematically.

Martens (1975) has depicted competition as a process consisting of four interrelated stages that filter through the individual. The stages include the objective competitive situation, subjective competitive situation, response, and consequences.

The *objective competitive situation* (OCS) refers to those "real factors in the physical or social environment that are arbitrarily defined as constituting a competitive situation" (Martens, 1975, p. 69). The OCS is based on social evaluation rather than on reward and is defined as a situation in which the comparison of an individual's performance is made with some standard in the presence of at least one other person who is aware of the criterion for comparison and can evaluate the comparison process (p. 71). The comparison standard can be an individual's past performance level, an idealized performance level, or another individual's performance.

The second stage of the competition process is the *subjective competitive situation* (SCS) and involves how the individual perceives, appraises, and accepts the OCS. The SCS is very important, as it is the manner in which the individual perceives reality. Therefore, it is from this base that the individual operates. The resultant *response* emitted in Stage 3 is a direct function of the SCS. Responses can be made on a psychological, physiological, or behavioral level. Possible responses include the decision to compete or to avoid competition, attempts to modify the objective competitive situation, and overt competitive behavior.

The fourth stage of the competition process involves the short- or long-term *consequences* arising from the comparison process, which can be perceived as positive, negative, or neutral. The perceived consequences provide important information that updates the SCS and affects future competitive responses.

Beginning with this framework, which identifies social evaluation as a key component of the competition process, it is now possible to detail the social evaluation potential in the naturalistic objective competitive situation encountered by children engaged in competitive youth sport. The subjective competitive situation and response stages can be examined to determine whether children perceive the social evaluation potential in the OCS and, if it is perceived, how children then respond with information-seeking and self-protective behavior. The potential long-term consequences of the competition process can then be analyzed in terms of implications for social psychological development. Figure 17.1 provides a schematic overview of the analytic strategy.

The Nature of Social Evaluation in the Naturalistic Objective Competitive Situation (OCS)

The naturalistic OCS that children typically encounter encompasses considerable social evaluation potential. *Social evaluation* is the appraisal of one's ability based on information received from other persons (Jones & Gerard, 1967). Children have been found to be active information seekers who derive information from both social and nonsocial sources, with much of their information coming from social sources (Jones & Gerard, 1967; White, 1959). The developing child has limited past experience upon which to draw and, consequently, is very dependent on significant adults and peers for information about reality and the adequacy of his or her abilities for dealing with this reality (Harter, 1978; Horn & Hasbrook, 1986; Jones & Gerard, 1967). As depicted in figure 17.1, the typical OCS includes at least three separate social evaluation processes: comparative appraisal, reflected appraisal, and consultation.

The Comparative Appraisal Process

Comparative appraisal is the process of comparing with others to determine one's own relative standing on a specific ability (Jones & Gerard, 1967). Comparative appraisal occurs in the OCS when the comparison standard is another individual's performance rather than a past or idealized performance standard. The developmental findings clearly indicate that comparative appraisal becomes very important to children at approximately 4 to 5 years of age and intensifies through the elementary school years (Masters, 1972; Veroff, 1969). The following developmental progression indicates why this seems to occur.

Very young children do not compare themselves or compete with others (Greenberg, 1932; Masters, 1972; Veroff, 1969). Instead, their time is spent autonomously accruing information about their own personal abilities. This is accomplished through exploration, solitary play, mastery attempts, striving to attain autonomous achievement goals, and feedback from adults (Cook & Stingle, 1974; Harter, 1978; Veroff, 1969; White, 1959). Eventually, however, personal or absolute ability is placed into a larger relative framework through comparative appraisal to achieve an accurate, meaningful, and complete assessment of ability. Developmentally the child appears to be ready to engage in this process around 4 or 5 years of age, when the first signs of comparative and competitive behavior are evidenced (Cook & Stingle, 1974; Greenberg, 1932; Leuba, 1933; Masters, 1972; Ruble et al., 1980; Veroff, 1969). Further, an increase in comparative and competitive behavior occurs with age throughout the elementary school period, with the greatest intensity occurring around grades 4, 5, and 6 (Cook & Stingle, 1974; Horn & Hasbrook, 1986; Kagan & Madsen, 1972; McClintock & Nuttin, 1969; Nelson, 1970; Nelson & Kagan, 1972; Veroff, 1969). During this important age span, many children are engaged in competitive youth sport activities, where much of the comparative appraisal occurs. Further, the focus of the appraisal is on motor ability. To excel motorically is one of the most prized and esteemed abilities of children of this age level. For example, personal perceptions of physical competence are positively related to self-esteem (e.g., Ebbeck & Stuart, 1993), sport enjoyment (e.g., Scanlan & Simons, 1992), motivation (e.g., Brustad, 1993a; Weiss & Chaumeton, 1993), and peer relations (Brustad, 1993b; Evans &

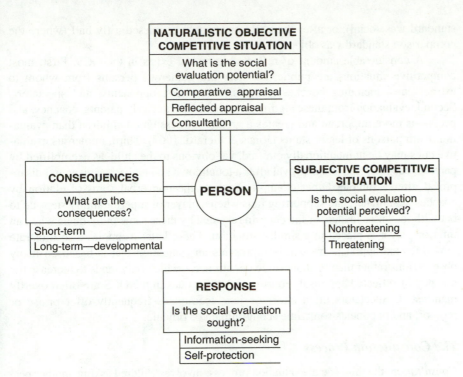

FIGURE 17.1

The role of social evaluation in the sport competition process.

From "Social Evaluation and the Competition Process: A Developmental Perspective" by T. K. Scanlan. In *Children in Sport* (3rd ed., p. 139) by F. L. Smoll, R. A. Magill, and M. J. Ash (Eds.). Champaign, IL: Human Kinetics Publishers. Copyright 1988 by F .L. Smoll, R. A. Magill, and M. J. Ash. Reprinted by permission.

Roberts, 1987). Therefore, the comparative appraisal process involves a central ability, making the outcomes of this process potentially very important.

The Reflected Appraisal Process

Reflected appraisal is the second social evaluation process that can occur in the OCS. This is the process by which the child "derives an impression of his position on some attribute through the behavior of another person toward him" (Jones & Gerard, 1967, p. 321). Children can obtain extensive information about their motor abilities by attending to the overt or covert cues emitted by one who is in the position to evaluate their abilities. Comparative and reflected appraisal are similar in that evaluative ability information is derived from a social source. However, the two processes differ in certain ways. First, in comparative appraisal, children evaluate their relative abilities by comparing with another person's ability but do not make any reference to the other person's direct behavior toward them (Jones & Gerard, 1967). Reflected appraisal involves the evaluation being "mediated by the behavior of the other person toward the person himself" (Jones & Gerard, 1967, p. 324). In this sense, the evaluation is inferred from the emitted behavior. Second, comparative appraisal involves evaluation through comparison with social standards, whereas reflected appraisal includes comparison with either social or objective standards. For example, a coach might unintentionally transmit reflected appraisal cues to a child after the child has won or lost a wrestling match (where the comparison standard was social), or after the child has caught or missed a fly ball (where the comparison standard was objective rather than social).

A considerable amount of reflected appraisal exists in the OCS. First, most competitive situations are public, so there are numerous persons from whom to extract cues, including coaches, parents, teammates, opponents, and spectators. Second, evaluation from these significant others—particularly parents, coaches, and peers—is more important and creates a greater impression on children than evaluation from persons of lesser status (Jones & Gerard, 1967). Third, numerous evaluative cues may be unintentionally emitted, yet obvious to the child, as exemplified by parental cues of pride and approval after a touchdown and embarrassment and disapproval after a fumble. Other examples include the nonverbal signs of elation by coaches, teammates, and supporting fans when a player of superior ability steps up to bat with the bases loaded, or the chagrin revealed by these same individuals when an inferior player is placed in a similar situation. These latter examples also illustrate how reflected appraisal frequently represents an evaluation that is based on many observations rather than on a one-time occurrence—which only tends to increase the potency of reflected appraisal. Fourth, evaluative cues in the OCS are often overtly manifested. Spectators often cheer or jeer, teammates frequently offer praise or reproof, and opponents sometimes congratulate or ridicule.

The Consultation Process

Consultation, the third social evaluation process, involves children asking another person for an ability appraisal or receiving an evaluation without explicitly requesting one (Jones & Gerard, 1967). The evaluation is direct rather than inferred and, again, is typically received from significant others. For example, parents often place great value on their child's motor ability; consequently they have much to say about his or her performance. It is the coach's job to evaluate ability, and players receive extensive information during practices that indicates their strengths, progress, and areas requiring improvement. Frequently coaches make overt evaluations that indicate their appraisal of a player's ability compared with other players. Selecting a team, choosing the starters, and picking all-star candidates are all examples of evaluations coaches make that reinforce important comparative appraisal information for the youth.

In sum, the OCS encompasses extensive potential social evaluation through the processes of comparative appraisal, reflected appraisal, and direct consultation. Therefore, much information is available to participants from which to establish accurate and complete ability assessments. Involvement in the competition process occurs during the age period when the social evaluation process is particularly intense and important. Furthermore, the specific ability being appraised—motor ability—is of central importance to developing youths. Therefore, it is contended that the social evaluation potential in the OCS is high.

The Subjective Competitive Situation

The subjective competitive situation (SCS) requires examination to determine whether the social evaluation in the OCS is actually perceived by the competitors (see fig. 17.1). Evidence of this perception would establish that social evaluation is a real and salient factor to the competition process.

The SCS is difficult to assess because it is a cognitive variable, requiring inference. One indicant used to assess the social evaluation potential in the SCS has been the perception of threat to self-esteem. Potential threat to self-esteem generally increases when social evaluation potential is high, when success and failure are clearly defined, and when negative outcomes and evaluation can be incurred. This perceived threat can induce psychological stress as manifested by state anxiety. *State anxiety* is defined by Spielberger (1966) as "subjective consciously perceived feelings of apprehension and tension, accompanied by or associated with activation or arousal of the autonomic nervous system" (p. 17). State anxiety is a *right-now* reaction to the immediate situation and can be assessed by physiological measures of autonomic arousal, by observation, and by psychological inventories. Two of the most commonly used psychological inventories employed to study youth are Spielberger's (1973) State Anxiety Inventory for Children (SAIC) and the Competitive State Anxiety Inventory for Children (CSAI-C) developed by Martens and his associates (Martens et al., 1980). Studies from three related lines of research provide insight into the SCS and the perception of threat.

The first line of research was initiated in a laboratory experiment designed to assess threat in the SCS and to determine the factors that induce it (Scanlan, 1975, 1977). Specifically, the effects of competitive trait anxiety (A-trait) and success-failure on state anxiety (A-state) manifested prior to and after a highly socially evaluative competition were investigated. An overview of this experiment is provided because it was the first study to assess perceived threat resulting from high social evaluation potential in the OCS.

Competitive A-trait, assessed by the Sport Competition Anxiety Test (SCAT; Martens, 1977), is an important intrapersonal factor related to perceived threat. It is a "relatively stable personality disposition that describes a person's tendency to perceive competitive situations as threatening or non-threatening" and to respond with varying A-state levels (Martens & Gill, 1976, p. 699). Findings in the general and test anxiety literatures consistently have shown that high A-trait individuals exhibit greater A-state than low A-trait individuals when in evaluative or psychologically stressful situations (Hodges & Durham, 1972; Lamb, 1972; Phillips et al., 1980; Sarason, 1968; Wine, 1982). Therefore, it was hypothesized in this study that high competitive A-trait children would evidence higher A-state than low competitive A-trait children when facing a socially evaluative competitive situation.

The degree of success or failure experienced during competition, defined in terms of win-loss outcomes, is an important situational determinant of perceived threat to self. Individuals achieving successful outcomes should be less threatened by the information about their ability, should expect greater positive evaluation from others, and should be more confident in their ability to effect positive outcomes in similar future encounters than individuals incurring failure. Individuals attaining moderately successful outcomes receive little definitive evaluative information and should approximate their precompetitive perceptions. Results from the general anxiety literature have indicated consistently that A-state decreases with success and increases with failure (Hodges & Durham, 1972; Ishiguro, 1965). Therefore, it was hypothesized that children experiencing more successful competition outcomes would evidence lower postcompetition A-state than children experiencing fewer successful outcomes.

The experimental design was a competitive A-trait × success-failure (2 × 3) factorial. The two levels of the first factor were high and low competitive A-trait. The Sport Competition Anxiety Test (SCAT) was administered to 306 boys between 10 and 12 years of age several weeks prior to the experimental phase of the study. The 41 high competitive A-trait boys and the 42 low competitive A-trait boys, representing the respective upper and lower quartiles on SCAT, were selected as participants. The three levels of success-failure were induced by manipulating win percentage. The success group won 80 percent (W80), the moderate-success group won 50 percent (W50), and the failure group won only 20 percent (W20) of the 20 contests. Both high and low A-trait boys were randomly assigned to success-failure conditions.

A-state was assessed by Spielberger's State Anxiety Inventory for Children (SAIC) at four different time periods. An initial basal measure was taken after a lengthy rest period. Assessments also were made just prior to competition, immediately after competition, and after a final debriefing session.

The findings demonstrated that competitive A-trait and success-failure are important factors in the perception of threat and, thereby, provided support for the two hypotheses. Competitive A-trait was found to be a significant predictor of precompetitive A-state, with high competitive A-trait individuals indicating greater A-state than low competitive A-trait individuals. The results also indicated that increases in postcompetition A-state levels were greatest in the failure (W20) group and smallest in the successful (W80) group.

The results of this study have been shown to be internally and externally valid; they have been successfully replicated under similar laboratory conditions (Martens & Gill, 1976) and in the natural field setting of competitive youth sport (Scanlan & Lewthwaite, 1984; Scanlan & Passer, 1978, 1979). Extensive social evaluation potential existed in the objective competitive situation of each study, and the evidence suggests that this social evaluation is actually perceived. Moreover, it is perceived by participants of both genders and in individual as well as team sports.

Evidence that the social evaluation in the OCS is perceived by young competitors has been supported by two additional lines of research. First, studies have indicated that even greater precompetition state anxiety is manifested in the particularly evaluative individual sport context than in the team sport domain (Griffin, 1972; Johnson, 1949; Simon & Martens, 1979; see Scanlan, 1984 for an elaboration of this issue). Second, it has been demonstrated that participants evidence concern about performance failure and negative social evaluation. These cognitions have been shown to be predictors of higher competitive trait anxiety (Gould, Horn, & Spreemann, 1983; Lewthwaite & Scanlan, 1989; Passer, 1983) and precompetition state anxiety levels (Scanlan & Lewthwaite, 1984). Brustad (1993a) provides a thorough review of perceived parental and coach evaluative reactions related to threat to self-esteem; and Scanlan, Stein, and Ravizza (1991) report similar appraisal factors related to threat in elite performers.

In sum, the findings of the three lines of research reviewed provide insight into threat in the subjective competitive situation. The evidence indicates that the social evaluation potential in the OCS is actually perceived and, therefore, is a salient factor in the competition process. The manner in which the subjective competitive situation is responded to in terms of seeking the available ability information and subsequent evaluation is examined next.

Response

It has been shown that children are very aware of and can feel threatened by the social evaluation potential in the objective competitive situation. Referring again to figure 17.1, the next point of interest is determining how children respond to this social evaluation. Do they actively seek the ability information that emanates from evaluation, or do they avoid this information, when possible, to protect themselves? Answers to these questions are needed to further establish the importance and pervasiveness of social evaluation information.

A matter of particular relevance to this discussion is determining how children, under different levels of perceived threat, structure the competitive situation when given the opportunity to select their own future opponents. Do they structure the situation to maximize or minimize information about their abilities? Festinger's social comparison theory provides some insight into the issue.

Festinger (1954) developed a theory of social comparison based on the premise that human beings are motivated to obtain evaluative information about their abilities and, in the absence of objective standards, seek comparative appraisal. Further, comparison is made with similar-ability others to maximize information gain. The paradigm usually employed to assess this hypothesis has been structured in the following way. Subjects are told that their score, representing performance on a positively or negatively valued attribute, has fallen at the median of a list of scores ordered by rank. Subjects are then asked which score in the ranked list they would like to see. Typically, if the extreme scores have been established and the trait is positive, subjects choose to see the score of a similar or slightly superior other in the rank order (Gruder, 1971; Hakmiller, 1966; Radloff, 1966; Singer & Shockley, 1965). This consistent finding indicates support for Festinger's information-seeking hypothesis.

However, several findings have demonstrated that when threat to self exists in social evaluation situations, self-protective behavior occurs. Further, such behavior increases as the probability of incurring threatening ability information increases. Results indicate that individuals reduce the probability of receiving this threatening information by comparing with individuals of lesser relative ability, thereby ensuring successful comparative appraisal (Dreyer, 1954; Friend & Gilbert, 1973; Hakmiller, 1966).

The following hypotheses can be derived from the social comparison findings. First, successful, unthreatened subjects structure the situation to maximize information gain by selecting opponents of equal or slightly greater relative ability. Conversely, unsuccessful, threatened subjects minimize information gain by selecting opponents of lesser relative ability. In this way, they protect themselves from incurring further negative appraisal information.

Scanlan (1977) tested these two hypotheses in the competition laboratory experiment presented earlier. Opponent preference questions were administered during the postcompetition period immediately after postcompetition A-state was assessed. The results supported the first hypothesis but not the second. Children in all three success-failure groups (W80, W50, W20) indicated a strong preference for opponents who equaled their abilities. These findings indicate that children engage in maximum information-seeking behavior during competition, regardless of their level of perceived threat.

Consequences

The final stage of the competition process involves the short- and long-term consequences, which may be positive, negative, or neutral (see fig. 17.1). Whenever social evaluation of ability occurs, positive or negative consequences can result during any given competition. The child might receive successful comparative appraisal information and positive reflected and/or consultation evaluation from significant others. Conversely, unsuccessful comparative appraisal and negative social evaluation might be incurred. It is probable that the consequences of any one *isolated* competitive experience will have minimal effect on social psychological development—unless, perhaps, the consequences are particularly aversive. The important point is that many children engage in intense competition over extended periods of time with similar consequences potentially being repeated over and over again. This repetition makes developmental considerations, such as self-esteem development, relevant. Through this repetition the potential accrual of primarily successful or primarily unsuccessful experiences, as perceived by the participant, can result. Also through this repetition, success-failure experiences might somewhat balance out, leading to relatively neutral long-term consequences.

The second important point is that the consequences of the competition process must be kept within the perspective of the total socialization process. The extensive evaluative information available in the objective competitive situation can result in children establishing an accurate assessment of an ability that is very important to them. Whether this information, be it positive or negative, results in favorable, neutral, or adverse consequences largely depends on the perspective provided by significant others. For example, children who continually receive negative comparative appraisal but gain support and guidance from their parents and coaches might benefit considerably from the competitive experience. The potential negative consequences might be neutralized or even supplanted with more positive outcomes. The children might learn to put comparative appraisal outcomes in perspective, learn to accept their capabilities and limitations within this particular achievement arena, and learn to define success and failure in terms of accomplishing realistic personal performance and effort goals. The potential negative impact of the consequences might further be reduced if the children can demonstrate other abilities, function competently in other evaluative achievement settings, and receive positive evaluation from significant others regarding their abilities.

In sum, the competition process must be placed within the larger socialization process to be adequately understood. Although competition is an important process, it cannot be isolated from the child's greater social context. The role of significant others and competence in other situations must be considered as they influence the positive, negative, or neutral long-term consequences of competition.

References

Brustad, R. J. (1993a). Youth in sport: Psychological considerations. In R. N. Singer, M. M. Murphey, & L. K. Tennant (Eds.), *Handbook of sport psychology* (pp. 695–717). New York: Macmillan.

———. (1993b). Who will go out and play? Parental and psychological influences on children's attraction to physical activity. *Pediatric Exercise Science, 5,* 210–223.

Church, R. M. (1968). Applications of behavior theory to social psychology: Imitation and competition. In E. C. Simmel, R. H. Hoppe, & G. A. Milton (Eds.), *Social facilitation and imitative behavior* (pp. 135–168). Boston: Allyn & Bacon.

Cook, H., & Stingle, S. (1974). Cooperative behavior in children. *Psychological Bulletin, 81,* 918–933.

Dreyer, H. S. (1954). Aspiration behavior as influenced by expectation and group comparison. *Human Relations, 7,* 175–190.

Ebbeck, V., & Stuart, M. E. (1993). Who determines what's important? Perceptions of competence and importance as predictors of self-esteem in youth football players. *Pediatric Exercise Science, 5,* 253–262.

Evans, J., & Roberts, G. C. (1987). Physical competence and the development of children's peer relations. *Quest, 39,* 23–35.

Festinger, L. A. (1954). A theory of social comparison processes. *Human Relations, 7,* 117–140.

Friend, R. M., & Gilbert, J. (1973). Threat and fear of negative evaluation as determinants of locus of social comparison. *Journal of Personality, 41,* 328–340.

Gould, D., Horn, T., & Spreemann, J. (1983). Sources of stress in junior elite wrestlers. *Journal of Sport Psychology, 5,* 159–171.

Greenberg, P. J. (1932). Competition in children: An experimental study. *American Journal of Psychology, 44,* 221–248.

Griffin, M. R. (1972). An analysis of state and trait anxiety experienced in sports competition at different age levels. *Foil* (Spring), 58–64.

Gruder, C. L. (1971). Determinants of social comparison. *Journal of Experimental Social Psychology, 7,* 473–489.

Hakmiller, K. L. (1966). Threat as a determinant of downward comparison. *Journal of Experimental Social Psychology Supplement, 2*(1), 32–39.

Harter, S. (1978). Effectance motivation reconsidered. *Human Development, 21,* 34–64.

Hodges, W. F., & Durham, R. L. (1972). Anxiety, ability and digit span performance. *Journal of Personality and Social Psychology, 24,* 401–406.

Horn, T. S., & Hasbrook, C. (1986). Informational components influencing children's perceptions of their physical competence. In M. R. Weiss & D. Gould (Eds.), *Sport for children and youths* (pp. 81–88). Champaign, IL: Human Kinetics.

Ishiguro, S. (1965). Motivational instructions and GSR on memory, especially as related to manifest anxiety. *Psychological Reports, 16,* 786.

Johnson, W. R. (1949). A study of emotion revealed in two types of athletic contests. *Research Quarterly, 20,* 72–79.

Jones, E. E., & Gerard, H. B. (1967). *Foundations of social psychology.* New York: Wiley.

Kagan, S., & Madsen, M. C. (1972). Rivalry in Anglo-American and Mexican children of two ages. *Journal of Personality and Social Psychology, 24,* 214–220.

Lamb, D. H. (1972). Speech anxiety: Towards a theoretical conceptualization and preliminary scale development. *Speech Monographs, 39,* 62–67.

Leuba, C. (1933). An experimental study of rivalry in children. *Journal of Comparative Psychology, 16,* 367–378.

Lewthwaite, R., & Scanlan, T. K. (1989). Predictors of competitive trait anxiety in male youth sport participants. *Medicine and Science in Sports and Exercise, 21,* 221–229.

Martens, R. (1975). *Social psychology and physical activity.* New York: Harper & Row.

———. (1976). Competition: In need of a theory. In D. M. Landers (Ed.), *Social problems in athletics* (pp. 9–17). Urbana: University of Illinois Press.

———. (1977). *Sport competition anxiety test.* Champaign, IL: Human Kinetics.

Martens, R., Burton, D., Rivkin, F., & Simon, J. (1980). Reliability and validity of the Competitive State Anxiety Inventory (CSAI). In C. H. Nadeau, W. R. Halliwell, K. M. Newell, & G. C. Roberts (Eds.), *Psychology of motor behavior and sport—1979* (pp. 91–99). Champaign, IL: Human Kinetics.

Martens, R., & Gill, D. (1976). State anxiety among successful and unsuccessful competitors who differ in competitive trait anxiety. *Research Quarterly, 47,* 698–708.

Masters, J. C. (1972). Social comparison by young children. In W. W. Hartup (Ed.), *The young child* (pp. 320–339). Washington, DC: National Association for Education of Young Children.

McClintock, C., & Nuttin, J. (1969). Development of competitive game behavior in children across two cultures. *Journal of Experimental Social Psychology, 5,* 203–218.

Nelson, L. L. (1970). *The development of cooperation and competition in children from ages five to ten years old: Effects of sex, situational determinants, and prior experiences.* Unpublished doctoral dissertation, University of California, Los Angeles.

Nelson, L. L., & Kagan, S. (1972). The star-spangled scramble. *Psychology Today, 6,* 53.

Passer, M. W. (1983). Fear of failure, fear of evaluation, perceived competence, and self-esteem in competitive trait anxious children. *Journal of Sport Psychology, 5,* 172–188.

Phillips, B. N., Pitcher, G. D., Worsham, M. E., & Miller, S. C. (1980). Test anxiety and the school environment. In I. G. Sarason (Ed.), *Test anxiety: Theory, research, and applications* (pp. 327–346). Hillsdale, NJ: Lawrence Erlbaum.

Radloff, R. (1966). Social comparison and ability evaluation. *Journal of Experimental Social Psychology Supplement, 2*(1), 6–26.

Ruble, D., Boggiano, A., Feldman, N., & Loebl, J. (1980). Developmental analysis of the role of social comparison in self-evaluation. *Developmental Psychology, 16,* 105–115.

Sarason, I. G. (1968). Verbal learning, modeling, and juvenile delinquency. *American Psychologist, 23,* 254–266.

Scanlan, T. K. (1975). *The effects of competition trait anxiety and success-failure on the perception of threat in a competitive situation.* Unpublished doctoral dissertation, University of Illinois, Urbana-Champaign.

———. (1977). The effects of success-failure on the perception of threat in a competitive situation. *Research Quarterly, 48,* 144–153.

———. (1984). Competitive stress and the child athlete. In J. M. Silva, III & R. S. Weinberg (Eds.), *Psychological foundations of sport* (pp. 118–129). Champaign, IL: Human Kinetics.

Scanlan, T. K., & Lewthwaite, R. (1984). Social psychological aspects of competition for male youth sport participants: I. Predictors of competitive stress. *Journal of Sport Psychology, 6,* 208–226.

Scanlan, T. K., & Passer, M. W. (1978). Factors related to competitive stress among male youth sports participants. *Medicine and Science in Sports, 10,* 103–108.

———. (1979). Sources of competitive stress in young female athletes. *Journal of Sport Psychology, 1,* 151–159.

Scanlan, T. K., & Simons, J. P. (1992). The construct of sport enjoyment. In G. C. Roberts (Ed.), *Motivation in sport and exercise* (pp. 199–215). Champaign, IL: Human Kinetics.

Scanlan, T. K., Stein, G. L., & Ravizza, K. (1991). An in-depth study of former elite figure skaters: III. Sources of stress. *Journal of Sport and Exercise Psychology, 13,* 103–108.

Simon, J., & Martens, R. (1979). Children's anxiety in sport and non-sport evaluative activities. *Journal of Sport Psychology, 1,* 160–169.

Singer, J. E., & Shockley, V. L. (1965). Ability and affiliation. *Journal of Personality and Social Psychology, 1,* 95–100.

Spielberger, C. D. (1966). *Anxiety and behavior.* New York: Academic Press.

———. (1973). *Preliminary test manual for the state-trait anxiety inventory for children ("How I feel questionnaire").* Palo Alto, CA: Consulting Psychologists Press.

Veroff, J. (1969). Social comparison and the development of achievement motivation. In C. P. Smith (Ed.), *Achievement-related motives in children* (pp. 46–101). New York: Russel Sage Foundation.

Weiss, M. R., & Chaumeton, N. (1993). Motivational orientations in sport. In T. S. Horn (Ed.), *Advances in sport psychology* (pp. 61–99). Champaign, IL: Human Kinetics.

White, R. W. (1959). Motivation reconsidered: The concept of competence. *Psychological Review, 66,* 297–334.

Wine, J. D. (1982). Evaluation anxiety. In H. W. Krohne & L. Laux (Eds.), *Achievement, stress and anxiety* (pp. 207–219). Washington, DC: Hemisphere.

18

PERCEIVED COMPETENCE IN YOUNG ATHLETES: RESEARCH FINDINGS AND RECOMMENDATIONS FOR COACHES AND PARENTS[1]

—Thelma S. Horn and Amy Harris

Imagine that you are watching a youth sport soccer practice. In particular, your attention is captured by two of the children, both of whom are very highly skilled. Not only do they appear to have a lot of general physical and motor ability, but they also are very competent in the basic soccer skills. After the practice, you talk to their coach, who verifies your positive evaluations of these two children. Specifically, the coach tells you that these two children have both been playing soccer for several years and have considerable talent for the game. As part of a project you are doing for a coaching theory class, you interview these two children. After extensive conversations with each of them separately, you find that they have quite different perceptions of their sport ability. One child tells you, somewhat matter-of-factly, "Yeah, I think I'm pretty good at soccer. Actually, I'm pretty good at most sports. Usually I'm one of the best players on the team." The other child is considerably more hesitant about her soccer and sport ability. She says, "Well, I don't think that I'm really all that good at soccer. There are a lot of skills I can't do, and I wish that I could be a lot better." It is obvious to you that these two children, who are very similar in their level of *actual* soccer ability, differ considerably in their *perceptions* of their own ability. One child has a very high perception of her soccer (and sport) ability, while the other child has a lower perception of her ability. Do these differences in perceived competence or perceived ability matter? Should we, as interested adults, be concerned about what children think about their ability in a sport or physical activity?

As the example in the previous paragraph suggests, perceived sport or physical competence can be defined as the child's belief concerning how competent or capable she or he is at a particular sport or physical activity. Perceived competence can be measured or assessed in relatively broad or general terms (i.e., "How good are you at sports?") or in regard to a more specific sport (i.e., "How good are you at baseball, or tennis, or gymnastics?") or even a more specific skill within a sport (i.e., "How good are you at batting a softball or shooting a free throw?"). Researchers and practitioners alike are very much aware that considerable variability exists between children in their perceptions of sport competence. As the example in the first paragraph illustrates, even if two children appear (to the adult) to have the same level of sport competence, they may have quite different perceptions of their competence.

In recent years, researchers in the sport psychology area have found that children's perceptions of competence are very important because they are very much related to, and can even predict, children's performance and behavior in sport and other physical activity situations. Specifically, researchers have found that children who have high perceptions of their sport or physical competence are more apt than are children with lower perceptions of competence to experience positive affect in sport situations (e.g., more enjoyment, pride, and happiness) and less apt to experience negative affect (e.g., less boredom, anxiety, and anger) (Ebbeck & Weiss, 1992; Scanlan & Lewthwaite, 1986). Similarly, high perceptions of competence are related to such other positive achievement cognitions as an internal locus of control, an intrinsic motivational orientation, and high self-esteem (Ebbeck & Weiss, 1992; Weiss, Bredemeier, & Shewchuk, 1986). Behaviorally, children with high perceptions of competence have been found to be more persistent after they experience failure at a physical task and to have higher expectancies for performance success than do children with low perceptions of competence (Rudisill, 1989). Thus, the research to date clearly indicates that perceived competence is an important factor that affects children's performance and behavior in sport situations.

Given the important role that perceived competence plays in regard to children's sport performance and behavior, it would seem reasonable that we, as interested adults (e.g., parents, teachers, coaches, researchers) would want to facilitate positive perceptions of competence in all children. The issues we need to address, then, include: What can we do to help each child believe that he or she is competent? What techniques can we, as coaches, use in practices and games to help each child feel good about her or his sport performance? How should we, as parents, respond to a child who has just missed a crucial free throw in a basketball game in order to "protect" her or his perception of competence?

To identify answers to the preceding questions, we first need to understand how children form their perceptions of competence. That is, we need to know what processes they use to make judgments about their sport ability and/or what information they use to determine whether they are good or not so good at a particular sport or sport skill. Similarly, we need to know how information such as a missed free throw affects children's feelings about themselves and their basketball ability.

Over the last 15 years, researchers have conducted a considerable amount of research in the sport psychology area to examine perceptions of competence in children (see recent reviews by Weiss & Chaumeton, 1992; Weiss & Ebbeck, in press). The results of this research have provided important information concerning the correlates, consequences, and antecedents of perceived competence in children. A critical review of this research, however, clearly indicates that these results need to be examined and interpreted from a developmental perspective. That is, the available research and theory indicate that children's perceptions of their sport competence change both quantitatively and qualitatively over the childhood and adolescent years. These changes may certainly be (and probably to a large extent are) caused by the maturational changes that occur in regard to children's physical, cognitive, and emotional capabilities. As children grow and develop physically, cognitively, and emotionally from birth to age 18, it would make sense that the processes they use to evaluate their sport competence would correspondingly change. However, it is also true that the sport environment (i.e., the program structure and philosophy, the coach's behavior, the training demands, the reward system) changes as the child's age increases. Thus, the changes that we see in regard to children's perceptions of sport competence may be due not only to maturation (i.e., changes in physical, cognitive, and emotional capabilities) but also as a response to changes in the sport and/or broader social environment itself.

This chapter reviews and describes the developmental progressions that tell us how children of different ages form their perceptions of sport competence. Because of the interrelationships between maturational processes and the sport environment, these developmental progressions must be examined within the context of the youth sport setting. Finally, this information is combined to identify possible techniques that can be used to facilitate high perceptions of sport competence in all children.

Perceived Sport Competence: Developmental Patterns

Researchers who have studied perceived competence in children from a developmental perspective have basically asked three questions. First, does the level of children's perceived competence change with age (i.e., do younger children have higher or lower perceptions of competence than do older children)? Second, does the accuracy with which children judge their sport ability change with age (i.e., are older children better at estimating or judging their ability at a sport than are younger children)? Third, do the processes children use to judge their performance change with age (i.e., do younger children use different information or different processes to judge their performance and their ability at a sport than do older children)?

The simple answer to all three of these questions is yes. Children's perceptions of their competence do change in all of the preceding ways with age. In the next sections of this chapter, these developmental changes, and the corresponding socioenvironmental changes, are identified and discussed. For purposes of conceptual ease, the age-related changes in children's self-perceptual processes are somewhat arbitrarily broken up into three developmental stages: early childhood (ages 3 to 6), middle and late childhood (ages 7 to 12), and adolescence (ages 13 to 18).

Early Childhood

Although relatively little research has been conducted in the physical or sport domain with children in this age group (ages 3 to 6), comparable research in the developmental and educational psychology areas (e.g., Harter, 1988; Stipek & MacIver, 1989; Stipek, Recchia, & McClintic, 1992) indicate that children as young as 2 or 3 do engage in the self-evaluation process (i.e., they do evaluate or judge their performance at a task) and that by 3 or 4 they already have a rudimentary conception or perception of personal competence that can be measured at least to some degree by using interview and/or observational techniques. Harter's (1988) work with children at this age indicates, however, that their perceptions of competence in the various achievement domains (physical, cognitive, social) are not nearly as well delineated or differentiated from each other as they are in older children.

Researchers in the educational and developmental psychology literatures (e.g., Harter, 1988; Stipek & MacIver, 1989) have also found that young children's perceptions of competence are generally high and quite inaccurate. That is, children at this age tend to have very high perceptions of their ability as compared with measures of their actual ability. Thus, although certainly some exceptions occur, most children in this age range tend to be eternal optimists in regard to their capabilities. As Stipek & MacIver (1989) caution, however, the positive bias young children show may be evident only when the assessments are made in regard to general competence (e.g., How good are you at sports? How smart are you?). When young children are asked to rate their competence in regard to specific skills (e.g., Can you catch a baseball? How good are you at batting? Can you count to 100?), they may be more realistic (and perhaps more accurate) in their self-assessments.

As noted earlier, relatively few research studies have been conducted by researchers in the sport or physical activity domain to examine the perceived competence of very young children. One exception to this is the work done by Beverly Ulrich (1987; Ulrich & Ulrich, in press). To measure perceived competence in young children, Ulrich uses an adapted version of a pictorial scale developed by Harter and her colleagues (Harter et al., 1983). This scale consists of a series of line drawings showing children engaged in a variety of motor, sport, or play-oriented tasks. The researcher shows each child the set of drawings and asks the child to indicate how good he or she is at each task. These ratings are then used to calculate a score representing the child's perceived physical competence.

Ulrich's research with this scale (Ulrich, 1987; Ulrich & Ulrich, in press) shows that children in kindergarten and first grade do have relatively high perceptions of their physical competence. Some gender differences in perceived competence were also found, but these differences varied somewhat depending on what kinds of skills were being assessed. Specifically, girls were higher than boys in perceived competence when the depicted skills were more play-oriented and primarily locomotor in nature (e.g., skipping, running, hopping). However, when children were asked to judge their competence in regard to fundamental motor skills (e.g., jumping, throwing, catching) or sport-specific skills (e.g., batting a baseball; dribbling a basketball; kicking a soccer ball), then the boys were higher than the girls in perceived competence. Thus, it appears that already in early childhood, gender differences occur in some aspects of children's self-assessments.

Although it is certainly important for us to know how high (or how low) children's perceptions of their competence are and/or how accurate they are in judging their sport and motor ability, it may be more valuable for us to know how they go about judging their performance. That is, what information do they use to judge whether they are good or not so good at a particular skill or activity? How do they explain or justify their judgments concerning their competence? Based on research and theory from the developmental and educational psychology literatures (Stipek & MacIver, 1989; Stipek et al., 1992), it appears as if young children's perceptions of competence (or their judgments concerning their performance) are based primarily on simple task accomplishment. Specifically, children in this age range are most apt to feel competent or successful when they complete a task that has a visually salient and intrinsically defined standard of success (e.g., completing a puzzle, stacking a set of blocks, running from one spot to another). Thus, if a preschooler who has stated that she is really good at jumping is asked how she knows she is so good at that skill, she might cite a particular jumping task she can do to justify her high self-competence rating (e.g., "I know I am good at jumping because I can jump across the creek that is behind my house"). This child is basing her perception of jumping ability on successful task accomplishment or completion (i.e., being able to jump across a creek) with no consideration for the objective difficulty of the task (how wide or narrow the creek is) or the subjective difficulty of it (i.e., whether or not most children her age can do the same thing).

Recently Stipek et al. (1992) have demonstrated that children as young as 3 years may certainly be aware of and/or able to compare their performance with that of their peers (i.e., to know who came in first in a race or who stacked the most blocks). However, their affective reactions to their performance appear to be primarily dictated by their ability to accomplish (or finish) the task rather than by whether or not their performance was better or worse than their peers. If, for example, a group of children in this age range are running a race, the child who is in the lead may actually stop to wait for her friends to catch up with her so that they can all cross the finish line together. When they do so, all of these children will then show joy with their performance simply because all of them accomplished the task (i.e., crossed the finish line). Stipek et al. did find that age has some impact on children's reactions to a competitive situation. Specifically, the older children in their sample of subjects (age range 24 to 60 months) showed greater affective reactions to winning (i.e., finishing a task first) than did the younger children. However, even for the oldest children, finishing the task appeared to be a more critical determinant of how they felt about themselves than did winning.

A second source of competence information for young children is the feedback they receive from significant adults (Stipek et al., 1992; Stipek & MacIver, 1989). Thus many children may base their perceptions of competence on what their parents, teachers, or coaches say. Example statements would be: "I know that I am a good runner because my mom says I am" or "My teacher says I can bat really good!" These children are basing their competence judgments on evaluative feedback they receive from significant adults concerning their performance. It is important to note here that young children take adult praise at "face value." Thus, even if a particular child obviously cannot bat as well as other children in her or his class, the positive feedback from the teacher appears to supersede or override other competence information.

Third, research with young children suggests that they equate effort and ability (Nicholls & Miller, 1984). Thus, working hard at a task indicates or signifies high ability as in the statement, "I know that I am good at jumping because I tried and tried to jump high, and then I did." Similarly, a child may say, "Well, I know that I am good at basketball because I practice a lot." These children are equating effort and ability (i.e., If I work hard at a task, then I must be good).

As noted earlier, several research studies have found that children in the preschool and early school years may exhibit generally high perceptions of competence.

This finding may be understandable given that most (but certainly not all) caregivers are generally positive in their feedback to children in achievement contexts (Ames, 1992; Stipek & MacIver, 1989; Stipek et al., 1992). Thus teachers in preschool gymnastics programs and academically oriented programs may tend to praise children for all of their task efforts. Furthermore, performance feedback to individual children may typically be given based on task accomplishment or mastery (e.g., finishing a task) or on effort (e.g., trying to kick the ball into the goal) rather than on task quality, performance outcome, or peer comparison. Generally, too, most parents (but certainly not all) may tend to respond positively to children's academic and physical task attempts. If adults criticize children at this age level, it is typically for behavioral or rules violations (e.g., failing to stay in line, not waiting for one's own turn, not following directions) rather than for lack of achievement on the task. Thus, at this stage of development, the sport or physical activity environment generally may tend to support high perceptions of competence in children. Recently Stipek and Daniels (1988) have provided evidence to show that kindergarten children who are exposed to a normatively based classroom environment (i.e., classrooms where a high emphasis is placed on peer comparison, and grades are given in a highly public manner) have lower perceptions of academic competence than do kindergarten children in classrooms described as less peer comparison-oriented (i.e., emphasis is placed on individual progress within the curriculum and more of the work is done in small-group format). Based on these results, it could be hypothesized that young children enrolled in sport or motor skill programs that place heavy emphasis on "being the best" and on "winning" would also acquire or develop lower perceptions of their physical competence.

Assuming that we, as interested adults, want to facilitate high perceptions of competence in children who are in the early childhood years, recommendations to individuals working with children of this age would include two primary things. First, try to provide children with multiple opportunities to demonstrate mastery or task accomplishment experiences. In a preschool movement education program, for example, if the task is to complete an obstacle course, the teacher should make sure that all children (even the later maturing and less well physically developed) can accomplish the task (i.e., finish the course). Because children at this age (especially those at preschool age) do not really use peer comparison to evaluate their competence, it doesn't matter that some children (the less motorically proficient) may need some assistance from the teacher to complete the obstacle course and/or may take longer to finish the course. It only matters that each child accomplish the task (i.e., complete the course). These mastery experiences do not necessarily have to be provided within an instructional context but certainly can be facilitated by parents or other caregivers in unstructured or play-oriented settings. Again, what is important here is that the child is given many opportunities to demonstrate mastery of some aspect of her or his physical environment—whether that is kicking a soccer ball from one point to another, walking on a low balance beam, or running from here to the wall.

Second, all children need to get positive feedback from significant adults (e.g., parents, teachers, coaches) for their performance accomplishments. As Stipek et al. (1992) suggest in their recent monograph, positive adult feedback given in response to a child's successful task accomplishment may enhance, or add to, the intrinsic pleasure the child already felt at the accomplishment itself. Thus praise by significant adults can certainly facilitate the child's perception of her or his physical competence. However, it is important to point out that adult praise at this stage should be contingent on (or given in response to) task accomplishment or completion rather than on other factors, such as peer comparison or on adult-determined task criteria (e.g., doing a skill "correctly"). That is, adults should not, at this stage of the game, subvert the emphasis that the children themselves place on simple task accomplishment or completion. Personally, we have seen 4-year-old children enrolled in a tennis instructional program get as much enjoyment out of hitting the ball into the net as they did when they hit the ball into the right service court. The simple joy was in hitting the ball with their rackets and not on the "correctness" of the response. Similarly, we have seen young soccer players (ages 4–6) not only take great pleasure in kicking their own soccer ball into the goal but also celebrating the fact that their friend can do it even harder. Thus, even though children at this stage are able to compare their performance with that of their peers, it is not a very critical source of competence information (i.e., they do not appear to use this information to judge their performance competence). If, however, parents, teachers, or coaches place very high emphasis on the results of the peer comparison process, then the child's natural or intrinsic joy at hitting a ball or jumping on a trampoline may be subverted. If, for example, a kindergartener comes home from school and says excitedly, "Guess what, Mom, I did 15 sit-ups in gym class today," and the mother responds with "How many did the other kids do?" the child is learning that performance is best judged by comparing it with that of peers. In contrast, if the mother responds with, "That's great. You must have worked hard to get that many," the child is learning that performance is best judged by whether or not he or she tried to do as many as he or she could. It is true, then, that the type, frequency, and intensity of the feedback adults give to young children not only tells them how good they are at that task but also how valuable that competency is relative to other aspects of life (i.e., sport competency is more important than music, reading, etc.) and how their performance in each domain will be or should be evaluated. Thus, even if the children themselves tend to emphasize task accomplishment as a primary source of competence information, adult feedback can be critical in either enhancing or subverting this competence information source.

Childhood Years

Over the elementary and middle school years (ages 7 to 12), children exhibit a number of developmental changes in regard to their perceptions of sport or physical competence. First, the generally high perceptions of competence that are seen in preschoolers and early elementary age children (kindergarten and first grade) appear to diminish somewhat over the next couple of years (second and third grade) (Ulrich, 1987; Ulrich & Ulrich, in press) but then remain fairly stable from age 8 to 12 years (Feltz & Brown, 1984; Horn & Hasbrook, 1986). In regard to accuracy, however, the available research suggests that children's ability to judge the quality of their performance increases linearly over this same age range (i.e., they become more accurate with increasing age) (Feltz & Brown, 1984; Horn & Weiss, 1991). These age-related changes in children's perceptions of their physical competence should be interpreted with some caution, however, as they are based predominantly on cross-sectional research and on statistical techniques that compare one age group mean with that of other age groups. As Duncan and Duncan (1991) have argued, longitudinal research designs that allow for an examination of developmental changes in the same group of children over time and that use measures of biological age rather than chronological age may reveal considerably different developmental trends in regard to children's perceptions of physical competence. Further research of this type is certainly necessary if we are to get a clear picture of the changes that may occur within any age range.

Although some researchers have found gender differences (males higher than females) in children's perceptions of physical or sport competence during the childhood years (e.g., Brustad, 1993; Eccles & Harold, 1991), others have not (e.g., Horn & Hasbrook, 1987). This inconsistency in research findings may be due to variability across studies in subject samples and/or in the context within which the self-assessments are taken. That is, it is possible that gender differences in perceived competence or perceived ability are more apt to be found when the study sample is drawn from a more general population (i.e., students in a required physical education class or in a very recreationally based sport program) but less likely to be found when the study sample is drawn from a more homogeneous population (i.e., male and female athletes who are engaged in a competitive sport program or who are enrolled in a voluntary instructionally based sport program such as a summer camp). This possibility is supported by research indicating that females tend to show more situational variability in self-assessments than do males (e.g., Lenney, 1977; Ulrich & Ulrich, in press). Thus it appears that gender differences in regard to perceived physical or sport competence, although evident in certain subject groups and in certain sport contexts, may not be consistently found across all ages or in all sport situations.

In regard to the processes children in this age range use to form their perceptions of physical or sport competence, the available research shows considerable change from the preschool years but also reveals changes that occur across this particular age range itself. To begin with, toward the end of the preschool years or early in the childhood years (e.g., ages 4 through 7), children begin using the peer comparison process to evaluate their own performance. That is, they judge their own competence or ability in a physical task or sport based on how their performance at the task or sport compares with that of their peers. Children may reason that "I know that I'm good at running because I can beat all of my friends" or "I'm not really good at basketball because I am always the last one picked for a team in gym class." Our research in this area (Horn & Hasbrook, 1986; Horn & Weiss, 1991) shows that the use of peer comparison to judge one's own competence increases steadily in importance until for many, if not most, children it becomes by the age of 12 the most important source of ability information.

Correspondingly, we have found that children's use of feedback from parents declines in importance from age 8 to 14, whereas children's use of evaluative feedback from peers and possibly from coaches increases in importance (Horn & Hasbrook, 1986; Horn & Weiss, 1991). Interestingly, it also appears as if children at the older end of this age range (11 and 12 years) may no longer take an adult's feedback at "face value" but, rather, evaluate that feedback relative to other sources of information (e.g., Meyer et al., 1979). Assume, for example, that a child, whose performance on a soccer drill is not as good as that of his teammates, receives very positive feedback from his coach in the form of a general statement such as "Good job, Jimmy" while his teammates, who are actually performing at a higher level of competence, get no praise. In this instance, Jimmy does not take his coach's comment at face value but, rather, evaluates it relative to peer comparison and comes up with the conclusion that "I must be really bad if my coach thinks this is a good performance for me." Thus the coach's positive feedback is actually interpreted by Jimmy as negative ability information. Similarly, a child who receives criticism from an adult for a particular performance attempt may perceive higher personal ability than does a child who exhibits the same level of performance but gets no feedback. Thus it appears that children at this age do use adult feedback as a source of competence information but that this feedback is interpreted relative to other performance indicators.

In addition to the preceding points, the available research (e.g., Horn & Hasbrook, 1986; Watkins & Montgomery, 1989) has also indicated that children (especially those at the younger ages) within this age range use performance outcomes (winning/losing) as important sources of ability information. Not only does this mean that they use personal performance outcomes (i.e., whether I win or lose a wrestling or tennis match) but also that they may use team performance outcomes to judge their own ability. Thus it would not be unusual for a 9-year-old child to say, "I guess I'm a really bad soccer player, and I know that because my team loses all the time." It may be, then, that children (especially those under 10 years) are not very good at separating their own personal competence from that of their team.

The developmental changes in regard to the processes children use to form perceptions of competence that have been described in the previous paragraphs can be interpreted from a broader developmental perspective. Specifically, given that children in the early and middle childhood years tend to be very concrete thinkers, it is understandable that their primary sources of competence information (e.g., peer comparison; evaluative feedback from teachers, coaches, peers, and parents; win-loss outcomes) tend to be very concrete in nature. That is, these sources of information are readily available in most sport-oriented contexts and provide easily visible and interpretable evaluations of personal competence.

Second, the broader developmental literature supports the notion that peers gradually become a more important source of information for children as they reach the end of the childhood years and progress into early adolescence (Adams, 1980). Finally, given that children at the older end of this age range (ages 10–12 years) may show great variability in regard to body size, shape, and composition because of differences in rate of maturation, it is not surprising that the peer comparison process may become progressively more pertinent as a source of ability information.

In addition to maturational issues, the developmental changes that we see in the processes that children in this age range use to form their perceptions of competence must also be interpreted relative to changes in the sport environment. One of the primary changes that occurs for children moving from very early youth sport programs to childhood and junior high programs is that the emphasis in such programs changes from an instructional orientation to that which is more competitive in nature.

Specifically, many (but certainly not all) sport-oriented programs for children in the early childhood years (ages 3 to 6) are conducted in a more instructional way. That is, more emphasis is placed on teaching children the fundamental sport skills and on encouraging the participation of all children. Beginning around the age of 6 or 7, however, the emphasis switches to a progressively more competitive orientation. Now leagues are formed, team and/or individual standings are kept, end-of-season trophies are awarded, all-star teams are added, tryouts are introduced, and some children may be "cut" from programs or at least tracked into a "lower" ability level. Even a cursory analysis of these changes suggests that the primary basis for decision making in regard to children's status within these programs is on peer comparison and performance outcomes. That is, children are cut from teams or tracked into a lower ability level on the basis of personal performance scores (e.g., batting averages, shooting percentages, agility run scores) that are compared with those of their peers (i.e., children with higher scores are kept on the team or placed in higher ability programs). Furthermore, awards (team trophies, individual awards) are most often given based either on win-loss outcomes (e.g., which team has the best win-loss record) or, again, on the peer comparison process. Thus the sport environment increasingly conveys to children the idea that their sport competence is best evaluated or judged by using performance outcomes and peer comparison (Chaumeton & Duda, 1988). Therefore, the increasing age-related tendency of children to use peer comparison and win-loss outcomes may certainly be due to maturational changes in cognitive and psychological abilities but can also be a function of relevant changes in the sport environment.

A second important change that occurs in regard to the sport environment is that coaches become a more credible source of ability information for children as they progress from early childhood sport-oriented programs into youth sport and then junior high programs. Adults who coach at the early youth sport levels (e.g., preschool and early elementary levels) may be selected (or recruited) for their coaching roles more for their nurturing and emotionally supportive skills (i.e., they are parents) than for their technical knowledge of the sport. Also, the program philosophies for children at this age tend to emphasize the notions that all children should play in all games and in all field positions and that the primary goal is to have fun. Thus the coaches are presented more as supporters or facilitators of children's sport experience. However, when children move up in youth sport programs (i.e., go from early instructional to the more competitive levels), the coach is presented as more of an authority figure. He (or, less often, she) may be marketed to parents and children as particularly "knowledgeable" about sport and/or as "experienced" (as an athlete or coach) in the sport process. In addition, now that players are cut or tracked on the basis of ability and that all kids may not have equal playing time (i.e., some will be regular starters and/or play a lot and some will not), the coach is necessarily perceived by the athletes (and their parents) as the controller of important resources (i.e., as the determiner of who will make the team, who will play, what positions each child will play). Given this important environmental change, it is not surprising that young athletes show an increasing tendency from ages 8 to 14 years to base their perceptions of sport competence on their coach's feedback and a corresponding decrease in use of feedback from parents.

Based on the information provided in the previous paragraphs concerning the way in which children think about sport and their position within it, what can we, as interested adults, do to facilitate positive self-perceptions in all children? First, because so much variation occurs between children in their maturation rates, it is important that we provide each of them with optimally challenging skill activities. Children in this age range appear to be very sensitive to performance successes and failures (e.g., how many free throws they can make out of 10; how many tennis serves they can get in the service court) as ways to evaluate their sport competence. Therefore, if a child is engaged in a sport activity in which the task demands greatly exceed her or his actual motor ability, then that child will have difficulty seeing any objective performance success (i.e., if a child does not have enough upper body strength to shoot a basketball from the 10-foot line, the child cannot ever "see" the shot go into the basket). The slower-maturing child, then, is at risk for developing a low perception of competence. Thus, the physical facilities, the equipment, and the game rules must be modified to provide children with optimal challenges so that they can achieve at least some performance success.

Second, it would be helpful to reduce or decrease the emphasis on peer comparison and performance outcomes as a means to evaluate personal competence. As noted earlier, the use of peer comparison appears to begin in the early elementary years (ages 4 to 7) and then increases in importance until by age 12 or 13 years, it becomes for many, if not most, children the primary source of competence information. As researchers and practitioners, we need to recognize that peer comparison and performance outcomes are not necessarily bad sources of information (We, as adults, use them all the time to judge our competence!). The problem, however, arises when one and/or the other become the *only* source (sources) of information that children use to judge their sport ability. Because only a few children within any group (team, physical education class) can fare well in the peer comparison process (i.e., only a few can be picked first for athletic teams, selected to all-star teams, receive most-valuable-player awards), the majority of children within that group are not receiving positive information about their competence via the peer comparison process. Therefore, if any single child is almost solely dependent on peer comparison as a means to judge sport ability, then that child is really at risk for low perceptions of competence.

As noted earlier in this chapter, part of the reason children at the upper end of this age range may rely so heavily on these two sources of information is because they constitute very concrete sources of information in the sport setting. That is, although an individual child's low test score in the academic classroom can, with some effort, be hidden from other children, a strike-out by a batter in a softball game or a missed free throw in a basketball game is very easily visible not only to the child her- or himself but also to everyone else. In addition, of course, as was noted earlier, youth sport programs (especially at the older ages) are very much structured to emphasize peer comparison and performance outcomes as primary ways to evaluate each child's sport ability.

Given this socioenvironmental situation, what can coaches or parents do to de-emphasize the use of these two sources of competence information? We can work with the individual child or groups of children to help them decrease their individual dependence on the peer comparison and performance outcomes. We can do that by encouraging them to turn instead to the use of self-comparison. Self-comparison involves the use of skill improvement over time or the achievement of self-set goals. We might help the child to see that even though she may not be in the starting lineup for her club volleyball team, she has improved her skill performance from last season or she is acquiring some very nice skill patterns. What we are trying to do here is help the child see that other ways can be used to evaluate or judge personal competence.

It is important to note again that most children may not spontaneously use self-comparison. The fact that they don't is likely due to the fact that the sport environment is structured to enhance the peer comparison and performance outcome process. In addition, because children at this stage are very concrete thinkers, it may be more difficult for them to use a comparison process that requires a time element (i.e., individual child must compare performance in today's game with her/his performance in a game that occurred last week). Given that individual children may even have difficulty remembering what they had for lunch today or where they left their shoes, it is understandable that self-comparison is more difficult for them. Coaches and parents can, however, make the self-comparison process more concrete. Examples include: (a) use of a personal performance improvement chart that maps individual children's progress at specific skills across the season; (b) incorporation of practice drills in which individual or group progress or improvement can be concretely measured across time; (c) use of individual accomplishment awards (e.g., skill mastery awards) for each game rather than best offensive or best defensive player awards; (d) use of goal-setting techniques; (e) provision of opportunities within each practice session to show children in concrete and easily visible ways that they have improved. These programmatic techniques can facilitate or promote what Ames (1992; in press) has referred to as a mastery motivational climate. This type of climate characterizes a sport environment in which success is defined by the individual child's progress on a skill continuum rather than as a function of normative comparison or performance outcomes (see also Duda, 1992 and Weiss & Ebbeck, in press).

Third, parents, teachers, and coaches, as well as the children themselves, must be taught about the wide variability in maturation that occurs between children during this age range. Because some children on a youth sport team are early maturers and others are late maturers, considerable differences are bound to exist between these children not only in size, speed, and strength but also in motor and sport skill proficiency. This situation, again, may encourage children to use peer comparison to evaluate personal competence and place the later-maturing children at particular risk for low perceived competence. As detailed elsewhere (Horn & Lox, 1993), coaches who are unaware that wide variability exists among children in maturation rates may assume that late-maturing children are just unathletic (i.e., that they have no innate athletic ability and never will have) and thus act toward these children in ways that impede their skill progress. If coaches (and parents) are made aware of the variation in maturation, then such expectancy-biased behavior on the part of the coaches and parents may be at least somewhat alleviated.

As a final recommendation for this age range, coaches and parents must provide children with appropriate and contingent performance feedback. That is, feedback should be given contingent to the level of performance that is exhibited. As previously noted, children at the upper end of this age range no longer take adults' praise and criticism at face value but, rather, evaluate it relative to other sources of competence information. Coaches who give inappropriate and/or noncontingent praise and criticism not only risk losing credibility as information givers but can also be exerting a negative effect on their athletes' self-perceptions (see Horn, 1987 and Horn & Lox, 1993 for further discussion of this topic). Therefore, coaches, teachers, and parents must be careful in regard to the type of feedback they give young athletes (see recommendations provided in chapter 9 of this volume).

In addition, adults need to remember that their performance feedback to children (i.e., the praise and criticism they direct to individual children or groups of children in response to performances) not only provides children with information concerning the coach's judgment of their performance ability but also informs kids as to how their performance will be judged within that sport context. For example, coaches who give praise and criticism to players contingent only on performance outcomes (e.g., whether a shot is made, a runner is thrown out, a rally point is won or lost) are telling their players that their personal competence can only be judged on the basis of outcome (i.e., if you win, you are talented and if you lose, you are a failure). In contrast, coaches who give praise and criticism contingent on skill technique (e.g., whether player used correct movement pattern regardless of whether the outcome was successful) are telling their players that their performance will be judged on the basis of skill learning, performance improvement, amount of effort exerted, and/or basic skill execution.

Given the vast differences between children in this age range in regard to physical maturation, motor skill proficiency, body control, and sport background, it makes sense that coaches' feedback would place greater emphasis on skill technique than on performance outcomes. That is, from a long-term goal perspective, for children at this age, learning the fundamental motor (throwing, catching, kicking) and sport skills (shooting layups, hitting a baseball, serving a tennis ball) is more important than winning. A corollary to this is that skill technique is something that almost all children (with few exceptions) can control. That is, an individual child on a Little League Baseball team may not yet have enough strength or speed to beat out a bunt, but she can learn and execute the correct skill pattern. Similarly, another child may not yet have the height, upper body strength, or jumping ability to be a powerful hitter in volleyball, but he can learn and execute the correct skill pattern. Thus, from multiple perspectives, it makes greater sense for coaches and parents to emphasize skill development rather than performance outcomes in youth sport settings.

Adolescence

During the adolescent years (ages 13–18), many additional changes occur in regard to children's perceptions of competence. Although researchers in the educational and developmental psychology literature have found that a rather significant decline occurs in children's perceptions of competence and control from late childhood to early adolescence (see Stipek & MacIver, 1989), no comparable age-related declines have yet been reported in regard to perceptions of physical competence. In fact, a few researchers have found increases in perceived competence from early to later adolescence (Duncan & Duncan, 1991; Petlichkoff, 1993). In addition, gender differences in self-perceptions have been found in several adolescent subject samples (e.g., Black & Weiss, 1992; Eccles & Harold, 1991). Specifically, males have been found to exhibit higher scores on perceived competence or perceived ability than did their female peers. However, as Vealey (1988) pointed out, gender differences in self-perceptions may not be consistently found across all subject samples. In her study, gender differences in the trait of sport-confidence, although evident in high school and college athletes, were not found in elite athletes. Thus, again, the degree of gender differences may vary as a function of the subjects and the situational sport context.

In regard to the processes adolescents use to judge their performance competence, Horn, Glenn, & Wentzell (1993) recently found a number of developmental changes that occur between the ages of 14 to 18 years. First, athletes in the younger end of this age range (athletes from freshman and sophomore teams) showed a greater tendency than did older athletes (high school juniors and seniors) to use evaluative feedback from peers to judge their sport ability. Second, athletes in the older group showed greater use of self-comparison processes (skill improvement over time), internalized or self-determined performance standards (achievement of self-set goals) and internal information (e.g., pre-event self-confidence, ability to motivate self, enjoyment of sport activity) to evaluate how competent they are at a particular sport.

A similar age-related trend was found in research by Vealey and Campbell (1988) who examined the competitive orientations of 13- to 18-year-old elite ice skaters. Examination of this data showed that a performance orientation (i.e., tendency to base performance satisfaction and feelings of competence on performing well) increased with age, whereas an outcome orientation (a tendency to base performance satisfaction and feelings of competence on winning) declined. Also, Watkins and Montgomery (1989), in a recent study examining children's and adolescents' reasoning about athletic excellence, found that adolescents showed a greater tendency than did younger children to use covert, or more abstract, factors (e.g., cognitive and attitudinal skills such as concentration, confidence, strategies) to explain differences between excellent athletes and others. Thus, there appears to be an increasing trend over the adolescent years to use more internally based criteria as a means to evaluate sport competence.

In addition to these age differences, consistent gender differences have also been found (e.g., Gill, 1992; Horn et al., 1993; Petlichkoff, 1993) in this adolescent age group. Specifically, male athletes are more oriented toward the use of winning and peer comparison as means to evaluate their sport ability, whereas female athletes are more apt to use self-comparison (skill improvement) processes, internalized performance standards (e.g., achievement of self-set goals), and the feedback of others (coaches, peers) to judge their sport ability. The fact that gender differences exist in the criteria adolescents use to judge their sport competence is particularly interesting given that few, if any, differences are found in younger children. These gender differences appear to emerge, or perhaps intensify, sometime during the early adolescent years.

The age-related changes that occur during the adolescent years in perceptions of competence must be examined in light of other broader developmental changes that are occurring within the individual and within the context of the sport environment. In regard to maturational changes, it is important to understand that many changes are occurring from early to late adolescence in regard to body size, shape, composition, and functioning (see chapter 11 of this volume). In addition, the variability between children in regard to rate of maturation continues. Some are early maturers, and others are late maturers. What complicates things now, however, is that this variability becomes uniquely obvious. We can, for example, have an early maturing 14-year-old boy on a freshman basketball team whose physique is already similar to that of an adult male while his teammate still has the size and linear physique that is characteristic of a prepubescent child. Similar variability occurs in regard to early- and late-maturing girls. The intensity, visibility, and variability of the physical changes that occur in the early adolescent years may contribute to early adolescents' tendencies to use peer comparison and peer feedback as primary sources of competence information.

From a cognitive perspective, children between the ages of 11 and 18 years develop more abstract reasoning or processing skills. Such cognitive maturation could certainly cause, or at least be associated with, corresponding changes in the processes/information adolescents use to judge their sport ability. For example, although researchers have found that adolescents continue to use peer comparison as a means to evaluate their sport competence, it has been hypothesized (but not yet tested) (Horn et al., 1993; Stipek & MacIver, 1989) that whereas children in the earlier age range (ages 8 to 12) may use a familiar or "known" peer comparison group (i.e., all the players on my team or in my league or my fifth-grade class), adolescents begin using a more extended peer comparison group, a group that includes known peers but is also expanded to include abstract peers (i.e., how do I compare with all high school juniors in the state?). This expanded comparison process may be more likely for adolescents because of their increased ability to reason in a more abstract form.

Another possible correlate of adolescents' cognitive maturation is their increasing ability to internalize achievement standards (Adams, 1980; Harter, 1981). That is, during the period from late childhood through adolescence, children acquire the ability to develop an internal set of performance criteria or standards that they can then use in subsequent performance situations to make independent judgments of their skill competence. The result of such internalization is that older adolescents probably become less dependent on such external sources of information as win-loss outcomes and evaluative feedback from others.

Third, a more abstract reasoning ability may also explain the fact that adolescents are able to integrate information concerning their sport ability from multiple sources. That is, unlike children in the earlier age group, who may depend on only one or two of the most visible information sources, adolescents may be able to integrate and synthesize information from a variety of sources. Along these same lines, adolescents may show less dependence on group performance outcomes (i.e., team win-loss record) to evaluate their own ability because they are now cognitively able to dissociate personal performance from that of the group.

Fourth, the use of effort as a source of competence information appears to undergo a change during the early adolescent years. As noted earlier, young children view effort as a primary indicator of ability (e.g., "If I try hard, I must be good"). Thus, the two constructs (effort and ability) are not well differentiated by young children (Nicholls & Miller, 1984). By the age of 11 or 12, however, children begin to see that ability and effort are independent entities. Furthermore, ability may now be perceived to be a stable, even innate, trait which is unaffected by effort (Dweck & Leggett, 1988). Such perceptions can certainly affect how adolescents judge their performance abilities. For example, an adolescent who perceives that she had to exert a considerable amount of effort to achieve success at a fairly easy task may conclude that she must have low competence. Similarly, such reasoning may affect how the adolescent interprets evaluative feedback. If, for example, two adolescents achieve the same level of performance, but one receives effort-related criticism from his or her coach (e.g., "You didn't try hard enough."), whereas the other one does not, the individual who receives no feedback may conclude that she or he is low in ability (i.e., "My coach does not think I can get better even with more effort. Thus, I must have low ability").

In addition to developmental changes that occur over the adolescent years in physical and cognitive abilities, numerous changes also occur in the sport environment. Specifically, the emphasis on competition (and winning) increases. In addition, membership on athletic teams gets increasingly more selective. That is, although many children may "make" their junior high basketball team, relatively few will "make" their high school varsity team. This increased selectivity may account for the higher perceptions of physical competence that have been found in varsity-level athletes (high school juniors and seniors) as compared with their younger counterparts (Petlichkoff, 1993). Over the high school years, too, the emphasis on extended peer groups increases. For example, early in an athlete's high school career (e.g., freshman level), coaches, parents, and others may compare individual athletes with their peers within the program (i.e., "Are you the best shooter on your team?") or maybe even within the league (i.e., "Are you the best point guard in the league?"). But, at the varsity level, the comparison may be extended. That is, we now not only have all-league teams (best athletes within a league) but also all-city and all-state teams. Obviously this represents an extension of the peer comparison group. Furthermore, those athletes who are superstars on their own high school team and even within their own city and state are additionally compared with an even larger peer group (all nation) for purposes of college recruitment (i.e., Who are the top 25 high school players in the country?). Thus, again the sport environment facilitates the progressive expansion of the peer group in regard to the evaluation of each athlete's sport competence.

Along with this, we also see an increase in training demands, and participation becomes increasingly more regimented. That is, athletes cannot miss practices or games, and they must follow prescribed training rules in regard to diet, bedtime, social life, and others. Based on anecdotal evidence (informal conversations with youth sport and adolescent athletes), it also may be that coaches become more controlling as their athletes increase in age. Specifically, coaches of adolescent athletes may be more apt than are coaches of younger athletes to act in practices and games in ways that are designed to show athletes that the coach is "in control." These behaviors not only include making the athletes do everything the coach says without providing an opportunity to discuss and/or respond but also giving the athletes noncontingent feedback. That is, if a very highly skilled athlete executes a good play, the controlling coach may give her or him critical feedback anyway just to show the player who is "in control" and/or to "reduce the superstar player down to size." Not all coaches of adolescent athletes are controlling in their behavior, but the percentage of such coaches may increase as athletes get older, more knowledgeable, and more skilled, and as the pressure on the coach to win increases. Thus, the socioenvironmental climate may change as the athletes progress from junior high to high school programs. These environmental changes may cause athletes to perceive that their behavior and their performance are no longer under their own control. Such perceptions may cause a decrease in the athlete's intrinsic motivation and also interfere with the athlete's ability to internalize a set of performance standards (Ames, in press; Horn & Hasbrook, 1987; Vallerand, Deci, & Ryan, 1987).

Finally, it is also likely that the sport and social environment may change in unique ways for girls during this adolescent period. Specifically, female athletes, especially those in the early adolescent years, may be given conflicting messages concerning the appropriateness of sport participation. As their bodies mature, girls may be overtly discouraged from continuing their sport participation or given subtle messages suggesting that they should not become too competent in sport. As Gill (1992) and Greendorfer (1992) explain, gender stereotypes concerning both male and female athletes abound in both the broader social and the more specific sport context. Thus girls who continue to participate in sport throughout the adolescent years may be subjected to different environmental conditions than are boys. Since sport is perceived to be more appropriate and more suited to boys, the expectations that coaches hold for adolescent girls may be significantly lower than that of which they are capable (see Horn & Lox, 1993). Therefore, girls at this age level may be given messages that suggest they have less competence in the sport context. Such socioenvironmental messages may leave adolescent girls at risk for lower perceptions of sport competence, which may help to explain why more gender differences appear to exist in competence perceptions during the adolescent years than in the earlier childhood years.

The developmental and socioenvironmental patterns that have been described in the previous paragraphs can be used to identify the techniques and strategies that adults should use in working with adolescent athletes. Some of these techniques are described in the following paragraphs.

First, we, as adults, should hold high expectations for all adolescents (e.g., males and females, early and late maturers, low- and high-skilled performers). However, and this is very important, our expectations for each child should be realistic or achievable, and these expectations should be held only for controllable skills and behaviors. As a baseball coach, for example, it would be unrealistic for me to expect all of my junior high players to be able to bat above .300 or to hit 20 home runs. I can, however, expect all players to use the correct batting techniques. Similarly, due to variable maturation rates, not all of my ninth-grade volleyball players may yet be tall enough or strong enough to execute a good block, but they can all be expected to learn the correct skill pattern and to get themselves into good position at the net. The key point here is that we, as adults, must be careful not to convey low expectations for certain players (e.g., females, late maturers) by "letting them get away with sloppy techniques."

Second, we should try to encourage each adolescent to develop an internalized set of performance standards. The internalized performance standards must be challenging but realistic. Adolescents who internalize a performance standard that is too low will be satisfied with a lower level of exhibited performance, and motivation will be low. Conversely, adolescents whose standard for performance is too high will likely experience anxiety because failure is almost virtually assured, and perceptions of competence will be consistently low. As a corollary to this, it should also be noted that some children do not develop an internalized structure but continue to depend on external sources of competence information (Horn & Hasbrook, 1987). The inability of some children to develop an internalized set of performance standards may be due either to the absence of performance feedback during the childhood and early adolescent years or to the inconsistency of such feedback. Either situation may make it more difficult for an individual child to internalize a consistent set of standards for his or her performance.

One way to encourage all children to develop an internal structure may be to incorporate specific classroom or practice (and game) strategies that teach children to assume more responsibility for both their practice effort and for the evaluation of their performance. These strategies have been referred to by various labels including self-regulatory learning (Schunk, 1989; Weiss, in press) and mastery motivational orientation strategies (Ames, 1992; in press). The primary emphasis of these techniques is to involve children (adolescents) in the learning process and to encourage them to engage in self-monitoring, self-evaluative, and self-rewarding behaviors. Research has supported the value of these strategies in regard to adolescents' performance and behavior in achievement contexts.

Third, as coaches, we should try to develop a more autonomous, rather than a controlling, coaching style. As suggested earlier, the primary goal of controlling coaches is to demonstrate and exert "control" over their athletes. In contrast, the primary goal of an autonomous coach is to get athletes to take responsibility for their own behavior (i.e., to "internalize" motivation so that athletes are working hard because they want to get better or to achieve a certain self-set goal). Thus, an autonomous coaching style is more consistent with the strategies identified in the previous paragraph. Initial research in the athletic setting (e.g., Vallerand & Pelletier, 1985) has revealed that an autonomous coaching style is associated with higher intrinsic motivation in athletes than is a controlling coaching style.

Fourth, because adolescents have the cognitive ability to integrate information from multiple sources, we need to help them do so. At this age, they should no longer focus exclusively on only one source of competence information but should be able to use multiple pieces of information to evaluate individual progress and competence in their sport.

Finally, as coaches, teachers, and parents, we need to continue to provide effective performance feedback. Our research clearly shows that adult feedback is an important factor in facilitating positive self-perceptions in children at all developmental levels. However, as noted earlier, children above the age of 10 no longer take adults' praise and criticism at face value but evaluate it relative to other sources of competence information. Thus, it is strongly recommended that coaches give feedback that is contingent to athletes' performances (e.g., athletes get praise if they executed a skill well and corrective feedback if they did not). Based on anecdotal evidence athletes themselves have provided, it appears as if controlling coaches do not give contingent feedback but, rather, use their feedback to play "mind games" with their athletes (i.e., they "mess with the minds" of superstar athletes so that they begin to doubt personal competence). In contrast, autonomous coaches give feedback that is directly related to the performance itself (i.e., such coaches are more consistent in how they evaluate athletes' performance). Thus, the way in which adults give performance feedback may be critical in either facilitating or undermining athletes' perceptions of their sport competence.

Conclusion

As this chapter has illustrated, children's perceptions of their physical and sport competence change both quantitatively and qualitatively with age. Such developmental changes or patterns are important to identify and to understand because of the impact that perceptions of competence have on children's and adolescents' performance and behavior. Given the importance of perceived competence for children of all ages, further developmentally based research on this topic is certainly warranted. We have probably only begun to understand how children's self-perceptions change as they grow and develop.

Notes

1. We would like to thank Ms. Carla Beatley, elementary physical education teacher at Westlake Elementary School in Dayton, Ohio, whose ideas concerning the facilitation of children's motor skills and self-esteem were incorporated into this chapter.

References

Adams, J. (1980). Understanding adolescents. In J. F. Adams (Ed.), *Understanding adolescence: Current developments in adolescent psychology* (pp. 2–29). Boston: Allyn & Bacon.

Ames, C. (1992). Achievement goals, motivational climate, and motivational processes. In G. C. Roberts (Ed.), *Motivation in sport and exercise* (pp. 161–176). Champaign, IL: Human Kinetics.

Ames, C. (in press). Classrooms: Goals, structures, and student motivation. *Journal of Educational Psychology.*

Black, S. J., & Weiss, M. R. (1992). The relationship among perceived coaching behaviors, perceptions of ability, and motivation in competitive age-group swimmers. *Journal of Sport and Exercise Psychology, 14,* 309–325.

Brustad, R. (1993). Who will go out and play? Parental and psychological influences on children's attraction to physical activity. *Pediatric Exercise Science, 5,* 210–223.

Chaumeton, N., & Duda, J. (1988). Is it how you play the game or whether you win or lose?: The effect of competitive level and situation on coaching behaviors. *Journal of Sport Behavior, 11,* 157–174.

Duda, J. (1992). Motivation in sport settings: A goal perspective approach. In G. C. Roberts (Ed.), *Motivation in sport and exercise* (pp. 57–91). Champaign, IL: Human Kinetics.

Duncan, T., & Duncan, S. (1991). A latent growth curve approach to investigating developmental dynamics and correlates of change in children's perceptions of physical competence. *Research Quarterly for Exercise and Sport, 62,* 390–398.

Dweck, C., & Leggett, E. (1988). A social-cognitive approach to motivation and personality. *Psychological Review, 95,* 256–273.

Ebbeck, V., & Weiss, M. (1992, October). *Antecedents of children's self-esteem: An examination of perceived competence and affect in sport.* Paper presented at the meeting of the Association for the Advancement of Applied Sport Psychology, Colorado Springs, CO.

Eccles, J., & Harold, R. (1991). Gender differences in sport involvement: Applying the Eccles expectancy-value model. *Journal of Applied Sport Psychology, 3,* 7–35.

Feltz, D., & Brown, E. (1984). Perceived competence in soccer skills among young soccer players. *Journal of Sport Psychology, 6,* 385–394.

Gill, D. (1992). Gender and sport behavior. In T. S. Horn (Ed.), *Advances in sport psychology* (pp. 143–160). Champaign, IL: Human Kinetics.

Greendorfer, S. (1992). Sport socialization. In T. S. Horn (Ed.), *Advances in sport psychology* (pp. 201–218). Champaign, IL: Human Kinetics.

Harter, S. (1981). A model of intrinsic mastery motivation in children: Individual differences and developmental change. In W. A. Collins (Ed.), *Minnesota symposium on child psychology* (Vol. 14, pp. 215–255). Hillsdale, NJ: Erlbaum.

———. (1988). Causes, correlates, and the functional role of global self-worth: A lifespan perspective. In J. Kolligian & R. Sternberg (Eds.), *Perceptions of competence and incompetence across the lifespan.* New Haven, CT: Yale University Press.

Harter, S., Pike, R., Efron, C., Chao, C., & Bierer, B. (1983). *Pictorial scale of perceived competence and social acceptance for young children.* Denver: University of Denver.

Horn, T. (1987). The influence of teacher-coach behavior on the psychological development of children. In D. Gould & M. Weiss (Eds.), *Advances in pediatric sport sciences* (Vol. 2, pp. 121–142). Champaign, IL: Human Kinetics.

Horn, T., & Hasbrook, C. (1986). Informational components influencing children's perceptions of their physical competence. In M. Weiss & D. Gould (Eds.), *Sport for children and youths: Proceedings of the 1984 Olympic Scientific Congress* (pp. 81–88). Champaign, IL: Human Kinetics.

———. (1987). Psychological characteristics and the criteria children use for self-evaluation. *Journal of Sport Psychology, 9,* 208–221.

Horn, T., & Lox, C. (1993). The self-fulfilling prophecy theory: When coaches' expectations become reality. In J. M. Williams (Ed.), *Applied sport psychology: Personal growth to peak performance* (pp. 68–81). Mountain View, CA: Mayfield.

Horn, T., & Weiss, M. (1991). A developmental analysis of children's self-ability judgments in the physical domain. *Pediatric Exercise Science, 3,* 310–326.

Horn, T. S., Glenn, S. D., & Wentzell, A. B. (1993). Sources of information underlying personal ability judgments in high school athletes. *Pediatric Exercise Science, 5,* 263–274.

Lenney, E. (1977). Women's self-confidence in achievement settings. *Psychological Bulletin, 84,* 1–13.

Meyer, W., Bachmann, M., Biermann, V., Hempelmann, P., Ploger, F., & Spiller, H. (1979). The informational value of evaluative behavior: Influence of praise and blame on perceptions of ability. *Journal of Educational Psychology, 71,* 259–268.

Nicholls, J., & Miller, A. (1984). Development and its discontents: The differentiation of the concepts of ability. In J. Nicholls (Ed.), *Advances in motivation and achievement: The development of achievement motivation* (pp. 185–218). Greenwich, CT: JAI.

Petlichkoff, L. (1993). Relationship of player status and time of season to achievement goals and perceived ability in interscholastic athletes. *Pediatric Exercise Science, 5,* 242–252.

Rudisill, M. (1989). Influence of perceived competence and causal dimension orientation on expectations, persistence, and performance during perceived failure. *Research Quarterly for Exercise and Sport, 60,* 166–175.

Scanlan, T., & Lewthwaite, R. (1986). Social psychological aspects of competition for male youth sport participants: IV. Predictors of enjoyment. *Journal of Sport Psychology, 8,* 25–35.

Schunk, D. (1989). Social-cognitive theory and self-regulated learning. In B. J. Zimmerman & D. H. Schunk (Eds.), *Self-regulated learning and academic performance* (pp. 83–110). New York: Springer-Verlag.

Stipek, D., & Daniels, (1988). Declining perceptions of competence: A consequence of changes in the child or in the educational environment? *Journal of Educational Psychology, 80,* 352–356.

Stipek, D., & MacIver, D. (1989). Developmental change in children's assessment of intellectual competence. *Child Development, 60,* 521–538.

Stipek, D., Recchia, S., & McClintic, S. (1992). Self-evaluation in young children. With commentary by Michael Lewis. *Monographs of the Society for Research in Child Development, 57* (1, Serial No. 226).

Ulrich, B. (1987). Perceptions of physical competence, motor competence, and participation in organized sport: Their interrelationships in young children. *Research Quarterly for Exercise and Sport, 58,* 57–67.

Ulrich, B., & Ulrich, D. (in press). Young children's perceptions of their ability to perform simple play and more difficult motor skills. In M. Roberton (Ed.), *Advances in motor development.* New York: AMS Press.

Vealey, R. (1988). Sport-confidence and competitive orientation: An addendum on scoring procedures and gender differences. *Journal of Sport and Exercise Psychology, 10,* 471–478.

Vealey, R., & Campbell, J. (1988). Achievement goals in adolescent figure skaters: Impact on self-confidence, anxiety, and performance. *Journal of Adolescent Research, 3,* 227–243.

Vallerand, R., & Pelletier, L. (1985). *Coaches' interpersonal styles, athletes' perceptions of their coaches' styles and athletes' intrinsic motivation and perceived competence: Generalization to the world of swimming.* Paper presented at the meeting of the Canadian Society for Psychomotor Learning and Sport Psychology, Montreal.

Vallerand, R. J., Deci, E. L., & Ryan, R. M. (1987). Intrinsic motivation in sport. In K. B. Pandolf (Ed.), *Exercise and sport sciences reviews* (Vol. 15, pp. 389–425). New York: Macmillan.

Watkins, B., & Montgomery, A. (1989). Conceptions of athletic excellence among children and adolescents. *Child Development, 60,* 1362–1372.

Weiss, M. (1994). Enhancing children's enjoyment and intrinsic motivation through sport: An educational model. In S. Murphy (Ed.), *Sport psychology interventions.* Champaign, IL: Human Kinetics.

Weiss, M., Bredemeier, B., & Shewchuk, R. (1986). The dynamics of perceived competence, perceived control, and motivational orientation in youth sports. In M. R. Weiss & D. Gould (Eds.), *Sport for children and youths: Proceedings of the 1984 Olympic Scientific Congress* (pp. 89–101). Champaign, IL: Human Kinetics.

Weiss, M., & Chaumeton, N. (1992). Motivational orientations in sport. In T. S. Horn (Ed.), *Advances in sport psychology* (pp. 61–99). Champaign, IL: Human Kinetics.

Weiss, M., & Ebbeck, V. (in press). Self-esteem and perceptions of competence in youth sport: Theory, research, and enhancement strategies. In O. Bar-Or (Ed.), *The encyclopaedia of sports medicine: Vol. 5. The child and adolescent athlete.* Oxford: Blackwell Scientific.

ENHANCING CHILDREN'S SPORT EXPERIENCES

—Terry D. Orlick and Louise Zitzelsberger

A child's early sport experiences are extremely important. Positive beginnings nourish future involvement in sport whether for pleasure or as a career. Early sport experiences have an enormous impact on how a child feels about himself or herself not only in relation to sport but also in relation to global self-esteem. Children want and need positive experiences in sport. They want to play, not watch others play; they want to achieve their own goals, not adult goals; they want less emphasis on winning and more freedom to have fun (Orlick, 1986). Unfortunately, what children want from sport is often overshadowed by what some adults have done to children's sport. A recent newspaper series on youth hockey describes a neglect of skill development and emphasis on winning; recruitment of bigger, more intimidating players by coaches of young teams; high dropout rates; early specialization; and discrimination in team selection against children born late in the year who are less physically mature (MacGregor, 1993). Some children face enormous pressure by coaches and parents to perform and, if they do not, are subjected to what borders on child abuse: being yelled at, ignored, left out, made to feel like a failure, and so on. Clearly this is not what children want and need from sport. To help children fully benefit from their sport experience, change can come from a number of directions. This chapter targets two areas: (1) providing an alternative to the competitive environment and (2) enhancing a child's capacity to cope with and benefit from the sport experience through mental skill training.

Alternatives to the Competitive Model

One way we can help children benefit from sport is to change the environment in which they play and compete. Problems surface when children's recreational time is monopolized by competitive activities with no playtime to balance their lives and values. By turning everything into a competition or quest for mastery, we rob children of an important life perspective. Cooperative games provide an alternative structure where children can play without judgment and without having to live up to the expectations of others. Competitive sport can be played in a healthier manner as well.

One of the best ways to help children keep competition in perspective is to teach them positive ways of coping with the potential stresses of competition.

Cooperative Sport and Games

Whether promoted through sport or experiences in the school or home, children often receive the message that all that matters is the product—winning. Children funneled through a high achievement system often learn to live only for the future, to evaluate their overall worth by numbers, and to accept that there is no place for play free from evaluation. They learn that they are always being judged and must always do their best or suffer the consequences of being a failure. One way to eliminate the problems experienced in intense or irrational competition is to simply alter the basic game structure, for example, by removing the need to compete and the rewards for demonstrating mastery over others.

The distinctive feature of cooperative games, which separates them from all other games, is their structural makeup. For example, in the traditional game of Musical Chairs, children not quick enough to sit on the remaining chairs when the music stops are eliminated until one winner is left. The game has a competitive structure in that players act against one another to win, and in the end only one child attains the object of the game.

In the cooperative version, as the number of chairs decreases, the people sitting on those chairs increase until all the children are either sitting on the last chair or sitting on or touching someone who is sitting on the last chair. This version frees the players from the pressure to compete, eliminates the need for destructive behavior, includes everyone for the duration of the game, and by design encourages helpful and fun-filled interaction (Orlick, 1982).

The concept is simple: People play *with* one another rather than *against* one another; they play to overcome challenges; not to overcome other people; and they are freed by the very structure of the activity to enjoy the game itself. No player need find himself or herself a benchwarmer nursing a bruised self-image. Because the games are designed so that cooperation among players is necessary to achieve the objective(s), children play together for common ends rather than against one another for mutually exclusive ends. In the process, they learn in a fun way how to become more considerate of one another, more aware of how other people are feeling, and more willing to operate in one another's best interests.

Over the past 20 years we have developed hundreds of cooperative games for various age groups. Most of the games are outlined in *The Cooperative Sports and Games Book* (Orlick, 1978a), *The Second Cooperative Sports and Games Book* (Orlick, 1982), and *Nice on My Feelings* (Orlick, 1992). People of every size, shape, age and ability—from infants to the aged—can enjoy these games, which can be played virtually anywhere with almost no equipment. When these games are appropriately selected or adapted for a specific age group, they almost always result in total involvement, feelings of acceptance, cooperative contribution by all players, and lots of smiling faces (Orlick, 1979a; Orlick & Pitman-Davidson, 1989). Several other books have addressed the competition issue and have presented practical alternatives that most children really enjoy (Michaelis & Michaelis, 1977; Morris, 1980; Orlick, 1978a, 1978b; Weinstein & Goodman, 1980).

Cooperative Values in Day-to-Day Living

Cooperative game studies have shown significant positive effects on behavior and suggest that physically active learning has great potential for humanistic development outside of sport (Jensen, 1979; Orlick, 1981a, 1981b; Orlick & Foley, 1976; Orlick, McNally, & O'Hara, 1978; Pines, 1979; Provost, 1981; Witt, 1980). However, some pervasive problems exist that may negate potential long-term impact. First, the number of children currently exposed to active cooperative learning opportunities is relatively low, children's time involvement is minimal, and programs are usually not continued from one age group to the next (or from year to year).

Second, those children who do experience cooperative learning opportunities live in a society that often supports contrary models of behavior (e.g., violent heroes in television programming, in professional sport, in movies, and in highly competitive structures in school and sport programming). The mediums of television, school, and sport provide a powerful, yet largely insensitive, model to overcome with respect to the promotion of cooperative and empathetic living (Orlick, 1983).

Many positive skills can be learned within cooperative structures and fostered in everyday life. The way we react to and with children from the very beginning can embellish humanistic qualities. These qualities—shared empathy, flexibility of thought, creativity, and the search for humor and fun—can be nurtured through the medium of cooperative play. These qualities surface naturally in young children. The only reason they fade as children grow is that they are not nurtured.

The paths to help children grow in warm and loving ways are numerous. Here are some suggestions for parents, teachers, or coaches (Orlick, 1983, 1992):

- Acknowledge and encourage any positive gestures exhibited by children toward others.
- Discuss with children how others might feel when someone is not nice to their feelings. For example, if you witness an inconsiderate act during a game, or when it is obvious that someone is being abused or feeling rejected, point it out and discuss it. Seize teachable moments to do this wherever they occur.
- Firmly voice your dissatisfaction with inconsiderate or disrespectful behavior on the part of any child. For example, if one child hits or hurts another child, physically or emotionally, tell him or her that it is unacceptable and respectfully explain why. Wherever possible, suggest and have children practice a more positive response that is nicer on other people's feelings; for example, they can practice requesting or sharing as an alternative to hitting or excluding.
- Recognize, respect, and express appreciation for the contributions, perspectives, and personal needs of others and encourage children to do likewise.
- Freely demonstrate your affection toward your children (and other children) so that children experience people as kind and loving.

Cooperation during Competition

In many present day games and sports, a basic structural problem exists where two or more people or teams want what only one of them can have—the goal, the ball, the space, or the victory. In such situations the question becomes, How far will each go to achieve these goals? The issue of reactions by and toward the "losers" may also become a problem. One way to alleviate such problems is to work within the competitive structure in an attempt to view competition in a healthier manner.

At its best, competition can be a forum for the positive pursuit of personal excellence—a way for participants to explore their personal potential. At its worst, competition pits person against person in destructive rivalry, resulting in high levels of anxiety, self-depreciation, insensitivity toward others, cheating, and destructive aggression.

Competitive games can be played in a more cooperative and humanistic fashion by showing children how to gain control over themselves and over the game. Within competitive structures are countless opportunities for teaching important human values. What better place than in the midst of a game to discuss the true meaning of such values as winning, losing, success, failure, anxiety, rejection, fair play, acceptance, friendship, cooperation, and healthy competition? What better place to help children become aware of their own feelings and more sensitive to the feelings of others? What better place to encourage children to help one another learn how to cope constructively with some of the problems and concerns they face? A time-out can be called to take advantage of a meaningful learning opportunity. The value (or devaluation) can be discussed quickly, the behavior can be reinforced or a change in behavior recommended, and play can resume. With little direction, children can decide for themselves what they want to get out of a game. They can discuss what other children do that makes them feel good or bad, how they think children should treat one another, how to help one another, and how to encourage one another to follow the values or behavior guidelines they feel are important. Orlick (1979a, 1979b, 1979c, 1980, 1981b, 1990, 1992, 1993), Orlick & Botterill (1975), Botterill (1978), and Halas (1987) have some good practical suggestions on how to carry out activities that promote cooperation, respect, and healthy competition.

Cooperative games are one way of meeting children's needs from sport. They have the additional benefit of teaching prosocial values that can be applied outside of the sport context. Competition can also be a positive experience if it is kept in perspective and guided by personal goals or personal mastery. Unfortunately, healthy competitive sport environments are not always what children face. Dealing with a world they cannot change may require enhanced coping resources on the part of children.

Mental Training with Children

Although modifications to the competitive model are occurring in a number of areas, it will take greater personal commitment on the part of coaches, teachers, and parents to influence the values promoted in children's sport. Positive changes take time and many are beyond the direct control of children. Teaching children how to deal with the sport environment that they find themselves facing is another important consideration.

In the sport world, the importance of mental training has been established at the elite level. Personal excellence and satisfaction with performance achievements are largely due to mental readiness (Orlick & Partington, 1988). Mental skill training not only helps athletes maximize their potential, it also helps them deal with the potential stress of competition, victory, loss, errors, and unmet goals. Young athletes can also benefit from mental skill training. The skills of relaxation, imagery, focusing, and refocusing are more than sport skills. They provide positive alternatives for handling stressful situations and for enhancing the quality of daily life.

Teaching Mental Skills to Young Athletes

In the past 20 years we have implemented many mental training programs with young athletes. The emphasis of these programs is on teaching skills of relaxation, imagery, focusing, refocusing, and constructive evaluation to assist children with mental and physical skill learning and in maximizing their potential. Helping children maintain a healthy perspective toward sport is also an important focus.

Our work in providing mental training services for young athletes has shown that children are highly capable of learning and applying a variety of mind/body skills (Zhang et al., 1992). We have found that many of the skills and techniques we teach high-performance athletes are relevant for children in sport, as long as the strategies and perspectives are explained, adapted, simplified, and presented in terms the children understand. For example, most children enjoy doing imagery and simple relaxation procedures. They gain from developing simple individualized plans or routines for prepractice and precompetition situations and have some very creative ideas for dealing with hassles, stress, or distractions. We have also found that their mental skills improve dramatically with practice. For this reason we try to integrate mental skill refinement into their daily practice sessions.

The ideal situation is to incorporate mental skills (such as imagery or focusing) into the execution of technical/physical skills during practice sessions. For example, a young diver can be encouraged to get into a routine of correctly "feeling" the take-off and dive in his or her mind and body before doing every dive and then fully focus on executing it. Consistent input and positive reminders are often necessary to ensure that the integration of mental with physical skills happens on a daily basis (Orlick & McCaffrey, 1991).

Teaching Mental Skills in the School System

Our focus in the past few years has been on developing a mental skill program to teach to elementary school classes from kindergarten to Grade 6. The program consists of fun games and activities that emphasize helping children develop their mental strengths and stress control skills. Activities cover relaxation, imagery, focusing, and refocusing. We also help children develop a positive perspective toward themselves and life through teaching them to think in positive ways, to look for highlights (the good things in the day, small or large), and ways to put away small stresses and switch to a more positive frame of mind (Orlick, 1993).

In 1993 the program was tested in a number of elementary schools. We received very positive feedback from teachers and students alike. The children not only found the games and activities fun, but they also were able to take the concepts and strategies and use them in school, at home, or in sport. We are now amalgamating the best games and activities into a comprehensive program for teachers. The teachers will then have the tools to integrate the program into their daily lesson plans. Not only do the children benefit, but also the teachers benefit from a class of students who are positive, cooperative, and more capable of managing stressful situations in a healthy way (Orlick, 1993).

Approaches That Work with Children

When we are effective with children, whether they are young athletes or children in another setting (e.g., school, hospital, summer camps), we have a meaningful impact with respect to enhancing life skills, coping skills, performance skills, self-confidence, and/or quality of living. To have an effect on children's lives, certain approaches, which are explained in the following sections, appear to work best.

Simple Strategies

Use simple approaches that allow children to form a clear image or feeling of what they are attempting to accomplish. For example, a child can pretend he is a piece of cooked spaghetti to relax, imagine she is changing channels of a TV to change the focus in her mind, use a little marble bag ("stress bag") to place worries in, create internal performance images and feelings while watching a video of someone performing a skill, practice focusing on cornflakes by focusing on one flake and then finding it among a number of others (for additional examples see Orlick, 1993).

Keep It Fun

When working with children, it is important to keep an element of fun in your approach or integrate some fun into the strategy itself. A young child does not have fun going through a dry, matter-of-fact progressive muscle relaxation procedure. However, children do have fun pretending they are a piece of warm, cooked spaghetti curling up on a plate. Turning an exercise into playing a game is the best way to get concepts across to children and ensure they will continue to practice them.

Concrete, Physical Component

Strategies that allow a child to physically act out the removal of stress or physically act out an image seem to work best. For example, with respect to refocusing or shifting the focus away from worry, children relate well to putting "it" into a tree, a match box, or a stress bag. In a sport like gymnastics, putting the handgrips used for one event into a gym bag is an effective way to "put away" the last event and focus on the next.

Individualized Approach

Getting to know a child as a unique individual is very important. The better you get to know a child, the better you can understand her specific needs, draw upon her input, and adapt your approach to fit the reality of her situation.

Multiple Approaches

If one approach does not work for a particular child, try another. As you get to know children better and they begin to understand their options more clearly, approaches that fit the situation become more prevalent.

Be Positive and Hopeful

Whether you are working with children in sport or in another setting (e.g., school, hospital), it is important that you project a positive belief in that child, in his or her strengths, and in his or her capacity to overcome obstacles and pursue personal goals.

Use Role Models

Most children respond well to the use of role models. If well chosen, a role model can set a positive example to emulate with respect to mental skills, physical skills, a healthy perspective, persistence, or anything else one might want to pursue. We often use videos of respected high-performance athletes to help younger athletes form a clearer image of moves they might like to do.

Involve Parents

Draw upon all the support systems possible when working with children. Parents are central. Wherever possible, solicit their support for reinforcing the concepts, positive approaches, and healthy perspectives you are attempting to teach. Talk with parents about what you are attempting to do, explain why it is important, and request their ongoing assistance in encouraging these important objectives.

Until our current societal values change in a substantial way, children will be forced to deal with stress in sport, school, and life. As concerned coaches, teachers, parents, or mental trainers, we need to continue to push for ways to improve the sport and life experiences of children—to place them more in keeping with what children themselves want. Providing children with opportunities to play free from expectation and evaluation is very important, as is helping them develop positive mental skills for stress control and self-growth.

Our ultimate goal with children is to teach them relevant cooperative values, mental skills, and positive perspectives that will enhance their quality of living. There is a great advantage in beginning this process at an early age to establish a concrete foundation of belief in themselves and in their capacity to directly influence the course of their lives. Children who learn positive mental skills and healthy perspectives early have more time to apply them to living their lives and pursuing their goals.

References

Botterill, C. (1978, July). Psychology of coaching. *Coaching Review,* pp. 45–57.

Halas, J. (1987). *The effect of a social learning intervention program on a grade seven physical education program.* Unpublished master's thesis, University of Ottawa, Ontario.

Jensen, P. (1979). *The effect of a cooperative games programme on subsequent free play of kindergarten children.* Unpublished doctoral dissertation, University of Alberta, Edmonton.

MacGregor, R. (1993, November 20). The great Canadian dream fades. *The Ottawa Citizen,* pp. B1–B2.

Michaelis, B., & Michaelis, D. (1977). *Learning through noncompetitive activities and play.* Palo Alto, CA: Learning Handbooks.

Morris, G. (1980). *How to change the games children play* (2nd ed.). Minneapolis: Burgess.

Orlick, T. (1978a). *The cooperative sports and game book.* New York: Pantheon.

———. (1978b). *Winning through cooperation: Competitive insanity, cooperative alternatives.* Washington, DC: Acropolis Press.

———. (1979a). Children's games: Following the path that has heart. *Elementary School Guidance and Counseling, 114,* 156–161.

———. (1979b). Cooperative games: Cooperative lives. *Recreation Research Review, 6,* 9–12.

———. (1979c, January). What do parents want for their kids, coach? *Coaching Review,* pp. 19–21.

———. (1980). Cooperative play and games. In J. Knight (Ed.), *All about play: A handbook of resources on children's play* (pp. 46–59). Ottawa, Ontario: Canadian Council on Children and Youth.

———. (1981a). Cooperative play socialization among preschool children. *Journal of Individual Psychology, 37,* 54–64.

———. (1981b). Positive socialization via cooperative games. *Developmental Psychology, 17,* 426–429.

———. (1982). *The second cooperative sports and games book.* New York: Pantheon.

———. (1983, June). Enhancing love and life mostly through play and games. *Humanistic Education,* pp. 153–164.

———. (1986). Evolution in children's sport. In M. Weiss & D. Gould (Eds.), *Sport for children and youths* (pp. 169–178). Champaign, IL: Human Kinetics.

———. (1990). *In pursuit of excellence: How to win in sport and life through mental training.* Champaign, IL: Leisure Press.

———. (1992). *Nice on my feelings.* Sacramento, CA: ITA Publications.

———. (1993). *Free to feel great: Teaching children to excel at living.* Carp, Ontario: Creative Bound Inc.

Orlick, T., & Botterill, C. (1975). *Every kid can win.* Chicago: Nelson-Hall.

Orlick, T., & Foley, C. (1976). Pre-school cooperative games: A preliminary perspective. In A. Yiannakis, T. McIntyre, M. Melnick, & D. Hart (Eds.), *Sport sociology: Contemporary themes* (2nd ed., pp. 266–273). Dubuque, IA: Kendall/Hunt.

Orlick, T., & McCaffrey, N. (1991). Mental training with children for sport and life. *The Sport Psychologist, 5,* 322–334.

Orlick, T., & Partington, J. (1988). Mental links to excellence. *The Sport Psychologist, 2,* 105–130.

Orlick, T., & Pitman-Davidson, A. (1989). Enhancing cooperative skills in games and life. In F. Smoll, R. Magill, & M. Ash (Eds.), *Children in sport* (3rd ed., pp. 149–160). Champaign, IL: Human Kinetics.

Orlick, T., McNally, J., & O'Hara, T. (1978). Cooperative games: Systematic analysis and cooperative impact. In F. Smoll & R. Smith (Eds.), *Psychological perspectives in youth sports* (pp. 203–225). Washington, DC: Hemisphere.

Pines, M. (1979, January). Good samaritans at age two. *Psychology Today,* pp. 66–77.

Provost, P. (1981). *Immediate effects of film-mediated cooperative games on children's prosocial behaviour.* Unpublished master's thesis, University of Ottawa, Ontario.

Weinstein, M., & Goodman, J. (1980). *Play fair: Everybody's guide to non-competitive play.* San Luis Obispo, CA: Impact.

Witt, W. (1980). *Comparison of a traditional program of physical education and a cooperative games program on the cooperative classroom behaviour of kindergarten children.* Unpublished master's thesis, Temple University, Philadelphia.

Zhang, L., Ma, Q., Orlick, T., & Zitzelsberger, L. (1992). The effect of mental-imagery training on performance enhancement with 7–10 year old children. *The Sport Psychologist, 6,* 230–242.

20

EXPERTISE IN YOUTH SPORT: RELATIONS BETWEEN KNOWLEDGE AND SKILL

—Jere D. Gallagher, Karen E. French, Katherine T. Thomas,
and Jerry R. Thomas

In recent years, motor development researchers have analyzed how children learn and perform sport skills in complex and varying environments (Campos & Gallagher, 1991; DelRio, 1989; French & Thomas, 1987; McPherson & Thomas, 1989). Emphasis has been placed on the evaluation of motor and cognitive skills and their role in children's development of sport expertise. In this paradigm, the development of cognitive (perception, attention, decision making, knowledge base, etc.) and motor skill (response selection, paramaterization, response execution, etc.) components of sport performance are considered to be closely linked, both being necessary if the goal is for children to achieve higher levels of sport performance.

Since the goal of youth sport should be to improve the skills of young athletes, this chapter focuses on the factors that impact on the development of expertise in athletes of varying ages. First we present a sport acquisition research model that establishes a link between the development of motor and cognitive skills. We then review the development of memory and the influence of memory strategy use on knowledge base. Next we focus on the contents of knowledge base and how a well-developed knowledge base facilitates memory strategy use even in young children. We conclude with application for youth sport coaches to suggest the development of skill and cognition during practice.

Sport Acquisition Research Model

A sport-specific research model contributes both theoretical and applied benefits to the study of children's skill acquisition (Thomas, French, & Humphries, 1986). Each sport has a complex set of rules, strategies, and skills that provide opportunities to gain understanding about how competence is developed. In fact, Ornstein and Naus (1985) make this very point when they indicate the need to determine what children of various ages know about specific content domains. Further, the sport-specific rules, strategies, and skills (a specific content domain for each sport) are of great interest to children over many years—in some instances over the life span. Thus motivation, interest, and persistence are inherent in the sport.

Sports can be classified as team or individual while skills can be categorized into open and closed. An integration of the data obtained from these various categories of sports and skills can result in substantial opportunities to develop and expand theories about acquisition of cognitive knowledge and strategies as well as theories of motor skill acquisition and control. Additionally, integration of cognitive knowledge and motor skill performance follows.

Coaches, instructors, and performers also benefit in applied ways from a sport-specific research model. Much information is acquired about ways to structure practice; how knowledge can be organized for effective instruction; techniques for teaching sport-specific strategies; and rates at which skills, knowledge, and strategies are learned and how they interact. This chapter integrates research using a sport-specific model to contribute to both theory and application.

Memory Development

Past research in the cognitive literature has investigated the role of children's memory processes on acquisition and retention of information (Bjorklund, 1985; Bjorklund & Thompson, 1983; Brown & Deloach, 1978; Chi, 1976, 1977, 1978, 1981; Ornstein & Naus, 1985; Piaget, 1969). These researchers have indicated three factors affecting memory development: capacity, strategies, and knowledge. The capacity hypothesis states that the improvement in memory performance with increasing age can be partially explained by an increase in memory capacity. The predominant explanation is that as children mature, memory capacity increases, allowing them to retain more (Piaget, 1969). The underlying metaphor was to view the mind as a container. As posited by Brown and Deloach (1978): "Little people have little boxes or jars in their heads, and bigger people have bigger ones" (p. 45). According to this view, any developmental difference in memory performance could be attributed to the capacity limitations of the younger groups.

The capacity hypothesis was challenged in the early 1970s by human information-processing theory. In this paradigm, cognitive researchers (Craik & Lockhart, 1972; Flavell, 1970) argued for a more active role of the memory system. Memory was viewed as a sequence of elaborate mental processes beginning with an initial stimulus and concluding with a response. The information received from the environment (perception) is held in various successive and temporary stores (working memory) until, through recoding and other transformations, it reaches a permanent store (long-term memory). The next sections review the research on perception, developmental strategy use changes, and long-term memory.

Perception

The use and interpretation of information in sensory store is termed *perception*. With age, intrasensory discrimination increases (Thomas & Thomas, 1987) and intersensory integration improves (Williams, 1983). An improvement in intrasensory discrimination has been well documented. As children age they are more accurate with positioning a limb (Thomas & Thomas, 1987; Williams, Temple, & Bateman, 1979), tactile point discrimination (VanDyne, 1973), and anticipation timing (Dunham & Reid, 1987; Thomas, Gallagher, & Purvis, 1981). Improved discrimination within a sensory system gives the individual higher quality information with which to make decisions for response selection, adaptation of the response to meet environmental demands, and detection and correction of errors.

Intersensory development parallels improvements in intrasensory development. The use of better processing strategies (Millar, 1974) and improved intrasensory functioning (Bryant, 1968) are the basis for improved intersensory functioning. After perception of the information, the individual must then manipulate the information, which occurs as an interaction of short- and long-term memory. Short-term memory processes are covered next.

Short-Term Memory

The concept of short-term memory (STM) is controversial, and the need for a separate STM system has been questioned (Dempster, 1988). *Short-term memory* has historically been defined as a passive rehearsal buffer for information (Atkinson & Shiffrin, 1968), but current research approaches STM as the active portion of long-term memory (Dempster, 1988). A dynamic, integrated memory system emphasizes active processing as opposed to merely a separate store. Thus the term *short-term memory* has been replaced by the term *working memory* to convey the idea of more than just a warehouse of information. The processing of information in working memory is accomplished through memory strategy use.

Of concern to contemporary researchers are developmental questions relating to the effectiveness of a particular strategy and conditions under which a strategy will be used and generalized. Difficulty with the research, however, is that there is not a single, agreed upon definition for a strategy (Bjorklund & Buchanan, 1989), and the factors responsible for emergence of memory strategies in early childhood have not been identified (Ornstein, Baker-Ward, & Naus, 1988).

Ornstein et al. (1988) view development of children's memory strategies as a process analogous to the development of skill. With increases in age and experience, the various cognitive operations that are involved in strategy production and execution become increasingly routinized and thus less demanding of attentional capacity and effort. The memory strategies reviewed here include attention, labeling, rehearsal, and organization.

Attention

A global term, *attention,* has been used to address a variety of processes, ranging from concentration and vigilance to mental set and arousal (Abernethy, 1993). When performing a motor skill, the individual must deal with a wealth of exteroceptive and proprioceptive information. While moving, performers at times need to focus their attention on selected information and at other times divide their attention between several items of information, often shifting attention from one stimulus to another, all while ignoring irrelevant information (Kay & Ruskin, 1990). Throughout the performance the individual must scan the environment, since the important cues appear at various locations. In this section we review the information-processing viewpoint of attention to include attentional capacity, attention span, and selective attention.

Attentional capacity has been used interchangeably with memory capacity. As mentioned previously, the increase in the physical aspects of the memory system appear to be minimal, with memory strategies and the amount of information in long-term memory playing a greater role (Gallagher, 1980; Gallagher & Fisher, 1983). Kail (1988) argues that a general developmental change in memory is due to the efficient allocation of processing resources and mental effort. The reasons for the capacity demands of strategy use decreasing with age are: practice, growth, and/or reorganization of the general knowledge base or more efficient and effective resource allocation of strategies (Guttentag & Ornstein, 1990). Younger children are regarded as less capable of controlling their attentional resources than are older children and adults (Barrett & Shepp, 1988).

Reviewing the developmental literature, Guttentag and Ornstein (1990) concluded that the capacity demands of strategy execution generally decline with age, thereby affecting the complexity of the strategies that children are able to deploy. Guttentag (1989) found that young children must exert greater mental effort than older children to execute the same procedures or use a less effective procedure than older children while exerting the same level of mental effort. Spontaneous strategy deployment for children in Grades 3 through 5 was predicted by the attentional demands of the strategy (Guttentag, 1989). These findings suggest that the high capacity demands of strategy execution did not prevent the younger children from being able to execute the strategy effectively; however, spontaneous strategy use was affected.

Paris (1988) suggests that age-related changes in spontaneous strategy selection are also influenced by interactions among the childrens' changing judgments of the effort required to use the strategy, their perceptions of the relative effectiveness of the strategy, and in their perceived level of required performance. Since young children have higher perceived costs of strategy use than older children, they may be unwilling to use the strategy due to the mental effort required.

A concept related to mental effort is *metamemory*. Research on metamemory determines the child's understanding of the workings of the memory system and also determines whether the understanding of memory facilitates memory strategy use. Young children have some degree of awareness of the usefulness of memory strategies (Schneider & Sodian, 1988). Results from a study by Fabricius and Cavalier (1989) on labeling task-appropriate cues demonstrated that children's conceptions of how labeling worked predicted their self-initiated use of a labeling strategy. The results suggest that the effects of increasing accessibility and increasing strategy effectiveness on strategy acquisition are mediated through children's causal theories of memory. However, when faced with novel situations, children tend to abandon a strategy if they do not understand the benefits of the strategy (Rao & Moley, 1989). Bjorklund and Buchanan (1989) and Rabinowitz (1988) indicate a higher probability of training effectiveness for familiar material.

Ornstein et al. (1988) suggest that future research be longitudinal to provide within-subject skill development. Individual variation needs to be related to varying task demands, and the mental effort required of the various strategies needs to be determined. Thus children's perception of mental effort and their knowledge of their memory strategies (metamemory) influence their performance.

A concept related to attentional effort is attention span. *Attention span* refers to the amount of time that an individual focuses on a task. Typically, older children and adults have longer attention spans than younger children. However, given motivation and interest, younger children can attend for long periods of time.

Once the child attends to the task, the next question is, Does the child know what to attend to? *Selective attention* serves in the perceptual encoding of task-appropriate cues and as a control process to continually maintain relevant information in working memory. Research has moved from a description of the development of selective attention (Ross, 1976; Stratton, 1978) to determining the mechanisms of selective attention and the relationship between perception and attention. We cover the development of selective attention followed by the mechanisms of selective attention and the relationship between perception and attention.

Ross (1976) has proposed three levels in the development of selective attention: overexclusive, overinclusive, and selective attention. Up to 5 or 6 years of age, the child focuses on a limited number of cues that are not necessarily related to task appropriateness (overexclusive phase). The overinclusive child attempts to attend to a larger amount of environmental cues (between 6 and 7, and 11 and 12 years of age), and environmental distractors significantly impact task performance. At approximately 11 years of age the child develops the ability to selectively attend to task-appropriate cues and ignore irrelevant information.

Since elementary school children have not developed a selective attention strategy, the question is, How do we teach children to attend to task-appropriate cues? The environment surrounding any movement task is complex, with high levels of irrelevant information present. Do children need to be taught the skill under low or high levels of interference? Thomas and Stratton (1977) and Ladewig and Gallagher (1992) have conducted research manipulating levels of interference during practice. The results from these studies demonstrated that low interference early in practice had a positive result during acquisition, but subjects exposed to high levels of interference early in practice had poor performance. During a retention test with high levels of interference, results indicated a reversal. Subjects exposed to high interference early in practice performed the retention task better. These results demonstrate the benefit of providing high interference early in practice as long as the subjects are given cues to focus attention. For this research, the task-appropriate information remained in the same location throughout the study. The next question is, When the task complexity is increased such that the relevant information can be found in various locations in the environment, can the children still deal with the high amount of interference during early learning?

An important factor in determining the development of selective attention is understanding the mechanisms of selective attention and the relationship between perception and attention. Investigating the mechanisms of selective attention, Tipper, MacQueen, and Brehaut (1988) have proposed a model in which the environment is initially screened for familiar items regardless of task appropriateness. Two mechanisms of selective attention are then utilized: an excitatory process, where the representations of the selected object receive further analysis, and an inhibitory process, where the responses are actively inhibited. Other researchers (Lorch, Anderson, & Well, 1984; Lorch & Horn, 1986; Reisberg, Barron, & Kemler, 1980) include a habituation response; the inhibitory process, because the environment is familiar, does not have to be evoked and attention is not distracted by irrelevant stimuli (Tipper et al., 1989).

During the past 10 years the joint development of perceptual organization and attention has been researched (Barrett & Shepp, 1988). One finding that has dominated the research is that young children perceive objects as integral wholes, whereas older children and adults perceive the same objects as aggregates of features. An implication from the interaction of perception and attention is that questions about the development of attention must also address the issue of perceived structure. If aspects of the stimuli are perceptually independent, the development of attention can be directly assessed. If, however, a child perceives an object as a whole, the failure to attend to a feature of the object cannot be attributed to an inability to attend but must be attributed to the nature of the perceived structure. Research supports this linkage of perceptual and attentional development (Shepp, Barrett, & Kolbert, 1987). Most stimuli are integral for young children but become increasingly separate with increasing age. A series of studies by Shepp et al. (1987) concluded that the development of perceived structure is enhanced by the flexibility of attention that accompanies perceptual development. Accordingly, the young child attends primarily to holistic properties; but with increasing age and experience the child becomes increasingly proficient in extracting either featural or holistic properties.

Labeling

A strategy related to the development of selective attention is labeling. *Labeling* is one aspect of perception, and increasing the meaningfulness of the label improves performance. The use of labels has improved children's recall performance for memory of location (Winther & Thomas, 1981), movement series (Miller, 1990; Weiss, 1983; Weiss & Klint, 1987), and head stands and forward rolls (Masser, 1993). Additionally labels have facilitated the performance of learning disabled children (Miller, 1990).

Rehearsal

Another strategy in working memory that facilitates performance is rehearsal. *Rehearsal* is important to maintain information in memory and transfer it to the knowledge base. The importance of active rehearsal has been demonstrated in a study by Gallagher and Thomas (1984). Given a series of eight movements, 5- and 7-year-old children chose to rehearse on an instance-by-instance basis, whereas 11- and 19-year-old subjects grouped the movements for recall. When forced to rehearse in an adult fashion, the 5- and 7-year-old children's performance improved. Similar findings have been reported with mentally retarded children (Reid, 1980; Schroeder, 1981).

Organization

Organization is a strategy used to combine information that is meaningful to reduce cognitive demands. Instead of thinking of separate pieces of information, the individual groups and recodes the information into one unit. Using a series of eight movements and manipulating the degree of organization in the material, Gallagher and Thomas (1986) found that 5-year-old children were unable to increase performance regardless of organization strategy or input of information. The 7-year-old children were able to use organized input to facilitate recall, but the strategy failed to transfer to a new task. Eleven-year-old children's performances, with the exception of the unorganized input group, conformed to the predictions. It was anticipated that the 11-year-old children used organized input and showed some transfer of strategy. However, they could not restructure the information or produce a self-generated organizational strategy. Nineteen-year-old subjects organized the information regardless of input.

Integrating the studies on rehearsal and organization of input, Gallagher and Thomas (1986) indicated that forcing the use of the strategies was of greater importance to younger children; it had less effect on older children and adults. The older children and adults were using the strategies when not forced to do so, whereas the younger children were not. Even though the 5-year-old children were given organizational cues, they failed to recall the movements in order (from short to long). Forcing rehearsal, on the other hand, aided recall of the 5-year-old children. The 7-year-old children used the organizational strategy to recall eight movements. The older children and adults in the self-determined strategy were similar in recall to the organizational strategy. They rehearsed spatially similar groups of movement.

Thus, younger children do not spontaneously use memory strategies. However, as Chi (1982) has suggested, this could be due to an inefficient knowledge base. Children's earliest successful memory strategies begin with highly familiar information as do successful training efforts. The automatization of these strategies occurs as a result of practice and experience reducing mental effort required to perform the strategy and lead to a functional enlargement of the space available in working memory for the handling of information-processing operations.

Long-Term Memory

Age-related changes in both the contents and familiarity of the knowledge base (long-term memory) have significant implications for the deployment of strategies. Knowledge base theorists postulate that knowledge is represented more elaboratively with increased practice; thus, information is accessed with less mental effort, leaving more mental resources available for the execution of strategies.

To this point, the various aspects of memory have been discussed with adult/child differences highlighted. Bjorklund (1985) and Ornstein and Naus (1985) have suggested there are long-term effects of changes in knowledge base on the developmental use of strategies, whereas Chi (1985) suggests that the relationship between strategy and knowledge is interdependent.

How Knowledge May Be Represented

This section deals with the type of information stored in the knowledge base, or long-term memory (LTM), and the quality of that information. Sport information is placed in LTM purposefully as a result of practice and experience. Increased knowledge is believed to be related to increases in skill level and experience (Abernethy, Thomas,

& Thomas, 1993). Two dimensions of sport performance are execution (motor skill) and decision making (cognitive). Information about each of these must be represented in memory. Execution knowledge is information about the mechanics of movement and movement parameters. Decision making includes selecting a response and evaluating the outcome. As skill level improves from novice to expert, the quantity and quality of information in the knowledge base increases (McPherson, 1993b; McPherson, Dovenmuehler, & Murray, 1992; McPherson & Thomas, 1989).

Research on expertise has been conducted in many domains, for example, dinosaurs (Chi & Koeske, 1983), chess (Chase & Simon, 1973), teaching (Berliner, 1986), resulting in a consensus that knowledge falls into three categories. These are declarative, procedural, and strategic knowledge (Chi, 1981). Research on sport has used the same categories to define knowledge (Chiesi, Spilich, & Voss, 1979; French & Thomas, 1987; McPherson & Thomas, 1989).

Declarative knowledge includes factual information. Rules, definitions, and other facts about the sport are categorized as declarative knowledge. Experts typically have more declarative knowledge than novices, including more concepts and more information describing each concept (Chase & Simon, 1973; Chi, 1978; Chi & Koeske, 1983; French & Thomas, 1987). Declarative knowledge is consistent and typically organized in similar patterns among experts within a domain (Chiesi et al., 1979; Murphy & Wright, 1984). Declarative knowledge is possessed by all experts but can be observed in novices. In other words, to become an expert, an athlete must know the rules, facts, and other basic information about the sport and the movements in the sport. However, this information does not guarantee that the athlete will become an expert.

Experts also have greater procedural knowledge than novices (Adelson, 1984; Chi, Feltovich, & Glaser, 1981; French & Thomas, 1987). *Procedural knowledge* is knowing how to do something. This is related specifically to problem solving and decision making but is based on declarative knowledge. Experts have more potential solutions and organize these in a way that leads to a logical solution. McPherson and Thomas (1989) called the connections between situations and outcomes linkages. Linkages were found to be a potent force in expert tennis players' ability to make good decisions. The tennis players had if-then statements that allowed them to select potential responses that were appropriate. The accuracy, number, and size of their selections increased with expertise. In some sports the number of concepts is more similar between experts and novices, but the experts have more connections among concepts and complexity within concepts (McPherson, 1993b). Athletes who have more potential solutions to problems in their sport, with greater depth of understanding to those solutions tend to be more expert. The organization of these representations is critical to ensuring expertise. Once again, procedural knowledge is required for expertise but does not guarantee expertise.

Strategic knowledge is the use of general rules or control processes to facilitate cognitive processing. Chi and Koeske (1983) found that a child who was an expert on dinosaurs would use rehearsal and encoding strategies, within the domain of dinosaurs, that were beyond what a child of that age should use. However, those same control processes were not used by that child in other domains. This suggests a relationship among the three types of knowledge, indicating that strategic knowledge may be linked more to experience rather than being age dependent. The three types of knowledge are viewed as hierarchical in nature. Each succeeding level is somewhat dependent upon the previous level and more complex than the preceding level(s).

Movement information is stored or represented first as declarative—facts and rules. The movements become increasingly automatic, so the performer may be relatively unaware of response programming (e.g., selecting movement parameters). One thing is clear: Experts have considerable information about how to execute their sport skills and they are able to translate this into action, even when some experts have difficulty verbalizing the motor skill knowledge (Davis, Thomas, & Thomas, 1991; Thomas & Lee, 1992). In studies of golfers and swimmers, experts had more declarative and procedural knowledge about execution than novices. Thus skill execution and knowing about skill appear to be limiting factors in sport performance. This means that athletes must have cognitive representations of the efficient motor patterns associated with their sport and be able to execute those patterns to become experts.

Coaches and teachers may have limited influence over skill execution due to a wide variety of biological factors such as size, muscle type, and physique, but the potential of athletes should not be limited by skill knowledge (Davis et al., 1991). Compelling evidence from swimmers and golfers suggests the importance of skill knowledge. All experts in both sports were able to recognize or recall many concepts about execution; this information was represented differently, however, depending on the age of the individual. Child experts could pantomime or demonstrate the important points of form and efficiency. Adults could distinguish between written statements of correct and incorrect form. Novices in both sports had fewer facts, or incorrect facts, about execution and were less often able to actually execute the correct form. The novice golfers were often confident that they knew the correct form, even when they did not. These golfers were often doing exactly what they believed to be correct, when in fact that movement was not effective or efficient. Age-group swimmers often commented that coaches did not care how they swam, as long as it was fast. For athletes to maximize their talent, coaches and teachers must help them to build correct cognitive representations of the important skills (Davis et al., 1991; Thomas & Lee, 1992).

In sum, information represented in long-term memory can be about the motor skill (execution) or decision making process (cognitive). Knowledge can be categorized as either declarative, procedural, or strategic. Higher levels of knowledge are associated with expertise, and lower levels limit sport performance. The next section reviews differences between expert and novice sport performers.

Expert/Novice Differences in Sport

Research has documented numerous differences in perceptual and cognitive abilities of adult expert and novice sport performers. Adult experts exhibit superior perceptual skills in anticipating the flight of objects (Abernethy, 1988; Abernethy & Russell, 1987, badminton; Bard & Fleury, 1981, ice hockey; Jones & Miles, 1978, tennis), use different visual cues or visual search strategies (Abernethy, 1988; Abernethy & Russell, 1987, badminton; Bard & Fleury, 1976, basketball; Helsen & Bard, 1989, soccer), detect the presence or absence of game-related stimuli (Allard & Starkes, 1980, volleyball), and recognize sequences of movements more accurately (Vickers, 1986, gymnastics).

A number of cognitive differences between expert and novice adult performers have also been determined. For example, experts recall game structured information more accurately than novices (Allard & Burnett, 1985; Allard, Graham, & Paarsula, 1980; Garland, 1989; Starkes, 1987), make faster and more accurate sport decisions (Bard & Fleury, 1976, basketball; Helsen & Bard, 1989, soccer; Starkes, 1987, field hockey), and employ different problem representations and cognitive processes to monitor current game situations, predict possible game scenarios, and plan actions in advance (McPherson, 1993a).

Laboratory Sport Studies

Fewer studies have examined expert-novice differences from a developmental perspective. In the discussion that follows, three laboratory studies are summarized that illustrate the paradigms and findings relevant to developmental changes in expertise. Starkes et al. (1987) compared verbal and motor recall of videotaped ballet movements by 11-year-old expert and novice performers. The years of experience in ballet was equated between the groups. Subjects viewed videotaped sequences of eight movement elements presented in a serial order. One series of movements (structured) was professionally choreographed. The order of elements was randomized in a second series of movement so that elements appeared in an unstructured manner. Subjects viewed each sequence twice and immediately recalled the sequence motorically or verbally. Expert-novice differences in motoric and verbal recall were found for structured sequences but no differences existed for unstructured sequences. Differences were largest for movement elements that occurred later in the movement sequence. The authors noted that strategies employed during recall were different for experts and novices. Novices tended to rush to recall the sequence immediately, whereas experts asked if they could think about the sequence before both types of recall. Experts rehearsed the elements, often using hand and foot movements in conjunction with verbalization prior to both verbal and motor recall. However, these rehearsal strategies were not used consistently for the unstructured sequences. Thus, strategic behavior (rehearsal strategies) may develop first as task-related or task-specific strategies (Chi, 1981).

A common paradigm to examine perceptual skill in expert and novice performers is film occlusion. Short sequences of game performance are filmed. Films are constructed to manipulate the length of exposure to the visual display (temporal occlusion) or visual events or cues (event occlusion) present on the film. Speed of processing can be inferred from temporal occlusion. Inferences regarding cue selection can be determined from event occlusion.

Abernethy (1988) and Abernethy and Russell (1987) used both temporal and event occlusion methods to study anticipation of the flight of a shuttlecock in expert and novice badminton players ages 11, 15, 18, and adult. Expert-novice differences in predicting shuttlecock flight during temporal occlusion did not emerge until adulthood. Adult experts performed better than younger age groups, whereas novices performed similarly regardless of age. Event occlusion trials eliminated single elements from the visual display on given trials (arm and racket, racket, opponent's head, opponent's lower body). Accuracy of prediction of the landing position of the shuttlecock was used as a dependent variable. The results showed that experts of all ages were able to use racket and arm cues to enhance their accuracy. The accuracy of performance for novices of all ages was enhanced by use-of-racket information only. Similar superiority of visual cue selection has been documented in young expert ice hockey players as well (Bard & Fleury, 1981). Thus, young expert performers tend to use different visual cues in predicting the flight of objects in sport environments. However, speed of processing as measured by temporal occlusion tasks do not show differences between experts and novices during childhood and adolescence.

Laboratory studies have also compared the accuracy and speed of decision making in adult and novice sport performers (Bard & Fleury, 1976; Helsen & Bard, 1989; Starkes, 1987). Typically these studies have involved decisions made by performers who had possession of the ball (e.g., decisions to pass, dribble, or shoot in basketball, soccer, or field hockey). The only developmental studies reported to date that examine the accuracy and speed of sport decisions were conducted by Johnson (1991) and Johnson, French, and Spurgeon (1992). These experiments compared the accuracy and speed of decisions regarding *where to run without the ball in soccer* in experienced 11- and 15-year-old soccer players with college-age experienced and novice soccer players. (In soccer and other invasion games, movement without the ball is often more important than movement with the ball.) All experienced players belonged to programs that selected players based on skill level (11-year-old local select team, 15-year-old South Carolina Olympic Development Team, University of South Carolina soccer team). Since some experience was necessary for this task, novice subjects were college-age physical education majors who had recently completed a semester of instruction in soccer but had no prior playing experience in soccer.

Twelve short videotaped sequences were selected from World Cup matches. Four sequences involved combination play, four were attack situations, and four were defensive situations. Subjects were required to view the sequence, wait for the identification of a specific player (identified during the sequence by a circle surrounding the player), and respond as quickly and accurately as possible where the identified player should run on the field in this situation. Reaction time and accuracy were recorded.

Across all situations, college players responded faster than college novices, followed by 15-year-old players and 11-year-old players. Differences in accuracy were situationally specific. Only a summary of trends is reported here. College novices and 11-year-old players exhibited similar patterns for accuracy. For complex patterns of play (overlaps, takeovers, curved run behind the defense, offside rule restricted runs), college players were the most accurate, followed by 15-year-old players, 11-year-old players, and college novices. In most situations, with the exception of long-pass situations, novices and 11-year-olds responded in similar ways. Long passes that were beyond the subjects' skill level were not considered as viable options. Thus their response selections were biased by the constraints of their skill level.

Naturalistic Sport Studies

Three studies (French & Thomas, 1987, basketball; McPherson & Thomas, 1989, tennis; and Nevett et al., 1993, baseball) have used the sport acquisition research model to examine the development of expertise in naturalistic sport environments. The sports selected for these studies fall along a continuum from continuous sports (basketball) to discrete sports (baseball). For example, play is relatively continuous in basketball, with limited opportunities for planning and preparation of responses in advance. Pauses in action are common in baseball (discrete), and many of the responses for defense can be planned in advance. Tennis involves a combination of continuous play and pauses between points that can be used for planning strategy for the next point.

Each study compared skilled and novice players at different ages on measures of sport-specific knowledge, sport-specific skills, game performance, and interviews of game situations. Game performance was videotaped and analyzed to determine the accuracy of cognitive decisions and sport skill execution during actual game play.

The first study to use this approach was conducted by French and Thomas (1987). The hypothesis for Experiment 1 was that sport-specific declarative knowledge was necessary to make appropriate decisions within the context of game play (procedural knowledge or response selection within game play), whereas a foundation of sport-specific skills were necessary to execute sport skills during game play.

The observational instrument developed for this study measured the accuracy of game decisions, the success rate of motor execution of sport skills and control of the ball during game play. Child experts scored significantly higher in measures of dribbling skill, shooting skill, and basketball knowledge. Child experts also exhibited a higher percentage of successful decisions made during game play, superior control of the ball, and a higher percentage of successful execution of sport skills during game play. The component of game performance that maximally discriminated expert and novice performance in basketball was the decision-making component. Children's ability to make appropriate decisions within the context of game play was related to their basketball knowledge, whereas successful execution of motor skills during game play was related to dribbling and shooting skill.

In Experiment 2, French and Thomas (1987) measured 8- to 10-year-old expert and novice basketball players on dribbling skill, shooting skill, basketball knowledge, and game performance at the beginning and end of the season. Both expert and novice players improved the quality of decisions and control of the basketball during game play from pretest to posttest. Subjects also improved their scores on the basketball knowledge test. Dribbling skill, shooting skill, and sport-skill execution during game play did not improve. The scores of the basketball knowledge test remained significantly related to the accuracy of decisions made during game play at the end of the season.

These experiments indicated that both cognitive and motor skills play a salient role in the development of basketball performance in young children. The development of cognitive skills progressed at a faster rate than the development of motor skills. Children were learning what to do in the context of the game faster than they were learning the motor skills necessary to carry out these actions. The authors noted that coaches tended to focus more instructional time during practices toward organization for competition (cognitive components such as rules, offensive plays and positioning, defensive alignments, out-of-bounds plays, etc.) than practice or drills of basketball skills.

A subsequent follow-up study examined changes in basketball knowledge and skills from the beginning of the season to the end of the season in a youth basketball league. No improvement in basketball skills or basketball knowledge was found. Game performance was not measured in this study. However, it clearly demonstrates that improvement in cognitive components of performance or skill components is not guaranteed by participation alone and points to further study of the instruction that youth sport coaches and parents provide.

McPherson and Thomas (1989) compared 10- to 11-year-old and 12- to 13-year-old expert and novice tennis players. Tennis knowledge, tennis skills, and game performance were measured. Serve decisions were positively related to both serve and tennis knowledge. Tennis knowledge and serve skill influenced player's decisions concerning how and where to serve. However, serve execution was not related to tennis knowledge or serve skill. Game decisions were related to tennis knowledge and skill in ground strokes. Subjects who made better decisions possessed more tennis knowledge and higher skill in the forehand and backhand.

In the second phase of their study, McPherson and Thomas (1989) used the procedures of protocol analysis to examine the structure of tennis knowledge. Two types of interviews were conducted. A situation interview was conducted using procedures similar to "think aloud" protocols (Ericsson & Simon, 1984). Subjects were asked to describe what they were thinking about in open-ended situations simulating the serve, backcourt, and net game situations. The point-by-point interview was a combination of "think aloud" and retrospective accounts (Ericsson & Simon, 1984) of thought processes used during and between points of game play. Subjects were asked the probe, "What were you thinking about on that point?", between points during their actual game play. Transcripts of the verbal protocols from each interview were coded to determine the content and structure of knowledge. Content was measured by the number of concepts (goal, condition, action), number of different concepts, and quality of each concept. Structure was inferred from the number of connections between concepts and linkages of concepts.

In both interviews, experts had more condition concepts and more alternative actions than novices. The variety of action concepts was the variable that maximally discriminated expertise. Experts also possessed a greater number of connections and linkages of goal, condition, and action concepts. Experts were more likely to elaborate action concepts by including parameterization of the action concepts (i.e., spin, direction, placement). McPherson and Thomas (1989) refer to these discriminations of action concepts as "do" statements. Experts also included more verbalizations that indicated monitoring and self-regulation strategies to detect errors. In other work with tennis and other sports, McPherson (1994) has found adult experts to have fewer "do" statements than adult novices. Thus, parameterization of action concepts may be accessed into working memory at certain stages of learning (including younger experts) during the development of expertise, but at higher levels of expertise these concepts cease to be accessed into working memory and drop out of verbalizations (Anderson, 1982; Fitts & Posner, 1967).

Nevett et al. (1993) compared different skill level baseball players, ages 7, 8, 9, and 10 years. The 7- and 8-year-olds were grouped together for competition and played coaches pitch. Nine- and 10-year-olds hit player-pitched balls, but stealing was restricted. Player position tended to be confounded with skill level. Higher-skilled players were more often pitchers, shortstops, and first basemen. Lower-skilled players most often played in the outfield. All but two 7-year-olds played in the outfield. All other ages could be divided into three skill levels.

Skill tests for throwing distance, fielding, and throwing accuracy were obtained for all subjects. A baseball knowledge test was given to the 9- and 10-year-old subjects. The reading level of the younger players precluded any meaningful paper-pencil measure of baseball knowledge. Many of the 7-year-olds were in first grade and had never taken a multiple-choice test. Game performance for five games was videotaped. Measures of baseball skill (catching, fielding, batting, throwing accuracy, throwing force) and cognitive components (game decisions, proper positioning on the field) were determined from the videotaped game play.

Several multivariate analyses were conducted to examine relations among age, years of playing experience, skill level, and game performance. Both age and skill level were significantly related to measures of baseball execution during game play. Neither age nor skill level were related to cognitive performance measures of game decisions and positioning. There were differences between skill levels on the baseball knowledge test at ages 9 and 10 years. However, execution of baseball skills, not cognitive components as in other sports, maximally discriminated game performance.

There are two reasons the cognitive decision-making component does not discriminate skill levels in baseball game performance. First, the frequency of occurrence of complex decisions in baseball is low. Outfield decisions are often limited to throw to the cutoff, home, or possibly another base. Throwing to the cutoff is the most frequent decision. In the infield, throwing to first or second base occurs much more often than other decisions, such as looking a runner back to the occupied base, then throwing to first. Thus, the low frequency of complex decisions may have influenced the lack of discrimination of baseball decisions. However, often winning and losing is determined by low frequency of occurrence situations during games. For example, two playoff games were lost by one team in this league within three days when the same player decided to try to make a play at home with a runner on third, two outs, and scoring one run would determine the game. In both cases, throwing the ball to first would have ended the inning and the game would have continued. However, in both cases the player chose to throw home with no chance of a play at the plate.

A second reason cognitive decision making does not discriminate skill levels is that coaches cue players concerning what to do between pitches. Field notes taken during games involving both leagues indicated that coaches of all age groups routinely cued and prompted players regarding where to throw the ball in a given game situation between pitches. Also, frequently parents and spectators would loudly verbalize where to throw during a given play. On numerous occasions, players would hesitate, hear the spectators, and then execute the decision the spectators vocalized. This type of cuing and constant reinforcement of what to do before the ball is hit was very effective in producing higher percentages of correct game decisions. In a sport like baseball, these techniques are very effective for *immediate* enhancement of performance. We do not know, however, whether this is the most effective way to produce knowledgeable players who can make good decisions without prompting.

Preliminary analyses of game situation interviews (French et al., in preparation) indicate that children often do not know what the correct action is in a given baseball situation. Several children responded by saying "they would do what the coach told them to do." One subject said that "if the coach didn't say anything, he would throw to first, if he said something, he would throw to second." Notice he was waiting to hear instructions during the play while he was fielding the ball.

It appears likely that overreliance on coaches' and spectators' prompting encourages players to wait for coaches' prompts and not internalize or process game information at levels that lead to more effective knowledge representations (KR). Like instances where more frequent feedback or KR can lead to poorer motor skill learning, high frequencies of prompting may lead to the same type of shallow processing that deters long-term benefits to knowledge and decision development. Coaches should provide practice opportunities for players to generate decisions in situations that occur frequently and infrequently. The emphasis should be on players *choosing* the correct response themselves (choice of responses) without prompts, rather than just drilling the appropriate response to one situation over and over.

Several other trends are important from the baseball studies. Many players had previous experience playing T-ball prior to entering this league. Correlations were calculated at each age between years of playing experience and each of the skill tests and measures of skill execution to determine whether years of playing experience increased skill level. Years of playing experience was not related to increased skill development until 9 or 10 years of age. These findings were consistent across all baseball skills measured. Thus, at younger ages (7 and 8), playing T-ball did not significantly increase children's baseball skills.

The type of experience that did seem to discriminate skilled players from lesser-skilled players was the amount of practice time outside of organized practices and games. Parents estimated the amount of time their child spent practicing skills with a number of significant others (e.g., father, mother, brother, friend). Across all ages, skilled players spent almost twice the amount of time practicing with a friend than the lesser-skilled players. Practice time with fathers was virtually equal in all skill groups. This suggests that the skilled players were initiating practice of skills themselves rather than being externally motivated by a parent or father to practice.

Which Develops First: Cognitive or Motor Skill?

Development of both cognitive and motor skill components takes hours of practice and years to develop to high levels of performance. Few studies have been conducted longitudinally, following changes in cognitive and motor skills, over some period of time (season) or instruction. Some findings suggest that cognitive decision-making skills at low sophistication levels develop faster than motor skills (French & Thomas, 1987, basketball; McPherson & French, 1991, tennis). However, more recent analyses of available data suggest that what develops is at least in part determined by the focus of instruction or practice. Cognitive skills progressed faster in the French and Thomas (1987) study because players focused on cognitive skills more frequently in practice. Adult novices followed over a period of skill instruction and tactical instruction improved tennis skill only when direct instruction of the skills became a focus of practice (McPherson & French, 1991). Some improvement in low-level cognitive skills was made when instruction was primarily skill oriented. However, the development of procedural knowledge structures in tennis were much more advanced when instruction focused on building cognitive decision-making skills (McPherson, 1991).

Some developmental limitations appear to influence both cognitive and sport skill development. Anticipation timing and reaction time show developmental trends that are not always overcome by expertise at young ages as evidenced by Nevett et al. (1993, batting, catching performance), Abernethy (1988, temporal occlusion), and Johnson (1991, reaction time). Also, maturation constrains skill improvement in sport skills that require force production (throwing, kicking, etc.). As evidenced by the long-pass situations in soccer (Johnson, 1991), response selection may be biased due to elimination of some alternatives that are not acknowledged as potential choices due to insufficient skill.

Thus, constraints on cognitive and skill development exist during childhood and early adolescence. For some sports, readiness for certain sport skills and sport tactics is an issue. Most youth sport leagues modify the rules, equipment, and game to accommodate the skill levels of age-grouped participants (i.e., T-ball, coaches pitch, player pitch). Some sports, such as soccer, have specified age-appropriate skills and tactics in a youth coaches manual (Rees, 1987). In some cases, coaches modify the game strategies in a positive way to meet the skill levels of their individual players; for example, positioning a teammate to help relay the ball to the cutoff when outfielders can not throw all the way to second base.

The problem with modifying strategies to accommodate skill levels at young ages is that many coaches end up with strategies that eliminate lesser-skilled players from full participation in the game (e.g., instructing outfielders to avoid throwing by requiring the center fielder, a better thrower, to make all throws; or avoiding passing to certain players because they do not catch or dribble well). Therefore, coaches need to carefully think about the reasons for modifying strategies and the potential impact of these modifications on every child's opportunity to learn the skills and tactics of the game.

Application for Youth Sport Coaches

Throughout this chapter, we have stressed the interaction of cognitive and motor skill performance. When planning practice, the youth sport coach needs to emphasize both, in addition to providing situations in which the athletes are given practice at decision making. Skill execution and knowing how and when to execute the specific skills appear to be limiting factors in sport performance. The coach needs to be aware that athletes make decisions that are biased by skill constraints.

During practice the athlete needs to learn how to execute the skill while developing the decision-making skills to translate knowledge into action. The correct cognitive representation of the important skills needs to be provided to develop an error detection and correction mechanism. Links between gamelike situations and outcomes are important for the athlete to appropriately parameratize the skill.

Improvement in a cognitive or skill component is not guaranteed by participation alone. Coaches need to provide practice opportunities that allow athletes to generate decisions to situations that occur both frequently and infrequently. Cueing and constant reinforcement by the coach during practice and game situations might be good for immediate performance but not for learning.

Motivation is important. Skilled players initiate practice of the skills with other players, rather than being externally motivated by a parent or coach. Thus coaches need to assist athletes in developing intrinsic motivation. Finally, children need to perceive the sporting experience as challenging yet fun!

References

Abernethy, B. (1988). The effects of age and expertise upon perceptual skill development in a racket sport. *Research Quarterly for Exercise and Sport, 59,* 210–221.

———. (1993). Attention. In R. Singer, M. Murphey, & K. Tennant (Eds.), *Handbook of research on sport psychology* (pp. 127–170). New York: Macmillan.

Abernethy, B., & Russell, D. G. (1987). Expert-novice differences in an applied selective attention task. *Journal of Sport Psychology, 9,* 326–345.

Abernethy, B., Thomas, J., & Thomas, K. (1993). Strategies for improving understanding of motor expertise. In J. Starkes & F. Allard (Eds.), *Cognitive issues in motor expertise* (pp. 317–356). Amsterdam: Elsevier Publishing.

Adelson, B. (1984). When novices surpass experts: The difficulty of the task may increase with expertise. *Journal of Experimental Psychology: Learning, Memory, and Cognition, 10,* 483–495.

Allard, F., & Burnett, N. (1985) Skill in sport. *Canadian Journal of Psychology, 2,* 14–21.

Allard, F., Graham, S., & Paarsula, M. E. (1980). Perception in sport: Basketball. *Journal of Sport Psychology, 2,* 15–21.

Allard, F., & Starkes, J. (1980). Perception in sport: Volleyball. *Journal of Sport Psychology, 2,* 22–23.

Anderson, J. R. (1982). Acquisition of cognitive skill. *Psychological Review, 89,* 369–406.

Atkinson, R., & Shiffrin, R. (1968). Human memory: A proposed system and its control process. In K. Spence & J. Spence (Eds.), *The psychology of learning and motivation* (Vol. 2, pp. 90–197). New York: Academic Press.

Bard, C., & Fleury, M. (1976). Analysis of visual search activity during sport problem situations. *Journal of Human Movement Studies, 3,* 214–222.

———. (1981). Considering eye movement as a predictor of attainment. In I. M. Cockerill & W. W. MacGillivary (Eds.), *Vision and sport* (pp. 28–41). Cheltonham, England: Stanley Thomas.

Barrett, S., & Shepp, B. (1988). Developmental changes in attentional skills: The effect of irrelevant variations on encoding and response selection. *Journal of Experimental Child Psychology, 45,* 382–399.

Berliner, D. C. (1986). In pursuit of the expert pedagogue. *Education Researcher, 15*(7), 5–13.

Bjorklund, D. (1985). The role of conceptual knowledge in the development of organization in children's memory. In C. Brainerd & M. Pressley (Eds.), *Basic processes in memory development: Progress in cognitive development research* (pp. 103–142). New York: Springer-Verlag.

Bjorklund, D., & Buchanan, J. (1989). Developmental and knowledge base differences in the acquisition and extension of a memory strategy. *Journal of Experimental Child Psychology, 48,* 451–471.

Bjorklund, D., & Thompson, B. (1983). Category typicality effects in children's memory performance: Qualitative and quantitative differences in the processing of category information. *Journal of Experimental Child Psychology, 35,* 329–344.

Brown, A., & Deloach, J. (1978). Skills, plans, and self-regulation. In R. Siegler (Ed.), *Children's thinking: What develops?* (pp. 3–35). Hillsdale, NJ: Erlbaum.

Bryant, P. (1968). Comments on the design of developmental studies of cross-modal matching and cross-modal transfer. *Cortex, 4,* 127–137.

Campos, W., & Gallagher, J. (1991). *Knowledge base and sport skill performance.* Paper presented at the meeting of the American Alliance for Health, Physical Education, Recreation and Dance, San Francisco, CA.

Chase, W. G., & Simon, H. A. (1973). Perception in chess. *Cognitive Psychology, 4,* 55–81.

Chi, M. (1976). Short-term memory limitations in children: Capacity of processing deficits? *Memory and Cognition, 4,* 559–572.

———. (1977). Age differences in memory span. *Journal of Experimental Child Psychology, 23,* 266–281.

———. (1978). Knowledge structures and memory development. In R. Siegler (Ed.), *Children's thinking: What develops?* (pp. 73–105). Hillsdale, NJ: Erlbaum.

———. (1981). Knowledge development and memory performance. In M. Friedman, J. Das, & N. O'Connor (Eds.), *Intelligence and learning* (pp. 221–229). New York: Plenum Press.

———. (1982). Knowledge development and memory performance. In M. Friedman, J. Das, & N. O'Connor (Eds.), *Intelligence and learning* (pp. 221–230). New York: Plenum Press.

———. (1985) Interactive roles of knowledge and strategies in the development of organized sorting and recall. In S. Chipman, J. Segal, & R. Glaser (Eds.), *Thinking and learning skills: Vol 2 Research and open questions* (pp. 457–483). Hillsdale, NJ: Erlbaum.

Chi, M., Feltovich, P. J., & Glaser, R. (1981). Categorizations and representation of physics problems by experts and novices. *Cognitive Science, 5,* 121–152.

Chi, M., & Koeske, R. D. (1983). Network representation of a child's dinosaur knowledge. *Developmental Psychology, 19,* 29–39.

Chiesi, H. L., Spilich, G. J., & Voss, J. F. (1979). Acquisition of domain related information in relation to high and low domain knowledge. *Journal of Verbal Learning and Verbal Behavior, 18,* 257–273.

Craik, F., & Lockhart, R. (1972). Levels of processing: A framework for memory research. *Journal of Verbal Learning and Verbal Behavior, 11,* 671–684.

Davis, C. M., Thomas, K. T., & Thomas, J. R. (1991). *Relations between knowledge and expertise in breaststroke swimming.* A paper presented at the Annual Meeting of the North American Society for the Psychology of Sport and Physical Activity, June 15, 1991, Asilomar, CA.

DelRio, L. (1989). *Content knowledge: Its influence on baseball performance at four age levels.* Unpublished doctoral dissertation, University of Pittsburgh.

Dempster, F. (1988). Short-term memory development in childhood and adolescence. In C. Brainerd & M. Pressley (Eds.), *Basic processes in memory development: Progress in cognitive development research* (pp. 209–248). New York: Springer-Verlag.

Dunham, P., & Reid, D. (1987). Information processing: Effect of stimulus speed variation on coincidence-anticipation of children. *Journal of Human Movement Studies, 13,* 151–156.

Ericsson, K. A., & Simon, H. A. (1984). *Protocol analysis: Verbal reports as data.* Cambridge, MA: MIT Press.

Fabricius, W., & Cavalier, L. (1989). The role of causal theories about memory in young children's memory strategy choice. *Child Development, 60,* 298–308.

Fitts, P. M., & Posner, M. I. (1967). *Human performance.* Belmont, CA: Brooks/Cole.

Flavell, J. (1970). *Cognitive development.* Englewood Cliffs, NJ: Prentice-Hall.

French, K. E., Nevett, M. E., McPherson, S. L., & Spurgeon, J. H. (in preparation). *Development of procedural knowledge in baseball.* Manuscript in preparation, University of South Carolina.

French, K. E., & Thomas, J. R. (1987). The relation of knowledge development to children's basketball performance. *Journal of Sport Psychology, 9,* 15–32.

Gallagher, J. (1980). *Adult-child motor performance differences: A developmental perspective of control processing deficits.* Doctoral dissertation, Louisiana State University.

Gallagher, J., & Fisher, J. (1983). A developmental investigation of the effects of grouping on memory capacity. In C. Branta & D. Feltz (Eds.), *Psychology of motor behavior and sport* (Abstracts from NASPSPA and CSPSLP, p. 60). East Lansing, MI: Michigan State University.

Gallagher, J., & Thomas, J. (1984). Rehearsal strategy effects on developmental differences for recall of a movement series. *Research Quarterly for Exercise and Sport, 55,* 123–128.

———. (1986). Developmental effects of grouping and recoding on learning a movement series. *Research Quarterly for Exercise and Sport, 57,* 117–127.

Garland, D. J. (1989). *The nature of chunking in recall of schematic sport diagrams: Perceptual chunking or conceptual chunking.* Unpublished doctoral dissertation, University of Georgia, Athens.

Guttentag, R. (1989). Age differences in dual-task performance procedures assumptions and results. *Developmental Review, 9,* 146–170.

Guttentag, R., & Ornstein, P. (1990). Attentional capacity and children's memory strategy use. In J. Ennis (Ed.), *The development of attention: Research and theory* (pp. 305–319). North-Holland: Elsevier Science Publishers.

Helsen, W., & Bard, C. (1989). *The relation between expertise and visual information processing in sport.* A paper presented at the International Conference on Youth, Leisure, Physical Activity, and Kinathropometry IV, Brussels, Belgium.

Johnson, D. L. (1991). *Off the ball decision making in soccer.* Unpublished master's thesis, University of South Carolina.

Johnson, D. L., French, K. E., & Spurgeon, J. H. (1992, March). *Age differences in the speed and accuracy of decision making among experienced soccer players.* A paper presented at the annual meeting of the American Alliance for Health, Physical Education, Recreation and Dance, Indianapolis, IN.

Jones, C. M., & Miles, T. R. (1978). Use of advance cues in predicting the flight of a lawn tennis ball. *Journal of Human Movement Studies, 4,* 231–235.

Kail, R. (1988). Developmental functions for speeds of cognitive processes. *Journal of Experimental Child Psychology, 45,* 339–364.

Kay, D. B., & Ruskin, E. M. (1990). The development of attentional control mechanisms. In J. Ennis (Ed.), *The development of attention: Research and theory* (pp. 227–244). North-Holland: Elsevier Science Publishers.

Ladewig, I., & Gallagher, J. (1992). *Development of selective attention strategies in children.* Paper presented at the Annual Convention of North American Society for the Psychology of Sport and Physical Activity. Pittsburgh, PA.

Lorch, E., Anderson, D., & Well, A. (1984). Effects of irrelevant information on speeded classification tasks: Interference is reduced by habituation. *Journal of Experimental Psychology: Human Perception and Performance, 10,* 850–864.

Lorch, E., & Horn, D. (1986). Habituation of attention to irrelevant stimuli in elementary school children. *Journal of Experimental Child Psychology, 41,* 184–197.

Masser, L. (1993). Critical cues help first grade student's achievement in handstands and forward rolls. *Journal of Teaching in Physical Education, 12,* 301–312.

McPherson, S. L. (1991, June). *Changes in knowledge content and structure in adult beginner tennis players: A longitudinal study.* A paper presented at the Annual Meeting of the North American Society for the Psychology of Sport and Physical Activity, Asilomar, CA.

———. (1993a). The influence of player experience on problem solving during batting preparation in baseball. *Journal of Sport and Exercise Psychology, 15,* 304–325.

———. (1993b). Knowledge representation and decision-making in sport. In J. L. Starkes & F. Allard (Eds.), *Cognitive issues in motor expertise* (pp. 159–188). Amsterdam: Elsevier.

———. (1994). The development of sport expertise: Mapping the tactical domain. *Quest, 46,* 223–240.

McPherson, S. L., Dovenmuehler, A., & Murray, M. (1992). *Player differences in representation of strategic knowledge and use during a modified volleyball game situation.* A paper presented at the Annual Meeting of the North American Society for the Psychology of Sport and Physical Activity, Pittsburgh, PA.

McPherson, S. L., & French, K. E. (1991). Changes in cognitive strategies and motor skill in tennis. *Journal of Sport and Exercise Psychology, 13,* 26–41.

McPherson, S. L., & Thomas, J. R. (1989). Relation of knowledge in boy's tennis: Age and expertise. *Journal of Experimental Child Psychology, 48,* 190–211.

Millar, S. (1974). Tactile short-term memory by blind and sighted children. *British Journal of Psychology, 65,* 253–263.

Miller, M. (1990). *The use of labeling to improve movement recall involving learning-disabled children.* Doctoral dissertation, University of Pittsburgh.

Murphy, G., & Wright, J. (1984). Changes in conceptual structure with expertise: Differences between real-world experts and novices. *Journal of Experimental Psychology: Learning, Memory, and Cognition, 190,* 144–155.

Nevett, M. E., French, K. E., Spurgeon, J. H., Rink, J. E., & Graham, K. C. (1993, March). *Skill and cognitive contributions to children's baseball performance across age and player positions.* A paper presented at the Annual Meeting of the American Alliance for Health, Physical Education, Recreation, and Dance, Washington, DC.

Ornstein, P., Baker-Ward, L., & Naus, M. (1988). The development of mnemonic skill. In F. Weinert & M. Perlmutter (Eds.), *Memory development: Universal changes and individual differences* (pp. 31–50). Hillsdale, NJ: Erlbaum.

Ornstein, P., & Naus, M. (1985). Effects of knowledge base on children's memory strategies. In H. Reese (Ed.), *Advances in child development and behavior* (pp. 113–148). New York: Academic Press.

Paris, S. (1988). Motivated forgetting. In F. E. Weinert & M. Perlmutter (Eds.), *Memory development: Universal changes and individual differences.* Hillsdale, NJ: Erlbaum.

Piaget, J. (1969). *On the development of memory and identity.* Worchester, MA: Clark University Press and Barre.

Rabinowitz, M. (1988). On teaching cognitive strategies: The influence of accessibility of conceptual knowledge. *Contemporary Educational Psychology, 13,* 229–235.

Rao, N., & Moley, B. (1989). Producing memory strategy maintenance and generalization by explicit or implicit training of memory knowledge. *Journal of Experimental Child Psychology, 48,* 335–352.

Rees, R. (1987). *The manual of soccer coaching.* Spring, TX: Annbon, Inc.

Reid, G. (1980). The effects of motor strategy instruction in the short-term memory of the mentally retarded. *Journal of Motor Behavior, 12,* 221–227.

Reisberg, D., Barron, J., & Kemler, D. (1980). Overcoming Stroop interference: The effects of practice on distractor potency. *Journal of Experimental Psychology: Human Perception and Performance, 6,* 140–150.

Ross, A. (1976). *Psychological aspects of learning disabilities and reading disorders.* New York: McGraw-Hill.

Schneider, W., & Sodian, B. (1988). Metamemory—memory behavior relationships in young children: Evidence from a memory-for-location task. *Journal of Experimental Child Psychology, 45,* 209–233.

Schroeder, R. (1981). *The effects of rehearsal on information processing efficiency of severely/profoundly retarded normal individuals.* Unpublished doctoral dissertation, Louisiana State University, Baton Rouge, LA.

Shepp, B., Barrett, S., & Kolbert, L. (1987). The development of selective attention: Holistic perception versus resource allocation. *Journal of Experimental Child Psychology, 43,* 159–180.

Starkes, J. L., (1987). Skill in field hockey: The nature of the cognitive advantage. *Journal of Sport Psychology, 9,* 146–160.

Starkes, J. L., Deakin, J. M., Lindley, S., & Crisp, F. (1987). Motor versus verbal recall of ballet sequences by young expert dancers. *Journal of Sport Psychology, 9,* 222–230.

Stratton, R. (1978). Information processing deficits in children's motor performance: Implications for instruction. *Motor Skills: Theory into Practice, 3,* 49–55.

Thomas, J., French, K., & Humphries, C. (1986). Knowledge development and sport skill performance: Directions for motor behavior research. *Journal of Sport Psychology, 48,* 592–597.

Thomas, J., Gallagher, J., & Purvis, G. (1981). Reaction time and anticipation time: Effects of development. *Research Quarterly for Exercise and Sport, 52,* 359–367.

Thomas, J., & Stratton, R. (1977). Effect of divided attention on children's rhythmic response. *Research Quarterly, 48,* 428–435.

Thomas, K., & Thomas, J. (1987). Perceptual development and its differential influence on limb positioning under two movement conditions in children. In J. E. Clark (Ed.), *Advances in motor development research* (pp. 83–96). Baltimore: AMS Press.

Thomas, K. T., & Lee, C. (1992). *A description of skill, knowledge, selected fitness measures and golf play in women over 50 years of age.* A paper presented at the Annual Meeting of the North American Society for Psychology of Sport and Physical Activity, June 12, 1992, Pittsburgh, PA.

Tipper, S., Bourque, T., Anderson, S., & Brehaur, J. (1989). Mechanisms of attention: A developmental study. *Journal of Experimental Child Psychology, 48,* 353–378.

Tipper, S., MacQueen, G., & Brehaut, J. (1988). Negative priming between response modalities: Evidence for the central locus of inhibition in selective attention. *Perception and Psychophysics, 43,* 42–52.

VanDyne, H. (1973). Foundations of tactical perception in three to seven year olds. *Journal of the Association of Perception, 8,* 1–9.

Vickers, J. N. (1986). The resequencing task: Determining expert-novice differences in the organization of a movement sequence. *Research Quarterly for Exercise and Sport, 57,* 260–264.

Weiss, M. (1983). Modeling and motor performance: A developmental perspective. *Research Quarterly for Exercise and Sport, 54,* 190–197.

Weiss, M., & Klint, K. (1987). "Show and tell" in the gymnasium: An investigation of developmental differences in modeling and verbal rehearsal of motor skills. *Research Quarterly for Exercise and Sport, 58,* 234–241.

Williams, H. (1983). *Perceptual and motor development.* Englewood Cliffs, NJ: Prentice-Hall.

Williams, H., Temple, J., & Bateman, J. (1979). A test battery to assess intrasensory and intersensory development of young children. *Perceptual and Motor Skills, 48,* 643–659.

Winther, K., & Thomas, J. (1981). Developmental differences in children's labeling of movement. *Journal of Motor Behavior, 13,* 77–90.

21

COMPETITIVE ANXIETY: SOURCES, CONSEQUENCES, AND INTERVENTION STRATEGIES

—Frank L. Smoll and Ronald E. Smith

Athletic competition places numerous demands on the participants' physical and psychological resources. Consequently, it is not surprising that three fundamental requirements of sports have considerable importance for psychosocial development. First, sports involve the demonstration of athletic prowess, which is a highly prized attribute among children and youth. Second, an opportunity for comparison of athletic ability with that of peers exists, which provides athletes with information about their physical competence. Third, youth sport participants are extensively evaluated by highly significant people, including coaches, parents, and peers (Brustad, this volume; Passer, 1988; Scanlan, this volume). These features of the athletic environment not only attract youngsters to sports but also serve as potential sources of stress. The physical and mental tests that are opportunities and challenges to some can be psychological threats to others. Some athletes have a positive drive to succeed; they regard pressure situations as challenges and rise to the occasion. Others, unfortunately, are motivated primarily by a fear of failing. When faced with the trials of competition, they are likely to be paralyzed by their fear and to "choke."

Perhaps because of the commonly held belief that the sport setting is highly stressful, youth sport authorities have been concerned with understanding the nature of stress, its antecedents, its consequences, and methods for alleviating it. This concern was reflected in the results of a questionnaire administered to sport psychologists and to nonschool youth sport coaches and administrators; "competitive stress placed on young athletes" and "helping young athletes cope with competitive stress" were among the five topics rated most important for study (Gould, 1982). In view of this, it is not surprising that competitive stress in youth sports has been the focus of considerable empirical attention.

This chapter begins with an analysis of the dynamics of competitive anxiety within the framework of a conceptual model of the stress process. We then discuss the determinants of athletic stress. Next the consequences of stress for young athletes are addressed. Consideration is then given to the question of whether sports are too stressful for youngsters. Finally, we present several intervention strategies that are designed to reduce stress in youth sports.

The Dynamics of Athletic Stress

Although numerous models and definitions of psychological stress have been proposed, some recurrent themes appear and a basic attempt at integration can be made. The term *stress* is used in two different but related ways. First, it is used in relation to situations that tax the physical and/or psychological capabilities of the individual (R. S. Lazarus & Folkman, 1984). For example, running a race against a superior opponent may be referred to as a stressor. The focus here is on the balance between the demands of the situation and on the personal and social resources of the person to cope with these demands. Such situations are likely to be labeled stressful when their demands test or exceed the resources of a person. The second use of the term stress refers to the individual's cognitive, emotional, and behavioral responses to situational demands. For example, "We have an important game tonight, and I feel nervous and uptight about it." Clearly the two uses of the word are not synonymous, for people vary widely in how "stressful" they find the same objective situations to be, as well as in their idiosyncratic responses to stressful situations. In our discussion, we use the term in the second sense to refer to a range of aversive emotional states, such as anxiety, depression, and anger.

An understanding of the nature of athletic stress may be facilitated by briefly exploring the factors that interact to produce it. Figure 21.1 presents a conceptual model of stress that encompasses relations among (a) the situation, (b) the person's cognitive appraisal of various aspects of the transaction between the person and the situation, (c) physiologic responses, and (d) instrumental behaviors (R. E. Smith, 1986a). Each of these components is, in turn, influenced by personality and motivational variables.

The Situational Component

The first component of the model, the *situation,* involves interactions between demands and personal and environmental resources. Demands can be external, as when an athlete confronts a strong opponent in an important contest, or they can have an internal origin in the form of desired goals, personal performance standards relating to values or commitments, or unconscious motives and conflicts. Resources include personal characteristics of the athlete that contribute to coping with the demands, as well as people in the social environment who provide help and support. Stress results from a significant imbalance between demands and resources. When demands are not met, costs in the form of anxiety, guilt, anger, and self-derogation may occur.

Stress is usually thought to occur in "overload" situations, where demands greatly exceed resources. However, psychological stress can also result when resources greatly exceed demands, or when the person is not challenged to use his or her resources. Feelings of boredom, stagnation, and staleness are common responses to this state of affairs. A condition of "underload" may also take a toll on a young athlete. Thus, both over- and undertaxing situations have been hypothesized to cause athletes to burn out (R. E. Smith, 1986b).

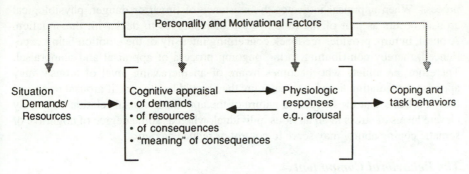

FIGURE 21.1

A conceptual model of stress showing hypothesized relations among situational, cognitive, physiologic, and behavioral components. Motivational and personality variables are assumed to affect and interact with each of the components.

Note. From "A Component Analysis of Athletic Stress" by R.E. Smith. In *Sport for Children and Youth: 1984 Olympic Scientific Congress Proceedings, Vol. 10* (p. 108) by M.R. Weiss and D. Gould (Eds.). Champaign, IL: Human Kinetics Publishers. Copyright 1986 by Human Kinetics Publishers. Reprinted by permission.

The Cognitive Component

Of all the components of the stress model, *cognitive appraisal* may be the most important. Although athletes often view their emotional reactions as being triggered directly by situational demands, situations usually exert their effects through the intervening influence of thoughts (R. S. Lazarus, 1982; C. A. Smith & Ellsworth, 1985). Through their own thought processes, people create the psychological reality to which they respond. In other words, what people tell themselves about situations and about their ability to cope with situational demands influences their emotional responses. Cognitive appraisal processes play a central role in understanding stress because the nature and intensity of emotional responses are a function of at least four different elements: appraisal of the situational demands; appraisal of the resources available to deal with them; appraisal of the nature and likelihood of potential consequences if the demands are not met; and the personal meaning of those consequences, which derive from the person's belief system, self-concept, and conditions of self-worth.

It is important to note that excessive or inappropriate stress responses can result from errors in any of the cognitive appraisal elements. For example, an athlete with low self-confidence may misappraise the balance between demands and resources so that failure seems imminent. Likewise, appraisal errors may occur in relation to the subjective likelihood of the potential consequences, as when an athlete anticipates that the worst is certain to happen. Finally, personal belief systems and internalized standards influence the ultimate meaning of the situation for the athlete. For example, an athlete who believes that his or her self-worth depends on success will attach a different meaning to sport outcomes than will an athlete who can divorce self-worth from success or failure. Many young athletes appear to be victimized by irrational beliefs concerning the meaning and importance of success and approval of others, and such beliefs predispose them to inappropriate stress reactions.

The Physiologic Component

Physiologic responses are linked in a bidirectional or reciprocal fashion to cognitive appraisal and thus constitute another aspect of the mediational portion of the stress process. When appraisal indicates the existence of threat or danger, physiological arousal occurs as part of the mobilization of resources to deal with the situation. Arousal, in turn, provides feedback concerning intensity of the emotion being experienced, thereby contributing to the ongoing process of appraisal and reappraisal. Therefore, an athlete who becomes aware of an increasing level of arousal may appraise the situation as more threatening than would be the case if arousal remained low. It follows that the reciprocal nature of the appraisal-arousal relation can easily elevate levels of stress in an anxious individual, whereas some degree of cognitive or somatic coping ability may serve to control or reduce anxiety.

The Behavioral Component

The fourth component of the model consists of output *behaviors* that constitute the person's attempt to cope with a given situation. The model emphasizes that task-oriented, social, and other classes of coping behaviors are mediated by cognitive appraisal processes and by the nature and intensity of physiologic responses that may occur. Furthermore, the adequacy, or success, of these behaviors affects the balance between demands and resources as well as the ongoing appraisal process.

This component analysis of stress indicates that a variety of elements interact with one another in complex ways. A change in any one of the components can influence all of the others, and all of the components can be strongly influenced by *personality and motivational factors.* Individual differences in personality and motivation influence the kinds of situations to which people expose themselves; the manner in which internal and external stimuli, as well as response capabilities and the meaning of potential consequences, are appraised; the intensity and duration of physiologic reactions; and the ways in which people attempt to cope with the situation as perceived.

Determinants of Athletic Stress

A substantial amount of research has been devoted to examining situational and intrapersonal factors associated with the anxiety young athletes experience prior to, during, and following competitive events. Most of the field studies investigating pre- and postcompetition anxiety have employed variations of the following methodological paradigm: Individual difference factors (e.g., competitive trait anxiety, self-esteem) thought to be predictive of anxiety were assessed several weeks before a competitive event. On the day of competition, characteristic pregame thoughts and worries as well as youngsters' perceptions of adults were assessed a few hours before the contest. Ten to 20 minutes prior to the event, young athletes completed measures of personal and team performance expectancies and either the State Anxiety Inventory for Children (Spielberger, 1973) or the children's version of the Competitive State Anxiety Inventory-1 (Martens et al., 1980). Postevent measures of state anxiety and assessments of the amount of fun experienced during the competition were made immediately after the contest. A smaller number of studies have employed psychophysiological measures to assess arousal during actual youth sport competition. The findings are highlighted in the next sections and are discussed in greater detail elsewhere (see Passer, 1988; Smith & Smoll, 1990).

Precompetition Anxiety: Situational Factors

Research has been conducted to determine whether certain types of sports are more anxiety-inducing than others. The results of Griffin (1972) and those of Simon and Martens (1979) are consistent in revealing that individual sports, which maximize the social evaluation potential of competition, generally elicit higher levels of precompetition anxiety than team sports. In addition to the type of sport, the criticality of the contest is another situational factor that has been found to influence precompetition anxiety. Studies have generally shown that more important events (e.g., championship games or matches) are more stressful than less important events (Feltz & Albrecht, 1986; Gould, Horn, & Spreeman, 1983b; Lowe & McGrath, 1971). The temporal countdown to competition is a third factor that affects precompetition anxiety. As one might expect, anxiety increases as the time of competition nears (Gould, Horn, & Spreeman, 1983a; Gould, Petlichkoff, & Weinberg, 1984).

Precompetition Anxiety: Intrapersonal Factors

The amount of anxiety experienced in a particular sport setting varies considerably from one athlete to another. Some youngsters, for example, may feel very anxious before the start of a contest, whereas others feel relatively calm and relaxed. This has prompted researchers to identify intrapersonal factors that might account for the individual differences. One such factor is competitive trait anxiety. In several laboratory experiments and field studies, findings consistently indicated that prior to competition, high competitive trait anxious boys and girls experience higher state anxiety than low competitive trait anxious children (Gill & Martens, 1977; Martens & Gill, 1976; Scanlan & Lewthwaite, 1984; Scanlan & Passer, 1978, 1979). Similarly, low self-esteem children experience more competitive anxiety than high self-esteem children (Scanlan & Passer, 1978, 1979).

Precompetition anxiety is also related to several intrapersonal factors that do not represent personality dispositions. Specifically, research with team (soccer) and individual (wrestling) sports has revealed that young athletes who experience high levels of state anxiety are characterized by low team and individual performance expectancies (Scanlan & Lewthwaite, 1984; Scanlan & Passer, 1978, 1979); they tend to worry more about failure, adult expectations, and social evaluation; and they perceive more parental pressure to participate (Scanlan & Lewthwaite, 1984).

Finally, precompetition state anxiety appears to be *unrelated* to certain intrapersonal factors. Research has shown that neither gender (Gill & Martens, 1977; Martens & Gill, 1976; Scanlan & Passer, 1978, 1979), nor age (Gould et al., 1983a), nor amount of sport experience (Gould et al., 1984) influence young athletes' competitive stress.

Anxiety during Competition

As we have seen, several situational factors are related to how much anxiety youngsters experience prior to competing. Other investigations have examined how specific situational factors that accompany or occur within a particular contest affect young athletes' anxiety during competition. Lowe and McGrath (1971) examined the effects of game and situation criticality on the pulse and respiration rates of 60 boys throughout an entire season of Little League Baseball. As predicted, players showed greater arousal as the criticality of the contest increased (e.g., when opposing teams were closer in ranking, as fewer games remained in the season) and as the criticality of the situation within the contest increased (e.g., when players were on base, when the score was close). Overall, game criticality seemed to have a greater effect on players' arousal than did situation criticality, which led Lowe and McGrath (1971) to suggest that the importance of the total situation (i.e., the game) may be a greater determinant of arousal than specific events within the situation.

In a study by Hanson (1967), the heart rates of 10 Little League Baseball players were monitored by telemetry during the course of a single game. Recordings were taken when the player was at bat, standing on base after a hit, sitting in the dugout after making an out, standing in the field, and sitting at rest before and after the game. When at bat, players' heart rates escalated dramatically to an average of 166 beats per minute (bpm), which was 56 bpm above their mean pregame resting rate. No other game situation caused arousal increases that even closely approximated the levels experienced when batting.

The studies by Hanson (1967) and Lowe and McGrath (1971) provided information about young athletes' physiological reactions to various game conditions. Several laboratory experiments, however, have used self-report measures to assess children's anxiety during competition. For example, Martens and Gill (1976) and Gill and Martens (1977) had children compete at a motor skills task over a series of trials, with the experimenters controlling the won-lost outcome of each trial. State anxiety was measured during midcompetition by Spielberger's (1973) State Anxiety Inventory for Children. The findings indicated that children who lost the early trials became more anxious than children who found themselves ahead.

A final factor affecting anxiety during competition merits attention, namely, competitive trait anxiety. The studies cited earlier indicated that prior to competition, high competitive trait anxious children experience greater state anxiety than low competitive trait anxious children. During competition, a similar but slightly weaker relation has been obtained as ongoing success-failure outcomes begin to influence youngsters' anxiety (Gill & Martens, 1977; Martens & Gill, 1976).

Postcompetition Anxiety

Two major predictors of postcompetition anxiety have been identified. These include (a) the situational factor of victory versus defeat, and its various gradations, and (b) the individual difference variable involving the amount of fun athletes report having had during the event. The effects of won-lost outcomes were examined in research with male and female youth soccer players (Scanlan & Passer, 1978, 1979) and with male junior wrestlers (Scanlan & Lewthwaite, 1984). The studies found that boys and girls who lose a contest experience greater postcompetition stress than children who win. Relatedly, children who lose experience a significant increase in pre- to postcompetition stress, whereas children who win manifest a significant decrease.

In their study of male players, Scanlan and Passer (1978) also examined the relation between game closeness and postcompetition anxiety. The closeness of the game did not influence the postgame anxiety of winners, suggesting that a victory by any margin was sufficient to minimize anxiety. Game closeness, however, did affect losers' anxiety. Boys who lost a game by a very close margin had higher postgame anxiety than boys who lost by greater margins.

Because several games in Scanlan and Passer's studies happened to end in a tie, this allowed them to examine the effects of a tied outcome on players' anxiety. Players experienced a significant increase in pre- to postgame state anxiety after tie matches; they had greater postcompetition anxiety than winners but less than losers (Passer & Scanlan, 1980; Scanlan & Passer, 1978). The findings thus suggested that a tie is perceived as an aversive outcome, not a neutral one.

In addition to won-lost outcome, the amount of fun experienced while competing has been found to be a strong and consistent predictor of postcompetition anxiety for both genders across diverse sport contexts. Boys and girls who report having less fun during a game or match experience greater postcompetition anxiety than children who report having more fun (Scanlan & Lewthwaite, 1984; Scanlan & Passer, 1978, 1979). Moreover, and perhaps most important, the inverse relation between fun and anxiety is independent of victory or defeat. In other words, it is not simply the case that winners have more fun than losers. This suggests that even among losing athletes, anxiety might be reduced by making the process of competition as enjoyable as possible.

Consequences of Athletic Stress

As noted earlier, sport is an important achievement arena where ability is publicly tested, scrutinized, and evaluated. Because of this, youngsters must learn to cope with the demands and pressures of competition if they are to enjoy and succeed in sports. Some athletes fortunately develop effective ways of coping with potential sources of stress. Others, who are not so fortunate, are prone to suffer adverse psychological, behavioral, and health-related effects. Consideration is now given to the negative consequences of excessive stress.

Effects on Participation, Enjoyment, and Withdrawal from Sports

Competitive stress affects youngsters in many different ways. Studies by Orlick and Botterill (1975) and by Pierce (1980) have indicated that some children actually avoid playing sports because of anticipated stresses. In addition to influencing the decision about entering a sport program, competitive stress can detract from children's enjoyment of sports. Youngsters who play for relatively punitive or critical coaches perceive more pressure and negative responses from their mothers and feel that their parents and coaches are less satisfied with their overall sport performance. They also view themselves as having less skill, express less enjoyment from their participation, and like their sport less (Scanlan & Lewthwaite, 1986; Smith, Smoll, & Curtis, 1978; Wankel & Kreisel, 1985).

Whether stress causes young athletes to withdraw from competition is another important issue. Pooley (1980) found that 33 percent of 10- to 15-year-old youth soccer dropouts attributed quitting to an overemphasis on competition and negative coaching behaviors (e.g., frequent criticism of players, pushing them too hard).

Similarly, a study of 10- to 18-year-old former swimmers by Gould et al. (1982) revealed that more than half of the youngsters rated "did not like the pressure" as either a very important (16%) or somewhat important (36%) reason for dropping out, and many rated "did not like the coach" as a very important (20%) or somewhat important (24%) factor. In a study of more than 1,000 age-group swimmers, McPherson et al. (1980) found that too much pressure, conflict with coaches, and insufficient success were among the reasons that swimmers reported for why their teammates dropped out of competition. Finally, in a study of 8- to 17-year-old wrestlers, a theoretically based comparison of dropouts' versus participants' won-lost records, performance expectancies, attributions, and sport values led Burton and Martens (1986) to conclude that youngsters appeared to drop out when their perceived ability was threatened by consistent failure. Existing evidence thus suggests that competitive stress contributes significantly to the dropout rate in youth sports.

Effects on Performance

Because of practical implications, the manner in which emotional arousal affects performance has received a great deal of theoretical and empirical attention. It is widely recognized that stress can have adverse effects on motor skill and athletic performance (see Smith & Smoll, 1990). In empirical investigations of the stress-performance relation, sport psychologists have assessed anxiety prior to or during competition and related it to actual measures of performance. For example, Klavora (1978) obtained pregame state anxiety scores for male high school basketball players and related the measures to coaches' evaluations of the individual player's performance. The results indicated that approximately 10 percent of the time the players were overexcited, during which time their ability to function up to normal capacity was inhibited. Although results of other studies are less consistent than one might expect (Lowe & McGrath, 1971; Scanlan & Lewthwaite, 1984), it is generally held that stress causes performance impairment in young athletes.

Another approach to assessing the stress-performance relation involves having youngsters report how they feel their performance typically is affected by stress. Pierce (1980) found that 31 percent of a sample of youth sport participants and 50 percent of sport dropouts reported that various worries prevented them playing up to their capabilities. On the other hand, 39 percent of a sample of elite wrestlers (Gould et al., 1983a) and 50 percent of junior elite runners (Feltz & Albrecht, 1986) reported that anxiety and nervousness helped their performance. Thus, although results are equivocal, it appears that some young athletes feel anxiety usually hurts their performance.

Effects on Physical Well-Being: Illness and Injuries

A vast amount of research has demonstrated positive, though modest, relations between high levels of stress and the onset of a variety of medical and psychological dysfunction in children (Coddington, 1972; Dohrenwend & Dohrenwend, 1981; Rabkin & Struening, 1976; Rahe & Arthur, 1978). The unfortunate effects of severe competitive pressures are all too frequently seen in young athletes who develop stress-related dermatological and gastrointestinal problems (Nash, 1987; Olerud, 1989). Reflex sympathetic dystrophy is an extreme example of a physical malady that may be linked with athletic anxiety. This ailment involves an abnormal response of the sympathetic nervous system to an injury, such as a sprain. An entire arm or leg may swell up, turn blue, and become blotchy, and the muscles of that limb may atrophy and the bone may be reabsorbed. A sports medicine specialist, Lyle J. Micheli, reported treating this condition in 30 to 40 youngsters per year over a span of four or five years. He attributes the disorder to the stressful conditions of youth sports, stating that "very few children ever get reflex sympathetic dystrophy, but the ones who do are almost always involved in organized sports training and stressful competition, especially in individualized sports like gymnastics, dance, and figure skating" (Nash, 1987, p. 131).

In addition to the preceding, some data indicate that involvement in sports disrupts youngsters' eating and sleeping patterns (Gould et al., 1983a; Skubic, 1956). The Michigan Youth Sports Study (Universities Study Committee, 1978) provides the most definitive data on sleep disruption. This comprehensive survey included a statewide sample of 1,118 male and female youth sport participants. Twenty-one percent of the children indicated that there were times when they did not receive enough sleep because of sports. Of the athletes experiencing sleep loss, 46 percent rated worrying about performance as a contributing factor and 25 percent indicated that being upset after losing was a cause. It should be noted, however, that other sources of sleep disruption were not directly related to competitive stress. Moreover, youngsters' sleep was disrupted somewhat less by sports involvement than by other achievement-oriented recreational activities (e.g., music, drama, clubs).

The widely recognized contribution of life change to the development of physical illness and psychological distress has stimulated research on the possible role of stress in athletic injuries (see Williams & Roepke, 1993). Several studies have examined whether athletes who experience a high degree of "life stress" are at greater risk for athletic injury. Studies of college football players have shown injury rates of 68 to 73 percent in athletes who had recently experienced major life changes, compared with rates of 30 to 39 percent in athletes who had not experienced such events (Bramwell et al., 1975; Cryan & Alles, 1983). In another study of college football players, Passer and Seese (1983) obtained partial support for an association between injury and object loss (a subgroup of negative life events involving the actual or threatened loss of a close personal relationship). In a study of younger athletes, Coddington and Troxell (1980) found no association between overall life stress and injury rates among high school football players. Athletes who suffered the actual loss of a parent, however, were five times more likely to be injured than teammates who had experienced no object loss.

The most compelling suggestions of an association between life stress and injuries have occurred in studies of football players. However, May et al. (1985) reported life change units to be related to injuries in a diverse group of male and female athletes, including gymnasts, figure skaters, basketball players, and biathletes. Unfortunately, the injury data were derived from athlete self-reports rather than from medical records, introducing the possibility of reporting bias.

There appears to be a reasonable basis for considering life stress as a potential risk factor in athletic injuries. However, stressors do not affect people in a uniform fashion; some people are highly susceptible, whereas others are quite resilient. In attempting to understand the bases for such variability, researchers have examined a number of potential moderator variables. Social support (Sarason & Sarason, 1985) and psychological coping skills (Lazarus & Folkman, 1984; Rosenbaum & Ben-Ari, 1985) are among the situational and individual difference variables considered most important in buffering the impact of life stress. Results from a study involving 451 high school male and female athletes suggest that the stress-injury relation may be enhanced dramatically by a combination of poor psychological coping skills and low social support (Smith, Smoll, & Ptacek, 1990). Major negative life changes in themselves were essentially unrelated ($r = .09$) to a measure of subsequent injury (time loss from participation). However, among athletes in the lower quartiles in *both* classes of psychosocial assets, a correlation of .55 was found between the number of major negative life events experienced in the six months prior to the start of the season and subsequent injury. No other low-high combination of social support and coping skills yielded a statistically significant stress-injury correlation. Thus coping skills and social support operated as moderator variables in an interactive manner; low levels of both variables were required for injury vulnerability in the face of high life stress.

In addition to being at greater risk for injury, sports medicine specialists have observed that athletes who find participation to be stressful and unpleasant often appear to take longer to recover from injuries (May & Sieb, 1987; Rotella & Heyman, 1993). Injured athletes frequently experience depression, anxiety, and anger, but the impact of such reactions on recovery are unclear. Speculation exists that athletes who are high in fear of failure might find an injury a socially acceptable means of avoiding exposure to the sources of stress, resulting in a longer required recovery period. In other words, some athletes may find an injury to be a temporary and legitimate haven from the stresses of competition.

Are Youth Sports Too Stressful?

In approaching the question of how stressful youth sports are, investigators have employed either physiological arousal or self-report measures to assess young athletes' stress. As discussed earlier, Hanson (1967) used telemetry to monitor the heart rates of 10 Little League Baseball players during various game situations. The most striking finding was the magnitude of response shown when players came to bat. As compared with an average pregame resting rate of 110 beats per minute (bpm), the average rate when batting was 166 bpm. The highest heart rate recorded while at bat was 204 bpm; the lowest was 145 bpm. Whether this arousal reflected an aversive emotional reaction, simple excitement or elation, or something else cannot be determined on the basis of physiological data alone. Indeed, after the game, most players reported that they did not feel particularly nervous while batting. This suggests that the arousal increases reflected stress reactions for some players and more positive emotional states for others.

Several studies have relied on self-report measures of state anxiety that require subjects to rate how tense, anxious, or worried they are at a particular moment. Scanlan and Passer (1978) obtained state anxiety measures from 11- and 12-year-old boys 30 minutes before and immediately after soccer matches. For the majority of

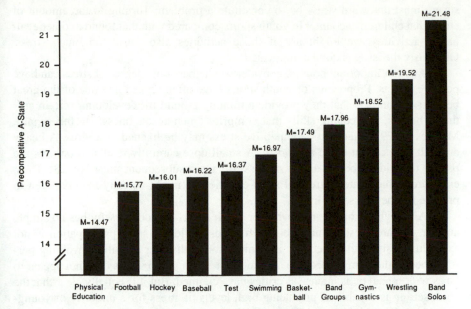

FIGURE 21.2

Children's precompetitive state anxiety in 11 sport and nonsport evaluative activities (scale range is 10 to 30).

Note. From "Children's Anxiety in Sport and Nonsport Evaluative Activities" by J. A. Simon and R. Martens, *Journal of Sport Psychology* 1 (Vol. 1, No. 2), p. 165. Copyright 1979 by Human Kinetics Publishers. Reprinted by permission.

these young athletes, only slightly higher anxiety levels were reported in comparison with preseason baseline measures. Some children, however, showed a preseason to pregame increase of as much as 20 points. Similar results were obtained in Scanlan and Passer's (1979) follow-up research with 10- to 12-year-old girl soccer players.

How stressful are sports compared with other evaluative activities in which children participate? In a landmark study, Simon and Martens (1979) administered a self-report state anxiety inventory to 9- to 14-year-old boys within 10 minutes before they competed in one of seven nonschool sports ($n = 468$) and four other activities ($n = 281$): interclass physical education softball games, academic tests, band group competitions, and music solo competitions. As shown in figure 21.2, none of the sports elicited as much anxiety as band solos. Moreover, wrestling was the only sport that was significantly more anxiety-arousing than school classroom tests. However, like Scanlan and Passer (1978, 1979), Simon and Martens (1979) reported that a minority of the young athletes experienced extremely high levels of anxiety before competing.

The studies described herein provide important information about the stress that young athletes experience, but they do not determine whether competitive stress is excessive. In this regard, Martens (1978) noted that no absolute standards exist by which to judge how great a physiological response or anxiety test score must be to indicate that a child is too psychologically stressed. Passer's (1988) analysis reveals other salient considerations. Specifically, children who experience the same operational level of stress (e.g., heart rate or anxiety score) may differ not only in how aversive they perceive that stress to be but also in their behavioral responses. Furthermore, when evaluating the consequences of stress, we might ask how many children must drop out, endure sleep loss, or undergo performance impairment for youth sports to be declared too stressful, or, for an individual child, how chronic or severe must untoward stress be to constitute a problem. Turning to the amount of stress that children encounter in youth sports compared with that found in other evaluative activities, we might ask if those activities also cause too much stress. Obviously the issue is quite complicated!

Another important point to consider is whether some degree of stress can have positive effects. Proponents of youth sports have often argued that one of the great benefits of sports is that they provide a training ground for developing certain attitudes, beliefs, and coping skills that comprise "mental toughness." In this regard, Martens (1979) stated that "competitive stress may be likened to a virus. A heavy dose all at once can make a child ill. A small dose carefully regulated permits the psyche to build antibodies and to successfully resist subsequent stress" (p. 28). Thus, exposure to moderately stressful sport experiences might actually help children to prepare for the stresses in life.

Although the question of whether youth sports are too stressful has no simple answer, research results indicate that for most children, sport participation is not exceedingly stressful, especially in comparison with other activities involving performance evaluation. Indeed, the amount of stress in youth sports does not appear to be as widespread or as intense as critics have claimed. But it is equally clear that the sport setting is capable of producing high levels of stress for a minority of youngsters. And, Gould (1993) and Passer (1988) have emphasized, if only 5 to 10 percent of the more than 25 million youth sport participants in the United States and Canada experience excessive stress, this would involve a significant number of children and adolescents. Instead of finding athletic competition enjoyable and challenging, these young athletes undoubtedly endure anxiety and discomfort, which can have harmful psychological, behavioral, and health-related effects. Because of this, priority should be given to minimizing sources of undue stress in youth sports and to identifying individuals who are at high risk for suffering adverse effects of competitive anxiety.

Stress Reduction Strategies

The conceptual model of stress not only provides a frame of reference for analyzing the dynamics of athletic stress but also suggests a number of points at which intervention strategies might be applied. In a general sense, any of the model's components may be a target for intervention. It is important to reiterate, however, that the model is a reciprocally interactive and recursive one; thus, measures taken to modify any one of the components will almost certainly affect others as well. Consideration is now given to how intervention might be directed at each of the four components of the model.

The Situational Component

The most practical and economical approach to solving stress-related problems involves using measures at the situational level to alter a situation's capacity to generate stress. Reduction of situational sources of stress is addressed relative to (a) changes in certain features of the sport itself, (b) the role of coaches in creating a psychologically healthy environment, and (c) the role of parents in combating competitive stress.

Modification of the Sport

The organization and administration of a sport program can be the focus of environmental change aimed at eliminating potential sources of stress. In this regard, it is well known that children vary greatly in physical and psychological maturation. Diverse programs should therefore be offered to provide for varied levels of athletic skill as well as degrees of competitive intensity. With adult counseling and guidance, youngsters can then select the level at which they prefer to play.

Other methods of matching children to the appropriate level of competition can serve to combat stress associated with inequity of competition and risk of injury. Some youth leagues utilize various homogeneous grouping procedures so that athletes compete against others of their own ability and size. Examples of homogeneous grouping procedures include (a) keeping the age range as narrow as possible (i.e., leagues for 9- and 10-year-olds and 11- and 12-year-olds rather than 9- to 12-year-olds), (b) using measures of height and weight in conjunction with chronological age for grouping purposes, and (c) using sport-skills tests to group participants (Martens & Seefeldt, 1979).

Organizational modification might also involve attempts to minimize situational demands that many youngsters find stressful. For example, to eliminate the stress-related emphasis on winning, some programs do not keep game scores, league standings, or individual performance statistics.

A more direct approach to change at the situational level involves modification of the sport itself. The purpose here is to decrease performance demands on growing children, thereby maximizing their chances of success and enjoyment. For example, Potter (1986) identified four categories in which sports are modified in the Eugene (Oregon) Sports Program: equipment, dimensions of the playing area, length of the contest, and rules changes. Examples of equipment changes include reduced ball size and lowered hoops in basketball and lowered nets in volleyball. In addition to reducing the overall dimensions of the playing area, appropriate scaling modifications are applied to restraining lines for particular skills, such as serving in volleyball, and shooting free throws in basketball. The length of the contest for all sports is shortened until at least the middle-school grades. Finally, specific rule changes are implemented to reduce demands on players. Examples include no press defense in basketball, no fumble recovery in football (i.e., ball is dead), and no stealing in baseball and softball.

The kinds of sport modifications described herein are highly desirable improvements. However, they may not be entirely appropriate for adolescent-level athletics. Additionally, because administrators are often reluctant to implement change, proposals to modify a particular policy or practice should include a rationale based on (a) growth and developmental status of young athletes, (b) biomechanics of young athletes' skill performance, and/or (c) systematically obtained empirical evidence substantiating the benefits of the modification (Haywood, 1986). For example, research has shown that the use of a smaller basketball results in better ball-handling skills and slightly better shooting for 9- to 13-year-old children (Haywood, 1978).

Coaching Roles and Relationships

Youth coaches typically occupy a central and critical position in the sport setting. The manner in which coaches structure the athletic situation, the goal priorities they establish, and the ways in which they relate to athletes are primary determinants of the outcomes of participation (Martens, 1978; Seefeldt & Gould, 1980; Smith & Smoll, this volume; Smoll & Smith, 1989). With specific reference to stress, Roberts (1986) and Scanlan (1986) identified coaches among the significant others who have a profound influence in shaping athletes' perceptions of achievement demands and capabilities. Thus, the ways in which coaches relate to their athletes can markedly influence how athletes appraise the situation and the amount of stress they experience.

As indicated in chapter 9 (Smith & Smoll, this volume), Coach Effectiveness Training (CET) is a proven and economical intervention, which provides instruction for coaches in creating a more positive interpersonal environment for athletes. The core of CET consists of a series of coaching guidelines based primarily on social influence techniques that involve (a) principles of positive control rather than aversive control and (b) the conception of success or "winning" as giving maximum effort. Field research has confirmed that this educational program favorably impacts the behaviors of coaches and the experiences of young athletes. Experimental group coaches who attended a preseason CET workshop were later judged by trained observers and by their players as behaving in a manner consistent with the coaching guidelines. In comparison with control group (untrained) coaches, CET coaches were better liked and rated as better teachers, and players on their teams liked one another more. Children who played for these coaches enjoyed their sport experience more, exhibited an increase in self-esteem, and had a lower attrition rate than players of control group coaches (Barnett, Smoll, & Smith, 1992; Smith, Smoll, & Curtis, 1979; Smoll et al., 1993). Moreover, youngsters who played for CET coaches showed a significant reduction in competitive trait anxiety over the course of the season, whereas a nonsignificant decline was found in players of untrained coaches (Smith, Smoll, & Barnett, in press).

An understanding of how CET affects athletes' competitive anxiety is important for both theoretical and practical reasons. In this regard, several features of the program might serve to reduce the anxiety-arousing potential of the sport environment. First, CET might be viewed, at least in part, as a social support enhancement program (Smith & Smoll, 1991), and considerable evidence indicates that social support has stress-reducing properties (Cutrona & Russell, 1990; Heller & Swindle, 1983; Linder, Sarason, & Sarason, 1988; Windle, 1992). Second, the program's emphasis on encouraging and positively reinforcing effort as opposed to outcome might also reduce stress, for it is generally recognized that increasing perceptions of personal control is one method of reducing stress (Folkman, 1984; Holahan & Moos, 1990). By encouraging coaches to focus on personal effort and improvement rather than on winning, the CET guidelines emphasize an area over which children have relatively greater personal control. Third, the more supportive environment, coupled with effective instructional strategies the coaches learn, may increase the skill level of the athletes and create a more favorable balance between the demands of the situation and the personal coping resources of the athletes, thus reducing stress (Lazarus & Folkman, 1984). Finally, a strong emphasis is placed on the outcome of "having fun," a factor that has been found to be inversely related to competitive stress (Scanlan & Lewthwaite, 1984; Scanlan & Passer, 1978, 1979). Thus, to the extent that the behavioral guidelines of the CET program are implemented by coaches, the two major sources of performance anxiety—fear of failure and fear of negative social evaluation—should be reduced. At this time, it is not known which of the four factors has the greatest stress-reducing effect, nor is it known whether the factors operate independently or in some combination. These issues await further empirical attention.

Parent-Induced Stress

Although coaches have the most direct contact with children within the sport environment, parents also play an important role. The literature on sport socialization confirms that parents are instrumental in determining children's sport involvement (Greendorfer, Lewko, & Rosengren, this volume; McPherson & Brown, 1988). Moreover, the negative impact that parents can have on young athletes is all too obvious. Some parents assume an extremely active role in their children's sport involvement, and in some instances, their influence becomes an important source of stress (Brustad, this volume; Passer, 1984; Scanlan, 1986; R. E. Smith, 1984).

What might constitute the underlying basis of parent-induced stress? All parents identify with their children to some extent and thus want them to do well. Unfortunately, in some cases, the degree of identification becomes excessive. The child becomes an extension of the parents. When this happens, parents begin to define their own self-worth in terms of their son or daughter's successes or failures. The father who is a "frustrated jock" may seek to experience through his child the success he never knew as an athlete. The parent who was a star may be resentful and rejecting if the child does not attain similar achievements. Some parents thus become winners or losers through their children, and the pressure placed on the children to excel can be extreme. The child *must* succeed or the parent's self-image is threatened. Much more is at stake than a mere game, and the child of such a parent carries a heavy burden. When parental love and approval depend on how well the child performs, sports are bound to be stressful.

Because of the harmful consequences that overzealous and unknowing adults cause, some youth leagues have banned parents from attending games to reduce the stress placed on young athletes and officials (Martens, 1978). We view this as an unfortunate example of situational change, as parents can strongly and positively affect the quality of their children's sport experience. More desirable and constructive efforts are reflected in an increasing number of publications concerning parent responsibilities toward youth sport participation (e.g., Galton, 1980; McInally, 1988; Rotella & Bunker, 1987). With specific reference to stress, *Parents' Complete Guide to Youth Sports* (Smith, Smoll, & Smith, 1989) attempts to educate parents about the nature and consequences of athletic stress. This volume provides information on how parents might teach their children stress management relaxation skills as well as how to prevent the development of fear of failure.

In spite of recent literary contributions, no attempt has been made to systematically develop and assess the effects of a sport-oriented educational program for parents. Many of the concepts and guidelines contained in CET would assist parents in facilitating their children's personal growth through athletics. For example, the philosophy of winning is as relevant for parents as it is for coaches. Indeed, the notion may be more important for parents to grasp because they can apply it to many areas of life outside athletics. The basic principles contained in the positive approach to coaching also apply to parents. By encouraging youngsters to do as well as they are currently able, by reinforcing effort as well as outcome, and by avoiding the use of criticism and punishment, parents might foster the development of positive motivation to achieve and help prevent fear of failure.

The Cognitive and Physiologic Components

Given that the amount of stress the young athlete experiences is a joint function of the intensity of environmental stressors and the way the individual appraises and copes with them, it follows that actively assisting youngsters in developing coping skills can increase their ability to deal effectively with athletic stress. Reduction of stress at the cognitive and physiological levels is the focus of stress management programs that seek to teach specific cognitive and physiological coping skills. Stress Management Training (SMT), developed by R. E. Smith (1980), consists of a number of clinical treatment techniques combined into an educational program for self-control of emotion. SMT was originally developed for individual and group psychotherapy clinical populations. The program components have been adapted to form a training package that has been used successfully with a variety of populations, including preadolescent, college, and professional athletes (Crocker, 1989; Crocker, Alderman, & Smith, 1988; R. E. Smith, 1984; Ziegler, Klinzing, & Williamson, 1982), test-anxious college students (Smith & Nye, 1989), problem drinkers (Rohsenow, Smith, & Johnson, 1985), and medical students (Holtzworth-Munroe, Munroe, & Smith, 1985).

When presented to athletes, the SMT program is labeled "mental toughness training," the latter being defined as the ability to control emotional responses that might interfere with performance and to focus attention on the task at hand. Ordinarily, the training involves six 1-hour group training sessions held twice a week, a series of specific homework assignments geared to self-monitoring, and the development and rehearsal of coping skills.

Part of SMT is directed at helping athletes to acquire specific coping skills at the physiologic level. Specifically, athletes are taught muscle relaxation skills that can be used to prevent or lower excessive arousal. The rationale underlying relaxation training is that the relaxation response is incompatible with physiologic arousal, and to the extent that athletes can voluntarily control their level of relaxation, they can also control stress responses. It is important to note that the purpose is *not* to eliminate arousal completely, because some degree of arousal enhances athletic performance. Rather, the goal of the training is to give young athletes greater control over emotional responses, enabling them to reduce or prevent high and aversive levels of arousal that interfere with performance and enjoyment.

Because of their generally superior ability to control motor responses, athletes tend to learn relaxation skills rather quickly. Acquiring such skills also helps athletes to become more sensitive to their bodily arousal, so that they can apply their coping skills before their level of arousal becomes excessive and difficult to manage.

In SMT a variant of progressive muscle relaxation (Jacobson, 1938) and deep breathing are taught as methods of lowering physiologic arousal. Individual muscle groups are tensed, slowly relaxed halfway, and then slowly relaxed completely. This procedure is designed to enhance discrimination of slight changes in muscle tension. The written training exercises are presented elsewhere (Smith et al., 1989, pp. 130–134). As training proceeds, athletes are taught to breathe slowly and deeply and to emit the mental command, "Relax," while they exhale and voluntarily relax their muscles. The mental command is repeatedly paired with the relaxation that occurs with exhalation; with time, the command becomes a cue for inducing relaxation.

In SMT, training in cognitive coping skills is carried out concurrently with relaxation training. This part of the program is targeted at dysfunctional thoughts that play a major role in the stress process. As noted earlier, stress responses are not directly triggered by the situation but rather by what people tell themselves about the situation and about their ability to cope with it. SMT thus includes two related procedures to modify cognitive processes. *Cognitive restructuring* (Goldfried & Davison, 1976; A. Lazarus, 1972) is directed at identifying and altering irrational beliefs that cause athletes to appraise the competitive situation as threatening. Dysfunctional stress-producing ideas (e.g., "It would be awful if I failed or if someone disapproved of me") are rationally analyzed, challenged, and replaced with self-statements that are both rationally sound and likely to reduce or prevent a stress response (e.g., "All I can do is give 100%. No one can do more"). In *self-instructional training* (Meichenbaum, 1977), athletes are taught to emit specific covert instructions designed to enhance attentional and problem-solving processes. In so doing, they are assisted in developing and using specific self-commands that can be employed in relevant situations (e.g., "Don't get shook up. Just focus on what you have to do").

Eventually, the relaxation and cognitive coping responses are combined into an *integrated coping response* that ties both into the breathing cycle. As the athlete inhales, an antistress self-statement is emitted (e.g., "I'm in control"). At the peak of inhalation, the word *So* is mentally said. Then, during exhalation, the athlete gives the mental self-command, "Relax," which was built into the relaxation training. This cognitive-behavioral coping response can be utilized instantaneously and as often as necessary in stressful situations.

Stress-coping skills are no different than any other kind of skill. To be most effective, they must be practiced under conditions that approximate real-life situations. For this reason, the skill-rehearsal phase of SMT includes a variant of a psychotherapeutic procedure known as *induced affect* (Smith & Ascough, 1985). With this technique, athletes are asked to imagine as vividly as possible stressful sport situations. They are then asked to focus on the feeling that the imagined situation elicits. The trainer suggests that when focused upon, the feeling becomes increasingly stronger. When a heightened state of arousal is produced, the athlete is asked to "turn it off" with the relaxation-coping skill. In a later rehearsal, antistress self-statements alone are used. Finally, the integrated coping response is used.

The SMT program ends with training in Benson's (1976) meditation procedure. The meditation technique cannot ordinarily be used in stressful athletic situations, but it is a general relaxation and tension-reducing technique that can be used in situations that do not require the athlete to perform. Many athletes find it useful in reducing pre-event stress.

The Behavioral Component

At the behavioral level, it is intuitively obvious, as well as theoretically consistent, that increasing the young athlete's physical prowess can make athletic demands easier to cope with (Roberts, 1986). It follows that training to improve sport skills should be one way to reduce competitive stress, as youngsters' anxiety reactions are derived in part from perceived deficits in ability. Specifically, feelings of insecurity and heightened anxiety might arise because of perceived lack of skill to cope with a situation. Support for this assumption is provided by research indicating that all-star athletes had significantly lower competitive trait anxiety scores than playing substitutes (T. Smith, 1983). Other research, however, is equivocal as to whether high competitive trait anxious athletes experience competitive stress due to a lack of athletic ability (Gould et al., 1983a; Magill & Ash, 1979; Passer, 1983; Passer & Scanlan, 1980). For some youngsters, increasing their level of skill may serve to reduce the perceived imbalance between athletic demands and resources, but for others skill improvement may not be sufficient to reduce anxiety. For the latter, assistance may be required in changing excessively high performance standards or distorted fears of the consequences of possible failure.

Concluding Comments

Some degree of stress is inherent in all competitive situations. Like striving for victory, it is an integral part of sports. But some young athletes experience excessive chronic stress that can contribute to a variety of psychological as well as physical maladies. This chapter has emphasized that an understanding of the antecedents, dynamics, and consequences of athletic stress can pave the way for preventive and remedial measures. Sport psychologists can play an important role in helping coaches, parents, and athletes to keep competition within a healthy perspective. Through our professional efforts, we can help to alleviate needless stress within sports and thus provide child and adolescent athletes with enjoyment and personal growth.

References

Barnett, N. P., Smoll, F. L., & Smith, R. E. (1992). Effects of enhancing coach-athlete relationships on youth sport attrition. *The Sport Psychologist, 6,* 111–127.

Benson, H. (1976). *The relaxation response.* New York: Avon.

Bramwell, S. T., Masuda, M., Wagner, N. N., & Holmes, T. H. (1975). Psychosocial factors in athletic injuries: Development and application of the Social and Athletic Readjustment Rating Scale (SARRS). *Journal of Human Stress, 1,* 6–20.

Brustad, R. J. (1995). Parental and peer influence on children's psychological development through sport. In F. L. Smoll & R. E. Smith (Eds.), *Children and youth in sport: A biopsychosocial perspective* (pp. 112–124). Dubuque, IA: Brown & Benchmark.

Burton, D., & Martens, R. (1986). Pinned by their own goals: An exploratory investigation into why kids drop out of wrestling. *Journal of Sport Psychology, 8,* 183–195.

Coddington, R. D. (1972). The significance of life events as etiologic factors in disease of children: 2. A study of a normal population. *Journal of Psychosomatic Research, 16,* 205–213.

Coddington, R. D., & Troxell, J. R. (1980). The effect of emotional factors on football injury rates: A pilot study. *Journal of Human Stress, 6,* 3–5.

Crocker, P. R. E. (1989). A follow-up of cognitive-affective stress management training. *Journal of Sport and Exercise Psychology, 11,* 236–342.

Crocker, P. R. E., Alderman, R. B., & Smith, F. M. R. (1988). Cognitive-affective stress management training with high performance youth volleyball players: Effects on affect, cognition, and performance. *Journal of Sport and Exercise Psychology, 10,* 448–460.

Cryan, P. D., & Alles, W. F. (1983). The relationship between stress and college football injuries. *Journal of Sports Medicine, 23,* 52–58.

Cutrona, C., & Russell, D. W. (1990). Type of social support and specific stress: Toward a theory of optimal matching. In B. R. Sarason, I. G. Sarason, & G. R. Pierce (Eds.), *Social support: An interactional view* (pp. 319–366). New York: Wiley.

Dohrenwend, B. S., & Dohrenwend, B. P. (1981). Life stress and illness: Formulation of the issues. In B. S. Dohrenwend & B. P. Dohrenwend (Eds.), *Stressful life events and their contexts* (pp. 1–27). New York: Prodist.

Feltz, D. L., & Albrecht, R. R. (1986). Psychological implications of competitive running. In M. R. Weiss & D. Gould (Eds.), *Sport for children and youths* (pp. 225–230). Champaign, IL: Human Kinetics.

Folkman, S. (1984). Personal control and stress and coping processes: A theoretical analysis. *Journal of Personality and Social Psychology, 46,* 839–852.

Galton, L. (1980). *Your child in sports.* New York: Franklin Watts.

Gill, D. L., & Martens, R. (1977). The role of task type and success-failure in group competition. *International Journal of Sport Psychology, 8,* 160–177.

Goldfried, M. R., & Davison, G. (1976). *Clinical behavior therapy.* New York: Holt, Rinehart, & Winston.

Gould, D. (1982). Sport psychology in the 1980s: Status, direction, and challenge in youth sports research. *Journal of Sport Psychology, 4,* 203–218.

———. (1993). Intensive sport participation and the prepubescent athlete: Competitive stress and burnout. In B. R. Cahill & A. J. Pearl (Eds.), *Intensive participation in children's sports* (pp. 19–38). Champaign, IL: Human Kinetics.

Gould, D., Feltz, D., Horn, T., & Weiss, M. (1982). Reasons for discontinuing involvement in competitive youth swimming. *Journal of Sport Behavior, 5,* 155–165.

Gould, D., Horn, T., & Spreeman, J. (1983a). Competitive anxiety in junior elite wrestlers. *Journal of Sport Psychology, 5,* 58–71.

———. (1983b). Sources of stress in junior elite wrestlers. *Journal of Sport Psychology, 5,* 159–171.

Gould, D., Petlichkoff, L., & Weinberg, R. S. (1984). Antecedents of, temporal changes in, and relationships between CSAI-2 subcomponents. *Journal of Sport Psychology, 6,* 289–304.

Greendorfer, S. L., Lewko, J. H., & Rosengren, K. S. (1995). Family and gender-based influences in sport socialization of children and adolescents. In F. L. Smoll & R. E. Smith (Eds.), *Children and youth in sport: A biopsychosocial perspective* (pp. 89–111). Dubuque, IA: Brown & Benchmark.

Griffin, M. R. (1972, Spring). An analysis of state and trait anxiety experienced in sports competition at different age levels. *Foil,* 58–64.

Hanson, D. L. (1967). Cardiac response to participation in Little League Baseball competition as determined by telemetry. *Research Quarterly, 38,* 384–388.

Haywood, K. M. (1978). *Children's basketball performance with regulation and junior-sized basketballs.* St. Louis: University of Missouri-St. Louis. (ERIC Document Reproduction Service No. ED 164 452).

———. (1986). Modification in youth sport: A rationale and some examples in youth basketball. In M. R. Weiss & D. Gould (Eds.), *Sport for children and youths* (pp. 179–185). Champaign, IL: Human Kinetics.

Heller, K., & Swindle, R. W. (1983). Social networks, perceived social support, and coping with stress. In R. D. Felner, L. A. Jason, J. N. Moritsugu, & S. S. Farber (Eds.), *Preventive psychology: Theory, research, and practice* (pp. 87–103). Elmsford, NY: Pergamon Press.

Holahan, C. J., & Moos, R. H. (1990). Life stressors, resistance factors, and improved psychological functioning: An extension of the stress resistance paradigm. *Journal of Personality and Social Psychology, 58,* 909–917.

Holzworth-Munroe, A., Munroe, M., & Smith, R. E. (1985). Effects of a stress-management training program on first- and second-year medical students. *Journal of Medical Education, 60,* 417–419.

Jacobson, E. (1938). *Progressive relaxation.* Chicago: University of Chicago Press.

Klavora, P. (1978). An attempt to derive inverted-U curves based on the relationship between anxiety and athletic performance. In D. M. Landers & R. W. Christina (Eds.), *Psychology of motor behavior and sport—1977* (pp. 369–377). Champaign, IL: Human Kinetics.

Lazarus, A. (1972). *Behavior therapy and beyond.* New York: McGraw-Hill.

Lazarus, R. S. (1982). Thoughts on the relation between emotion and cognition. *American Psychologist, 37,* 1019–1024.

Lazarus, R. S., & Folkman, S. (1984). *Stress, appraisal, and coping.* New York: Springer.

Linder, K. C., Sarason, I. G., & Sarason, B. R. (1988). Assessed life stress and experimentally provided social support. In C. D. Spielberger & I. G. Sarason (Eds.), *Stress and anxiety* (Vol. 11, pp. 231–240). Washington, DC: Hemisphere.

Lowe, R., & McGrath, J. E. (1971). *Stress, arousal and performance: Some findings calling for a new theory* (Report No. AF 1161-67). Washington, DC: Air Force Office of Strategic Research.

Magill, R. A., & Ash, M. J. (1979). Academic, psycho-social, and motor characteristics of participants and nonparticipants in children's sport. *Research Quarterly, 50,* 230–240.

Martens, R. (1978). *Joy and sadness in children's sports.* Champaign, IL: Human Kinetics.

———. (1979). An examination of some frequent concerns in youth sports from a psychological perspective. In N. J. Smith (Ed.), *Sports medicine for children and youth* (pp. 24–32). Columbus, OH: Ross Laboratories.

Martens, R., Burton, D., Rivkin, F., & Simon, J. (1980). Reliability and validity of the Competitive State Anxiety Inventory (CSAI). In C. H. Nadeau, W. R. Halliwell, K. M. Newell, & G. C. Roberts (Eds.), *Psychology of motor behavior and sport—1979* (pp. 91–99). Champaign, IL: Human Kinetics.

Martens, R., & Gill, D. L. (1976). State anxiety among successful and unsuccessful competitors who differ in competitive trait anxiety. *Research Quarterly, 47,* 698–708.

Martens, R., & Seefeldt, V. (1979). *Guidelines for children's sports.* Washington, DC: American Alliance for Health, Physical Education, Recreation and Dance.

May, J. R., & Sieb, G. E. (1987). Athletic injuries: Psychosocial factors in the onset, sequelae, rehabilitation, and prevention. In J. R. May & M. J. Asken (Eds.), *Sport psychology: The psychological health of the athlete* (pp. 157–185). New York: PMA Publishing.

May, J. R., Veach, T. L., Southard, S. W., & Herring, M. (1985). The effects of life change on injuries, illness, and performance in elite athletes. In N. K. Butts, T. T. Gushikin, & B. Zarins (Eds.), *The elite athlete* (pp. 171–179). Jamaica, NY: Spectrum.

McInally, P. (1988). *Moms and dads, kids and sports.* New York: Macmillan.

McPherson, B. D., & Brown, B. A. (1988). The structure, processes, and consequences of sport for children. In F. L. Smoll, R. A. Magill, & M. J. Ash (Eds.), *Children in sport* (3rd ed., pp. 265–286). Champaign, IL: Human Kinetics.

McPherson, B., Marteniuk, R., Tihanyi, J., & Clark, W. (1980). The social system of age group swimmers: The perception of swimmers, parents and coaches. *Canadian Journal of Applied Sport Sciences, 4,* 142–145.

Meichenbaum, D. (1977). *Cognitive-behavior modification.* New York: Plenum.

Nash, H. L. (1987). Elite child-athletes: How much does victory cost? *The Physician and Sportsmedicine, 15,* 128–133.

Olerud, J. E. (1989). Acne in a young athlete. In N. J. Smith (Ed.), *Common problems in pediatric sports medicine* (pp. 219–221). Chicago: Year Book Medical Publishers.

Orlick, T. D., & Botterill, C. (1975). *Every kid can win.* Chicago: Nelson-Hall.

Passer, M. W. (1983). Fear of failure, fear of evaluation, perceived competence, and self-esteem in competitive-trait-anxious children. *Journal of Sport Psychology, 5,* 172–188.

———. (1984). Competitive trait anxiety in children and adolescents: Mediating cognitions, developmental antecedents and consequences. In J. M. Silva & R. S. Weinberg (Eds.), *Psychological foundations of sport* (pp. 130–144). Champaign, IL: Human Kinetics.

———. (1988). Determinants and consequences of children's competitive stress. In F. L. Smoll, R. A. Magill, & M. J. Ash (Eds.), *Children in sport* (3rd ed., pp. 203–227). Champaign, IL, Human Kinetics.

Passer, M. W., & Scanlan, T. K. (1980). The impact of game outcome on the postcompetition affect and performance evaluations of young athletes. In C. H. Nadeau, W. R. Halliwell, K. M. Newell, & G. C. Roberts (Eds.), *Psychology of motor behavior and sport—1979* (pp. 100–111). Champaign, IL: Human Kinetics.

Passer, M. W., & Seese, M. D. (1983). Life stress and athletic injury: Examination of positive versus negative events and three moderator variables. *Journal of Human Stress, 9,* 11–16.

Pierce, W. J. (1980). *Psychological perspectives of youth sport participants and nonparticipants.* Unpublished doctoral dissertation, Virginia Polytechnic Institute and State University, Blacksburg.

Pooley, J. C. (1980). Dropouts. *Coaching Review, 3,* 36–38.

Potter, M. (1986). Game modifications for youth sport: A practitioner's view. In M. R. Weiss & D. Gould (Eds.), *Sport for children and youths* (pp. 205–208). Champaign, IL: Human Kinetics.

Rabkin, J. G., & Struening, E. L. (1976). Life events, stress, and illness. *Science, 194,* 1013–1020.

Rahe, R. H., & Arthur, R. J. (1978). Life changes and illness studies: Past history and future directions. *Journal of Human Stress, 4,* 3–15.

Roberts, G. C. (1986). The perception of stress: A potential source and its development. In M. R. Weiss & D. Gould (Eds.), *Sport for children and youths* (pp. 119–126). Champaign, IL: Human Kinetics.

Rohsenow, D. J., Smith, R. E., & Johnson, S. (1985). Stress management training as a prevention for heavy social drinkers: Cognitions, affect drinking, and individual differences. *Addictive Behaviors, 10,* 45–54.

Rosenbaum, M., & Ben-Ari, K. (1985). Learned helplessness and learned resourcefulness: Effect of noncontingent success and failure on individuals differing in self-control skills. *Journal of Personality and Social Psychology, 48,* 198–215.

Rotella, R. J., & Bunker, L. K. (1987). *Parenting your superstar.* Champaign, IL: Human Kinetics.

Rotella, R. J., & Heyman, S. R. (1993). Stress, injury, and the psychological rehabilitation of athletes. In J. M. Williams (Ed.), *Applied sport psychology: Personal growth to peak performance* (2nd ed., pp. 338–355). Mountain View, CA: Mayfield.

Sarason, I. G., & Sarason, B. R. (Eds.). (1985). *Social support: Theory, research, and application.* Boston: Nijhoff.

Scanlan, T. K. (1986). Competitive stress in children. In M. R. Weiss & D. Gould (Eds.), *Sport for children and youths* (pp. 113–118). Champaign, IL: Human Kinetics.

———. (1995). Social evaluation and the competition process: A developmental perspective. In F. L. Smoll & R. E. Smith (Eds.), *Children and youth in sport: A biopsychosocial perspective* (pp. 298–308). Dubuque, IA: Brown & Benchmark.

Scanlan, T. K., & Lewthwaite, R. (1984) Social psychological aspects of competition for male youth sport participants: I. Predictors of competitive stress. *Journal of Sport Psychology, 6,* 208–226.

———. (1986). Social psychological aspects of competition for male youth sport participants: IV. Predictors of enjoyment. *Journal of Sport Psychology, 8,* 25–35.

Scanlan, T. K., & Passer, M. W. (1978). Factors related to competitive stress among male youth sports participants. *Medicine and Science in Sports, 10,* 103–108.

———. (1979). Sources of competitive stress in young female athletes. *Journal of Sport Psychology, 1,* 151–159.

Seefeldt, V., & Gould, D. (1980). *Physical and psychological effects of athletic competition on children and youth* (Report No. SP 015398). Washington, DC: ERIC Clearinghouse on Teacher Education.

Simon, J. A., & Martens, R. (1979). Children's anxiety in sport and nonsport evaluative activities. *Journal of Sport Psychology, 1,* 160–169.

Skubic, E. (1956). Studies of little league and middle league baseball. *Research Quarterly, 27,* 97–110.

Smith, C. A., & Ellsworth, P. C. (1985). Patterns of cognitive appraisal in emotion. *Journal of Personality and Social Psychology, 48,* 813–838.

Smith, R. E. (1980). A cognitive-affective approach to stress management training for athletes. In C. H. Nadeau, W. R. Halliwell, K. M. Newell, & G. C. Roberts (Eds.), *Psychology of motor behavior and sport—1979* (pp. 54–72). Champaign, IL: Human Kinetics.

———. (1984). Theoretical and treatment approaches to anxiety reduction. In J. M. Silva & R. S. Weinberg (Eds.), *Psychological foundations of sport* (pp. 157–170). Champaign, IL: Human Kinetics.

———. (1986a). A component analysis of athletic stress. In M. R. Weiss & D. Gould (Eds.), *Sport for children and youths* (pp. 107–111). Champaign, IL: Human Kinetics.

———. (1986b). Toward a cognitive-affective model of athletic burnout. *Journal of Sport Psychology, 8,* 36–50.

Smith, R. E., & Ascough, J. C. (1985). Induced affect in stress management training. In S. R. Burchfield (Ed.), *Stress: Psychological and physiological interactions* (pp. 359–378). New York: Hemisphere.

Smith, R. E., & Nye, S. L. (1989). A comparison of induced affect and covert rehearsal in the acquisition of stress-management coping skills. *Journal of Counseling Psychology, 36,* 17–23.

Smith, R. E., & Smoll, F. L. (1990). Sport performance anxiety. In H. Leitenberg (Ed.), *Handbook of social and evaluation anxiety* (pp. 417–454). New York: Plenum.

———. (1991). Behavioral research and intervention in youth sports. *Behavior Therapy, 22,* 329–344.

———. (1995). The coach as a focus of research and intervention in youth sports. In F. L. Smoll & R. E. Smith (Eds.), *Children and youth in sport: A biopsychosocial perspective* (pp. 125–141). Dubuque, IA: Brown & Benchmark.

Smith, R. E., Smoll, F. L., & Barnett, N. P. (1995). Reduction of children's sport performance anxiety through social support training and stress-reduction training for coaches. *Journal of Applied Developmental Psychology, vol. 16,* 125–142.

Smith, R. E., Smoll, F. L., & Curtis, B. (1978). Coaching behaviors in Little League Baseball. In F. L. Smoll & R. E. Smith (Eds.), *Psychological perspectives in youth sports* (pp. 173–201). Washington, DC: Hemisphere.

———. (1979). Coach effectiveness training: A cognitive-behavioral approach to enhancing relationship skills in youth sport coaches. *Journal of Sport Psychology, 1,* 59–75.

Smith, R. E., Smoll, F. L., & Ptacek, J. T. (1990). Conjunctive moderator variables in vulnerability and resiliency research: Life stress, social support and coping skills, and adolescent sport injuries. *Journal of Personality and Social Psychology, 58,* 360–370.

Smith, R. E., Smoll, F. L., & Smith, N. J. (1989). *Parent's complete guide to youth sports.* Reston, VA: American Alliance for Health, Physical Education, Recreation and Dance.

Smith, T. (1983). Competitive trait anxiety in youth sport: Differences according to age, sex, race, and playing status. *Perceptual and Motor Skills, 57,* 1235–1238.

Smoll, F. L., & Smith, R. E. (1989). Leadership behaviors in sport: A theoretical model and research paradigm. *Journal of Applied Social Psychology, 19,* 1522–1551.

Smoll, F. L., Smith, R. E., Barnett, N. P., & Everett, J. J. (1993). Enhancement of children's self-esteem through social support training for youth sport coaches. *Journal of Applied Psychology, 78,* 602–610.

Spielberger, C. D. (1973). *Preliminary test manual for the state-trait anxiety inventory for children.* Palo Alto, CA: Consulting Psychologists.

Universities Study Committee. (1978). *Joint legislative study on youth sports programs: Phase II. Agency sponsored sports.* East Lansing, MI: Michigan Institute for the Study of Youth Sports.

Wankel, L. M., & Kreisel, P. S. J. (1985). Factors underlying enjoyment of youth sports: Sport and age group comparisons. *Journal of Sport Psychology, 7,* 51–64.

Williams, J. M., & Roepke, N. (1993). Psychology of injury and injury rehabilitation. In R. N. Singer, M. Murphey, & L. K. Tennant (Eds.), *Handbook of research on sport psychology* (pp. 815–839). New York: Macmillan.

Windle, M. (1992). A longitudinal study of stress buffering for adolescent problem behaviors. *Developmental Psychology, 28,* 522–530.

Ziegler, S. G., Klinzing, J., & Williamson, K. (1982). The effects of two stress management training programs on cardiorespiratory efficiency. *Journal of Sport Psychology, 4,* 280–289.

22

MORAL DEVELOPMENT AND CHILDREN'S SPORT

—Brenda Jo Light Bredemeier and David Lyle Light Shields

Children's sport is a social arena brimming with moral dilemmas. As a rule-governed activity, many of the moral decisions that take place in sport concern the rules. Young sport participants must decide whether to surreptitiously violate the rules of play, whether to "stretch" the rules, whether to commit a strategically advantageous intentional foul, and so on. And even if a young athlete decides to observe the rules scrupulously, other moral decisions need to be made. Should one play when injured? Should one use aggressive but legal tactics? Should one employ harassing techniques designed to disrupt the opponent's concentration? These are just a few examples of the kinds of dilemmas the sport participant faces. A similar list could be generated reflecting the moral decisions that coaches, parents and fans, and others involved in the world of children's sport need to make.

In this chapter, our focus is children's morality. In short, we attempt to respond to two critical questions. The first question addresses the antecedents of children's moral actions in sport: What are the processes that underlie children's ethical behavior? The second question probes the potential impact of sport on children's moral growth: How does sport influence the processes and competencies that underlie children's moral behavior? With these two questions as our scaffolding, we will outline the current state of knowledge of this field of inquiry. Unfortunately the answers are quite incomplete. Most of the research has yet to be done. But the good news is that a growing number of sport psychologists have begun to address this important dimension of children's sport experience. We hope this chapter will help to indicate some directions for future research that might be pursued fruitfully.

Understanding Children's Moral Actions in Sport

Before we can begin to answer the question of how sport experience influences children's moral development, we need to have a conceptual framework for understanding the psychological processes and competencies that undergird moral behavior. The importance of beginning with such a framework can be illustrated by an interesting study conducted by Kleiber and Roberts (1981). In a field experiment with 54 fourth- and fifth-grade boys and girls, subjects were given the Social Behavior Scale (Knight & Kagen, 1977) before and after participating in a two-week "Kick-Soccer

World-Series." The Social Behavior Scale provides children 10 opportunities to obtain rewards for themselves and others. Responses are classified into four categories along a single continuum: "rivalry and superiority," "superiority," "equality," and "altruism." At the time of the pretest, it was found that those boys and girls with the most sport experience were significantly more likely to deny rewards to other children. After controlling for the initial differences in scores, Kleiber and Roberts found that the two-week intensive kick-ball experience had no reliable impact on the giving pattern of participants when all 10 test trials were considered. However, when only the last trial was examined (arguably the most significant), then the boys (but not the girls) displayed a significant decrease in generosity as a result of participation in the sport tournament. For boys, at least, the study suggested that a weak causal relationship may have existed between participation in the sport tournament and decreased altruism.

The Kleiber and Roberts (1981) study found that (a) both girls and boys who had extensive sport experience previous to the pretest were less altruistic than their peers, and (b) for boys, some evidence indicated that participation in a two-week sport tournament had a detrimental impact on their altruistic behavior. Though the study had some methodological difficulties (cf. Shields & Bredemeier, 1994), let us assume the legitimacy of these findings. What we still do not know is what psychological processes or competencies accounted for the lower scores on altruism. Did participation in sport impact on how the children perceived the task contained in the Social Behavior Scale? Alternately, did prolonged participation in sport detrimentally influence the development of moral concepts and reasoning? Or, perhaps, moral reasoning competency was unaffected but the sport experience activated other nonmoral motives that simply overwhelmed the young athletes' moral inclinations. Finally, perhaps the young sport participants intended to act altruistically but did not possess the psychological skills needed to sustain their intended action through completion.

Rest's Four-Component Model of Moral Action

James Rest (1983, 1984) has elaborated an approach to conceptualizing moral action that we have found useful. He began with a straightforward question: "What do we have to suppose went on in the head of a person who acts morally in some situation?" (1984, p. 25). In answer, Rest suggested that at least four major processes are implicated in moral action; deficiencies in any process can result in a failure to behave morally. In brief, a person must interpret the situation and the action possibilities (Process I), form a moral judgment about what should be done (Process II), choose a value (moral or nonmoral) to seek through action (Process III), and carry out the intended act (Process IV). These four processes, summarized in table 22.1, define Rest's four-process model for understanding moral behavior.

Rest's model is useful for at least three reasons. First, it renders the complexity of moral behavior more manageable by organizing moral constructs and research into meaningful components. Second, rather than dividing cognition and affect, it enables the investigator to consider cognitive-affective interactions within and

TABLE 22.1 Rest's Four-Component Model of Morality[*]

Process One

Major function: To interpret the situation in terms of how one's actions affect the welfare of others.

Cognitive-affective interactions: Drawing inferences about how the other will be affected, and feeling empathy, disgust, and so on, for the other.

Situational factors influencing component: Ambiguity of people's needs, intentions, and actions; familiarity with the situation; amount of time available; degree of personal danger and susceptibility to pressure; sheer number of elements involved and the saliency of crucial cues; complexity of cause-effect links; preconceptions and prior expectations.

Process Two

Major function: To formulate what a moral course of action would be.

Cognitive-affective interactions: Both abstract-logical and attitudinal-valuing aspects are involved in the construction of moral meaning; moral ideals are composed of both cognitive and affective elements.

Situational factors influencing the process: Factors affecting the application of particular social norms or moral ideals; delegation of responsibility to someone else; prior conditions or agreements; the particular combination of moral issues involved; preempting of one's sense of fairness by prior commitments to some ideology or code.

Process Three

Major function: To select from among competing value outcomes or ideals the one to act on.

Cognitive-affective interactions: Calculation of relative utilities of various goals; mood influencing outlook; defensive distortion of perception.

Situational factors influencing the process: Factors that activate different motives other than moral motives; factors that influence estimates of costs and benefits; factors that influence subjective estimates of the probability of certain occurrences; factors that affect one's self-esteem and willingness to risk oneself, defensively reinterpreting the situation by blaming the victim, denying need or deservingness.

Process Four

Major function: To execute and implement what one intends to do.

Cognitive-affective interactions: Task persistence as affected by cognitive transformation of the goal.

Situational factors influencing the process: Factors that physically prevent one from carrying out a moral plan of action; factors that distract, fatigue, or disgust a person; cognitive transformations of the goal; timing difficulties in managing more than one plan at a time.

[*]Adapted from Rest (1984)

among component processes. Finally, and perhaps most important, the model is built around a descriptive analysis of the necessary processes that flow into moral action. The description, however, is rooted in everyday language so that it remains as theory-independent as possible. As a result, scholars can use the model to coordinate insights from different research traditions without requiring that integrated approaches have no incompatible assumptions.

To clarify and illustrate the four processes, let's reflect on a hypothetical subject in the Kleiber and Roberts (1981) study. Suppose Phoumara finished playing the Kick-Soccer tournament and is now faced with the Social Behavior Scale. After being removed from his classroom, Phoumara finds himself in another room with an unfamiliar adult explaining an unfamiliar task. The adult explains that he is to do "a little exercise" for which prizes can be earned. By selecting from among a set of four alternatives depicted on a large cardboard chart, he can gain poker chips that he can later exchange for prizes for himself and another child in another school. Oddly, no matter which of the four alternatives he selects, he will receive three chips for himself, but the number of chips that he can gain for the mysterious other child varies from one to four. Thus, with alternative one, he gains three chips for himself and one for the other child. With alternative two, he gains three chips for himself, and two for the other child, and so on. He will have 10 opportunities to choose.

Imagine that Phoumara is internally assessing the situation. Let's peek in on his thinking:

> Hey, why did this guy pull me out of class? What's this "little exercise" really about? Let's see, what are the alternatives? Ok, I get it. No matter which one I pick, I get the same. The other kid, though, gets more or less than me depending on my choice? Who is this kid anyway? Am I suppose to beat him? Is this a game like the Kick-Soccer games? Can't be; it's too easy. Maybe it's not a contest. Then what is it? Maybe the guy's a pen salesman. I wonder if the other kid likes pens. Probably.

In brief, Rest's first process reflects a recognition that moral action builds on a particular understanding or interpretation of a given situation. Implicit in that interpretation are the actor's views of the varying alternative actions that might be taken and the anticipated consequences of those actions for oneself and for the others involved.

Let us assume that Phoumara has decided that the "little exercise" is not a competitive game and that he clearly understands the action alternatives. Let's again observe his thinking:

> Those are some nice pens, but what should I do? I get 10 choices and, no matter what, I get three chips with each choice. Let's see, that's 30 chips. Darn, I can only get the second-best pen. But I could get 40 chips for the other kid and he could get the best pen. But the other kid doesn't have to do anything. Maybe I should get him only enough chips to earn a crummy pen since I'm the one who has to do this exercise. On the other hand, why not go ahead and get the best prize for the other kid even though it doesn't help me at all? Then again, maybe I should just pick the choice where we each get three chips. That's fair, I guess.

Process II of Rest's model involves consideration of "what is right" in a given situation. Moral concepts such as fairness, truthfulness, welfare, and keeping promises are likely to be featured in the forefront of thinking during Process II.

But moral options are never selected in a vacuum, and this is indicated by Rest's third process. Let us suppose that Phoumara has decided that from a purely moral standpoint the best option is to go for equality. His reflections may continue:

> The prizes are just some pens, no big deal. Maybe I should just have some fun. Let's see, I get 10 picks. Why not mix them up. Maybe that will confuse this guy and he'll keep me out of class longer. On the other hand, maybe the other kid really would like a pen. I guess I'll stick with Option Three and get us both similar pens.

Phoumara is weighing what is really important to him in this situation. The moral values elevated in Process II compete with a host of nonmoral values for priority. Process III is about selecting a value on which to act.

Phoumara chose to act in an egalitarian manner. But a decision to act in a particular way does not always translate into corresponding action. Let's again follow Phoumara's thinking:

> Ok, Option Three is the equal reward choice. I'll just keep picking that one. Now that I've decided that, what was it I was supposed to tell Maya about Joshua? . . . I can't remember. I hate it when I forget things. Why did Mom ask me to tell her anyway? Oops, time to pick again, let's see. Yeah, option three. . . . Now, Mom's gonna be upset if I don't remember to tell Maya, . . . Oh, what was it? Time to pick again? Darn it, I think I'll go for Option 1, this is silly anyway!

Process IV of Rest's model reflects the fact that even after a moral action has been decided on, the successful completion of that action requires a number of personal skills. Such constructs as ego strength or self-regulation skills refer to what colloquially is often termed "having the strength of one's convictions." Phourmara in our hypothetical example got distracted and frustrated by something his mother asked him to do and the frustration led him to abandon his intended course of action.

We hope that this brief hypothetical example helped the reader better understand the four processes of Rest's model of morality. Even if we were successful in that effort, however, our illustration has several misleading features. First, we have presented the processes as if they occurred in an orderly temporal sequence. In reality, they may be experienced in varying order and often more than one can be operative simultaneously. No doubt there are feedback and feedforward loops in sociomoral processing; partially completed aspects of one process influence how another process is being handled, and so on (Rest, 1983, 1984). Sociomoral processing often includes detours, dead ends, and conceptual and emotional gyrations that cannot be represented in a simple model. Nonetheless, there is a kind of logical progression among the processes so that it makes sense—for purposes of analysis—to divide the processes leading to moral action in the manner described.

In addition, we have described the processes as if they were composed primarily of conscious ruminations. But a considerable amount of sociomoral processing occurs outside awareness and is not as explicit as our illustration implied. Finally, our illustration emphasized cognitive processing. Rest, however, has emphasized that each process involves both cognitive and affective dimensions, together with cognitive-affective interactions. Moral action is guided by moral reasoning that is infused with and partially motivated by such feelings as empathy, sympathy, pride, and guilt.

Four Moral Competencies

Rest's model of moral action provides a highly useful tool for exploring moral action. We believe, however, that the model can be made more useful by elaborating a tripartite description of influences that impact on each of Rest's four processes. The three main sources of influence that we believe should be systematically integrated into a model of moral functioning are: (a) contextual influences, (b) personal competencies, and (c) ego processing variables (i.e., competency-mediators). Elsewhere, we elaborate a 12-component model of moral action in a sport context that details these three sets of influences that impact on each of Rest's four moral action processes (cf. Shields & Bredemeier, 1994). For our present purposes, we are concerned with how sport involvement might influence children's moral development. To respond to this issue, we limit our discussion to four sets of psychological competencies that undergird moral action. The competencies discussed are not the only relevant ones, but we believe they are critical competencies undergirding their corresponding processes. The competencies, together with their correlated processes, are identified in table 22.2.

We adhere to the main tenets of the structural-developmental approach to psychology. In this approach to investigating human development and behavior, the active, creative, and meaning-construing capacities of the person are emphasized together with social influences stemming from the environment. Thus, in an investigation of moral action, an articulation of the cognitive and affective competencies that make moral action possible is essential. A description of a person's relevant competencies provides a window into how that person might behave when she lives up to her full potential. Sometimes these competencies can be described in structural terms. Structural competencies, however, are theoretical abstractions that can be studied and understood only through an analysis of specific contents. For example, knowing a person's moral stage is useful in understanding moral action only as that stage is manifest through particular moral beliefs, attitudes, and values (aspects of moral "content"). In the following sections, we briefly describe selected competencies underlying each process of moral action.

Role-Taking and Perspective-Taking Ability

Role-taking and perspective-taking abilities are the structural competencies that we believe most clearly underlie Process I, interpreting the context. The associated content pertains to whose perspective is taken and what information is gleaned.

To accurately interpret moral situations, a person must be able to infer from relevant cues how the situation appears to others (role taking) and how multiple views are related and coordinated (perspective taking). For example, if a pitcher considers hurling a fastball at the head of a batter, she must be able to anticipate how the batter would feel and how others, including teammates, coaches, game officials, opponents, and fans, would view the action. The pitcher must coordinate all these pieces of information to anticipate the likely outcomes of a behavioral option, in this case, throwing at the batter's head.

Role taking is really a collective name for at least three separate though interrelated processes (Kurdek, 1978; Shantz, 1975; Staub, 1979). *Perceptual role taking*

TABLE 22.2 Moral Processes and Psychological Competencies

Process	1. Interpretation	2. Judgment	3. Choice	4. Implementation
Psychological Competencies	Role taking; Perspective taking	Moral reasoning	Self structure	Self-regulation & social problem-solving skills

refers to the ability to understand that others have different visual fields from oneself and to comprehend the nature of the differences. More important from the perspective of moral action are skills in *cognitive role taking* and *affective role taking,* defined respectively as the ability to understand that others have different cognitions or affects from oneself, and to comprehend the nature of the differences. Even affective role taking is essentially cognitive, since it refers to the task of understanding or intuiting another's affective state. The intercorrelations among these different types of role-taking ability are generally low to moderate (Kurdek, 1978; Shantz, 1975).

Selman (1976, 1980) has offered an elaborate description of the development of social perspective-taking ability, and it has been used extensively by moral development theorists (e.g. Enright, Lapsley, & Olson, 1986; Keller & Edelstein, 1991; Kohlberg, 1976; Walker, 1980). Kohlberg (1984), for example, believed that a particular stage of social perspective taking is *necessary but not sufficient* for obtaining a parallel stage of moral development, though his position on the nature of social perspective taking vacillated (cf. Keller & Edelstein, 1991).

Selman defined social perspective taking in terms of the way the individual differentiates his or her perspective from other perspectives and relates these perspectives to one another. In Selman's five-level model, each advance represents a shift, qualitative in nature, in the child's understanding of persons and of the relationship between the points of view of self and others. Based on his research, Selman identified five levels of social perspective-taking ability and approximate ages. Brief descriptions are provided in table 22.3.

Selman has maintained that his depiction of social perspective-taking development fits the criteria for a universal, invariant stage sequence. That is, the stages are organized hierarchically, with each stage more encompassing and advanced than the previous stage; in addition, each higher stage represents a structural reorganization of the preceding stage based on a new operational principle.

If role taking and perspective taking are key constructs within Process I of the moral action model, then we should expect to find empirical support for a positive relation between these abilities and measures of prosocial behavior. Since the two constructs overlap and have not always been clearly distinguished in the literature, we discuss them together. In a meta-analysis of a large number of studies relating role taking (and/or perspective taking) to prosocial behavior, a positive and

TABLE 22.3 Selman's Levels of Social Perspective Taking

Level 0: Undifferentiated and Egocentric Perspective Taking (about ages 3–6)

The child is able to distinguish the physical self from other selves but unable to distinguish the social perspectives (thoughts, feelings) of other and self. The child can correctly label the manifest feelings of another but does not comprehend psychological cause-effect relations. The child assumes that another person interprets social reality in the same way as the self does and has difficulty distinguishing another's intentional and unintentional acts.

Level 1: Differentiated and Subjective Perspective Taking (about ages 5–9)

The youngster now recognizes that each person has a unique covert psychological life. This advance is based on the differentiation between physical and psychological characteristics of persons. The child can appreciate the distinction between intentional and unintentional acts. The main limitation of this level is that social perspectives are not yet able to be coordinated. The child's experience is still the model for understanding others' perspectives. Thus, if playing marbles makes the self happy, it will also appeal to the self's playmates.

Level 2: Self-reflective and Reciprocal Perspective Taking (about ages 7–12)

The youth is now able to step mentally outside himself or herself and take a second-person perspective on her or his own thoughts and action. At the same time, the youth realizes that others can be self-reflective as well. These advances enable the youth to differentiate between the self-presentation of another and the inner, truer reality of the other. The youth is also aware that each person is conscious of the other's perspective and that this awareness influences self and other's view of each other. This level of social perspective taking is prerequisite for youngster's understanding of competition.

Level 3: Third-Person and Mutual Perspective Taking (about ages 10–15)

Persons are now seen as holding organized attitudes and values that have continuity across time, as opposed to randomly changeable assortments of mental states as was true in the previous level. The critical conceptual advance is toward the ability to take a true third-person perspective, to step outside not only one's own immediate perspective, but outside the self as a totality. The budding adolescent can now view himself or herself both as subject and object. Interactions with others can now be seen from the perspective of a "generalized other" outside the interaction.

Level 4: Societal-Symbolic Perspective Taking (about age 12 to adult)

The adolescent now recognizes that there are limits to the understanding that both self and others have of themselves and of each other and that actions may arise from motives not understood by the actor. People are now seen as complex, multifaceted, and potentially internally contradictory agents. In addition, at Level 4 a new idea of personality as a historically evolved complex of traits, beliefs, values, and attitudes emerges. In terms of the coordination of perspectives, the adolescent is now able to perceive how relations can be coordinated within systems that rely on a generalized other perspective, such as legal, conventional, and moral systems.

significant relationship between the two was found (Underwood & Moore, 1982). The relationship between role taking and prosocial behavior is strongest when multiple measures of role taking and prosocial behavior are employed as indices (Elder, 1983; Kurdek, 1978).

Moral Reasoning

Moral reasoning refers to the psychological competence underlying the second process. The best-known moral stage theory is that of Lawrence Kohlberg (1981, 1984), who proposed a six-stage model of moral reasoning development. The brief descriptions of Kohlberg's stages are well known and will not be reviewed here. In fact, one problem with Kohlberg's theory may be its overexposure. Though most psychologists are familiar with the basic tenets of Kohlberg's theory and the summary descriptions of his stages, few have taken the effort to study the nuances and complexities of his theory (cf. Rest, 1994). As a result, many shallow critiques have been promulgated that do not genuinely engage the theory.

Kohlberg's important stage theory of moral reasoning development is not the only viable approach, however. For example, we have found the work of Norma Haan (1978, 1983, 1985, 1986, 1991; Haan, Aerts, & Cooper, 1985) useful in examining moral reasoning development in physical activity contexts. Elsewhere we have described her theory and research in detail and have contrasted it with Kohlberg's model (Shields & Bredemeier, 1994). For now, let us simply observe that whereas Kohlberg focused on the logic an individual applies to resolve moral dilemmas, Haan focused more on how an individual negotiates moral agreements with others that all can live with.

Ample evidence indicates that moral reasoning development is an important influence on moral action (Blasi, 1980; Rest, 1986). The importance of investigating moral reasoning, however, extends beyond the amount of variance it may explain with regard to moral behavior. A person's moral reasoning supplies the moral meaning to their action. The structure and content of a person's moral reasoning is the generator of the moral significance that a person attaches to behavior. Thus, to understand a young soccer player's decision to trip an opponent, for example, it is essential to investigate the player's moral reasoning about the action.

The Self Structure

Process III in Rest's model of moral action focuses on value choice. What type of value will be chosen, in turn, reflects the motives activated and how these are coordinated or prioritized. The self structure—the person's organized perceptions and evaluations of the self—is a dynamic psychological organization that underlies Process III. Two critical dimensions of the self structure are particularly important to the theme of moral motivation: motivational orientation and the moral self.

Motivational Orientation

Nicholls's influential work on achievement motivation focuses on how the individual constructs the value of achievement activities (cf. Nicholls, 1983, 1989, 1992). Fundamentally, different motivational (or goal) orientations involve differing understandings of the self-in-relation. All people, according to Nicholls, are motivated to experience competence. For some, feelings of competence arise from a favorable comparative stance toward others. For others, competence is self-referenced. For example, in academic settings, some students are motivated primarily by the challenge to perform well relative to others, whereas other students are motivated by the challenge to exceed their own previous performance. An *ego orientation* is one in which a person is motivated to display competence in relation to others, seeking to demonstrate superiority at the task at hand. In contrast, a concern for self-referenced personal achievement characterizes a *task orientation*.

Nicholls (1989) has maintained that "different motivational orientations are not just different types of wants or goals. They involve different world views" (p. 102). Thus, a person's goal orientation (task or ego) will correspond with a set of attitudes, beliefs, and values that are congruent with the trajectory of achievement calibration that the goal orientation defines. A person with a high ego orientation calibrates achievement through referencing self against others, and this approach to defining success is likely to correlate with a relative lack of concern for moral issues like justice or fairness. A person with a high task orientation, on the other hand, defines success in terms that are self-referenced and is likely to emphasize such values as fairness and cooperation.

Both individual differences and features of the social context influence the type of motivational orientation that a person has. In a competitive situation, most people become more ego oriented and less task oriented (Nicholls, 1989). Consequently, sports tend naturally to stimulate an emphasis on the ego orientation, which can have negative consequences for moral behavior. Moreover, the more important winning becomes, the more strong will become the contextual pull toward adopting an ego orientation. Thus, youth sport coaches may be well advised to deemphasize competitive outcome and emphasize instead the self-referenced improvement of skills.

The Moral Self

A second major construct of the self structure that we believe is crucial to a model of influences on moral action is the moral self. The moral self refers to the saliency of moral concerns in one's core identity and the specific moral qualities that one uses to define oneself. Our thesis can be stated simply: The more one defines oneself in moral categories, the more committed one becomes to living morally, and the more likely one's moral actions will cohere with one's moral judgments.

The organized totality of concepts and constructs that an individual uses to interpret the self can be called a person's self-understanding. Included in people's self-understandings are their interpretations of diverse aspects of self: one's physical self; one's activities and skills; one's psychological, social, and moral characteristics; and so on. But what dimensions of the self are at the core of self-understanding appear to vary developmentally and individually.

William Damon (1984) has proposed that during some periods of development the two conceptual systems comprising self-understanding and morality operate as distinct psychological structures with little direct bearing on one another. At other times more integration and reciprocal influence occur between the two. The relationship between self-understanding and morality has tremendous significance for Process III because moral ideals that belong to a conceptual system perceived as peripheral to one's self-understanding are not likely to carry much motivational weight.

Damon (1984) reported on a series of investigations in which he asked children a number of self-definitional questions, such as "What kind of person are you?" or "How would you describe yourself?" In addition, he probed children's descriptions of their own self-interest—what was important to them. He found that children of all ages had self-understandings that reflected some appreciation for the physical, active, social, and psychological aspects of themselves. However, regular changes in the saliency and sophistication of these different self-perceptions accompanied children's development. Two developmental trends are especially relevant to our discussion. First, as children develop they tend toward integrating and systematizing their self-conceptions. With maturity the physical self and the psychological self, for example, become less dualized. Second, though children have some awareness of all the various dimensions of themselves throughout development, the domain of self-perception that children use to define their core identity changes in a consistent developmental progression. Young children focus their self-definitions on the physical self. The active, social, and psychological dimensions of self are, in turn, favored respectively as development progresses.

The major area of focus for self-definition has important implications for moral action. Because the self is construed first physically ("I'm big") and then in terms of one's activities ("I'm athletic") during childhood, Damon contends, children's moral cognitions are only minimally integrated into their concepts of self. One consequence of the split between the peripheral "moral self" and the central "physical or active self" is that children often conceive of their self-interests as in opposition to the demands of morality. This may help to explain the inconsistencies so common in children's moral thought and action. Children may know what is right, but moral concerns are not critical to how they define who they are or what they want for themselves; consequently, moral knowledge lacks the motivational force necessary to propel moral action. A Little League player, for example, who defines himself primarily in terms of his "active" self may place little emphasis on moral concerns, and morality may quickly be superseded when needed to maintain a positive image of physical competency.

In contrast, the moral and self systems become increasingly coordinated in adolescence when self-understanding is construed primarily in social and psychological terms. The psychological focus allows young adults to define themselves morally and to develop an awareness of the ways self and moral interests are related to one another. As adolescents move toward moral definitions of self, we might anticipate an increasing tendency to choose moral values over nonmoral ones when there is a conflict among values (cf. Damon, 1977, and Gerson & Damon, 1978 for support of this thesis).

Damon's view of self-understanding is compatible with Blasi's interpretation of how personal identity mediates the relationship between moral knowledge and practical moral decisions. The role of morality in one's identity, Blasi claims, is a function of both development (cf. Damon, 1984) and individual differences. Individual differences include how important being moral is to a person's identity and which moral aspects are emphasized in one's moral identity. Mark, a high school football player, for example, sees compassion as essential to his identity; correspondingly, he refuses to act in ways he perceives to be aggressive, but he sometimes cheats when he doesn't see that as really hurting anyone. A friend of his, Tonya, sees fairness and justice as central to her self-identity; she steadfastly refuses to violate any rule but engages in aggressive acts whenever she can do so legally. Thus, people with a similar stage of moral reasoning development may accent different moral content and this may influence their moral choices.

For Blasi, moral identity is the key source of moral motivation. One's sense of personal moral integrity—that is, one's view of oneself as a moral person who both believes in and acts on fairness, justice, compassion, and/or some other moral construct—provides the motivational dynamic to choose moral values over nonmoral values. Blasi appeals to Erikson's notion of fidelity, the basic virtue that Erikson considers inherently tied to the development of identity, and suggests that the connection between moral identity and moral functioning is expressed by a perceived obligation to act with self-consistency, according to one's judgment of what is right.

Self-Regulation and Social Problem-Solving Skills

Two major clusters of psychological constructs are particularly relevant to Process IV: self-regulation and social problem-solving skills. The first set pertains to marshalling one's own interior resources for persisting at difficult tasks. The second set of competencies pertains more to negotiating problems with others.

Self-Regulation

Self-regulation skills incorporate those intrapersonal competencies related to the monitoring and managing of one's own psychology-in-action. Self-regulation skills include such interrelated constructs as ego strength, ego resiliency, impulse control, and the ability to delay gratification. The literature relating self-regulation skills to moral action is sparse, but existing studies generally support a link between these skills and prosocial or moral behavior (Alterman et al., 1978; Block & Block, 1973; Grim, Kohlberg, & White, 1968; Lind, Sandberger, & Bargel, 1981; Long & Lerner, 1974; Mussen et al., 1970; Strayer & Roberts, 1989).

Perhaps the concept that best subsumes and summarizes the self-regulation skills, as operative in moral contexts, is autonomy. According to Lindley (1986), "the underlying idea of the concept of autonomy is self-mastery" (p. 6). Autonomy encompasses an ability to define goals, to take responsibility for action, and to assert oneself, when needed, in order to not conform to social expectations or pressures counter to one's views. A player, for example, who is high in autonomy may refuse to obey a coach's instructions to take performance-enhancing drugs, commit an intentional foul, or join a fight. Not surprisingly, autonomy has been postulated by many as a central element mediating between moral reasoning and moral behavior (Erikson, 1950, 1968; Hodge, 1988; Hogan, 1970, 1973; Kurtines, 1974, 1978; Meakin, 1982).

Social Problem Solving

Self-regulation skills are necessary to deal with internal obstacles to moral action, such as paralyzing fear, fatigue, and lack of confidence. In moral action contexts, people also must be able to negotiate interpersonal problems that may arise. Social problem-solving skills are important in the process of carrying out moral action (e.g., Shure, 1980, 1982; Soloman et al., 1985). Though a number of specific social problem-solving skills have been isolated (cf. Shure, 1982; Spivack, Platt, & Shure, 1976), two in particular have been found to relate significantly to prosocial behavior: alternative solution and means-end thinking. Alternative solution thinking—the ability to generate multiple solutions to an interpersonal conflict—has been demonstrated to have a positive relationship with low social withdrawal (Olson et al., 1983a) and positive peer interactions (Olson et al., 1983b) in 4- to 5-year-olds, and peer or teacher ratings of prosocial behavior (Shure, 1980). Means-end thinking refers to the ability to articulate the steps necessary to carry out a solution to an interpersonal problem, and the recognition that obstacles might interfere with goal completion and that goal satisfaction may be delayed. Low means-end thinking has been related to psychiatric and acting-out problems in adolescents and adults (cf. Butler & Meichenbaum, 1981) and, conversely, high means-end thinking has been related to low aggression in girls (Marsh, Serafica, & Barenboim, 1981). Finally, means-end thinking has been related positively to a number of indices of prosocial behavior (Marsh et al., 1981; Shure, 1980).

Having briefly identified the key psychological processes and underlying competencies that feed into moral action, we are in position to turn to the second question: How does sport experience influence children's moral development?

Sport and Moral Development

Moral development is sometimes used as a shorthand phrase for the development of moral reasoning. For our purposes, this definition of moral development is inadequate. We are interested in investigating how sport experience influences the full set of psychological competencies that undergird moral action. Using our model of moral action, we can amplify on the question of the impact of sport on moral development by addressing four separate questions: (1) How does sport impact on participants' role-taking and perspective-taking ability? (2) How does it impact on their moral reasoning development? (3) How does it impact on their self structure? And, finally, (4) How does it impact on their self-regulatory and social problem-solving skills?

Before we turn to a summary of the literature, some preliminary remarks are in order. Most of the existent research does not allow cause-effect relationships to be determined. Consequently, we are not able to determine whether sport experience impacts on the psychological competencies undergirding moral behavior. But a number of intriguing correlations between various types of sport experience and relevant psychological competencies have been found. It is certainly possible and in some instances quite likely that a causal relationship exists between sport experience and the correlated phenomena, but this will need to be determined through use of different research methodologies than the ones employed.

It is also important to emphasize that sport experience is not uniform. The important dimension of sport experience, from a moral standpoint, is the nature of the social relationships and interactions that occur. Tossing a ball through a hoop, running on a track, or kicking a ball through two up-right posts have no intrinsic moral significance. The quality and dynamics of the social relationships and interactions, however, vary considerably from one sport to another, from one team to another, and from one level of competition to another. The impact of children's participation in youth sport programs on their moral development will vary according to the sport structure (e.g., team or individual, level of contact), the quality and style of coaching (e.g., decision-making style, motivational orientation), the social support (e.g., parental and peer inputs), and a host of other variables. This variety should be kept in mind throughout the following discussion.

Sport and Perspective Taking

The relationship between sport participation and role taking or perspective taking is relatively unexplored. On a theoretical level, we might anticipate that sport experiences promote social perspective-taking ability (cf. Coakley, 1983, 1984; Martens, 1976; Mead, 1934). Sport interactions, particularly in team sports, are predicated on an ability to coordinate actions and such coordinations, in turn, require an ability to comprehend the game through multiple frames of reference. For example, to play shortstop effectively, one must be able to anticipate what each teammate is likely to do in any number of fielding situations. That involves complex coordinations of different perspectives on the game. In addition, most sports involve a strategy component that draws on the participants' abilities to anticipate the behavior of the opponent. Successful employment of game strategy quickly spirals up the perspective-taking ladder.

Despite the potential that sport may have for promoting social perspective-taking skills, competition generally appears to impede role and perspective taking (cf. Johnson & Johnson, 1983). For example, Tjosvold, Johnson, and Johnson (1984) placed undergraduate students in dyads and assigned them a negotiation task. Some dyads were structured cooperatively, some competitively. In the competitively structured dyads, participants were less accurate in understanding each other's perspectives.

Sport and Moral Reasoning

If moral reasoning is vital to responsible moral decision making, then it is important to know whether those heavily invested in sport differ in any systematic way from the general population in their moral reasoning. Of course, the line separating athletes from nonathletes is somewhat fictitious because most people are involved in physical activity to one degree or another. But for those who are active, dedicated athletes, the sport experience can be emotionally intense, quite demanding of one's time and energy, and central to one's self-definition. For these reasons, the sport experience may provide a sufficiently potent influence on the participants' psychosocial lives to impact on the development of their moral reasoning maturity.

In one study (Bredemeier & Shields, 1984b) employing an objective measure of moral reasoning maturity derived from Kohlberg's stage theory, we found that both male and female intercollegiate basketball players were below reported college norms, though females scored significantly higher than males. Similarly, Hall (1986) found that intercollegiate male and female basketball players scored lower on a Kohlbergian measure of moral development. In a more elaborate study using Haan's model of morality (Bredemeier & Shields, 1986c), we found once again that intercollegiate basketball players of both genders had less mature moral reasoning patterns than their peers, but the same was not true at the high school level. Interscholastic basketball players did not differ from their high school peers on moral reasoning maturity. Furthermore, we found that college swimmers did not differ from nonathletes in their moral reasoning maturity.

In another study, we examined the relationship between children's sport participation and interest, on the one hand, and their moral reasoning maturity and aggression tendencies, on the other (Bredemeier, Weiss, Shields, & Cooper, 1986). Analyses revealed that boys' participation and interest in high-contact sports and girls' participation in medium-contact sports (the highest level of contact sport experience girls reported) were associated with less mature moral reasoning and greater tendencies to aggress.

In some of our research, we have presented specially-designed dilemmas that contain parallel moral problems in sport and nonsport settings to both athletes and nonathletes (Bredemeier & Shields, 1984a, 1986a, 1986b, 1986c). Beginning around the dawn of adolescence, both sport participants and students who do not compete in organized athletics begin to use divergent patterns of reasoning for the two types of dilemmas, though athletes tend to diverge more than the nonathletes (Bredemeier, in press; Bredemeier & Shields, 1984a). When structural scoring procedures are applied, the reasoning in response to the sport-specific dilemmas appears, on average, less mature or adequate than corresponding reasoning about everyday life settings.

The discrepancy we have found between life and sport moral reasoning may be one aspect of a larger phenomenon. Huizinga (1955) has described play as a "stepping out of 'real life' into a temporary sphere of activity with a disposition all of its own" (p. 8). Several philosophers, anthropologists, sociologists, and psychologists also have suggested that play and/or sport exists in a unique sphere and that entry into that sphere involves cognitive, attitudinal, and value adjustments (cf. Bateson, 1955; Corsaro, 1981; Giffin, 1982; Schmitz, 1976; Sutton-Smith, 1971). Referring to sport, Firth (1973) discusses how rituals and conventions serve to mark temporal boundaries and symbolize the reconstitution of people into players and players back into people.

If entry into sport involves a transformation of cognition and affect, then it is reasonable to hypothesize that moral reasoning undergoes some change in its underlying organization when one moves from general life into sport. The divergence in moral reasoning scores described earlier partially supports this hypothesis. We have labeled the type of moral reasoning that occurs in sport "game reasoning."

The transition in moral perspective from life to sport is attested to by numerous informal observations as well. Consider, for example, a comment by former heavyweight boxing champion Larry Holmes. Before he enters the ring, he said, "I have to change, I have to leave the goodness out and bring all the bad in, like Dr. Jekyll and Mr. Hyde" (quoted in Bredemeier & Shields, 1985, p. 23). Ron Rivera of the Chicago

Bears described the personality transformation he undergoes when entering his sport. The off-field Ron, he said, is soft-spoken, considerate, and friendly. When asked to describe the on-field Ron, he replied, "He's totally opposite from me. . . . He's a madman. . . . No matter what happens, he hits people. He's a guy with no regard for the human body" (quoted in Bredemeier & Shields, 1985, p. 24). Rivera's comment is echoed continually by sport commentators who frequently note a perceived discrepancy between the on-field athlete and the off-field athlete.

Unfortunately, we currently know little about the genesis, developmental course, and behavioral implications of game reasoning. Entry into the realm of sport clearly stimulates, at least for many, a change in moral reasoning patterns, but the phenomenon is not yet well understood. At least until we understand this phenomenon better, we would encourage youth sport coaches not to use language or techniques that might encourage participants to separate their sport experience from "real life." For example, opponents should not be depersonalized or vilified in an attempt to "psych up" youngsters.

Sport and the Self Structure

Two dimensions of the self structure particularly important to the theme of moral motivation—the dominant theme of Process III—are motivational orientation (cf. Nicholls, 1983, 1989, 1992) and the moral self (cf. Blasi, 1984, 1989; Damon, 1984).

Motivational Orientation

A study by Joan Duda (1989) examined the relationship between goal orientation in sport and beliefs about the purposes of sport participation among high school athletes. Her main findings revealed a positive association between athletes' task orientation and their view that sport should teach people such values as trying hard, cooperation, rule-obedience, and being good citizens. In contrast, athletes who were predominantly ego orientated tended to believe that sport should increase one's social status and show people how to survive in a competitive world.

One's goal orientation logically would be associated with one's view of the relative importance of moral values in an achievement context. As Nicholls (1989) writes: "A preoccupation with winning (beating others) may well be accompanied by a lack of concern about justice . . . and fairness" (p. 133). Duda empirically investigated this logical connection and found, indeed, a strong relationship between goal orientation and behaviors perceived as legitimate in the pursuit of victory (Duda, Olson, & Templin, 1991). Athletes who were more task oriented endorsed less cheating behavior and expressed greater approval of "sportsmanlike" actions; high ego orientation scores related to higher approval ratings of intentionally injurious behavior, a finding replicated with a sample of high school and college-level football players (Huston & Duda, 1992).

Dawn Stephens's (1993) dissertation work extended Duda's investigation of motivational orientations and moral behavior factors (Stephens et al., 1991). Stephens administered a test battery to 214 female soccer players, ages 10 to 14, that included a sport-specific achievement orientation scale, a measure of participants' perceptions of their coaches' motivational orientation, a "sportspersonship" inventory, and a self-report measure assessing participants' temptation to violate moral norms during a sport contest (lie to an official, hurt an opponent, and break one of the rules). Stephens found that players who described themselves as experiencing high temptation to play unfairly differed significantly from those experiencing low temptation. Specifically, players who were more tempted were more ego than task oriented and perceived their coaches as being more ego oriented and less task oriented. Also, high temptation was associated with: (a) greater approval of behaviors designed to obtain an unfair advantage over an opponent, (b) belief that more of their teammates would play unfairly in the same situation, and (c) longer involvement with current team. Stephens's work points to the need to study directly the relationships among moral atmosphere variables (e.g., perceptions of coaches' goal orientation, and beliefs about the likelihood of teammates engaging in unfair sport practices), moral reasoning level, motivational achievement orientation, and sport behavior.

The Moral Self

No empirical data are yet available on the relationship between the moral self and sport involvement. On theoretical grounds, however, it might be hypothesized that sport experience will decrease the saliency of moral concerns in participants' thinking, and then, over time, decrease the saliency of the moral self in one's self-understanding. The process of competition by its very structure tends to focus attention away from moral concerns (Johnson & Johnson, 1989; Kohn, 1986; Nicholls, 1989) and may actually positively promote cheating and aggression (Kohn, 1986). Initially, moral concerns may be only deemphasized in the sport realm, but for those who define athletics as core to their identity, the deemphasis on morality in sport may generalize to other dimensions of their lives. On the other hand, sport may be an optimal medium for learning to sustain one's moral integrity in a competitive context (cf. Shields & Bredemeier, 1994); that is, precisely because sport may tempt participants to violate moral norms, it may be a good context for practicing moral integrity. At least some empirical evidence supports the contention that physical activity experiences can help participants grow morally (Beller & Stoll, 1992; Bredemeier, Weiss, Shields, & Shewchuk, 1986; Romance, Weiss, & Bockoven, 1986).

Sport, Self-Regulation, and Social Problem-Solving Skills

Unfortunately, we know very little about the relations between sport participation and the development of children's self-regulatory and social problem-solving skills. It is possible that the kinds of psychological skills necessary for focused sport performance may transfer (particularly with transfer training) to the moral domain. If so, sport may provide a medium for learning self-regulatory skills useful to moral action, but this possibility remains theoretical. No empirical evidence supports such a link. With reference to social problem-solving skills, it is clear that informal games may provide a highly useful context for the development of such skills (cf. Devereux, 1976; Coakley, 1990), but it is less clear how adult-organized and adult-controlled youth sport programs might be similarly beneficial.

Conclusion

Does sport build character or characters? There can be no unequivocal answer to that question. Sport is a multidimensional social practice that varies considerably from one sport to another, from team to team, and from one competitive level to another competitive level. In this chapter, we have attempted to identify key variables that underlie moral behavior in a sport context. In short, these are role taking and perspective taking, moral reasoning, the self structure (especially motivational orientation and the moral self), and self-regulatory and social problem-solving skills. We have identified key literature related to each and have indicated possible directions for future research. In the interest of all children and youth, we hope that many more researchers and practitioners will pick up the challenge to explore the potential of sport to enhance participants' moral development.

References

Alterman, A., Druley, K., Connolly, R., & Bush, D. (1978). A comparison of moral reasoning in drug addicts and nonaddicts. *Journal of Clinical Psychology, 34,* 790–794.

Bateson, G. (1955). A theory of play and fantasy. *Psychiatric Research Reports, 2,* 39–51.

Beller, J. M., & Stoll, S. K. (1992). A moral reasoning intervention program for student-athletes. *The Academic Athletic Journal,* Spring, 43–57.

Blasi, A. (1980). Bridging moral cognition and moral action: A critical review of the literature. *Psychological Bulletin, 88,* 1–45.

———. (1984). Moral identity: Its role in moral functioning. In W. Kurtines & J. Gewirtz (Eds.), *Morality, moral behavior, and moral development* (pp. 128–139). New York: Wiley.

———. (1989). The integration of morality in personality. In I. E. Bilbao (Ed.), *Perspectivas acerca de cambio moral: Posibles intervenciones educativas.* San Sebastian: Servicio Editorial Universidad del Pais Vasco.

Block, J., & Block, J. H. (1973, January). *Ego development and the provenance of thought: A longitudinal study of ego and cognitive development in young children.* Progress report for the National Institute of Mental Health (grant no. MH16080).

Bredemeier, B. J. (in press). *Divergence in children's moral reasoning about issues in daily life and sport specific contexts. International Journal of Sport Psychology.*

Bredemeier, B. J., & Shields, D. L. (1984a). Divergence in moral reasoning about sport and life. *Sociology of Sport Journal, 1,* 348–357.

———. (1984b). The utility of moral stage analysis in the investigation of athletic aggression. *Sociology of Sport Journal, 1,* 138–149.

———. (1985). Values and violence in sport. *Psychology Today, 19,* 22–32.

———. (1986a). Athletic aggression: An issue of contextal morality. *Sociology of Sport Journal, 3,* 15–28.

———. (1986b). Game reasoning and interactional morality. *Journal of Genetic Psychology, 147,* 257–275.

———. (1986c). Moral growth among athletes and nonathletes: A comparative analysis. *Journal of Genetic Psychology, 147,* 7–18.

Bredemeier, B. J., Weiss, M. R., Shields, D. L., & Cooper, B. (1986). The relationship of sport involvement with children's moral reasoning and aggression tendencies. *Journal of Sport Psychology, 8,* 304–318.

Bredemeier, B. J., Weiss, M. R., Shields, D. L., & Shewchuk, R. M. (1986). Promoting moral growth in a summer sport camp: The implementation of theoretically grounded instructional strategies. *Journal of Moral Education, 15,* 212–220.

Butler, L., & Meichenbaum, D. (1981). The assessment of interpersonal problem-solving skills. In P. Kendall & S. Hollon (Eds.), *Assessment strategies for cognitive-behavioral assessment.* New York: Academic Press.

Coakley, J. J. (1983). Play, games, and sport: Developmental implications for young people. In J. C. Harris & R. J. Park (Eds.), *Play, games and sports in cultural contexts* (pp. 431–450). Champaign, IL: Human Kinetics.

———. (1984). *Mead's theory on the development of the self: Implications for organized youth sport programs.* Paper presented at the Olympic Scientific Congress, Eugene, OR.

———. (1990). *Sport in society: Issues and controversies* (4th ed.). St. Louis: Times Mirror/Mosby.

Corsaro, W. A. (1981). Friendship in the nursery school: Social organization in a peer environment. In S. R. Asher & J. M. Gottman (Eds.), *The development of children's friendships* (pp. 117–134). Cambridge: Cambridge University Press.

Damon, W. (1977). *The social world of the child.* San Francisco: Jossey-Bass.

———. (1984). Self-understanding and moral development from childhood to adolescence. In W. M. Kurtines & J. L. Gewirtz (Eds.), *Morality, moral behavior, and moral development* (pp. 109–127). New York: Wiley.

Devereux, E. (1976). Backyard vs. little league baseball: The impoverishment of children's games. In D. Landers (Ed.), *Social problems in athletics* (pp. 37–56). Urbana, IL: University of Illinois Press.

Duda, J. L. (1989). The relationship between task and ego orientation and the perceived purpose of sport among male and female high school athletes. *Journal of Sport and Exercise Psychology, 11,* 318–335.

Duda, J. L., Olson, L. K., & Templin, T. J. (1991). The relationship of task and ego orientation to sportsmanship attitudes and the perceived legitimacy of injurious acts. *Research Quarterly for Exercise and Sport, 62,* 79–87.

Elder, J. L. D. (1983-April). *Role-taking and prosocial behavior revisited: The effects of aggregation.* Paper presented at the biennial meeting of the Society for Research in Child Development, Detroit.

Enright, R., Lapsley, D., & Olson, L. (1986). Moral judgment and the social cognitive developmental research programme. In S. Modgil & C. Modgil (Eds.), *Lawrence Kohlberg: Consensus and controversy* (pp. 313–324). Philadelphia: Falmer.

Erikson, E. H. (1950). *Childhood and society.* New York: Norton.

———. (1968). *Identity: Youth and crisis.* New York: Norton.

Firth, R. (1973). *Symbols public and private.* New York: Cornell University Press.

Gerson, R., & Damon, W. (1978). Moral understanding and children's conduct. In W. Damon (Ed.), *New directions for child development* (Vol. 1, pp. 41–59). San Francisco: Jossey-Bass.

Giffin, H. L. N. (1982). *The metacommunicative process in a collective make-believe play.* Unpublished doctoral dissertation, University of Colorado, Boulder.

Grim, P., Kohlberg, L., & White, S. (1968). Some relationships between conscience and attentional processes. *Journal of Personality and Social Psychology, 8,* 239–253.

Haan, N. (1978). Two moralities in action contexts: Relationship to thought, ego regulation, and development. *Journal of Personality and Social Psychology, 36,* 286–305.

———. (1983). An interactional morality of everyday life. In N. Haan, R. Bellah, P. Rabinow, & W. Sullivan (Eds.), *Social science as moral inquiry* (pp. 218–250). New York: Columbia University Press.

———. (1985). Processes of moral development: cognitive or social disequilibrium? *Developmental Psychology, 21,* 996–1006.

———. (1986). Systematic variability in the quality of moral action as defined by two formulations. *Journal of Personality and Social Psychology, 50,* 1271–1284.

———. (1991). Moral development and action from a social constructivist perspective. In W. Kurtines & J. Gewirtz (Eds.), *Handbook of moral behavior and development, Vol. 1: Theory* (pp. 251–273). Hillsdale, NJ: Erlbaum.

Haan, N., Aerts, E., & Cooper, B. B. (1985). *On moral grounds: The search for a practical morality.* New York: New York University.

Hall, E. R. (1986). Moral development levels of athletes in sport-specific and general social situations. In L. Vander Velden & J. H. Humphrey (Eds.), *Psychology and sociology of sport: Current selected research* (Vol. 1, pp. 191–204). New York: AMS Press.

Hodge, K. P. (1988). *A conceptual analysis of character development in sport.* Unpublished doctoral dissertation, University of Illinois at Urbana-Champaign.

Hogan, R. (1970). A dimension of moral judgment. *Journal of Consulting and Clinical Psychology, 35,* 205–212.

———. (1973). Moral conduct and moral character: A psychological perspective. *Psychological Bulletin, 79,* 217–232.

Huizinga, Johan. (1955). *Homo ludens: A study of the play element in culture.* Boston: Beacon Press.

Huston, L., & Duda, J. (1992). *The relationship of goal orientation and competitive level to the endorsement of aggressive acts in football.* Unpublished paper.

Johnson, D. W., & Johnson, R. T. (1983). The socialization and achievement crisis: Are cooperative learning experiences the solution? In L. Bickman (Ed.), *Applied social psychology annual 4.* Beverly Hills, CA: Sage.

———. (1989). *Cooperation and competition: Theory and research.* Edina, MN: Interaction Books.

Keller, M., & Edelstein, W. (1991). The development of socio-moral meaning making: Domains, categories, and perspective-taking. In W. M. Kurtines & J. L. Gewirtz (Eds.), *Handbook of moral behavior and development Vol. 2: Theory* (pp. 89–114). Hillsdale, NJ: Erlbaum.

Kleiber, D. A., & Roberts, G. C. (1981). The effects of sport experience in the development of social character: An exploratory investigation. *Journal of Sport Psychology, 3,* 114–122.

Knight, G. P., & Kagen, S. (1977). Development of prosocial and competitive behaviors in Anglo-American and Mexican-American children. *Child Development, 48,* 1385–1394.

Kohlberg, L. (1976). Moral stages and moralization: The cognitive-developmental approach. In T. Lickona (Ed.), *Moral development and behavior: Theory, research and social issues* (pp. 31–53). New York: Holt, Rinehart and Winston.

———. (1981). *Essays on moral development: Vol. 1: The philosophy of moral development.* San Francisco: Harper & Row.

———. (1984). *Essays on moral development: Vol. 2: The psychology of moral development.* San Francisco: Harper & Row.

Kohn, A. (1986). *No contest: The case against competition.* Boston: Houghton Mifflin.

Kurdek, L. A. (1978). Perspective taking as the cognitive basis of children's moral development: A review of the literature. *Merrill-Palmer Quarterly, 24,* 3–28.

Kurtines, W. (1974). Autonomy: A concept reconsidered. *Journal of Personality Assessment, 38,* 243–246.

———. (1978). A measure of autonomy. *Journal of Personality Assessment, 42,* 253–257.

Lind, G., Sandberger, J., & Bargel, T. (1981). Moral judgment, ego strength, and democratic orientations: Some theoretical contiguities and empirical findings. *Political Psychology, 3,* 70–110.

Lindley, R. (1986). *Autonomy.* London: Macmillan.

Long, G. T., & Lerner, M. J. (1974). Deserving the "personal contract" and altruistic behavior by children. *Journal of Personality and Social Psychology, 29,* 551–556.

Marsh, D. T., Serafica, F. C., & Barenboim, C. (1981). Interrelationships among perspective taking, interpersonal problem solving, and interpersonal functioning. *Journal of Genetic Psychology, 138,* 37–48.

Martens, R. (1976). Kid sports: A den of iniquity or land of promise. In R. Magill, M. Ash, & F. Smoll (Eds.), *Children in sport: A contemporary anthology* (pp. 201–216). Champaign, IL: Human Kinetics.

Mead, G. H. (1934). *Mind, self, and society.* Chicago: University of Chicago Press.

Meakin, D. C. (1982). Moral values and physical education. *Physical Education Review, 5,* 62–82.

Mussen, P., Rutherford, E., Harris, S., & Keasey, C. (1970). Honesty and altruism among preadolescents. *Developmental Psychology, 3,* 169–194.

Nicholls, J. G. (1983). Conceptions of ability and achievement motivation: A theory and its implications for education. In S. G. Paris, G. M. Olson, & H. W. Stevenson (Eds.), *Learning and motivation in the classroom.* Hillsdale, NJ: Erlbaum.

———. (1989). *The competitive ethos and democratic education.* Cambridge, MA: Harvard University Press.

———. (1992). The general and the specific in the development and expression of achievement motivation. In G. C. Roberts (Ed.), *Motivation in sport and exercise.* Champaign, IL: Human Kinetics.

Olson, S. L., Johnson, J., Parks, K., Barrett, E., & Belleau, K. (1983a, April). *Behavior problems of preschool children: Dimensions and social and cognitive correlates.* Paper presented at the biennial meeting of the Society for Research in Child Development, Detroit, MI.

———. (1983b, April). *Social competence in preschool children: Interrelations with sociometric status, social problem-solving, and impulsivity.* Paper presented at the biennial meeting of the Society for Research in Child Development, Detroit, MI.

Rest, J. R. (1983). Morality. In P. Mussen (Gen. Ed.), *Manual of child psychology,* volume *Cognitive development* (pp. 556–629), J. Flavell & E. Markman (Eds.), 4th ed., New York: John Wiley & Sons.

———. (1984). The major components of morality. In W. Kurtines & J. Gewirtz (Eds.), *Morality, moral behavior, and moral development* (pp. 356–629). New York: John Wiley & Sons.

———. (1986). *Moral development: Advances in research and theory.* New York: Praeger.

———. (1994). Background: Theory and research. In J. R. Rest (Ed.), *Moral development in the professions* (pp. 1–26). Hillsdale, NJ: Lawrence Erlbaum.

Romance, T. J., Weiss, M. R., & Bockoven, J. (1986). A program to promote moral development through elementary school physical education. *Journal of Teaching in Physical Education, 5,* 126–136.

Schmitz, K. (1976). Sport and play: Suspension of the ordinary. In M. Hart (Ed.), *Sport in the sociocultural process.* Dubuque: Wm. C. Brown.

Selman, R. L. (1976). Social-cognitive understanding: A guide to educational and clinical practice. In T. Lickona (Ed.), *Moral development and behavior* (pp. 299–316). New York: Holt, Rinehart, & Winston.

———. (1980). *The growth of interpersonal understanding.* New York: Academic.

Shantz, C. U. (1975). The development of social cognition. In E. M. Hetherington (Ed.), *Review of child development research* (Vol. 5, pp. 257–323). Chicago: University of Chicago.

Shields, D. L. L., & Bredemeier, B. J. L. (1994). *Character in action: Moral development and physical activity.* Champaign, IL: Human Kinetics.

Shure, M. B. (1980). *Interpersonal problem solving in ten-year-olds.* Final grant report to the National Institute of Mental Health (Grant # R01 MH 27741).

———. (1982). Interpersonal problem solving: A cog in the wheel of social cognition. In F. C. Serafica (Ed.), *Social-cognitive development in context.* New York: Guilford Press.

Solomon, D., Watson, M., Battistich, V., Schaps, E., Tuck, P., Solomon, J., Cooper, C., & Ritchey, W. (1985). A program to promote interpersonal consideration and cooperation in children. In R. Slavin, S. Sharan, S. Kagan, R. Hertz-Lazarowitz, C. Webb, & R. Schmuck (Eds.), *Learning to cooperate, cooperating to learn.* New York: Plenum.

Spivack, G., Platt, J. J., & Shure, M. B. (1976). *The problem solving approach to adjustment.* San Francisco, CA: Jossey-Bass.

Staub, E. (1979). *Positive social behavior and morality: Vol. 2: Socialization and development.* New York: Academic.

Stephens, D. (1993). *Goal orientation and moral atmosphere in youth sport: An examination of lying, hurting, and cheating behaviors in girls' soccer.* Unpublished doctoral dissertation, University of California at Berkeley.

Stephens, D. E., Bredemeier, B. J. L., Shields, D. L. L., & Ryan, M. K. (1991). *Relation of motivational and leadership variables to temptation to play unfairly.* Presentation made at the International Conference for Physical Activity, Fitness and Health (ICAPFH), Toronto, Ontario, Canada, May 10–13, 1992.

Strayer, J., & Roberts, W. (1989). Children's empathy and role taking: Child and parental factors, and relations to prosocial behavior. *Journal of Applied Developmental Psychology, 10,* 227–239.

Sutton-Smith, B. (1971). Boundaries. In R. E. Herron & B. Sutton-Smith (Eds.), *Child's play.* New York: John Wiley & Sons.

Tjosvold, D., Johnson, D., & Johnson, R. (1984). Influence strategy, perspective-taking, and relationships between high- and low-power individuals in cooperative and competitive contexts. *Journal of Psychology, 116,* 187–202.

Underwood, B., & Moore, B. (1982). Perspective-taking and altruism. *Psychological Bulletin, 91,* 143–173.

Walker, L. J. (1980). Cognitive and perspective-taking prerequisites for moral development. *Child Development, 51,* 131–139.

FUTURE DIRECTIONS

The first part of the book presented a historical account of the development of youth sports in America and a view of their current status. In the parts that followed, youth sports were considered from a variety of perspectives. The main thrust was to synthesize information about children's readiness for participation, the social processes involved, anatomical and physiological concerns, and psychological issues. Consideration was given to the effects of participation on young athletes as well as how to deal with some of the problems associated with youth sports. Although significant progress has been made, one of the common conclusions was that we do not know enough about youth sport phenomena, either in terms of knowledge about the participants or about the appropriate role of youth sports in society. These concerns are the focus of the concluding part, the ultimate goal of which is to promote changes that will enable youth sports to fulfill their potential as a valuable developmental experience for children and youth.

In chapter 23, Daniel Gould looks at the future from the perspective of sport psychology research. If we are to understand the psychological effects of youth sport participation, and if we are to effectively deal with problematic psychological issues, more research-based information is clearly needed. Gould's analysis of this need begins with an examination of studies that have had a significant practical and theoretical impact. Four lines of past youth sport research are identified, and two of these areas are reviewed (coaching effectiveness research; predictors of state and trait anxiety in young athletes). These investigations were characterized by several features that enabled them to yield the most useful and meaningful information. From this base, Gould concludes that if sport psychologists are to conduct socially relevant research that will make contributions to youth sports, three issues must be addressed. First, critical questions of practical significance must be identified. Second, he argues that descriptive, evaluation, and systems research are all needed (and examples of each type of research are presented). The third issue is the need for sport psychologists to realize that no single method is always best and that varied as well as innovative methodological procedures must be employed. In this regard, a shift is suggested from traditional methodologies (i.e., linear causation and ANOVA categories models) to multivariate longitudinal designs and to employment of qualitative research methods to a greater degree.

A different view of the future is provided by Vern Seefeldt in the final chapter. Rather than being solely concerned with future research, he prophesies about what is needed if youth sport proponents are to be proactive in seeking solutions to problems. In this regard, four categories of adult leaders are identified as primary agents of change—administrators and professors from institutions of higher learning, directors of recreation, administrators of single-sport agencies, and public school physical education teachers and coaches. Consideration is given to what each "agent of reform" must do to bring about progress. Seefeldt then predicts what the future holds with respect to several salient issues, including the following: the increasing role of scientific inquiry in deriving answers to critical questions, the proliferation of educational programs for volunteer coaches, greater reliance on programs conducted under the auspices of municipal recreation departments, greater dependence on volunteer workers, and the integration of mentally and physically handicapped individuals. The result is a chapter that provides a stimulating basis for discussion about the direction of youth sport programs in the next decade and why modifications are imminent.

CHAPTER

SPORT PSYCHOLOGY: FUTURE DIRECTIONS IN YOUTH SPORT RESEARCH[1]

—Daniel Gould

Historical research by Berryman (this volume) and by Wiggins (this volume) has shown that competitive athletic programs for children have existed in North America since the early 1920s. Although these programs have a long heritage, their period of greatest growth has occurred within the last two decades. It has been estimated that 16 to 20 million children between the ages of 6 and 16 years participate in a wide variety of organized sport programs (Martens, 1978, 1986). Not only is participation in these programs enormously popular, but also the participants are intensely involved. Gould and Martens (1979), for example, found that, on the average, young athletes participate in these programs 12 hours a week during an 18-week season. Clearly the youth sport setting involves a large proportion of the population and constitutes an important part of children's lives.

Sport psychology researchers paid only scant attention to the study of youth sport throughout much of the twentieth century. More recently, however, the topic has drawn considerable psychological interest. Unfortunately, increased empirical efforts in the area have not necessarily guaranteed beneficial results of either a theoretical or an applied nature, nor will they in the future. To adequately examine psychological aspects of youth sport participation, long-range, systematic, well-conducted research programs are needed. Before such projects can be initiated on a more frequent basis, however, it will be necessary to examine the existing literature and determine current lines of research that have provided the greatest empirical and applied benefits. Thus, this chapter examines key lines of past youth sport research, identifies critical research questions, outlines appropriate theoretical and methodological approaches, and suggests future research directions.

Meaningful Lines of Youth Sport Research

In the late 1970s and early 1980s, the number of youth sport psychological studies greatly increased, as evidenced by the large number of review articles summarizing existing research and outlining practical implications for coaches, parents, and administrators (e.g., Gerson, 1977; Roberts, 1980; Thomas, 1978). The majority of implications made in these reviews were based on research from the parent discipline of psychology and not from sport-psychology research. Consequently, one found oneself asking why many of the sport psychological studies were telling us so little about youth sport! Although the youth sport research provided little practical information for a number of reasons (e.g., scant amount of research, infancy of the field), one of the primary reasons stemmed from the questions being asked. Many times we did not ask the most appropriate questions. To identify the most important research questions we needed to more closely examine the objectives of our research.

Three of the various objectives that sport psychologists may have for studying youth sport seemed most prevalent. These included the following:

1. *To provide psychological information that will help those involved in youth sport provide its young participants with positive and productive experiences.* Specifically, the methods of the behavioral sciences could be used to identify and evaluate behavioral guidelines and strategies that adult leaders could use to more effectively communicate with, reinforce, and instruct young athletes. Providing this type of information is important because most nonschool youth sport coaches have little formal coaching education and develop coaching guidelines based on experiences of trial and error or through the modeling of college and professional coaches, who work with vastly different populations.

2. *To test existing psychological theory in a sport setting.* Theory is the ultimate goal of science, and psychologists (Bronfenbrenner, 1977) and sport psychologists (Martens, 1987; Smith & Smoll, 1978) alike have emphasized the need for the behavioral scientist to test existing psychological theory in complex and diverse social settings. The youth sport domain provides a readily accessible, naturalistic field setting where this can be accomplished.

3. *To develop new theory.* Although it is extremely important to test existing theory, a number of investigators (Martens, 1979, 1987; Siedentop, 1980) have suggested that existing psychological theory will not have all the answers for the sport psychologist. New theories that account for multivariate, highly complex athletic settings must be identified and tested. The youth sport setting is ideal for this purpose.

Given these objectives for conducting youth sport research, the body of knowledge in the area was examined.[2] Key studies were identified based on two criteria: (a) their practical significance and (b) their contribution to the development or extension of psychological theory. Characteristics of these studies were also identified. The four key lines of research identified were: (a) the coaching effectiveness research of Smith, Smoll, and their associates; (b) predictors of state and trait anxiety in young athletes initiated by Scanlan and her associates and later continued by a number of investigators; (c) young athlete self-esteem and motivation research best reflected in the work of developmental sport psychologist Maureen Weiss; and (d) investigations examining moral development and sportspersonship in young athletes spearheaded by Bredemeier, Shields, and Weiss. Space limitations prevent an examination of all four of these lines of research, so only the first two areas will be described here. For information about the latter two areas, the reader is referred to in-depth reviews by Weiss (1993), Weiss and Chaumeton (1992), Weiss and Bredemeier (1990) and Bredemeier and Shields (this volume).

Coaching Effectiveness Research

The original coaching effectiveness research of Smith, Smoll, and their associates (Curtis, Smith, & Smoll, 1979; Smith, Smoll, & Curtis, 1978, 1979; Smith, Smoll, & Hunt, 1977; Smith et al., 1979; Smoll et al., 1978) can be categorized into three distinct phases. First, a Coaching Behavior Assessment System (CBAS) was developed over several years. This observational system consisted of behavioral categories derived from social learning theory and assessed individual differences in behavioral profiles of coaches. Both reactive and spontaneous coaching behaviors were assessed and included behaviors such as positive reinforcement, nonreinforcement, mistake-contingent encouragement, mistake-contingent technical instruction, punishment, punitive technical instruction, ignoring mistakes, keeping control behaviors, general technical instruction, general encouragement, organization, and general communication. The CBAS inventory was found to be a highly reliable and valid assessment instrument.

In a second phase of the project, the relationship between coaching behaviors of Little League Baseball coaches as assessed by the CBAS instrument ($N = 51$), and player perceptions ($N = 542$) of coaching behaviors, attitudes, and self-esteem were examined. It was found that coaches who were rated more positively by the children gave more technical instruction than general encouragement, gave more reinforcement and mistake contingent feedback, and engaged in more behaviors associated with keeping control. Negatively evaluated coaches generally were more punitive and gave more punitive technical instruction. Finally, children who played for the positively evaluated coaches had higher general and athletic self-concepts.

Because the results of this second phase were descriptive and no causal inferences could be made, a third phase was conducted. In this phase, 31 Little League Baseball coaches were randomly assigned to either an experimental group that received training in a positive approach to coaching (e.g., were given behavioral guidelines derived in the previous phase that emphasized the desirability of reinforcement, encouragement, and technical instruction) or to a control condition in which they coached as they normally would. The intervention program received by the experimental group of coaches consisted of a 2.5-hour coaching clinic, self-assessment of coaching behaviors, and observer feedback concerning emitted coaching behaviors. Dependent variables observed included coaching behaviors, self-perceived coaching behaviors, player perceptions of coaching behaviors, as well as attitudinal and self-esteem measures of 325 of their players. Findings revealed that the behavioral profiles of the experimental coaches differed from the control coaches in the expected direction. Moreover, the children who played for the experimental coaches, as compared with children who played for the control coaches, demonstrated greater enjoyment, a greater desire to play, rated their coaches as more knowledgeable, and rated their team higher in attraction.

The fourth phase of this line of research has recently been conducted and focused specific attention on how coaching behaviors affect self-esteem development and attrition rates in young athletes (Barnett, Smoll, & Smith, 1992; Smith & Smoll, 1990; Smoll et al., 1993). The relationship between self-esteem enhancement and coaching behaviors was examined in 51 male Little League Baseball coaches and 542 of their players (Smith & Smoll, 1990). Children with low self-esteem responded most positively to coaches who exhibited reinforcing and encouraging behaviors as measured by CBAS and most negatively to coaches who were low on supportiveness. Similarly, high levels of technical instruction were positively associated with enhanced self-esteem, whereas low levels of supportiveness were associated with lowered self-esteem. Hence, a strong association was exhibited between high levels of technical instruction, encouragement, supportive behaviors, and self-esteem enhancement.

Next, Smoll, Smith, Barnett, and Everett (1993) compared 8 youth baseball coaches, who attended a preseason workshop designed to increase supportiveness and instructional effectiveness, to 10 control group coaches, who did not participate in such a workshop. One hundred fifty-two boys who played for these coaches were interviewed pre- and postseason. The findings revealed that boys with low self-esteem showed significant increases in general self-esteem across the season whereas low self-esteem children who played for control group coaches did not. As was the case with other studies in the series, players who played for the trained coaches also evaluated their coaches more positively, had more fun, and exhibited higher team attraction. No differences in won-loss records were evident between the trained and control group coaches.

As a follow-up to the previous study, Barnett, Smoll, and Smith (1992) examined dropout rates in the children who played for the trained and control coaches. Results revealed that control group children exhibited a 26 percent dropout rate, whereas the attrition rate for experimental group players was only 5 percent. Interestingly, no differences were evident in won-loss records of the teams, and it was concluded that dropout rates were associated with negative sport experiences brought about by coaching behaviors exhibited during the previous season.

Taken together, then, the investigations in this four-phase project continued to add significantly to our understanding of the influence that coaching behaviors have on the affective reactions of young athletes. First, coaching behaviors were consistently associated with a variety of psychological reactions of players, including such attributes as the amount of fun experienced, liking of the coach, and liking of the game. Positive, instructional, and supportive coaching behaviors were also associated with enhanced self-esteem, especially for low self-esteem players. Second, these same patterns of coaching behaviors were also associated with motivation levels as players who played for coaches taught to be more positive, supportive, instructive, and encouraging evidenced lower dropout rates. Finally, it was shown that coaches could be trained to exhibit desirable coaching behaviors and, in turn, have positive effects on their young athletes motivation and psychological states.

Competitive Anxiety Research

The second important line of research was initiated by Scanlan and her colleagues (Passer & Scanlan, 1980; Scanlan & Lewthwaite, 1984; Scanlan & Passer, 1978a,

1978b, 1979). These investigators examined the relationships between competitive trait anxiety, self-esteem, team performance expectancies, personal performance expectancies, worries about failure, worries about adult expectations and social evaluation, parental pressure to participate, game or match outcome, perceived fun, and pre- and postcontest state anxiety in youth sport participants. In all, a series of three interrelated field studies were conducted using a similar methodological format. Competitive stress or state anxiety was assessed just prior to and immediately following competition and was correlated to various individual difference factors (e.g., trait anxiety, self-esteem, worries about adult expectations) taken well before the contests. In the first investigation, male youth soccer players, ages 10 to 12 years, were used as subjects (Scanlan & Passer, 1978b). The second investigation replicated and extended the first by employing female youth soccer players of the same age (Scanlan & Passer, 1979). Finally, the latest study in the series (Scanlan & Lewthwaite, 1984) extended the results of the soccer studies to the sport of wrestling, examining male youth wrestlers, ages 10 to 14.

Overall, the findings of these studies have shown that sport competition is perceived as anxiety-producing by *some* children in some situations. In particular, the findings demonstrate that competitive trait anxiety, performance expectancies pertinent to the particular sport context, victory versus defeat and its varying degrees, and the amount of fun experienced while competing are strong and consistent predictors of competitive stress for both genders across diverse sport contexts. Self-esteem also was found to be a significant, although relatively weak, predictor of stress for boys and girls in the soccer studies and was significantly correlated with but not predictive of stress in wrestling. The latest study in this series (Scanlan & Lewthwaite, 1984) has identified several new factors associated with stress that focus on children's characteristic prematch thoughts and worries, as well as their perceptions of the significant adults in their lives (Scanlan, 1986, p. 117). Finally, many of these findings were recently replicated in an independent youth wrestling investigation conducted by Gould et al. (1991).

Although the previous studies focused on predictors of state anxiety in young athletes, several investigators have also begun to focus attention on factors associated with heightened competitive trait anxiety in young athletes; that is, factors that influence their personality disposition to perceive socially evaluative environments like competition as more or less threatening and respond with varying levels of state anxiety. And this is important because youngsters who experience the most state anxiety in competitive sports environments have been consistently shown to be high trait anxious.

Passer (1983) was the first investigator to examine this issue when he compared 163 high and low trait anxious 10- to 15-year-old soccer players on performance expectancies, criticism for failure, self-esteem, perceived competence, and evaluative- and performance-related worries. His findings demonstrated that high as compared with low trait anxious players worried more frequently about losing; coach, parent, and teammate evaluations; and not playing well.

In a follow-up study, Brustad and Weiss (1987) compared 55 male and 55 female youth softball participants and found that high versus low trait anxious boys reported more performance worries and lower self-esteem. High versus low trait anxious girls, however, were not found to differ on any of these variables. Similar results for male and female participants did emerge in a second investigation of 207 youth basketball players conducted by Brustad (1988). Hence, both male and female high competitive trait anxious young athletes differed from their low trait anxious counterparts in that they exhibited higher levels of evaluative- and performance-based worries and lower self-esteem.

An important recent investigation by Newton and Duda (1992) also looked at predictors of competitive trait anxiety in young athletes. Male and female youth tennis players (*M* age = 12 years) were studied and it was found that an ego goal orientation (a tendency to base one's goals on winning or beating others versus self-improvement) was related to higher levels of multidimensional trait anxiety. Hence, youth tennis players whose goals focus on contest outcome (versus self-improvement) to judge athletic success are more threatened by social evaluation and competition.

Last, in an investigation linking the previously discussed coaching behavior research with the research on factors influencing trait anxiety in young athletes, Smith, Smoll, and Barnett (in press) found that the youth league coaches who took part in their Coach Effectiveness Training intervention were not only effective in positively influencing their athletes motivation and self-esteem but in lowering their trait anxiety as well. This is certainly an important finding as it suggests that high trait anxious children can gain much from the youth sport experience.

In summary, then, the research examining factors associated with increased trait anxiety in young athletes shows that high trait anxious children perceive failure and negative evaluation from significant others as more emotionally aversive and worry more about such concerns than their low trait anxious counterparts. These children also tend to adopt outcome, as opposed to mastery or self-referenced, goal orientations. An encouraging finding that needs replication is that coaches trained to be more encouraging, supportive, and instructive have positive effects in lowering trait anxiety in young athletes. Factors associated with heightened state anxiety include low self-esteem, low personal and team performance expectancies, and heightened trait anxiety. Children who experience high state anxiety during competition also report having less fun and satisfaction and frequently worry about adult evaluation and expectations.

Lessons to Be Learned

Both of these comprehensive research projects, as well as the motivation and moral development lines of research that have proven to be fruitful in the area of youth sport, are characterized by several features. First and foremost, they asked important questions of practical concern for youth sport personnel. What effect do coaching behaviors have on the psychological development of young athletes? What causes stress and anxiety in youth sport participants? How is self-esteem and motivation developed in young athletes? And how, and under what conditions, does moral development occur in young athletes?

Second, these studies integrated previous research and directly tested theory or attempted to generate new theory to explain the relationships between variables. For example, Smoll and Smith (1989) have developed a theoretical model of leadership in youth sports. This cognitive-behavioral model specifies how situational factors, individual difference factors, and cognitive processes mediate overt coaching behaviors and young athletes's reactions to them. Similarly, much of the youth sport anxiety research has been guided by anxiety theories developed in general psychology.

Third, these lines of research were methodologically sound. They examined more than a few isolated teams (entire leagues), were multivariate in nature, and involved more than one assessment.

Finally, these projects were part of a systematic series of studies, not isolated, single studies. The research of Smith, Smoll, and associates, for instance, was conducted in four distinct phases (Phase 1—development of assessment instruments; Phase 2—descriptive hypothesis-generating research; Phase 3—hypothesis-testing experimental research; Phase 4—special focus on understanding the coaching behavior self-esteem relationship) and provides a good model for future researchers to follow. Similarly, the factors related to competitive-stress investigations represent how a line of research can be conducted by groups of independent authors examining similar issues. It is also interesting to note that the initial state anxiety research that Scanlan and her associates conducted was part of a series of field studies, where the researchers tested theoretical principles derived from a line of laboratory research on competitive anxiety in a field setting. Conducting these three studies also allowed the investigators to replicate and extend their findings to young female athletes and across sports.

In contrast, a review of the literature revealed that youth sport studies that did not have the same impact as these lines of investigation did not reflect many of these characteristics. Investigations with less impact, for example, did not ask questions of practical importance, were often methodologically weak, and were not multivariate in their approach. Moreover, these investigations typically were not part of a systematic series of studies, nor did they integrate previous research into the design.

Conducting Youth Sport Research That Counts

Boring (1963), eminent historian of psychology, wrote that "one finds that he [or she] needs to know about the past, not in order to predict the future, but rather in order to understand the present" (p. 89). Thus, historically examining the youth sport literature will not let us predict what the future will bring. However, understanding the past research may help us design studies that have a higher probability of having greater impact and may help make our research efforts more fruitful and economical. If we agree with some of the leaders in the field (Martens, 1979, 1987; Siedentop, 1980; Smith & Smoll, 1978) and assume that one of the sport psychologist's major objectives is to conduct socially significant research that will make meaningful contributions to those involved in sport, then we must address three issues:

1. What questions should we ask if we are to have the greatest impact in providing information that ensures productive and healthful programs for children?
2. What types of research settings are needed if answers to these questions are to be derived?

3. What methodological approaches should be employed if valid and reliable answers are to be provided to these questions?

What Questions Should We Ask?

Do we ask important questions? Does our research really make a difference? All too often the answer to these questions has been no. Locke (1969), for example, has indicated that

> if you wiped out the last 50 years of research in physics or chemistry or medicine, life in our world would instantly change. If you wiped out the last 50 years of research in physical education, would physical education and physical educators continue to function as usual? The answer is usually an emphatic "yes." (p. 6)

Psychologists like Bronfenbrenner (1977) and, more recently, sport scientists like Martens (1979, 1987) and Siedentop (1980) have suggested that the time has come for sport psychologists to spend less time in their laboratories and more time on the playing fields, in the gymnasiums, and natatoriums. In essence, we must establish ecological validity for our theories (Bronfenbrenner, 1977). Siedentop (1980) warns that all too often applied research has been thought of as only extending laboratory research to practical settings. Behaviorists like Baer, Wolf, and Risely (1968), however, suggest that "the label applied is not determined by the research procedures used but by the interest which society shows in the problems being studied" (p. 12). Thus, if the sport psychologist conducting youth sport research is to have practical impact, then questions of practical importance must be identified.

To identify these issues, a content analysis of the practical and empirical youth sport literature was conducted by the author and topics of psychological significance in youth sport were identified. A brief questionnaire was then formulated and administered to 23 sport psychologists working in youth sport throughout North America, as well as to 33 nonschool youth sport coaches and administrators. The results of this survey revealed that the following 10 topics were rated as most important by the combined sample:

- Reasons why young athletes stop participating
- Competitive stress placed on young athletes
- Helping young athletes cope with competitive stress
- Effects of competition on the psychological health and development of children
- Skills for enhancing communication with young athletes
- Strategies for developing self-confidence
- Why young athletes participate in sport
- Effects of winning and losing on young athletes
- What young athletes like and dislike about sport
- Effects of parent-child relationships on sport involvement and success

Moreover, no differences were found between the groups on their ratings of the 10 topics ranked as most important for study.

These findings identify a number of sport psychological topics of practical significance for the youth sport researcher. However, asking questions of a practical significance does not mean the abandonment of theory, be it the testing of existing theory in youth sport field settings or the development of a new theory. Theory is the major goal of science, whether it be of basic or applied nature (Kerlinger, 1973). Moreover, it has often been said that if one is interested in practical implications, nothing is more practical than good theory. The previously mentioned work of Scanlan and her associates, as well as the motivation and perceived competence research of Weiss (1991), are excellent examples of research that tests existing theory in youth sport settings while addressing practical problems.

It is also important to recognize that applying existing theory to sport can advance knowledge in sport psychology only so far. The sport psychologist must not only test existing theory but must also develop new sport-specific theories that better explain the complex interaction of personal and environmental variables in the naturalistic youth sport field setting (Martens, 1979, 1987; Siedentop, 1980; Smith & Smoll, 1978; Thomas, 1980). The need to test existing theory and to develop new theory is of paramount importance because we are sometimes blinded by the *zeitgeist* in which we work. For example, the early research on attributions in the youth sport setting primarily consisted of an extension of laboratory research findings to naturalistic environments. Although these findings were important in that they further verified previous research, the scientists were often blinded by the theory's assumptions and limitations.

One should have asked, are the four basic attributions found in the laboratory appropriate for sport settings? Some research (Roberts & Pascuzzi, 1979) indicated that alone they may not have been and, interestingly, attribution theory was later revised to be more inclusive (Weiner, 1985). In a related matter, why has the critical link between attributions and performance or participation in youth sport not been assessed to a greater degree? Is it that we assume that attributions will automatically influence behavior because this is what is predicted from the general theoretical notions? Similarly, the feasibility of identifying learned-helpless young athletes and modifying their helpless states through attributional retraining has not been examined. Finally, the effects of extrinsic rewards on the young athlete's intrinsic motivation have not been examined in the field, although the author and a number of other reviewers have based practical implications on laboratory research within the attributional framework. In essence, whether we are testing existing theory and/or developing new theory, from time to time we must be able to step back and examine whether the *zeitgeist* or paradigm in which we are working is blinding us—preventing us from testing basic assumptions or asking theoretically important but forgotten questions.

When testing existing theory and developing new theory, the youth sport researcher must also remember that the young athlete is not a miniature adult. Too often we erroneously assume that psychological processes and theories that have been based on research with adults automatically transfer to younger age groups. Weiss and Bredemeier (1983) and Weiss (1991), however, have presented convincing evidence that shows that psychological processes systematically vary with age or the developmental level of the child. Thus, when testing existing theory and developing new sport-specific theories in youth sport, developmental factors must be considered.

The present review of the existing youth sport research clearly showed that the areas that have provided the most impact are ones where the investigators pursued a series of interrelated questions. Thus, in planning youth sport research, it is more fruitful for investigators to think in terms of lines of research, focusing on a number of interrelated questions and subquestions rather than on single, isolated questions. It may be fruitful to adopt elements of the method of strong inference developed by Platt (1964). That is, we should conduct lines of research in a logical fashion by attempting to devise and test alternative hypotheses, critically examining the results of previous studies and formulating questions in future investigations that will eliminate rival hypotheses.

A good example of this approach in the youth sport research is the work of Smith and Smoll and their associates. As already mentioned, this series of investigations was carried out in four phases. Phase 1 focused on the question of whether coaching behaviors could be reliably and validly assessed. After this was established, the question of what relationship exists between coaching behaviors and player attitudes was explored. The authors did not stop here, however. When stable relationships were found between coaching behaviors and player attitudes and motivation, the next interrelated question was posed. Can coaching behaviors be changed, and will these changes result in changes in attitudes and motivation on the part of players? This question was answered in Phase 3. Presently, Phase 4 is taking place and is focusing on examining the effects of coach behaviors and behavioral training on development of self-esteem and other psychological variables. Although not currently under way, strong inference would suggest that a next logical series of questions would focus on what specifically caused the changes in coaching behaviors and player affect. For instance, were the results of Phase 3 due to a placebo effect associated with the training program? Were they caused by the 2.5-hour coaching clinic, the self-assessment procedures employed, or the feedback given to the coaches about their actual behavior?

Although the strong inference process has much to offer the youth sport researcher, its limitations also must be recognized. Hafner and Presswood (1965), for example, suggest that the notion of strong inference is idealistic because alternative hypotheses do not always appear. Moreover, if we encounter an occasional mistake in observation, the idea that a systematic series of interrelated questions results in valid answers to a problem may be false. We may be systematically pursuing subquestions in the wrong direction! Similarly, Feltz (1989) convincingly argues that the strong inference notion that science can only advance by disproofs is faulty. In contrast, she contends that the sport psychology researcher must employ a planned critical multiplism approach, where a series of investigations are planned using multiple ways to formulate research questions, measure variables, design investigations, analyze results, and interpret findings. Consequently, sport psychologists conducting youth sport research must simultaneously consider sets of contending theoretical ideas, design and evaluate experiments with the greatest care, use multiple methods, replicate results, and view results from a single investigation with great care.

What Types of Research Settings Are Needed?

In preparing this chapter, a number of papers on the philosophy of science (Boring, 1955, 1963; Bronowski, 1973; Hafner & Presswood, 1965; Kuhn, 1970; Patton, 1990; Platt, 1964), the future direction of social psychology (Gergen, 1973; Helmreich, 1975; McGuire, 1973; Schlenkar, 1974), and direction of the research in sport psychology

(Martens, 1979, 1987; Siedentop, 1980; Smith & Smoll, 1978; Thomas, 1980) were reviewed. One common theme in all of these papers was that we should beware of those who employ one method or instrument, either experimental or theoretical. If the state of knowledge in a field is to be advanced, diverse methods must be employed. Descriptive studies, evaluation research, and systems approach research are all types of research that are applicable in the psychological study of youth sport.

Descriptive Research

In the early 1970s, if a particular sport psychological investigation was not theoretical, highly controlled, and conducted in the laboratory, it was more than likely not highly evaluated. Times have changed and we have come a long way since then. More and more field research is being conducted, and we now encourage new and different approaches to the field. We are still not completely open-minded, however. For example, the utility of descriptive research needs to be recognized and more highly supported, especially in the area of youth sport. Although theory is our ultimate goal, we must recognize that youth sports are conducted in a highly complex physical and social environment. We know little about this environment; some feel it cannot be explained with existing laboratory-generated theories (Martens, 1979, 1987; Siedentop, 1980; Smith & Smoll, 1978). Thus, descriptive research could play an important role in helping us understand this complex setting and, in so doing, provide us with the groundwork needed for the development of new theory.

Descriptive research could also be extremely useful in answering practical problems. At the Michigan Youth Sports Institute, for example, a three-year descriptive study of the children's sport scene was conducted (Universities Study Committee, 1976, 1978a, 1978b). A descriptive study was selected because little was known about children's sport in Michigan. The number of participants involved; participation patterns; player attitudes toward sport, coaching, and officiating; and parental attitudes toward a variety of issues had never been extensively examined. The results of these investigations have provided a wealth of data. For example, it was found that children's sport participation steadily increased up to the ages of 12, 13, and 14, after which it markedly declined, with approximately 35 percent of the children discontinuing participation at this time. Information also was obtained on the reasons for children's involvement and discontinuation of participation. These findings have provided the staff of the Youth Sports Institute with valuable athletic motivation information to convey to youth sport coaches.

Descriptive research can also be extremely useful in solving controversial youth sport issues. Critics of youth sport, for example, suggest that coaches' overemphasis on winning places children under too much stress, that adult leaders demonstrate unsporting behavior, and that parents often stifle fun in children's sport programs. The sport psychologist could develop behavioral observation systems for assessing behaviors like these and examine the relationships among these factors.

Finally, descriptive research does not have to be atheoretical. Descriptive methods could be used to provide support for theoretical formulations. For example, Bandura (1977) suggests that performance accomplishments are one primary means of influencing an individual's self-efficacy to be associated with various performance accomplishments over the course of a season. Similarly, changes in Harter's (1981) perceived competence scale scores could be examined over the course of several seasons, and relationships between competence and various environmental factors (coaching behavior assessments, success) could be made.

Evaluation Research

Edward Suchman (1967) indicates that "evaluation research is a specific form of applied research whose primary goal is not the discovery of knowledge but rather a testing of the application of knowledge" (p. 75). Evaluation research includes the process of determining the value or amount of success in achieving some predetermined program objective or objectives (Patton, 1990; C.H. Weiss, 1972). In essence, evaluation research involves the careful planning of specific program objectives, the identification of criteria to measure the success of these objectives, determination and exploration of the degree of success, and recommendations for further program activity.

Although little has been conducted by sport psychologists, evaluation research holds great promise for those interested in youth sport. A number of sport psychologists, for example, have been involved in making sport psychological presentations in clinics and workshops held for youth coaches. Although it is easy for us to assume that we are contributing to the betterment of children's sport by conducting these programs, little empirical evidence exists outside of that of Smith, Smoll, and their associates to support this assumption. Do youth coaches conduct themselves in a more socially acceptable manner after receiving information on the psychology of sportspersonship? If so, do these behaviors affect the young athlete's moral attitudes and behaviors? Evaluation research could be used to answer these and related questions.

Evaluation research could also be used to provide information that could assist program administrators in ending controversies in children's sport. Martens, Rivkin, and Bump (1984) and Spieth (1977), for instance, compared the amount of activity youngsters experience in traditional versus nontraditional baseball leagues. Specifically, in both studies it was found that young athletes who played in a nontraditional league where their own coach pitched to them had more swings at pitches, made more contact with the ball, and had more balls hit to them in the field than children who played in traditional leagues. Similarly Corbin and Laurie (1980) used evaluation research to assess the effects of rule changes in children's baseball on parental attitudes toward those rule changes. Specifically it was found that parents generally supported program changes designed to reduce competition and focus attention on fun and skill development. These initial efforts demonstrate the practical implications that youth sport evaluation research can have.

Systems Approach Research

A third type of research that could be useful to the sport psychologist conducting youth sport research is systems approach research. Smith and Smoll (1978) indicate that because the youth sport setting involves the extensive interplay of a variety of social systems and subsystems, to fully understand the setting one must examine the various systems. Specifically, in the systems approach, the investigator (a) identifies all social systems and subsystems, (b) focuses on system change and factors related to change, (c) develops a model that describes causal patterns between systems and factors affecting systems, and (d) manipulates model elements to test their predicted effect on the system. This model would be especially appropriate in studying socialization into and through sport. Systems such as the child, teammates, and parents could be identified and observed simultaneously and longitudinally. Relationships between systems could be examined, models developed, and predictions of the model tested.

What Methodological Approach Should Be Employed?

The sport psychologist can pose the appropriate and socially relevant questions and conduct research in the most appropriate setting to answer these questions, but unless good methodological procedures are utilized, all of his or her efforts are in vain. What is the best methodological format to follow when conducting naturalistic research in field settings? There is no one *best* method. The problem at hand determines which methods are most appropriate. For example, when conducting research in an underdeveloped area (e.g., parental relationship issues in youth athletes), noncausal survey techniques may be the most appropriate methods to employ. In essence, the primary purpose of this type of investigation would be the description of the phenomenon of concern and the identification of variables that covary with it. After a number of noncausal relationships are established, however, the manipulation of various independent variables thought to influence the behavior of concern may be in order (e.g., parental educational strategies designed to develop positive parent-child athlete relationships), or statistical techniques such as structural or path analyses may be employed, which will allow one to test theoretically derived paths or relationships between variables.

It is becoming more apparent, however, that the same procedures that have guided both social psychologists in general and sport psychologists in particular are not always appropriate for field settings (Martens, 1979, 1987; Patton, 1990). Because we are investigating a complex phenomenon where a large number of internal and external factors are affecting the populations we sample, the traditional methodology of linear causation and convenient ANOVA categories are often inappropriate. For instance, in studying the effects of coaching behaviors on the attitudinal development of young athletes, isolating and assessing the effects of one particular coaching behavior (e.g., positive reinforcement) on attitudinal development will not be enough. Numbers of behaviors (e.g., positive reinforcement, punishment, technical instructions) of coaches and other role models (e.g., parents, peers) will need to be assessed in a variety of settings (games and practices) across time. Consequently, the sport psychologist interested in providing valid answers to many of the questions posed in this manuscript must consider multivariate longitudinal designs, use regression analyses that look at all subjects—not just dichotomized or trichotomized groups—and employ a wide range of quantitative and qualitative assessment procedures. In addition, answers to many of the complex questions involving children in sport do not reside in the psychological domain alone. Instead they are influenced by the complex interplay of psychological, physiological, and kinesiological factors (Weiss, 1991). Thus, team research of a multidisciplinary nature is also needed.

Pediatric sport psychology researchers should also employ qualitative research methods to a much greater degree. Patton (1990), for instance, has convincingly shown that qualitative research methods such as in-depth interviews, case studies, and field observations provide a wealth of detailed information and depth of understanding not resulting from traditional quantitative methods. Using participant observation and interview techniques, for instance, Harris (1983) studied two youth baseball teams differing in their ethnic makeups. Her results revealed that few ethnic group differences emerged between the teams. Moreover, players from both teams reflected their coaches' characterizations (most important concepts regarding the goals of the youth baseball experience) of youth baseball, partially redefining and adding to them. More recently, Donnelly (1993) conducted in-depth interviews with former elite young athletes who had taken part in high-performance sports. In doing so, a number of important and previously undocumented negative side effects of participation, such as troubled family relationships, social relationship problems, identity concerns, and excessive behaviors like recreational drug use, were identified. Clearly, then, these initial studies show how conducting qualitative youth sport research can supplement and extend the excellent quantitative research knowledge base that has begun to develop in the area.

A final methodological issue that cannot be ignored focuses on sampling concerns. Too often youth sport researchers select the most convenient sample of young athletes for their investigations rather than choosing the most appropriate sample available for answering the questions posed. For example, Feltz and Ewing (1987) have indicated that many of the controversies surrounding sport competition for children are most prominent at the elite levels of involvement. They indicate, however, that few investigators have examined critical issues, such as burnout and excessive competitive stress, with samples of elite young athletes. Similarly, in a follow-up investigation to the previously discussed work of Smith, Smoll, and their colleagues, Horn (1985) has found that behaviors emitted by youth sport coaches differ depending on the sampling context; that is, whether coaching behaviors were observed in practices or competitions. These sampling context findings are of critical importance, as it was previously assumed that the pattern of observed coaching behaviors was similar across both practices and competitions. Hence, sport psychologists conducting youth sport research must pay particular attention to sampling issues and the effects of these issues on both their findings and their interpretation of findings.

A Final Comment

Social philosopher Herbert Marcuse (1964) has indicated that many times societal issues and problems remain unanswered, but not because those in the society are incapable of answering them. On the contrary, answers to these problems could be successfully achieved if the societal members only took the time to ask the appropriate questions. In many ways, the sport psychologist interested in studying youth sport is in a similar situation. We are in an emerging area and have the opportunity before us to conduct research that can have a tremendous impact on the estimated 16 to 20 million children involved in youth sport. However, to conduct research that will have this practical significance, we need to stop, step back, and examine the major practical and theoretical issues in the field.

Notes

1. This is an abridged and updated version of a manuscript by Gould (1982) titled "Sport Psychology in the 1980's: Status, Direction and Challenge in Youth Sports Research" that appeared in the *Journal of Sport Psychology, 4,* 203–218.
2. Due to space limitations it is not possible to include a comprehensive review of the psychological investigations conducted in the youth sport area. Therefore, the interested reader is referred to related reviews (Gould, 1993; Gould & Seefeldt, 1981; Gould & Weiss, 1987; Seefeldt & Gould, 1980; Weiss, 1993; Weiss & Bredemeier, 1983) and, upon request from the author, may receive a detailed listing of the references reviewed.

References

Baer, B., Wolf, M., & Risely, T. (1968). Current dimensions of applied behavior analysis. *Journal of Applied Behavior Analysis, 1,* 91–97.

Bandura, A. (1977). Self-efficacy: Toward a unifying theory of behavioral change. *Psychological Review, 84,* 191–215.

Barnett, N. P., Smoll, F. L., & Smith, R. E. (1992). Effects of enhancing coach–athlete relationships on youth sport attrition. *The Sport Psychologist, 6,* 111–127.

Berryman, J. W. (1995). The rise of boys' sports in the United States, 1900 to 1970. In F. L. Smoll & R. E. Smith (Eds.), *Children and youth in sport: A biopsychosocial perspective* (pp. 4–14) Dubuque, IA: Brown & Benchmark.

Boring, E. G. (1955). Dual role of the zeitgeist in scientific creativity. *Scientific Monthly, 80,* 101–106.

———. (1963). Science and the meaning of its history. In R. I. Watson & D. T. Campbell (Eds.), *History, psychology and science: Selected papers* (pp. 87–91). New York: Wiley.

Bredemeier, B. J. L., & Shields, D. L. L. (1995). Moral development and children's sport. In F. L. Smoll & R. E. Smith (Eds.), *Children and youth in sport: A biopsychosocial perspective* (pp. 381–401) Dubuque, IA: Brown & Benchmark.

Bronfenbrenner, U. (1977). Toward an experimental ecology of human development. *American Psychologist, 32,* 513–531.

Bronowski, J. (1973). *The ascent of man.* Boston: Little, Brown.

Brustad, R. J. (1988). Affective outcomes in competitive youth sport: The influence of intrapersonal and socialization factors. *Journal of Sport and Exercise Psychology, 10,* 307–321.

Brustad, R. J., & Weiss, M. R. (1987). Competence perceptions and sources of worry in high, medium and low competitive trait anxious young athletes. *Journal of Sport Psychology, 9,* 97–105.

Corbin, C. B., & Laurie, D. R. (1980, May). *Parental attitudes concerning modifications in baseball for young children.* Paper presented at the North American Society for Psychology of Sport and Physical Activity Conference, Boulder, CO.

Curtis, B., Smith, R. E., & Smoll, F. L. (1979). Scrutinizing the skipper: A study of leadership behaviors in the dugout. *Journal of Applied Psychology, 64,* 391–400.

Donelley, P. (1993). Problems associated with youth involvement in high performance sport. In B. R. Cahill, & A. J. Pearl (Eds.), *Intensive participation in children's sports* (pp. 95–126). Champaign, IL: Human Kinetics.

Feltz, D. (1989). Future directions in theoretical research in sport psychology: From applied psychology toward sport science. In J. S. Skinner, C. B. Corbin, D. M. Landers, P. E. Marlin, & C. L. Wells (Eds.), *Future directions in exercise and sport research* (pp. 435–452). Champaign, IL: Human Kinetics.

Feltz, D. L., & Ewing, M. E. (1987). Psychological characteristics of elite young athletes. *Medicine and Science in Sport and Exercise, 19*(5), S98–S105.

Gergen, K. J. (1973). Social psychology as history. *Journal of Personality and Social Psychology, 26,* 309–320.

Gerson, R. (1977). Redesigning athletic competition for children. *Motor Skills: Theory into Practice, 2,* 3–14.

Gould, D. (1982). Sport psychology in the 1980's: Status, direction and challenge in youth sports research. *Journal of Sport Psychology, 4,* 203–218.

———. (1993). Intensive sport participation and the prepubescent athlete: Competitive stress and burnout. In B. R. Cahill & A. J. Pearl (Eds.), *Intensive participation in children's sports* (pp. 19–30). Champaign, IL: Human Kinetics.

Gould, D., Eklund, R., Petlichkoff, L., Peterson, K., & Bump, L. (1991). Psychological predictors of state anxiety and performance in age-group wrestlers. *Pediatric Exercise Science, 3,* 198–208.

Gould, D., & Martens, R. (1979). Attitudes of volunteer coaches toward significant youth sport issues. *Research Quarterly, 50,* 369–380.

Gould, D., & Seefeldt, V. (1981). Youth sports research and practice: A selected bibliography. *Physical Educator,* (Suppl.).

Gould, D., & Weiss, M. R. (1987). (Eds.). *Advances in pediatric sport sciences Vol. 2: Behavioral issues.* Champaign, IL: Human Kinetics.

Hafner, E. M., & Presswood, S. (1965). Strong inference and weak interactions. *Science, 149,* 503–510.

Harris, J. C. (1983). Interpreting youth baseball player's understanding of attention, winning and playing the game. *Research Quarterly for Exercise and Sport, 54,* 330–339.

Harter, S. (1981). The development of competence motivation in the mastery of cognitive and physical skills: Is there a place for joy? In G. C. Roberts & D. M. Landers (Eds.), *Psychology of motor behavior and sport—1980* (pp. 3–29). Champaign, IL: Human Kinetics.

Helmreich, R. (1975). Applied social psychology: The unfulfilled promise. *Personality and Social Psychology Bulletin, 1,* 548–560.

Horn, T. S. (1985). Coaches' feedback and changes in children's perceptions of their physical competence. *Journal of Educational Psychology, 77,* 174–186.

Kerlinger, F. N. (1973). *Foundations of behavioral research.* New York: Holt, Rinehart & Winston.

Kuhn, T. S. (1970). *The structure of scientific revolutions.* Chicago: University of Chicago Press.

Locke, L. F. (1969). *Research in physical education.* New York: Teachers College Press.

Marcuse, H. (1964). *One-dimensional man.* Boston: Beacon.

Martens, R. (1978). *Joy and sadness in children's sports.* Champaign, IL: Human Kinetics.

———. (1979). About smocks and jocks. *Journal of Sport Psychology, 1,* 94–99.

———. (1986). Youth sport in the USA. In M. R. Weiss & D. Gould (Eds.), *Sport for children and youths: 1984 Olympic Scientific Congress Proceedings* (Vol. 10, pp. 27–33). Champaign, IL: Human Kinetics.

———. (1987). Science, knowledge and sport psychology. *The Sport Psychologist, 1,* 29–55.

Martens, R., Rivkin, F., & Bump, L. A. (1984). A field study of traditional and nontraditional children's baseball. *Research Quarterly for Exercise and Sport, 55,* 351–355.

McGuire, W. J. (1973). The yin and yang of progress in social psychology: Seven koans. *Journal of Personality and Social Psychology, 26,* 446–456.

Newton, M. L., & Duda, J. L. (1992, June). *The relationship of goal perspectives to multidimensional trait anxiety in adolescent tennis players.* Paper presented at the North American Society for the Psychology of Sport and Physical Activity Conference, Pittsburgh, PA.

Passer, M. W. (1983). Fear of failure, fear of evaluation, perceived competence and self-esteem in competitive-trait anxious children. *Journal of Sport Psychology, 5,* 172–188.

Passer, M. W., & Scanlan, T. K. (1980). The impact of game outcome on the post competition affect and performance evaluations of young athletes. In C. H. Nadeau, W. R. Halliwell, K. M. Newell, & G. C. Roberts (Eds.), *Psychology of sport and motor behavior—1979* (pp. 100–111). Champaign, IL: Human Kinetics.

Patton, M. Q. (1990). *Qualitative evaluation and research methods* (2nd ed.). Newbury Park: Sage.

Platt, J. R. (1964). Strong inference. *Science, 146,* 347–352.

Roberts, G. C. (1980). Children in competition: A theoretical perspective and recommendations for practice. *Motor Skills: Theory into Practice, 4,* 37–50.

Roberts, G. C., & Pascuzzi, D. (1979). Causal attributions in sport: Some theoretical implications. *Journal of Sport Psychology, 1,* 203–211.

Scanlan, T. K. (1986). Competitive stress in children: In M. R. Weiss & D. Gould (Eds.), *Sport for children and youths: 1984 Olympic Scientific Congress Proceedings* (Vol. 10, pp. 113–118). Champaign, IL: Human Kinetics.

Scanlan, T. K., & Lewthwaite, R. (1984). Social psychological aspects of competition for male youth sport participants: I. Predictors of competitive stress. *Journal of Sport Psychology, 6,* 208–226.

Scanlan, T. K., & Passer, M. W. (1978a). Anxiety inducing factors in competitive youth sports. In F. L. Smoll & R. E. Smith (Eds.), *Psychological perspectives in youth sports* (pp. 107–122). Washington, DC: Hemisphere.

———. (1978b). Factors related to competitive stress among male youth sports participants. *Medicine and Science in Sports, 10,* 103–108.

———. (1979). Sources of competitive stress in young female athletes. *Journal of Sport Psychology, 1,* 151–159.

Schlenkar, B. R. (1974). Social psychology and science. *Journal of Personality and Social Psychology, 29,* 1–15.

Seefeldt, V., & Gould, D. (1980). *The physical and psychological effects of youth sports competition.* Washington, DC: Eric Clearinghouse on Teacher Education.

Siedentop, D. (1980). Two cheers for Rainer. *Journal of Sport Psychology, 2,* 2–4.

Smith, R. E., & Smoll, F. L. (1978). Sport and the child's conceptual and research perspectives. In F. L. Smoll & R. E. Smith (Eds.), *Psychological perspectives in youth sports* (pp. 3–13). Washington, DC: Hemisphere.

———. (1990). Self-esteem and children's reactions to youth sport coaching behaviors: A field study of self-enhancement processes. *Developmental Psychology, 26,* 987–993.

Smith, R. E., Smoll, F. L., & Barnett, N. P. (1995). Reduction of children's sport performance anxiety through social support training and stress-reduction training for coaches. *Journal of Applied Developmental Psychology, 16,* 125–142.

Smith, R. E., Smoll, F. L., & Curtis, B. (1978). Coaching behaviors in Little League Baseball. In F. L. Smoll & R. E. Smith (Eds.), *Psychological perspectives in youth sports* (pp. 173–201). Washington, DC: Hemisphere.

———. (1979). Coach effectiveness training: A cognitive-behavioral approach to enhancing relationship skills in youth sport coaches. *Journal of Sport Psychology, 1,* 59–75.

Smith, R. E., Smoll, F. L., & Hunt, E. (1977). A system for the behavioral assessment of athletic coaches. *Research Quarterly, 48,* 401–407.

Smith, R. E., Smoll, F. L., Hunt, E., Curtis, B., & Coppel, D. B. (1979). Psychology and the bad news bears. In G. C. Roberts & K. M. Newell (Eds.), *Psychology of motor behavior and sport—1978* (pp. 109–130). Champaign, IL: Human Kinetics.

Smoll, F. L., & Smith, R. E. (1989). Leadership behaviors in youth sports: A theoretical model and research paradigm. *Journal of Applied Sport Psychology, 19,* 1522–1551.

Smoll, F. L., Smith, R. E., Barnett, N. P., & Everett, J. J. (1993). Enhancement of children's self-esteem through social support training for youth sport coaches. *Journal of Applied Psychology, 78,* 602–610.

Smoll, F. L., Smith, R. E., Curtis, B., & Hunt, E. (1978). Toward a mediational model of coach-player relationships. *Research Quarterly, 49,* 528–541.

Spieth, W. R. (1977). Investigation of two pitching conditions as determinants for developing fundamental skills of baseball. *Research Quarterly, 48,* 408–412.

Suchman, E. A. (1967). *Evaluation research: Principles and practice in public service and social action programs.* New York: Russell Sage Foundation.

Thomas, J. R. (1978). Attribution theory and motivation through reward: Practical implications for children's sports. In R. A. Magill, M. J. Ash, & F. L. Smoll (Eds.), *Children in sport: A contemporary anthology* (pp. 149–157). Champaign, IL: Human Kinetics.

———. (1980). Half a cheer for Rainer and Daryl. *Journal of Sport Psychology, 2,* 266–267.

Universities Study Committee. (1976). *Joint legislative study on youth sports programs: Agency sponsored sports—Phase I report.* Lansing: State of Michigan.

———. (1978a). *Joint legislative study on youth sports programs: Agency sponsored sports—Phase II report.* Lansing: State of Michigan.

———. (1978b). *Joint legislative study on youth sports program: Agency sponsored sports—Phase III report.* Lansing: State of Michigan.

Weiner, B. (1985). An attribution theory of achievement motivation and emotion. *Psychological Review, 92,* 548–573.

Weiss, C. H. (1972). *Evaluative research: Methods of assessing program effectiveness.* Englewood Cliffs, NJ: Prentice-Hall.

Weiss, M. R. (1991). Psychological skill development in children and adolescents. *The Sport Psychologist, 5,* 333–354.

———. (1993). Psychological effects of intensive sport participation on children and youth: Self-esteem and motivation. In B. R. Cahill & A. J. Pearl (Eds.), *Intensive participation in children's sports* (pp. 39–69), Champaign, IL: Human Kinetics.

Weiss, M. R., & Bredemeier, B. J. (1983). Developmental sport psychology: A theoretical perspective for studying children in sport. *Journal of Sport Psychology, 5,* 216–230.

———. (1990). Moral development in sport. *Exercise and Sport Sciences Reviews, 18,* 331–378.

Weiss, M. R., & Chaumeton, N. (1992). Motivational orientations in sport. In T. S. Horn (Ed.), *Advances in sport psychology* (pp. 61–99). Champaign, IL: Human Kinetics.

Wiggins, D. K. (1995). A history of highly competitive sport for American children. In F. L. Smoll & R. E. Smith (Eds.), *Children and youth in sport: A biopsychosocial perspective* (pp. 15–30). Dubuque, IA: Brown & Benchmark.

THE FUTURE OF YOUTH SPORTS IN AMERICA

—Vern Seefeldt

Youth sports have attracted the attention of parents, educators, and physicians ever since their emergence and phenomenal growth during the period following World War II. During the ensuing years such issues as the exclusion of unskilled athletes, exploitation of children for personal and commercial gain, and an undue emphasis on winning at the expense of other values have consistently kept the proponents of youth sports in a defensive position. The serious nature of these accusations also implies that agencies would be obligated to address them. Herein lies one of the controversies associated with youth sports. Proponents contend that any organizational event involving children in which the activity is largely conducted by adults who serve as volunteers is likely to have some problems. Moreover, the problems are being addressed in a systematic way. Detractors have responded by claiming that the increased accessibility and opportunities in youth sports have merely extended the problems to a larger group of clients.

The continuing popularity of organized athletics for children implies that a significant number of adults believe that the inherent benefits of sport participation outweigh the potential detrimental effects. The popularity of selected sports is reflected in the number of registered participants even during times when no increases occurred within the age ranges of youth sport participants in the general population. These increases in participation suggest that parents who enroll their children in competitive athletic programs either agree with the current philosophy and operation of the programs or they have sufficient confidence in the programs' sponsors to assume that the required changes will take place as soon as the conflict between tradition and new information can be resolved.

Whether the promoters of children's sport deserve the annual vote of confidence they receive from millions of parents who enroll their children in competitive athletics is an issue that has aroused considerable controversy. The media's persistent attention to the problems of youth sports has stimulated the scientific community to conduct investigations regarding the benefits and consequences of children's involvement in sport. Specialists in sports medicine, sport psychology, sport sociology, sport physiology, biomechanics, and motor behavior now consider children to be legitimate subjects in their investigations (Burton, 1988; Coakley, 1992; Doucherty, Wenger, & Collins, 1987; Goldberg, 1989; Lohman, 1989; Sewall & Micheli, 1986).

The attention of scientists to the alleged problems of youth sports has resulted in two important outcomes that have been missing heretofore in its turbulent history: (a) An interdisciplinary account of what happens to children as a result of their athletic participation has gradually emerged, and (b) the conditions that have been proven to be detrimental to the welfare of children have prompted changes in the rules and policies of the various sponsoring agencies. On the basis of the modifications made in youth sports during the last decade, proponents of youth sports have reason to believe that additional changes in the structure and conditions under which competition takes place will be forthcoming.

History of Youth Sports

Children's sport programs that are supervised by adults have been immersed in controversy almost from their modest beginning on the playgrounds of New York City at the turn of the century. Berryman (this volume) chronicled the growth of sport for children from the time sports emerged as an after-school recreational activity that was designed to prevent juvenile delinquency to the time nearly a century later when groups are again turning to youth sports and recreation as a means of structuring the nonschool hours of children and youth (Carnegie Corporation of New York, 1992). Berryman's review reveals several important historical facts that are commonly lost in the debate of the relative merits of school-based versus agency-sponsored sports: (a) that youth sports were an outgrowth of the regular public school curriculum; (b) that sports were initiated as a diversionary activity to meet the perceived competitive needs of boys; and (c) that certain sports became highly competitive in a matter of years, even when they were under the auspices of public school personnel. Therefore the argument that youth sports are beset with problems because they are under the auspices of volunteers, primarily parents, does not seem to have historical validity.

The withdrawal of support for competitive athletics prior to high school age by public school educators in the 1930s has had a lasting influence on youth sport programs. The elimination of athletic competition from many elementary school programs ushered in an increase in the number of programs in physical education and intramural sports. The new school-based programs were to emphasize the acquisition of skills for all children, in lieu of the specialized attention that was reputed to be directed to a few highly skilled athletes in the interscholastic sports. However, withdrawal of public school sponsorship of competitive sports for children and youth prompted a number of family-oriented agencies such as the YMCA, YWCA, and the Police Athletic League to begin offering competitive athletics in private facilities. These offerings became more numerous and diverse as additional agencies, created for the sole purpose of offering sport competition for children, were established.

The creation of nonschool agencies in the 1930s through 1950s for the specific purpose of teaching sports skills to children and youth created a paradox that persists to the present day. Schools that employ personnel who are educated to teach movement skills and to serve as coaches are offering limited opportunities for children and youth to learn the sports skills of their culture, whereas nonschool agencies are spending substantially greater amounts of time teaching sports skills to children—

but under the direction of administrators and coaches who are generally not well qualified to conduct such programs. This estrangement is also reflected in memberships of professional organizations. For example, the professional organizations of physical educators and coaches have few members whose primary interest is recreational sports. Concomitantly, organizations that serve professional recreation seldom attract physical educators and coaches as members.

The indifference of public school personnel to the agency-sponsored sport programs that sprang up as replacements for elementary school athletic programs frequently led to animosity and hostility between the two groups. This unfriendly attitude was fueled periodically by policy statements from the American Medical Association and the National Education Association, which opposed highly organized sports activities for children before the ninth grade. Despite these statements of position by educational and medical associations, the number of programs and participants in youth sports continued to grow, unmindful of the unsolicited advice that was directed at them.

By 1970 the opportunities for regional and national competition in children's athletics had expanded to include virtually every sport in which competition was available at the adult level. National sponsorship of programs also seemed to increase the intensity of competition to the point where even the agencies who proclaimed a philosophy of "everyone plays" contradicted their own mottos by supporting national tournaments in which the elimination of all teams except the eventual victor was inherent in the structure of the competition. Children also became involved in sport at younger ages. Data from the *Joint Legislative Study on Youth Sports,* Phase II (1978) indicated a modal age of 8 years for boys and 10 years for girls (see table 24.1) as the time when competition in a specific sport began, with many children already competing at 4 or 5 years of age. These data were supplemented by a study conducted nearly a decade later (Ewing & Seefeldt, 1989) that indicated the dropout or attrition in youth sports was well under way by 10 years of age in both boys and girls (see table 24.2).

Evidence of a changing attitude about youth sports by physicians, educators, and administrators began to emerge in the 1970s. The culmination of this conciliatory position occurred at a meeting sponsored by the National Association for Sport and Physical Education in Washington, DC (R. Merrick, personal communication, November 5, 1976) in 1977. Two documents, *Youth Sports Guide for Coaches and Parents* (Thomas, 1977) and *Guidelines for Children's Sports* (Martens & Seefeldt, 1979), summarize the content of the historic meeting between two groups: those who formerly opposed children's sport and those who represented the nonschool sport agencies.

In essence, the two groups agreed to recognize that athletic competition for children had become an enduring part of our culture. The conditions under which healthful competition should occur were described in a "Bill of Rights for Young Athletes" (Martens & Seefeldt, 1979). A significant change in the attitudes that physicians and educators held about youth sports was now a matter of record. Instead of their previous disapproval of athletic competition for children, its former antagonists and protagonists now agreed to work together for more desirable conditions under which competition for children and youth should be organized and implemented.

TABLE 24.1 Percentages Reflecting Ages When Children First Enrolled in an Organized Sport[1]

Chronological Age	Boys	Cumulative Total	Girls	Cumulative Total
Before age 3	4	—	2	—
3	3	7	3	5
4	6	13	6	11
5	13	26	9	20
6	10	36	10	30
7	16	52	11	41
8	17	69	15	56
9	13	82	12	68
10	9	91	14	82
11	4	95	8	90
12	3	98	6	96
13	1	99	2	98
14	1	100	2	100

[1]From *Joint Legislative Study on Youth Sports: Phase II* (1978). Copyright 1978 by the Michigan State University Youth Sports Institute. Reprinted by permission.

Agents of Reform

Changes in youth sports primarily depend on the degree to which the attitudes of its adult leaders can be modified. These modifications have generally received their impetus from the leadership at the institutions where teachers, recreation directors, sport managers, and coaches receive their formal education. This section identifies four categories of agents who are primarily responsible for the education and experiences of individuals who control youth sports in the United States. These four categories include administrators and professors from institutions of higher learning, directors of recreation, administrators of single-sport agencies, and public school physical education teachers and coaches.

Educators and Administrators in Higher Education

The attitudes and values concerning sport competition that coaches, teachers, and recreation directors support and advance are likely to have been derived from their former instructors. To the degree that curricula reflect the importance of subject matter, as determined by faculty in colleges and universities, the management of youth sports holds a relatively low priority in the minds of those who prepare professional workers in recreation, athletics, and physical education. Few courses in the curricula of students who choose physical education, recreation, or sport management as areas of concentration are devoted specifically to the problems and proposed solutions of age-group athletic competition. In situations where the topic is included in course

TABLE 24.2 Percentage of Participants, by Chronological Age, Who Indicated That They Will Not Play Next Year, a Sport They Played This Year

Sport	10	11	12	13	14	15	16	17	18
Baseball	8.5	12.5	14.9	14.0	13.9	13.8	9.7	6.6	2.7
Basketball	5.0	6.8	11.5	13.8	19.4	18.6	11.5	8.3	3.3
Football	3.3	8.1	9.6	12.1	14.8	17.7	13.4	13.3	5.6
Gymnastics	10.6	17.1	17.1	15.0	13.2	11.9	5.7	3.9	1.7
Softball	6.3	11.1	13.5	12.5	15.8	16.9	10.0	8.2	2.7
Swimming	9.7	14.7	12.8	12.1	14.1	11.3	10.9	8.3	2.5
Tennis	6.0	12.0	11.6	14.6	12.3	16.0	10.5	8.8	5.3
Volleyball	2.9	5.4	10.0	12.6	22.2	18.5	13.4	10.2	2.9
Wrestling	6.2	7.6	9.2	9.7	12.9	17.7	12.9	15.2	6.6
Ice Hockey	2.9	6.7	11.5	19.2	15.4	10.6	15.4	12.2	4.8

From Ewing, M. and Seefeldt, V. (1989). *Participation and Attrition Patterns in America's Agency-Sponsored and Interscholastic Sports: An Executive Summary.* Sports Goods Manufacturer's Association, North Palm Beach, Florida.

offerings, it receives the superficial treatment that is generally reserved for unimportant content. This direct or subtle omission of information about youth sports in the undergraduate preparation of students who will eventually be responsible for guiding the athletic activities of children is an inexcusable form of negligence on the part of those in charge of academic programs.

In addition to providing current information about children's athletic competition, administrators and faculty members in higher education can influence the attention directed at youth sport by: (a) providing students with practical day-to-day experiences in planning, conducting, and evaluating sport programs, (b) encouraging students to become involved in basic and field-based research involving young athletes, and (c) placing students as interns into programs that are conducted according to an acceptable philosophy, with sound operating procedures. Placing students into situations where they can be closely supervised as they learn their profession is a model that has been used successfully for decades. Every indication suggests that this model would serve an equally useful purpose in the education of coaches and directors of youth sport programs in the future (Murphy, 1985).

Although research pertaining to the problems in youth sports has not kept pace with the phenomenal increase of participation in such programs, many scientists who had previously concentrated on adults are now attempting to learn more about the effects of athletic participation on youthful competitors (Coakley, 1992; Goldberg, 1989; Pillemer & Micheli, 1988). As the intensity and duration of training programs for children have increased, we have learned that children encounter problems of a physiological and psychological nature similar to those observed for decades in adult competitors. Scientists, when working in the area of childhood, face the problems of defining additional intervening variables and determining their influence on an immature, growing system. Educators should apprise their students of the potential problems that exist in children's sport and, whenever possible, enlist their assistance in conducting research that seeks basic and practical solutions to these problems.

Directors of Recreational Programs

Directors of recreation are essential agents in any attempt to change youth sports because they usually have a direct involvement with the coaches and officials who actually conduct the practices and contests. Although sport-specific agencies with regional or national affiliations conduct many programs at the local level, the vast majority of youth sport programs exist under the auspices of the local recreation department. Even programs that are controlled under a national affiliation often depend on local facilities, administrators, and coaches for their implementation. Therefore, the philosophy and operational procedures promoted by the local recreation directors have the potential of exerting a profound influence on youth sports, even when the programs are not initiated or maintained by the Recreation Department.

Frequently, recreation directors have been accused of acting as "activity brokers" by relinquishing their responsibility for youth sports to the first agency or service club that requests permission to sponsor the programs (Greenslit, 1981). The criticism that recreation directors are more concerned about the number who participate than the quality of their participation seems unfair, but criticism seems appropriate when recreation directors permit other agencies to conduct programs of youth sports on municipal properties even when the philosophies of the two groups are incompatible.

Desirable changes in youth sports depend on the acknowledgment by recreation directors that athletic competition involving children is here to stay, that it has potentially beneficial and detrimental effects, and that the potential for beneficial results can be influenced by strong leadership within the local recreation program. The abdication of responsibility for youth sport programs to other agencies by recreation directors will usually generate more problems than it solves.

Managers of Single-Sport Agencies

Single-sport agencies are defined here as organizations that promote and sponsor competition in a specific sport for children of designated age ranges (Seefeldt, Ewing, & Walk, 1992). Examples of single-sport agencies are Little League Baseball, Pop Warner Football, USA Hockey, and the American Youth Soccer Organization. Single-sport agencies have been instrumental in elevating certain sports for children to their present levels of popularity and deserve much of the credit for the uniformity of rules and playing conditions throughout the nation. However, these agencies have also received much of the criticism for conducting programs in ways that some adults consider to be unacceptable to the welfare of children.

Single-sport agencies have generally been responsible for the standard rules and modifications that distinguish children's sport from the sport of their adult prototypes. They have also been instrumental in developing a system of adult volunteer leadership that permits these programs to operate at low overhead costs to local communities. Also ascribed to single-sport agencies by their detractors is a desire to maintain complete control over programs, to impose a set of inflexible playing conditions on local programs, to conduct "elitist" programs wherein only the skillful athletes are retained, and to extract membership fees in exchange for providing little more than playing rules and a tournament structure, while imposing the responsibility of instruction and implementation on local residents. The amplified intensity associated with competition in interleague, regional, and national play is also attributed to sponsors of nationally affiliated programs.

If single-sport agencies are to maintain their roles as leaders in the organization and promotion of sport for children, they must adjust more readily to the suggestions for change that research supports. In an era where litigation is the common recourse for negligent acts, the safety and welfare of youthful competitors is likely to receive greater attention in the next decade. The current inflexibility of rules and lack of a willingness to adopt the safety features that accompany many of the modifications in equipment and playing rules for youthful competitors will become increasingly intolerable to adult leaders in local programs as they become more knowledgeable about the potential to promote greater safety through modifications. A philosophy that places the single-sport agency in a role that facilitates, rather than controls, the leadership of local communities in sport-program management is likely to become the modus operandi at the local level in the future.

Public School Personnel

The concessions that educators made in the last decade to the involvement of children in athletic competition (Martens & Seefeldt, 1979) were based on the assumption that great changes would occur in current operating procedure by organizers of sport programs. Implicit in these changes was the important role that physical education teachers, coaches, and public school administrators would have in bringing about the cooperation between personnel in the public school and the youth agencies. Central to such negotiations were the resolution of such problems as overlapping seasons, eligibility of participants, frequency and intensity of competition, age when competition should begin, and the emphasis to be placed on the athlete's skill acquisition versus winning as the primary criterion for success. There are indications that some resolution to these problems has occurred, but changes have been slower than anticipated (Brown & Branta, 1988; Hill & Simons, 1988).

Evidence of changes that are designed to affect the safety of young athletes is most prominent in the design of equipment. For example, in baseball such changes as the visor on the batter's helmet, adjustable personalized helmets, low-compression baseballs and softballs, progressive-release bases, and the double base at first base have all been introduced in the last decade. The low rate of acceptance of these safety features is an indication of the traditional and conservative nature of adults who control children's sports.

Much of the control over athletic facilities and the expertise for teaching and managing sport programs currently lies with the coaches and administrators of public schools. Consequently, it appears that they are also in a position to make the greatest contribution to the youth sport movement. The "Bill of Rights for Young Athletes" argues distinctly that such a contribution is possible without compromising the principles upon which physical education, interscholastic athletics, and youth sport programs are based. Agency-sponsored youth sport programs can no longer be viewed as desirable substitutes for physical education programs or as farm systems for the interscholastic athletic program. If the emphasis in youth sport programs is to be on maximum participation and skill acquisition for all individuals, there is no need to fear that overexposure and exploitation will occur in agency-sponsored sports or that children's participation in them will be detrimental.

Projections for the Future of Youth Sports

The history of youth sports suggests that the future has room for both optimism and pessimism. The following projections for changes in youth sports are overwhelmingly optimistic. This does not imply, however, that youth sports are in a position where any change would be an improvement. In fact, any changes would be detrimental to the degree that they emulate the adult model of sport participation and ignore what has been learned about training, motivation, goal setting, and other parameters of competition as they relate to children and youth. The optimism is generated by the emerging information from the scientific community and the widespread desire of individuals currently involved in youth sports to provide the best possible experiences for children. These predictions are also influenced by variables such as population migration, energy costs, structure of the family, attitudes toward persons with handicapping conditions, and childbearing practices of the various racial and ethnic groups. To the degree that these variables are incorporated into the plans of program providers, they will be instrumental in determining the direction of youth sport programs in the next decade.

Scientific Inquiry

The influence of science on youth sports eclipses the importance of any other variable because of our previously depressed status of knowledge concerning the development of children involved in intensive physical activity. Many training programs for children formerly were modeled after those of adults, but without the associated experimental evidence to support them. Our knowledge about adults in stressful situations is relatively sophisticated because of the research that has been conducted during the past three decades. However, the influence of competitive stress on children has just begun to be the focus of scientific inquiry (Boileau, 1984; Gould, 1993; Smoll & Smith, this volume). Consequently, the changes that will be made in children's sport programs in the future are more likely to be stimulated by scientific evidence.

Two issues appear to have paramount importance in athletic competition for children: (a) the influence of physical stress on biological structure and function and (b) the psychological consequences and benefits of highly competitive situations. Many questions have been raised: How much physical and psychological stress is essential for optimum development and at what point does it become excessive? At what age should athletic competition begin? At what ages and in what sports can boys and girls compete on an equal basis on the same teams? What are the immediate and latent consequences of specific physically and emotionally stressful activities? Answers to such questions are becoming more numerous in the scientific literature. To hasten this process the leaders in youth sports must communicate their concerns to the scientific community, which must then conduct the applied kinds of research that will lead to solutions that can be incorporated into defensible practices.

Formal Education and Certification of Volunteer Coaches

The availability of new information about children in sport must be interpreted and made available to volunteer coaches at a more rapid rate. Establishment of numerous organizations that have as their purpose the education of volunteer coaches will expedite the flow of materials in a form that hitherto has been inaccessible to them. As managers of sport programs become aware of the information available to coaches, they must provide inducements for their coaches to become involved in programs that lead to certification. Minimum knowledge and competency in various subject matter areas has been identified (National Association for Sport and Physical Education, 1994). Credits or equivalent competencies that volunteer coaches acquire should be transferable across state and regional boundaries, similar to the transfer of certification in the Red Cross Lifesaving Program.

Local Ownership of Programs

As local managers become more knowledgeable about conducting sport programs for children, they will rely more on their own abilities to make sound decisions and depend less on regionally or nationally based agencies for guidance. To compete with locally controlled programs, nationally based agencies will have to restore to the local communities a greater share of the funds that they currently extract in the form of memberships and registrations. Increased services and education for coaches and administrators are two ways in which an infusion of resources would result in immediate changes. Providing educational programs for coaches, conducting research, and furnishing inducements such as insurance, certification, and newsletters are other examples of how a portion of the membership fees could be returned to communities. Greater representation in decisions that affect local programs and increased flexibility of rules to ensure greater participation in relation to local needs are additional concessions that nationally affiliated programs will have to make if they are to retain their status at the local level.

Greater Reliance on Municipal Sport Programs

Reduction of federal and state revenues to finance public school operations will reduce the number of school-sponsored sport programs available to elementary, middle school, and high school students. When school-sponsored sport programs are eliminated, the burden of providing comparable opportunities is usually shifted to community recreation departments and service-oriented agencies. Of these two groups, the service-oriented agencies will be in the most advantageous position to provide temporary relief for curtailed school athletic programs because their present operating procedure already includes fund-raising and fees as means of acquiring revenue. Unless municipal recreation directors procure funds from extramural sources, they too will face many of the same budgetary problems as the public schools.

Municipal recreation programs will not only receive more frequent demands for competitive programs from displaced public school athletes, but their adult clients will demand more time and space as well. Parents are having fewer children and having them at a later age, thus freeing adults for their own recreation pursuits. The provisions of athletic programs for women in high schools and colleges has resulted in greater numbers who seek single-gender athletic experiences beyond their formal education. The demands for coeducational sport programs for adults are also likely to increase as more women become involved in physical activities. Increased longevity has resulted in an additional generation of older, healthier adults competing for the facilities and personnel of local recreation departments. These demands for facilities and administrative expertise to conduct programs for adults poses potential problems for children and youth unless directors of recreation become more aggressive advocates for clients who are unable, financially and politically, to protect their own interests.

Increased Role for Volunteers

Financial constraints and the increased demand for services will cause municipal recreation departments to seek even more volunteer assistance for their professional staff members in the future. Dependence on volunteers creates a new series of problems, foremost of which will be the need for programs to educate the volunteers. Sport programs that depend on volunteers, whether locally controlled or offered by national sports governing bodies, must gradually demand certain levels of competence from their coaches and officials. The threat of lawsuits resulting from injuries, both physical and psychological, will force sponsoring agencies to require certain levels of competence that can most easily be assessed or certified through a formal instructional program. For this reason, required competence on the part of coaches will become commonplace by the twenty-first century (National Association for Sport and Physical Education, 1994).

Coaching as a Male-Dominated Profession

A unique problem arises when youth sport programs are conducted by volunteers. Today many children are being raised in single-parent homes, most frequently by the mother (Carnegie Corporation of New York, 1992). However, with the exception of gymnastics, swimming, and figure skating, most of the youth sport coaches are males, including those in interscholastic programs.

The lack of females as youth sport coaches may be to some degree associated with the lower participation rates and higher attrition rates of girls, but extenuating circumstances most likely account for the disparity. Convincing a single-parent female, who also works full time, that she should devote several evenings a week, plus weekends, to attend coaching workshops and to coach her child's athletic team may challenge the persuasive powers of any recreation director. The later age of child bearing also reduces the number of years a parent may be willing to assist as a volunteer coach, official, or administrator in a youth sport program.

Changes in Activity Patterns

The trend for adults to engage in activities that offer personal autonomy and less regimentation will also be evident in children's sport (Ewing & Seefeldt, 1989). Due to a prevailing philosophy that emphasizes personal needs, the shift to local ownership and control by recreation departments will bring a greater emphasis on personal growth and participation, with less emphasis on a philosophy that stresses "win at all costs." Goals of sport programs will be readjusted to incorporate the qualities of social development, fun, skill acquisition, and personal fitness that have historically been a part of children's motivation for participation but that have not always been evident in the conditions imposed on them by adults (Ewing & Seefeldt, 1989).

Sports that permit the attainment of personal goals and individual styles of play will become more popular, and those that require a high degree of regimentation will decrease in popularity. Racial and ethnic preferences will also determine the popularity of certain sports. An increasing proportion of children from African American and Latino origins and a decreasing proportion of Caucasian children in the population of the United States suggests that sports that are part of the culture of minority groups, namely, soccer, baseball, and basketball, will have an increase in the proportion of child participants, whereas football, ice hockey, wrestling, and swimming will decrease in popularity. Due to an increase in the number of young children who are eligible for memberships, the absolute number of youth sport competitors will increase through the remainder of this decade. As a point of reference, Martens's (1986) projection of youth sport participation from 1977 to 1984 is shown in table 24.3 in contrast to newer projections into the twenty-first century.

Integration of Mentally and Physically Handicapped Children

Despite the mandates of PL 94-142, Education for All Handicapped Children Act, and PL 93-112, Section 504 of the Rehabilitation Act, little evidence shows that attempts to incorporate handicapped persons into youth sport programs have been successful. Recent inquiries to representatives of six nationally affiliated sports governing bodies confirmed that all of these organizations welcome handicapped persons into their competitive programs (Seefeldt, Ewing, & Walk, 1992). However, only one of the programs had special provisions in its rules to accommodate such individuals, and only one provided incentives and encouragement for the enrollment of special populations.

The positive attitude of program leaders from national sports governing bodies indicates that the merger of sport programs for handicapped and able-bodied individuals is possible, but progress in this area will depend on how aggressively the advocates for persons with handicapping conditions pursue this opportunity (American Academy of Pediatrics, 1987; Shephard, 1990). Modification of rules involving equipment, playing conditions, eligibility, and skill requirements must occur prior to such a merger. Although the long-standing image that sport is reserved for the able-bodied will be difficult to overcome, the remainder of the twentieth century will result in a gradual blending of available facilities and programs to accommodate more children and youths who have handicapping conditions.

TABLE 24.3 Estimated Participation Patterns in Nonschool Sports (1977–1984) for Children Aged 6–18 Years (in Millions)[1]

Sport	Boys		Girls		Combined		Percent Gain-Loss (Boys)	Percent Gain-Loss (Girls)
	1977	1984	1977	1984	1977	1984		
Baseball	4.20	3.91	0.79	0.62	4.99	4.53	−7	−12
Softball	1.97	2.10	2.41	2.62	4.38	4.72	+6	+9
Swimming	1.71	1.85	1.91	2.08	3.62	3.93	+8	+9
Bowling	2.07	2.07	1.51	1.50	3.58	3.57	0	−1
Basketball	2.13	2.13	1.22	1.22	3.35	3.35	0	0
Football (tackle)	1.56	1.16	0.29	0.10	1.85	1.26	−26	−66
Tennis	0.88	1.35	0.95	1.24	1.83	2.59	+53	+30
Gymnastics	0.59	0.75	1.17	1.50	1.76	2.25	+27	+28
Football (flag)	1.11	1.20	0.36	0.45	1.47	1.65	+8	+25
Track & field	0.76	1.00	0.54	0.75	1.30	1.75	+32	+39
Soccer	0.72	2.20	0.52	1.70	1.24	3.90	+305	+327
Wrestling	——	0.25	——	0.00	——	0.25	——	——
Other	1.24	1.00	0.79	0.80	2.03	1.80	−19	+1
Totals	18.94	20.97	12.46	14.58	30.41	35.55		
Percent by sex	62%	59%	38%	41%				

[1]From "Youth Sport in the USA" by R. Martens. In *Sport for Children and Youths* (p. 28) by M. R. Weiss and D. Gould (Eds.), 1986, Champaign, IL: Human Kinetics. Copyright 1986 by Human Kinetics. Adapted by permission.

Summary

Youth sport programs are at a place in their natural history where change is imminent. Plagued by controversies brought on by rapid growth and lack of a firm knowledge base, proponents of youth sports have frequently been defensive in their reactions to criticism rather than proactive in seeking solutions to problems. Four categories of adult leaders have been identified as the primary agents of change in youth sport. Variables likely to influence the impending changes are (a) the availability of scientific information about the effects of stressful competition on children and (b) the proliferation of educational programs for volunteer coaches. Additional changes will include a greater emphasis on athletic programs offered by recreation departments, a greater dependence on volunteer workers to conduct the programs, and the integration of individuals with handicapping conditions into programs that have previously been reserved for able-bodied competitors.

References

American Academy of Pediatrics. (1987). Exercise for children who are mentally retarded, policy statement, *The Physician and Sportsmedicine, 15,* 141–142.

Berryman, J. W. (1995). The rise of boys' sports in the United States, 1900 to 1970. In F. L. Smoll & R. E. Smith (Eds.), *Children and youth in sport: A biopsychosocial perspective.* (pp. 4–14). Dubuque, IA: Brown & Benchmark.

Boileau, R. (1984). *Advances in pediatric sports science.* Champaign, IL: Human Kinetics.

Brown, E., & Branta, C. (1988). *Competitive sports for children and youth: An overview of research and issues.* Champaign, IL: Human Kinetics.

Burton, D. (1988). The dropout dilemma in youth sports: Documenting the problem and identifying solutions. In R. Malina (Ed.), *Young athletes: Biological, psychological and educational perspectives* (pp. 245–266). Champaign, IL: Human Kinetics.

Carnegie Corporation of New York. (1992). *A matter of time: Risk and opportunity in the nonschool hours.* New York: Carnegie Council on Adolescent Development.

Coakley, J. (1992). Burnout among adolescent athletes: A personal failure or social problem? *Sociology of Sport Journal, 9,* 271–285.

Doucherty, D., Wenger, H., & Collins, M. (1987). The effects of resistance training in aerobic and anaerobic power of young boys. *Medicine and Science in Sports and Exercise, 19,* 389–392.

Ewing, M., & Seefeldt, V. (1989). *Participation and attrition patterns in America's agency-sponsored and interscholastic sports: An executive summary.* North Palm Beach, FL: Sporting Goods Manufacturer's Association.

Goldberg, B. (1989). Injury pattern in youth sports. *The Physician and Sportsmedicine, 17,* 175–186.

Gould, D. (1993). Intensive sport participation and the prepubescent athlete: Competitive stress and burnout. In B. R. Cahill & A. J. Pearl (Eds.), *Intensive participation in children's sports* (pp. 19–38). Champaign, IL: Human Kinetics.

Greenslit, J. (1981, April). *Youth sports programs: Whose responsibility?* Paper presented at the Second Annual Youth Sports Forum, East Lansing, MI.

Hill, G., & Simons, F. (1989). A study of sport specialization of high school athletes. *Journal of Sport and Social Issues, 1,* 1–13.

Lohman, T. (1989). Assessment of body composition in children. *Pediatric Exercise Science, 1,* 19–30.

Martens, R. (1986). Youth sport in the USA. In M. R. Weiss & D. Gould (Eds.), *Sport for children and youths* (pp. 27–34). Champaign, IL: Human Kinetics.

Martens, R., & Seefeldt, V. (1979). *Guidelines for children's sports.* Reston, VA: American Alliance for Health, Physical Education, Recreation and Dance.

Murphy, P. (1985). Youth sports coaches: Using hunches to fill a blank page. *The Physician and Sportsmedicine, 13,* 136–142.

National Association for Sport and Physical Education. (1994). *National standards for athletic coaches.* Reston, VA: Author.

Pillemer, F., & Micheli, L. (1988). Psychological considerations in youth sports. *Clinics in Sports Medicine, 7,* 679–689.

Seefeldt, V., Ewing, M., & Walk, S. (1992). *An overview of youth sports programs in the United States.* Washington, DC: Carnegie Council on Adolescent Development.

Sewall, L., & Micheli, L. (1986). Strength training for children. *Journal of Pediatric Orthopedics, 6,* 143–146.

Shephard, R. (1990). *Fitness in special populations.* Champaign, IL: Human Kinetics.

Smoll, F. L., & Smith, R. E. (1995). Competitive anxiety: Sources, consequences, and intervention strategies. In F. L. Smoll & R. E. Smith (Eds.), *Children and youth in sport: A biopsychosocial perspective* (pp. 359–380). Dubuque, IA: Brown & Benchmark.

Thomas, J. R. (Ed.). (1977). *Youth sports guide for coaches and parents.* Washington, DC: American Alliance for Health, Physical Education, Recreation and Dance.

Universities Study Committee. (1978a). *Joint legislative study on youth sports–Phase II report.* Lansing: State of Michigan.

Weiss, M. R., & Gould, D. (Eds.). (1986). *Sport for children and youths.* Champaign, IL: Human Kinetics.

CONTRIBUTORS

The Editors

Frank L. Smoll, Ph.D., Professor, Department of Psychology, University of Washington, Seattle
Ronald E. Smith, Ph.D., Professor, Department of Psychology, University of Washington, Seattle

The Authors

David I. Anderson, M. A., Doctoral Candidate and Graduate Assistant, Department of Kinesiology, Louisiana State University, Baton Rouge

Donald A. Bailey, Ph.D., Professor, College of Physical Education, University of Saskatchewan, Saskatoon

Jack W. Berryman, Ph.D., Associate Professor, Department of Medical History and Ethics, University of Washington, Seattle

Brenda Jo Light Bredemeier, Ph.D., Associate Professor, Department of Human Biodynamics, University of California, Berkeley

Robert J. Brustad, Ph.D., Assistant Professor, School of Kinesiology and Physical Education, University of Northern Colorado, Greeley

Martha E. Ewing, Ph.D., Associate Professor, Department of Physical Education and Exercise Science, Michigan State University, East Lansing

Karen E. French, Ph.D., Associate Professor, Department of Physical Education, University of South Carolina, Columbia

Jere D. Gallagher, Ph.D., Associate Professor, Department of Health, Physical and Recreation Education, University of Pittsburgh, Pittsburgh

Daniel Gould, Ph.D., Professor, Department of Exercise and Sport Science, University of North Carolina, Greensboro

Susan L. Greendorfer, Ph.D., Professor, Department of Kinesiology, University of Illinois, Urbana

Amy Harris, M. S., Department of Physical Education, Health, and Sport Studies, Miami University, Oxford

Thelma S. Horn, Ph.D., Associate Professor, Department of Physical Education, Health, and Sport Studies, Miami University, Oxford

Mimi D. Johnson, M. D., Clinical Assistant Professor, Division of Adolescent Medicine, Department of Pediatrics, University of Washington, Seattle

Bill Kozar, Ph.D., Professor, Department of Health, Physical Education, and Recreation, Boise State University, Boise

John H. Lewko, Ph.D., Director of Child and Development Studies, Centre for Research in Human Development, Laurentian University, Sudbury, Ontario

Russell H. Lord, Ed.D., Professor, Department of Educational Foundations, Montana State University, Billings

Richard A. Magill, Ph.D., Professor, Department of Kinesiology, Louisiana State University, Baton Rouge

Robert M. Malina, Ph.D., Professor, Department of Kinesiology and Health Education, University of Texas, Austin

Norman Morra, M. A., Doctoral Candidate and Research Assistant, Department of Sociology and LaMarsh Centre for Research on Violence and Conflict Resolution, York University, North York, Ontario

Terry D. Orlick, Ph.D., Professor, School of Human Kinetics, University of Ottawa, Ontario

Michael W. Passer, Ph.D., Senior Lecturer, Department of Psychology, University of Washington, Seattle

Lynda B. Ransdell, M. S., Doctoral Candidate and Graduate Assistant, Physical Education Research Laboratory, Arizona State University, Tempe

Roy L. Rasmussen, Ph.D., Associate Professor, Department of Physical Education, St. Francis Xavier University, Antigonish, Nova Scotia

Karl S. Rosengren, Ph.D., Assistant Professor, Department of Kinesiology, University of Illinois, Urbana

Tara Kost Scanlan, Ph.D., Professor, Department of Psychology, University of California, Los Angeles

Vern Seefeldt, Ph.D., Professor and Director of the Institute for the Study of Youth Sports, Department of Physical Education and Exercise Science, Michigan State University, East Lansing

David Lyle Light Shields, Ph.D., University of California, Berkeley

Michael D. Smith, Ph.D., Professor of Sociology and Physical Education and Director of the LaMarsh Centre for Research on Violence and Conflict Resolution, York University, North York, Ontario

Jerry R. Thomas, Ed.D., Associate Dean of the Graduate College, Arizona State University, Tempe

Katherine T. Thomas, Ph.D., Assistant Professor, Department of Exercise Science and Physical Education, Arizona State University, Tempe

David A. Van de Loo, M. D., Senior Fellow, Adolescent Medicine and Sports Medicine, Division of Adolescent Medicine, Department of Pediatrics, University of Washington, Seattle

David R. Webb, M. D., Medical Director, Center for Sports Medicine, The Duluth Clinic, Duluth

Christine L. Wells, Ph.D., Professor, Exercise and Sport Research Institute, Arizona State University, Tempe

David K. Wiggins, Ph.D., Professor, College of Nursing and Health Science, George Mason University, Fairfax

Louise Zitzelsberger, M. S., Doctoral Candidate and Research Assistant, School of Human Kinetics, University of Ottawa, Ontario

INDEX

Motivation, 354
  as an optimal readiness factor, 62–64
  and readiness for competition, 75–78
  role of, 63–64
Motivational orientation, 389–90,
    396–97
Motor skills
  acquisition of, 51–55
  and cognitive skills, 51–52
  development of, 352–53
  and expertise development, 346–52
  generality vs. specificity, 52–53
Movement skills, acquisition of, 50
Multidimensionality, 113–14
Multisensory integration, 66–67
Municipal sport programs, 431–32
Muscle action (types of), 249–51
Muscular Christianity, 16–17
Muscular endurance, 251–52

National Association for Sport and
    Physical Education Youth Sports
    Task Force, 23
National Council of Youth Sports
    Directors (NCYSD), 23
National Recreation Association survey
    (1950), 7–8
National Youth Sports Coaches
    Association, 23–24, 126
North American Society for the
    Psychology of Sport and Physical
    Activity (NASPSPA), 22
North American Youth Sport Institute
    (NAYSI), 23

Objective competitive situation (OCS),
    299, 300–302
Olympic weight lifting, 255–56
Open skills, 67
Optimal readiness periods, 62–64
Organization memory strategy, 343–44
Organized youth sports. *See* Youth
    sports, organized
Orlick, Terry D., essay by, 330–37
Osgood-Schlatter's disease, 263, 284
Osteochondritis disease, 284
Overload, 253, 256
Overuse injuries, 283
  and athletes' developmental history,
    288
  contributing factors to, 286–90
  and fitness level, 289
  intrinsic causes of, 283–84

nature and incidence of, 283–86
recommendations to reduce, 290–92
Oxygen-carrying capacity, 206–7
Oxygen transport system, 191

Pain perception, 290
Parental action characteristics, 69–71
Parent-induced stress, 373–74 (*see also*
    Stress)
Parents, 93–98, 112–18, 120–21
  and history of youth sports, 8, 11, 19
  See also Sport socialization
Participation, 1, 434
  patterns of, 31–44
Pascuzzi, D.L., 76
Passer, Michael W., essay by, 73–86
Patriarchy, 96
Peer comparison, 315–19, 323
Peer influences, 118–121, 239
Perceived competence, 309
  developmental patterns of, 311–27
  recommendations for improving,
    314–15, 319–21, 325–27
Perception, 339–40
Perceptual role taking, 386–87 (*see also*
    Role taking)
Performance
  strength training and, 257–58
  stress and, 366
Performance economy, 208
  relative to menstrual cycle, 217
Performance outcomes, 317–18
Periodization, 291
Perspective taking, 386–89, 394
Perspiration, 193
Phosphokinase, 235
Physique, 163–64
Piaget, J., 60–61
Pitching, 63
Place-holding, 52
Play, theory of, 17
Playground movement, 17–18
Plyometrics, 254–55
Postcompetition anxiety, 364–65 (*see*
    also Stress)
Postmenarcheal female athlete,
    200–212
Posture control, 66–67
Power, 251
  measurements of, 252–53
Power lifting, 255
Preadolescence
  boys competition in, 5–6
  and sport socialization, 94–97

Precompetition anxiety, 363, 369 (*see*
    also Stress)
Preparticipation exam, 288–89, 291
Prerequisite skills, 62–63, 66
Primary sex characteristics, 54
Procedural knowledge, 345
Public School Athletic League (PSAL),
    15, 18

Q angle, 202

Ransdell, Lynda B., essay by, 200–225
Rasmussen, Roy L., essay by, 187–99
Reactive behaviors, 128
Readiness, 49, 177
  and athletes' developmental history,
    288
  cognitive, 78–81
  for competition, 73–86
  and overuse injuries, 286–88
  for participation, 49–71
Recreation directors, 428
Reflected appraisal process, 301–2
Reflexes, 53
Reflex sympathetic dystrophy, 366–67
Rehearsal memory strategy, 343
Relaxation, 334–35
  and Stress Management Training
    (SMT), 375
Research, 26–27, 430–31
  future directions in, 405–18
Resistance exercises, 253–56
Respiratory ventilation (V_E), 217
Response stage of competition, 299
Rest, James (model of morality),
    382–85
Reward approach (for studying
    competition), 298–99
Role models, 336
Role taking, 80–81, 386–89, 394
Rosengren, Karl S., essay by, 89–111
Running
  early training and, 194
  gender differences and, 212–13
Running economy, 208

Scanlan, Tara Kost, essay by, 298–308
Scientific inquiry, 430–31
Secondary sex characteristics, 54, 203
Seefeldt, Vern
  essays by, 31–45, 49–56, 423–35
  and Youth Sport Institute (YSI), 23